A Conceptual History of Psychology

A Conceptual History of Psychology

John D. Greenwood

City College & Graduate Center
City University of New York

McGraw-Hill
Higher Education

Boston   Burr Ridge, IL   Dubuque, IA   New York
San Francisco   St. Louis   Bangkok   Bogotá   Caracas   Kuala Lumpur
Lisbon   London   Madrid   Mexico City   Milan   Montreal   New Delhi
Santiago   Seoul   Singapore   Sydney   Taipei   Toronto

McGraw-Hill
Higher Education

Published by McGraw-Hill, an imprint of The McGraw-Hill Companies, Inc., 1221 Avenue of the Americas, New York, NY 10020. Copyright © 2009. All rights reserved. No part of this publication may be reproduced or distributed in any form or by any means, or stored in a database or retrieval system, without the prior written consent of The McGraw-Hill Companies, Inc., including, but not limited to, in any network or other electronic storage or transmission, or broadcast for distance learning.

This book is printed on acid-free paper.

1 2 3 4 5 6 7 8 9 0 DOC/DOC 0 9 8

ISBN: 978-0-07-285862-4
MHID: 0-07-285862-1

Editor-in-Chief: *Michael Ryan*
Publisher: *Beth Mejia*
Sponsoring Editor: *Suzanna Ellison*
Marketing Manager: *James Headley*
Developmental Editor: *Emily Pecora*
Production Editor: *David Blatty*
Manuscript Editor: *Joan Pendelton*
Design Manager: *Margarite Reynolds*
Production Supervisor: *Randy Hurst*
Composition: *ICC Macmillan Inc.*
Printing: *45# New Era Matte, R. R. Donnelley & Sons/Crawfordsville, IN*

Cover art: Computer Image of Street Lights on Pier. © Royalty-Free/Corbis

Library of Congress Cataloging-in-Publication Data

Greenwood, John D.
    A conceptual history of psychology/John Greenwood.—1st ed.
       p. cm.
    Includes bibliographical references and index.
    ISBN-13: 978-0-07-285862-4 (alk. paper)
    ISBN-10: 0-07-285862-1 (alk. paper)
  1. Psychology—History. I. Title.
BF81. G73 2009
150. 9—dc22   2007046130

The Internet addresses listed in the text were accurate at the time of publication. The inclusion of a Web site does not indicate an endorsement by the authors or McGraw-Hill, and McGraw-Hill does not guarantee the accuracy of the information presented at these sites.

www.mhhe.com

For my brother Malcolm

BRIEF CONTENTS

CONTENTS

CHAPTER 8   *Psychology in Germany   295*

PREFACE

The study of the history of psychology, like the study of psychology itself, should be an intellectual adventure. This is the course in which the serious student of psychology can engage with the basic concepts that structure the field, in all its range and variation. Whether you plan a career in clinical psychology, experimental psychology, academics, or any of the other fields for which a degree in psychology helps to prepare you, this course will provide invaluable preparation. Your engagement with the assumptions, associations, and constructions that have shaped the development of psychology will help you to look beneath the surface to see how conceptual frameworks drive theory and practice—skills that you'll find are valuable and useful throughout your life.

WHY A CONCEPTUAL HISTORY OF PSYCHOLOGY?

This textbook is a *conceptual* history of psychology; it traces the continuities and discontinuities in our theoretical conceptions of human psychology and behavior from the speculations of the ancient Greeks to the institutionalized scientific psychology of the 20th century. I highlight some of the remarkable continuities that reach across centuries and millennia, such as those between Aristotle's psychology and contemporary cognitive psychology, as well as fundamental discontinuities between superficially similar theoretical positions, such as those between supposedly "liberalized" forms of neobehaviorism and cognitive psychology. I also try to tease apart historically associated positions that have no essential connection, such as the common association between materialism and the view that human psychology is continuous with animal psychology. I have found in my own teaching experience that these conceptual continuities, discontinuities, and relationships are what engage students, and help them see the significance of the subject for their own contemporary theory and practice.

INCIDENTS AND ACCIDENTS

I have made a serious attempt to illustrate the *contingency* of many of the conceptual principles and associations that have informed the historical development of psychology and that continue today to shape our conception of the contemporary discipline. I demonstrate that the general acceptance of certain conceptions of human psychology and behavior has often been the idiosyncratic product of personal, social, cultural, economic, political, religious, and institutional factors, which made certain conceptions and associations appealing to theorists at the time, even if there were no compelling theoretical or empirical reasons for accepting them. I do not dispute that many developments in the history of psychology were the product of genuine advances in theory, methodology, or empirical evidence. However, I also demonstrate that many of the conceptions of human psychology and behavior associated with them were not mandated by these advances but were rather the product of independent factors often peculiar to that time or place, such as the late-19th-century conception of humans and animals as "conscious automata," which was supported but not established by developments in experimental physiology. To illustrate this contingency, I have included short histories of the development of the subdisciplines of clinical, social, and developmental psychology, which did not follow the general pattern of the development of psychology in the 20th century (from structural to functional psychology, and from the various phases of behaviorism to contemporary cognitive psychology).

A CRITICAL APPROACH

I have also written a work that challenges students to think *critically* about the development of psychology over the centuries; without such a critical approach, a history of psychology is not worth its salt. I hope that students will come to recognize that contemporary conceptions of scientific psychology—including their own—are powerfully shaped by the particular and sometimes peculiar manner in which the study of psychology developed. I hope that they therefore will learn to critically examine the conceptual principles and associations informing their own future theory and practice, whether as academics, clinicians, experimentalists, or everyday students of human psychology and behavior. This is essential to their creative development and to that of their discipline.

CONCEPTS AND CATEGORIES

This history of psychology is distinctive in other ways. In organizing the material, I have avoided forcing it into distorting philosophical categories, such as rationalism versus empiricism, or making it accord with schools of psychology such as structuralism, functionalism, and behaviorism (although some of the latter is inevitable, given that certain historical developments were partly driven by the rhetoric of competing schools, notably in the 1920s and 1930s). I have instead focused on the conceptual relations between attempts to understand human psychology and behavior at different historical periods, whatever the avowed or assigned "isms" of their advocates.

Philosophical differences over theories of knowledge obscure fundamental psychological agreement between theorists, such as the commitment by rationalists such as Descartes and empiricists such as Hume to the view that human thought is essentially imagistic and necessarily conscious. Although many histories of psychology treat the psychology of Wilhelm Wundt in Germany and Edward B. Titchener in America as forms of structural psychology, in contrast to the forms of functional psychology that developed in America shortly afterward, there are radical differences between the psychology of Wundt and Titchener and fundamental affinities between Wundt's "voluntaristic" psychology and functional psychology. For this reason, I have not followed the convention of including separate chapters on Gestalt and Freudian psychology, although these were recognized as distinctive schools of psychology in the 1930s, along with structuralism, functionalism, behaviorism, and the like. While I recognize the significance of these forms of psychology, I have accorded them the coverage I think they deserve in their historical context, given their limited influence (for better or worse) on the development of institutional scientific psychology in the 20th century.

I have not made any special attempt to represent the history of psychology as progressive and integrated, for the simple reason that often enough it was not. I have rather tried to let the historical record reveal whatever degree of progression or integration (or lack thereof) there was during any historical period. I think that any critical and honest student of the history of psychology must recognize that it represents a complex web of conceptual relations that reaches backward and forward across the centuries, including the 20th century. Instead, I have explored these conceptual relations through critical comparisons and contrasts that highlight their continued relevance for contemporary debates about the foundational principles of the discipline.

This work is intended for students taking upper undergraduate and graduate courses in the history of psychology, who have sufficient background in theories and methods of psychology to come to grips with the conceptual contours of the history of their discipline. I have included discussion questions at the end of each chapter, conceived of as food for thought. They are designed to stimulate critical thinking about some of the concepts and principles discussed within the chapters. I find that such questions arise naturally when students engage the issues raised by a conceptual history of psychology, and most of those included have come from my own students. I have also provided sets of conventional review questions and multiple-choice assessments on the book's Web page for those who wish to use them, as well as what I hope are creative suggestions for student essays and projects.

THE NEW HISTORY OF PSYCHOLOGY

I have done my best to take into account the excellent scholarship in the history of psychology produced in the last four decades, in professional journals such as the *Journal of the History of the Behavioral Sciences* and (more recently) *History of Psychology* and in specialist monographs such as those included in the Cambridge University Press series *Studies in the History of Psychology*. As a result, I challenge many of the myths that have established themselves through repetition in traditional histories, such as the claim that during the medieval period hundreds of thousands of neurotic and psychotic women were burned at the stake because they were misdiagnosed as witches; that Wilhelm Wundt held that experimentation was inappropriate for the study of higher cognitive and social processes; that functional and behaviorist psychologies were a natural development of Darwin's theory of evolution; that John B. Watson was fired from Johns Hopkins University because of his affair with Rosalie Rayner and consequent divorce; and that contemporary cognitive psychology marks a return to the structural or "introspective" psychology of the early 20th century. I hope that as a result students will find the accounts of individuals and movements covered in this work refreshingly thought-provoking and reflective of current scholarship. While I do not expect that everyone will agree with my characterizations, I hope they will agree that I have usually made a good case for them.

I have tried to make the work critically challenging, but have also done my best to present the material in a clear and engaging style (with great help from my editors and reviewers). While I focus on conceptual continuity and discontinuity, I have also included interesting, intriguing, and sometimes downright salacious details about the personal lives of individual psychologists—not in order to sensationalize the history of psychology, but because they are integral parts of it. Students will learn how Aristotle spent his honeymoon collecting biological specimens, about the strange fate of Descartes' skull, of Dr. "Monsterwork" and his lying machine, and of John B. Watson's measurement of the female orgasm (the real reason he was fired from Johns Hopkins University). I have also included illustrations drawn from the excellent archival material that is now available, which I hope will further enliven the text and make a welcome change from collections of dead white heads.

HISTORY OF PSYCHOLOGY AND SCIENCE

I trace the development of our conception of human psychology and behavior over the past two millennia, with particular emphasis on the period of the scientific revolution in the 16th and 17th centuries, and the development of institutional scientific psychology in the 19th and 20th centuries. I also examine the development of our conception of *science* and how this has shaped our conception of a scientific psychology. I try to show that the development of scientific psychology has been powerfully shaped by commitment to a number of principles that have been historically associated with physical science, such as the principles of atomism, invariance, and universality, but whose relevance for psychology remains an open and empirical question.

I hope that this text stimulates you to reflect upon the manner in which your discipline has been powerfully shaped by its conceptual history and challenges you to cast a critical eye upon your own assumptions and associations. This is why a course in the history of psychology is important and valuable for any student of the subject: It should expand your intellectual horizon beyond your immediate theoretical, empirical, or professional interests, to the concepts that drive psychological inquiry. I hope that this text inspires you to embark on your own personal quest.

ACKNOWLEDGEMENTS

I would like to thank my reviewers for their invaluable suggestions for improving the text: Mark Hatala, Truman State University; Gerard D. Hoefling, The University of Delaware; Kevin Keating, Florida Atlantic University; David Leary, University of Richmond; Vanessa McKinney, SUNY–Fredonia; John A. Mills; Jill Morawski, Wesleyan University; Susan L. O'Donnell, George Fox University; Terry F. Pettijohn, Ohio State University; Philip Tolin, Central Washington University; William Tooke, SUNY–Plattsburgh; Charles Trimbach, Roger Williams University; David Zehr, Plymouth State University; Robert Lana, Temple University; Laura Schneider, Texas Wesleyan University; Marc Lindberg, Marshall University; Victor Bissonnette, Berry College.

I would also like to thank the following persons and institutions for helping to make this book a reality: to the hundreds of students who have taken my classes in the history of psychology at City College and the CUNY Graduate Center for the past fifteen years, whose searching questions have kept the subject alive for me; to David Leary, for his encouragement, conversations, and Jamesian spirit; to Kurt Danziger, for setting the standard of scholarship to which all historians of psychology aspire, and for suggesting the title of this book; to my friends and colleagues at Cheiron (The International Society for the History of the Behavioral and Social Sciences), for their intellectual hospitality over the years; to Ken King, my original sponsoring editor, for persuading me to write the book; to Suzanna Ellison, my final sponsoring editor, for seeing it through to completion; to David Blatty, my production editor, for gracefully indulging all my last minute changes; to Joan Pendleton, my manuscript editor, for revealing the mysteries of the English language and APA style; to the editors and publishers of *Journal of the History of the Behavioral Sciences* (Wiley), *History and Psychology* (American Psychological Association), *History of the Human Sciences* (Sage), and *Journal for the Theory of Social Behavior* (Blackwell) for their permission to employ material published in these journals; to Bill Kelly and the CUNY Graduate Center for providing me with a semester leave from my duties as executive officer, without which this book could not have been completed; and to Shelagh, Robert, and Holly, for keeping me on the bright side of the road.

CHAPTER 1

History, Science, and Psychology

I N 1877 JAMES WARD AND JOHN VENN PETITIONED THE UNIVERSITY OF
Cambridge in England to have experimental psychology introduced as an academic discipline. The University Senate refused to do so on the grounds that it
would "insult religion by putting the soul on a pair of scales" (Hearnshaw, 1989,
p. 125). In a 1907 paper published in *American Medicine*, Dr. Duncan Macdougall
of Haverhill, Massachusetts, described his attempt to put the soul on a scale
(Macdougall, 1907). He persuaded six dying patients to spend their last hours in
a special bed that rested on a platform beam scale. By comparing the weight of
the individual (plus bed) before and immediately after death, Macdougall estimated the weight of the human soul to be about "three-fourths of an ounce."
He repeated this experiment with 15 dying dogs, who manifested no weight
loss upon expiration, confirming the popular belief that animals have no soul
(Roach, 2003).

From the dawn of recorded civilization, humans have not only speculated
about the nature and causes of mind and behavior, but have also employed their
ingenuity to put these speculations to empirical test. In the seventh century BCE,
the Egyptian King Psamtik I supposed that children with no opportunity to learn a
language from other people would spontaneously develop the natural and universal language of humankind, which he presumed to be Egyptian (Hunt, 1994). He
tested this hypothesis by having one of his subjects seclude a number of infants
and observe which language they first spoke; he was disappointed to learn that
they did not speak Egyptian. As the centuries progressed, critical thinkers continued to speculate about the nature and causes of mind and behavior and to subject their theories to empirical test. The process was accelerated by the scientific
revolution in Europe in the 16th and 17th centuries and by the development
of experimental physiology and evolutionary theory in the 19th century, which
promoted the growth of the institutional science of psychology in the late 19th
and 20th centuries. The story of this progression, development, and growth is the
history of psychology.

WHY STUDY THE HISTORY OF PSYCHOLOGY?

In high school many years ago, I was an enthusiastic student of history and did fairly well in the subject. Once, when persuaded to serve on a student opinion panel to pass the days between final examinations and summer vacation, I was asked the question "Why study history?" At a loss for an answer, I responded "Because it's there!"

In later years I came to recognize other answers. By studying the past we are better able to anticipate the future. Or, as the philosopher George Santayana put it, "Those who cannot remember the past are condemned to repeat it" (1905, p. 284). Unfortunately, knowledge of past errors is no guarantee against their repetition, as is attested by the continuing horrors of war. History also broadens our intellectual horizons, by introducing us to historically distant social and cultural forms of life, in much the same way as anthropology broadens our intellectual horizons by introducing us to alternative contemporary social and cultural forms of life. As in anthropology, however, there is always the danger of interpreting historically or culturally different forms of life in terms of our own cultural categories.

Still, both answers are legitimate reasons for studying the history of psychology. By learning about the overreaching ambitions of early American psychologists with respect to mental testing and eugenics, which supported restrictive immigration programs and compulsory sterilization, we hopefully insulate ourselves against similar ambitions. By learning about the theoretical visions of early psychologists such as René Descartes (1596–1650), Wilhelm Wundt (1832–1920), and John B. Watson (1878–1958), we come to appreciate the radically different ways in which past theorists conceived of mind and behavior.

In the case of the history of scientific disciplines such as psychology, there is another justification, which also answers a question naturally expressed by students: Why does the contemporary psychologist need to study the history of psychology? While it is possible to function as a psychologist without knowing the history of psychology, there are real dangers in doing so. Practitioners who neglect the history of their discipline fail to appreciate the historical contingency of the assumptions that have shaped their discipline, often via peculiar and accidental combinations of social circumstance and personality. This is especially true of the history of psychology, which in recent centuries has been significantly shaped by assumptions about the defining features of scientific thought.

Still, there was some point to my original response. The best reason for studying the history of psychology (like the history of anything) is because of its intrinsic interest. Anyone who finds psychological theory and experiment interesting, and most students who take courses in the history of psychology already do so, cannot fail to be engaged by the history of psychology.

Internal and External History

Contemporary **historiography**, the theory and methodology of history, recognizes a variety of approaches to the history of disciplines such as psychology. Traditional histories of psychology, such as Edwin G. Boring's (1886–1968) classic *A History of Experimental Psychology* (1929), have tended to be **internal histories**, largely devoted to the development of psychological theories and methods within the discipline. Such histories are generally written by "insiders," that is, by psychologists themselves, and are thus sometimes characterized as "house histories" (Woodward, 1987). In contrast, more recent histories have tended to be **external histories**, which aim to account for the development of psychological science in terms of social, economic, political, and cultural conditions that promoted certain forms of psychological theory and practice and constrained others (Buss, 1975; Furumoto, 1989). Some of these histories have also been written by "outsiders," that is, by professional historians rather than psychologists (e.g. Smith, 1997), although this remains relatively rare.

Of course, few histories of psychology adopt an exclusively internal or external approach, and the appropriate form of historical analysis ought to be determined by the historian's judgment about whether internal or external factors played a more influential role during any significant period (cf. Boakes, 1984, pp. xiii–xiv). For example, the different internal intellectual traditions of Great Britain and Germany probably best explain the differences between British associationist psychology and the German holistic psychology of Wilhelm Wundt (1832–1920) and the Gestalt psychologists. In contrast, external factors such as the pragmatic and utilitarian orientation of turn-of-the-century America clearly play a major role in accounting for the development of functionalist and behaviorist psychology in America in the early decades of the 20th century. Yet this can scarcely be the whole story, since institutional psychology also became increasingly applied in Germany and France at around the same time.

Zeitgeist and Great Man History

Histories of psychology also differ in how much influence they attribute to major psychologists, or **great men**, as opposed to the **zeitgeist**, or "spirit of the times" (Boring, 1929). Again, how much attention ought to be paid to either factor ought to be determined by the historian's judgment about the respective influence of these factors during any historical period. While Wundt deserves credit for founding the first experimental laboratory at the University of Leipzig in 1879, it may be argued that psychology would have developed in Germany in much the same way that it did if Wundt had never lived. On the other hand, although behaviorism no doubt would have developed in America even if John

B. Watson had never lived, it likely would not have taken the specific form that it did in the 1920s.

Sometimes a major historical development is a product of both a significant individual and the spirit of the times, of someone being the right person in the right place at the right time. Ivan Pavlov (1849–1936) is famous for his "discovery" of what is now known as classical conditioning. He demonstrated that the salivatory reflex of dogs and other animals could be conditioned to the presentation of a neutral stimulus when it is regularly paired with food. Yet this form of learning was identified centuries earlier. For example, it was described by the Edinburgh physician Robert Whytt (1714–1766), who cited conditioned salivation (to the smell of a lemon) as an illustration. Edwin B. Twitmyer (1873–1943), an early pioneer of speech pathology, discovered that the patellar (knee-jerk) reflex could be classically conditioned and made it the subject of his doctoral dissertation at the University of Pennsylvania. When he completed his thesis, "A Study of the Knee Jerk," in 1902, he arranged to have it published privately, but it attracted little attention. Twitmyer recognized the significance of this form of conditioned learning and delivered a paper on his research at the 1904 meeting of the American Psychological Association, but it fell on deaf ears.

It was only with Pavlov's investigations that this form of learning was adopted as an explanatory paradigm by behaviorist psychologists. Pavlov had the scientific prestige, having won the Nobel Prize in physiology for his work on digestion. His investigations were based upon rigorously controlled experiments conducted by a team of researchers at a scientific institute, at a time when rigorous experimentation was treated as the distinctive mark of genuinely scientific psychology. Pavlov's work became known in translation to American psychologists at precisely the time when they were developing explanations of animal and human behavior in terms of correlations between observable stimuli and responses (Logan, 2002).

Sometimes the influence of certain psychologists is a product of fortuitous circumstances. Thus Watson was fortunate to attain the chairmanship of the Johns Hopkins department of psychology and the editorship of *Psychological Review* as a result of James Mark Baldwin's (1861–1934) being forced to resign these positions after being arrested in a brothel. Clark L. Hull's (1884–1952) neobehaviorist theories of learning may have been superior to those of Edward C. Tolman (1886–1959), but the success of Hull's research program was at least partly due to the fact that it received generous funding from the Laura Spelman Rockefeller Memorial Fund during the Depression, whereas Tolman's did not.

Presentist and Contexualist History

Historians also distinguish between what has been called **presentist history** of psychology, sometimes also known as "Whig" history, in which the history of psychology is represented as approaching and approximating (idealized) contemporary theory and practice, and **contextualist history**, sometimes also known as "historicism," in which each historical episode or epoch is explicated neutrally in its own terms (Stocking, 1965). Presentist approaches have long been popular and generally represent the history of psychology as a long evolution from primitive theories about immaterial souls or spirits to the modern scientific endeavor. Yet although it is certainly true that many early theorists believed in immaterial souls or spirits, it does a great injustice to pioneers such as Hippocrates (c. 460–377 BCE) and Descartes to represent early psychologists as primitive thinkers.

The Greek physician Hippocrates rejected traditional accounts of epilepsy in terms of spirit possession and advanced his own account in terms of brain damage and dysfunction. Although Descartes did maintain that the mind is an immaterial substance, he also proposed the first systematic reflex theory of animal and (some) human behavior. Medieval Christians did not burn hundreds of thousands of psychotics and schizophrenics whom they ignorantly misdiagnosed as witches. Rather, 17th- and 18th-century hysterics in Europe and America did that, *after* the scientific revolution in Europe that began in the 16th century. Indeed, it may be reasonably argued that the persecution of witches in Europe and America was itself largely a product of the scientific revolution of the 16th century (Cohen, 1975; Kirsch, 1978).

Although the general movement from a "primitive" to an empirically based psychology marked an intellectual advance, the development of scientific psychology did not proceed in as smooth or linear a fashion as is normally supposed. Indeed, one may reasonably maintain that at certain critical periods, including the 20th century, psychological science regressed. For example, Aristotle is conceptually closer to contemporary cognitive psychologists than many of the late-19th- and early-20th-century pioneers of psychological science.

On the other hand, there are serious problems associated with contextual approaches that profess to adopt a completely neutral attitude to the history of psychology. It is certainly appropriate, for example, to try to explain why behaviorism appealed to many American psychologists in the 1920s: to try to explain why, given their intellectual and social institutional background, it was *reasonable* for many psychologists to adopt behaviorism in the 1920s. However, it is doubtful that one can determine the significance of this important episode in the history of psychology without some working conception of the nature and potential of psychological science and thus of whether the behaviorist period represented an advance or regression in the general development of psychological theory and practice.

Conceptual History of Psychology

While historians of psychology have vexed over these historiographic matters, they have tended to neglect another project. This is the identification of significant conceptual continuities and discontinuities in the history of psychological theory and practice, such as the conceptual continuity between the approaches of

Aristotle and contemporary cognitive psychology and the conceptual discontinuity between "liberalized" neobehaviorist theories and those of contemporary cognitive psychology. Without some grasp of these continuities and discontinuities, any explanatory history of psychology is theoretically blind. In the **conceptual history** of psychology that follows, I focus on these continuities and discontinuities, offering explanations of thematic developments based upon contemporary scholarship.

The history of psychology is still in its infancy as an academic discipline. Although the first histories of psychology were written in the early decades of the 20th century (Baldwin, 1913; Brett, 1912–1921), the history of psychology became established as a subdiscipline of psychology only in the 1960s, with the founding of the *Journal of the History of the Behavioral Sciences* in 1965 and the establishment of the Division of the History of Psychology of the American Psychological Association that same year. Cheiron: The International Society for the History of the Behavioral and Social Sciences was formed in 1969; the NSF summer institute that led to its formation was held at the University of New Hampshire in 1968, where the first PhD program in the history of psychology was instituted. Consequently, the explanations in this work should be recognized as partial and tentative and

Participants at the NSF summer institute at the University of New Hampshire in 1968, which led to the formation of Cheiron: The International Society for the History of the Behavioral and Social Sciences in 1969.

relative to the level of analysis. Deeper levels of analysis may reveal richer conceptual strands, and readers are encouraged to pursue them.

While the early history of psychology ranges over the Mediterranean, the Middle East, and Europe, and 19th-century history focuses upon developments in Britain, France, and Germany, the 20th-century history of psychology is very much the history of American psychology. Although institutional scientific psychology originated in Germany at the end of the 19th century, by the beginning of the 20th century American psychology came to dominate other national psychologies in terms of the number of psychologists, institutions offering degrees, books, journals, and student populations. It maintained its dominance throughout the 20th century (Brandt, 1970; Koch, 1992; Rosenzweig, 1984), especially after the Second World War, when it effectively "colonized" the national psychologies of many European states (van Strein, 1997) and Japan.

SCIENCE AND PSYCHOLOGY

One of the distinctive features of early scientific psychology and later forms of academic psychology is the degree to which they were shaped by prevalent conceptions about the nature of science. Psychology, perhaps more than any other discipline, self-consciously modeled itself upon successful sciences such as physics, chemistry, and biology. In consequence, many contemporary psychologists embrace a number of principles that are of questionable relevance to psychological science.

To illustrate this important point, it is useful to distinguish between those principles that are generally agreed to be essential features of empirical science (as opposed to formal sciences such as logic and pure mathematics) and those principles whose relevance is an open question.

Objectivity

It is generally acknowledged that a minimal condition of an intellectual discipline constituting a science is that the propositions it offers are **objective**. Propositions are objective if their truth or falsity is determined by independent facts. Thus, the propositions that *bodies of different weight fall with equal acceleration* and that *electrons have a negative electric charge* are objective because they are true if and only if bodies of different weight do fall with equal acceleration and electrons do have a negative electric charge (and false otherwise). Analogously, the propositions that *the patellar reflex can be classically conditioned* and that *humans employ prototypes in category formation* are objective because they are true if and only if the patellar reflex can be classically conditioned and humans do employ prototypes in category formation (and false otherwise).

The objectivity of scientific propositions should be distinguished from the objectivity of the judgments of scientists about the best theories in any domain (the best theories of molecular bonding, neural transmission, or human aggression, for example). Such judgments are objective if they are *unbiased*, and **subjective** if they are biased by individual or collective preferences or by social, political, or religious interests in the advocacy of certain theories (for example, that the earth is the center of the universe, that evolution is progressive, or that there are racial and gender differences in intelligence). The objectivity of propositions is also not equivalent to **materialism**: the view that ultimate reality is material. Although many propositions are rendered true or false by independent facts about the existence (or nonexistence) and properties of material bodies, others may be rendered true or false by independent facts about abstract objects such as numbers or by independent facts about the existence (or nonexistence) of immaterial or spiritual entities such as immortal souls or a benevolent God.

Causal Explanation

Of course, the requirement of propositional objectivity does not distinguish the propositions of scientific disciplines from those of everyday life or religion. The propositions that *cats like milk* and that *God is good and all powerful* are likewise objective because they are also true if and only if there are cats that like milk and there is a God that is good and all powerful (otherwise they are false). Another essential requirement of a scientific discipline, and one that goes some way to distinguishing scientific disciplines from other forms of speculation, is *causal explanation:* the propositions of scientific disciplines advance causal explanations of how certain events, regularities, or structures are generated or produced. Thus biologists explain patterns of embryonic development in terms of genetic programming, and psychologists explain systematic errors in probabilistic reasoning in terms of cognitive heuristics.

Causal explanations of classes of events, regularities, or structures cite factors that are held to be conditions for them: Their existence is held to be *conditional* upon the prior (or simultaneous) existence of such factors. To explain rusting in terms of oxidation is to claim that the presence of oxygen is a condition for rusting; to explain learning in terms of reinforcement is to claim that reinforcement is a condition for learning. All causal explanations cite conditions that are held to be sufficient for the generation of an effect, given other enabling conditions. Such conditions are sometimes also held to be necessary for the generation of an effect, but not always. For example, a source of ignition is often held to be both necessary and sufficient for combustion, given other conditions such as the presence of oxygen. However, the presence of a violent stimulus is not held to be necessary for aggressive behavior, even if it is held to be sometimes sufficient, given other enabling conditions (Berkowitz & Le Page, 1968), since there are other recognized causes of aggressive behavior such as frustration and anger.

Causal explanations are often couched in terms of functional relations between variables, when one variable is held to increase or decrease with another: Thus the increased volume of a gas (at constant pressure) is held to be functionally explained in terms of increased temperature, and increased levels of "destructive obedience" are held to be functionally explained in terms of the increased proximity of commanding authorities (Milgram, 1974).

Empirical Evaluation

Of course, everyday folk also offer causal explanations of events, regularities, and structures, so an appeal to causal explanation is insufficient to distinguish scientific physics and psychology from so-called folk-physics and folk-psychology. What does distinguish most folk descriptions and explanations from scientific ones is that the latter are subject to empirical evaluation. Scientific descriptions and explanations are tested either directly by observation or, in the case of theoretical descriptions and explanations about unobservables such as electrons or repressed thoughts, indirectly via their observational implications. This condition goes a long way to account for the fact that scientific disciplines are also generally held to be objective in the sense that the judgments of scientists are *unbiased*. Systematic methods of empirical evaluation, including experimentation, are held to enable scientists to adjudicate between alternative causal explanations independently of personal, social, political, or religious biases. Thus, properly scientific judgments are held to be adjudicated (ideally) by empirical data alone.[1]

Karl Popper (1963) has claimed that the testability, or **falsifiability**, of scientific theories is what distinguishes genuine sciences such as physics and biology from **pseudosciences** such as astrology, psychoanalysis, and Marxism. According to Popper, genuine scientific theories do not merely accommodate known empirical data, but make risky predictions which, if falsified by consequent observations, would lead to their rejection; an example is Einstein's risky prediction that light rays traveling to Earth from distant stars would be deflected by the gravitational force of the sun (a prediction corroborated by Eddington in 1917). In contrast, pseudosciences either do not generate risky predictions (in the case of astrology and psychoanalysis) or accommodate failed predictions by ad hoc modifications of the theory designed to protect it from falsification (in the case of Marxist theory).

The practice of phrenology in the early 19th century was frequently pseudoscientific. Franz Joseph Gall (1758–1828) and his followers maintained that innate

---

[1]In conjunction with other theoretical desiderata such as simplicity, fertility, and the like.

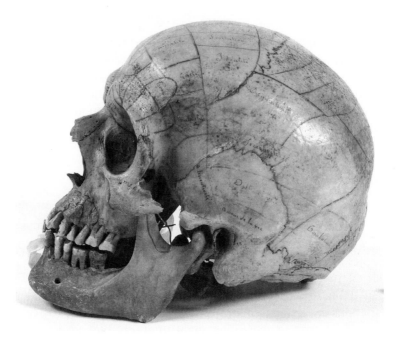

Skull with phrenological markings.

psychological faculties are manifested as protrusions or indentations of the skull, caused by the over- or underdevelopment of the region of the brain associated with the faculty. Phrenologists were quick to seize on evidence that supported their theoretical localization of psychological faculties to regions of the brain, but explained away negative evidence in a variety of ad hoc ways. For example, brain protrusions not associated with superior development of the associated faculty were explained away in terms of brain damage. Original estimates of the development of a psychological faculty were sometimes revised to accord with those predicted by the degree of protrusion or indentation of the skull. When phrenologists discovered that Descartes' skull was indented in the area of the brain where the rational faculty was supposed to be located, phrenologists concluded that Descartes could not have been as great a thinker as was commonly supposed (Young, 1990, p. 43).

While these three conditions seem clearly necessary for any scientific discipline, it may be doubted whether they are sufficient. It may be argued that scientific explanations should also be quantitative: that they should describe mathematical relations between variables, such as Boyle's law (at constant temperature the volume of a given mass of gas is inversely proportional to its pressure) or Fechner's law (the intensity of a sensation is a logarithmic function of the intensity of the physical stimulus). Yet although quantification is normally a virtue, it is doubtfully necessary, since empirically well-supported qualitative explanations, such as Charles Darwin's (1809–1882) account of the evolution of species through natural selection (Darwin, 1859) and Jean Piaget's (1896–1980) account of cognitive development in children (Piaget, 1926) seem valuable contributions to scientific knowledge. It may be argued that a certain amount of systematicity is also required: that scientific explanations should fit within some coherent general theory, such as the explanations of the properties of the elements that make up the periodic table in terms of differences in their composition and structure. However, it is difficult to specify what this amounts to and seems to dogmatically presuppose some predetermined degree of system in nature (including human nature).

Moreover, even if such conditions were considered sufficient for a discipline to count as scientific, many questions would remain unanswered. One such question concerns the nature of causality and causal explanation. Is causality more than conditionality, and do causal explanations do anything more than cite empirical conditions that enable scientists to predict empirical outcomes, such as combustion and conformity? How does causation relate to correlation? It is generally agreed that causality is not equivalent to correlation, even though the identification of causality is based upon the observed correlation of conditions and effects. Two factors may be highly correlated, but not causally related, because they may be joint effects of independent conditions (the propensity to watch violent television and engage in aggressive behavior may be joint effects of childhood abuse) or cyclical processes that happen to be sequentially related (such as the correlation between the population of mules and PhD students in southern California, which rise and fall together). Conversely, some causal conditions may be rarely correlated with their effects, because of interference (lead screening ensures that humans are rarely affected by plutonium sickness, and parents and the police may discourage aggression in children inclined to it by exposure to violence on television or the street).

The distinction between experimental studies, designed to identify causal conditions in artificially isolated and controlled "closed" systems, and correlational studies, designed to identify the degree of correlation between factors in naturally occurring "open" systems (Bhaskar, 1975), was popularized in psychology through Robert Session Woodworth's (1869–1962) *Experimental Psychology* (1938), and institutionalized in "The Two Disciplines of Scientific Psychology," Lee J. Cronbach's presidential address to the American Psychological Association in 1957.

Another question concerns the status of theoretical claims about unobservable entities such as electrons or motives. Should theoretical claims about such entities be treated as potential descriptions of possibly real entities or as merely useful (or useless) fictions? **Realism** is the view that scientific theories about entities that are not observable—or not directly observable (in the case of electrons) or intersubjectively observable (in the case of motives)—are potentially true descriptions of them. **Instrumentalism** is the view that scientific theories "about" unobservable entities such as electrons or motives are not potentially true descriptions of them, but merely linguistic devices that facilitate the prediction of the behavior of observable entities, such as electric circuits or human behavior. The realist view holds that there are objective conditions for the truth of theoretical claims over and above the truth of the empirical predictions that can be derived from them. The instrumentalist view holds that there are no such conditions: The truth of the empirical predictions that can be derived from theoretical claims is sufficient for the "truth" of these theoretical claims. Realism has been the favored position among natural scientists, but instrumentalism was a popular position among 20th-century neobehaviorist psychologists (e.g., Kendler, 1952).

Some of these questions are considered in later chapters of this work. However, it is not important for our present purposes to provide a complete definition of science or final answers to these questions. What is important is to distinguish essential features of science from a set of principles that are frequently associated with science but cannot be considered essential to it. Many psychologists adopted these principles, which embody assumptions about the subject matter and scope of explanations in science, because they were associated with early exemplars of successful physical science, even though it is an open question whether they are appropriate for psychological science. One of the aims of this work is to document how psychologists came to adopt these principles.

Atomism

One of the principles associated with science is **atomism**, which holds that the entities that form the subject matter of scientific disciplines can be individuated and exist independently of other entities to which they may be related. That is, they can be theoretically described without making reference to other entities and can exist in the absence of (or in isolation from) other entities. This principle holds for elements such as carbon, which can be theoretically described in terms of its composition, structure, and properties without citing any other elements or their properties. Carbon could in principle exist even if no other element existed, and samples of carbon can be isolated from other elements to which they may be related (causally or spatially).

However, this principle does not hold for entities such as quarks (the constituents of protons, neutrons, and electrons) or parts of electromagnetic fields, which appear to be **relational** in nature: They can be individuated and exist only in relation to other entities. Individual quarks or parts of electromagnetic fields can be theoretically described only by reference to other quarks or parts of electromagnetic fields, and individual quarks or parts of electromagnetic fields cannot be isolated from other quarks or parts of electromagnetic fields. For this reason sciences such as physics have abandoned the principle of atomism.

Many psychologists have assumed that psychological states and behavior are atomistic in nature, the notable exception being the Gestalt psychologists.

They have assumed that psychological states and behavior can be theoretically described and experimentally isolated independently of their relation to other psychological states and behavior. However, it may be reasonably doubted whether this principle holds for certain psychological states and behavior. Cognitive states such as beliefs seem to be relational in nature, because they presuppose a network of other beliefs. It may be doubted, for example, that a person could be ascribed only a *single* belief, such as the belief that the Empire State Building is in New York City. The true ascription of such a belief would appear to presuppose that the person has other beliefs about New York City (such as where it is), a grasp of the semantics of the linguistic contents of the belief (what the terms *building* and *in* mean, for example), and so forth. Analogously, certain forms of social behavior, such as serving on a jury or engaging in altruistic or aggressive behavior, seem to be relational in nature: They appear to presuppose an institutional context and relationship to other persons. However, it ought to be stressed that the question of whether psychological states and behavior are atomistic or relational in nature (or the degree to which they are atomistic or relational) is an open question. The point is only that there is nothing unscientific about supposing that some psychological states and behavior are *not* atomistic in nature.

Universality of Causal Explanation

Another principle associated with science is the **universality of causal explanation**, sometimes known as the *singularity* of causality. According to this principle, the same causal explanation applies to each and every instance of a class of events, regularities, or structures. This seems to be true of rusting, superconductivity, and biological death, which appear to have only one kind of cause. However, it is not obviously true of physical motions, which may be caused by either gravitational or electromagnetic (or strong or weak nuclear) forces, or of some cancers, which may be caused by either genetic or environmental factors.

Nevertheless, from the time of Isaac Newton (1642–1727) to the present day, psychologists have regularly insisted that universality is the measure of the scientific adequacy of psychological explanation (Kimble, 1995; Shepard, 1987, 1995): They have assumed that there is one and only one causal explanation of aggression, depression, or learning, for example. However, it may be reasonably supposed that some psychological states and behaviors have more than one cause. It does not appear unscientific or absurd to suppose, for example, that some aggressive behaviors are products of motives of revenge, whereas others are caused by the presence of "violent stimuli" such as weapons (Berkowitz & Le Page, 1968) and others by overexcitation of the lateral hypothalamus (brought on by drugs or diet). It does not appear unscientific to suppose that some forms of depression are the product of genetic predisposition and others a function of environmental pressures. Again, it should be stressed that it is an open question whether aggression or depression do have more than one cause. The point is that there is nothing unscientific about supposing that they do.

Ontological Invariance

A closely related principle is **ontological invariance** in space and time. According to this principle, the kinds of entities that constitute the subject matter of scientific disciplines can be re-identified in all regions of space and time. This principle appears to hold for fundamental physical particles and forces, which we believe to have been around for all time (or at least since the big bang) and to be found in all regions of space, and possibly also for many chemical elements and compounds. However, it does not appear to hold for organic life forms, some of which are later evolutionary developments and some of which are not found in many regions of space (for example, on planets too hot or too cold to sustain them). Thus, while fundamental branches of physics and chemistry embrace this principle, sciences such as biology do not, since species and viruses transform themselves (and become extinct) in historical time and are not to be found in all regions of the earth (far less the universe).

Once again, the point is not to prejudge open questions, but to note that there is nothing unscientific about supposing that certain entities are not invariant in space and time. Consequently, there is nothing unscientific about supposing that certain psychological states and behaviors are not invariant in cultural space and historical time. For example, it appears that the behavioral practice of couvade, in which husbands empathetically simulate the birth pangs of their wives, may be unique to a small number of Amazonian tribes. The emotion of *amae*, a kind of "fawning" dependency, may be distinctively Japanese (Doi, 1973), and *fago*, a complex emotion involving elements of death, going on a journey, and being in the presence of an admirable person, may be unique to the Ifaluk (Lutz, 1982). The pathological emotion of accidie, a debilitating form of disgusted boredom, may have been restricted to medieval times (Altschule, 1965).

Although natural scientists have been prepared to abandon the principle of ontological invariance, psychologists have been reluctant to do so. Indeed, many contemporary psychologists oppose the notion that psychological explanation may vary cross-culturally and transhistorically because the psychologies of different cultural and historical communities may be distinct. The suggestion that there might be "indigenous psychologies" localized to specific cultural or historical communities (Heelas & Lock, 1981; Moghaddam, 1987) has met with a vigorous critical response from psychologists (Kimble, 1989; Staats, 1983; Spence, 1987), many of whom have insisted that any form of psychology that implies the cultural or historical restriction of psychological explanation is unscientific.

Testing for cross-cultural differences in visual acuity (The Torres Strait Expedition, 1898).

Of course, it is often very difficult to determine whether a certain emotion such as accidie or a disorder such as schizophrenia varies cross-culturally or trans-historically, since accidie may be present in contemporary cultures even though they do not have a word for it (Findley-Jones, 1986), and the identification of schizophrenia in medieval times is hampered by the limited availability of clinical descriptions from that period (Heinrichs, 2003). However, acknowledging that it is difficult to determine cross-cultural and transhistorical variance in psychology and behavior does not mean that it is unscientific to suppose it exists.

Explanatory Reduction

Another influential principle is **explanatory reduction**, according to which the best explanation of a complex entity, property, or process is given by an analysis of its material components. This principle has served some physical sciences very well. The causal properties of the elements of the periodic table are best explained in terms of their electronic components and chemical bonds, and the thermody-namic properties of gases are best explained in terms of statistical mechanics (by treating gases as collections of molecules in random motion). Yet not all physical scientific explanations proceed in this fashion. Sometimes the best explanation operates by specifying relations on the same level as the entities or processes explained. Thus contemporary physics does not treat the mass of a physical body as a function of the autonomous masses of its components, but as a function of its relation to other physical bodies. Evolutionary processes in contemporary biology are partially explained in terms of genetics and partially explained in terms of the environments in which organisms are situated.

The same is true of psychological science. It might turn out that neurophysiology and biology will ultimately furnish the best explanations of mind and behavior, as generations of theorists have hoped and anticipated. Yet this might not turn out to be the case. The best explanations might turn out to be those that develop theories of the relational integration of our cognitive architecture and behavior. The development of Sigmund Freud's (1856–1939) theory of neurosis is an interesting example. Freud was originally trained as a physiologist and developed his theory of neurosis in terms of repressed memories after he realized he could not provide a reductive physiological explanation of *conversion hysterias*: instances of physical paralysis in which there is no discernible physiological abnormality. Freud explained these cases of paralysis by treating them as manifestations of anxiety symbolically related to past traumatic episodes. As Freud put it in his paper, "The Unconscious":

> Research has given irrefutable proof that mental activity is bound up with the function of the brain as it is with no other organ. . . . But every attempt to go from there to discover a localization of mental processes, every endeavor to think of ideas as stored up in nerve-cells and of excitations as traveling along nerve-fibers, has miscarried completely. . . . *Our psychical topography has for the present nothing to do with anatomy*; it has reference not to anatomical localities, but *to regions in the mental apparatus*, wherever they may be situated in the body.
>
> —(1915/1957, pp. 174–175, my emphasis)

Of course one might question the adequacy of Freud's account of conversion hysterias, and Freud himself originally tried to develop a reductive physiological theory (which he later abandoned) in "Project for a Scientific Psychology" (1895/1950). But once again, the point is only that there is nothing unscientific about the supposition that the best explanation of psychological states and behavior might not be reductive.

Determinism

Another principle much favored by psychologists is **determinism**. According to this principle, for every event there is a set of prior conditions whose combination is sufficient to generate that event, such that no other outcome is possible. For example, if a billiard ball is struck by another and moves off with a certain velocity, it is presumed that it does so because the force of the ball colliding with it is sufficient to propel it and, given the force of the colliding ball, no other outcome is possible. Although physical scientists embraced this principle for many centuries, contemporary physicists have abandoned it. According to contemporary quantum mechanical theory, radioactive decay is not uniquely determined by prior conditions: These conditions ensure that there is a certain (fairly high) probability that a beta particle will be emitted, but do not ensure that a beta particle will be emitted. Analogously, it does not appear to be unscientific to suppose that the conditions responsible for human aggression or depression merely incline or promote (or render probable) instances of aggression or depression without determining them.

Psychologists are strangely reluctant to embrace such a possibility, insisting that determinism is a presumption of science. Yet for most practical purposes it does not matter whether psychologists embrace this principle, since psychologists would advance and test explanations in much they same way whether they thought conditions determine or simply promote psychological or behavioral outcomes. They would proceed in the same way whether they thought "violent stimuli" determine or merely incline people to be aggressive, for example. They would still predict that people would tend to become aggressive in the presence of violent stimuli and that there would be statistically significant differences between the behavior of subjects who are exposed to "violent stimuli" and those who are not.

Two other features are often treated as essential to science. The first is commitment to experimentation as the mark of a genuinely scientific discipline, and the second is commitment to empiricism.

Experimentation

Experimental sciences are those in which scientists are able to create situations in which causal conditions can be isolated and causal explanations evaluated. For example, at Camp Lazear in Havana in 1900, Walter Reed and James Carroll determined that the bite of the tiger mosquito is the cause of yellow fever by experimentally isolating human volunteers and exposing them to "noxious vapors" from swamps, contact with fellow sufferers (strictly speaking, their soiled clothing), and tiger mosquitoes—the three then-prevalent hypotheses about the cause of yellow fever. Since after 30 days in isolation, only subjects exposed to tiger mosquitoes contracted yellow fever, the researchers concluded that tiger mosquito bites are the cause of yellow fever and that contact with "noxious vapors" and contagion are not.

The logic of experimentation is directly related to the conception of causality as conditional. Given this conception, scientists attempt to identify conditions that are regularly present when a certain effect is present and regularly absent when a certain effect is absent or to identify variables that regularly increase or decrease when other variables increase or decrease. John Stuart Mill's (1806–1873) methods of agreement, difference, and concomitant variation, often known as "Mill's methods" (Mill, 1843), describe situations in which such conditions can be identified.

According to Mill's **method of agreement**, if instances of an effect have only one condition in common, then that condition is the cause of the effect. According to **Mill's method of difference**, if an instance in which an effect occurs and an instance in which it does not occur differ with respect to only one condition, then that condition is the cause, or an essential part of the cause, of the effect. According to the **method of concomitant variation**, if one condition increases or decreases while an effect increases or decreases, then that condition is the cause of the effect.

Since correlation is not equivalent to causality, no amount of positive instances of correlation between conditions and effects—between, for example, a form of psychological treatment and the elimination or attenuation of neurotic symptoms—can establish a causal connection. However, one negative instance of the presence of a condition in the absence of an effect—a case, for example, of excessive masturbation not followed by blindness—can demonstrate the absence of a causal connection. The method of eliminating competing causal hypotheses until only one viable hypothesis remains is known as **eliminative induction**, a method Francis Bacon (1561–1626) promoted during the scientific revolution in Europe. According to this method, it is not sufficient to observe that yellow fever is commonly preceded by exposure to tiger mosquito bites to establish that tiger mosquito bites are the cause of yellow fever. One has first to eliminate alternative causal hypotheses in terms of exposure to noxious vapors and contagion, by demonstrating the absence of yellow fever in the presence of noxious vapors and contact with other victims of yellow fever. Analogously, it is not enough to observe elimination or attenuation of neurotic symptoms commonly preceded by a form of psychological therapy to establish the causal efficacy of that form of psychological therapy. One must first eliminate alternative causal hypotheses in terms of spontaneous remission (most neurotics get better anyway) or a placebo effect (engendered by client or therapist expectations of improvement).

Of course such characterizations are idealized. Since causal conditions can be counteracted by interference conditions (protective paint can prevent rusting, even if oxygen and water are present, and parents and the police can suppress aggressive behavior, even in the presence of violent stimuli), causal investigations presuppose that potential conditions of interference are absent in naturally occurring situations or have been eliminated or controlled for in experimental situations. Thus, experimental observations are usually preferred to naturalistic observations when they can be obtained, since experimental isolation and control can help to eliminate or attenuate potential interference conditions.

The ability to create experimental situations is a great convenience for sciences that are enabled to do so, but experimentation is not an essential feature of science, since causal explanations can be evaluated via forms of observation that do not involve experimental manipulation and control. Many highly successful sciences such as astronomy and geology are not experimental sciences, and one may contrast the relatively few repetitions of controlled experiments commonly employed in physics and chemistry with the mass of observations patiently gathered in astronomy and ethology. However, scientific psychology was instituted as an academic discipline in Germany in the 1880s in large part through its commitment to experimentation, and generations of 20th-century psychologists have seen commitment to experimentation as the sine qua non of scientific psychology; this has been especially true of social psychologists (Greenwood, 1994). Robert S. Woodworth, who popularized the distinction between experimental and correlational studies in *Experimental Psychology* (1938), also promoted the notion that experimentation is the best, if not the only, reliable means of evaluating causal explanations (Winston & Blais, 1996).

Many psychological states and behaviors can be objects of experimental analysis, yet it is not obvious that they all can. Although psychologists clearly have the ability to manipulate and control human psychology and behavior, it is not clear that they can experimentally isolate all aspects of it. In the case of social-psychological states and behavior, for example, it may not be possible to re-create social attitudes or jury behavior in isolation from their everyday social contexts. As Chapanis (1967, p. 558) put it, with respect to many social-psychological states and behavior, "the very act of bringing a variable into the laboratory usually changes its nature."

The familiar definition of experiments in terms of the active manipulation of "independent variables" is a 20th-century psychological construction, common to textbooks of psychology but rarely found in textbooks of physics and biology (Winston & Blais, 1996). The source of this definition is Edwin G. Boring's *The Physical Dimensions of Consciousness* (1933, pp. 8–9), although it was popularized in psychology in Woodworth's *Experimental Psychology* (1938), known as the "Columbia Bible" (Winston, 1990).

Empiricism

Science is often held to be founded on empiricism. In one clear sense it is. The principle of **methodological empiricism** requires that all scientific descriptions and explanations be subject to observational evaluation (the term *empiricism* comes from the Greek *empeirikos*, which means "experience") and is just the third condition earlier identified as essential to science. In this respect, all scientists are empiricists. However, this principle should be carefully distinguished from **dogmatic empiricism**, the highly contentious view that scientific theory and causal explanation are restricted to the description of the correlation of observables.

It should also be carefully distinguished from the doctrine of **meaning empiricism**, according to which linguistic terms derive their meaning through association with observables (that can be seen, touched, or otherwise experienced through the senses). The most contentious version of this doctrine, popular in psychology from the 1930s onward, is the doctrine that theoretical propositions "about" unobservable entities such as protons or repressed memories must be operationally defined in terms of observables. Despite its popularity among psychologists, the **operational definition** of the meaning of theoretical propositions is virtually unknown outside of the social sciences and thus cannot be reasonably maintained as an essential feature of science. Later chapters of this work chart the historical adoption of this doctrine by psychologists.

This doctrine became popular among psychologists in part because in its original form it was linked to a particular theory about the origin of concepts or ideas. According to the theory of **psychological empiricism**, all concepts or ideas are derived from experience. In this view, only someone who has experienced the color red can form the concept or idea of "red."

Scientific Method

Psychological scientists regularly appeal to their employment of the scientific method in justifying the scientific status of their discipline, conceived either as a method of deriving theories from observations or as a method of postulating theories and testing them via their deductive or predictive implications. The former is usually characterized as the **inductive method**, the latter as the **hypothetico-deductive method**. Galileo Galilei's (1564–1642) derivation of his law of falling bodies from his measurement of the velocities of balls rolling down an inclined plane and Jean Piaget's descriptions of the stages of cognitive development based upon his observations of the development of his own children (Piaget, 1926) exemplify the inductive method. Johannes Kepler's (1571–1630) postulation of elliptical orbits to explain planetary motions and Leon Festinger's (1919–1989) prediction that subjects committed to certain beliefs will continue to maintain these beliefs in the face of contradictory evidence as a consequence of "cognitive dissonance" (Festinger, Riecken, & Schachter, 1956) exemplify the hypothetico-deductive method.

Francis Bacon is usually held to be the principal advocate of the inductive method, conceived of as a systematic means of ascending from observations to increasingly more general theories. Although some natural scientists and psychologists do seem to have developed their theories in this fashion, as in the case of Galileo and Piaget, later methodologists came to hold that such a method is not necessary and maintained that many successful theories are based upon hunches, lucky guesses, or prior speculation.

For example, Otto Loewi (1873–1961) had a peculiar dream. He imagined a tank of water in which two frog hearts were suspended. He dreamed that he stimulated the vagus nerve of one heart, causing it to beat, and lo and behold, the second also began to beat! Perplexed but intrigued, he set about reproducing the conditions of his dream. He suspended two frog hearts in separate tanks of fluid connected by tubing, and found that stimulation of the vagus nerve of one produced heartbeat in both. He recognized immediately that some chemical transmitted from one heart to the other must have produced the stimulation of the second heart, and the theory of neurotransmitters was born.

It is doubtful that Galileo developed his law of falling bodies from observations of balls rolling down an inclined plane. The mathematical formulation of Galileo's law of falling bodies, the so-called mean-speed theorem, was stated by mathematicians associated with Merton College, Oxford, in the 14th century. Galileo admitted as much, claiming that he did his experiments "in order to be assured that the acceleration of heavy bodies falling naturally does follow the ratio expounded above" (1638/1974, p. 169), where the "ratio expounded above" is a proof of the Merton mean-speed theorem (Harré, 1981). Yet this does nothing to belittle Galileo's achievement, which was to empirically evaluate and consequently establish this formula.

Later scientific methodologists came to reject the Baconian notion of a "logic of discovery." John Herschel (1792–1871) distinguished between the "context of discovery" and the "context of justification" of scientific theories (Herschel, 1830). He noted that although many theories are formulated as a result of some form of inductive assent, the source of a theory is irrelevant to its scientific acceptability. Theories are accepted on the basis of their conformity with observation and experiment, and a lucky theoretical guess that is superior to an inductively derived theory in terms of its predictive success is always preferred. Hershel's contemporary, William Whewell (1794–1866), also maintained that many of the most significant advances in science, such as Kepler's postulation of elliptical orbits, were a product of "felicitious and explicable strokes of inventive talent" (1858, p. 64).

These critical responses evolved into the 20th-century position known as hypothetico-deductivism. According to this position, the source of a scientific theory is irrelevant to its empirical adequacy, which is a function of its confirmed empirical implications:

> There are . . . no generally applicable "rules of induction," by which hypotheses or theories can be mechanically derived or inferred from empirical data. The transition from data to theory requires creative imagination. Scientific theories are not *derived* from observed facts, but *invented* to account for them. . . . Scientific objectivity is safeguarded by the principle that while hypotheses and theories may be freely invented and *proposed* in science, they can be accepted into the body of scientific knowledge only if they pass critical scrutiny, which includes in particular the checking of suitable test implications by careful observation and experiment.
>
> —(Hempel, 1966, pp. 15–16)

According to this view, science develops through a process of hypothesis postulation and empirical testing or a series of "conjectures and refutations" (Popper, 1963).

Since the time of Herschel and Whewell, methodologists have also stressed the significance of **novel predictions** in establishing scientific theories: predictions that go beyond the established empirical data that a theory is introduced to explain, such as Einstein's prediction (derived from the theory of relativity) that light rays traveling to Earth from distant stars would be deflected by the gravitational force of the sun. These predictions are especially important in adjudicating conflicts between competing theories that explain the same range of empirical data. Thus, the conflict between the corpuscularian (particle) and wave theories of light, which both explained and predicted the established laws of reflection, refraction, and the rectilinear propagation of light, was adjudicated by Foucault's experiment, which demonstrated that light decelerates when moving from a less dense to a denser medium (for example, from air to water), as the wave theory predicted, but contrary to the acceleration predicted by the corpuscularian theory. Such adjudicating instances are often characterized as **crucial instances** or **crucial experiments**.

Both the inductivist and hypothetico-deductivist positions have proved popular with scientific psychologists. It would be hard to find a more forceful advocation of inductive ascent than Watson's characterization of behaviorist psychology in *Behaviorism* (1924) or a clearer illustration of hypothetico-deductivism than the system of theoretical postulates and derived empirical predictions in Hull's *Principles of Behavior* (1943).

PHILOSOPHY AND PHYSIOLOGY

Many of the early theorists discussed in this work, such as Aristotle, Augustine, Aquinas, Descartes, Hume, and Kant, are usually characterized as philosophers rather than psychologists, and their work forms the basis of courses in philosophy and history of philosophy. However, although such early theorists were deeply concerned with **ontological** and **epistemological questions** about the fundamental nature of reality and our knowledge of it, they also developed substantive theories of perception, cognition, and behavior. Thus the Scottish philosopher David Hume (1711–1776), who argued that we cannot have knowledge of fundamental entities such as material substance or the self, developed detailed psychological explanations of how we come to believe in material bodies and enduring selves and conceived of his project as "an attempt to introduce the experimental method of reasoning into moral subjects" (Hume, 1739/1973).

To describe such theorists as philosophers or psychologists is anachronistic, since our conception of philosophy as a conceptual discipline and psychology as an empirical discipline is a product of the separate institutional development of the academic disciplines of philosophy and psychology in the early 20th century

(Reed, 1987). University academics concerned with both philosophical and psychological questions were designated as professors of philosophy for generations before, and Wundt held chairs in philosophy throughout his career at the universities of Heidelberg, Zürich, and Leipzig.

For this reason I have avoided trying to organize the historical narrative of this work in terms of traditional philosophical categories, such as the distinction between rationalists and empiricists or idealists and materialists. Theorists such as Descartes and John Locke (1632–1704) did disagree about whether we can have knowledge through pure reason. Descartes, the **rationalist**, maintained that we can have **a priori knowledge**, independently of experience, based upon reason; Locke, the **empiricist**, maintained that we can have only **a posteriori knowledge**, based upon experience. However, they also shared fundamental psychological theories about the imagistic nature of ideas and the conscious accessibility of all mental states.

Many of the early theorists discussed in this work are characterized as scientists or physiologists. Such characterizations are also anachronistic. Our conception of science as a social and professional institution, whose practitioners are committed to the empirical evaluation of formalized theories, is a relatively recent invention. The term *scientia,* from which the English term *science* is derived, originally referred to any form of knowledge, theoretical or practical. The science of physiology in its modern sense is tied to 18th- and 19th-century conceptions of cellular organization and the central and peripheral nervous system. The ancient Greeks originally used the term *physiology* to reference the study of nature in general; the medical restriction of the term to theories of nature employed to explain the functions of the human body was for centuries tied to the theory of the "four humors" (Hatfield, 1992).

However, we can recognize anticipations of our conception of science in the early naturalistic and mathematical speculations of the ancient Greeks, in the increasing emphasis on the empirical evaluation of theories from the 16th century onward, and in the development of scientific societies in the 17th century. Analogously, we can recognize discussions of the functions of the human organism and its components from the ancient Greeks to present-day physiologists. Although it is anachronistic to talk about early science and scientists and early physiology and physiologists, it is justified to the degree that many early thinkers developed theories about the structures and processes that still form part of the subject matter of contemporary sciences such as physiology.

The same is true of psychology. Although the institutional science of psychology is a late-19th-century creation (in Europe and America), many of the mental states and processes studied by contemporary psychologists (such as sensation, perception, emotion, memory, dreaming, learning, language, and thought) were objects of theoretical interest and empirical study for many early theorists or, as they are sometimes called in this work, proto-psychologists.

DISCUSSION QUESTIONS

1. Do you think that psychologists have more reason to study the history of their discipline than physicists or biologists? Is the history of psychology intrinsically more interesting because it is the history of attempts to attain a scientific understanding of our own mentality and behavior?

2. Could there be an internal contextualist history of psychology? Could there be an external presentist history of psychology? A history of psychology in terms of the prevailing zeitgeist is usually an external history, and a history of psychology in terms of the contributions of "great men" is usually internal. But must this be the case?

3. If a discipline is objective and advances causal explanations that are subject to systematic empirical evaluation, is that sufficient to constitute it as a scientific discipline? If not, what other features do you think are necessary?

4. Can you think of a psychological state or process that is not atomistic, not invariant in cultural space and historical time, and figures in causal explanations that are not universal?

5. Why do you think psychologists are so committed to experimentation? Should they be? Why do you think that social psychologists are so committed? Is experimentation especially suited to social psychology? Or especially problematic in social psychology?

GLOSSARY

a posteriori knowledge Knowledge based upon (after) experience.

a priori knowledge Knowledge independent of (prior to) experience.

atomism The principle that entities can be individuated and exist independently of other entities to which they may be related.

conceptual history A history of significant conceptual continuities and discontinuities in the development of a discipline.

contexualist history A history that attempts to explicate historical episodes and epochs neutrally in their own terms.

crucial instance/crucial experiment An empirical outcome enabling the adjudication of competing theories via their different predictions about the same empirical domain.

determinism The principle that there is a set of prior conditions sufficient for the production of any event, such that no other outcome is possible.

dogmatic empiricism The view that scientific theory and causal explanation are restricted to the description of the correlation of observables.

eliminative induction The method of eliminating competing causal hypotheses until only one viable hypothesis remains.

empiricist Someone who maintains that all knowledge is a posteriori, based upon experience.

epistemological question A question concerning our knowledge of reality. From the Greek *episteme*, meaning "knowledge."

explanatory reduction The principle that the best explanation of a complex entity, property, or process is given by an analysis of its material components.

external history A history of a discipline in terms of (external) social, economic, political, and cultural conditions.

falsifiability The characteristic of a scientific theory that allows it to be falsified by observation; also called testability. According to Popper, the falsifiability of scientific theories is what distinguishes science from pseudoscience.

great men history A history that ascribes major developments to the influence of individuals.

historiography The theory and methodology of history.

hypothetico-deductive method The method of postulating theories and testing them via their deductive or predictive implications.

inductive method The method of deriving theories from observations.

instrumentalism The view that scientific theories "about" unobservable entities are not potentially true descriptions of them, but merely linguistic devices that facilitate the prediction of the behavior of observable entities.

internal history A history of a discipline in terms of the development of theories and methods within the discipline.

materialism The view that ultimate reality is material.

meaning empiricism The doctrine that linguistic items derive their meaning by association with—or their definition in terms of—observable entities.

method of agreement The methodological principle that if instances of an effect have only one condition in common, then that condition is the cause of the effect.

method of concomitant variation The methodological principle that if one condition increases or decreases while an effect increases or decreases, that condition is the cause of the effect.

method of difference The methodological principle that if an instance in which an effect occurs and an instance in which it does not occur differ with respect to only one condition, then that condition is the cause, or an essential part of the cause, of the effect.

methodological empiricism The principle that requires that all scientific descriptions and explanations be subject to observational evaluation.

novel predictions Predictions that go beyond the established empirical data that theories are introduced to explain and whose confirmation plays a significant role in establishing the theories.

objectivity 1. A characteristic of propositions when their truth or falsity is determined by independent facts. 2. A characteristic of the theoretical judgments of scientists when they are unbiased, when they are based only upon empirical evaluation.

ontological invariance The principle that kinds of entities in a scientific domain can be re-identified in all regions of space and time.

ontological question A question concerning the fundamental nature of reality. From the Greek *ontos*, meaning "being."

operational definition A definition of the meaning of theoretical propositions in terms of observables.

presentist history A history in which a discipline is represented as approaching and approximating (idealized) contemporary theory and practice.

pseudoscience A discipline in which theoretical propositions are untestable or unfalsifiable.

psychological empiricism The doctrine that all concepts or ideas are derived from experience.

rationalist Someone who maintains that it is possible to have a priori knowledge, independently of experience, based upon reason.

realism The view that scientific theories about entities that are not observable are potentially true descriptions of them.

relational An entity is relational if it can be individuated and exist only in relation to other entities.

subjectivity A characteristic of the theoretical judgment of scientists when they are biased by individual or collective preferences or by social, political, or religious interests in the advocacy of certain theories.

universality of causal explanation The principle that one and the same causal explanation applies to every instance of a class of events, regularities, or structures.

zeitgeist history A history that ascribes major developments to the "spirit of the times."

REFERENCES

Altschule, M. D. (1965). Acedia: Its evolution from deadly sin to psychiatric syndrome. *British Journal of Psychiatry, 111,* 117–119.

Baldwin, J. M. (1913). *History of psychology.* New York: Putnam.

Berkowitz, L., & Le Page, A. (1968). Weapons as aggression-eliciting stimuli. *Journal of Personality and Social Psychology, 7,* 202–207.

Bhaskar, R. (1975). *A realist theory of science.* London: Leeds Books.

Boakes, R. (1984). *From Darwin to behaviorism: Psychology and the minds of animals.* Cambridge: Cambridge University Press.

Boring, E. G. (1929). *A history of experimental psychology.* New York: Century.

Boring, E. G. (1933). *The physical dimensions of consciousness.* New York: Century.

Brandt, L. W. (1970). American psychology. *American Psychologist, 25,* 1091–1093.

Brett, G. S. (1912–1921). *A history of psychology* (Vols. 1–3). London: Macmillan.

Buss, A. R. (1975). The emerging field of the sociology of psychological knowledge. *American Psychologist, 30,* 988–1002.

Chapanis, A. (1967). The relevance of laboratory studies to practical situations. *Ergonomics, 10,* 557–577.

Cohen, N. (1975). *Europe's inner demons.* London: Chatto/Heinemann.

Cronbach, L. J. (1957). The two disciplines of scientific psychology. *American Psychologist, 12,* 671–684.

Darwin, C. (1859). *On the origin of species by means of natural selection.* London: John Murray.

Doi, T. (1973). *The anatomy of dependence.* Tokyo: Kodansha International.

Festinger, L., Riecken, H. W., & Schachter, S. (1956). *When prophecy fails.* Minneapolis: University of Minnesota Press.

Findley-Jones, R. (1986). Accidie and melancholia in a clinical context. In R. Harré (Ed.), *The social construction of emotions.* Oxford: Blackwell.

Freud, S. (1950). Project for a scientific psychology. In J. Strachey (Ed. & Trans.), *The standard edition of the works of Sigmund Freud* (Vol. 1). London: Hogarth. (Original work published 1895)

Freud, S. (1957). The unconscious. In J. Strachey (Ed. & Trans.), *The standard edition of the works of Sigmund Freud* (Vol. 14). London: Hogarth. (Original work published 1915).

Furumoto, L. (1989). The new history of psychology. In I. S. Cohen (Ed.), *The G. Stanley Hall Lecture Series* (Vol. 9). Washington, DC: American Psychological Association.

Galileo, G. (1974). *Dialogues concerning two new sciences* (S. Drake, Trans.). Madison, WI: University of Wisconsin Press. (Original work published 1638)

Greenwood, J. D. (1994). *The disappearance of the social in American social psychology.* New York: Cambridge University Press.

Harré, R. (1981). *Great scientific experiments.* Oxford: Phaedon.

Hatfield, G. (1992). Descartes's physiology and its relation to his psychology. In J. Cottingham (Ed.), *The Cambridge companion to Descartes*. Cambridge: Cambridge University Press.

Hearnshaw, L. S. (1989). *The shaping of modern psychology: An historical introduction*. London: Routledge.

Heelas, P., & Lock, A. (Eds.). (1981). *Indigenous psychologies*. London: Academic Press.

Heinrichs, R. W. (2003). Historical origins of schizophrenia: Two early madmen and their illness. *Journal of the History of the Behavioral Sciences, 39,* 349–363.

Hempel, C. G. (1966). *Philosophy of natural science*. Englewood Cliffs, NJ: Prentice-Hall.

Herschel, J. (1830). A *preliminary discourse on the study of natural philosophy*. London: Longman, Rees, Orne, Brown & Green and John Taylor.

Hull, C. L. (1943). *Principles of behavior*. New York: Appleton-Century-Crofts.

Hume, D. (1973). *Treatise on human nature* (L. A. Selby-Bigge, Ed.). Oxford: Clarendon Press.

Hunt, M. (1994). *The story of psychology*. New York: Anchor Books.

Kendler, H. H. (1952). What is learned?—A theoretical blind alley. *Psychological Review, 59,* 269–277.

Kimble, G. A. (1989). Psychology from the point of view of a generalist. *American Psychologist, 44,* 491–499.

Kimble, G. A. (1995). Discussant's remarks: From chaos to coherence in psychology. *International Newsletter of Uninomic Psychology, 15,* 34–38.

Kirsch, I. (1978). Demonology and the rise of science: An example of the misperception of historical data. *Journal of the History of the Behavioral Sciences, 14,* 149–157.

Koch, S. (1992) Postscript. In S. Koch & D. E. Leary (Eds.), *A century of psychology as a science*. Washington, DC: American Psychological Association.

Logan, C. (2002). When scientific knowledge becomes scientific discovery: Classical conditioning before Pavlov. *Journal of the History of the Behavioral Sciences, 38,* 393–403.

Lutz, C. (1982). The domain of emotion words among the Ifaluk. *American Ethnologist, 9,* 113–128.

Macdougall, D. (1907). Hypothesis concerning soul substance together with experimental evidence of the existence of such substance. *American Medicine, 2,* 240–243.

Milgram, S. (1974). *Obedience to authority*. New York: Harper & Row.

Mill, J. S. (1843). *A system of logic, rationative and inductive, being a connected view of the principles of evidence, and the methods of scientific investigation*. London: Longmans, Green.

Moghaddam, F. M. (1987). Psychology in three worlds as reflected by the crisis in social psychology and the move toward indigenous third-world psychology. *American Psychologist, 42,* 912–920.

Piaget, J. (1926). *The language and thought of the child*. London: Routlege.

Popper, K. R. (1963). *Conjectures and refutations*. London: Routledge & Kegan Paul.

Reed, E. S. (1997). *From soul to mind*. New Haven, CT: Yale University Press.

Roach, M. (2003). *Stiff: The curious lives of human cadavers*. New York: Norton.

Rosenzweig, M. R. (1984). U.S. psychology and world psychology. *American Psychologist, 39,* 877–884.

Santayana, G. (1905). *The life of reason: Vol. 1. Reason in common sense*. New York: Scribner's.

Shepard, R. N. (1995). Mental universals: Towards a twenty-first century science of mind. In R. L. Solso & D. W. Massaro (Eds.), *The science of the mind: 2001 and beyond*. New York: Oxford University Press.

Shepard, R. N. (1987). Toward a universal law of generalization for psychological science. *Science, 237,* 1317–1323.

Smith, R. (1997). *The human sciences*. New York: Norton.

Spence, J. T. (1987). Centrifugal versus centripetal trends in psychology: Will the center hold? *American Psychologist, 42,* 1052–1054.

Staats, A. W. (1983). *Psychology's crisis of disunity: Philosophy and method for a unified science*. New York: Praeger.

Stocking, G. W. (1965). Editorial: On the limits of "presentism" and "historicism" in the historiography of the behavioral sciences. *Journal of the History of the Behavioral Sciences, 1,* 211–218.

van Strein, P. J. (1997). The American "colonization" of northwest European social psychology after World War II. *Journal of the History of the Behavioral Sciences, 33,* 349–363.

Watson, J. B. (1924). *Behaviorism*. New York: Norton.

Whewell, W. (1858). *Novum organum renovatum*. London: Parker.

Winston, A. S. (1990). Robert Sessions Woodworth and the "Columbia Bible": How the psychological experiment was redefined. *American Journal of Psychology, 103,* 391–401.

Winston, A. S., & Blais, D. J. (1996). What counts as an experiment?: A transdisciplinary analysis of textbooks, 1930–1970. *American Journal of Psychology, 109,* 599–616.

Woodward, W. R. (1987). Professionalization, rationality, and political linkages in twentieth-century psychology. In M. G. Ash & W. R. Woodward, (Eds.), *Psychology in twentieth century thought and society*. New York: Cambridge University Press.

Woodworth, R. S. (1938). *Experimental psychology*. New York: Holt.

Young, R. M. (1990). *Mind, brain and adaptation in the nineteenth century*. New York: Oxford University Press.

CHAPTER 2

Ancient Greek Science and Psychology

Folk

THE ORIGINS OF PSYCHOLOGICAL KNOWLEDGE MAY BE SAID TO BE AS old as humankind. From as early as recorded time, men and women have speculated about the nature and source of psychological states and processes and their relationship to human behavior. Theoretical reflections on sensation, memory, and dreaming, for example, are to be found in many ancient works, such as the Hindu sacred texts known as the Vedas (which precede the first millennium BCE) and the Assyrian "dream books" (from around the fifth millennium BCE).

Many early cultures, such as the Egyptian and Babylonian, tried to understand human psychology and behavior in terms of the activity of some immaterial "spirit" or "soul," usually intimately associated with breath and with the action of the heart and lungs. The Greek term *psyche*, from which the term *psychology* is derived, is etymologically tied to words signifying breath (*pneuma*) or wind (Onians, 1958). There is nothing especially remarkable about this. At a basic level of observation, it is obvious that whatever enables the human organism to act in a purposive fashion is intimately associated with the action of the heart and lungs. When activity in these organs ceases, so also does the activity of the human organism.

Many early theories that postulated immaterial spirits or souls also maintained that such entities could enjoy a life after death in some spiritual realm. However, not all early theories were committed to the notion of an afterlife, and for those that were, it was often an impoverished and literally shady sort of thing. In Greek mythology, for example, the dead survived as shadows of their former selves, which could only be temporarily revived via blood sacrifice.

Beliefs in immaterial spirits or souls are often characterized as **animistic** and are to be found in many so-called primitive cultures today. However, we should guard against the rather condescending assumption that all earlier cultures explained mind and behavior in terms of immaterial spirits or souls and that humans came to a proper understanding of these matters only with the development of psychological science, since such assumptions can seriously prejudice our approach to the history of psychology. Although many ancient thinkers did

30

embrace theories about immaterial spirits or souls, their psychological understanding was far more sophisticated—and materialistic—than is usually acknowledged. Indeed, as will be argued in this chapter, Aristotle's conception of mental states and processes as the functional capacities of complex material bodies approximates our contemporary cognitive psychological conception in critical respects.

This is not to presume the superiority of our contemporary cognitive psychology, which is a matter of lively contention, still less to maintain that modern conceptions of the psychological developed in tandem with historical advances in scientific methodology. On the contrary, as will be noted in later chapters, Aristotle's sophisticated conception of the psychological was one of the casualties of the scientific revolution in Europe during the 16th and 17th centuries.

GREEK SCIENCE

Although beliefs about mind and behavior are as old as humankind, systematic accounts only began to emerge with the development of theoretical science in ancient Greece. The origins of Greek science can be traced to earlier developments in Babylon, Egypt, and Phoenicia, where arithmetic, geometry, and astronomy flourished, and in India and China, where astronomy was well advanced by the second millennium BCE. Some time around the seventh century BCE, the Greeks exploited these developments to forge a mental set that we recognize as a precursor to scientific thinking. This involved a new level of abstract, critical, and speculative thought that within three centuries transformed the intellectual environment of the ancient world. The reasons why such protoscientific thought emerged in ancient Greece are obscure. Increased literacy, facilitated by the appropriation of the Phoenician alphabet, no doubt played a role, as did the unusually liberal (for the time) political structure of the federation of city-states that formed ancient Greece. However, such features seem insufficient in themselves to explain the intellectual revolution that the ancient Greeks produced. As Bertrand Russell once remarked, "nothing is so surprising or difficult to account for as the sudden rise of civilization in Greece" (1945, p. 3).

A distinctive feature of many early Greek thinkers was their rejection of supernatural or religious forms of explanation and their advocacy of naturalistic and mathematical forms of explanation. Yet early Greek "science" was largely speculative. It was loosely based upon empirical evidence and rarely based upon experimentation in the modern sense of manipulative intervention and control. One reason for this, which appears to have extended into the medieval period, is that the forms of intervention required for empirical studies in physics, chemistry, and biology were dismissed as "mechanical" or "servile" arts, suitable only for slaves,

mechanical activity demeaning

as opposed to "liberal arts" such as logic and rhetoric, the approved pursuits of freemen. The Greek historian Xenophon (c. 431–c. 355 BCE) epitomized this attitude: "The mechanical arts carry a social stigma, and are rightly dishonored in our cities."

Nonetheless, early Greek science was often directed to the explanation of puzzling empirical effects and occasionally did employ simple forms of manipulative experimentation, especially in medicine (Lloyd, 1964). The early Greeks advanced very general theories about the nature of reality that appeared to accommodate their sensory experience of the world. If their practice sometimes appears questionable, it is well to remember that they were just starting out. There was already a wealth of empirical effects to be explained, and experimentation was premature given the tentative nature of their theories.

Early Greek science was also critical only in a limited sense. Early Greek theorists offered their theories as speculative hypotheses and expected other theorists to offer alternative hypotheses. Although they offered arguments and analogies in support of their speculative hypotheses, only a few criticized the arguments of their opponents. The systematic criticism of arguments was a later Greek development pioneered by Socrates, Plato, and Aristotle, and the rigorous empirical testing of competing theories was a much later historical development.

However, in early Greek science we find the development of two broad theoretical perspectives that are important components of scientific thought. **Naturalism** is the view that the universe is best explained in terms of material elements and processes. **Formalism** is the view that the universe is best explained in term of formal or mathematical relations. These two perspectives, in conjunction with the later emphasis on the empirical and experimental evaluation of theories, constitute our modern conception of science.

While one should not exaggerate the degree to which these early Greek thinkers anticipated modern science, many of the conceptual features of their theoretical systems are common to modern scientific theories: for example, the exploratory and explanatory use of analogies and the assumption that all apparent change and development is ultimately the alteration of fundamental enduring elements, be they material particles or forms of energy. These early Greek thinkers also extended their theoretical systems to offer rudimentary explanations of biological development and psychological functioning.

Although the Greek term *psyche* is generally translated as "soul," the reader should guard against associations with the contemporary English term. The Greeks conceived of the **psyche** as the general principle of life in animate beings, which included but was not restricted to psychological capacities. The Greek psyche cannot be presumed to be immaterial in nature, like the enduring entities of religions committed to a spiritual afterlife. Although some Greek theorists did maintain that the psyche is immaterial and capable of surviving the destruction of the material body, others denied that this was the case.

THE NATURALISTS

Many early Greek thinkers tried to explain the workings of the universe in terms of its material elements and processes, as opposed to supernatural or religious explanations in terms of immaterial spirits or gods. They represented the beginning of the naturalistic or materialist tradition in science, which attempts to identify the fundamental elements of the natural world. The Greeks characterized the fundamental element as **physis**, and persons who developed systematic theories about the fundamental element (or elements) came to be known as *physicists*.

fundamental element
"
physis

Thales

Thales (c. 624–c. 546 BCE) of Miletus is generally considered to be the first major theorist in this tradition. He was the founder of what has come to be known as the **Ionian school**, because its principal advocates came from the Ionian federation of city-states, located in what is now the southwest coast of Turkey. Thales declared that the fundamental element is water. This was not an unreasonable speculation, since water can manifest itself as a liquid, solid (frozen), or gas (evaporated) and is essential to all forms of life. It seemed a plausible enough candidate for the basic element that composed all other complex entities.

Thales gained a reputation, common to many abstract thinkers, as a man with his head in the clouds. Aristotle recounts the story of how Thales walked into a well because he was so preoccupied with his study of the stars (Kirk, Raven, & Schofield, 1983, p. 80). Yet he was no ivory tower theorist. Using astronomical calculations to anticipate a record olive crop, he cornered the market in olive presses and made a small fortune leasing them out. He served as an army engineer and was famous in antiquity for having predicted an eclipse of the sun during a battle between the Medes and Lydians. He also is credited with having introduced geometry to ancient Greece, although much of his grounding in the subject was likely derived from his travels in Egypt and Babylon.

The distinguishing feature of Thales' thought was his introduction of abstract, critical, and speculative modes of theorizing. The theses he advanced were offered as hypotheses, not as religiously grounded dogmas. In this respect he may be said to have initiated the critical tradition of scientific thinking. Other Ionian theorists felt free to reject his speculations and to offer their own in critical competition.

Anaximenes

Anaximenes (c. 588–c. 524 BCE) of Miletus postulated that the fundamental element is air, possibly because he was impressed by the infinite malleability of air and the phenomenon of condensation. He developed his theory to explain some puzzling empirical effects, such as the fact that we blow slowly on our hands with an open mouth to warm them, but blow quickly on hot drinks with pursed lips to cool them (Barnes, 1979a, p. 49). Anaximenes accounted for these effects by claiming that properties such as temperature are a function of the density of the constitutive air: The rarefied air from our open mouths is warm, whereas the condensed air from our compressed lips is cooler.

Anaximenes was one of the first to offer explanations of the nature and properties of physical particulars in terms of modifications of an underlying primary element. He explained the nature and properties of clouds, rocks, and human bodies, for example, in terms of their composition by air of different densities, through the processes of rarefication and condensation. According to Anaximenes, rarefied air becomes fire; progressively condensed air becomes wind, then cloud, then water, stone, and so forth. He claimed that the earth itself was formed by the condensation of a vast mass of air, which is ever present in unlimited quantity, and that especially rarefied air constitutes the psyche of living beings. His rudimentary attempt to explicate differences in *qualitative* properties such as temperature and color in terms of *quantitative* properties such as density presaged the distinctively quantitative foundations of modern physical science.

Heraclitus

Heraclitus of Ephesus (c. 540–c. 480 BCE) declared that the fundamental element is fire (or firelike) and maintained that all physical particulars are modifications and alterations of the fundamental and enduring fiery element:

> This world neither any god nor man made; but it always was and is and will be, an ever-living fire, kindling in measures and being extinguished in measures.
>
> —(Barnes, 1979a, p. 61)

For Heraclitus, this included other "elements" such as water, air, and earth, as well as more complex physical particulars such as rocks, trees, animals, and planets. He maintained that condensed fire becomes moist and forms water; solidified water turns to earth; and so forth. The psyche of a human being is composed of fire: It comes from water and returns to water at death, except for a few particularly virtuous souls (such as soldiers slain in battle) who join the cosmic fire. Heraclitus characterized the dry psyche as healthy and the wet psyche as unhealthy: The drunken man behaves like a foolish boy because his psyche is moist.

Heraclitus was primarily concerned to explain the phenomenon of change. He maintained that the natural world is in constant flux, like the waters of a river:

> On those who step into the same rivers, different and different waters flow.
>
> —(Barnes, 1979a, p. 66)

We ordinarily distinguish between enduring physical particulars, such as stones and trees, and transient entities, such as rivers and clouds. However, Heraclitus maintained that the apparent stability and continuity of physical particulars is illusory, because everything is constantly changing:

> And some say not that some existing things are moving, and not others, but that all things are in motion all the time, but that this escapes our perception.
>
> —(Kirk, Raven, & Schofield, 1983, p. 195)

He claimed that the engine of flux is the constant strife or "war" between polar opposites such as hot and cold, wet and dry, and light and dark.

Heraclitus's fundamental vision of the natural world is now commonplace in scientific thought. We recognize that multiplicity and change underlie apparent unity and continuity: We believe that the solid oak chair is really constituted by a multiplicity of atoms (or atomistic wave-packets) and that the cells of our enduring bodies are continuously being replaced.

Empedocles

Empedocles (c. 495–c. 435 BCE) of Acragas denied that any of the four observable physical elements are more fundamental than any other and developed his theory of the "four elements" (Figure 2.1). He held that fire, air, earth, and water are the eternal and irreducible "roots" that constitute all physical particulars: Combined in one proportion they constitute bone, in another proportion they constitute blood, and so forth (Kirk, Raven, & Schofield, 1983, p. 302). He maintained that the processes of combination and dissolution of these elements are governed by the cosmic principles of love and strife, in a continuous cycle of change and development.

Like Heraclitus, Empedocles held that these basic elements and forces are eternal. They account for the creation, temporary endurance, and destruction of all physical

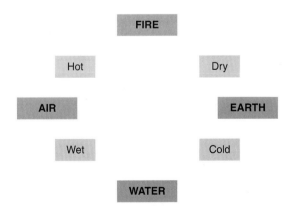

FIGURE 2.1   Empedocles: the four elements.

particulars, such as planets, oceans, and animals, which are merely the successive combination and separation of these basic elements in different proportions:

> Double is the birth of mortal things and double their failing; for the one is brought to birth and destroyed by the coming together of all things, the other is nurtured and flies apart as they grow apart again. And these things never cease their continual interchange, now through love all coming together into one, now again each carried apart by the hatred of strife.
>
> —(Kirk, Raven, & Schofield, 1983, p. 287)

Like Heraclitus and Anaximenes, Empedocles maintained that all apparent creation and destruction in the natural world is merely the alteration of the fundamental enduring elements of the material substratum: "insofar as they never cease their continual interchange, thus far they exist always changeless in the cycle" (Kirk, Raven, & Schofield, 1983, p. 287).

His theory was enormously influential, especially in medicine and psychology. Empedocles maintained that health consists of the proper balance of the four elements in our physical bodies and blood. The Greek and Roman physicians Hippocrates and Galen developed this account into the theory of physiological and psychological "humors," and similar principles of equilibrium or homeostasis are to be found in a great many later biological and psychological theories.

Empedocles held that blood contains the four elements in almost perfect combination and consequently identified blood as the medium of perception and thought. According to Empedocles, physical bodies emit effluences, or **eidola**, in the form of faint copies of themselves. Perception occurs when eidola enter the blood through the pores of the skin and their compositional elements match up with like elements in the blood (fiery elements of the eidola match up with fiery elements in the blood, and so forth), generating images in the heart:

> *Nourished in a sea of churning blood*
> *where what men call thought is especially found—*
> *for the blood about the heart is thought for men.*
> —(Barnes, 1987, p. 191)

In his account of the origin of animals and humans, Empedocles developed a rudimentary theory of evolution. He described how the parts of animals (constituted by the elements in different proportions) were originally combined in a random fashion, resulting in a variety of hybrid forms:

> But as one divine element mingled further with another, these things fell together as each chanced to meet other . . . , and many other things besides these were constantly resulting.

Many creatures were born with faces and breasts on both sides, man-faced ox-progeny, while others sprang forth as ox-headed offspring of man, creatures compounded partly of male, partly of the nature of female, and fitted with shadowy parts.

—(Kirk, Raven, & Schofield, 1983, p. 304)

Empedocles' theory anticipated some of the distinctive features of Darwin's later theory of evolution, such as the random mutation of biological forms described above (albeit fantastically). More significantly, as Aristotle clearly recognized, Empedocles provided an account of how "suitably formed" combinations that developed *by chance* would be naturally selected over time and produce adapted species that appeared, but *only* appeared, to have been purposely created:

Wherever, then, everything turned out as it would have if it were happening for a purpose, there the creatures survived, being accidentally compounded in a suitable way; but where this did not happen, the creatures perished and are perishing still, as Empedocles says of his "man-faced ox-progeny."

—(Kirk, Raven, & Schofield, 1983, p. 304)

Empedocles was acclaimed as a great thinker during his lifetime, attaining almost godlike status. He believed that the psyche was composed of all four elements, which could be recombined to constitute a different psyche in different generations (the principle of metempsychosis). Thus Empedocles believed that he had been different beings in his former lives:

> For already have I once been a boy and a girl
> And a bush and a bird and a silent fish in the sea.
> —(Barnes, 1987, p. 196)

The Atomists: Leucippus and Democritus

The theories of the Greek atomists Leucippus (c. 500–c. 450 BCE) and his disciple Democritus (c. 460–c. 370 BCE) represent the culmination of the naturalist tradition in early Greek thought. They maintained that the ultimate constituents or elements are "atoms and the void." Of Leucippus little is known, and most of what we know of Greek atomism is based upon the views attributed to his pupil Democritus. Democritus was called the "laughing philosopher," supposedly because he was so amused by human folly. According to a contested legend, he blinded himself in order to secure his happiness, in the belief that his blindness would eliminate his desire for women.

The Greek atomists maintained that atoms are solid particles that differ only in their properties: "some of them are scalene, some hooked, some hollow, some convex" (Barnes, 1979b, p. 41). They bind together on contact, through "overlappings and interlockings of the bodies" (Barnes, 1979b, p. 41). They are infinite, indivisible, and invisible, and their movements and bindings in the void are responsible for the creation and destruction of physical particulars:

> They move in the void . . . and when they come together they cause coming to be, and when they separate they cause perishing.
>
> —(Kirk, Raven, & Schofield, 1983, p. 407)

They held that the combination of atoms in empty space explains the properties of physical particulars. For example, they explained the different weights of different types of physical particulars in terms of their different densities and claimed that the celestial bodies were formed by the ignition of dense masses of atoms compressed into rapidly moving vortexes.

Democritus developed a theory of perception similar to Empedocles', based upon the atomic hypothesis. He claimed that thin films of atoms shaped in the form of physical bodies emanate from their surface. Our sense organs receive these eidola and interact with (highly mobile) fire atoms in our brain, which form copies of physical bodies. We perceive physical bodies and their properties when similar arrangements of atoms form in our sense organs and brain. Democritus maintained that the psyche is itself composed of fine fiery atoms, which are dispersed with the dissolution of the living body.

Like Empedocles and Heraclitus, the Greek atomists claimed that all perceived creation and destruction in the natural world is merely the alteration of the fundamental and enduring elements of the material substratum and that complexity and change underlie the apparent unity and stability of physical particulars. However, they went one step further, anticipating a distinctive feature of modern science.

Most Greek naturalists accepted the perceived properties of physical particulars at face value and attempted to explain them in terms of the arrangement and alteration of their fundamental material components. They maintained that our senses do not reveal the fundamental nature of reality, but they did not generally deny the reality of the empirical appearances they tried to explain. However, the Greek atomists claimed that many of the perceived properties of physical particulars are not genuine properties but are only their effects on our sense organs and nervous systems.

They made a distinction between those properties that physical particulars have independently of our perception of them, such as size, shape, and motion, and those "properties" that are merely the effects they produce in the sense organs and nervous systems of sentient beings, such as color, taste, and smell. Consequently, they maintained that while there are atoms with shapes, sizes, and motions in the void, there are strictly speaking no colors, smells, tastes, sounds, or textures. Democritus famously maintained that

> By convention sweet and by convention bitter, by convention hot, by convention cold, by convention color: in reality atoms and void.
>
> —(Barnes, 1987, p. 253)

This distinction between what later came to be known as **primary qualities** and **secondary qualities** was made by most of the pioneers of the scientific revolution in Europe in the 16th and 17th centuries. Like these later scientists, the Greek atomists explained the generation of secondary qualities such as taste as a causal product of the primary qualities of atoms, such as their shape and size:

> Sour taste comes from shapes that are large and multi-angular and have very little roundness; for these, when they enter the body, clog and bind the veins and prevent their flowing. . . . Bitter taste comes from small, smooth, rounded shapes whose periphery does have joints; that is why it is viscous and adhesive.
>
> —(Barnes, 1979b, p. 71)

The Greek atomists also maintained that the universe is governed by rigidly deterministic laws. Whatever happens in the natural world is determined by natural necessity, as an inevitable consequence of the arrangements and motions of the constituent atoms. There is no room for randomness or choice in the purely mechanistic universe of the Greek atomists: There are only atoms and the void. Still, Democritus was no fatalist. He maintained that happiness is the goal of life, which is best attained through self-control and moderation, including the general avoidance of the pleasures of the flesh: "For men gain contentment from moderation in joy and a measured life" (Barnes, 1987, p. 269). Epicurus (341–271 BCE) later developed this sophisticated form of hedonism, although the position now popularly known as epicureanism bears little relation to the doctrines of either, being commonly associated with the maximal satisfaction of sensual desires.

THE FORMALISTS

Although the early Greek naturalists generally accepted the evidence of sense experience, they gradually came to conceive of theoretical knowledge as the discernment of the underlying reality beyond or "behind" sensory appearances. A similar notion seems to have motivated many of the theorists of the formalist schools developed by Parmenides (b. c. 515 BCE) and Pythagoras (b. c. 570 BCE), who were more deeply skeptical of our sense experience of the world. According to these formalist theorists, the changing world of sense experience is illusory, and

The natural philosopher discovers the reality beyond sensory appearances. *The Heavens.* Camille Flammarion. From *L'atmosphére metorologie populaire,* 1898, in the style of the 1500s, woodcut.

the changeless reality beyond or "behind" sensory appearances can be grasped only by reasoning and logic. Formalist theories were based mainly upon logical deduction and argument, in contrast to the empirical puzzles and theoretical analogies exploited by naturalists.

Parmenides

Many formalists denied the reality of change. According to Parmenides of Elea, reality is unitary, unchanging, motionless, indivisible, and eternal. In his extended poem *On Nature*, he claimed that we can deduce that reality is an eternal unity:

> . . . *that being, it is ungenerated and undestroyed,*
> *whole, of one kind and motionless, and balanced.*

Nor was it ever, nor will it be; since now it is, all together,
one, continuous.

—(Barnes, 1979a, p. 178)

Parmenides contrasted the "way of truth" with the "way of opinion," the way reality appears to our sense experience, as a created multiplicity of moving, changing objects.

Parmenides was acutely conscious of the conflict between reason and sense experience and maintained that sense experience is illusory. He claimed that the perfect, eternal, and unchanging intelligible world, unlike the imperfect, temporary, and changing sensible world, can be known only through the exercise of reason, which gets us to the reality beyond or "behind" sensory appearances. Parmenides is often credited with the development of the **dialectic method**: the systematic exploration of arguments for and against opposing positions. He was the primary theorist of what came to be known as the **Eleatic school**, so-called because its members came from Elea, a Greek settlement in southern Italy. Other members of the school included Zeno of Elea (b. c. 490 BCE) and Xenophanes (b. c. 570 BCE), who famously ridiculed the petty foibles and frailties of the Greek gods.

Since Parmenides maintained that reality is unchanging, he is often characterized as a theorist of *being*, in contrast to Heraclitus, who maintained that reality is constantly changing and who is often characterized as a theorist of *becoming*; the contrast between their theories is often referred to as the debate between **being vs. becoming**.

Zeno of Elea

Zeno of Elea developed a famous series of arguments in support of the Parmenidian position. These arguments were designed to demonstrate the illusory nature of sense experience and commonsense assumptions about multiplicity and change based upon it. According to Plato, Zeno tried to protect the Parmenidian "affirmation of the one" from critical ridicule by demonstrating that the "hypothesis of the existence of many, if carried out, appears to be still more ridiculous than the hypothesis of the existence of one" (Barnes, 1979a, p. 233).

Zeno advanced a number of **reductio ad absurdum** arguments, which purport to demonstrate the falsity of commonsense assumptions about multiplicity, change, and motion by demonstrating that they lead to false or absurd consequences. The most famous of these, commonly known as Zeno's paradoxes, purport to demonstrate the illusory nature of motion. The best known is the tale of the race between Achilles and the tortoise, who is given a head start because he cannot move as fast as Achilles. Whenever Achilles reaches the tortoise's starting point, the tortoise has moved on to another point; whenever Achilles reaches that point, the tortoise has moved on to another; so Achilles can never catch up with the tortoise. As Aristotle put it:

> This says that the slow will never be caught in running by the fastest. For the pursuer must first get to where the pursued started from, so that it is necessary that the slower should always be some distance ahead.
>
> —(Barnes, 1979a, p. 273)

Pythagoras

Parmenides, Zeno, and other members of the Eleatic school maintained that theoretical understanding could be attained only through abstract reasoning. Pythagoras (c. 572–497 BCE) and his followers agreed, but went one step further and maintained that ultimate reality *is itself abstract in nature*, being constituted by mathematical harmonies and ratios. They maintained that the illusory world of sense experience is merely the manifestation of fundamental mathematical harmonies and ratios. In contrast to the naturalists, who sought theoretical understanding of the basic material constituents of the universe, the Pythagoreans sought understanding of its basic formal principles.

Pythagoras formulated ontological and epistemological distinctions between the abstract objects of mathematics and logic and the concrete physical particulars of the natural world that are the objects of sense experience. He claimed that mathematical and logical relations are perfect, eternal relations that exist independently of physical particulars and that knowledge of the abstract truths of mathematics and logic can be attained directly through the exercise of pure reason, independently of sense experience. For example, it is eternally true that the angles of a triangle add up to 180°, whether or not any physical triangles have ever existed or been perceived by sentient beings. Moreover, this truth can be known (at least in principle) by a rational being without any sense experience of physical triangles. In contrast, the objects of sense experience, which are subject to creation, destruction, and change, are imperfect and cannot be truly known. Pythagoras's distinction between the "intelligible" and the "sensible" worlds exerted a powerful influence on many later thinkers, including Plato.

Pythagoras was a **dualist**, who maintained that mind and body are distinct entities. He distinguished between the immortal psyche, which can rationally apprehend the intelligible world, and the corruptible material body in which it is temporarily imprisoned. This conception of the relation between the psyche and the material body, which likely had its origins in the mystery religions of Greece and Egypt, influenced many ancient and medieval theorists, such as Plato, Plotinus, Saint Augustine, and Avicenna.

Pythagoras and his followers made major contributions to mathematics, astronomy, and physics. They formulated the basic principles of arithmetic and geometry later described in Euclid's *Elements*. Pythagoras explained the formation of the universe in mathematical terms, as an imposition of limit on the limitless, and one of his followers Philolaus is reputed to have been one of the first to conceive of Earth as a moving planet. Pythagoras is also credited with the discovery of the musical scale, by developing a set of mathematical laws describing the harmonic ratios of vibrating strings of different lengths. This latter achievement seems to have inspired his view that everything in the universe can be explained in terms of the principles of mathematical harmony.

Pythagoras was a charismatic leader. The school he founded, while dedicated to the study of mathematical harmonies and ratios, was as much a moral as an intellectual brotherhood. His rational depreciation of the sensible world and sense experience was matched by a moral depreciation of the material body and sensual pleasure. Pythagoras and his followers believed in the immortality and transmigration of the psyche. According to Pythagoras, each human psyche is possessed of its own divinity and goes through cycles of rebirth in vegetable, animal, and human form, which it can remember. Release from the bodily prison and cycle of rebirth can be attained only by the purification of the psyche through rational contemplation of the intelligible world, by which it may attain eventual union with the "world soul."

Pythagoras and his followers repudiated the sensual pleasures of the material body, and committed themselves to an ethic of abstinence and self-discipline. This included the prohibition of meat or beans, since both might include transmigrated souls, and adoption of various measures designed to liberate the psyche from its bodily prison. Their conception of the body as a temporary prison subject to physical and moral decay through age and sensual corruption exerted a powerful influence in the following centuries, most notably on early Christian theology.

Pythagoras and his followers took their commitment to mathematical harmony to mystical extremes. They associated justice with the number four and reason with the number one; and they reputedly drowned Hippasus of Metapontum, a fellow Pythagorean, because of his discovery of irrational numbers (Blackburn, 1996, p. 173). Nonetheless, the Pythagorean school marks the beginning of the mathematical tradition that inspired Galileo to characterize mathematics as the language of science, Kepler to try to compose the "harmony of the celestial spheres" based upon the geometry of the regular solids, and Newton to spend much of his life working on the numerology of the biblical Book of Daniel.

Although Pythagoras treated the psyche as an entity capable of surviving bodily death, he identified the brain as the bodily organ of thought. He also developed an account of physical and psychological health based upon the harmonious blending of bodily elements. Since Pythagoras maintained that physical and psychological disorders derived from the disruption of bodily harmony, his recommended treatments were designed to restore harmony and included regulated diet, exercise, and music. Empedocles' treatment of health as harmony between the "four elements" was likely based upon the Pythagorean account.

THE PHYSICIANS

Early Greek medicine was based upon religious mysteries and practiced by temple priests who kept the secrets of Asclepius, the Greek god of medicine. Treatments consisted largely of sleep, suggestion, diet, and exercise. These forms of **temple medicine** were challenged by the schools of Alcmaeon and Hippocrates, who rejected religious beliefs and mystical practices in favor of naturalistic theories and treatments based upon observation (however rudimentary).

Alcmaeon

Alcmaeon (fl. c. 500 BCE) founded a school of medicine in Croton, in southern Italy, but rejected the theory and practice of temple medicine. He established that the brain is the center of perception and cognition: He dissected the human eye and brain and traced the optic nerves from the retina to the brain (Lloyd, 1991). Alcmaeon also developed the influential theory of **animal spirits**, conceived of as the material carriers of nerve impulses.

Alcmaeon rejected mystical and religious medical accounts and advanced a theory of health and disease based upon the properties associated with the four elements of Empedocles, such as hot and cold, dry and moist, and so forth. He claimed that health consists of the proper balance of these properties and that disease is caused by imbalance. Since an excess of heat causes fever, it should be treated by cooling the patient; since an excess of dryness causes dehydration, it should be treated by increasing the intake of liquids. Alcmaeon believed that extremes of the elemental properties are the cause of death.

Hippocrates

Hippocrates (c. 460–377 BCE), who is often called the father of medicine, was born on the Greek island of Cos, off the coast of modern Turkey. He studied at the great center of temple medicine there, but founded his own medical school when he later came to reject temple medicine and attained a celebrated reputation as a healer and teacher. Only a few of the medical writings attributed to Hippocrates, the *Corpus Hippocraticum*, were probably written by him, so it is hard to distinguish his individual contribution from those of his followers. Accordingly, it is best to treat him as the representative leader and spokesman of the medical school of Cos.

Like Alcmaeon, Hippocrates claimed that the brain is the center of psychological capacities:

It ought to be generally known that the source of our pleasure, merriment, laughter and amusement, as of our grief, pain, anxiety and tears is none other than the brain . . . it is the brain too which is the seat of madness and delirium.

—(Lloyd, 1983, p. 248)

He maintained that epilepsy, the so-called sacred disease, is a disorder of brain function and that popular explanations in terms of divine possession are pseudo-explanations grounded in ignorance:

I do not believe that the "Sacred Disease" is any more divine or sacred than any other disease, but, on the contrary, has specific characteristics and a definite cause. . . . It is my opinion that those who first called this disease "sacred" were the sort of people we now call witch-doctors, faith-healers, quacks and charlatans. . . . By invoking a divine element they were able to screen their own failure to give suitable treatment and so called this a "sacred" malady to conceal their ignorance of its nature.

—(Lloyd, 1983, pp. 237–238)

Hippocrates developed Alcmaeon's conception of health as balance into the influential theory of the **four humors**—yellow bile, blood, black bile, and phlegm—supposedly formed from the four elements postulated by Empedocles (Figure 2.2). According to this theory, yellow bile is formed from fire, blood from air, black bile from earth, and phlegm from water. According to Hippocrates, health derives from the proper balance of these humors, and disease from their imbalance:

Health is primarily that state in which these constituent substances are in the correct proportion to each other, both in strength and quantity, and are well mixed. Pain

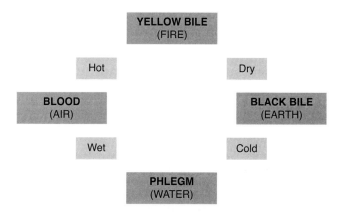

FIGURE 2.2 Hippocrates: the four humors.

occurs when one of the substances presents either a deficiency or an excess, or is separated in the body and not mixed with the others.

—(Lloyd, 1983, p. 262)

Consequently Hippocrates recommended treatments designed to restore humoral balance, such as appropriate diet, rest, exercise, bathing, massage, and laughter.

Hippocrates is often characterized as an early practitioner of **holistic medicine**, because he emphasized the natural healing power of the body and the need to treat physical and psychological disorders as disorders of the whole body. However, he was not averse to medical intervention. He recommended trepanning for the relief of brain tumors and bloodletting to treat disorders supposedly caused by an excess of blood, a popular medical practice that continued until the 18th century. Hippocrates also recognized that physical and psychological diseases and disorders could sometimes be relieved through mere faith in the competence and commitment of the physician (see Frank, 1973, for a modern account):

For some patients though conscious that their condition is perilous, recover their health simply through their contentment with the goodness of the physician.

—(Jones, 1923, p. 319)

Hippocrates' accounts of physical and psychological disease and disorder are remarkable in their diagnostic detail. In the *Art of Healing,* he provided extensive descriptions of arthritis, epilepsy, mumps, and tuberculosis and of paranoia, phobia, depression, mania, and hysteria. On the basis of his studies of brain damage and paralysis, he established the contralateral control of the body by the hemispheres of the brain.

Hippocrates and his followers developed a code of ethics for physicians, now known as the Hippocratic oath, which contemporary physicians vow to follow. This includes the injunction not to refuse treatment to patients who cannot afford to pay for it and to decline payment for the treatment of patients in financial straits.

THE PHILOSOPHERS

As Greece and Athens entered their "golden age," many thinkers came to reflect on the epistemological foundations of naturalism and formalism. In an intellectual arena in which competing theories were supported by arguments, skill in argumentation came to be appreciated and valued for its own sake.

The **Sophists** were professional teachers of rhetoric and logic, who charged their students for instruction in the art of persuasion. They were skeptical about the possibility of human knowledge, although they also professed it for a fee. The term *Sophist* was originally applied to any wise man, but it acquired negative connotations when Plato caricatured some Sophists as money-grabbing charlatans. Yet they offered practical advice as well as instruction in argument. For example, Antiphon is reputed to have offered an early form of "verbal" psychotherapy based upon interactive dialogue to those suffering from grief and melancholy (Pivnicki, 1969; Walker, 1991).

They also raised troubling questions about claims to knowledge of the natural world based upon sense experience. Protagoras of Abdera (c. 490–c. 420 BCE) based his claim that "Of all things man is the measure" (Barnes, 1979b, p. 239) upon the variability of sense experience: What seems cold or loud to one person may seem warm or quiet to another person, or to the same person at a later time. His intent may have been only to affirm the authority of immediate sense experience, but he is commonly taken to have advocated a form of **relativism**, according to which what is true is relative to what any individual perceives or judges to be the case. Gorgias of Leontini (c. 485–380 BCE) argued that we could not have knowledge of anything beyond or "behind" sense experience. It was against such forms of relativism and skepticism that Socrates and Plato advanced their accounts of objective knowledge.

Socrates

Socrates (c. 469–399 BCE) gave Western philosophy its distinctive focus on the critical analysis of concepts and arguments. His single-minded commitment to the pursuit of wisdom is best exemplified by his famous claim that "the unexamined life is not worth living." Apart from short periods of military service and occasional work as a stonemason, he devoted his life to philosophical disputation with the Sophists, his aristocratic friends, and the people of Athens. Indifferent to fame and fortune, he accepted no fees for his teaching, since he professed not to know anything worthwhile. In 399 BCE he was charged with corrupting the Athenian youth. His consequent trial, imprisonment, and death are movingly described in Plato's *Apology, Crito,* and *Phaedo.*

Socrates focused on ethical questions and taught that virtue is knowledge. He tried to discover the objective essence of courage, justice, knowledge, and virtue through critical examination of proposed definitions in terms of properties common to all their instances. For example, in *Theaetetus,* Plato has him defining knowledge in terms of justified true belief. His method of critical examination has come to be known as the Socratic method.

Plato

Plato (429–347 BCE) was born in Athens of an aristocratic family. His disgust with the politics of his day reputedly led him to conclude that only philosophers are fit to rule, a position that he defended at length in the *Republic.* After the death of his teacher Socrates, Plato traveled extensively. He returned to Athens and founded his Academy in 387 BCE; he enjoyed a successful career as a teacher until his death at the age of 82.

Many of Plato's doctrines were developments of Pythagorean theory. He was a dualist who believed that the psyche is an immortal and immaterial entity temporarily imprisoned in a material body, and he claimed that true knowledge can be attained only when the purified psyche surmounts the corruption of the material body (through self-discipline or death). In the *Republic*, Plato maintained that justice or well-being in the individual and the state is founded upon the harmony of the parts of the hierarchic and tripartite psyche, comprising reason, passion, and appetite. Psychological harmony is achieved when reason controls the passions and appetites; psychological disorder and immorality result when the passions and appetites gain control. In his description of the conflict between reason and the passions and appetites, Plato anticipated the later Freudian contrast between the rational and irrational elements of human personality (Simon, 1972).

Like Pythagoras, Plato distinguished between the intelligible and sensible worlds. He claimed that the abstract forms or ideas elicited via the Socratic method of critical examination are more real than the concrete physical particulars supposedly revealed through sense experience. According to Plato's **theory of Forms**, such abstract ideas are perfect, eternal, and unchanging, in contrast to imperfect, transient, and changing physical particulars. Plato maintained that physical particulars are imperfect copies of the Forms and exist only via derivative "participation" in them. Consequently he distinguished genuine knowledge (*episteme*) derived from rational apprehension of the Forms from mere belief or opinion (*doxa*) based upon sense experience.

In maintaining that knowledge of the Forms can be attained through the exercise of reason independently of sense experience, Plato defended a nativist conception of knowledge based upon the Pythagorean doctrine of the transmigration of the psyche. According to Plato's **theory of recollection**, all knowledge is remembrance of knowledge possessed by the immortal psyche, but temporarily forgotten with each cycle of reincarnation. In a famous passage in the *Meno*, Plato described how Socrates managed to elicit innate knowledge of geometry from an untutored slave boy.

Like Socrates, Plato was grappling with the threats posed to objective knowledge by the relativism and skepticism of the Sophists. Yet his own solution was almost as bad as the original relativist and skeptical threats. The notion that sense experience is illusory and impedes the attainment of genuine knowledge through pure exercise of the intellect cast a dead hand on the development of scientific reasoning in the ensuing centuries, particularly when it was taken up by the early Christian Church fathers.

ARISTOTLE: THE SCIENCE OF THE PSYCHE

Aristotle (384–322 BCE) was born in Macedonia, the son of a royal physician. He entered Plato's Academy at the age of 17 and remained there until Plato's death. After a period of traveling, during which he married and served as tutor to the young Alexander the Great (from 343–340 BCE), he returned to Athens in 335 BCE and founded his own school, the Lyceum. There he instituted research on a wide variety of subjects and created the first great library of antiquity. After the death of Alexander the Great in 323 BCE, Aristotle felt obliged to retire to Chalcis because of the level of anti-Macedonian feeling, lest Athens "sin twice against philosophy" (the first sin being the trial and execution of Socrates). He died a year later.

Aristotle's theoretical contributions range across a wide variety of subjects and cover most of the sciences known in his day (although some parts of his extensive body of work are attributed to his Lyceum students). His theory of the syllogism provided the justificatory basis of logical inference until the late 19th century, when its limitations were finally realized. He was the first Greek theorist to devote a whole work to psychology (*De Anima*), although his psychological contributions range across a variety of works, such as *On Memory*, *On Dreams*, and *Nicomachean Ethics*. He was also the first theorist to reflect critically on the nature of psychological explanation, and the subtlety and sophistication of his account has scarcely been rivaled since.

Yet what was distinctive about Aristotle, and what distinguished him from early naturalists and formalists, was his strong empirical bent. His researches in biology, for example, were based upon a wealth of careful observations of the flora and fauna of the natural world. His detailed descriptions of the embryology of the chick in the *History of Animals*, which were based upon his dissection of eggs and embryos at different stages of incubation, took the subject pretty much as far as it could be taken prior to the development of the microscope.

Aristotle was not afraid to get his hands dirty and was a great collector of biological specimens. According to legend, he spent most of his honeymoon extending his collection of seashells. He got many things wildly wrong, although he usually had some reason for adopting the views he did. We may scoff at Aristotle's belief that the heart rather than the brain is the organ of perception and cognition. Yet it was based upon his observation that the heart is the first organ to manifest activity in the embryological development of the chick and that humans and other animals recover with greater frequency from wounds to the head than wounds to the heart. More important, Aristotle kept an open mind on most theoretical matters. He emphasized that his own theoretical contributions were provisional and based upon the limited development of the sciences of his day and that the last court of appeal for any theory was observation. For example, in discussing the generation (procreation) of bees in the *Generation of Animals* (III, 760b29–33), he qualified his tentative theoretical claims:

> Such appears to be the truth about the generation of bees, judging from theory and from what are believed to be the facts about them; the facts, however, have not yet been sufficiently grasped; if ever they are, then credit must be given rather to observation than to theories, and to theories only if what they affirm agrees with the observed facts.[1]

Theoretical Science

For Aristotle, the goal of theoretical science was the classification of substances and explanation of their properties. He claimed that essential form (*morphe*) constitutes matter (*hule*) as particular substances—a doctrine known as **hylomorphism** (Jager & VanHoorn, 1972). For Aristotle, matter is the basic constituent of all substances, which are individuated as distinct substances—as individual frogs as opposed to individual roses, for example—by their essential form. Thus a rose is matter in the form of a rose; a frog is matter in the form of a frog; a human being is matter in the form of a human being, and so forth.

Aristotle held that the essential form of a substance is only conceptually distinct from its matter. Although the different forms of different types of substances can be identified and distinguished, they do not and cannot exist independently of matter. Plato had maintained that forms exist as autonomous abstract particulars in a realm of ideas, which can be apprehended only through pure reason. In contrast, Aristotle held that forms exist only as the forms of matter. For example, sphericality (the essential property of spheres) can be conceptually distinguished from cubicality (the essential property of cubes), but only exists as the sphericality of materially instantiated substances. Aristotle also claimed that knowledge of forms could be gained only through sense experience, by abstraction from the perceived common properties of classes of substances, such as roses, frogs, and human beings. He consequently denied that we have innate knowledge of common properties or **universals**.

Aristotle also distinguished between potentiality and actuality. He accounted for all change in nature in terms of the process of **entelechy**, by which what is merely potential becomes actual through the realization of its form. This conception of change as a process in which determinate potentiality becomes actualized was best suited to the explanation of biological development, in which what is potentially an oak, an acorn, becomes an oak; what is potentially a chick, an embryo, becomes a chick; and what is potentially an adult human being, a

---

[1]All quotations from Aristotle are from Barnes (1995).

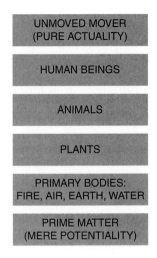

FIGURE 2.3   Aristotle: the scala naturae.

neonate, becomes an adult human being. However, Aristotle also extended this account to other natural changes, such as changes in the motion of physical bodies.

Aristotle represented nature as a hierarchically structured order of existents, or **scala naturae**, in which simpler forms of being, or formed matter, serve as the matter for higher forms of being, such as plants and animals (Figure 2.3). At the bottom of the scale is prime matter: It has the potential for form, but in its unformed state is mere potentiality. The simplest types of formed matter or substances, the primary bodies, are the four elements identified by earlier Greek physicists: fire, air, earth, and water. These combine in successively more complex forms to constitute inanimate bodies and living organisms such as plants, animals, and human beings, organized according to genus and species. At the very top of the scale is the **unmoved mover,** or pure actuality, which is responsible for the realization of all things and whose form does not itself require material instantiation. This hierarchical conception of nature as a **great chain of being** (Lovejoy, 1936) exerted a powerful influence on later theorists and served as the foundation of most systems of biological classification until the 18th century.

Aristotle placed human beings at the midpoint of the scala naturae and placed Earth at the center of the universe. According to Aristotle's geocentric (Earth-centered) theory, the sun and other planets traverse concentric orbits around Earth. Aristotle postulated a set of hollow and transparent crystalline spheres that carry the planets in their constant circular orbits. The outermost sphere, the celestial sphere, carries the fixed stars and marks the finite boundary of the universe. Aristotle claimed that celestial objects, unlike objects in the sublunar region that are composed of fire, air, earth, and water, do not undergo substantive change and are composed of a fifth element, which he called the ether.

Aristotle claimed that scientific knowledge is knowledge of first principles, which he held to be necessary truths. He believed that scientific knowledge is originally based upon generalization from observed instances, or **induction by enumeration**; for example, we come to know that "all ruminants with cloven hooves are animals with missing incisor teeth" on the basis of observing instances of ruminants with cloven hooves that have missing incisor teeth. However, he maintained that knowledge of substantial forms is based upon the direct rational intuition of first principles, which enables humans to discriminate the essential from the accidental properties of substances (Losee, 1980). Essential properties of substances are those properties that members of a class must have in order to count as members of that class; accidental properties are properties that members of a class happen to have, but need not have in order to be members of that class. For example, sentience and rationality are essential properties of human beings, whereas differences in their complexion are accidental properties.

Causality and Teleology

Aristotle distinguished four types of causality, which he claimed play a role in the explanation of all existents in the natural world. The **material cause** of an existent is the material in which it is realized. The material cause of a statue of Zeus would be the marble or bronze from which it is created. The **formal cause** of an existent is its essential form, which distinguishes this type of existent from all others. The formal cause of a statue of Zeus would be the structure or shape of the statue, sculpted in the image of Zeus. The **efficient cause** of an existent is the agency responsible for its generation. The efficient cause of a statue of Zeus would be the artist who created it. The **final cause** of an existent is the end or function or purpose for which it exists. The final cause of a statue of Zeus could be the glorification of the gods. Although the preceding example is useful for illustrative purposes, Aristotle maintained that the **four causes** are only distinct in the case of artifacts such as statues. In the case of all other natural existents, the formal cause is also the efficient and final cause.

Modern conceptions of causality tend to equate causality with efficient causality: that is, with conditions sufficient to bring about an effect. Contemporary scientists continue to employ material and formal causal explanations, insofar as they explain the powers and properties of chemical compounds and biological organisms in terms of their composition and structure, but have abandoned final causal explanations in physical and biological science. One of the distinctive features of the scientific revolution in Europe in the 16th and 17th centuries was the rejection of final causal explanations in favor of efficient causal explanations in physics and medicine. Yet Aristotle's science was a comprehensively **teleological science**, in which all natural processes were explained in terms of an ascribed end or goal state (*telos*).

To get the flavor of this, consider how an explanation of photosynthesis in plants might proceed in terms of Aristotle's four causes. We might say that the material cause of photosynthesis is the organic molecules out of which plants are composed. We might say that the formal cause of photosynthesis is the biological structure that distinguishes plants from other types of entities (including the fact that they contain the enzyme chlorophyll), which explains their ability to perform photosynthesis. We might say that the efficient cause of photosynthesis is the action of sunlight on plants, which, given their composition and structure, is sufficient for photosynthesis. And we might say that the final cause of photosynthesis, its end state or function or purpose, is the maintenance of atmospheric oxygen, which sustains those life forms that depend upon oxygen.

Now the material, formal, and efficient causal components of this complex explanation are relatively unproblematic. They map easily onto contemporary forms of explanation in chemistry and biology, which specify enabling and stimulus conditions that are jointly sufficient for an effect or process. However, the last component, the final cause, is alien to modern science, which would treat references to the end or function or purpose of photosynthesis as redundant from the point of view of scientific explanation. Modern biologists would insist that while it is a fortunate consequence for humans and other oxygen-dependent species that photosynthesis contributes to the maintenance of atmospheric oxygen, this is nothing more than a fortuitous effect: It is not the end or function or purpose of anything or anyone.

Similarly, post-Darwinian biologists dismiss explanatory references to the function of the human eye or the long neck of the giraffe. They maintain that the human eye and the giraffe's neck have no function or purpose in themselves, and that their existence can be exhaustively explained in terms of the survival advantages conferred upon organisms possessing them in particular environments. Although modern biologists retain talk of functions as an informal convenience, they hold that such talk can be eliminated from biology without any loss of scientific insight.

Yet Aristotle maintained that all existents have ends or functions or purposes. For Aristotle, this was as true of the motion of physical bodies as it was for biological processes and human behavior. He explained "natural" motion in terms of the "natural resting place" of each of the primary bodies, to which they move when unopposed: Earth moves to the center; and water, air, and fire move to successive spheres about the center (he explained "unnatural motion" in terms of impressed forces). Aristotle maintained that the scala naturae is purposively ordered, with every existent having its fixed place and function, and rejected the evolutionary theory of Empedocles.

Aristotle treated natural processes as **intrinsically teleological**, since he maintained that the ends or purposes are inherent in the processes themselves. Later generations of Christian and Islamic scholars treated them as **extrinsically tele-ological**, as a product of the ends or purposes of separate beings, such as a super-natural God conceived of as the intelligent designer of the natural world. Yet this formed no part of Aristotle's account. His commitment to teleological science was not a product of his commitment to a belief about intelligent creation, but a gen-eralization of his belief in the inherent directionality of biological development.

Aristotle's Psychology

The basic principles of Aristotle's psychology were developed in *De Anima* ("on the soul"), and are the product of the application of his causal schema to human beings. According to Aristotle, the psyche is the formal cause of a human being, the set of functional properties that constitute certain substances as human beings. The material cause of human beings is the organized organic material out of which they are composed. According to the principle of entelechy, the psyche is the actuality of a material body that potentially has life: It actualizes the potential of the human body to be the living creature that is a human being. As Aristotle put it, the psyche is "the form of a natural body having life potentially within it" (*De Anima*, II, 1, 412a20–21). As in the case of other natural existents, the formal cause of human beings, the psyche, is also their efficient and final cause. Aristotle likened the functional properties that constitute the psyche of a human being to the capacity for sight that is the function of the eye: "Suppose that the eye were an animal—sight would have been its soul" (*De Anima*, II, 1, 412b18–19).

Aristotle claimed that plants and animals also have a psyche, ordered according to the hierarchical scale of nature. At the lowest level, there is the **nutritive psy-che**, the essence of plants, which serves the functions of growth, self-maintenance through nutrition, and reproduction. The **sensitive psyche**, which is the essence of animals, is responsible for sensation, the experience of pleasure and pain, imagination and memory, and locomotion through sensuous desire. The **rational psyche** or mind (*nous*), which is the essence of human beings, serves a variety of cognitive functions, such as abstraction, deliberation, and recollection.

The functions of the rational psyche in human beings presuppose the functions of the sensitive psyche, which in turn presuppose the functions of the nutritive psyche, since the functions of each lower-level psyche serve as enabling conditions for the functions of each higher-level psyche. The self-maintenance of organisms through nutrition, for example, serves as an enabling condition for sensations received by the sensitive psyche, which in turn serve as an enabling condition for the cognitive functions of the rational psyche (since for Aristotle, all thought requires images derived from sensation). Thus, human beings have three types of psyche: a nutritive psyche by virtue of which they are self-sustaining beings, a sensitive psyche by virtue of which they are sentient beings, and a rational psyche by virtue of which they are cognitive beings.

Materialism and Psychological Explanation

Aristotle was a materialist who denied that the psyche could exist independently of the material body. Since he treated the psyche as the functional form of materially instantiated substances such as plants, animals, and humans, the question of whether the psyche could survive the destruction of the material body did not arise. It was inconceivable to him that the form of any substance could exist independently of the material it constituted *as* that particular kind of substance. For Aristotle, the rational (or sensitive or nutritive) psyche could no more exist independently of the material body it constituted as the substance of a human being than the shape of a statue of Zeus could exist independently of the marble it constituted as a statue of Zeus or than the seeing of the eye could exist apart from the material of the eye:

> As the pupil *plus* the power of sight constitutes the eye, so the soul plus the body constitutes the animal.
>
> > From this it is clear that the soul is inseparable from its body.
>
> > > —(*De Anima*, II, 1, 413a2–4)

Although Aristotle was a materialist who held that psychological properties and capacities are instantiated in material bodies, he was not a *reductive explanatory materialist*. He did not claim that psychological states and processes could be reductively explained in terms of their material components. This comes out clearly in Aristotle's discussion of emotions such as anger, for example:

> Anger should be defined as a certain mode of movement of such and such a body (or part or faculty of a body) by this or that cause and for this or that end. . . . Hence a physicist would define an affection of soul differently from a dialectician; the latter would define e.g. anger as an appetite for returning pain for pain, or something like that, while the former would define it as a boiling of the blood or warm substance surrounding the heart. The one assigns the material conditions, the other the form or account; for what he states is the account of the fact, though for its actual existence there must be embodiment of it in a material such as it is described by the other.
>
> > —(*De Anima*, I, 1, 403a26–403b4)

Although Aristotle denied that psychological functions could be reductively explained in terms of their material components and processes, he insisted that theories of psychological functions must be constrained by theories of their material instantiation (although he mistakenly believed that they are instantiated in the heart rather than the brain, whose function he believed was to cool the blood). Thus Aristotle defended the autonomy of psychological explanation while insisting that it is not divorced from the material conditions of the natural world. For Aristotle, this was a distinctive virtue of his theoretical position in contrast to dualist accounts of the immateriality of the psyche: Such accounts were not constrained in any way by the material conditions of psychological functioning. As Aristotle put it, such accounts merely "join the soul to a body, or place it in a body, without adding any specification of the reason of their union, or of the bodily conditions required for it" (*De Anima*, I, 3, 407b15–17).

Sensation, Perception, and Cognition

In his account of sensation and perception, Aristotle claimed that there are **special sensibles**, objects of sense that are only discernible by a single sense. Color is the special object of sight, sound the special object of hearing, and so on for smell, touch, and taste, the five senses recognized by Aristotle. He also claimed that there are **common sensibles**, such as movement and magnitude, which can be perceived by more than one sense. Each of the five senses requires a sense organ and a medium between the sensible quality and that organ. In the case of sight, for example, the object seen must possess color, and there must be a transparent medium containing light between the object and the eye. Aristotle maintained that error is possible with respect to judgments about common sensibles, but not with respect to judgments about the special objects of sense.

Aristotle also postulated a **common sense** that combines information about special and common sensibles to form an integrated perception of substances in the external world, such as apples and antelopes. He does not seem to have conceived of common sense as an additional sense requiring a separate organ, but as an emergent function of the five senses working in unison at a complex level of organization. Aristotle held that the most rudimentary form of sense perception is touch. He claimed that touch is linked to basic forms of desire, which are in turn linked to the capacity to experience pleasure and pain.

Aristotle believed that cognition is dependent upon imagery: "Without an image thinking is impossible" (*On Memory*, 1, 450a1). He conceived of images as representations of substances and their properties derived from our sensory experience, as faint copies or traces of sensory experience that survive in memory:

> Memory . . . is the having of an image, related as a likeness to that of which it is an image; and . . . it has been shown that it is a function of the primary faculty of sense-perception.
>
> —(*On Memory*, 1, 451a16–18)

Aristotle distinguished between simple memory, the ability to recognize an image as a representation of something in the past, and recollection, which involves the active search of memory images. He claimed that animals have the capacity for simple memory, but that only humans with a rational psyche have the capacity for recollection, which involves deliberation. According to Aristotle, deliberation is the capacity to comprehend the common form of different instances of the same type of substance by abstraction from sense experience (for example, to comprehend the common form of statues or swans by abstraction from perceived instances of them), which is the basis of all theoretical knowledge, including psychological knowledge.

Aristotle claimed that deliberative reason is a capacity unique to humans, which distinguishes them from animals and plants. Although he held that plants, animals, and humans are part of a hierarchically graded system of nature, he did not maintain that differences between humans and animals are merely differences in degree of complexity. He claimed that humans have psychological capacities such as deliberation that are not instantiated to any degree in animals, but that are different in kind from the capacities shared by humans and animals, such as sensation and desire.

In his discussion of recollection, Aristotle identified a number of principles that came to form the basis of later psychological theories. He noted that recollection is facilitated by the meaningful ordering of material to be recollected, one of the phenomena explored in Wundt's Leipzig laboratory in the late 19th century. He also noted that recollection is based upon relations of similarity, contrast, and contiguity (togetherness in space and time):

> Whenever, therefore, we are recollecting, we are experiencing one of the antecedent movements until finally we experience the one after which customarily comes that which we seek. This explains why we hunt up the series, having started in thought from the present or some other, and from something either similar, or contrary, to what we seek, or else from that which is contiguous with it.
>
> —(*On Memory*, 2, 451b17–19)

These principles, in particular the principle of contiguity (with repetition), became the mainstay of associationist psychology in Europe in the 18th and 19th centuries and of behaviorist psychology in America in the 20th century.

Like his contributions to theoretical science in general, Aristotle's contributions to psychology were wide ranging. He devoted a whole work to dreams (*On Dreams*), which he explained naturalistically in terms of the free operation of images, unconstrained by sensory inputs and rational judgment. He rejected the popular notion that dreams have religious or prophetic significance, although he acknowledged the diagnostic value of certain dreams as indicators of developing medical conditions, such as dreams of walking on fire as indicators of developing fever. He emphasized the critical role of habituation in the development of psychological traits and capacities. In his account of our aesthetic appreciation of theatrical tragedy (in the *Poetics*), he described the psychological relief produced by the cathartic expression of emotion, a notion that later played a central role in psychoanalytic theory.

In his ethical writings, Aristotle maintained that happiness derives from the proper exercise of the faculties of appetite, passion, and reason. He emphasized the virtue of mediation (the "golden mean") and held that the good life is to be attained through the subordination of appetite and passion to the control of reason. The *Nicomachean Ethics* includes subtle discussions of the psychological basis of failures of rational self-control, such as intemperance, incontinence, and weakness of will (*akrasia*). Aristotle was also the first psychological theorist to recognize the social dimensions of human psychology and behavior and famously remarked that "man is by nature a political [social] animal" (*Politics*, I, 2, 1253a2).

Active and Passive Reason

Aristotle complicated matters by maintaining that although the faculty of **passive reason** is responsible for the apprehension of universals and comprehension of first principles, it cannot achieve knowledge on its own. In a difficult set of passages in *De Anima*, he claimed that potential knowledge of universals and first principles is actualized by the operation of **active reason**. Since active reason is pure actuality, it is unchangeable and unconstrained by any temporally delimited material substance. Consequently, it can and does survive the death and destruction of those formed material substances that are human beings. As Aristotle put it, active reason is "immortal and eternal" (*De Anima*, III, 5, 430a23). Christian apologists later exploited these sorts of comments, and identified active reason with the immaterial soul that is distinct from the material body, survives death, and enjoys eternal bliss or damnation. They also identified the unmoved mover, which Aristotle postulated in the *Metaphysics* as pure form and pure actuality, with the Christian God.

Yet there is no ground for such identifications in Aristotle, and Christian notions of an immortal immaterial soul and God are quite alien to the Aristotelian worldview. Aristotle seems to have introduced both active reason and the unmoved mover to satisfy metaphysical requirements in his system, since he maintained that actuality is always prior to potentiality. He maintained that active reason, for example, enables the cognitive functions of passive reason, without which "nothing thinks" (*De Anima*, III, 5, 430a25), in much the same way as light enables colors to be seen, or "makes potential colors into actual colors" (*De Anima*, III, 5, 430a, 17).

As conceived by Aristotle, active reason and the unmoved mover are as amorphous and undifferentiated as prime matter and have none of the traditional properties that Christians ascribe to the immortal soul or God. With respect to active reason, Aristotle took pains to stress that although it survives the destruction of the material body, it retains no knowledge or memories, no pleasures or pains, and no desires, emotions, motives, or personality characteristics.

Psychology and Teleology

Although Aristotle's account of the psychology of human beings was intimately linked to his general teleological account of the natural world, it did not depend upon it. His general account of the subject matter and appropriate modes of explanation in psychology can stand alone, independently of the adequacy of his particular theories in biology and physics, which have long since been rejected on empirical grounds.

There is a very real temptation, influential in the 20th century, to suppose that the attribution of ends or purposes to human agents is no more legitimate than the attribution of ends or purposes to the motion of physical bodies or the evolution of biological species and that psychology will become properly scientific only when it abandons all explanatory references to ends and purposes (Blumberg & Wasserman, 1995). Yet many of the pioneers of the scientific revolution in the 16th and 17th centuries, such as Galileo and Newton, who rejected final causal explanations in physics in favor of efficient causal explanations, acknowledged the legitimacy of final causal explanations of human and animal behavior. Although the Darwinian revolution in biology displaced purpose from the realm of biological development in the late 19th century, many evolutionary theorists (including Darwin himself) maintained that ends and purposes play a critical role in the individual adaptation of humans and animals to their environments.

The development of modern science did involve a general displacement of final causal explanation by efficient causal explanation, but teleological explanation cannot be dismissed as inherently unscientific or irrelevant in psychology. The pioneers of information theory in the 1940s, whose work presaged the cognitive revolution in psychology of the 1950s, maintained that teleological explanation is necessary to account for the "intrinsically purposive" behavior of living organisms and machines such as torpedoes, which modify their behavior in accord with information feedback (Rosenbleuth, Wiener, & Bigelow, 1943, pp. 19–20). Contemporary cognitive psychologists recognize that a great deal of human and animal behavior is intrinsically purposive, and some maintain that this is also the case with respect to the "artificially intelligent" behavior of modern computers (Boden, 1977).

Functionalism

In treating psychological states and processes as the capacities of complex material bodies, Aristotle anticipated the modern **functionalist** account of mentality (Nussbaum & Putnam, 1992; Wilkes, 1992), in which mental states are conceived of as internal states of an organism that are caused by environmental stimuli and which in turn cause other mental states and behavior. By this account, mental states such as pain, anger, and the belief that there is an object in one's path are defined as internal states with characteristic stimulus causes, mental effects, and behavioral consequences.

A distinguishing feature of the functionalist account of mental states and processes is the recognition that they can be **multiply realized** in different material systems, such as human brains or the control units of digital computers, just as the functional form of a clock can be multiply realized in sundials, water clocks, and various other mechanical devices composed of different materials. Aristotle also recognized this feature when he claimed that *different materials* could be constituted as the *same type of substance* by sharing the *same essential form:*

> In the case of things which are found to occur in specifically different materials, as a circle may exist in bronze or stone or wood, it seems plain that these, the bronze or the stone, are no part of the essence of the circle, since it is found apart from them.
>
> —(*Metaphysics*, VII, 11, 1036a30–34)

Thus a circular shape may exist in bronze, wood, or stone, and a statue of Zeus may be sculpted out of limestone, marble, or quartz.

Although Aristotle knew nothing of computers, the same principle applies to the essential forms, or computational functions, involved in cognitive operations such as addition or the memorization of serial lists. Cognitive operations such as addition may be performed on abacuses, mechanical adding machines, and digital computers, and by the human brain, composed of different materials with different modes of organization. Serial lists may be memorized by computers and by human beings, despite their differences in material composition and organization. In modern terminology, the same programs or software can be run on different forms of hardware or biological wetware.

Aristotle dismissed as "absurd" the view that the rational psyche could be instantiated in any material substance, such as that of a mouse, a tree, or a pebble. In particular, he opposed the dualist view that the psyche could be temporarily "imprisoned" in any form of physical body: "as if it were possible, as in the Pythagorean myths, that any soul could be clothed in any body" (*De Anima*, I, 3, 407b21–22). This was simply a consequence of Aristotle's claim that theoretical accounts of psychological states and processes must be constrained by our best theories of their material instantiation. For similar reasons, modern functionalists, including cognitive psychologists, deny that psychological states and processes can be realized in just any physical medium. They recognize the complexity of physical architecture required for cognitive processing.

Aristotle did maintain that we have knowledge of the rational psyche only as materially instantiated in human beings (Green, 1998). Yet he was careful to note that this contingent fact does not undermine the distinction between functional forms and their material instantiation, even though we are liable to mistakenly equate them when a functional form is as a matter of fact materially instantiated in only one known manner, as in the case of the rationale psyche:

> Of things which are *not* seen to exist apart, there is no reason why the same may not be true, e.g. even if all circles that had ever been seen were of bronze (for none the less the bronze would be no part of the form); but it is hard to effect this severance in thought. e.g. the form of man is always found in flesh and bones and parts of this kind: are these then also parts of the form and the formula? No, they are matter; but because man is not found in other matters we are unable to effect the severance.
>
> —(*Metaphysics*, VII, 11, 1036a34–1036b6)

Aristotle never considered the real possibility of full-blown rational agents other than biological human beings, since he had no knowledge of computers and did not reflect on the possibility of Martian life forms, the favored examples of modern functionalists. Yet his claim that the rational psyche is as a matter of fact instantiated only in human biological systems is entirely consistent with his functionalist position, since it is a claim maintained by a good many contemporary cognitive psychologists who recognize the limitations of computer simulations of human perception and cognition. They maintain that although rudimentary psychological capacities have been actualized in computer simulations of vision and problem solving, the only known examples of organized physical bodies capable of full-blown sentience, perception, cognitive processing, and consciousness are biological human beings.

Yet like Aristotle, such theorists still maintain the functionalist emphasis on the *autonomy* of psychological explanation. They do not feel obliged to reduce theoretical accounts of cognitive functions to theories of their neurophysiological realization, although they recognize the critical constraints imposed by such theories. In this respect they are thoroughly Aristotelian: They are materialists but not reductive explanatory materialists.

Consciousness and Vitality

Aristotle's psychology has a distinctively modern ring, insofar as he anticipated the functional form of 20th-century cognitive psychology. However, some modern commentators have complained about his neglect of the concept of consciousness:

> Concepts like that of consciousness do not figure in his conceptual scheme at all; they play no part in his analysis of perception, thought, etc. (Nor do they play any significant role in Greek thought in general.) It is this perhaps that gives his definition of the soul itself a certain inadequacy for the modern reader.
>
> —(Hamlyn, 1968, p. xiii)

Aristotle does seem to have recognized the concept of consciousness:

> He who sees perceives that he sees, and he who hears that he hears . . . so that if we perceive, we perceive that we perceive, and if we think, that we think.
>
> —(*Nicomachean Ethics*, IX, 9, 1170a29–32)

Yet it is true that he had little use for it. Still, his neglect of the concept cannot be presumed to be an inadequacy of his psychology. Although many modern theorists did come to treat consciousness as an essential feature of mentality, this is not the case with respect to contemporary cognitive psychologists, who regularly appeal to unconscious mental states and processes.

Another virtue of Aristotle's psychology was his location of theories of psychological functioning within a general biological framework. In this respect he anticipated the form of functional psychology developed by early-20th-century psychologists at the University of Chicago. James R. Angell (1869–1949), the acknowledged leader of this movement, claimed that aspects of functional psychology were "plainly discernable in the psychology of Aristotle" (Angell, 1907, p. 61). Yet in conceiving of both vital biological and cognitive psychological functions as the actuality of "bodies that have life potentially," Aristotle treated the psyche as the active principle of both life and mind. It was not until the period of the scientific revolution in Europe, when principles of mechanical (efficient causal) explanation were first extended to the "vital functions" of the "body-machine" (such as respiration and digestion), that psychological theorists first came to distinguish between the explanatory principles of life and mind.

THE ARISTOTELIAN LEGACY

The death of Aristotle marked the end of the "golden age" of Greece and Athens. His student Theophrastus (c. 371–c. 286 BCE) succeeded him as head of the Lyceum. Although a prolific writer and popular teacher, Theophrastus was overshadowed by the brilliance of his master and initiated what turned out to be a long tradition of scholarly commentary on the work of Aristotle and other Greek theorists. As the centuries progressed and Christianity arose, Aristotle's work was neglected. It was rediscovered and developed by later Islamic and medieval Christian scholars, ironically to the point that much of Aristotle's naturalistic and empirically inspired science came to be treated as religious dogma.

DISCUSSION QUESTIONS

1. Early Greek scientists and physicians frequently conceived of physical and psychological health as a form of harmony or balance, and this idea has remained popular with many later psychologists. Why do you think this is so? Why should we presume that psychological health in particular involves any form of harmony or balance?

2. Leucippus and Democritus advanced an atomic theory of nature: They maintained that all physical objects (such as planets, trees, and animals) are combinations of independent atoms. Yet unlike later scientific psychologists influenced by 18th-century atomism, they did not claim that the "elements" of perception are atomistic in nature. Democritus's theory of perception focused on the reception of form elements (such as shape) rather than perceptual atoms. Were the Greek atomists being inconsistent in this respect? Or is there no essential connection between physical and psychological atomism?

3. The Greek atomists Leucippus and Democritus conceived of a cold, hard mechanistic universe of atoms and the void, governed by rigid deterministic laws. Such a conception has proved abhorrent to many later humanistic and religious thinkers (including humanistic psychologists), who maintain that such a conception renders life meaningless and purposeless. Yet Democritus himself was not driven to despair, and maintained that the goal of human life is happiness, which he thought best achieved through self-discipline and moderation. Was he being inconsistent? Must nature be meaningful and purposive in order for us to lead meaningful and purposive lives?

4. Aristotle thought that teleological explanation applies to all physical, biological, and psychological processes, but many think that such explanations have no place in science. Some have tried to restrict teleological explanation to the explanation of biological and/or psychological processes, while others have claimed that teleological explanation applies to the behavior of some physical systems (machines) and some biological and psychological systems.

Do you think that teleological explanations have any place in contemporary science, including psychological science? If so, where do you think they apply?

5. Aristotle noted how the forms of substances can be multiply realized in different materials (a statue of Zeus may be made of marble, wood, or ice) and suggested that the same is true in principle of the functional form of the rationale psyche, even though as a matter of fact we are acquainted only with the rationale psyche of human beings. Do you think that psychological states and processes can be multiply realized—for example, in suitably developed robotic computers or alien life-forms of different material constitution? Is it just a contingent fact that the only full-blown sentient, cognitive, and conscious beings known to psychological science are human beings?

GLOSSARY

active reason In Aristotle, pure actuality that enables knowledge of universals and first principles.

animal spirits According to Alcmaeon, the material carriers of nerve impulses.

animism The belief in immaterial spirits or souls.

being vs. becoming The contrast between the view that reality is unchanging (held by Parmenides) and the view that it is constantly changing (held by Heraclitus).

common sense According to Aristotle, the faculty that combines information from the special senses into unified perception.

common sensibles According to Aristotle, properties that can be discriminated by more than one sense (e.g., movement can be discriminated by both sight and touch).

dialectic method A method of argument involving the systematic exploration of arguments for and against opposing positions.

dualism The view that the psyche (or soul or mind) and material body are distinct entities.

efficient cause The agency responsible for an existent.

eidola Faint copies of physical objects that some early Greek theorists such as Empedocles and Democritus believed emanated from physical objects and explained our perception of them.

Eleatic school The group of early Greek formalist theorists associated with Elea in southern Italy, whose members included Parmenides, Zeno of Elea, and Xenophanes.

entelechy According to Aristotle, the process by which what is merely potential becomes actual, through the realization of its form (e.g., the embryo developing into a chick).

final cause The end or function or purpose for which something exists.

formal cause The essential form of an existent.

formalism The view that the universe is best explained in terms of formal or mathematical relations.

Forms, theory of In Plato, the theory that ultimate reality is constituted by abstract ideas or Forms, in which concrete physical particulars derivatively "participate."

four causes According to Aristotle, the material, formal, efficient, and final causes of an existent.

four humors According to Hippocrates, the bodily substances that are formed from the four elements of Empedocles. Yellow bile is formed from air, blood from fire, black bile from earth, and phlegm from water. He maintained that health derives from the proper balance of these humors, and disease from their imbalance.

functionalism Theory in which mental states are conceived of as internal states of an organism that are caused by environmental stimuli and that in turn cause other mental states and behavior.

great chain of being The term used by the historian of ideas Arthur Lovejoy to describe hierarchical conceptions of nature such as Aristotle's *scala naturae.*

holistic medicine A form of medicine that emphasizes the natural healing power of the body and treats physical and psychological disorders as disorders of the whole body.

hylomorphism Aristotle's view that substances are constituted by matter (*hule*) with substantial form (*morphe*).

induction by enumeration Generalization on the basis of observed instances. For example, generalization to "All A's are B's" on the basis of observed instances of A's that are B's.

Ionian School The group of early Greek naturalistic theorists associated with the Ionian federation of city-states, whose members included Thales and Anaximenes.

material cause The material in which an existent is realized.

multiple realizability The capacity of functionally defined entities or properties to be realized in a variety of different material systems.

naturalism The view that the universe is best explained in terms of material elements and processes.

nutritive psyche According to Aristotle, the essential functional properties of plants.

passive reason According to Aristotle, the faculty responsible for the apprehension of universals and comprehension of first principles.

physis The Greek word for the fundamental element(s) (from which the term *physics* is derived).

primary qualities Qualities that physical objects have independently of our perception of them, such as size, shape, and motion.

psyche The Greek term usually translated as "soul," but without any presumed reference to an immaterial entity.

rational psyche According to Aristotle, the essential functional properties of human beings.

recollection, theory of According to Plato, knowledge is a form of remembrance of knowledge possessed by the immortal immaterial psyche, but temporarily forgotten with each cycle of reincarnation.

reductio ad absurdum argument An argument that purports to demonstrate the falsity of assumptions by demonstrating that they lead to false or absurd consequences.

relativism Theory that truth is relative to what any individual perceives or judges to be the case.

scala naturae Aristotle's hierarchical conception of nature, ranging from prime matter (pure potentiality) through increasingly complex levels of natural substances to the unmoved mover (pure actuality).

secondary qualities Qualities that are merely the effects that physical objects produce in the sense organs of sentient beings, such as color, taste, and smell.

sensitive psyche According to Aristotle, the essential functional properties of animals.

Sophists Professional teachers of rhetoric and logic in ancient Greece.

special sensibles According to Aristotle, the special objects of the individual senses, discernible by those senses alone (e.g., color is the special object of sight).

teleological science Form of science that employs explanations in terms of ends or goal states.

teleology, extrinsic Ends or purposes of a separate being (such as God).

teleology, intrinsic Ends or purposes inherent in natural processes.

temple medicine An early form of Greek medicine based upon religious beliefs and mystical practices.

universal Common property of a class of particulars (e.g., redness, the common property of red things).

unmoved mover According to Aristotle, the first cause or principle that is pure form and pure actuality, responsible for the actualization of all things.

REFERENCES

Angell, J. R. (1907). The province of functional psychology. *Psychological Review, 14,* 61–91.

Barnes, J. (1979a). *The presocratic philosophers: Volume 1. Thales to Zeno.* London: Routledge & Kegan Paul.

Barnes, J. (1979b). *The presocratic philosophers: Volume 2. Empedocles to Democritus.* London: Routledge & Kegan Paul.

Barnes, J. (1987). *Early Greek philosophy.* New York: Penguin.

Barnes, J. (Ed.). (1995). *The complete works of Aristotle: The revised Oxford translation* (Vols. 1–2). Princeton, NJ: Princeton University Press.

Blackburn, S. (1996). *The Oxford dictionary of philosophy.* Oxford: Oxford University Press.

Blumberg, M. S., & Wasserman, E. A. (1995). Animal mind and the argument from design. *American Psychologist, 50,* 133–144.

Boden, M. (1977). *Artificial intelligence and natural man.* New York: Basic Books.

Frank, J. D. (1973). *Persuasion and healing.* Baltimore: Johns Hopkins University Press.

Green, C. D. (1998). The thoroughly modern Aristotle: Was he really a functionalist? *History of Psychology, 1,* 8–20.

Hamlyn, D. (1968). Introduction. In D. W. Hamlyn (Trans.), *Aristotle's De Anima Books II and III (With Certain Passages from Book I).* Oxford: Clarendon Press.

Jager, M., & VanHoorn, W. (1972). Aristotle's opinion on perception in general. *Journal of the History of the Behavioral Sciences, 8,* 321–327.

Jones, W. H. S. (1923). *Hippocrates* (Vol. 1). New York: Putnam.

Kirk, G. S., Raven, J. E., & Schofield, M. (1983). *The presocratic philosophers: A critical history with a selection of texts.* Cambridge: Cambridge University Press.

Lloyd, G. E. R. (1964). Experiment in early Greek philosophy and medicine. *Proceedings of the Cambridge Philological Society,* n.s. *10,* 50–72.

Lloyd, G. E. R. (1983). *Hippocratic writings.* New York: Penguin.

Lloyd, G. E. R. (1991). *Methods and problems in Greek science.* Cambridge: Cambridge University Press.

Losee, J. (1980). *A historical introduction to the philosophy of science.* Oxford: Oxford University Press.

Lovejoy, A. O. (1936). *The great chain of being.* Harvard: Harvard University Press.

Nussbaum, M. C., & Putnam, H. (1992). Changing Aristotle's mind. In M. C. Nussbaum & A. O. Rorty (Eds.), *Essays on Aristotle's De anima.* Oxford: Clarendon Press.

Onians, R. B. (1958). *The origins of European thought*. Cambridge: Cambridge University Press.

Pivnicki, D. (1969). The beginnings of psychotherapy. *Journal of the History of the Behavioral Sciences, 5*, 238–247.

Rosenblueth, A., Wiener, N., & Bigelow, J. (1943). Behavior, purpose and teleology. *Philosophy of Science, 10*, 18–24.

Russell, B. (1945). *A history of Western philosophy*. New York: Simon & Schuster.

Simon, B. (1972). Models of mind and mental illness in ancient Greece: II. The Platonic model. *Journal of the History of the Behavioral Sciences, 8*, 389–404.

Walker, C. E. (Ed.) (1991). *Clinical psychology: Historical and research foundations*. New York: Plenum.

Wilkes, K. V. (1992). Psyche versus the mind. In M. C. Nussbaum & A. O. Rorty (Eds.), *Essays on Aristotle's* De anima. Oxford: Clarendon Press.

CHAPTER 3

Rome and the Medieval Period

W ITH THE DEFEAT OF ATHENS BY SPARTA IN THE PELOPONNESIAN WAR (431–404 BCE), the Greek city-states began to disintegrate. By the time Aristotle died in 322 BCE, they had become part of the short-lived Macedonian Empire, founded by Alexander the Great. Republican Rome invaded shortly afterward, and they were eventually incorporated into the Roman Empire. The center of learning shifted from Athens to Alexandria in Egypt. In the uncertain years that followed, the confident theoretical speculations of the Greek naturalists and formalists became the object of Skepticism and Cynicism. The Hellenistic and later Roman period witnessed a turn to more practical philosophies of life, such as Epicureanism and Stoicism.

The Romans were great technologists and administrators, but contributed little to the development of science. Mystical forms of Neoplatonism became popular and informed the emergence of Christianity in the early days of the Roman Empire. When Christianity was accepted as the state religion, the works of pagan scholars such as Pythagoras and Aristotle were denigrated and condemned. With the decline of the Roman Empire, Western Europe entered what is known as the Dark Ages, a time when many of the classical Greek texts were destroyed or lost. Alexandrian scholars fled to Constantinople, then to Persia, where the classical texts were rediscovered by Islamic scholars and eventually by Christian scholars with the advent of the Crusades. During the middle and later medieval period, Aristotle's natural philosophy was integrated with Christian theology, effectively fossilizing his theories as church dogma.

Although science developed little during the medieval period, the medievals were not as hostile to it as is commonly supposed. They did not generally persecute practicing scientists and did not burn hundreds of thousands of neurotic and psychotic women whom they misdiagnosed as witches. What was distinctive about the medieval period was the general lack of interest in the empirical evaluation of scientific theories, including psychological theories. Most medieval scholars were content to develop their theories based upon classical and theological authorities.

THE ROMAN AGE

The Roman Age began with the 500 years of the Roman Republic prior to the time of Julius Caesar (100–44 BCE), during which the Senate governed Rome. After Caesar's assassination, Rome was governed by a series of emperors, beginning with Augustus (63 BCE–14 CE). The Roman Empire, which at the height of its power stretched from the British Isles to the Middle East, brought stability and order to the Mediterranean world for nearly 400 years, until it collapsed due to internal pressures and external invasions.

The Hellenistic Period

During the Hellenistic period (the time between the dissolution of the Greek city-states and the emergence of the Roman Empire), the theoretical speculations of early Greek thinkers were rejected. **Skeptics,** such as Pyrrho (c. 365–c. 275 BCE), repudiated all pretensions to knowledge. They advocated the suspension of belief and recommended that people follow the local moral and religious practices prevalent in society at any particular time and place. The **Cynics** Antisthenes (c. 445–c. 364 BCE) and Diogenes (c. 412–323 BCE) dismissed classical learning and conventional morality and recommended a life of natural independence, free of government, custom, and tradition. They were called Cynics by virtue of the extremely primitive form of life they advocated and exemplified. *Cynic* means "doglike," and Diogenes is reputed to have behaved like a dog, using the public square as his toilet and venue for masturbation.

Hellenistic thinkers turned from theoretical speculation to more practical philosophies of life. These had a significant impact on Roman religious practices and moral attitudes, but contributed little to science and psychology. Epicurus (c. 341–270 BCE) and his Roman disciple Lucretius (c. 99–55 BCE) developed a philosophy of individual happiness grounded in Democritean atomism and the denial of the possibility of an afterlife. **Epicureanism** was not a simple hedonism of maximizing pleasure through wine, women, and song, but a philosophy of moderation based upon reason, choice, and discipline, which would supposedly ensure the greatest amount of genuine happiness over the long term. The highest form of pleasure was held to be friendship, and rich food and drink (especially in excess) were to be avoided. As for sex, according to Epicurus, it never did anyone any good, and you should count yourself lucky if you were not harmed by it!

The philosophy of Zeno of Citium (c. 333–264 BCE) was also based upon Democritian atomism and came to be known as **Stoicism** (because the school in which Zeno taught had a *stoa poikile,* or multicolored covered gallery). According to Zeno, everything in nature is predetermined according to a divine plan. Everyone is assigned a role and destiny prescribed by God, and virtue consists in acting in accord with this natural law and adopting the right attitude toward it. The good life consists of freely accepting one's fate, whether it be good or ill, with indifference. Stoicism had widespread appeal among the Romans and seemed especially suited to their moral, social, and practical temperament. Emperors (Marcus Aurelius, 121–180 CE), states-men (Seneca, c. 4 BCE–65 CE), and slaves (Epictetus, c. 55–c. 135 CE) embraced it.

Alexandrian Science

As theoretical speculation declined in Greece, the center of science and learning shifted from Athens to Alexandria, founded by Alexander the Great and completed by Ptolemy, one of his generals. The Ptolemaic dynasty created a great university and a famous library. The Great Library of Alexandria, which contained over a quarter of a million volumes, was one of the seven wonders of the ancient world.

Herophilus of Chalcedon (335–280 BCE), a Hippocratic disciple, founded the anatomical school at the Museum of Alexandria, where medical research and teaching were based upon the dissection of human cadavers and the vivisection of animals. Herophilus distinguished between the sensory and motor nerves (von Straden, 1989), and with his colleague Erasistratus (c. 304–c. 250 BCE) he explored the functions of the nervous system. By exposing and severing nerve bundles, they determined that the nerves are responsible for transmitting impulses (or "motions") from the senses to the brain and from the brain to the muscles; they speculated that these impulses were borne by animal spirits (very small material particles) passing through otherwise hollow nerves. The Roman physician Galen later developed this speculation into a detailed theory of nervous transmission that remained influential until the 17th century. Herophilus is sometimes called the father of anatomy (and Erasistratus the father of physiology), but his pioneering work also brought dissection into disrepute. The Christian father Quintus Septimius Florens Tertullian (c. 160–230 CE) accused him of having dissected live criminals, supplied by King Ptolemy I, who reputedly also participated in many dissections (Roach, 2003). The Romans consequently prohibited the practice in Alexandria and throughout the empire.

Euclid (c. 325–c. 265 BCE) was curator and librarian of the Great Library of Alexandria. His *Elements* integrated and organized the body of arithmetic and geometric knowledge developed by the Egyptians, Babylonians, and Pythagoreans, within which he derived theorems such as Pythagoras's theorem from self-evident axioms. Euclid's deductive system of demonstration, in which the truth of theorems is shown to follow logically from the assumed truth of axioms, became a popular model for theoretical explanation in natural science. Isaac Newton (1642–1727) later employed it in his statement of the theory of universal gravitation (Newton, 1687/1969), as did Thomas Hobbes (1588–1679) in his mechanistic theory of human psychology and behavior (Hobbes, 1640/1966) and Clark L. Hull (1884–1952) in his neobehaviorist theory of learning (Hull, 1943).

Archimedes (c. 287–c. 212 BCE) founded the science of hydrostatics with his treatise *On Floating Bodies*. He was reputedly in the public baths when he invented a method for measuring the specific gravities of substances by displacement (in order to identify forgeries among the royal jewelry) and ran naked through the streets shouting "Eureka!" ("I have it!"). In *On Plane Equilibriums*, he organized the known principles of mechanical equilibrium into a deductive system, from which he derived theorems governing the (idealized) operation of mechanical levers. Archimedes put his theoretical knowledge to practical use in his design of military catapults, when he returned to his native Syracuse (in Sicily) to serve as a military engineer in the defense of the city as the Romans besieged it. According to legend, he was slain by Roman soldiers while he contemplated a geometric problem.

It was also in Alexandria that Claudius Ptolemy (c. 100–c. 170 CE) developed Aristotle's geocentric (Earth-centered) theory of the heavens in his *Almagest*. He claimed that the planets maintain circular orbits around a fixed Earth, but introduced a system of epicycles (circles within circles) to account for the retrograde motion of some of the planets (which appear to slow down, stop, reverse, and then move on again in the original direction). Ptolemy dispensed with Aristotle's crystalline planetary spheres, but retained his celestial sphere, which supposedly carried the fixed stars. This astronomical system was generally accepted (with only minor modifications) until the 16th century, when it was challenged by pioneers of the scientific revolution in Europe such as Nicholaus Copernicus (1473–1543), Johannes Kepler (1571–1630), and Galileo Galilei (1564–1642). Ptolemy also did pioneering experiments on color and the reflection and refraction of light, which are documented in his *Optics* (Smith, 1996).

Rome and Science

Although the Romans produced many technological marvels, such as aqueducts, baths, roads, and military machines, they created little in the way of developed natural or psychological science. The Romans were great engineers and mechanics, insofar as it suited them in the practical world of everyday affairs, but they seem to have been constitutionally uninterested in the pursuit of abstract thought and speculative theory. They were not actively hostile to science and respected and preserved the works of the classical Greeks. Roman scholars transcribed the works of Plato and Aristotle and translated them into Latin, and aristocratic Romans sent their children to study in Alexandria. However, with few exceptions, such as the philosopher Lucretius (c. 99–c. 55 BCE), who developed the atomism of Epicurus in his poem *De Rerum Natura*, they expressed little interest in expanding on the works of their predecessors. Science entered a period of progressive decline and was eventually suffocated by the development of Christianity, which became the official religion of the Roman Empire in 380 CE.

Galen   Once again, the physicians were a notable exception. Galen (c. 130–c. 200 CE), who became personal physician to the Roman Emperor Marcus Aurelius, was trained in Alexandria, where medical science was originally based upon the dissection of human cadavers. Although by Galen's time human dissection was prohibited throughout the Roman Empire, he managed to supplement his theoretical medical training with experience as a gladiatorial surgeon and with his own dissection of animals such as goats, pigs, sheep, and cattle.

Like Aristotle, Galen maintained that every structural form, organ, and system of the human body has its own distinctive purpose or function, which he detailed in *On the Usefulness of the Parts of the Body*. One especially influential doctrine was Galen's account of the role of "vital" and "animal" spirits in supporting biological and psychological functions. According to Galen, the heart is responsible for the distillation of vital spirits drawn from the air, which regulate movement. When conveyed to the network of interwoven blood vessels in the brain known as the *rete mirabile* (the "marvelous net"), they are further refined to animal spirits, which are responsible for perceptual and cognitive functions. Galen claimed that the animal spirits fill the ventricles (cavities) of the brain and the nerves and that they issue from the eyes in vision.

The principles of Galen's anatomy and physiology dominated medical science in the ensuing centuries and became virtual dogmas during the medieval period. They persisted well into the 17th century: Theories referencing animal spirits are to be found in the mechanistic physiology of Hobbes and Descartes, for example. One particularly influential doctrine was Galen's development of Hippocrates' theory of the four bodily humors into a theory of personality types (Figure 3.1).

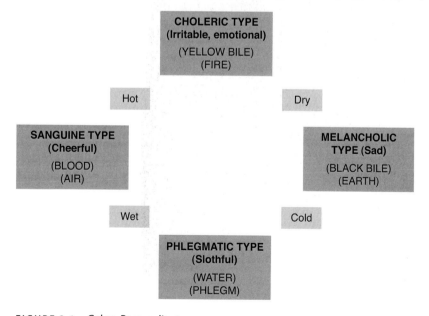

FIGURE 3.1   Galen: Personality types.

According to this theory, the cheerful, or **sanguine**, type of personality, has an excess of blood; the sad, or **melancholic**, type has an excess of black bile; the irritable and emotional, or **choleric**, type has an excess of yellow bile; and the slothful, or **phlegmatic**, type has an excess of phlegm. This theory has long since entered the vernacular and survives in everyday phrases such as "phlegmatic character" and "bad humor." In *On the Diagnosis and Cure of the Soul's Passions*, Galen recommended individual counseling for emotional problems and documented the physiological symptoms of the "love sickness," such as increased pulse and heart rate.

Neoplatonism

The Pythagorean elements of Plato's philosophy were also developed in the early years of the Roman Empire. **Neoplatonic** theories focused on the mystical and spiritual elements of Plato's philosophy rather than its critical rationalism and exerted a powerful influence on the early development of Christianity.

Philo of Alexandria (c. 20 BCE–50 CE) claimed that knowledge is revealed by God and cannot be attained through sense experience or reason. He maintained that both sense experience and reason are impediments to knowledge, which can be attained only via the passive reception of divine illumination by a purified mind, through meditation, trance, or dreams. Like Plato, Philo claimed that the immaterial soul is "imprisoned" in the inferior material body. Throughout a human life it can either rise above carnal experience and move toward the light (of divine illumination) or sink down to carnal experience and move away from the light.

The most influential Neoplatonist was Plotinus (c. 204–270 CE). Educated in Alexandria, he founded a philosophical school in Rome under the protection of the Emperor Gallienus (c. 213–268 CE). He also conceived of the immaterial psyche as imprisoned in the inferior material body, from which it could escape only through transcendental experiences, such as meditation and dreams. In the *Enneads*, Plotinus claimed that all reality is based upon a series of emanations from "the One," the original and eternal source of being. Next comes the realm of intelligence (a reflection of the One or ideas in the mind of the One), psyche, and finally matter. Like Plato, Plotinus claimed that the material world is an inferior copy of the divine abstract realm, although he was less critical of sense experience than Philo and Plato. He suggested that sense experience could be a source of beauty in art and music, as well as a source of ignorance and evil. He claimed that sense experience provides an accurate representation of external physical particulars, but since they are constantly changing, it is of little value. Genuine knowledge can be attained only through the apprehension of ideas in the realm of intelligence or, in rare cases, through mystical union with the One (O'Meara, 1995).

Like Philo, Plotinus maintained that the soul can ascend to spirituality and mystical unity or descend to the carnal degradations of the material body. He was so committed to the view that the soul is imprisoned in the material body that he took no care of his own body. He ate little, abstained from sex, and was indifferent to matters of personal hygiene. He left Rome after the assassination of Gallienus and died of leprosy shortly afterward.

The Decline of the Roman Empire

The Roman Empire lasted from approximately the first to the fifth century CE, although it was in serious decline by about the second century. Scientific thinking degenerated, even in Alexandria, after the Romans took over the administration of Egypt following the defeat of Cleopatra and Mark Anthony at Actium in 31 BCE (and their subsequent suicides). The government corruption, economic degeneration, and barbarian invasions that marked the decline of the Roman Empire led many to seek solace in "other-world" philosophies, such as Neoplatonism and Christianity.

Historians mark the end of the Roman Empire with the deposition of the Emperor Romulus Augustus in 476 CE. A remnant continued in the East, founded by the Emperor Constantine (c. 272–337 CE), with its center at Byzantium, which was later renamed Constantinople. The Byzantine Empire lasted until 1453 CE, when Constantinople fell to the Turks. It contributed little to the development of science, but for a period preserved much of the classical scholarship that was destroyed or lost in the West.

Christianity   The disintegration of the Roman Empire was paralleled by the development of "mystery" religions, which promised otherworldly salvation in times of great trouble and tribulation. The one that came to dominate was based upon the life and teachings of Jesus (c. 4 BCE–30 CE). Early doctrinal dissension, often extremely violent, was settled through the early church councils, such as the Council of Nicaea in 325 CE. Originally persecuted, Christians gained increasing power and influence after the Emperor Constantine's Edict of Milan in 313 CE, which granted religious toleration. The Emperor Theodosius (c. 346–395 CE) proclaimed Christianity as the official state religion in 380 CE and prohibited all pagan religions.

All this was extremely bad news for learning in general and scientific thought in particular. Pagan science was condemned along with pagan religion. The Archbishop Theophilus of Alexandria, who like many early Church fathers was zealous in his destruction of all pagan symbols, was responsible for the destruction of much of the Great Library at Alexandria in 391 CE. Hypatia (c. 370–415 CE), the distinguished female mathematician and astronomer, was murdered by a mob of

Christians. They dragged her into a church and ripped the flesh from her body with roof tiles, most likely on the orders of Cyril, the nephew of Theophilus, who had replaced him as patriarch of Alexandria. Cyril was later canonized. Many scholars fled Alexandria, which went into decline as a center of learning and science.

Some sought refuge in Athens, where Plato's Academy was still in operation, although by this time devoted almost exclusively to mystical speculation. However, Christian pressure persuaded the Emperor Justinian (483–565 CE) to close it down in 529 CE and to forbid the study of all "heathen learning." Other scholars migrated to Constantinople, taking many classical works with them. Despite Constantine's noble intention to create a virtuous Christian city in the East, the debauchery of the masses and the ferocity with which every new type of heresy was persecuted forced many Alexandrians to flee to Mesopotamia and eventually to Persia. There they translated the works of Plato, Aristotle, Euclid, Archimedes, and Ptolemy, making the works of these classical theorists available to the Islamic Empire that was soon to engulf them.

Christianity and Pagan Thought   One of the earliest debates within Christianity was whether to dismiss alternative philosophies and religions as pagan and heretical, the position championed by Saint Jerome (c. 345–420 CE), or whether to integrate at least some elements of them within Christianity, the position championed by Saint Ambrose (c. 340–397 CE). Although Jerome represented the original consensus, Ambrose and his followers eventually won the day. As a result, many Christians enjoy such originally pagan symbols, artifacts, and offices as holly wreaths, Christmas trees, incense, and the originally Druid roles of best man (strictly, next best man, since his duty was to take the place of the groom if the groom died or reneged) and maid of honor (whose virginity was sacrificed to the next best man if the groom did his duty). One significant consequence was that the bishop of Rome adopted the pagan office of Pontifex Maximus, a position that evolved into the authoritarian structures of the papacy. However, these early Church fathers did not look to Aristotle's empirical science and materialist psychology, but embraced the Neoplatonic conception of the psyche as an immortal spiritual entity temporarily imprisoned in an inferior material body.

Saint Augustine   Augustine of Hippo (354–430 CE) was largely responsible for the Neoplatonization of Christianity. He affirmed the conception of the soul as a separate spiritual entity temporarily imprisoned in an inferior material body. He reaffirmed Plotinus's view that knowledge can be attained only through acquaintance with the eternal forms or ideas and the illumination of God and that man should turn away from the world of the senses and carnal pleasure.

Born in North Africa to a pagan father and Christian mother, Augustine converted to Christianity at the age of 31. After years of debauchery, during which he "boiled over in . . . fornications," he experienced a revelation and dedicated the rest of his life to monastic devotion. He is often remembered for his prayer from the licentious days prior to his revelation in which he pleaded: "Give me chastity and continency, only not yet." Augustine became bishop of Hippo in 396 CE and advanced a number of doctrines that were to dominate Christian theology into the 12th century, such as the doctrines of free will, the reality of the fall, and original sin.

Augustine developed a form of **substance dualism** and a set of supporting arguments that later came to be associated with René Descartes (whom he almost certainly influenced). He maintained that the soul is a special and simple spiritual substance, which is distinct from material substance and can survive bodily death. Our knowledge of the distinctive nature of the soul as a special type of "thinking substance" is based upon the certainty of our beliefs about ourselves, in contrast to our often erroneous beliefs about physical objects in the external world. Augustine argued that he could not be mistaken about his existence, for he must exist in order to be mistaken:

> The certainty that I exist, that I know it, and that I am glad of it, is independent of any imaginary and deceptive fantasies.
>
> In respect of these truths I have no fear of the arguments of the Academics. They say, "Suppose you are mistaken?" I reply, "If I am mistaken, I exist." A non-existent being cannot be mistaken; therefore I must exist, if I am mistaken. Then since my being mistaken proves that I exist, how can I be mistaken in thinking that I exist, seeing that my mistake establishes my existence?
>
> —(*The City of God*, pp. 459–460)

Augustine extolled the potential of the "inner senses" to provide us with self-knowledge of the contents of experience, thought, and memory and maintained that self-knowledge of the soul leads to knowledge of God. He created a new literary art form in his biographical *Confessions,* which provided an exhaustive catalogue of his sins with an extensive psychological commentary upon them. It contains astute observations on emotion, the perception of time, memory, and dreams. Augustine maintained that certain forms of knowledge are innate, such as our knowledge of mathematical relations and moral principles, and noted that certain forms of memory, such as our memory of emotions, do not involve images.

Like Philo, Augustine depreciated reason and experience in the pursuit of knowledge. He maintained that they are of value only insofar as they accord with Christian theology:

> For whatever a man has learned elsewhere is censured there [Holy Scripture] if it is harmful; if it is useful, it is found there.
>
> —(*On Christine Doctrine*, p. 63)

Augustine advocated and exemplified a life of piety and humility. He championed faith and emotional communication with God over reason and sense experience and recommended that humankind turn away from the ways of the world and look to God and the promise of Heaven.

The Fall of the Roman Empire

It is not surprising that Augustine held these views or that many accepted his theological vision in the ensuing centuries. The Western Empire was in disarray, ravaged by war, famine, and disease. In 410 Rome was sacked by the Visigoths under Alaric and later by the Huns and the Vandals. Communication and the rule of law broke down in the West. Augustine wrote *The City of God* (from 413 to 427) in response to Alaric's sacking of Rome, contrasting the temporal earthly city dominated by materialism and evil with the eternal and spiritual city of God that embodies goodness and salvation.

The new tribes that settled the fragments of the Western Empire, such as the Vandals, the Angles, the Saxons, and the Jutes, could not maintain the commercial centers of the former empire, and western Europe became increasingly rural and feudal. City walls eroded, harbors silted, and roads fell to ruin. Treasuries were looted, and learned books were destroyed or lost. The social unit was the farm-estate, which sustained a subsistence agricultural economy. Trade diminished to a vanishing point, and populations declined. Rome was reduced from a population of 1,500,000 in the first century to 300,000 in the fifth century, and by the end of the sixth century only about 50,000 remained in the ruins and rubble. The money economy returned to a barter economy.

MEDIEVAL PSYCHOLOGY

It is customary to mark the beginning of the **medieval period** with the deposition of Romulus Augustus in 476 and its end with the fall of Constantinople to the Turks in 1453. There is, of course, a high degree of arbitrariness about these dates. The Roman Empire was in decline long before the deposition of Romulus Augustus, and there were anticipations of the return of scientific thought in the centuries before the fall of Constantinople. Still, these dates are not without foundation. By the end of the fifth century the money-based commercial empire of the Romans had dissolved into isolated feudal enclaves based upon a rural subsistence economy. Most of the classical works were destroyed or lost and did not become available to Western scholars until the 12th century. By the end of the 15th century the Renaissance and Reformation were in full swing in western Europe, and the antipathy to tradition that they represented was a harbinger for the scientific revolution that began in the 16th century.

In western Europe, the period from about 500 to 1000, during which commerce and learning declined, is usually characterized as the early medieval period (the term *medieval* means "middle ages"). The period between about 1000 and 1300, during which commerce and learning revived, is usually characterized as the middle medieval period. The period from about 1300 to 1600, during which the intellectual and social system of the medieval world broke down through internal inconsistencies and the pressure of the Renaissance and Reformation, is usually characterized as the late medieval period.

It is customary to represent the medieval Christian Church as hostile to scientific thinking, to the point of the active persecution of scientists. Although there is some truth in this picture, it is also somewhat of a caricature, and the real story is more complex and interesting. Moreover, whatever learning was preserved in the West, particularly during the early medieval period, sometimes known as the Dark Ages, was preserved by clerics in monastic enclaves. However, during this period civilization and learning stagnated in Europe, apart from a brief renaissance during the reign of Charlemagne (742–814).

Islam

It was the Islamic Empire that rediscovered, translated, and preserved the works of Aristotle and other Greek thinkers. The prophet Muhammad was born in 570 and experienced his first vision of the archangel Gabriel in 610. It was revealed to him that he had been chosen as the messenger of Allah (God), and he received the sacred writings that formed the basis of the Koran, the holy book of the new Islamic religion. His followers quickly captured the holy cities of Mecca and Medina. Spectacularly, within a hundred years of the death of the prophet in 632, the Islamic Empire extended over an area greater than the Roman Empire at its height, including North Africa and Spain, Syria, Egypt, Arabia, and Persia. This brought Islamic scholars into contact with the classical works lost to the Western world.

The Islamic conquerors initially condemned and rejected such pagan works with the zeal of the early Christians. They destroyed the remains of the Great Library at Alexandria in 642, using the classical volumes to fuel the city baths. In justification, Caliph Omar claimed that "if these writings of the Greeks agree with the book of God, they are useless, and need not be preserved; if they disagree, they are pernicious, and ought to be destroyed," an attitude almost identical to that of Augustine.

Later caliphs were less antagonistic. Around 800 Caliph Haroun-al-Raschid had the works of Aristotle, Hippocrates, and Galen translated into Arabic; and his successors sent missions to Constantinople and India to discover other scientific works suitable for translation. The works of Plato, Plotinus, Euclid, Archimedes, and other classical writers became available to the Islamic Empire when it conquered Persia (where the works had been preserved by Alexandrians who had fled to Persia from Constantinople), and scholars such as Yaqub ibn Ishaq al-Kindi (d. after 866) and Abu Nasr al-Farabi (c. 870–950) translated them into Arabic. In this fashion the Islamic Empire became the repository of classical learning and science. The most famous Islamic scholars were Abu Ali al-Husayn ibn Sina (c. 980–1037), known in the West as Avicenna, and Muhammad ibn Roshd (1126–1198), known in the West as Averroës, who produced translations of, and commentaries on, these classical works. Avicenna and Averroës tried to integrate the central features of Platonic and Aristotelian philosophy with Islamic theology. Abu Ali Hasan ibn al-Haitham (965–1039), known in the West as Alhazan, developed the first detailed and experimentally grounded theory of visual perception.

Avicenna: *Canon of Medicine*, Venice 1595.

Avicenna   Avicenna was a physician to several Persian princes. He developed Galen's theories in his encyclopedic *Canon of Medicine*, a text that was widely used in medical schools in Europe and Asia during the medieval period. He wrote extensive and influential commentaries on the works of Aristotle, including psychological treatises based upon Aristotle's *De Anima* (Gutas, 1988). He became known in the Islamic world as the "third Aristotle,"[1] although his general Aristotelian principles were heavily larded with Platonic modifications (Goodman, 1992).

Avicenna developed the hierarchical account of the nutritive, sensitive, and rational psyche to be found in Aristotle's *De Anima*. He also followed Aristotle in distinguishing between passive and active reason and maintaining that active reason is immortal. However, in contrast to Aristotle, who claimed that passive reason is materially instantiated,

---

[1]Abu Nasr al-Farabi, who introduced Aristotelian logic to Islam, was known as the "second Aristotle."

Avicenna was a dualist who claimed that passive reason is a capacity of the immaterial or spiritual psyche. This conception was famously developed in Avicenna's **flying man argument**, which, like Augustine's similar argument, anticipated the argument for substance dualism later developed by René Descartes. Avicenna claimed that if a full-grown person suddenly came into existence, suspended in space, with limbs separated and eyes covered, he would have no sensation but would nevertheless be aware of his existence as an entity distinct from his body:

> Suppose that he was just created at a stroke, fully developed and perfectly formed but with his vision shrouded from perceiving all external objects—created floating in the air or in space, not buffeted by any perceptible current of the air that supports him, his limbs separated and kept out of contact with one another, so that they do not feel each other. Then let the subject consider whether he would affirm the existence of his self. There is no doubt that he would affirm his own existence, although not affirming the reality of any of his limbs or inner organs, his bowels, or heart or brain, or any external thing. Indeed he would affirm the existence of this self of his while not affirming that it had any length, breadth or depth. And if it were possible for him in such a state to imagine a hand or any other organ, he would not imagine it to be part of himself or a condition of his existence.
>
> —(Rahman, 1958, p. 16)

Avicenna followed Plato in treating forms or universals as prior to individual substances and identified Aristotle's prime mover with the Islamic God, or Allah. He also adopted a variant of Plotinus's theory of emanations to describe the relation between God, the world of intelligible ideas, immaterial souls, and material bodies.

Averroës   Averroës was a judge and physician who spent most of his life in Spain. He wrote detailed commentaries on Aristotle, whom he greatly venerated, and became known as "The Commentator" (on Aristotle, who had become known as "The Philosopher"). He provided an interpretation of Aristotle that was generally devoid of the Platonic modifications made by Avicenna (Kogan, 1985). He followed Aristotle in treating individual substances as prior to forms or universals, and his interpretation became foundational for many medieval Christian apologists, save for one problematic aspect. Averroës treated active reason as immaterial and immortal, but did not equate it with the individual human psyche. He argued that there is no way to distinguish the active reason of different human beings if active reason has no physical properties or spatial location and consequently maintained that active reason in all humans is numerically identical: It is one and the same in all humans. This doctrine, "that the intellect of all men is one and the same in number," became known in the Christian world as the **Averroës heresy** and was condemned by the Bishop of Paris in 1270 (Thorndike, 1944). Since he followed Aristotle in treating the rational psyche of human beings as materially instantiated, Averroës maintained that he could not accept the immortality of the soul on rational grounds, although he embraced it as an act of faith (Leaman, 1988).

Alhazan   Alhazen was perhaps the first to maintain that vision occurs when light reflected from external objects enters the eye. He conducted original experiments on light reflection and refraction and atmospheric effects on vision. His *Book of Optics* (1021) contains detailed discussions of color perception, apparent size, and double vision. Alhazen explored the problem of image inversion and located binocular vision in the "common nerve" (the optic nerve). He distinguished between sensation and perception and was one of the first theorists to relate the physics of light reflection to the anatomy of the eye. His empirical work and the problems it raised set the medieval agenda of research in visual perception (Lindberg, 1968).

European Recovery: Reason and Faith

The so-called Dark Ages in western Europe came to an end around 1000. Economies began to improve; the population began to increase again, particularly in the cities; the feudal system and the papacy evolved into dominant and integrative social structures. Commerce and communication improved, and theory and learning experienced a revival of sorts. Teachers of law, grammar, rhetoric, and logic were in high demand in urban centers, as religious and civic authorities tested the limits of their jurisdictions. Students and masters formed themselves into corporate entities called universities, with defined powers and rights. These were founded at Bologna (1088), Paris (1150), Oxford (1167), Padua (1222), Salamanca (1218), Vienna (1365), Prague (1348), and other urban centers, often in conjunction with the expansion in cathedral construction. Toward the end of the medieval period universities began issuing certificates, such as the baccalaureate, master's, and doctoral degrees (Pyenson & Sheets-Pyenson, 1999).

The first Crusade (1095) brought the Western world in contact with Islamic scholarship, which had preserved the works of early Greek thinkers. The medical schools of many medieval universities adopted Avicenna's *Canon of Medicine* as their primary text, and the commentaries of Avicenna and Averroës introduced the medieval Christian world to the works of Aristotle. Although condemned in 1220 and 1277, the naturalism of Aristotle eventually came to displace the Neoplatonism of Augustine as the conceptual foundation of Christianity.

The Church had by this time become more open to forms of knowledge other than scripture and revelation. Saint Anselm (1033–1109) claimed that reason and sense experience can supplement faith and developed famous arguments purporting to demonstrate the existence of God. Peter Lombard (c. 1095–1160) claimed that knowledge of God can be obtained through knowledge of divine works, including the natural world and its human inhabitants. Saint Albertus Magnus (c. 1193–1280) produced a comprehensive review of the works of Aristotle and his Islamic commentators and recommended reason and sense experience as legitimate sources of knowledge, since he presumed that neither would conflict with scripture.

Peter Abelard   Peter Abelard (1079–1142) also produced translations and reviews of Aristotle's works. He raised the employment of reason and argument to new heights and is often credited with the revival of the dialectic method of the early Greek philosophers, notably in his *Sic et Non* ("For and Against"). Abelard was convinced that any method of argument, including critical dialectic, would affirm God's existence, goodness, and wisdom. However, in practice his arguments exposed a number of conflicting theological positions, which got him into trouble with the church authorities.

While a canon of Notre Dame Cathedral in Paris, he met Héloise (1101–1164). By his own account, Abelard immediately set out to seduce her. He could scarcely believe his own good fortune when Héloise's uncle, Fulbert, offered free room and board in his house if Abelard would agree to tutor his niece privately. According to Abelard, he might as well have "entrusted a tender lamb to a hungry wolf" (Robertson, 1972, p. 43). He seduced her, and for the next few months the lovers "left no phase of love untried" (Grane, 1970, p. 49). Eventually Fulbert figured out what was going on and threw Abelard out, although by this time Héloise was pregnant.

The lovers married in secret. When Fulbert publicized the marriage, Abelard made Héloise pretend to accept holy vows. He took her to a convent and dressed her in a nun's habit. Fulbert was infuriated by Abelard's shoddy attempt to hide his own transgression, and with some aides, attacked Abelard in bed one night and castrated him: "They cut off those parts of my body with which I had done the deed they deplored" (Robertson, 1972, p. 55).

The passion of the lovers continued unabated, although now on a rather more Platonic level, as testified by the love letters they exchanged in the following years. Héloise became abbess and prioress of the Paraclete Abbey, which Abelard founded. Héloise's letters to Abelard include the learned *Problemata Héloissae*, which took the form of philosophical questions (with some spicy interludes). Abelard continued to court controversy and attention. A church council condemned his work in 1121, and he barely survived an assassination attempt in 1132. He was censured by Pope Innocent II in 1140 and ordered to cease writing and teaching. He died two years later and was buried in the Paraclete Abbey; on her death, Héloise was buried beside him. Their remains were later transferred to a crypt in the Père-Lachaise cemetery in Paris.

The Christian Church and Aristotelian Philosophy

The Christian Church originally rejected the works of Aristotle, which were condemned by Saint Bonaventure (1221–1274). However, medieval **scholastics** quickly followed their Islamic counterparts by trying to integrate them with Christian theology. In the prevalent literary metaphor of the time, they tried to effect a kind of intellectual "marriage" of Aristotelian theory and Christian theology. Aristotle's active reason was identified with the immortal soul, and Aristotle's unmoved mover was identified with the Christian God.

Thomas Aquinas   The classic statement of this attempt to reconcile reason (or at least the reason of Aristotle) and faith is to be found in the work of Saint Thomas Aquinas (c. 1225–1274). Born in the Italian city of Roccasecca, he was known as the "dumb ox" to his fellow students and the "angelic doctor" to his later admirers. His original attempt to enter the Church was thwarted by his family, who imprisoned him in the hope of persuading him to change his mind. When all attempts (including sexual temptation) failed, they relented and allowed him to travel to Cologne and study with Albertus Magnus, who persuaded him of the virtues of Aristotelian philosophy. Aquinas attained his master's degree from the University of Paris, where he taught for a number of years. His major work, *Summa Theologica*, appropriated those elements of Aristotelian theory most congenial to Christian theology.

Aquinas: the "marriage" of Christian theology and Aristotelian philosophy.

It is not hard to understand why Aristotelian theory appealed to Christian theologians. Aristotle's universe was teleological and hierarchical. Every inanimate and animate object had its own end or function, and it was easy to interpret this in terms of divine purpose and creation. Aristotle's scala naturae was represented as a "great chain of being" (Lovejoy, 1936), beginning with inanimate objects and reaching up through the vegetative, animal, and human kingdoms to the angels and God above, with the earth at the physical center of the universe and man at its spiritual center. This fixed hierarchical conception of the natural order served conveniently to sanction the established social hierarchy of the Church and the feudal system, with the pope and kings at its apex and the laboring peasants at its base, everyone serving their proper and fixed purpose in the feudal structure of nobles, lords, and vassals. Although initially controversial, Aquinas's Aristotelian version of Christianity came to supplant the earlier Neoplatonic version promoted by Augustine and remains to this day the foundational theology of the Roman Catholic Church.

Aquinas revived the Aristotelian conception of the human psyche as the functional capacities of the human material body. He also went one step further and treated active reason as a functional capacity of the embodied human psyche (Abel, 1995; Haldane, 1992). Consequently, later Christian theology shaped by Aquinas has tended to focus on the sure and certain hope of resurrection rather than a spiritual afterlife. Like Aristotle, Aquinas claimed that thought is dependent upon sensory experience, since it is dependent upon the ability to form sensory images, and he consequently denied the existence of innate ideas (Davies, 1992).

Aquinas also recognized the **intentional** nature of psychological states such as thoughts, emotions, motives, and memories: The fact that such psychological states make reference to some object beyond themselves. Thus my thought that Aristotle was the first psychological scientist is directed to or about Aristotle. In the late 19th century, the German psychologist Franz Brentano (1838–1917) characterized intentionality as the distinctive "mark of the mental" (Brentano, 1874/1995).

The Inner Senses The early Christian fathers, such as Augustine, had followed Plato, Philo, and Plotinus in treating the soul as an immaterial spiritual entity temporarily imprisoned in the material human body, the view also embraced by Avicenna. Aquinas returned Christianity to the Aristotelian conception of the soul as the functional form of the material human body, the view embraced by Averroës, although both Christian and Islamic scholars in the medieval period tried valiantly to reconcile the two positions (Kemp, 1990). Given this significant change, neither Christian nor Islamic theological orthodoxy can be blamed for the substance dualism that dominated early psychological science. Post-medieval commitments to dualism were in a very real sense a by-product of the scientific revolution in Europe that began in the 16th century: This was the position championed by René Descartes, one of the primary advocates of the new mechanistic science.

In any case, although the differences between such theorists were theologically significant, they seem to have played a relatively minor role in the development of medieval psychological theories. Since so little was known about human physiology and neurophysiology, different views about the immaterial versus the material basis of the human psyche had little impact upon psychological theory, which may be one reason why few scientists were persecuted by religious authorities for their specifically psychological theories.

A good example is the popularity of the theory of the **inner senses** or "inner wits" throughout the medieval period (Harvey, 1975). This theory was an amalgamation of the psychology of Aristotle and the neurophysiology of Galen. The inner senses were usually identified as common sense, imagination, estimation, memory, and reason. They were held to be located in the **ventricles** (fluid-filled

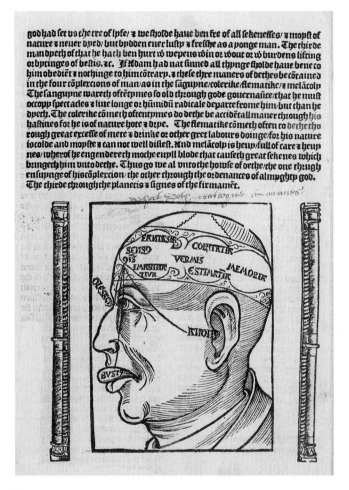

Medieval depiction of inner senses. Inner Wits: The Nobel Lyfe and Natures of Man (c. 1521).

cavities) of the brain, which were identified with reasonable accuracy by Galen (although Galen himself believed that psychological capacities were instantiated in the substance of the brain rather than the ventricles).

Early versions of the theory are to be found in Nemesius (a fourth-century Christian physician) and Augustine (Green, 2003). Avicenna developed the most popular and influential version in his *Canon of Medicine*, the standard medical text of the medieval period (Kemp, 1997). Avicenna claimed that the three ventricles of the brain perform five distinct cognitive operations. The anterior ventricle receives impressions from the various sensory organs and nerves, which are integrated by the common sense located at the front of the ventricle; the images produced are stored by the imagination at the rear. The middle ventricle is responsible for both the reconstruction of stored images to form complex representations (including representations of hitherto unobserved objects, such as men with wings or golden mountains) and estimation, based upon instinct or associative learning:

> Then there is the estimative faculty located at the far end of the middle ventricle of the brain, which perceives the non-sensible intentions that exist in the individual sensible objects, like the faculty that judges that the wolf is to be avoided and the child to be loved.
>
> —(Rahman, 1952, p. 31)

The posterior ventricle is responsible for memory of cognitive reconstructions and estimations produced in the middle ventricle.

The theory was employed to explain a variety of psychological phenomena beyond basic perception and cognition. The bizarre nature of dream images was explained in terms of imagination and memory operating independently of sense perception; and mania, melancholia, and accidie (a debilitating form of apathy) were attributed to disturbances of the different ventricles (Kemp, 1990). The theory was abandoned when the 16th-century anatomist Andreas Vesalius (1514–1564) demonstrated that the sensory nerves are connected to the rear of the brain and not to the anterior ventricle.

Medieval Christianity and Science

By the 13th century, Aristotle's works had been thoroughly assimilated by Christian theologians. This proved to be a mixed blessing. While Aristotle's achievements were duly recognized, the critical and empirical spirit behind them was not. Aristotle's generally cautious and qualified theories were elevated and fossilized into Christian dogma, to the point that it became a heresy to question those Aristotelian theories that were adopted by the Church, as Galileo, Bruno, and Descartes later learned to their cost.

However, it is a myth that the Church was actively hostile to science and used the Inquisition to stifle and inhibit those of a scientific and empirical bent. Few scientists are recorded as having being burnt at the stake by the Inquisition. The general response of the Church to problematic intellectual positions was the expurgation of printed works and excommunication of their authors (Thorndike, 1944). The Church was actively hostile to astrology, which was frequently practiced in conjunction with astronomy, but only one astrologer is recorded as having been condemned to death, one Cecco d'Ascoli in 1327 (Wedel, 1968).

It is also a myth that the medieval Church impeded the scientific study of medicine by prohibiting the dissection of human cadavers (Demaitre, 1975). The Council of Tours issued a prohibition against human dissection in 1163, but this was not directed toward medical science. It was introduced to discourage the convenient practice of dismembering the mortal remains of Crusaders before they were shipped home. In any case, many medical schools, such as the Hippocraticum Medicorum Collegium at Salerno, the leading medical school in the 12th century, simply ignored the prohibition, and there was no systematic ecclesiastical opposition to human dissection during the medieval period. At many universities, such as the University of Bologna, human dissection was mandatory (Bullough, 1958). The students resisted it, not the university or church authorities (Kemp, 1990).

Guglielmo da Saliceto (1210–1277), an Italian surgeon, published a record of his dissections in 1275, as did Mondino de' Luzzi (c. 1275–1326) in 1316. One of the few anatomists to be sentenced to death by the Inquisition was Vesalius, who pioneered the scientific revolution in medicine at the University of Padua in the 16th century, at the very end of the medieval period. However, Vesalius was accused of murder before the Inquisition by the parents of a man he had supposedly dissected while still alive, not for his medical dissection per se. His life was spared by the intervention of Phillip II, and his sentence was commuted to a religious pilgrimage.

Pope Gregory IX instituted the **Inquisition** in 1233 to repress the remains of the **Catharian heresy** in Spain and the south of France, which Pope Innocent II had earlier launched the Albigensian Crusade to combat. The Catharists were critical of the wealth and power hierarchy of the Church and maintained that since Christ was poor the Church should follow his example and abandon its wealth. Many perished for that dangerous belief, but not for advocating any controversial scientific theory.

Witches and Demons   Another myth is that the Church, largely through the offices of the Inquisition, condemned hundreds of thousands of unfortunate persons, mainly women, to burn as witches. The medieval period is often represented as a regressive period of reversion to superstitious theories of spirit possession and repressive treatments of psychological disorder. It is commonly supposed that during the medieval period symptoms of psychological disorder were treated as evidence of witchcraft or demon possession and that many innocents perished as a result of such ignorance (Altrocchi, 1980; Alexander & Selesnick, 1966; Suinn, 1975). Estimates of the human cost of this persecution are usually in the order of hundreds of thousands in Europe: "literally hundreds of thousands of women and children were condemned as witches . . . and burned at the stake" (Zax & Cohen, 1976, p. 41).

Yet, for most of the medieval period, the Church did not recognize the existence of witches and reserved the stake for unrepentant heretics (Kirsch, 1978). Although the Office of the Inquisition was undoubtedly repressive and employed secret investigations and torture, it was only employed to investigate witchcraft toward the end of the medieval period (Cohen, 1975). The famous tract against witchcraft, *Malleus Maleficarum* (*The Witches Hammer*), written by Jacob Sprenger

Burning witches.

and Heinrich Kramer, was published in 1487, years after the fall of Constantinople and the beginning of the European Renaissance, which are usually held to mark the end of the medieval period (Cohen, 1975).

Although this "huntsman's bible" is often held to have been responsible for "hundreds and thousands of women and children being burned at the stake" (Alexander & Selesnick, 1966), the numbers are greatly exaggerated (Schoeneman, 1977), possibly by a factor as high as 100 percent (Maher & Maher, 1985; Trevor-Roper, 1967). For example, the extremely active Grand Inquisitor Bernard Gui (c. 1307–1323) dealt with 930 cases in his lifetime, of which 80 accused were already deceased when they came to trial: in only 43 cases were the accused condemned to the stake (Coulton, 1961, cited in Kemp, 1990). It has been argued that the European witch craze was not a function of medieval superstition and ignorance, but a product of the scientific revolution of the 16th century, which encouraged the idea that there might be empirical indices of demon possession and witchcraft (Kirsch, 1978).

The European "witch craze" was real enough, but reached its zenith in the 16th , 17th, and 18th centuries. Critics such as Cornelius Agrippa (1486–1535) and Philippus Paracelsus (1493–1541) challenged explanations of abnormal behavior in terms of witchcraft from the moment they were embraced by later Protestant and Catholic zealots. Johann Weyer (1515–1588) in the *Deception of Demons* (1563) and Reginald Scott (c. 1538–1599) in the *Discovery of Witchcraft* (1584/1971) were among the first to suggest that some of the persons identified as witches might be suffering from some form of psychological disorder.

Still, it is doubtful if all those who were burned as witches were psychologically abnormal, since the motives of their persecutors appear to have been many and various. They included social, political, economic, legal, and personal as well as religious reasons (Schoeneman, 1977; Spanos, 1978). For example, while most of the witches burned in Britain were female and poor, a good number in continental Europe were male and rich, and this demographic distribution may have been not accidentally related to the more liberal laws of property seizure in continental Europe (Currie, 1968).

The medieval Church did recognize demon possession, which it distinguished from witchcraft. However, most clerics were skeptical of purported cases of demon possession, and there were few cases of prosecution because they believed possession to be a rare occurrence. Exorcisms were also infrequent and usually only performed in cases of convulsion and incoherence of speech (Neugebauer, 1978). Saint Francis of Assisi (c. 1182–1226) employed a variety of tests to discriminate the possessed from the psychologically disturbed, based upon the attributed powers and responses of demons (Kemp, 1990). Philipp Melanchthon (1497–1560) tried to achieve the same goal by splashing suspected persons with vials of ordinary well water and holy water. He judged only those few whose violent response was restricted to holy water to be possessed (Bodin, 1975).

The officers of the Inquisition were usually friars of the Franciscan order, founded by Saint Francis in the 13th century. The Franciscan order, like the Dominican order, was created in response to the Catharian heresy, which many believed could be countered only by clerics who preached orthodoxy while living lives of poverty and austerity. One of the paradoxes of the medieval period was that, while the Franciscans staffed the most oppressive office of the Church, their order also produced open-minded theorists such as Roger Bacon (c. 1214–1292), Duns Scotus (c. 1265–1308), and William of Occam (c. 1280–1349), whose work anticipated the scientific revolution of the 16th and 17th centuries (Kemp, 1990).

Natural Fools and Accidie   It is commonly supposed that the medievals had little understanding of psychological disorders and consequently treated those suffering from them in cruel and barbaric ways. It is often righteously assumed that it was only in the 20th century that scientific psychology developed an adequate classification system for psychological disorders and developed effective and humane means of treating them.

Yet medieval theories of psychological disorders were quite various. Most disorders were attributed to constitutional or environmental brain damage, as in the case of those identified as "natural fools" and those whose disorders were attributed to accidents such as blows to the head (Spanos, 1978). Psychological disorders were also attributed to the imbalance of humors brought about by noxious substances such as strong wine; to emotional stress induced by over-zealous work or study; and to various psychological and social causes, such as marriage problems, frustrated love or fortune, failed ambition, guilt, jealousy, fear, bereavement, economic problems, discord between parents and children, social abuse, and stigma (Neugebauer, 1978).

The medieval view of psychological disorders was neither narrow nor conceptually unsophisticated. To take but one example, in the fifth century, the Christian theologian John Cassian listed **accidie** as the eighth deadly sin. This was a form of depression characterized as a debilitating form of apathy or disgust with life, which came to be known as the "noonday sickness," because it drew monks away from their midday prayers. This form of depression was distinguished from the form of depression involving sadness associated with personal loss or feelings of inadequacy, which came to be known as melancholie. These different forms of depression, which were distinguished by Aristotle and Saint Paul, who thought only the former sinful, were much discussed in medieval times (Altschule, 1965). As late as the 17th century, the English physician Richard Napier (1559–1634) distinguished cases of accidie from melancholie and noted that the leisured upper classes suffered from it more frequently than the laboring lower classes (MacDonald, 1981).

Eventually the term and diagnosis fell out of use, and it was dropped from the list of deadly sins. Few people complain of accidie these days, and it is not recognized in any edition of the *Diagnostic and Statistical Manual of Mental Disorders* (DSM). Nonetheless, the medievals may not have been wildly off the mark. The psychiatrist Robert Findley-Jones (1986) has suggested that the General Health Questionnaire and the Present State Examination can be employed to discriminate accidie from regular depression and that accidie appears to be especially prevalent among housewives and the unemployed (in Melbourne, Australia, at least).

Medieval modes of treatment tended to be eclectic, ranging from rest and relaxation, controlled diet, music, medicines, and folk-compounds to bloodletting, purgatives, amulets, counseling, and prayer. Most of these were based upon a holistic conception of health derived from Hippocrates. It was only in the 18th and 19th centuries that "scientific" treatments such as spinning, water-dousing, and electrical stimulation became popular, along with primitive and often dangerous experiments in psychopharmacology, involving iron, arsenic, and strychnine (Jackson, 1986). The medievals generally treated those suffering from psychological disorders with the level of sympathy and care appropriate to these harsh times.

Empiriks

Although medieval Christian scholars were not actively hostile to science, they did little to promote it. Throughout the medieval period, real opportunities for the advancement of science were frequently not exploited, not because of clerical interference, but out of a general lack of interest in pursuing theoretical questions empirically.

A good illustration of this was the failure to empirically evaluate the theories of Galen, whose anatomy and physiology were taught at most medical schools during the medieval period. To take but one example, Galen had described a system of blood vessels at the base of the brain in humans and animals known as the *rete mirabile* (the marvelous net), which were believed to refine the animal spirits in the brain:

> The plexus called retiform [rete mirabile] by anatomists is the most wonderful of the bodies located in this region. It encircles the gland [the hypophysis] itself and extends far to the rear; for nearly the whole base of the encephalon has this plexus lying beneath it.
>
> —(*On the Usefulness of the Parts of the Body*, 1, p. 430)

His description of this system was regularly repeated in medieval medical texts (Kemp, 1990). However, fairly elementary neurophysiological examination would have established that this system does not exist in humans, although it does in ungulates, such as sheep and goats, upon which Galen practiced his dissections. Vesalius demonstrated this in the 16th century, when Padua and other Italian medical schools led the scientific revolution in medicine. Although dissection was not systematically prohibited or suppressed, and indeed was required in many medical schools, few physicians in medieval times seem to have bothered to empirically check the adequacy of Galen's account, just as few natural philosophers before Galileo seem to have bothered to empirically check the adequacy of Aristotle's false but intuitively plausible theory that bodies of different weight fall with different velocities.

For the medievals, theoretical knowledge was based upon scholarly tradition. Medical degrees at Oxford, for example, were awarded on the basis of three public lectures on the works of Galen (Kemp, 1990), not upon hours spent in biology labs or anatomy classes. If you were injured and needed surgical treatment during the medieval period, you did not consult a physician. You went to a butcher, one skilled in the practical art of the knife, or, as they were called in those days, an **empirik**. They were originally treated as charlatans, who ignored scientific theory and based their practice on observation alone.

Science as we know it today came about when theorists also became empiriks, when they began to subject their own and their predecessors' theories to empirical tests. This is what distinguishes the practice of the pioneers of the scientific revolution in Europe in the 16th century, such as Galileo and Vesalius, and eventually the practice of the first truly scientific psychologists.

Anticipations

The general tenor of the medieval mind was nonempirical: Theories were held to derive their support from tradition and scripture. Still, there were a number of medieval theorists who advanced principles of scientific methodology that were clearly ahead of their time and which have a distinctly modern resonance. Robert Grosseteste (c. 1168–1253), chancellor of the University of Oxford, produced detailed commentaries and analyses of Aristotle's *Posterior Analytics* and *Physics* and wrote extensively on the logic of the confirmation and falsification of scientific theories.

Roger Bacon (c. 1214–1292), a Franciscan who studied at Oxford and Paris (where he later taught), also wrote extensive commentaries on Aristotle and strove to achieve a unification of the various sciences of his day. In his *Opus Magnus* Bacon put forward what he called the first and second **prerogatives of experimental science**. He maintained that any theory developed to accommodate a range of observations should be further tested via additional novel predictions derived from the theory and that experimentation, in the form of controlled intervention, can augment the naturalistic observational basis of scientific theories. Bacon is often unfairly characterized as a necromancer (an enchanter) because of his interest in alchemy and his extravagant claims about its achievements. However, he clearly recognized the need for theoretical science to unite with technical craft traditions such as alchemy, which represented one of the few approximations to empirical science in medieval times.

Duns Scotus (c. 1265–1308), a Franciscan who studied at Oxford and Paris, and William of Occam (c. 1280–1349), a Franciscan who studied at Oxford, described the methods of comparative causal analysis later known as "Mill's methods." William of Occam enunciated a general principle of theoretical economy that has come to be known as **Occam's razor**: "Entities are not to be multiplied beyond necessity." Although the principle was originally introduced within the medieval debate about the ontological status of universals, it applies generally to the evaluation of any set of competing theories.

Occam claimed that one ought not to postulate any more entities or degrees of complexity than are necessary to explain a range of phenomena in any domain. When two or more theories are equivalent in terms of the empirical data they predict and purport to explain, Occam's razor reasonably enjoins us to choose the simplest theory. This principle eventually found its psychological expression in the methodological prescription formulated by the English comparative psychologist Conwy Lloyd Morgan (1852–1936), which came to be known as **Morgan's canon**. Morgan claimed that psychologists should not explain animal behavior by reference to complex cognitive states if it can be explained in simpler terms, such as in terms of instincts or learned habits (Morgan, 1894/1977).

These theorists were ahead of their time, and their work had little immediate impact. Few rushed to implement their principles, and many of them failed to follow their own methodological prescriptions, often regressing to appeals to tradition or the "naturalness" of their theories. Most continued to assimilate Aristotelian philosophy to Christian theology, and their development of the more empirically oriented elements of Aristotle's scientific writings brought them into conflict with the Church authorities. Bacon was confined for a number of years, and Occam fled to Bavaria when the Inquisition examined his writings, although he escaped condemnation.

THE END OF THE MEDIEVAL PERIOD

The end of the medieval period is conventionally dated by the fall of Constantinople to the Turks in 1453. This date is somewhat arbitrary. The forces of change were in motion long before, and recognizable anticipations of the scientific revolution can be traced back as early as the 12th century. Yet the date is not inappropriate. By 1453 the world was changing fast and expanding rapidly. Around this date Johann Gutenberg (c. 1397–1468) printed his first Bible. Forty years later Christopher Columbus (c. 1451–1506) discovered the Americas. The Renaissance and Reformation were in full swing, and the scientific revolution was about to begin.

DISCUSSION QUESTIONS

1. The theories of early Greek scientists had few practical or technological applications. The Romans were very practical and technological, but seemed constitutionally uninterested in science. Is there no connection between science and technology? In considering this question, remember that many 20th-century theorists saw scientific psychology as the basis of a technology of social control or "social engineering," through forms of education and treatment.

2. Theorists such as Plotinus and Avicenna followed Plato in maintaining that the psyche is immaterial and that some forms of knowledge (such as knowledge of mathematics and moral principles) are innate. Theorists such as Averroës and Aquinas followed Aristotle in maintaining that the psyche is materially incarnated and that there is no innate knowledge. Is there any connection between their views on the psyche and their views on the possibility of innate knowledge?

3. Have you ever experienced a debilitating emotion akin to accidie? Does the medieval characterization of this emotion bear any resemblance to contemporary clinical phenomena? Does the fact that we no longer talk about accidie mean that we no longer experience it?

4. Think of the scientific theories you know, in psychology and other natural and social sciences. Are they formulated, or formulable, as sets of axioms and theorems, in the manner in which they were presented by early theorists

such as Euclid and Archimedes and by later natural scientists and psychologists such as Isaac Newton and Clark L. Hull? Does such axiomization represent a desirable ideal for scientific theories (promoting scientific rigor) or an overly formal constriction (impeding the fertile development of theories)?

5. Consider the fact that the medieval theory of the "inner senses" was advocated by both materialists such as Averröes and Aquinas and by substance dualists such as Augustine and Avicenna. In this instance, commitment to an immaterial soul seems to have had no significant implications for specific psychological theories of perception and cognition. Does it have any implications for psychological theories?

GLOSSARY

accidie A form of depression recognized by ancient and medieval theorists, which they characterized as a debilitating form of apathy or disgust with life.

Averroës heresy Averroës's claim that the active reason in all humans is numerically identical. The Christian Church condemned it as heresy in 1270.

Catharian heresy The belief that since Christ was poor the Church should abandon its wealth.

choleric type According to Galen, the irritable and emotional personality type with an excess of yellow bile.

Cynics The followers of Antisthenes and Diogenes, who rejected classical learning and conventional morality and advocated a primitive and independent lifestyle.

empirik The medieval term for a butcher, skilled in the practical art of surgery.

Epicureanism Philosophy of happiness based upon moderation developed by Epicurus and his Roman disciple Lucretius.

flying man argument Avicenna's argument in support of substance dualism.

inner senses A medieval psychological theory that was an amalgamation of the psychology of Aristotle and the neurophysiology of Galen. The "inner senses" were identified as perceptual and cognitive faculties located in the ventricles of the brain.

Inquisition Office created by Pope Gregory IX in 1233 to combat heresy; its officers were generally friars of the Franciscan order.

intentionality The directedness or "aboutness" of psychological states such as thoughts, emotions, motives, and memories.

medieval period The period from approximately 500 to 1600 CE.

melancholic type According to Galen, the sad type of personality with an excess of black bile.

Morgan's canon Methodological prescription, advanced by the comparative psychologist C. Lloyd Morgan, that psychologists should not explain animal behavior by reference to complex cognitive states if it can be explained in simpler terms.

Neoplatonism Theories developed in the early years of the Roman Empire that emphasized the mystical and spiritual elements of Plato's philosophy.

Occam's razor Principle advanced by William of Occam, according to which no more entities or degrees of complexity should be introduced in a theoretical explanation than are necessary to explain the range of data in any domain. When empirically equivalent theories compete, Occam's razor enjoins us to choose the simplest theory.

phlegmatic type According to Galen, the slothful personality type with an excess of phlegm.

prerogatives of experimental science Methodological principles advanced by Roger Bacon, who maintained that theories should be evaluated by reference to their novel predictions and that experimentation should augment naturalistic observation.

sanguine type According to Galen, the cheerful personality type with an excess of blood.

scholasticism The term used to describe medieval attempts to integrate Aristotelian philosophy and Christian theology.

Skeptics The followers of Pyrrho, who repudiated all pretensions to knowledge.

Stoicism The philosophy of life advocated by Zeno of Citium, in which the good life is identified with acceptance of one's fate in a determined world.

substance dualism Theory that the soul (or mind) is a special and simple spiritual substance distinct from material substance, which can survive bodily death.

ventricles The fluid-filled cavities of the brain identified by Galen, which were held to be the location of perceptual and cognitive faculties according to the medieval theory of the "inner senses."

REFERENCES

Abel, D. C. (1995). Intellectual substance as form of the body in Aquinas. *American Catholic Philosophical Quarterly, 69* (Suppl.), 227–236.

Alexander, F. G., & Selesnick, S. T. (1966). *The history of psychiatry: An evaluation of psychiatric thought and practice from prehistoric times to the present.* New York: Harper & Row.

Altrocchi, J. (1980). *Abnormal behavior.* New York: Harcourt Brace Jovanovich.

Altschule, M. D. (1965). Acedia [accidie]: Its evolution from deadly sin to psychiatric syndrome. *British Journal of Psychiatry, 111*, 117–119.

Augustine, Saint. (1958). *On Christian doctrine.* (D. W. Robertson, Jr., Trans.) Indianapolis: Bobbs-Merrill. (Original work from fourth and fifth centuries CE).

Augustine, Saint. (1972). *The city of God* (H. Bettenson, Trans.). New York: Penguin. (Original work from fifth century CE)

Bodin, J. (1975). *Colloquium of the seven about secrets of the sublime* (Marion Kuntz, Trans.). Princeton: Princeton University Press.

Brentano, Franz. (1995). *Psychology from an empirical standpoint.* London: Routledge. (Original work published 1874)

Bullough, V. L. (1958). Medieval Bologna and the development of medical education. *Bulletin of the History of Medicine, 32*, 201–215.

Cohen, N. (1975). *Europe's inner demons.* London: Chatto/Heinemann.

Coulton, G. G. (1961). *Medieval panorama: Vol II. The horizon of thought.* London: Collins.

Currie, E. P. (1968). Crimes without criminals—Witchcraft and its control in Renaissance Europe. *Law and Society Review, 3*, 1026.

Davies, B. (1992). *The thought of Thomas Aquinas.* Oxford: Oxford University Press.

Demaitre, L. (1975). Theory and practice of medical education at the University of Montpelier in the thirteenth and fourteenth centuries. *Journal of the History of Medicine and Allied Sciences, 30*, 103–123.

Findley-Jones, R. (1986). Accidie and melancholie in a clinical context. In R. Harré (Ed.), *The social construction of emotion.* Oxford: Blackwell.

Galen. (1968). *On the usefulness of the parts of the body* (Vols. 1–2; M. T. May, Trans.). Ithaca, NY: Cornell University Press. (Original work from second century CE)

Goodman, L. E. (1992). *Avicenna.* New York: Routledge.

Grane, L. (1970). *Peter Abelard's philosophy and Christianity in the Middle Ages* (F. Crowley & C. Crowley, Trans.). New York: Harcourt, Brace & World.

Green, C. D. (2003). Where did the ventricular localization of mental faculties come from? *Journal of the History of the Behavioral Sciences, 39*, 131–142.

Gutas, D. (1988). *Avicenna and the Aristotelian tradition.* Leiden: Brill.

Haldane, J. (1992). Aquinas and the active intellect. *Philosophy, 67*, 199–210.

Harvey, E. R. (1975). *Inward wits.* London: Warburg Institute, University of London.

Hobbes, T. (1966). *On human nature.* In W. Molesworth (Ed.), *The English works of Thomas Hobbes.* Darmstadt, Germany: Scientia Verlag Aalen. (Original work published 1640)

Hull, C. L. (1943). *Principles of behavior.* New York: Appleton-Century-Crofts.

Jackson, S. W. (1969). Galen—On mental disorders. *Journal of the History of the Behavioral Sciences, 5*, 365–384.

Jackson, S. W. (1986). *Melancholia and depression: From Hippocratic to modern times.* New Haven, CT: Yale University Press.

Kemp, S. (1990). *Medieval psychology.* New York: Greenwood Press.

Kemp, S. (1997). The inner senses: A medieval theory of cognitive functioning in the ventricles of the brain. In W. G. Bringmann, H. E. Lück, R. Miller & C. E. Early (Eds.), *A pictorial history of psychology.* Chicago: Quintessence.

Kirsch, I. (1978). Demonology and the rise of science: An example of the misperception of historical data. *Journal of the History of the Behavioral Sciences, 14,* 149–157.

Kogan, B. (1985). *Averroës and the metaphysics of creation.* Albany: State University of New York Press.

Leaman, O. (1988) *Averroës and his philosophy.* (2nd ed.) Oxford: Clarendon Press.

Lindberg, D. (1968). Alhazan's theory of vision and its reception in the west. *Isis, 58,* 321–341.

Lovejoy, A. O. (1936). *The great chain of being.* Harvard: Harvard University Press.

MacDonald, M. (1981). *Mystical Bedlam—Madness, anxiety and healing in seventeenth-century England.* Cambridge: Cambridge University Press.

Maher, W. B., & Maher, B. A. (1985). Psychopathology: 1. From ancient times to the eighteenth century. In G. A. Kimble & K. Schlesinger (Eds.), *Topics in the history of psychology* (Vol. 2). Hillsdale, NJ: Erlbaum.

Morgan, C. L. (1977). *Introduction to comparative psychology.* In D. N. Robinson (Ed.), *Significant contributions to the history of psychology, 1750–1920.* Series D: *Comparative psychology* (Vol. 2). Washington, DC: University Publications of America. (Original work published 1894)

Neugebauer, R. (1978). Treatment of the mentally ill in medieval and early modern England: A reappraisal. *Journal of the History of the Behavioral Sciences, 14,* 158–169.

Newton, I. (1969). *Mathematical principles of natural philosophy.* (F. Cajori, Trans.). New York: Greenwood Press. (Original work published 1687)

O'Meara, D. J. (1995). *Plotinus: Introduction to the Enneads.* Oxford: Oxford University Press.

Pyenson, L., & Sheets-Pyenson, S. (1999). *Servants of nature: A history of scientific institutions, enterprises, and sensibilities.* New York: Norton.

Rahman, F. (Trans.) (1952). *Avicenna's psychology.* London: Oxford University Press.

Rahman, F. (Trans.). (1958). *Shifa De Anima (Avicenna).* Oxford: Oxford University Press.

Roach, M. (2003). *Stiff: The curious lives of human cadavers.* New York: Norton.

Robertson, D. W., Jr. (1972). *Abelard and Heloise.* New York: Dial Press.

Schoeneman, T. J. (1977). The role of mental illness in the European witch hunts of the sixteenth and seventeenth centuries: An assessment. *Journal of the History of the Behavioral Sciences, 13,* 337–351.

Scott, R. (1971). *Discovery of witchcraft.* New York: Walter J. Johnson. (Original work published 1584)

Smith, A. M. (1996). Ptolemy's theory of visual perception. *Transactions of the American Philosophical Society, 86,* Pt. 2.

Spanos, N. P. (1978). Witchcraft in histories of psychology: A critical analysis and an alternative conception. *Psychological Bulletin, 85,* 417–439.

Sprenger, J., & Kramer, H. (1989). *Malleus maleficarum* [*The witches hammer*] (M. Summers, Trans.). Mineola, NY: Dover. (Original work published 1487)

Suinn, R. (1975). *Fundamentals of behavior pathology* (2nd ed.). New York: Wiley.

Thorndike, L. (1944). *University records and life in the Middle Ages.* New York: Cambridge University Press.

Trevor-Roper, H. R. (1967). *The European witch-craze of the 16th and 17th centuries.* Harmondsworth, England: Penguin.

von Straden, H. (1989). *Herophilus: The art of medicine in early Alexandria.* Cambridge: Cambridge University Press.

Wedel, T. (1968). *The medieval attitude towards astrology, particularly in England.* Hamden, CT: Archon.

Weyer, J. (1563). *Deception of demons.* London.

Zax, M., & Cohen, E. L. (1976). *Abnormal psychology.* (2nd ed.). New York: Holt, Rinehart & Winston.

CHAPTER 4

The Scientific Revolution

O N OCTOBER 11, 1572, THE DANISH ASTRONOMER TYCHO BRAHE (1546–1601) observed a bright new object in the evening sky. This was "a miracle indeed," since this object did not move against the background of fixed stars and must itself have been a star. Yet Aristotle had taught that everything in the celestial region, the sphere of fixed stars, was perfect and unchanging. Brahe's observation of what we now believe to have been a supernova (a new star) was one of the many developments that led to the eventual overthrow of the Aristotelian geocentric (Earth-centered) astronomical system and the medieval worldview based upon it.

By the 14th century, the social, political, and intellectual order of the medieval world had begun to break down. Increased urbanization and the return to a money economy eroded the structure of the feudal system, and the rise of nation-states undermined the political authority of the papacy. Intermittent wars between the emerging nation-states led to a severe economic depression. This was followed by the plague of 1348–1350, later known as the "Black Death," which decimated the European population and bred doubt and resentment against the medieval Church, the dominant authority. Although the Church embraced Aristotle's philosophy, the threat posed by its naturalism and rationalism generated dissent and division, leading initially to attempts to divorce the separate realms of faith and reason and then to the autonomous emergence of naturalistic empirical science.

Various developments contributed to the transformation of the intellectual landscape. Marco Polo's (1254–1324) exploration of China, Christopher Columbus's (1451–1506) discovery of America in 1492, and Magellan's (1480–1521) circumnavigation of the globe expanded the horizons of the known world. Perhaps the most significant development was the invention of printing and the consequent transformation of communication. In the city of Mainz in southern Germany, Johann Gutenberg (c. 1397–1468) created movable type and published an edition of the Bible in 1450. The consequent explosion in printed works expanded intellectual horizons by broadening access to the Bible and classical works. By 1500, about 8 million volumes had been printed (Pyenson & Sheets-Pyenson, 1999); by 1600, about 20 million, with over a dozen presses established in European cities (Foote, 1991). The critical interpretation of these works by humanist scholars encouraged a more secular—and more skeptical—approach to the classical tradition and scriptural authority, and the reliable reproduction of works in physics, astronomy, and medicine transformed science into a public enterprise. In earlier centuries the works of Aristotle, Ptolemy, and Galen had been transcribed by hand by monastic clerics, with errors compounded over generations, and read only by the educated elite. From the mid-15th century onwards multiple copies of scientific works were critically scrutinized by the scientific community and educated members of the lay public.

Critical questioning of the classical tradition and scriptural authority was paralleled by the critical and empirical evaluation of the theories of Aristotle, Ptolemy, and Galen during the period of the 16th and 17th centuries in Europe known as the scientific revolution. As their theories were displaced by those of Nicholaus Copernicus (1473–1543), Johannes Kepler (1571–1630), Galileo, Newton, and Vesalius, empirical evaluation displaced the authority of tradition as the mark of modern science. Quantified efficient causal explanation of matter in motion displaced final causal explanation in the new physics, and eventually these mechanistic forms of explanation were extended to the realm of biology and psychology by theorists such as Gomez Pereira (1500–c. 1558), William Harvey (1578–1657), Descartes, Julien Offroy de La Mettrie (1709–1751), Thomas Hobbes (1588–1679), and Robert Whytt (1714–1766).

RENAISSANCE AND REFORMATION

The **Renaissance**, meaning "rebirth," originated in southern Italy in the 14th century, eventually spreading to Northern Europe. It promoted innovative developments in art, literature, architecture, music, mathematics, and—eventually—religion and science. Humanistic thinkers such as Francesco Petrarch (1304–1374), Giovanni Pico della Mirandola (1463–1494), and Desiderius Erasmus (c. 1466–1536) were highly critical of the institutional hierarchy and dogmatism of the established church and recommended a return to a more personal relationship with God. With greater access to classical literature, Renaissance humanists rediscovered the ancient Greek theorists and found much to admire in their focus upon the psychology of human life. They rediscovered Plato, who came to rival Aristotle as the classical authority, although Aristotle continued to be admired for his original works, as opposed to the sterile appropriations of his natural philosophy that had become fossilized as church dogma. Indeed, the Renaissance deserves to be characterized as a period of rediscovery as much as rebirth, since it was largely grounded in the recovery and retranslation of classical texts, which came to be admired for their intrinsic merits and celebration of humanity.

Petrarch is often treated as the founder of **Renaissance humanism**, insofar as his writings heralded the increased focus on the psychology of human individuals, including their place in the social and political order. Petrarch was critical of the sterility of scholastic thought and particularly the overly rigid Aristotelianism at the heart of Christian dogma. He celebrated the critical and naturalistic thought of the ancients and their focus on human capacities and potential. In religion, he recommended a return to the more personal and spiritual form of religion practiced by Augustine, presaging the later Protestant Reformation.

The Renaissance commitment to human potential was expressed in Pico's famous oration on the dignity of humanity, in which he located humankind as poised between the lower animals and the angels: capable of degenerating to bestiality, but also endowed with almost unlimited potential for creative intellectual, moral, and spiritual development. According to Pico, God had allowed humans to determine the limits of their own nature.

Somewhat paradoxically, in Renaissance humanism faith in the potential of humanity went hand in hand with skepticism about human pretensions to knowledge. Erasmus, in *The Praise of Folly* (1512), caricatured the dogmatic and superstitious beliefs of medieval scholasticism and contrasted the pretentious ceremony and hierarchy of the Church with the simple humility and humanity of Christ. Paracelsus rejected the classical authority of Galen and Avicenna in the realm of medicine, which he claimed should be founded upon empirical learning, although his own practice was heavily infused with astrology and mysticism.

The cautious skepticism of earlier humanists was eclipsed by the radical skepticism of Michel de Montaigne (1533–1592), who resurrected the arguments of Greek skeptics such as Pyrrho. He maintained that neither sense experience nor reason could yield knowledge of the natural and spiritual world. While few shared Montaigne's depth of skepticism, his advocacy of such an extreme position stimulated later defenses of autonomous rationality and the scientific method, notably those advanced by Descartes and Bacon.

The Renaissance promoted pioneering explorations of human nature in the art and anatomy of Leonardo da Vinci (1452–1519), the political writings of Niccolò Machiavelli (1469–1527), and the poetry and drama of William Shakespeare (1564–1616), but did little to advance the systematic scientific study of human psychology. However, it did witness the first attempts to apply medical and psychological theories to the development of education, most notably in the work of the Spanish humanist Juan Luis Vives (1492–1540). Born in Valencia, Vives was educated at the universities of Paris and Louvain, where he befriended Erasmus. His reputation as a teacher and scholar in the Netherlands later earned him a position at Oxford University (from 1523–1528), where he was supported by Thomas More and Henry VIII. After Henry's dispute with More over his divorce from Catherine of Aragon and More's subsequent execution, Vives returned to the Netherlands. There he completed *De Anima et Vita* (1538), in which he argued that knowledge of human physiology and psychology should be applied to the improvement of educational practice and the humane treatment of the insane.

Vives is best remembered for his comprehensive treatment of the associative principles of similarity, contrast, and contiguity (Brett, 1912–1921), which has led some to characterize him as the "father of modern psychology" (Clemens, 1967). Although his treatment of association followed Aristotle's general account, Vives tried to link the operation of memory to humoral physiology and cited many more examples of associationist principles than Aristotle. In many respects, Vives was a transitional figure, who retained great respect for classical authorities and deviated little from them in practice, but also conceived of the study of human psychology as a form of naturalistic knowledge grounded in observation:

> The study of man's soul exercises a most helpful influence on all kinds of knowl-
> edge. . . . This treatment of the development of knowledge within our souls will
> proceed parallel with the natural order.
>
> —(*De Disciplinis*, cited in Clemens, 1967, p. 221)

Reformation

Dissatisfaction with the sterility, pomp, and hierarchy of the medieval Church eventually produced the religious movement known as the **Reformation**, spearheaded by Martin Luther (1483–1546), the Augustinian monk and professor at Wittenberg University who initiated the movement by nailing his 95 objections to the door of Wittenberg Cathedral in 1517. Luther's revolt was motivated by his objections to the Church's sale of indulgences (papal pardons for sins), a form of fund-raising promoted by the revolution in printing, which also enabled Luther's objections to be rapidly disseminated throughout Europe. Luther advocated a simpler and more spiritual approach to God and initially hoped for internal reform within the Church. However, he later rejected the philosophy of Aristotle and the authority of the pope, which led to his excommunication in 1521.

The form of Protestant religion originally developed by Luther, who emphasized individual faith, conscience, and attention to scripture in contrast to the hierarchical pomp and ritual of the established Church, represented an intellectual liberation of sorts. However, it very quickly rigidified into its own forms of institutionalized dogma as Protestantism spread throughout Europe. The ideal of individual conscience was converted into the ideal of conscience in obedience to scripture as interpreted by Luther and John Calvin (1509–1564), whose uncompromising doctrines about predestination exemplified a harsh and unforgiving attitude to sin. As the reformers attained positions of authority and power in Protestant states and provinces, they were at least as zealous in their persecution of heretics and dissenters as the traditional medieval Church.

One consequence of the Protestant Reformation was the institutional confirmation of the Aristotelian theories of Aquinas as the doctrinal foundation of

Roman Catholicism, as affirmed by the Council of Trent (1545–1563). It also seems to have encouraged a more vigorous and violent response to heretics, witches, and other dissenters by the Catholic Inquisition. The late 15th and 16th centuries marked the high point of religious repression in Europe, including the suppression of scientific works and the persecution of individual scientists.

Michael Servetus (c. 1511–1533), the Spanish anatomist who rejected Galen's account of the circulation of the blood in the heart and who was one of the first to identify pulmonary circulation, made the mistake of sending a copy of his "On the Restoration of Christianity" to John Calvin in Geneva. Calvin denounced Servetus to the Catholic Inquisition, and he was arrested and sentenced to death by burning. Servetus managed to escape, but he was later recaptured in Geneva and burned by Protestant reformers, while the Catholic Inquisition burned his effigy and his books. Although Servetus was persecuted for his religious rather than his medical views, the Reformation did little to promote the spirit of intellectual curiosity that motivated him.

THE SCIENTIFIC REVOLUTION

The period characterized as the scientific revolution was marked by revolutions in theory, particularly in astronomy, physics, and medicine. The most famous of these was the overthrow of the Aristotelian and Ptolemaic **geocentric** (Earth-centered) **theory** in favor of the Copernican **heliocentric** (sun-centered) **theory**. According to Ptolemaic theory, the fixed Earth is the center of the universe, with the sun and other planets revolving in circular orbits around it. Yet since the time of Aristotle, it had been known that planets do not move in perfect circular orbits. As observed from Earth, their orbits appear to be erratic, looping backward in their paths from time to time. To accommodate this "wandering," or retrograde, motion, Ptolemy had introduced a system of **epicycles**, or circles within circles, and this system had been modified and extended to a level of great complexity by later astronomers. The Ptolemaic theory served as an effective predictive and navigational device for centuries and was in accord with common sense. The planets appear in motion to the naked eye, and everyday experience seems to confirm a stationary Earth (we don't feel it moving, and don't fall off).

The Copernican Revolution

Nicholaus Copernicus was a Polish monk who studied at the universities of Cracow, Bologna, Ferrara, and Padua. He advanced his heliocentric theory in *On the Revolution of the Celestial Spheres*, published in 1543. In this work, Copernicus argued that the motions of the planets might be better explained by supposing that the sun, not Earth, is the fixed center of the universe and that Earth and other planets traverse circular orbits around it.

This was not a new hypothesis. Aristarchus (c. 310–c. 230 BCE) had first advanced it about 1,800 years earlier. Copernicus noted this and also ascribed an earlier version of his theory to the Pythagorean mathematician Philolaus (b. c. 480–480 BCE). Many were skeptical of the Ptolemaic system, since its complexity seemed inconsistent with Pythagorean requirements of simplicity and harmony. This was the view, for example, of Domenico Novara, professor of mathematics and astronomy at the University of Bologna, during the period Copernicus was in attendance.

Copernicus's heliocentric theory accommodated the same observational data as the developed geocentric theory. However, Copernicus was not able to do away with Ptolemy's system of epicycles, although he was able to reduce their number. Copernicus eliminated one serious anomaly of the geocentric theory, concerning the orbital times of planets. According to the geocentric theory, the moon, the closest planet to Earth, completes its orbit in four weeks, whereas the sun, which is furthest from Earth, takes only one day. According to the heliocentric theory, the orbital times of the planets vary inversely with their distance from the sun. Copernicus also provided an explanation of observed changes in planetary brightness, a problem for the geocentric theory but a natural consequence of the heliocentric theory (Dolling, Gianelli, & Statile, 2003). However, the Copernican theory had its own problems, notably the failure to detect **stellar parallax**, the variation in the angular separation of the stars, which was a crucial implication of Earth's projected orbit around the sun.

Copernicus's work was published posthumously, although his delay in publishing appears to have had more to do with his anticipation of the incredulity with which he thought his theory was likely to be received than out of any fear of persecution by the Church. Summaries of his conclusions had been circulated for years before, and one was published in 1540. It was not until Kepler's forceful advocacy of the Copernican theory in the late 1590s and the publication of Galileo's *Letters on the Solar Spots* (1613/1957) that the Copernican theory encountered serious opposition from the Church.

Realism and Instrumentalism   The publication of *On the Revolution of the Celestial Spheres* initially encountered less opposition than might have been expected partly because the Lutheran theologian Andreas Osiander (1498–1552), who had been authorized to see Copernicus's work through the press after his death, added an introduction. Osiander suggested that Copernicus's work ought not to be read as a potentially true description of astronomical reality (of the relative positions and motions of the planets), but as a useful mathematical fiction that accommodated the planetary motions:

> For it is the job of the astronomer to use painstaking and skilled observation in gathering together the history of the celestial movements, and then—since he cannot by

any line of reasoning reach the true causes of these movements—to think up or construct whatever causes or hypotheses he pleases such that, by the assumption of these causes, those same movements can be calculated from the principles of geometry for the past and for the future too . . . For it is not necessary that these hypotheses should be true, or even probably; but it is enough that they provide a calculus which fits the observations.

—(1543/2003, p. 43)

Osiander was an *instrumentalist,* a proponent of the view that scientific theories are merely calculative devices or "fictions" employed to predict observations or "save the appearances" and that the best theory is simply the most economical predictive device. Copernicus himself was almost certainly a *realist,* a proponent of the view that theories purport to describe reality and that the best theory is the one that provides the most accurate description of reality, as were later defenders of the Copernican system such as Galileo and Kepler. Kepler, who revealed the identity of Osiander as the author of the introduction to *On the Revolution of the Celestial Spheres* in the *New Astronomy* (1609), claimed that he founded astronomy on real causes and not fictional hypotheses.

Not all theologians shared Osiander's instrumentalist views. The Jesuit Christopher Clavius (1538–1612), who was also a realist, argued that Copernicus had simply saved the appearances by deducing true observational predictions from *false* theoretical assumptions. Clavius noted that there was nothing remarkable about this, since true conclusions (or predictions) can be deduced from any number of false assumptions. Thus, to take a modern example, the true conclusion "all metals are conductors" can be deduced from the true premises "all metals are elements with free electrons in their outer shells" and "all elements with free electrons in their outer shells are conductors" *and* from the false premises "all metals are elements containing electronic fluids" and "all elements containing electronic fluids are conductors." According to Clavius, the Copernican theory was simply false and inferior to the Ptolemaic theory, which he held to be consistent with both the principles of astronomy and Christian theology.

The Reception of the Copernican Theory   These sorts of considerations led the Inquisition, under Cardinal Bellarmine (1542–1621), to adopt the view that the Copernican theory could be judged superior to the Ptolemaic theory only in terms of its economy as a mathematical model or calculation device and that to defend its physical truth was "formally heretical." *On the Revolution of the Celestial Spheres* was placed on the Catholic Index of Prohibited Books in 1616.

Galileo Galilei (1564–1642), who had indicated his support for the Copernican theory in *Letters on the Solar Spots* (1613/1957), was warned about the judgment of the Inquisition. For a few years he remained quiet, and the new Pope Urban VIII turned a blind eye to the unorthodox doctrines that Galileo advanced in *The Assayer* (1623/1957). However, in 1632 Galileo published *Dialogue Concerning the Two Chief World-Systems, Ptolemaic and Copernican*. This work was immediately prohibited, and the following year Galileo was imprisoned. Rheumatic and near blind at age 70, he was examined by the Inquisition and shown the instruments of torture. He was ordered to do penance for three years (while under house arrest) and to recant the Copernican doctrine. According to legend, at the end of his recantation he muttered under his breath "And yet it moves." The Catholic Church absolved him of his intellectual sins in 1992.

Others were not so lucky. It was bad enough that Copernicus had undermined the Aristotelian thesis, so congenial to Christian theology, that Earth and humankind are at the privileged center of creation, by suggesting that Earth is just one of the many planets orbiting the sun. The Dominican monk and astronomer Giordano Bruno (1548–1600) went one stage further and suggested that Earth is merely one (insignificant) planet among many in an infinite universe. In *On the Infinite Universe and Worlds* (1584/1950) Bruno declared that the debate between the Aristotelians and Copernicans about whether Earth or the sun is the center of the universe is vacuous, since "as the universe is infinite, no body can properly be said to be in the center of the universe or at the frontier thereof." In 1592, after many years of wandering Europe, Bruno unwisely let himself fall within the reach of the Inquisition. After seven years in prison, he was finally tried and condemned to death by burning at the stake (although it is unlikely that he was condemned to death for his scientific views—he also denied the Immaculate Conception and identified the pope with the Beast of Revelations).

Although the Copernican system eventually came to displace the Ptolemaic system, the "Copernican revolution" in astronomy was not an overnight affair. As late as 1669, the year Isaac Newton attained his professorship at Cambridge University, the Ptolemaic theory was still being defended, and opposition to the Copernican theory continued in France into the 18th century. At the time of Copernicus, there were no empirical grounds for preferring his system to that of Ptolemy, since both theoretical systems accommodated most of the available observational data.

Gradually fortunes shifted in favor of the Copernican theory. Johannes Kepler (1571–1630) was a dedicated Pythagorean who believed that God had created the world in accord with mathematical harmonies. He was employed as a research assistant to Tycho Brahe (1546–1601), the Danish astronomer, when the latter took up the position of royal mathematician at the court of the German King Rudolph II in Prague (where he was engaged in the preparation of military horoscopes). Working with Brahe's mass of accumulated observational data, which he inherited upon Brahe's death in 1601, Kepler eliminated many of the artificialities of the Copernican theory by supposing that the planets move in elliptical rather than circular orbits around the sun. In the *New Astronomy* (1609), he demonstrated that the orbital velocities of the planets vary with their distance from the sun, increasing as they approach the sun and decreasing as they move away from it.

In addition, after hearing of the invention of the telescope by Dutch lens crafters, Galileo immediately constructed his own and proceeded with record speed to observe the mountains and valleys of the moon, the moons of Jupiter, the phases of Venus, and the rings of Saturn, as well as a multitude of previously undetected stars. These observations undermined the general Aristotelian and Ptolemaic position. The mountains and valleys of the moon indicated that at least one celestial body is not perfectly spherical, and the observation of new stars indicated that the stars are at different distances from Earth and not fixed to a celestial sphere. The moons of Jupiter appeared to constitute a miniature Copernican system, since their orbits vary with their distance from Jupiter, and the phases of Venus could only be explained in terms of a sun-centered orbit.

None of this demonstrated the outright superiority of the Copernican theory, but it convinced many people. The crucial observation came with the telescopic observation of the stellar parallax predicted by the Copernican theory alone, although most astronomers had already abandoned the Ptolemaic theory by the time this was observed by Friedrich Bessel (1784–1846) in 1838, nearly 300 years after the publication of Copernicus's theory.

Galileo and the New Science

The scientific revolution was more than a revolution in astronomical—and physical and medical—theories: It amounted to a full-scale revolution in intellectual attitude. Prior to this time, many scholars were content to assess theoretical claims by reference to their consistency with classical and religious authorities. Famously, some of Galileo's colleagues at the University of Pisa refused to look through his telescope because they considered it redundant: They maintained that astronomical questions had already been settled by Aristotle and scripture. Yet from around the 16th century onward, natural philosophers came to adopt the view that theories ought not to be accepted until they have been empirically tested, ideally via what came to be known as a crucial experiment, enabling scientists to adjudicate between competing theoretical explanations of the same range of empirical data. They eventually became what the ancients and medievals had deplored, *empiriks*.

Galileo best epitomized this new empirical attitude. He was not prepared to accept or reject the Ptolemaic or Copernican theories on the basis of classical or religious authority and entered the astronomical debates only after he had developed the telescope and made what he believed to be crucial observations in support of the Copernican theory. Although earlier investigators anticipated him in both theory and practice, none matched his ability to integrate and propagate those elements that have since come to be treated as constitutive of modern science.

Galileo was appointed professor of mathematics at the University of Pisa at the age of 25. He served as professor of mathematics at the University of Padua from 1592 until 1610, when he became mathematician-in-residence to the Grand Duke of Tuscany. He made important contributions to astronomy and physics, subjecting entrenched Aristotelian theories to critical empirical scrutiny. He continued his scientific work right up to his death in 1642, albeit in secret, since his later years were spent under house arrest imposed by the Inquisition. His last work, *Dialogue Concerning Two New Sciences* (1638/1974), was smuggled out of Italy for publication.

Galileo was committed to the empirical evaluation of scientific theories and the development of instruments that enable and facilitate the testing of scientific theories. He constructed his first telescope in 1609 to test the Copernican theory. He also took a critical empirical look at Aristotle's theory of falling bodies, according to which bodies of different weight fall with different velocities. He demonstrated that bodies of different weight, such as a 100-pound cannon ball and 1-pound musket ball, fall with approximately the same velocity (according to legend, by dropping them off the Leaning Tower of Pisa). Using an improved water clock and a gently sloping inclined wooden plane down which he released polished bronze balls, Galileo developed and tested his own theory of falling bodies. This led him to recognize that forces act on bodies not to produce motion, as Aristotle had argued, but to change it, or produce acceleration.

Galileo not only rejected particular Aristotelian theories, but also the general form of Aristotelian explanation in physics. He renounced all attempts to explain the motion of bodies in terms of Aristotelian final causes, in terms of their propensity to move toward their "natural resting place," and employed only efficient causal explanations of matter in motion. This latter type of explanation, in terms of antecedent conditions sufficient to produce an effect, came to be characterized as **mechanistic explanation** and became associated with the popular 17th-century conception of the universe as a giant (usually clockwork) mechanism, governed by fixed laws of nature.

Galileo also insisted that the business of science is to explain quantitative and not merely qualitative changes and to do so by reference to quantitative changes in fundamental variables such as time, space, and motion, which led him to declare that mathematics is the language of science:

> Philosophy is written in this grand book, the universe, which stands continually open to our gaze. But the book cannot be understood unless one first learns to comprehend the language and read the letters in which it is composed. It is written in the language of mathematics.

> —(1623/1957, pp. 237–238)

Galileo also reprised the ancient distinction between primary and secondary qualities. He maintained that primary qualities, such as size, shape, and motion, are real properties of material bodies and explain how bodies affect our senses. Secondary qualities, such as colors, tastes, and smells, are nothing more than the manner in which material bodies affect our senses:

> Hence I think that tastes, odors, colors and so on are no more than mere names so far as the object in which we place them is concerned, and that they reside only in the consciousness. Hence if the living creature were removed, all those qualities would be wiped away and annihilated.
>
> —(1623/1957, p. 274)

Galileo explained differences in secondary qualities, such as tastes and smells, in terms of differences in primary qualities, such as the shapes, sizes, and velocities of microscopic particles:

> There are bodies which constantly dissolve into minute particles, some of which are heavier than air and descend, while others are lighter and rise up. The former may strike upon a certain part of our bodies that is much more sensitive than the skin, which does not feel the invasion of such subtle matter. This is the upper surface of the tongue; here the tiny particles are received, and mixing with and penetrating its moisture, they give rise to tastes, which are sweet or unsavory according to the various shapes, numbers and speeds of the particles.
>
> —(1623/1957, p. 276)

Galileo's new science represented an integration of the ancient naturalist (Ionian) and mathematical (Pythagorean) traditions. It also marked a new beginning, by combining these traditions with a new emphasis on empirical and experimental evaluation and the rejection of final causal explanation in favor of efficient causal or mechanistic explanation. These paradigmatic elements are also to be found in the work of the major scientists of the scientific revolution, such as Robert Boyle (1627–1691), Descartes, William Gilbert (1544–1603), William Harvey (1578–1657), Robert Hooke (1635–1703), Kepler, and Newton.

In these important respects, the work of such theorists was discontinuous with the work of most ancient and medieval theorists and marked a decisive break with the prior historical tradition. However, the scientific revolution was neither as sudden nor as revolutionary as its name might suggest. As noted earlier, anticipations of the new science can be found in the writings of scholastics such as Robert Grosseteste, Roger Bacon, and William of Occam; and empirical research played a significant role in the work of Aristotle, Alcmaeon, Hippocrates, and Galen. Although Galileo made much of his own break with the Aristotelian tradition, by his own day that tradition had become pretty eclectic. The doctrines that form the basis of Galileo's *Assayer*, for example, are to be found in his notes from his Aristotelian teachers at the Jesuit Collegío Romano (Wallace, 1984).

However, the rejection of classical orthodoxy came to play a major role in the rhetoric of the new science. Post-Galilean thinkers came to see themselves as making a new scientific beginning by breaking with tradition, rejecting ancient and medieval theories precisely because they were not empirically grounded. Thus, to take but one of many examples, Descartes felt obliged to preface his study of physiological psychology in *The Passions of the Soul* (1649) with the following remarks:

> The defects of the sciences we have from the ancients are nowhere more apparent than in their writings on the passions. . . . The teachings of the ancients about the passions are so meagre and for the most part so implausible that I cannot hope to approach the truth except by departing from the paths they have followed. This is why I shall be obliged to write just as if I were considering a topic that no one had dealt with before me.
>
> —(1649/1985, p. 328)

Andreas Vesalius and the Scientific Revolution in Medicine

Galileo did not reject Aristotle's astronomical and physical theories out of hand, but only when they failed to survive empirical evaluation. Similarly, Andreas Vesalius (1514–1564) subjected the classical medical theories of Galen to empirical evaluation and found them wanting. A native of Belgium, Vesalius came from a line of royal physicians. He studied at the universities of Louvain and Paris and was appointed professor of surgery and anatomy at the University of Padua.

The dissection of cadavers had become commonplace in medical teaching by the time Vesalius took up his professorship. However, a butcher or barber would usually conduct the dissections. They would cut portions from a cadaver for a demonstrator to display to students, while the lecturer read from Latin translations of Galen or Avicenna.

Vesalius: dissection; cover plate of *On the Fabric of the Human Body* (1543).

Vesalius performed his own dissections and demonstrations and quickly identified many errors in Galen, which led him to conclude that much of Galen's system was based upon the physiology of pigs and goats rather than that of humans.

In 1543 Vesalius published his revolutionary *On the Structure of the Human Body*, which contained detailed descriptions and illustrations of the bones, muscles, veins, arteries, viscera, and brain of the human body. Although his challenges to Galen generated the same reactionary response as Galileo's challenges to Aristotle, his pioneering studies transformed medical theory and practice. He abandoned his own research in 1544 when he was appointed court physician to the Emperor Charles V, but his work was continued by his student Realdo Columbus (c. 1516–1559), who made important contributions to the study of circulation and respiration, and by later generations of anatomists such as Giovanni Battista Morgagni of Padua (1682–1771), Hermann Boerhaave (1668–1738), Joseph Lieutaud (1703–1780), and William Hunter (1718–1783).

Francis Bacon and the Inductive Method

One of the most articulate advocates of the new science was the Englishman Francis Bacon (1561–1626), who titled his major work on scientific method the *New Organon*, or "new method," (1620/1994), in explicit contrast to the Aristotelian corpus, which had come to be known as the *Organon*. Bacon was educated at the University of Cambridge, which he entered at age 13, and was admitted to the bar after studying at Gray's Inn. Although his attempts to obtain a high government position were thwarted (or at least ignored) by Queen Elizabeth I, his star rose (at least temporarily) when James I gained the throne in 1603. Bacon acquired various titles, including a knighthood, and high government office; he was appointed Attorney General in 1613 and Lord Chancellor in 1618. In 1621 he was publicly disgraced and imprisoned for having accepted bribes during his tenure as Lord Chancellor. In his defense, Bacon claimed that although he had taken bribes, he had not allowed them to influence his judgment. He spent his last years in seclusion and died as a consequence of one of his own experiments. He caught a cold while stuffing a chicken with snow in order to assess its utility as a preservative.

Bacon was a harsh critic of ancient and medieval natural philosophy and an optimistic and spirited promoter of the new science. He argued that the veneration of the ancients and the contemplative ideals of scholastic thought were major obstacles to the progress of scientific knowledge. He recommended a more active and critical approach, in which "vexed nature" was interrogated through experimental intervention. He maintained that a true science of nature should be grounded in mechanical crafts such as alchemy rather than scholastic contemplation and reflection (although he was also critical of many alchemical practices, and practitioners such as Paracelsus).

Bacon was a committed realist and materialist, who believed that the "secrets of nature" could be revealed through observation and experiment. He was dismissive of Renaissance skepticism, which he thought could be overcome by the employment of a proper method for revealing the "subtlety of Nature." He followed Galileo in maintaining that final causality has no place in the explanation of the motion of physical bodies, although, like many other 16th- and 17th-century scientists (including Galileo), he acknowledged that final causal explanations are legitimate in their appropriate psychological domain:

> The final cause, so far from assisting the sciences, actually corrupts them, except for those concerned with human actions.
>
> —(1620/1994, p. 134)

Bacon is often treated as a champion of the inductive method, who abjured hypothetical speculation in favor of careful and systematic observation. He did claim that his own method involved cautious inferential ascent from carefully established "natural and experimental histories" to the establishment of theoretical axioms:

> But there will be hope for the sciences when, and only when, ascent is made by the right kind of ladder, through an uninterrupted, connected series of steps, from particulars to lesser axioms, one above the other, and last of all to the most general.
>
> —(1620/1994, p. 110)

However, Bacon was dismissive of the Aristotelian method of enumerative induction, through which general truths of nature are derived by generalization from the observation of positive instances of correlation (by generalizing that "All swans are white" on the basis of the observation of a number of white swans, for example). He insisted that true natural science should be based upon eliminative induction, in which causal conditions are identified via the falsification of alternative causal hypotheses:

> For induction that proceeds through simple enumeration is childish, its conclusions are precarious, and open to danger from a contradicting instance, and it generally makes its pronouncement on too few things, and on those only that are ready to hand. But induction that will be of use for the discovery and demonstration of the arts and sciences must analyse Nature by proper rejections and exclusions, and then, after a number of negatives, come to a conclusion on the affirmative instances.
>
> —(1620/1994, p. 111)

Bacon did not advocate a narrow empiricist science restricted to observational correlation. He was well aware of the need for creative invention in the formulation of hypotheses and championed the role of novel prediction in empirical evaluation. He claimed that hypotheses should be evaluated by their utility in "discovering new works": "axioms properly and methodologically applied can very well point to and indicate new particulars" (1620/1994, p. 50). He recognized that different hypotheses can provide formally adequate explanations of the same empirical data (as demonstrated by the Copernican debates) and recommended that such conflicts between hypotheses be adjudicated by a crucial instance (1620/1994, p. 210): a prediction affirmed by one hypothesis but denied by the other (such as the different predictions about whether light accelerates or decelerates in moving from a less dense to a denser medium offered by the particle and wave theories of light). Bacon characterized such a prediction as an **Instance of the Fingerpost**, which serves as a "pointer" to the correct theory (in England, signposts at rural crossroads often have wooden fingers pointing in the direction of nearby villages).

Bacon was opposed to the Aristotelian rational intuition of causal principles and essential forms, of proceeding directly to very general theories or axioms:

> The understanding must not be allowed to leap and fly from particulars to remote and nearly the most general axioms . . . and from their [supposed] unshakeable truth, to prove and deliver intermediate axioms.
>
> —(1620/1994, p. 110)

However, as Newton was shortly to demonstrate with his theory of gravitation, a speculative "leap" to very general principles could also be enormously productive.

Nevertheless, Bacon's account of inductive ascent from observations to increasingly general hypotheses and theories does describe the practice of many of the contributors to the scientific revolution. Robert Hooke and Robert Boyle derived their laws of elasticity and gas expansion from tables of correlation, and the works of William Gilbert on magnetism (*On Magnetism*, 1600/1958), William Harvey on the circulation of the blood (*On the Circulation of the Blood,* 1628/1989) and Isaac Newton on optics (*Opticks*, 1704/1952) include many careful descriptions of observed effects and tentative empirical laws, followed by conclusions that develop cautious speculative theories to integrate and explain these tentative laws.

Bacon was one of the first theorists to stress that scientific knowledge enables scientists to predict and control the natural world, or establish "dominion over nature." He famously claimed that

> Human knowledge and human power come to the same thing, for where the cause is not known the effect cannot be produced. We can only command Nature by obeying her, and what in contemplation represents the cause, in operation stands as the rule.
>
> —(1620/1994, p. 43)

He was greatly impressed by the technological potential of scientific discoveries, citing the recent inventions of printing, gunpowder, and the compass:

> It is worth noticing the great power and value and consequences of discoveries, in none more obvious than those three which were unknown to the ancients . . . namely, the arts of printing, gunpowder, and the compass. For these three have changed the whole face and condition of things throughout the world, in literature, in warfare and in navigation.
>
> —(1620/1994, pp. 130–131)

In claiming that scientific theories should be judged by the success of their "works," Bacon also stressed their contribution to the human condition. In the *New Atlantis* (1627/1966), he envisioned a developed inductive science capable of relieving human pain, curing disease, and extending the life span.

Like many other advocates of the new science, Bacon recommended that practitioners should abandon the theories of the ancients and medievals and begin anew:

> We can look in vain for advancement in scientific knowledge from the superinducing and grafting of new things on old. A fresh start must be made, beginning from the very foundations.
>
> —(1620/1954, p. 51)

In representing the new science as setting the course for new scientific discoveries, Bacon likened himself to Columbus setting out to discover the Americas:

> And so my conjectures, which make what is hoped for probable, are set out and made known; just as Columbus did, before his wonderful voyage across the Atlantic Ocean.
>
> —(1620/1954, p. 103)

The frontispiece of the *New Organon* depicted a ship setting out on uncharted waters.

Social Dimensions of Science Bacon was one of the earliest practitioners of the psychology

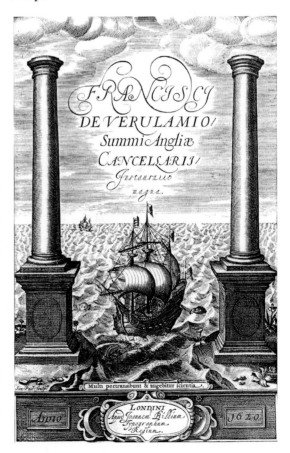

Frontispiece of Francis Bacon's *Novum Organum* (1620). Ship of Knowledge setting out on uncharted waters.

and sociology of science and documented a variety of cognitive deficits and social biases, which he called "idols which beset men's minds." He argued that the method of inductive ascent was the best means of surmounting these cognitive and social dimensions of human nature.

Bacon characterized as **Idols of the tribe** those innate human propensities to project a greater degree of regularity in nature than can actually be found, to presume that the "subtleties" of nature can be understood through familiar analogies, and to adhere to favored theories in the face of empirical falsification. The net result of such cognitive deficits was what Bacon called "wishful science." Bacon characterized as **Idols of the cave** those idiosyncratic products of individual human development that incline some men to fixate on novelty and others to overproject similarity or difference in nature. He cautioned scientists to be especially suspicious of any theoretical notion about which they were individually enthusiastic.

Bacon characterized as **Idols of the marketplace** those notions derived from common linguistic usage employed in the theoretical description of nature that impede the development of proper scientific terminology. He characterized as **Idols of the theatre** those theoretical systems that are socially maintained by the various schools of philosophy as received dogma (such as the Ptolemaic theory) and form the bases of most forms of education.

Although he identified some of the social dimensions of human nature that bias scientific thought, Bacon was also a forceful advocate of the social community of science. He recognized the benefits for scientific communication derived from the invention of printing and those that could be accrued through the social cooperation of scientists. In the *New Atlantis* (1627/1966) he envisioned a future society of scientists and technologists devoted to knowledge and discovery and petitioned King James I to finance the creation of cooperative research projects. Although personally unsuccessful in securing this goal in his own lifetime, the "Royal Society of London for Improving Natural Knowledge" was founded in London by Charles II in 1662 and implemented both Bacon's general vision and a number of his specific research projects.

Similar societies were founded in Europe at around the same time. The Academia del Cimento (Academy of Experiments) was founded in Florence in 1657, the Académie des Sciences in Paris in 1666, the Berlin Academy in 1700, and the St. Petersburg Academy in 1724 (Pyenson & Sheets-Pyenson, 1999). One consequence of the formation of these scientific societies was the development of the logic and practice of what came to be known as the experimental report. In the early meetings of the Royal Society, when the numbers were relatively small, members used to demonstrate their "effects" in front of their colleagues. When time constraints and the rapidly increasing membership made it impractical for most members to do so, they developed a convention that members should report their results by writing a "recipe" that would enable any other member to reproduce their effects. In this fashion the logic of experimental replication was born. These "recipes" were collected annually and published as the *Philosophical Transactions of the Royal Society* (Bazerman, 1988). Experimental reports in psychology, with their methods, design, and procedure sections, are direct descendants of these "recipes."

Philosophical Transactions, first published in 1665, became the model for later scientific journals, such as the German *Miscellanea Curiosa*, first published in 1670, and the French *Histoires et Mémoires*, first published in 1702. International scientific communication was also greatly enhanced by the emergence of scientific correspondents; these initial efforts developed into the institution of corresponding members of scientific societies. Henry Oldenburg (c. 1618–1647), the first secretary of the Royal Society, maintained an extensive correspondence network with members of the European scientific community, as did Marin Mersenne (1588–1648) in Paris.

The Newtonian Synthesis

In the conclusion of *On Magnetism* (1600/1958), William Gilbert had speculated that the planets are held in their orbits (and their matter held in cohesion) by a force analogous if not identical to magnetism. Isaac Newton (1642–1727) developed this speculation into the theory of universal gravitation. Born in Lincolnshire, Newton was educated at Trinity College, Cambridge, where he received his degree in 1665. In the two years following, he secluded himself in Lincolnshire to avoid the plague. This was perhaps Newton's most creative period: He developed the binomial theorem, invented the "method of fluxions" (calculus), and created the first reflecting telescope. It was also during this period that Newton first began to develop his theory of universal gravitation. He was appointed professor of mathematics at Cambridge in 1669. He became a fellow of the Royal Society in 1672 and was elected president in 1703. He published *Mathematical Principles of Natural Philosophy* (*Principia*) in 1687 and *Opticks* in 1704.

In 1696 Newton was appointed warden of the Royal Mint, in order that he might apply his mathematical talents to the reformation of the currency—although Voltaire maintained that he was appointed because the Treasurer, Lord Halifax, was besotted with Newton's niece. Throughout his life Newton engaged in running feuds with Robert Hooke and Gottfried Leibniz (1646–1716) over credit for the initial development of the "rectilinear inertial principle" and calculus. With respect to the development of calculus, an investigative committee of the Royal Society found in favor of Newton, but this was scarcely surprising, since Newton, in his capacity as president of the society, appointed the committee and authored its final report.

Newton's theory of universal gravitation was held to be a triumph of mechanistic explanation, since it integrated the laws of terrestrial and celestial motion propounded by Galileo and Kepler (or at least approximations of them) and successfully explained a wide range of empirical data, such as the motion of the tides and centrifugal motion. Newton also followed Galileo in assuming that quantified mechanistic laws could be extended to the atomistic components of material bodies, or **corpuscles** as Robert Boyle called them, and developed his own **corpuscularian theory of light** in *Opticks* (1704/1952), in which he treated light as a stream of material corpuscles. The triumph of the new mechanistic and mathematical science, based upon quantified efficient causal explanations of matter in motion, appeared complete.

Yet not everyone rushed to embrace Newton's gravitational theory, at least initially. It took almost 80 years for Newton's theory to displace Descartes' rival vortex theory on the continent of Europe. One of the advantages of Descartes' theory was that it explained why all the planetary orbits are in the same direction, which Newton's theory did not. However, Newton's theory eventually came to establish its supremacy, and deservedly so, since later Newtonians transformed what initially appeared to be empirical anomalies into substantive developments of Newtonian theory. For example, U. J. J. Leverrier (1811–1877) accommodated the initial failure of Newton's theory to correctly predict the orbit of Uranus by postulating another planet beyond Uranus, which led to the discovery of the planet Neptune.

Newton, who was a great admirer of Bacon, avowed that he had followed the method of inductive ascent in the development of his theories:

> Particular propositions are inferred from the phenomena, and afterwards rendered general by induction. Thus it was that the impenetrability, the mobility, and the impulsive force of bodies, and the laws of motion and gravitation, were discovered.
>
> —(1687/1969, p. 547)

Yet this was patently not the case with respect to the development of Newton's laws of motion, which involved the direct postulation of very abstract axioms. Newton's first law of motion states, "Every body continues in a state of rest, or of uniform motion in a right line, unless it is compelled to change that state by forces impressed upon it." Since no body actually moves in a right line, because every body is subjected to external forces, this cannot be established by induction (Losee, 1980).

MAN THE MACHINE

The mechanistic forms of efficient causal explanation that displaced teleological or final causal explanation in astronomy and physics were eventually extended to biology and psychology. One of the first and most influential mechanistic explanations of a biological process was William Harvey's account of the circulation of the blood (1628/1989), in which he claimed that the veins and arteries form closed loops through which the heart pumps blood.

The Spanish physician Gómez Pereira (1500–c.1559) extended mechanistic explanation to the whole human body. Pereira studied at the University of Salamanca, where he became acquainted with the work of the Merton mathematicians, notably Richard Swineshead's text on motion, *Liber Calculationum* (Bandrés & Llavona, 1992). In *Antoniana Margarita* (1554), Pereira employed Swineshead's theoretical system to explain the "vital" functions of animals in purely mechanistic terms. He explained all forms of animal behavior in terms of instincts and learned habits, without any reference to consciousness or reason, which he denied animals possessed. He provided a detailed account of reflexive behavior, in which he described how mechanical activation in sensory organs is transmitted by the nerves to the brain, which in turn activates nerves that produce mechanical movements in muscles. Pereira's account anticipated the theory of reflexive behavior later developed by Descartes.

René Descartes: Mind and Mechanism

René Descartes was born in La Haye, France, in 1596, and educated at the Jesuit College at La Flèche. He attained a degree in law from the University of Poitiers, but did not practice, since his share of the family fortune furnished him with independent financial means. He enlisted privately in the Dutch army in 1618 and, while serving at Ulm, had a dream "in a stove-heated room" that stimulated his interest in science and methodology. He traveled widely in Europe, returning to take up residence in Holland in 1628. During the next 20 years he changed his residence as many times, his whereabouts known only to his close friend in Paris, Marin Mersenne, with whom he corresponded but rarely saw. The reasons for his voluntary solitude are unclear, since few details of his private life are known. He never married, although he did have an illegitimate daughter, Francine, who died at the age of 5 in 1640.

Between 1629 and 1633 Descartes produced his major work on physics and mathematics, *The World*, but suppressed its publication when he heard of Galileo's troubles with the Inquisition. To no avail, as it turned out: Descartes' works were placed on the Catholic Index of Prohibited Books, as was *The World* when it was published posthumously in 1664. In this work Descartes presented his vortex theory of celestial motion, which dominated continental Europe in the late 17th and early 18th century, until it was eventually displaced by Newton's gravitational theory. Descartes introduced analytic geometry, with its system of what are now known as Cartesian coordinates, in *Discourse on Method* in 1637. His other major works on knowledge and the relation between mind and body were *Meditations on First Philosophy* (1641) and *The Passions of the Soul* (1649).

In 1649 Queen Kristina of Sweden (1626–1689) invited the now famous Descartes to be her personal philosopher in residence. He accepted, but it proved to be a fatal error. The philosopher who had developed many of his ideas in his bed (he created analytic geometry by meditating on a means of plotting the position of a fly on the roof above his bed) did not take kindly to Queen Kristina's tutorial schedule, which began at five in the morning, or the severe Swedish winter. He died of pneumonia within six months and was buried in a Swedish cemetery. His last words are reputed to have been "So, my soul, it is time to part."

Insult followed injury. In 1666 the French resolved to have Descartes' remains returned to his native land. The French ambassador to Sweden arranged to have the body exhumed and returned to France in a special copper coffin constructed for this purpose, but on exhumation it was discovered that the coffin was too short. The ambassador ordered that the head be severed from the body, to be returned to France separately. The body was shipped back to Paris, where it was buried in the church of Sainte-Genevieve-du-Mont, minus the right forefinger, which the ambassador had cut off as a souvenir. Unfortunately, the head did not make it back as quickly. It was purloined by a Swedish army captain and changed hands many times among private collectors of exotica before being returned to Paris in 1806. For many years it was shelved in the Musée de l'Homme, part of the National Academy of Sciences, where it remained until very recently (Boakes, 1984). The present curator was not happy that the head was being displayed among a collection of criminals and primitives and removed it from the shelf.

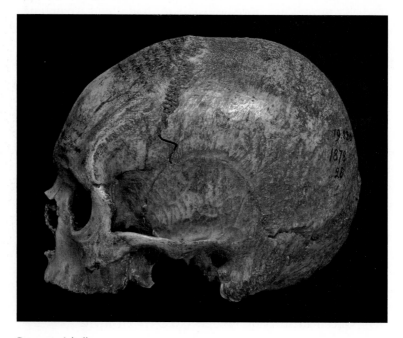

Descartes' skull.

According to the last report,[1] it is now housed in a drawer of one of his filing cabinets!

Descartes' Science   Like Bacon, Descartes aimed to reconstruct human knowledge and dismissed the "shaky foundations" upon which the ancient and medieval tradition was based. He resolved

> never to accept anything as true if I did not have evident knowledge of its truth . . . to avoid precipitous conclusions and preconceptions, and to include nothing more in my judgments than what is presented to my mind so clearly and so distinctly that I had no occasion to doubt it.
>
> —(1637/1985, p. 120)

Although he ended up affirming many doctrines that were congenial to the Catholic Church, such as the existence of God and the immortality of the soul, Descartes insisted that any form of knowledge worth its name ought to be independently demonstrable through reason or empirical evidence.

Also like Bacon, Descartes affirmed the potential of the new mechanistic science to extend the power of humans over nature and to improve the human condition, in contrast to the contemplative natural philosophy of the scholastics. As he put it, the new science "opened my eyes to the possibility of gaining knowledge which would be very useful in life, and of discovering a practical philosophy which might replace the speculative philosophy taught in the schools":

> Through this philosophy we could know the power and action of fire, water, air, the stars, the heavens and all the other bodies in the environment . . . and we could use this knowledge . . . for all the purposes for which it is appropriate, and thus make ourselves, as it were, the lords and masters of nature. This is desirable not only for the invention of innumerable devices which would facilitate our enjoyment of the fruits of the earth and all the goods we find there, but also, more importantly, for the maintenance of health, which is undoubtedly the chief good and the foundation of all the other goods in this life.
>
> —(1637/1985, pp. 142–143)

Like Galileo, Descartes was committed to the primary and secondary quality distinction and abjured final causal explanation in physics. Indeed, in one fundamental respect his physics represented more of a paradigm of mechanistic explanation than Newton's physics, since Descartes conceived of motion as the

---

[1]I owe this piece of information to a former graduate student, Mark Sheehan, who visited the Musée de l'Homme to view Descartes' skull.

rearrangement of bodies in space. According to Descartes' **vortex theory**, planets are held in their orbits by swirling vortices of "subtle matter," analogous to the motion of corks caught up in a whirlpool. Many held that such explanations in terms of "action-by-contact" were superior to explanations in terms of "action-at-a-distance," such as explanations postulating "occult" forces of gravitational or magnetic attraction, which seemed as dubious as Aristotelian final causal explanations in terms of bodies trying to reach their natural resting place.

In contrast to Bacon and Galileo, Descartes was a rationalist. He claimed that knowledge of the fundamental nature of material bodies could be attained only by rational intuition, since it is not given to us in the flux of sense experience. Thus Descartes maintained that some general theoretical principles are known a priori, independently of sense experience. For example, in his discussion of the melting of a piece of wax in the *Meditations* (1641/1985), he argued that we determine that extension (in space) is the essential property of material bodies through rational intuition rather than by sense experience, since we recognize that it is the only property that remains constant throughout changes in the perceived taste, smell, color, shape, and size of the wax (1641/1985, p. 20–21).

Descartes also claimed that very general principles of physics, such as "all motion is caused by impact or pressure" and "all bodies at rest remain at rest, and bodies in motion remain in motion, unless acted upon by some other body" (Newton's first law), could be rationally intuited, or deduced from rationally intuited principles (Buchdahl, 1969). He maintained that we have innate ideas and knowledge: that our ideas of God, infinity, and perfection, and our knowledge of the axioms of geometry and logic are so "clear and distinct" that they must be accepted as true, even though they may have no counterparts in our sense experience.

Descartes' ideal of knowledge was a deductive structure with rationally intuited axioms at its apex. His goal was to identify axioms, or "first principles," that were so certain that they were immune from error or doubt. Although he rejected Bacon's claim that such axioms must be established via inductive ascent, Descartes recognized that lower-level principles and laws have to be established by observation and experiment. For Descartes, rationally induced general laws place constraints on our theories of the motion of material bodies, but the particular content of laws governing their motion has to be empirically determined (Clark, 1982). Descartes' own work in optics and biology was based upon observation and experiment, and in the last chapter of *Discourse on Method* he acknowledged that competing scientific explanations can be adjudicated only by critical observations, or what Bacon called crucial instances:

> I know of no other means to discover this than by seeking further observations whose outcomes vary according to which of the ways provide the correct explanation.
>
> —(1637/1985, p. 144)

Animal Automatism One of Descartes' most significant contributions to the history of science and psychology was his application of the mechanistic principles of efficient causal explanation to the behavior of organic beings. In his *Treatise on Man* (the second part of *The World*), he advanced mechanistic explanations (in terms of matter in motion) of the biological and psychological functions of animals and humans. He maintained that

> the digestion of food, the beating of the heart and arteries, the nourishment and growth of the limbs, respiration, waking and sleeping, the reception by the external sense organs of light, sounds, smells, tastes, heat and other such qualities, the imprinting of the ideas of these qualities in the organ of the "common" sense and the imagination, the retention or stamping of these ideas in the memory, the internal movements of the appetites and passions, and finally the external movement of all the limbs . . . follow from the mere arrangement of the machine's organs every bit as naturally as the movements of a clock or other automaton [moving machine] follow from the arrangement of its counter-weights and wheels.
>
> —(1664/1985, p. 108)

One of Descartes' best known contributions in this area was his detailed description of **reflexive behavior**. Although Galen had identified simple reflexes such as the pupillary reflex, Descartes was the first to provide a detailed physiological account of reflexive behavior, which he characterized as automatic and involuntary:

> If someone suddenly thrusts his hand in front of our eyes as if to strike us, then even if we know he is our friend, that he is doing this only in fun, and that he will take care not to harm us, we still find it difficult to prevent ourselves from closing our eyes. This shows that it is not through the mediation of our soul that they close, since this action is contrary to our volition, which is the only, or at least the principle, activity of the soul. They close rather because the mechanism of our body is so composed that the movement of the hand towards our eyes produces another movement in our brain, which directs the animal spirits into our muscles that make our eyelids drop.
>
> —(1649/1985, pp. 333–334)

Descartes called such behavior reflexive because he believed that in the case of automatic and involuntary behavior, animal spirits are "reflected" in the brain in the fashion that light is reflected on the surface of a liquid (Boakes, 1984).

Descartes claimed that sensory organs are connected to pores in the brain via a system of "delicate threads" within the nerves and that the pores in the brain are capable of directing animal spirits though the nerves to the muscles. In the case of a person who withdraws a foot when it comes into contact with fire,

Descartes supposed that the moving particles of the fire interact with receptors in the foot, which pull on the nerve threads connected to the pores of the brain. This action in turn causes the release of animal spirits, which flow through the nerves to the muscles of the foot, causing it to be withdrawn from the fire:

> Next, to understand how the external objects which strike the sense organs can prompt this machine to move its limbs in numerous different ways, you should consider that the tiny fibres (which, as I have already told you, come from the innermost region of its brain and compose the marrow of the nerves) are so arranged in each part of the machine that serves as the organ of some sense that they can be easily moved by the objects of that sense. And when they are moved, with however little force, they simultaneously pull the parts of the brain from which

Man reflexively withdrawing foot from fire, illustrating nerve pathway to brain. From Descartes: *Treatise on Man* (1664).

they come, and thereby open the entrances to certain pores in the internal surface of the brain. Through these pores the animal spirits in the cavities of the brain immediately begin to make their way back into the nerves and so to the muscles which serve to cause movements in the machine.

—(1664/1985, p. 101)

Descartes claimed that this mechanistic reflexive form of explanation could be extended to all animal and much of human behavior and suggested that

> This will not seem at all strange to those who know how many kinds of automatons, or moving machines, the skill of man can construct with the use of very few parts, in comparison with the great multitude of bones, muscles, nerves, arteries, veins, and all the other parts that are in the body of any animal. For they will regard this body as a machine which, having been made by the hands of God, is incomparably better ordered than any machine that can be devised by man, and contains in itself movements more wonderful than those in any such machine.

—(1637/1985, p. 139)

Descartes' conception of the living body as an **automaton** or "moving machine" may have been inspired by the mechanical statues found in the royal gardens of his day, such as those in the chateau of Saint-Germain-en-Laye outside Paris (which Descartes may have visited), powered by water and triggered by mechanical plates embedded in footpaths. The general form of Descartes' account did not mark much of an advance over the medieval theory of the inner senses. He retained Aristotle's common sense and Galen's "animal spirits," and many of the details of his account were empirically falsified within his own lifetime. However, Descartes' account was revolutionary because he applied mechanistic reflexive explanation not only to innate reflexes such as the pupillary reflex and involuntary behavior such as digestion, yawning, and sleeping, but also to many forms of animal and human behavior based upon learning and memory: "movements which are so appropriate not only to the actions of objects presented to our senses, but also to the passions and the impressions found in memory" (1664/1985, p. 108). Like 20th-century behaviorist psychologists, he maintained that the learned behavior of animals, and much of the learned behavior of humans, is as automatic and involuntary as innate reflexes and instincts and can be explained *without reference to consciousness or cognition*. Like Gómez Pereira, Descartes held that animals lack consciousness and reason, which he believed justified his own practice of dissecting live animals, whose yelps and howls he treated as merely mechanical noises.

Mind and Body   Although Descartes believed that mechanistic reflexive forms of explanation could account for all animal behavior and some human behavior, he denied that they could account for voluntary human behavior. Descartes did not simply maintain, as many contemporary cognitive psychologists would maintain, that some human behaviors are nonreflexive because they involve some form of internal cognitive processing and thus require a more complex mechanistic explanation. Rather, he claimed that voluntary human behavior could not be explained mechanistically at all. According to Descartes, some human behavior is generated through the action of a distinct immaterial soul, whose essence is thought. Descartes was perhaps the most famous substance dualist and **interactionist**. He claimed that the immaterial mind, the seat of reason, consciousness, and will, interacts with the material body via the pineal gland in the brain, which enables the immaterial mind to direct the animal spirits to different muscles and generate different forms of behavior at will.

Why did Descartes hold such a view? It is easy to understand how he might have been motivated to do so. To extend mechanistic explanation to the human mind would have been to deny the existence of the immortal soul, still a danger-ous heresy in Descartes' day. He was well aware of the fate of Bruno and Galileo and withdrew his general mechanistic work *The World* when he learned of Galileo's condemnation by the Inquisition. Later critics have speculated that Descartes did not really believe that human psychology is exempt from mechanistic explanation, but only publicly advocated such a view to avoid persecution (Lafleur, 1956). Julien Offroy de La Mettrie (1709–1751), who did extend the principles of mechanistic explanation to human thought and voluntary behavior, was one of the first to accuse Descartes of being a closet materialist about the mind.

Descartes' primary argument for his ontological distinction between mind and body was epistemological in nature and was part of his general project to set knowledge upon firm and certain foundations. In reaction to ancient and Renaissance skepticism about beliefs derived from our sense experience of the world, Descartes sought a "first principle" for his knowledge system that was so certain that it was immune from error or doubt. He followed Augustine and Avicenna in claiming that although he could doubt that he had a material body, he could not doubt that he existed as a thinking being, since thinking presupposes existence and doubting is a form of thinking. Consequently,

> observing, that this truth "I am thinking, therefore I exist" was so firm and sure that all the most extravagant suppositions of the skeptics were incapable of shaking it, I decided that I could accept it without scruple as the first principle of the philosophy I was seeking.
>
> —(1637/1985, p. 127)

Given that he could without contradiction or absurdity doubt the existence of his body (however exaggerated this doubt might be, including the imagination of an "evil demon" intent on deceiving him), but could not doubt his existence as a thinking being, Descartes claimed that he could not be identical to his body, since "Otherwise, if I had doubts about my body, I would also have doubts about myself, and I cannot have doubts about that" (1643/1985, p. 412).

Whatever the merits of this argument, Descartes' interactionist account of the relation between mind and body created a serious problem. How could an immaterial mind, with no physical properties or spatial location, interact with a material body extended in space? This was an especially pressing problem for Descartes, given his commitment to the efficient causal explanation of the motion of material bodies in terms of action by contact and his recognition of the intimate connection between mind and body, particularly in relation to the appetites and emotions:

> Nature also teaches me, by these sensations of pain, hunger, thirst and so on, that I am not merely present in my body as a sailor is present in a ship, but that I am very closely joined and, as it were, intermingled with it, so that I and the body form a unit.
>
> —(1641/1985, p. 56)

This problem, which had vexed Queen Kristina of Sweden, was one that Descartes never resolved.

Materialist critics such as Pierre Gassendi (1592–1655), Hobbes, and La Mettrie maintained that the functions of the human mind, including language and reasoning, could be ascribed to the brain and extended mechanistic causal explanation to encompass all human thought and behavior. Other critics defended mind-body dualism but rejected interactionism. Arnold Geulincx (1625–1669) and Nicholas Malebranche (1638–1715) held that God directly causes the regular correlation between mental and bodily states, a view known as **occasionalism**, and Leibniz claimed that God maintains the regular correlation of mental and bodily states through a **pre-established harmony** between mental and bodily states. However, neither position proved popular with later dualists.

Machine and Animal Intelligence   Descartes offered arguments in support of his claim that mechanistic reflexive explanation could not be extended to voluntary human behavior that were independent of his epistemological arguments for mind-body dualism. He claimed that voluntary human behavior could always be distinguished from the behavior of animals or machines, even if such machines were physically modeled upon real people. These arguments are especially interesting because they anticipate late-20th-century debates about whether machines such as digital computers are capable of simulating language comprehension and problem solving.

According to Descartes, all machines, including animal automata, are incapable of language. Although suitable machines could be created (and animals such as parrots taught) to produce appropriate noises in appropriate stimulus situations—for example, to utter "I am in pain" when their receptors were damaged—Descartes claimed that

> it is not conceivable that such a machine should produce different arrangements of words so as to give an appropriately meaningful answer to whatever is said in its presence, as even the dullest of men can do.
>
> —(1637/1985, p. 140)

Although he acknowledged that machines could perform some complex tasks better than humans (a mechanical clock can measure time better than a person can), Descartes claimed that no machine is capable of problem solving in the form of rational adaptation to novel situations:

> Even though such machines might do some things as well as we do them, or perhaps even better, they would inevitably fail in others, which would reveal that they were acting not through understanding but only from the disposition of their organs.
>
> —(1637/1985, p. 140)

These arguments highlight the peculiar nature of Descartes' contribution to psychology. In claiming that mechanistic explanation could be extended to the realm of animal and human behavior, he emphasized the continuity of animal and human behavior with other material processes in nature. In denying that mechanistic reflexive explanation could be extended to human thought and voluntary behavior, he postulated a fundamental discontinuity between animals and human beings.

Descartes believed that the extension of mechanistic explanation to human thought and voluntary behavior undermined human freedom and claimed that the idea that humans are no different from animals posed a serious threat to morality and religion:

> For after the errors of those who deny God . . . there is none that leads weak minds further from the path of virtue than that of imagining that the souls of beasts are of the same nature as ours, and hence that after this present life we have nothing to fear or to hope for, any more than flies and ants.
>
> —(1637/1985, p. 141)

It is important to recognize that Descartes' arguments against animal and machine language and problem solving were independent of his arguments for mind-body dualism. Conwy Lloyd Morgan, the comparative psychologist, and John B. Watson, the behaviorist psychologist, were later materialists who also maintained that only humans have the capacity for language, and the question of whether machines such as digital computers are capable of genuinely creative problem solving remains a lively issue for contemporary psychologists and philosophers (Boden, 2003; Dreyfus, 1992).

Vitalism   Descartes extended the principles of mechanistic explanation to the functions of the Aristotelian nutritive and sensitive souls, but not to those of the rational soul. In so doing, he took the revolutionary step of separating the principles of life and mind.

From the time of the ancient Greeks, the psyche had been treated as the actualizing principle of both life and mind. By maintaining that vital processes such as digestion, respiration, and sensory-motor reflexes are a product of the organized matter of the body machine, Descartes denied that the rational soul or mind is responsible for the life of the material body:

> In order to explain these functions, then, it is not necessary to conceive of this machine as having any vegetative or sensitive soul or other principle of movement and life.
>
> —(*Treatise on Man*, 1664/1985, p. 108)

This was the fundamental idea behind the mechanistic conception of biological functions. Or, as Descartes put it,

> And let us recognize that the difference between the body of a living man and that of a dead man is just like the difference between, on the one hand, a watch or other automaton (that is, a self-moving machine), when it is wound up and contains in itself the corporeal principle of the movements for which it was designed, together with everything else required for its operation; and on the other hand, the same watch or machine when it is broken and the principle of its movement ceases to be active.
>
> —(1649/1985, pp. 329–330)

Thus Descartes did not treat the immaterial soul as the source of the vitality of the material body or the departure of the immaterial soul as the cause of bodily death. According to Descartes, this common error likely arose from "supposing that since dead bodies are devoid of heat and movement, it is the absence of the soul which causes this cessation of movement and heat":

> Thus it has been believed, without justification, that our natural heat and all these movements of our bodies depend upon our soul; whereas we ought to hold, on the contrary, that the soul takes its leave when we die only because this heat ceases and the organs which bring about bodily movement decay.
>
> —(1649/1985, p. 329)

This account of biological functions in terms of an emergent **vital force** of organized matter stimulated a fertile tradition of physiological research, although it later became the object of criticism by reductive physiologists, notably in the 19th century.

Introspection and Images Descartes claimed that we have infallible **introspective knowledge**: that our conscious apprehension of our own mental states such as sensations, beliefs, emotions, thoughts, and memories is direct and certain. In developing his system of knowledge from first principles, Descartes argued that although he could doubt that sense experience provides knowledge of the existence and properties of material bodies in the external world, he could not doubt the contents of his sense experience—of how things appeared to his senses. Consequently, even if his judgment that he was sitting by a bright and crackling fire was false because he was dreaming this while asleep in bed, he could at least be certain that this was how things *appeared* to his consciousness (1641/1985, p. 19). In this view, as long as we restrict our judgments to the contents of our consciousness they are immune from error. We err only when we make inferences about material bodies in the external world on the basis of our sense experience.

The view that our knowledge of mental states is direct and certain was maintained by most psychologists and philosophers throughout the succeeding centuries and remained popular until the early decades of the 20th century. Empiricists such as John Locke (1632–1704), George Berkeley (1685–1753), and David Hume (1711–1776), who rejected Descartes' rationalist claims about innate ideas and the rational intuition of fundamental scientific principles and maintained that all our ideas and knowledge are derived from experience, also embraced this account of self-knowledge of mental states.

Descartes also articulated the problem about our knowledge of the external world that vexed later empiricists: What justification do we have for making inferences about the existence and properties of material bodies in the external world on the basis of our sense experience? How do we know that there are material bodies in the external world that have the colors and shapes that we attribute to them on the basis of sense experience? This was not a problem generated by the mere possibility of doubting the existence and properties of material bodies in the external world, but was a product of Descartes' treatment of thoughts and ideas as images.

Descartes characterized the problem about our knowledge of the existence and properties of material bodies in the external world as a problem about the justification of our belief that our ideas of material bodies and their properties *resemble* material bodies and their properties:

> But the chief question at this point concerns the ideas which I take to be derived from things existing outside me: what is my reason for thinking that these resemble these things?
>
> —(1641/1985, p. 26)

This was a serious problem for Descartes, since his commitment to the distinction between primary and secondary qualities forced him to acknowledge that it was doubtful if our ideas of secondary qualities resemble the real qualities of material bodies:

> There may be a difference between the sensation we have of light (i.e. the idea of light which is formed in our imagination by the mediation of our eyes) and what is in the objects that produces that sensation within us (i.e. what is in the flame or the sun that we call by the name "light"). For although everyone is commonly convinced that the ideas we have in our minds are wholly similar to the objects from which they proceed, nevertheless I cannot see any reason which assures us that this is so.
>
> —(1664/1985, p. 81)

Later empiricists such as Locke, Berkeley, and Hume shared Descartes' conception of thoughts and ideas as images. They also recognized that this caused a problem for the justification of our claims to have knowledge of the existence and properties of material bodies in the external world, since we cannot directly compare imagistic thoughts with external reality, in the way that we can compare a representational painting to the actual physical scene it is intended to represent (a painting of the Grand Canal in Venice with the actual Grand Canal in Venice, for example). This conception of thoughts as images remained popular for many centuries, and impeded the development of a psychology of thought until the early 20th century.

Nevertheless, Descartes also deserves credit for being one of the earliest theorists to recognize that thoughts cannot be equated with images. He noted that although we can conceive of both a triangle and a chiliagon (a figure with a thousand sides) and can form an image of a triangle, we cannot form an image of a chiliagon (1641/1985, p. 50).

La Mettrie: Machine Man

Descartes had taken the revolutionary step of extending the principles of mechanistic explanation to all animal and some human behavior by treating such behavior as the product of matter in motion, but had resisted extending these principles to the human mind, whose material basis he denied. The French military physician Julien Offroy de La Mettrie had no such qualms and boldly declared that "man is a machine" and "there is in the whole universe only one diversely modified substance" (1748/1996, p. 39).

A native of Brittany, La Mettrie received his medical education at the University of Leiden in Holland. He practiced as a physician in Leiden for a number of years, publishing papers on smallpox, venereal disease, and vertigo until commissioned as an army physician during the Franco-Austrian war. He is reputed to have developed his materialist views as a consequence of a fever contracted during the siege of Freiburg: The disorders of thought and emotion induced by the fever left a lasting impression on him. La Mettrie published *The Natural History of the Soul* in 1745, in which he argued that humans are complex animals. This work created such an uproar amongst the French clergy that La Mettrie was forced to return to Holland. In 1748 he produced his major work *Man Machine*, in which he argued that the principles of mechanistic explanation should be extended to all human behavior, including human thought and language. When the blatant materialism and implicit atheism of this work proved too much even for the enlightened Dutch, La Mettrie moved to Berlin at the invitation of Frederick the Great, who became his biographer. There he died prematurely, through hedonistic overindulgence, according to his meaner critics. He expired during a bout of indigestion brought on by a surfeit of pheasant and truffles.

Organized Matter   La Mettrie believed that the organization of matter held the key to the understanding of all animal and human behavior:

> Since all the soul's faculties depend so much on the specific organization of the brain and of the whole body that they are clearly nothing but that very organization, the machine is perfectly explained!
>
> —(1748/1996, p. 26)

He claimed that "organized matter is endowed with a motive principle, which alone distinguishes it from unorganized matter" and that the gradations of complexity of animal and human behavior are "dictated by the diversity of this organization" (1748, p. 33). He consequently maintained that human thought is an emergent property of matter at a complex level of organization:

> I believe thought to be so little incompatible with organized matter, that it seems to be one of its properties, like electricity, motive power, impenetrability, extension, etc.
>
> —(1748/1996, p. 35)

The extension of mechanistic explanation to thought was so obvious and natural, according to La Mettrie, that Descartes must have been convinced of it. Although Descartes, who "understood animal nature and was the first to demonstrate perfectly that animals were mere machines," publicly avowed that mind and body are distinct substances, "it is obvious that it was only a trick, a cunning device to make the theologians swallow the poison hidden behind an analogy that strikes everyone and that they alone cannot see":

> For it is precisely that strong analogy which forces all scholars and true judges to admit that, however much these haughty, vain beings . . . may wish to exalt themselves, they are basically only animals and vertically crawling machines.
>
> —(1748/1996, p. 35)

La Mettrie claimed that the man machine is materially continuous with the animal machine: "From animals to man there is no abrupt transition" (1748/1996, p. 13). He maintained that the man machine differs from the animal machine only in terms of the degree of complexity of its material organization:

> We can see that there is only one substance in the universe and that man is the most perfect one. He is to the ape and the cleverest animals what Huygen's planetary clock is to one of Julien Leroy's watches.
>
> —(1748/1996, pp. 33–34)

La Mettrie held that physicians were "the only natural philosophers who have the right to speak on this subject" (1748, p. 5), since only their views were based upon "experience and observation alone" (1748, p. 4). He offered two forms of evidence in support of his materialist theory of mind and his claims about the continuity between animal and human machines. He documented the effects of various ingested substances, such as opium, wine, coffee, and red meat upon human thought and emotion and noted how damage caused to the "springs" of the human machine by fever or poisoning can produce severe disruption to mental functioning in the form of delusions and mania. He also appealed to the studies in "comparative anatomy" conducted by the Oxford neuroanatomist Thomas Willis (1621–1675), author of *The Anatomy of the Brain* (1664) and *Two Discourses Concerning the Soul of Beasts* (1672):

> In general, the form and composition of the quadruped's brain is more or less the same as man's. Everywhere we find the same shape and the same arrangement, with one essential difference: man, of all the animals, is the one with the largest and most convoluted brain, in relation to the volume of his body. Next come the ape, beaver, elephant, dog, fox, cat, etc.: these are the animals that are most like man, for we can also see in them the same graduated analogy concerning the corpus callosum.
>
> —(1748/1996, pp. 9–10)

However, La Mettrie's appeal to the effects of ingested substances, fever, and poisoning on mental functioning hardly established materialism. Although he demonstrated that many "states of the soul are . . . related to those of the body" (1748/1996, p. 9), regular correlation between mental and bodily states was entirely consistent with Descartes' interactionist dualism and was in fact presupposed by it. Although the evidence from comparative anatomy supported the hierarchical gradation of human and animal psychology and behavior, it did not demonstrate their continuity. Many ancient and medieval theorists acknowledged the hierarchical gradation of humans and animals, but maintained that some psychological capacities, such as abstract thought and language, are attributable only to humans.

Strong and Weak Continuity   La Mettrie avowed two forms of continuity between humans and animals, which should be carefully distinguished. One is the **weak continuity** between humans and animals presupposed by materialism: the notion that humans and animals, like vegetables and minerals, are composed of the same basic material, differently organized. La Mettrie rejected Descartes' claim that humans and animals are fundamentally discontinuous because humans have an immaterial mind and animals do not. As he put it,

> Man is not molded from a more precious clay; nature has used one and the same dough, merely changing the yeast.
>
> —(1748/1996, p. 20)

Thus he maintained that human thought is materially instantiated in the human brain.

However, La Mettrie also argued for **strong continuity** between human and animal psychology and behavior. He claimed that differences between human and animal psychology and behavior are merely differences in degree and not fundamental differences in kind. According to this view, human psychology and behavior are fundamentally *identical* to animal psychology and behavior. Human psychology and behavior may be re-identified in other animals, albeit in attenuated form, since human psychology and behavior are merely more complex forms of animal psychology and behavior. Thus La Mettrie argued that thought and language could be attributed to animals, although in attenuated form.

However, the weak continuity of materialism does not entail the strong continuity of human and animal psychology and behavior, any more than the weak continuity of the inorganic and organic presupposed by materialism entails strong continuity of structure and function between the inorganic and organic. Rocks and plants are both composed of organized matter, but plants have properties, such as the ability to perform photosynthesis, that are not instantiated *to any degree* in rocks. Consequently, although humans and animals are both composed of organized matter, it might still be the case that humans have some psychological capacities, such as the capacity for abstract thought or language, that are not instantiated *to any degree* in animals. Whether or not the capacity for abstract thought or language is in fact instantiated in animals is a separate empirical matter.

The weak continuity of materialism and strong continuity between human and animal psychology and behavior became associated historically because Descartes rejected both materialism and strong continuity and because most later evolutionary theorists, comparative psychologists, and behaviorists were materialists who, like La Mettrie, affirmed strong continuity. However, there is no intrinsic connection between materialism and strong continuity. Aristotle and other ancient and medieval theorists affirmed the weak continuity of materialism but denied strong continuity between human and animal psychology and behavior, as did the comparative psychologist Conwy Lloyd Morgan and the behaviorist psychologist John B. Watson, who were both materialists but maintained that only humans have the capacity for language.

Animals and Language   Although it was not mandated by his materialism, La Mettrie maintained that human and animal psychology and behavior are strongly continuous. He acknowledged that only humans speak a language, but denied that machines and animals are incapable of learning a language. He believed that language is the product of intelligence and learning, which he held to be a function of brain size. Given the anatomical and behavioral similarities between apes and humans, La Mettrie was convinced that apes are capable of learning language:

> The similarity of the ape's structure and functions is such that I hardly doubt at all that if this animal were perfectly trained, we would succeed in teaching him to utter sounds and consequently to learn a language. Then he would no longer be a wild man, nor an imperfect man, but a perfect man, a little man of the town, with as much substance or muscle for thinking and taking advantage of his education as we have.
>
> —(1748/1996, p. 12)

He suggested teaching apes language using the techniques developed by J. C. Amman (1700/1965) for teaching sign language to deaf-mutes. In the 20th century, Allen and Beatrice Gardner used similar techniques to teach the sign language of the deaf to chimpanzees (Gardner & Gardner, 1969).

La Mettrie claimed that the linguistic competencies of humans, like their developed forms of social and cultural behavior, are based upon interpersonal imitation or "mimicry," a form of reflexive learning that is as automatic as the pupillary reflex:

> We take everything—gestures, accents, etc.—from those we live with, in the same way as the eyelid blinks under the threat of a blow that is foreseen, or as the body of a spectator imitates mechanically, and despite himself, all the movements of a good mime.
>
> —(1748/1996, p. 9)

He maintained that animals are also capable of imitation or "mimicry," and noted how a monkey can learn "to put on and take off his little hat or to ride a trained dog" (1748/1996, p. 13). Similar accounts of imitative learning formed the basis of the theories of social behavior developed by Gustav Le Bon (1841–1931) and Gabriel Tarde (1843–1904) in the late 19th century, which played a major role in shaping the development of 20th-century American social psychology. Like 20th-century behaviorist psychologists, La Mettrie believed that the same basic principles of learning applied to animals and humans and that these principles could be exploited to improve their condition through training and education.

God, Nature, and Morality   Although La Mettrie affirmed the probability of the existence of a "supreme Being" (1748/1996, p. 22), he denied that it vouchsafed the doctrines of any established religion. He was scornful of academic arguments for the existence of God, particularly those based upon the diversity and functional adaptation of animal species, and the apparently purposive nature of biological development. He acknowledged that it was unlikely that such features were the product of blind chance, but claimed that "destroying chance does not prove the existence of a supreme Being" (1748/1996, p. 24). La Mettrie suggested another alternative, that functionality and apparent teleology are simply a product of the ordered development of nature itself:

> The eye sees only because it happens to be organized and placed as it is; and that, given the same rules of movement followed by nature in the generation and development of bodies, it was not possible for that wonderful organ to be organized and placed otherwise.
>
> —(1748/1996, p. 25)

Certainly La Mettrie took seriously the possibility that there is no purpose or design informing human existence:

> Who knows after all whether the reason for man's existence is not his existence itself. Perhaps he was thrown by chance on a point on the earth's surface without being able to say how or why, but simply that he has to live and die, like mushrooms which appear from one day to the next, or flowers which grow beside ditches and cover walls.
>
> —(1748/1996, p. 23)

Such an uncompromising materialist and mechanistic conception appeared to paint a very bleak picture of human nature. It suggested that humans are no better than animals, concerned only with the satisfaction of sensual desires, especially given La Mettrie's celebration of the sexual nature of the human machine. This was precisely the consequence of treating men as machines that Descartes had feared.

Yet La Mettrie was rather more sanguine about the prospects for humanity. He questioned the common assumption that humans are morally superior to animals, noting that animals rarely murder or torture each other or engage in religious wars and claimed that some animals are capable of moral emotions such as remorse. More significantly, he stressed that a materialist and mechanistic account of human thought and behavior does not preclude human virtue, since it treats human virtue as a product of material organization on a par with thought and digestion:

> Since thought clearly develops with the organs, why should not the matter that composes them not also be capable of remorse once it has acquired, with time, the faculty of feeling? . . .
>
> Given the slightest principle of movement, animate bodies will have everything they need to move, feel, think, repent, and in a word, behave in the physical sphere and in the moral sphere which depends upon it.
>
> —(1748/1996, p. 26)

According to La Mettrie, there is no special reason to suppose that human machines would pursue their own selfish interests at the expense of others. On the contrary:

> The materialist, convinced, whatever his vanity might object, that he is only a machine or an animal, will not ill-treat his fellows. . . . Following the law of nature given to all animals, he does not want to do to others what he would not like others to do to him.
>
> —(1748/1996, p. 39)

Although La Mettrie's work had a major impact in the 18th century, his name became associated with such odium that he was rarely cited and consequently had little effect on the later development of psychology. Although his commitment to strong continuity presaged a fundamental principle of evolutionary theory and behaviorist psychology, later evolutionists and behaviorist psychologists seem to have been unaware of his work. When Thomas Huxley (1825–1895) addressed the British Association in Belfast in 1874 on "The Hypothesis That Animals Are Automata, and Its History," he gave due credit to Descartes but made no mention of La Mettrie (Boakes, 1984).

Thomas Hobbes: Empiricism, Materialism, and Individualism

The Englishman Thomas Hobbes (1588–1679) shared La Mettrie's materialist vision of human psychology but took a rather more pessimistic view of its implications. Born in Malmesbury, England, Hobbes was educated at Oxford University and served as Francis Bacon's secretary for a short period. He entered the employment of William Cavendish, third Earl of Devonshire, and for most of the rest of his life served as secretary and tutor to the family. This put him in some danger during the period leading up to the English Civil War. Hobbes fled to France in 1640 and did not return until 1651. He made several tours of Europe, where he met many of the leading theorists of his day, such as Galileo and Descartes, with whom he became friends. He lived to age 91, producing translations of Homer's *Iliad* and *Odyssey* at age 87.

Hobbes's main interests were political, and his major work *Leviathan* (1651) is primarily an argument in favor of absolute monarchy. His aim was to devise a political system capable of avoiding the horrors of civil war, having been greatly affected by the English Civil War, albeit at a distance. His psychological theories are mainly to be found in *On Human Nature* (1640) and the preliminary chapters of *Leviathan*.

Hobbes claimed that his psychological interests were aroused after having read Euclid's *Elements* at age 40; it induced his reverence for the self-contained axiomatic systems of geometry. Consequently, he tried to deduce his claims about human psychology and society from a number of self-evident axioms, based upon the principles of the new mechanistic science. Although Hobbes followed Descartes in adopting a deductive approach to explanation, he rejected Descartes' rationalist account of knowledge and denied the existence of innate ideas.

Hobbes was a psychological empiricist who maintained that all our ideas or concepts are derived from sense experience:

> The original of them all is that which we call *sense*; for there is no conception in a man's mind which hath not at first, totally, or by parts, been begotten upon the organs of sense. The rest are derived from that original.
>
> —(1651/1966, p. 1)

Hobbes was also committed to the **homogeneity of cognition and sense perception**: He claimed that the difference between cognition and sense perception is a matter of degree (of intensity), but not a fundamental difference in kind. On this account, thinking of a tree in blossom is like seeing and smelling a tree in blossom, only fainter. Hobbes agreed with Descartes that ideas are like pictorial images, since he maintained, with later empiricists, that our ideas are copies or faint images of sense impressions of objects:

> For after the object is removed, or the eye shut, we still retain an image of the thing seen, though more obscure than when we see it. . . . *Imagination* therefore is nothing more than *decaying sense.*
>
> —(1651/1966, p. 4)

Hobbes derived his first principles from the materialism of the new mechanistic science. Adopting a reductive explanatory approach to human psychology, he claimed that mental states and processes are "nothing really, but motion in some internal substance of the head":

> which motion not stopping there, but proceeding to the heart, of necessity must either help or hinder the motion which is called vital; when it helpeth, it is called delight, contentment, or pleasure, which is nothing really but motion about the heart, as conception is nothing but motion in the head; and the objects that cause it are called pleasant or delightful.
>
> —(1640/1966, p. 31)

Hobbes also embraced a form of **psychological hedonism**, according to which all human behavior is determined by the desire to attain pleasure and avoid pain:

> This motion, in which consisteth pleasure or pain, is also a solicitation or provocation either to draw near the thing that pleaseth, or to retire from the thing that displeaseth; and this solicitation is the endeavor or internal beginning of animal motion, which when the object delighteth, is called appetite; and when it displeaseth, it is called aversion.
>
> —(1640/1966, p. 31)

Hobbes famously claimed that the unbridled pursuit of selfish interest would inevitably lead to the war "of every man, against every man" and that in such a "state of nature" the life of man would be "solitary, poor, nasty, brutish, and short" (1651/1966, p. 113). He believed that humans embrace systems of civic government out of self-interest, in order to avoid these anticipated consequences. He argued that an absolute monarchy, in which individuals abandon their rights to a sovereign power, is the most just and efficient form of government, although he maintained that any form of government is better than none.

Hobbes's explanatory reductionism is also manifest in his **individualism**, which formed the basis of his account of social community in *Leviathan*. According to Hobbes, societies or social groups are nothing more than collections of human individuals, and social behavior is nothing more than the aggregate behavior of collections of human individuals, determined by their pursuit of pleasure and avoidance of pain. This individualistic conception of the social was characteristic of later empiricist concepts of the social, from Adam Smith (1723–1790) to Floyd Allport (1890–1978), who determined the course of American social psychology in the early 20th century (Katz, 1991).

Frontispiece of Hobbes's *Leviathan* (1651). Body of state represented as aggregation of individual persons.

In advancing these materialist and mechanistic explanations of human psychology and behavior, Hobbes denied that humans have free will. He claimed that the "will" is just the most powerful appetite, or efficient cause, and is the same in animals and men. He thus reduced final causation in the realm of human psychology and behavior to efficient causation:

> A final cause has no place but in such things as have sense and will, and this also I . . . prove . . . to be an efficient cause.
>
> —(1655/1966, p. 132)

Like La Mettrie, Hobbes was condemned by the religious establishment for his materialist views. He was denied admission to the newly formed Royal Society, which is perhaps not that surprising, since although he was a vigorous advocate of the new mechanistic science, he did not make any substantive contribution to it. He did, however, take the first step in extending mechanistic forms of explanation to mental processes. He offered tentative explanations of "trains of thought," likening the "coherence" of thought to the "coherence" of matter. He suggested that ideas derived from sense experience are connected in our memory by their conjunction in our sense experience:

> The *cause* of the *coherence* or consequence of one conception to another, is their first *coherence* or consequence at that time when they are produced by *sense*.
>
> —(1640/1966, p. 15)

Hobbes is sometimes treated as the father of British empiricism and the founder of what later came to be known as associationist psychology. Yet although he was the first to clearly articulate many of the distinctive principles of British empiricism, such as the principles of psychological empiricism and the homogeneity of cognition and sense perception, and did suggest a mechanistic treatment of the association of thought, his contribution was more programmatic than substantive. It was John Locke who detailed the origin of complex ideas in sense experience and David Hume and David Hartley (1705–1757) who developed the principles of association that grounded the later development of associationist psychology.

MENTAL MECHANISM AND STIMULUS-RESPONSE PSYCHOLOGY

By the end of the 17th century the triumph of mechanism was complete in the physical sciences, and mechanistic explanation was extended to human psychology and behavior in the 18th and 19th centuries. However, this did not lead to a progressive acceptance of materialism, as might have been expected. Most of those who developed mechanistic explanations of mental states and processes did their best to avoid any association with materialism. Even those who explored the material basis of mentality in the brain avowed a form of dualism or a **neutral parallelism**, by maintaining that every mental state is correlated with a brain state, while carefully avoiding speculation about the basis of the correlation between mental and brain states. Although the power of organized religion declined over these centuries, the religious establishment still played a powerful role within society and civic administration, often determining royal or government patronage and university positions.

One of the peculiarities of Descartes' pioneering account of reflexive behavior in animals and humans was that he presumed that the nerves from sensory receptors are connected in the brain to the nerves that control motor behavior, even though it was common knowledge that animals often continue to display reflexive behavior after decapitation. For example, La Mettrie noted how

> A drunken soldier cut off the head of a turkey-cock with a sabre. The animal stayed upright, then it walked and ran; when it hit the wall it turned around, beat its wings, still running, and finally fell down.
>
> —(1748/1996, p. 27)

The English clergyman Stephen Hales (1677–1761) demonstrated that decapitated frogs continue to respond to stimulation so long as the marrow of their spinal cord remains intact (La Mettrie's *Man Machine* was provocatively dedicated to Hales). Robert Whytt (1714–1766), who taught in the medical school at the University of Edinburgh, confirmed these results in a careful series of experiments:

> When any of the muscles of the leg of a frog are irritated some time after cutting off its head, almost all the muscles belonging to the legs and thighs are brought into contraction, if the spinal marrow be entire.
>
> —(cited in Smith, 1992, p. 74)

He also noted that decapitation enhances reflexive activity (Smith, 1992) and that some reflexes can be preserved even if only a small portion of the spinal cord remains intact (Boakes, 1984).

Whytt maintained that such experiments demonstrated that

> a certain power of influence lodged in the brain, spinal marrow, and nerves, is either the immediate cause of the contraction of muscles of animals, or at least necessary to it.
>
> —(1751/1978, p. 3)

He claimed that decapitated animals respond selectively to stimulation and noted how a brainless frog will use its legs to relieve the irritation caused by an acid-soaked tissue applied to its skin, just as many intact animals use their legs to rid themselves of fleas and ticks (Reed, 1997).

Whytt suggested that such experiments demonstrated the existence of an unconscious "sensitive soul" in the spinal cord, capable of making adaptive responses to sensory stimulation. Like Thomas Willis, the Oxford neuroanatomist, he suggested that mentality is distributed throughout the nervous system and not restricted to the brain. This suggestion generated opposition as fierce as that for La Mettrie's claim that mentality is a property of the brain. However, it indirectly stimulated many 19th-century neurophysiologists, who often saw themselves as opponents of such crass materialism, to locate mentality in the higher regions of the brain, such as the cerebral cortex.

In his *Essay on the Vital and Other Involuntary Motions of Animals* (1751), Whytt identified a range of innate reflexive behavior, such as digestion, coughing, sneezing, and penile erection (Boakes, 1984). He introduced the notion of a **stimulus** into the theoretical vocabulary, defined as the application of any form of physical energy to a nerve (Reed, 1997). He also noted how certain originally neutral stimuli can acquire the capacity to generate innate reflexes by association with their precipitating stimuli (Boakes, 1984), anticipating Pavlov's account of conditioned reflexes, including the form of conditioned salivation that became the primary focus of his experimental studies:

> Thus the sight, or even the recalled idea of grateful food causes an uncommon flow of spittle into the mouth of a hungry person; and the seeing of a lemon cut produces the same effect in many people.
>
> —(cited in Boakes, 1984, p. 95)

DISCUSSION QUESTIONS

1. Bacon claimed that scientific theories should be judged by the utility of their "works" or "discoveries" and that genuine scientific knowledge leads to "dominion" over nature. What useful works or discoveries have scientific psychological theories promoted? Is dominion over humans an appropriate goal for scientific psychology? If so, to what degree? In what sense?

2. Descartes believed that animals lack sensory awareness and consciousness. Do you? How could you tell? Can you think of a "crucial instance" or "crucial experiment" that would demonstrate sensory awareness or consciousness in animals? Could a machine have sensory awareness or consciousness? How could you tell?

3. Does thinking of animals as machines incline us to think they are more or less likely to be capable of language and problem solving?

4. Does materialism imply strong continuity between human and animal psychology and behavior?

5. Hobbes was an individualist about social community. Are social attitudes and behavior just the common attitudes and behavior of a collection of individuals? Is contemporary social psychology individualist, or does it conceive of social attitudes and behavior as something more than (or different from) the aggregation of attitudes and behavior?

GLOSSARY

automaton A moving machine.

corpuscle Seventeenth-century term for the atomistic components of material bodies, coined by Robert Boyle.

corpuscularian theory of light Theory of light in which it is treated as a stream of material corpuscles, or atoms.

epicycles A system of circles within circles introduced by Ptolemy (and Copernicus) to accommodate the "wandering" motion of planets.

geocentric theory The theory that Earth is the fixed center of the universe, around which the sun and other planets orbit.

heliocentric theory The theory that the sun is the fixed center of the universe, around which Earth and other planets orbit.

homogeneity of cognition and sense perception The claim that cognition and sense perception differ in degree (of intensity) but not fundamental kind, usually via the claim that ideas are weaker images of sense impressions.

Idols of the cave Cognitive biases in scientific thinking that are idiosyncratic products of individual human development.

Idols of the marketplace Social biases in scientific thinking based upon notions derived from common linguistic usage.

Idols of the theatre Social biases in scientific thinking based upon theories maintained by schools of philosophy as received dogma.

Idols of the tribe Cognitive biases in scientific thinking based upon innate human propensities.

individualism The view that societies or social groups are nothing more than collections of human individuals and that social behavior is nothing more than the aggregate behavior of collections of human individuals.

Instance of the Fingerpost Francis Bacon's name for a crucial instance that enables the empirical adjudication of competing theories.

interactionism The view that mind and body causally interact.

introspective knowledge The conscious apprehension of mental states, usually held to be direct and certain.

mechanistic explanation Efficient causal explanation in terms of antecedent conditions sufficient to produce an effect, often associated with a conception of the universe as a giant (usually clockwork) machine.

neutral parallelism The view that every mental state is correlated with a brain state, without commitment to any theory about the nature of the relation between mental and brain states.

occasionalism The view that God directly causes the regular correlation between mental and bodily states.

pre-established harmony The view that God maintains the regular correlation between mental and bodily states.

psychological hedonism The view that all human behavior is motivated by the desire to attain pleasure and avoid pain.

reflexive behavior Automatic and involuntary behavior in response to stimulation.

Reformation The Protestant religious movement founded by Martin Luther.

Renaissance The cultural movement that began in southern Italy in the 14th century and promoted innovative developments in art, literature, architecture, and music, as well as in mathematics, religion, and science.

Renaissance humanism The Renaissance focus on human psychology and celebration of its potential.

stellar parallax The variation in the angular separation of the stars that was a crucial implication of the Copernican heliocentric theory.

stimulus Term introduced by the Edinburgh physician Thomas Whytt to describe the application of any form of physical energy to a nerve.

strong continuity The view that the differences between human and animal psychology and behavior are differences in degree and not fundamental differences in kind.

vital force An emergent force of organized matter held to explain biological functions such as bodily heat and movement.

vortex theory of motion Descartes' theory of motion in terms of "action by contact."

weak continuity The view that humans and animals are composed of the same basic material, differently organized.

REFERENCES

Amman, J. C. (1965). *A dissertation on speech* (C. Baker, Trans.). Amsterdam: North-Holland. (Original work published 1700; original translation 1873)

Bacon, F. (1966). *New Atlantis.* In *The advancement of learning and New Atlantis.* Oxford: Oxford University Press. (Original work published 1627)

Bacon, F. (1994). *Novum organum* (P. Urbach & J. Gibson, Eds. & Trans.). Chicago, IL: Open Court. (Original work published 1620)

Bandrés, J., & Llavona, R. (1992). Minds and machines in Renaissance Spain: Gómez Pereira's theory of animal behavior. *Journal of the History of the Behavioral Sciences, 28,* 158–168.

Bazerman, C. (1988). Reporting the experiment: The changing account of scientific doings in the *Philosophical Transactions of the Royal Society, 1665–1800.* In C. Bazerman, *Shaping scientific knowledge: The genre and activity of the experimental article in science.* Madison: University of Wisconsin Press.

Boakes, R. (1984). *From Darwin to behaviorism: Psychology and the minds of animals.* Cambridge: Cambridge University Press.

Boden, M. (2003). *The creative mind: Myths and mechanisms.* New York: Routledge.

Brett, G. S. (1912–1921). *A history of psychology* (Vols. 1–3). London: Macmillan.

Bruno, G. (1950). *On the infinite universe and worlds.* In D. W. Singer, *Giordano Bruno: His life and thought.* New York: Schuman. (Original work published 1584)

Buchdahl, G. (1969). *Metaphysics and the philosophy of science.* Oxford: Blackwell.

Clark, D. (1982). *Descartes' philosophy of science.* Manchester, England: Manchester University Press.

Clemens, R. D. (1967). Physiological-psychological thought in Juan Luis Vives. *Journal of the History of the Behavioral Sciences, 3,* 219–235.

Copernicus, N. (1976). *On the revolutions of the heavenly spheres* (A. M. Duncan, Trans.). New York: Barnes & Noble. (Original work published 1543)

Descartes, R. (1985). *Discourse on the method.* In J. Cottingham, R. Stoothhoff, & D. Murdoch (Trans.), *The philosophical writings of Descartes* (Vol. 1). Cambridge: Cambridge University Press. (Original work published 1637)

Descartes, R. (1985). *Meditations on first philosophy.* In J. Cottingham, R. Stoothhoff, & D. Murdoch (Trans.), *The philosophical writings of Descartes* (Vol. 2). Cambridge: Cambridge University Press. (Original work published 1641)

Descartes, R. (1985). *Search after truth.* In J. Cottingham, R. Stoothhoff, & D. Murdoch (Trans.), *The philosophical writings of Descartes* (Vol. 2). Cambridge: Cambridge University Press. (Original work published 1643)

Descartes, R. (1985). *The passions of the soul.* In J. Cottingham, R. Stoothhoff, & D. Murdoch (Trans.), *The philosophical writings of Descartes* (Vol. 1). Cambridge: Cambridge University Press. (Original work published 1649)

Descartes, R. (1985). *The world.* In J. Cottingham, R. Stoothhoff, & D. Murdoch (Trans.), *The philosophical writings of Descartes* (Vol. 1). Cambridge: Cambridge University Press. (Originally published 1664; includes *Treatise on Man*)

Dolling, L. M., Gianelli, A. F., & Statile, G. N. (Eds.). (2003). *The tests of time: Readings in the development of physical theory.* Princeton: Princeton University Press.

Dreyfus, H. (1992). *What computers still can't do: A critique of artificial intelligence.* Cambridge, MA: MIT Press.

Erasmus, D. (1979). *The praise of folly* (C. H. Miller, Trans.). New Haven: Yale University Press. (Original work published 1512)

Foote, T. (1991). Where Columbus was coming from. *Smithsonian* (December), 28–41.

Galileo, G. (1957). *Letters on the solar spots.* In S. Drake (Trans.), *Discoveries and opinions of Galileo.* Garden City, NY: Doubleday. (Original work published 1613)

Galileo, G. (1957). *The assayer.* In S. Drake (Trans.), *Discoveries and opinions of Galileo.* Garden City, NY: Doubleday. (Original work published 1623)

Galileo, G. (1967). *Dialogue concerning the two chief world-systems, Ptolemaic and Copernican* (S. Drake, Trans.). Berkeley: University of California Press. (Original work published 1632)

Galileo, G. (1974). *Dialogues concerning two new sciences* (S. Drake, Trans.). Madison: University of Wisconsin Press. (Original work published 1638)

Gardner, B. T., & Gardner, R. A. (1969). Teaching language to a chimpanzee. *Science, 165,* 664–672.

Gilbert. W. (1958). *On magnetism* (P. F. Mottelay, Trans.). New York: Dover. (Original work published 1600)

Harvey, W. (1989). *On the circulation of the blood.* In R. Willis (Trans.), *The works of William Harvey.* Philadelphia: University of Pennsylvania Press. (Original work published 1628)

Hobbes, T. (1966). *Leviathan.* In W. Molesworth (Ed.), *The English works of Thomas Hobbes.* Darmstadt, Germany: Scientia Verlag Aalen. (Original work published 1651)

Hobbes, T. (1966). *On human nature.* In W. Molesworth (Ed.), *The English works of Thomas Hobbes.* Darmstadt, Germany: Scientia Verlag Aalen. (Original work published 1640)

Hobbes, T. (1966). *On matter.* In W. Molesworth (Ed.), *The English works of Thomas Hobbes.* Darmstadt, Germany: Scientia Verlag Aalen. (Original work published 1655)

Katz, D. (1991). Floyd Henry Allport: Founder of social psychology as a behavioral science. In G. A. Kimble, M. Wertheimer, & C. White (Eds.), *Portraits of pioneers in psychology* (Vol. 1). Hillsdale, NJ: Erlbaum.

Lafleur, L. J. (1956). Introduction to Descartes' *Discourse on Method.* Indianapolis: Bobbs-Merrill.

La Mettrie, J. O. de la. (1996). *Machine man.* In A. Thompson (Trans. & Ed.), *Machine man and other writings.* Cambridge: Cambridge University Press. (Original work published 1748)

La Mettrie, J. O. de la. (1996). *Natural history of the soul.* In A. Thompson (Trans. & Ed.), *Machine man and other writings.* Cambridge: Cambridge University Press. (Original work published 1745)

Losee, J. (1980). *A historical introduction to the philosophy of science.* New York: Oxford University Press.

Newton, I. (1952). *Opticks; or, A treatise of the reflections, refractions, inflections & colors of light.* New York: Dover. (Original work published 1704)

Newton, I. (1969). *Mathematical principles of natural philosophy* (F. Cajori, Trans.). New York: Greenwood Press. (Original work published 1687)

Osiander, A. (2003). Preface to N. Copernicus, *On the revolutions of the heavenly spheres*. In L. M. Dolling, A. F. Gianelli, & G. N. Statile (Eds.), *The tests of time: Readings in the development of physical theory*. Princeton: Princeton University Press. (Original work published 1543)

Pyenson, L., & Sheets-Pyenson, S. (1999). *Servants of nature: A history of scientific institutions, enterprises, and sensibilities*. New York: Norton.

Reed, E. S. (1997). *From soul to mind*. New Haven, CT: Yale University Press.

Smith, R. (1992). *Inhibition: History and meaning in the sciences of mind and brain*. Berkeley: University of California Press.

Wallace, W. A. (1984). *Galileo and his sources: The heritage of the Collegio Romano in Galileo's science*. Princeton: Princeton University Press.

Whytt, R. (1978). *An essay on the vital and other involuntary motions of animals*. In D. N. Robinson (Ed.), *Significant contributions to the history of psychology, 1750–1920*. Series E: *Physiological Psychology*. Vol. 1. Washington, DC: University Publications of America. (Original work published 1751)

Willis, T. (1672). *Two discourses concerning the soul of brutes*. London.

Willis, T. (1965). *The anatomy of the brain* (W. Feindel, Ed.). Montreal: McGill University Press. (Original work published 1664)

CHAPTER 5

The Newtonian Psychologists

THE ACHIEVEMENTS OF THE SCIENTIFIC REVOLUTION REPRESENTED THE vanguard of the **Enlightenment**, that period in European thought in the 17th and 18th centuries when confidence in human reason and experience gradually came to supersede faith in religion and traditional authority. One central feature of Enlightenment thought, which flourished in France, Scotland, England, and Germany, was a commitment to human progress and an optimistic belief in the applicability of scientific knowledge, including social and psychological knowledge, to the improvement of the human condition. The Enlightenment saw the emergence of more liberal, secular, and utilitarian concepts of humanity and the development of more democratic societies, such as the United States. Although not universally embraced, these Enlightenment ideals continue to inform contemporary confidence in the theoretical progress and social utility of the sciences, including social and psychological science.

The rejection of the Aristotelian tradition was good news for the natural sciences. The rejection of Aristotle's geocentric theory and final causal explanations of motion led to advances in astronomy and physics. However, it was not so obviously good news for psychology. One of the casualties of the scientific revolution was Aristotle's biologically grounded functional psychology, which came to be replaced by a variety of mechanistic psychological theories. This was not the intent of the pioneers of the new science, such as Galileo, Bacon, and Newton. Although they maintained that final causal explanation has no place in physical science, most recognized that final causal explanation is entirely appropriate in the realm of human and animal behavior. Yet this qualification was generally ignored by the protopsychologists of the 17th and 18th centuries, who tried to create a science of psychology based upon the mechanistic forms of efficient causal explanation characteristic of the new science, for which Newton's physics came to serve as a paradigm.

Newton's theory of universal gravitation was hugely influential, not only in physical science, where it continued to reign supreme throughout the 18th and 19th centuries, but also with respect to the forms of psychological theory that developed during these centuries. These were either attempts to model psychological theory upon Newtonian science, such as associationist psychology, or reactions to them, such as "common sense" psychology, and rationalist, humanist, and romantic alternatives. Newton's theory remained influential in psychology into the 20th century (and remains influential in the 21st), even for those forms of functionalist and behaviorist psychology that were supposedly grounded in Darwin's evolutionary biology. For example, even though Newton's theory had been decisively rejected by natural scientists by the early decades of the 20th century, throughout his professional career the behaviorist psychologist Clark C. Hull prominently displayed a copy of Newton's *Principia* (1687) on his desk and made it required reading for his graduate students in psychology.

THE NEWTONIAN PSYCHOLOGISTS

Like many other social scientists, psychologists came to treat Newton's theory not only as a paradigm of scientific achievement, but also as a paradigm of scientific thought. They came to treat particular features of Newton's theory as essential conditions of scientific thought, which ought to be reproduced in any properly scientific psychology.

Newtonian Science

One of the central features of Newton's theory was that it provided a *universal* explanation of terrestrial and celestial motion in terms of gravitational forces. This feature of Newton's theory became fairly quickly elevated into an implicit criterion of adequacy for a scientific explanation. According to this criterion, an adequate scientific explanation must be universal: It must furnish an explanation of *all* the phenomena in any particular domain. Newton himself gave no more than a cautious and qualified endorsement of this principle, allowing that in at least some cases, we might have to recognize different causal explanations of the same range of phenomena: "Therefore to the same natural effects we must, *as far as possible*, assign the same causes" (1687/1969, p. 398, my emphasis). In his own case, he was prepared to introduce God's intervention as the cause of some celestial motions, over and above gravitational forces, and thought it entirely appropriate to do so "to discourse of whom [God] from the appearances of things does certainly belong to natural philosophy" (1687/1969, p. 546). Nonetheless, generations of psychologists since Newton have been committed to the notion that universality is the mark of a genuine scientific explanation (Kimble, 1995).

The objects of Newton's theory were material bodies, with mass and velocity, held to exist for all time and in all regions of space. Later generations of psychologists likewise presumed that human psychology and behavior are invariant in historical time and cultural space, to the point of claiming that it is unscientific to suppose that this might not be the case (Spence, 1987).

Two other principles that figured prominently in Newton's science were successfully adopted by later generations of physical scientists. These were the principle of *atomism,* which holds that entities that form the subject matter of scientific disciplines, such as atoms, planets, and cells, can be individuated without reference to other entities and can exist independently of them, and the principle of *explanatory reduction,* which holds that the best explanation of a complex entity is in terms of its material components. At the beginning of *Principia,* Newton speculated that the properties and behavior of complex material bodies might eventually be explained in terms of mathematical laws governing the material "corpuscles" (or atoms) that composed them, the **corpuscularian hypothesis** promoted by his colleague Robert Boyle:

> I wish we could derive the rest of the phenomena of nature by the same kind of reasoning from mathematical principles; for I am induced by many reasons to suspect that they may all depend upon certain forces by which the particles of bodies, by some causes hitherto unknown, are either mutually impelled toward each other, and cohere in regular figures, or are repelled and recede from each other.
>
> —(1687/1969, p. xvii)

This hypothesis, developed with great success in the physical sciences, led many psychologists to presume that an atomistic and reductive analysis of human psychology and behavior is also required to constitute psychology as a genuine science.

Newton's gravitational theory is often treated as a paradigm of a deterministic physical system: a system in which, for every event, there is an antecedent set of conditions sufficient to produce it. However, it was the French mathematician Pierre Simon de Laplace (1749–1827) who gave Newton's theory its deterministic interpretation, by demonstrating the stability of the solar system within Newtonian mechanics. Newton had postulated the intervention of God to maintain this stability, but Laplace famously remarked to Napoleon that he had no need of that hypothesis.

Laplace represented his deterministic thesis through the image of a superintelligence capable of knowing the position and velocity of all material bodies at any instant in time and thus able to calculate and successfully predict all consequent positions and motions according to Newton's laws. Later generations of psychologists came to treat the principle of determinism as a foundational assumption of scientific psychology, despite the fact that physicists abandoned it in the early part of the 20th century.

The success of Newtonian science also promoted a plausible legend, that progress in science is achieved through a process of continuous **theoretical unification**. Thus Galileo's law of free fall and Kepler's laws of planetary motion were independently developed and restricted to terrestrial and celestial motion respectively, but were later unified by integration within Newton's gravitational theory. The various gas laws relating pressure, temperature, and volume, Graham's law, Charles's law, and Boyle's law, were independently established by Thomas Graham (1805–1869), Jacques Alexandre Charles (1746–1823), and Robert Boyle but were later integrated within the kinetic theory of gases; and contemporary physicists look forward to the attainment of Grand Unified Theory (GUT), which they hope will eventually integrate the theories of the four known physical forces (gravitation, electromagnetism, strong nuclear, and weak nuclear). Similarly, psychologists have tried to develop theories of learning that integrate classical and operant conditioning (e.g., Hull, 1937) and regularly dream of developing a universal theory that will integrate the various explanatory principles of the different branches of psychology. Yet, as is often lamented, psychology still awaits its Newton.

Newton's achievement is often also associated with an **empiricist** or **positivist conception of scientific explanation**, according to which causal explanations and scientific laws are nothing more than descriptions of observational correlation, with references to causal forces and hypothetical entities dismissed as appeals to "occult" properties. At the end of *Principia*, Newton admitted that he did not know the nature or ultimate cause of gravity, and declared, "I frame no hypothesis" (1687/1969, p. 547). Yet Newton was no empiricist or positivist. He certainly conceived of gravity as a genuine force and was not averse in principle to postulating hypothetical entities to furnish causal explanations: For example, in *Opticks* (1704/1952) he postulated "multitudes of unimaginable small and swift corpuscles" to explain the transmission of light. Later 18th-century empiricist interpreters, such as George Berkeley and David Hume, and 19th-century positivists, such as Auguste Comte (1798–1857) and Ernst Mach (1838–1916), were the ones who characterized Newton's achievement in these terms and who mediated the adoption of the Newtonian paradigm for many psychologists.

Newton was, of course, an empiricist in the general sense that any post-Galilean scientist was a (methodological) empiricist. He maintained that scientific theories must be based upon empirical data rather than rational intuition or classical authority:

> Although the arguing from experiments and observations by induction be no demonstration of general conclusions, yet it is the best way of arguing which the nature of things admits of.
>
> —(1704/1952, p. 404)

Yet Newton did not claim that scientific explanations are nothing more than descriptions of observational correlation. He did not presume that all properly scientific explanations are universal and reductive or that the objects of all scientific disciplines are atomistic and invariant in space and time. And he never denied the legitimacy of final causal explanations of human behavior.

Yet all this was ignored by later generations of psychologists who tried to reprise Newton's achievement by reproducing these particular features of Newtonian theory. They strove to develop universal theories of mentality and behavior, conceived as atomistic entities invariant in (cultural) space and (historical) time. They sought to establish mechanistic laws describing the combination of mental elements into mental complexes and the correlation of mental states with other mental states and behavior, and they hoped to eventually explain them in terms of underlying laws of neurophysiological combination and correlation.

John Locke: The Underlaborer for Newtonian Science

The English philosopher John Locke (1632–1704) was the first to systematically apply the principles of Newtonian science to psychology and is generally credited as the father of British empiricism. Locke was greatly impressed by the "incomparable Mr. Newton" and his scientific achievements. They met in 1689 and remained friends and correspondents throughout the rest of their lives. Locke avowed that his intellectual ambition was to serve as a kind of "under-labourer" for Newtonian science, "clearing ground a little, and removing some of the rubbish, that lies in the way to knowledge" (1690/1975, p. 10).

Locke was born in Somerset, England, and educated at Oxford University, where he studied medicine and attained teaching appointments in Greek, moral philosophy, and rhetoric. He demonstrated his medical skill in 1668 when he supervised an operation to remove a hydatid cyst of the liver from the first Earl of Shaftesbury, who became his friend and patron (the silver tap inserted in Shaftesbury's liver made him the object of many contemporary witticisms).

While studying at Oxford, Locke met Robert Boyle, the pioneer of modern chemistry and primary advocate of the corpuscularian hypothesis. Locke served as Boyle's research assistant for some years, and both became members of the newly founded Royal Society (Boyle was one of its founders). Locke lived in France from 1675 to 1679, where he read the works of Descartes and Gassendi.

Like Hobbes before him, Locke was greatly influenced by the political upheavals of his day. He may have seen Charles I executed in the courtyard of the Palace of Whitehall. This is quite likely, since at the time the 17-year-old Locke was attending Westminster School, which borders on the Palace of Whitehall, and it was customary in his day for schoolchildren to be taken on outings to witness public executions (they were usually beaten afterward, to impress the event on their memory). Like his mentor Lord Shaftesbury, Locke was opposed to the Catholic Stuart kings of England and in particular to their defense of the doctrine of the "divine right" of kings. Locke claimed that political sovereignty depends upon the consent of the governed. He maintained that the power of a state should be constrained by a system of checks and balances, particularly between the executive, legislative, and judicial branches of government. His defense of the fundamental rights of citizens in a democratic state, developed in his *Two Treatises on Government* (1689/1988), played an influential role in the development of the United States Constitution and the state constitutions of Virginia and North Carolina.

Shaftesbury's opposition to the succession of the Catholic James II led to his imprisonment in the Tower of London. Fortunately, he escaped, and sought exile in Holland in 1681. Locke followed him into exile in 1683 but returned to England in 1688 after the accession of the Protestant William of Orange to the English throne (the "Glorious Revolution"). Two years later Locke published his major work, *An Essay Concerning Human Understanding* (1690), which he revised through five subsequent editions (the last in 1706, published posthumously). On his return to England, Locke served in a number of minor administrative positions in government. He spent his last years (1691–1704) in Essex at the home of Lady Masham (1658–1708), an early proponent of women's education.

Psychological and Meaning Empiricism   Locke's aim in the *Essay* was to determine the possibility and extent of human knowledge by exploring the origin of our ideas. Like Hobbes, he was a psychological empiricist, who held that all our ideas or concepts are derived from experience, either from sense experience, in the case of "ideas of sensation," or from inner experience, in the case of "ideas of reflection" (1690, pp. 104–105). He was also an **epistemological empiricist**, who maintained that all knowledge is derived from experience. This was a natural consequence of his psychological empiricism, since knowledge for Locke amounted to "nothing but the perception of the connection and agreement, or disagreement and repugnancy of any of our ideas" (1690/1975, p. 525).

Locke was a **psychological atomist**, who claimed that mental states and properties could be individuated independently of each other. He maintained that the basic materials of our psychology and knowledge are simple ideas of color, taste, smell, and the like, which are "perfectly distinct" from each other (1690/1975, p. 119). For Locke, simple ideas of sensation constitute the atoms or corpuscles of our complex ideas and knowledge of the external world. From these simple ideas, we can form an "almost infinite variety" of complex ideas, such as the ideas of "material substance," "identity," "infinity," and the like, via the mental operations of comparison, memory, discrimination, combination, enlargement, abstraction, and reasoning. All ideas are simple ideas or composed of simple ideas, just as material bodies are either elementary corpuscles or composed of elementary corpuscles. Thus our complex ideas of material substances such as apples and antelopes are "nothing but collections of simple *ideas*, with a supposition of something, to which they belong, and in which they subsist" (1690/1975, p. 316).

Locke maintained that it is not possible to have any simple idea that is not derived from experience or to invent any complex idea that is not constructed out of simple ideas derived from experience. Consequently he claimed that a congenitally blind person could not have any idea of a color such as red, and anyone who lacked experience of color, taste, and smell could not form the complex idea of a material substance such as an apple.

Locke was also a meaning empiricist, who claimed that words derive their meaning through their employment as "signs" for ideas derived from experience:

> *Man*, therefore, had by nature his organs so fashioned, as to be *fit to frame articulate sounds*, which we call words. But this was not enough to produce language; for parrots . . . will be taught to make articulate sounds distinct enough, which yet, by no means, are capable of language.
>
>   Besides articulate sounds, therefore, it was further necessary that he should be *able to use these sounds, as signs for internal conceptions*; and to make them stand as marks for the *ideas* within his own mind, whereby they might be made known to others, and the thoughts of men's minds be conveyed from one to another.
>
> —(1690/1975, p. 402)

Consequently Locke maintained that the meaningful use of language is also dependent upon experience. A congenitally blind person could not understand the meaning of the word *red*, and anyone who lacked experience of color, taste, and smell could not understand the meaning of the word *apple*.

Primary and Secondary Qualities   Locke's psychological theory was not only modeled upon Newton's theory, but also was employed to articulate and justify the central tenets of the Newtonian worldview. Thus Locke endorsed the ancient distinction between primary and secondary qualities championed by Newton and earlier pioneers of the scientific revolution such as Descartes and Galileo (although the terms of the distinction were coined by Boyle). Locke agreed that material substances have only primary qualities such as shape, size, and motion and that secondary qualities such as colors and tastes are merely the effects of our sensory interactions with material substances with primary qualities:

> The particular *bulk, number, figure, and motion of the parts of fire, or snow, are really in them*, whether any ones senses perceive them or no: and therefore they may be called *real qualities*, because they really exist in these bodies. But *light, heat, whiteness*, or *coldness, are no more really in them, than sickness or pain is in* manna [a form of bread].
>
> —(1690/1975, pp. 137–138)

However, Locke drew the distinction in a slightly different way from Newton and earlier scientists. He distinguished primary and secondary qualities in terms of the different powers of material substances to cause *ideas* of primary and secondary qualities. Locke claimed that although material substances really do have primary qualities that form the basis of their causal powers, they have secondary qualities only in the sense that they have the power to cause ideas of secondary or "sensible" qualities in us.

Since Locke believed that material substances really do have primary qualities but not secondary qualities, he claimed that only our ideas of primary qualities could be said to *resemble* the primary qualities of material substances themselves:

> From whence I think, it is easy to draw this observation, that the *ideas of primary qualities* of bodies, *are resemblances* of them, and their patterns do really exist in the bodies themselves; but the *ideas, produced in* us *by* these *secondary qualities, have no resemblance* of them at all. There is nothing like our ideas, existing in the bodies themselves. They are, in the bodies, we denominate from them, only a power to produce those sensations in us, and what is sweet, blue, or warm in idea, is but a certain bulk, figure, and motion of the insensible parts, in the bodies themselves, which we call so.
>
> —(1690/1975, p. 137)

The justification of this claim was another matter. Like Descartes and Hobbes, Locke claimed our ideas are like pictures, or images derived from sense experience:

> The *ideas* of the nurse and the mother, are well framed in their minds [children's]; and, like pictures of them there, represent only those individuals.
>
> —(1690/1975, p. 411)

Although it was reasonable to suppose that our ideas or concepts are images that resemble the contents of our sense perception (if they are simply weaker versions of them), it was much more problematic to suppose that our ideas are images that resemble the (primary) qualities of material substances in the external world, since we have no means of comparing our imagistic ideas of objects with the objects themselves (for example, our idea of the rectangular shape of a table with the shape of the table itself). Indeed, on this conception, it was very hard to justify the assumption that we could have knowledge of the material substances that formed the basic substratum of the Newtonian universe. Locke himself admitted that "of this supposed something, we have no clear distinct *idea* at all" (1690/1975, p. 316).

Consciousness   Like Descartes, Locke held that self-knowledge of mental states, including our sense experience, is direct and certain, because we are immediately conscious of our mental states. He claimed that consciousness accompanies all mental states and makes our psychology transparent to us:

> Consciousness . . . is inseparable from thinking, and as it seems to me, essential to it; it being impossible for anyone to perceive, without perceiving, that he does perceive. When we see, hear, smell, taste, feel, meditate, or will anything, we know that we do.
>
> —(1690/1975, p. 335)

Locke's reasons for holding this view may appear rather lame to the modern reader. He claimed that it is "hard to conceive, that any thing should think, and not be conscious of it":

> For to be happy or miserable without being conscious of it, seems to me utterly inconsistent and impossible.
>
> —(1690/1975, p. 110)

It is perhaps not so hard to conceive of this at all, and later theorists who were prepared to recognize unconscious mental states and processes challenged Locke's view. However, this conception of mental states as essentially conscious, and objects of direct and certain knowledge, remained popular among psychologists and philosophers until the early 20th century.

Locke seems to have held this view because he treated consciousness of mental states as a form of internal perception, or introspection. This notion of consciousness as a form of inner awareness, which also proved popular with later generations of psychologists and philosophers, was itself a 17th-century invention. The earliest recorded use of the English verb form *be conscious of* in this sense dates from 1620, and of the noun *consciousness* from 1678. *Self-consciousness* in this sense first appeared in 1690, the year in which Locke's *Essay* was first published. Of course, the term *consciousness* existed long before this, but meant something quite different; its original etymological meaning was "shared knowledge" (*con*, "with," + *scio*, "I know"). So too with the concept of introspection: The term "introspection" (*intro*, "within," + *specio*, "I look") made its first appearance in France and England toward the end of the 17th century (Wilkes, 1988).

Probable Opinion   Locke's commitment to direct and certain knowledge of mental states, including the contents of our sensory experience, left him with a problem about our knowledge of material substances in the external world. Our beliefs about such entities appeared to be nothing more than uncertain inferences based upon sensory experience.

However, Locke was quite prepared to embrace this conclusion, and it bothered him far less than it had Descartes. Descartes was vexed by this problem because he had retained the Aristotelian view that genuine scientific knowledge is necessarily true and demonstrable. However, scientists and philosophers gradually abandoned this view as the scientific revolution developed, for they came to recognize that scientific knowledge is fallible, revisable, and at best merely *probable*. The modern conception of probability was itself a late development of the scientific revolution (Hacking, 1975). Thus Locke, like Newton, was willing to accept that we can have only "probable opinion" about material substances and their properties and indeed with respect to any form of scientific knowledge.

The Association of Ideas Locke's psychological empiricism inclined him toward a rather naive and optimistic environmentalism, of the sort characteristic of 20th-century behaviorist psychologists such as John B. Watson and B. F. Skinner (1904–1990). Because he believed that most human failings are the product of poor upbringing, Locke stressed the critical importance of a good education in *Some Thoughts Concerning Education* (1693/1989).

It was in the course of considering unreasonable adult behavior and irrational childhood fears that Locke discussed the "association of ideas." He distinguished between associations based upon natural connections and those based upon contingent or "accidental" contiguity:

> Some of our *ideas* have a natural correspondence and connection one with another: It is the office and excellency of our reason to trace these, and hold them together in that union and correspondence which is founded in their particular beings. Besides this there is another connection of *ideas* wholly owing to chance or custom; *ideas* that in themselves are not at all of kin, come to be so united in some men's minds, that t'is very hard to separate them, they always keep in company, and the one no sooner at any time comes into the understanding but its associate appears with it.
>
> —(1690/1976, p. 395)

Locke claimed that ideas associated by contiguity lead to unreasonable, unnatural, and superstitious beliefs:

> Many children, imputing the pain they endured at school to their books they were corrected for, so join these *ideas* together, that a book becomes their aversion, and they are never reconciled to the study and use of them all their lives after; and thus reading becomes a torment to them, which otherwise possibly they might have made the great pleasure of their lives.
>
> —(1690/1976, p. 399)

Given that many "vain terrors" are based upon such contingent associations, Locke reasoned that they could be relieved by attenuating the association. In

Locke's explanation of the creation of "vain terrors" of the dark through "unnatural association" with stories of "Goblins and Sprights" (terrors that later afflicted the behaviorist John B. Watson).

explaining how to relieve a child's unnatural fear of frogs, Locke anticipated the behavioral therapy of "systematic desensitization" developed by Joseph Wolpe in the 1950s (Wolpe, 1969):

Your child shrieks, and runs away at the sight of a frog; let another catch it and lay it down a good distance from him; at first accustom him to look upon it, and see it leap without emotion; then to touch it lightly while it is held fast in another's hand; and so on till he can come to handle it as confidently as a butterfly, or a sparrow. By the same way any other vain terror may be removed if care be taken, that you go not too fast, and push not the child on to a new degree of assurance, till he be thoroughly confirm'd in the former. And thus the young soldier is to be trained on to the warfare of life.

—(1693/1989, p. 151).

Locke is often credited as the founder of the later tradition of associationist psychology, but this is misleading, since he did not believe that the principle of contiguity provided a universal explanation of human thought and behavior. On the contrary, he insisted that it only explained a limited range of "unreasonableness" within it. The point of education was not to manipulate thought and behavior on the basis of associations grounded in contiguity, but rather to "prevent the undue connection of ideas in the minds of young people" (1690/1976, p. 397).

Locke's *Essay* had a major impact in Britain and Europe, where it was favorably received. The favorable reception was at least partly due to Locke's careful refusal to speculate about the relation between mental states and material states of the brain. Although Locke entertained the "supposition" that mental states are states of material substance, he maintained that "the more probable opinion" is that they are states of an " individual immaterial substance" (1690/1976, p. 345).

George Berkeley: Idealism

George Berkeley was born in Kilkenny, Ireland, where he first attended college. He entered Trinity College, Dublin in 1700, at the age of 15. He received his bachelor's degree in 1704 and his master's degree in 1707. He became a fellow of the college in 1707 and was later ordained as a deacon of the Anglican Church. In 1709 he published *An Essay Towards a New Theory of Vision*, followed a year later by *A Treatise Concerning the Principles of Human Knowledge* (1710).

After traveling in Europe for some years, in 1724 Berkeley embarked on an ambitious scheme to found a Christian college in Bermuda for the education of both colonists and native peoples. He sailed for America in 1728 with his new wife, settling in Rhode Island to await financial support for his project from the British government. When it became clear that the promised support would not be forthcoming, he returned to London in 1731. He was appointed Bishop of Cloyne (in County Cork, Ireland) in 1734 and devoted the last years of his life to his parishioners, the intended audience of his last work *Siris: A Chain of Philosophical Reflections and Inquiries Concerning the Virtues of Tar-Water* (1744). The city of Berkeley, California, is named after him.

Idealism   Berkeley is best remembered as the philosophical advocate of **idealism**: the view that only immaterial minds and their ideas exist. The Irish poet William Butler Yeats enthused that Berkeley "proved the world a dream," and Dr. Johnson is reputed to have refuted Berkeley by kicking a stone: "I refute him thus!" When he visited the home of Jonathan Swift, Swift declined to open the door, declaring that it was merely an idea in Berkeley's mind. Berkeley was not moved by such responses but did take precautions to ensure that on his death his body would be laid out until it began to putrefy (he was afraid of being buried alive while in a comatose state).

Whatever the limitations of his idealism, Berkeley did highlight some serious problems with the Newtonian theoretical system. He questioned how primary qualities such as size, shape, and motion could be held to be objective properties of material substances if our only access to these properties is through our sense experience of subjective and variable secondary qualities such as color. He also developed some of the less palatable implications of the Lockean "way of ideas" and drew attention to a problem of perception that became a major focus of psychologists in the 19th and early 20th centuries.

Berkeley agreed with Locke's definition of knowledge in terms of the "agreement or repugnancy among ideas," but poured scorn on Locke's assumption that we can attain knowledge of the primary qualities of material substances through our ideas of them. Since according to Berkeley (and Locke) we have no independent access to material substances, we have no reason whatsoever to suppose that our ideas of primary qualities resemble qualities that material substances really do have. As Berkeley tersely put it, "an idea can be like nothing but an idea" (1710/1975, p. 79).

Thus Berkeley claimed that our ideas of material substances cannot make reference to entities held to be distinct from and independent of our sensory ideas, since all we have access to are complexes of sensory ideas that exhibit a certain "constancy and coherence" in our experience. Accordingly, our thought and talk about "material substances" such as apples, trees, and tables can only reference such complexes of ideas:

> I see this *cherry*, I feel it, I taste it. . . . Take away the sensations of softness, moisture, redness, tartness, and you take away the cherry. Since it is not a being distinct from sensations; a *cherry*, I say, is nothing but a congeries of sensible impressions, or ideas perceived by various senses: which ideas are united into one thing (or have one name given to them) by the mind; because they are observed to attend each other. . . . But if you mean by the word *cherry* an unknown nature, distinct from all these sensible qualities, and by its existence something distinct from its being perceived; then, indeed, I own, neither you nor I, nor anyone else, can be sure it exists.
>
> —(1713/1975, pp. 196–197)

According to Berkeley, it is meaningless to claim that such an object exists, since we have no sense impression or idea of it.

Consequently, Berkeley rejected as absurd the Newtonian program of explaining the perceived properties of material substances in terms of the properties of the corpuscles that compose them. He claimed that the notion that our sense impressions "are the effects of powers resulting from the configuration, number, motion and size of corpuscles, must certainly be false" (1710/1975, p. 84). He also employed the principle of meaning empiricism to reject central components of Newton's theory. For example, talk of an absolute space that could exist in the absence of material bodies is nonsense, according to Berkeley, since no one could perceive it:

> And so let us suppose that all bodies were destroyed and brought to nothing. What is left they call absolute space. . . . that space is infinite, immovable, invisible, insensible, without relation and without distinction. That is, all its attributes are privative or negative. It seems therefore to be mere nothing. . . .
>
> From absolute space then let us take away now the words of the name, and nothing will remain in sense, imagination or intellect. Nothing else then is denoted by these words than pure privation or negation, i.e. mere nothing.
>
> —(1721/1975, p. 222)

For similar reasons, he rejected "gravity" and other mechanical forces as "occult" qualities that explain nothing. According to Berkeley, references to mechanical efficient causes or "powers" are vacuous, since we have no sense impressions or ideas of them. Thus he maintained that "real efficient causes of the motion and existence of bodies or of corporeal attributes in no way belong to mechanics or experiment, nor throw any light on them" (1721/1975, p. 219).

For Berkeley, the only business of science, including Newtonian science, is to determine "by experiment and reasoning" the regularities to be found in our sensory experience. He denied that efficient causes can be identified in sense experience: The only efficient cause is God, the creator of sense impressions and ideas, who ensures that certain complexes are reliably conjoined in our experience. Scientific laws merely describe conjunctions between "sign" and "signified" that are useful in anticipating experience, and are maintained through the beneficence of God:

> The ideas of sense . . . are not excited at random . . . but in a regular train or series, the admirable connection whereof sufficiently testifies the wisdom and benevolence of its Author. Now the set rules or established methods, wherein the mind we depend upon [God] excites in us the ideas of sense, are called the *Laws of Nature:* and these we learn by experience, which teaches us that such and such ideas are attended with such and such other ideas, in the ordinary course of things.
>
> —(1710/1975, pp. 85–86)

Distance Perception   Berkeley also engaged a problem about visual perception that vexed later generations of psychologists and physiologists. How do we perceive the distance, shape, size, and motion of physical bodies in space and time? According to Berkeley, the primary objects of perception are simple and discrete (atomistic) sensory impressions or ideas: of color, smell, sound, and the like. Yet, if this is the case, we do not strictly perceive the distance, shape, size, and motion of physical bodies, since we do not have discrete (atomistic) sensory impressions of them, and our ideas or concepts of them cannot be derived from the mere aggregation or association of sensory impressions of color, smell, sound, and the like.

In *An Essay Towards a New Theory of Vision* (1709/1975), Berkeley maintained that distance is not visually perceived:

> It is, I think, agreed by all that distance, of itself and immediately, cannot be seen. For distance being a line directed end-wise from the eye, it projects only one point in the fund of the eye, which point remains invariably the same, whether the distance be shorter or longer.
>
> —(1709/1975, p. 9)

Berkeley rejected the account that Descartes and his followers championed. They claimed that the visual perception of distance is a "complicated reasoning process" involving calculations based upon differences in the angle of a triangle formed by imaginary lines from the eyes to the object perceived. Berkeley dismissed this account because the postulated cognitive process is not an object of experience:

> But those lines and angles, by means whereof some men pretend to explain the perception of distance, are themselves not at all perceived, nor are they in truth ever thought of by those unskillful in optics. I appeal to anyone's experience whether upon sight of an object he computes its distance by the bigness of the angle made by the meeting of the two optic axes? Or whether he ever thinks of the greater or lesser divergency of the rays, which arrive from any point to his pupil? Everyone is himself the best judge of what he perceives, and what not. In vain shall any man tell me that I perceive certain lines and angles which introduce into my mind the various ideas of distance, so long as I myself am conscious of no such thing.
>
> —(1709/1975, p. 10)

According to Berkeley, we make inferences about distance on the basis of associations between visual cues, bodily movements, and tactile sensations. We learn that bodies that appear smaller in our visual field and require a broader visual focus are at a greater distance than those that appear larger and require a narrower visual focus, based upon their correlation with past experience of moving through space to locate them:

> Looking at an object I perceive a certain visible figure and color, with some degree of faintness and other circumstances, which from what I have formerly observed, determine me to think, that if I advance forward so many paces or miles, I shall be affected with such and such ideas of touch.
>
> —(1709/1975, p. 20)

The inadequacy of Berkeley's account, on its own terms, is worth noting. If the idea or concept of distance cannot be derived from visual sense impressions (since distance cannot be seen), it cannot be derived from tactile sense impressions either (since distance cannot be touched). Berkeley only appeared to avoid the problem by supposing that distance is inferred, but this presupposes that we already have an idea or concept of distance that we employ in our inferential judgment. That is, although a learned correlation between visual and tactile sense impressions may explain our developed ability to estimate distance, it cannot explain the origin of our idea or concept of distance. Such considerations led later theorists such as Thomas Reid (1710–1796) and Immanuel Kant (1724–1804) to claim that our concepts of distance, shape, and size, and our concepts of substance and causality, are part of our innate endowment, and Herman von Helmholtz (1821–1894) to theorize that our "perception" of physical bodies and their properties is really a form of unconscious cognitive judgment.

David Hume: Mental Mechanism

David Hume (1711–1776) was born in Edinburgh, Scotland, the son of a minor landowner. He studied law at Edinburgh University, but never took a degree. In 1734 he traveled to La Flèche (where Descartes had studied at the Jesuit College), which he made his base for studying and writing. At the age of 28 he produced his major theoretical work, *A Treatise of Human Nature, Being an Attempt to Introduce the Experimental Method of Reasoning into Moral Subjects* (1739). Hume later complained that "it fell still-born from the press, without reaching such distinction as even to excite a murmur from the zealots." This was somewhat of an exaggeration, but it did not attract as much attention as Hume had wished. This motivated him to produce a shorter work in which he presented the main themes of the *Treatise* in a more accessible manner. In 1748 he published *An Enquiry Concerning Human Understanding*, followed by *An Enquiry Concerning the Principles of Morals* in 1751.

Hume's skeptical views did not recommend him to the establishment of his day. He was refused professorships at Edinburgh and Glasgow universities because of religious opposition. He returned to Edinburgh in 1739, where he produced *Essays Moral and Political* in 1742 and his *History of England* between 1754 and 1762. He served as an aide to General James St. Clair during the years 1746–1748 and became the darling of the French salons during the years 1763–1766, when he served as secretary to the embassy and later as chargé d'affaires in Paris.

Hume died in Edinburgh in 1776. The Scottish church fathers that had persecuted him throughout his lifetime tried to convert him as he lay in bed dying, but he chased them out. He was interred in a modest tomb in Edinburgh, and it was not until 1997 that a monument was finally erected to celebrate his contribution to the Scottish Enlightenment. Hume's last skeptical work on religion, *Dialogues Concerning Natural Religion*, which he withheld from publication during his lifetime, was published posthumously in 1779. He entrusted the work to the economist Adam Smith (1723–1790), who declined to publish it (it was eventually published by Hume's nephew).

Hume was perhaps the most consistent empiricist, pressing the consequences of psychological and meaning empiricism to their limit. Although he ranks as one of the major thinkers of the Western tradition, his recognition had been grudging within the philosophical community, at least until the 20th century. Hume's critical arguments were invariably destructive and skeptical. His devastating critiques of our pretension to have knowledge of material substances, causality, the future, and the self infuriated later generations of philosophers and scientists, who made valiant attempts to answer them, with doubtful success.

Much of the original antagonism to Hume derived from his atheism, which prevented him from obtaining any university position during his lifetime. However, much of it also derived from Hume's honestly avowed ambition to make a literary name for himself. Philosophers are supposed to be disinterested seekers of truth. It came hard to many that one with such seemingly base and selfish motives could have the best arguments. Hume's literary reputation was established in his own day primarily through his *History of England*, although his *Treatise* and *Enquiries* account for his enduring reputation.

Hume's primary aim in the *Treatise* and *Enquiries* was to provide naturalistic psychological explanations of how we come to hold those beliefs about material bodies, causality, and the self that he maintained are incapable of rational justification. In advancing these psychological explanations, Hume initiated the tradition of associationist psychology and developed a hugely influential account of causal explanation grounded in the principles of association.

Indeed, Hume saw himself primarily as a psychologist applying the principles of Newtonian science to the study of the human mind. He subtitled the *Treatise* as *An Attempt to Introduce the Method of Experimental Reasoning Into Moral Subjects,* and his investigations were very much in the spirit of the new science of Galileo and Newton. He never accepted any claim about human psychology at face value but always checked it for himself introspectively. For example, he rejected the claim that we have direct knowledge of a simple self by reporting his failed attempt to identify it through introspection:

> There are some philosophers, who imagine we are every moment intimately conscious of what we call our *self.* . . .
>
> For my part, when I enter most intimately into what I call *myself*, I always stumble upon some particular perception or another, of heat or cold, light or shade, love or hatred, pleasure or pain. I never can catch *myself* at any time without a perception, and never can observe anything but the perception.
>
> —(1739/1973, pp. 251–252)

Impressions and Ideas Hume embraced the standard empiricist principles expounded by Locke and Berkeley (and Hobbes). Hume was a psychological atomist, who maintained that all our complex ideas and impressions (of sense or feeling) are composed of discrete simple ideas and impressions:

> Simple perceptions or impressions and ideas are such as admit of no distinction nor separation. The complex are the contrary of these, and may be distinguished into parts. Tho' a particular colour, taste, and smell are qualities all united together in this apple, 'tis easy to perceive that they are not the same, but are at least distinguishable from each other.
>
> —(1739/1973, p. 2)

He was also committed to the principle of psychological empiricism. He affirmed that all the simple ideas that compose our complex ideas are derived from impressions of outer sense or inner feeling:

> *All* our simple ideas in their first appearance are deriv'd from simple impressions, which are correspondent to them, and which they exactly represent.
>
> —(1739/1973, p. 4)

Like Locke and Berkeley (and Hobbes), Hume treated ideas as fainter images of impressions (of sense or feeling):

> All the perceptions of the human mind resolve themselves into two distinct kinds, which I shall call *impressions* and *ideas*. The difference betwixt these consists in the degree of force and liveliness with which they strike upon the mind, and make their way into our thought or consciousness. These perceptions, which enter with most force and violence, we name impressions; and under this name I comprehend all our sensations, passions, and emotions, as they make their first appearance in the soul. By ideas I mean the faint images of these in thinking and reasoning.
>
> —(1739/1973, p. 1)

Like Berkeley, Hume was a meaning empiricist who recognized the critical implications of this principle. He claimed that words that cannot be related to ideas derived from experience are meaningless:

> When we entertain, therefore, any suspicion that a philosophical term is employed without any meaning or idea (as is but too frequent) we need to enquire *from what impression is that supposed idea derived?*
>
> —(1748/1975, p. 22)

> But if you cannot point out *any such impression*, you may be certain you are mistaken, when you imagine you have *any such idea*.
>
> —(1739/1973, p. 65)

Hume turned his critical eye on our ideas of beauty, causality, material substance, and the self. He declared that we have no ideas of material substance or the self and provided what he thought was the best psychological explanation for our belief in such "fictions." In the case of our ideas of beauty and causality, he offered a slightly different analysis. He did not deny that we have ideas of beauty or causality, but only that these ideas are derived from sense impressions of the properties of material bodies. Our idea of beauty, for example, is not derived from our sense impression of any property of external material bodies such as the Venus de Milo, for we have no sense impression of such a property. Instead, our idea of beauty is derived from positive *internal feelings* that are caused by our sensory experience of external material bodies such as the Venus de Milo:

> The beauty is not a quality of the circle. . . . It is only the effect which that figure produces upon the mind, whose peculiar fabric of structure renders it susceptible of such sentiments.
>
> —(1751/1975, pp. 291–292)

According to Hume, we mistakenly but quite naturally project this internal idea based upon feelings onto external bodies, as if material bodies themselves had the property of beauty. For Hume, this was just a basic fact about human psychology—we cannot help but project such ideas. Like Francis Hutcheson (1694–1746) before him, Hume treated our idea of beauty as a secondary quality, which is caused by but does not represent any quality of material bodies. Hume famously extended this type of analysis to our idea of causality.

Hume's Fork   Hume distinguished between propositions that are rendered true (or false) by relations between ideas, such as "a triangle has three sides" and propositions rendered true (or false) by virtue of corresponding sense impressions or feelings (or lack thereof), such as "all acids are corrosive" or "elation is regularly followed by disappointment." Propositions such as "a triangle has three sides" are *internally* true, since our idea of a triangle includes the idea of a three-sided figure. By contrast, propositions such as "all acids are corrosive" or "elation is regularly followed by disappointment" are *externally* true, since our ideas of acid and elation do not include the ideas of corrosion or disappointment. We have to discover via sensory or introspective experience whether they are invariably or regularly conjoined.

This distinction between **relation of ideas** and **matters of fact and existence** easily accommodated the propositions of logic and mathematics, "reasoning concerning quantity and number," whose truth or falsity is determined by internal relations between symbols, and the propositions of empirical science, the products of "experimental reasoning," whose truth or falsity is determined by independent facts about the world based upon experience (sense impressions or feelings). However, Hume claimed that these two types of propositions are the *only* types of meaningful proposition: If a claim is not identifiable as one of these types, it is meaningless. Thus Hume concluded his *Enquiry Concerning Human Understanding* by proclaiming

> When we run over libraries, persuaded of these principles, what havoc must we make? If we take in our hand any volume; of divinity or school metaphysics, for instance; let us ask, *Does it contain any abstract reasoning concerning quantity and number?* No. *Does it*

contain any experimental reasoning concerning matter of fact and existence? No. Commit it then to the flames: for it can contain nothing but sophistry and illusion.

—(1748/1975, p. 165)

Mental Mechanism Hume followed the Newtonian program in psychology by treating simple ideas as the mental atoms or corpuscles out of which all complex ideas are compounded. He took the Newtonian program one step further by employing the principle of the association of ideas as the foundation of mental mechanism. Hume developed universal explanations of mental association in terms of resemblance, contiguity, and cause and effect and conceived of the "uniting principle" of association as the mental analogue of gravity:

> Were ideas entirely loose and unconnected, chance alone wou'd join them; and t'is impossible the same simple ideas would fall regularly into complex ones (as they commonly do) without some bond of union among them, some associating quality, by which one idea naturally introduces another. This uniting principle among ideas is not to be consider'd as an inseparable connection; . . . but we are only to regard it as a gentle force, which commonly prevails. . . . The qualities, from which this association arises, and by which the mind is after this manner convey'd from one idea to another, are three, *viz,* RESEMBLANCE, CONTIGUITY in time or place, and CAUSE and EFFECT.
>
> —(1739/1973, pp. 10–11)

Given his commitment to a Newtonian program in psychology, it is probably no accident that Hume employed Newton's own description of gravity as a "gentle force" in his characterization of the principle of association. It is certainly no accident that Hume characterized the "associating quality" of ideas as a form of attraction, analogous to gravitational attraction:

> Here is a kind of ATTRACTION, which in the mental world will be found to have as extraordinary effects as in the natural, and to shew itself in as many and as various forms. Its effects are every where conspicuous; but as to its causes, they are mostly unknown, and must be resolv'd into *original* qualities of human nature, which I pretend not to explain.
>
> —(1739/1973, pp. 12–13)

Even Hume's modest pretense about his inability to ultimately explain this form of attraction echoes Newton's avowed ignorance of the ultimate nature of gravity. For example, in his letters to Dr. Bentley, Newton admitted:

> The cause of gravity is what I do not pretend to know.
>
> —(Cited in Leon, 1999, pp. 77–78)

Causality as Constant Conjunction   Hume's analysis of the idea of (efficient) causality followed the same lines as his analysis of the idea of beauty and exploited the associative principles of resemblance and contiguity. Hume asked his devastating question: From what impression is our idea of causality derived? If one considers a paradigm case of mechanical causation, in which a moving billiard ball collides with a stationary billiard ball and causes it to move, Hume noted that the only common observable features of this sequence are contiguity (togetherness) in space and time, the temporal priority of the motion that we call the cause, and that fact that the two observed motions are "constantly conjoined" in our experience.

Hume recognized that this analysis of the content of our idea of causality is intuitively unsatisfactory. When we believe that the motion of one body causes the motion of another, we do not simply believe that the motions are conjoined in space and time and that the first just happens to be constantly or regularly followed by the second. We believe that the second motion follows the first because the first *produces* or *generates* it: that the force of the collision has the "power" to generate motion in the second ball. As Hume put it, we believe that there is some "necessary connection" between the motion of the first and the second ball: The second ball *must* move, given the prior motion of the first ball. Yet according to Hume, there is no observable feature of causal sequences that corresponds to our idea of power or necessary connection:

> It follows that we deceive ourselves, when we imagine we are possest of any idea of this kind, after the manner we commonly understand it. All ideas are deriv'd from, and represent impressions. We never have any impression, that contains any power or efficacy. We never therefore have any idea of power.
>
> —(1739/1973, p. 161)

However, Hume did not really deny that we have any idea of causal power or necessary connection. All he denied is that we have such an idea "as we commonly understand it": that is, as derived from some observed property of material bodies. Instead, in line with his account of our idea of beauty, Hume claimed that our idea of causal power or necessary connection is derived from an internal *feeling*, produced by repeated observations of one event being followed by another. According to Hume, this repetition creates an internal *expectation* of the second event, given an impression or idea of the first. This expectation is based upon an internal feeling only, not upon any observable property of the sequence itself:

> For after we have observ'd the resemblance in a sufficient number of instances, we immediately feel a determination of the mind to pass from one object to its usual attendant. The several instances of resembling conjunctions leads us into the notion of power and necessity. These instances are in themselves totally distinct from each other, and have no union but in the mind, which observes them, and

collects their ideas. Necessity, then, is the effect of this observation, and is nothing but an internal impression of the mind, or a determination to carry our thoughts from one to another.

—(1739/1973, p. 165)

Although based upon an internal feeling, we naturally *project* the idea of causality upon external bodies, as if our idea of causal power or necessary connection represented some property of the bodies themselves.

In accord with this analysis, Hume produced two definitions of causality. The first was objective, or "philosophical":

We may define a CAUSE to be "an object precedent and contiguous to another, and where all the objects resembling the former are plac'd in like relations of precedency and contiguity to those objects, that resemble the latter."

—(1739/1973, p. 170)

This definition purports to represent the legitimate content of our ascriptions of causality to material bodies in the external world. To say that one thing is a cause of another is just to say that they are contiguous in space and time and constantly conjoined.

Hume's second definition was psychological, or "natural":

A CAUSE is an object precedent and contiguous to another, and so united with it, that the idea of the one determines the mind to form the idea of the other, and the impression of the one to form a more lively idea of the other.

—(1739/1973, p. 170)

This definition aimed to provide a psychological account of causal judgment, based upon the associative principles of resemblance and contiguity.

Hume's account of causal judgment was enormously influential in the development of psychological theories in the 19th and 20th centuries. Although Hume officially recognized three principles of association—namely, resemblance, contiguity, and cause and effect—his analysis of causality reduced the relation of cause and effect to contiguity and similarity with repetition (to the repetition of similar contiguous sequences). The principles of contiguity, similarity, and repetition played a major role in the development of associationist psychology in the 19th century and behaviorist theories of classical and instrumental conditioning in the 20th century.

The Empiricist Conception of Causal Explanation   Hume's objective definition of causality underwrote the later empiricist and positivist conception of causal explanation and scientific laws, including Newton's laws. In this view, causal explanations and scientific laws are just descriptions of observational correlation, which are sufficient for prediction and control. Putative explanatory references to "occult" forces or powers are vacuous and redundant. Thus to say that there is a gravitational "force of attraction" between two bodies is just to say that they will move toward each other unless impeded. To say that bodies move toward each other *because* of such a force is just to say that bodies move toward each other because they move toward each other, which is no news to anyone.

One may get the flavor of this type of empiricist and positivist analysis of causal explanation and scientific law by considering a famous example from a Molière play, in which a scholastic doctor offers an explanation of why the ingestion of opium is followed by sleep. Why is the ingestion of opium regularly followed by sleep? Because of the "soporific power" of opium. But wait: What does it mean to claim that opium has a "soporific power"? Well, it means that the ingestion of opium is regularly followed by sleep. Some explanation! But hold on, protests the scholastic doctor: There is more to it than that. Opium has a "soporific power" because of its "dormative nature." But what does it mean to claim that opium has a "dormative nature"? Well, it means that the ingestion of opium is regularly followed by sleep! According to Hume and later empiricists and positivists, references to "power," "force," and "nature" add nothing to causal explanation, and the business of science is just to describe those constant conjunctions of observables that we call scientific laws.

In many respects, Hume's critique was useful: It put the final nail in the coffin of the ancient (Aristotelian) and medieval notion, still to be found in Descartes, that causal explanations are necessary truths, capable of demonstration through some form of rational intuition—as if by reason alone we could determine that heated water will boil, in the fashion that we determine that the idea of a triangle contains the idea of three sides. For Hume and later generations of philosophers and scientists, causal sequences can only be determined empirically: Nobody can discover what bodies, acids, or human beings can or cannot do except by observation and experiment. Hume placed our knowledge of causality squarely in the realm of empirical "matters of fact and existence" rather than the realm of conceptual "relations of ideas."

This important contribution deserves due emphasis. However, the virtues of Hume's analysis have also been exaggerated. It is no doubt true that some explanatory references to "power" and "nature" are vacuous, as in the case of dispositional concepts such as solubility, which can be wholly explicated in terms of observable sequences. To say that something is soluble is just to say that if it is placed in a solvent it will dissolve. Yet this is not obviously true of all theoretical causal explanatory references. Theoretical explanations of the powers of chemical elements in terms of their natures are not mere redescriptions of how they are observed to behave, but descriptions of their underlying composition and structure that explain their observable behavior.

Even references to "gravitational force" need not be explanatorily vacuous, when they are employed to explain motion in terms of the exchange of fundamental particles such as "gravitons" (sometimes held to play the same role in gravitational theory as positrons in the theory of weak nuclear forces). However hesitant Newton may have been about his knowledge of the ultimate nature of gravity, he never doubted the legitimacy of causal explanations of the properties and behavior of material bodies in terms of the motions and interactions of the unobservable corpuscles that compose them (1687/1969, p. xvii).

Although Hume may have been correct in claiming that we have no sensory experience of causal power, it does not follow that causality is nothing but the correlation of observables. Most practicing scientists remain causal realists, who hold that causality is grounded in generative mechanisms, which support qualified conditionals (of the form "if . . . then . . . , unless . . .") but not descriptions of constant or regular conjunction. Causality cannot be equated with constant or regular conjunction, because although many entities have the causal power to produce certain effects, their action may be prevented or interfered with (Geach, 1975, p. 93). Tin has the power to act as a superconductor when subjected to a low temperature and potential difference, but will not do so in a magnetic field; the tubercle bacillus has the power to induce tuberculosis in humans, but its action can be prevented via inoculation.

For this reason, the frequency of an observed conjunction is no measure of the existence of a causal relation. The sounding of factory hooters regularly follows the sounding of school bells at the end of the day in many localities, but there is no causal relation between them. Conversely, the real power of plutonium rods in nuclear reactors to generate sickness and death in humans is rarely manifested because of lead screening. The frequency with which a particular manifests its causal power is a contingent matter, which depends upon how often the action of a particular is prevented or interfered with, which varies from place to place and over historical time. The incidence of tuberculosis upon exposure to the tubercle bacillus used to be very high in the West, but is now very low because of the development of prophylactics. It is considerably higher in Third World countries with limited vaccination programs and is now on the rise in the West, with the development of bacilli strains resistant to prophylactics.

This is of no small import for a potentially applied science such as psychology, whose practitioners do not merely aim to predict and control behavior, but also hope to be able to intervene to prevent or impede certain forms of behavior, such as aggression, child abuse, suicide, marital breakdown, and interracial conflict, even when causal conditions that promote such behavior are present. To be successful in applied science, it is not sufficient to identify the causal factors responsible for certain types of effects. One also needs to understand the mechanisms underlying causal processes in order to develop effective means of prevention and interference.

One might also have serious doubts about Hume's psychological account of causal judgment. Hume claimed that the strength of our belief in a causal relation is a function of the number of conjunctions we have observed:

> As the habit, which produces the association, arises from the frequent conjunction of objects, it must arrive at its perfection by degrees, and must acquire new force from each instance, that falls under the observation. The first instance has little or no force: the second makes some addition to it: the third becomes still more sensible, and 'tis by these slow steps, that our judgment arrives at a full assurance.
>
> —(1739/1973, p. 130)

Yet no amount of repetitions of the school bell being followed by the sounding of the factory hooter, or of the contiguous ringing of two spatially adjacent alarm clocks owned by those who have difficulty rising early, incline us to believe in a causal connection; and children learn that placing their hand in the fire is the cause of their consequent pain the first time around—they do not need to keep sticking their hands in the fire to convince themselves.

David Hartley: The Neurology of Association

David Hartley (1705–1757) extended the Newtonian program of psychology in two fundamental ways. He provided a neurophysiological account of the association of ideas, and he extended the principles of association to encompass behavior. Hartley trained as a minister at the University of Cambridge, but his naturalistic interests led him into medicine. His *Observations on Man: His Frame, His Duty, and His Expectations* were first published in 1749 and ran to six editions (the last published in 1834, almost a century after the original).

Hartley followed earlier empiricists in maintaining that all ideas are derived from experience and tried to explain all mental operations in terms of their association. However, he claimed that temporal contiguity with repetition is sufficient for association and distinguished between "synchronous" and "successive" association:

> Any sensations A, B, C, etc., by being associated with one another a sufficient number of times, get a power over the corresponding ideas a, b, c, etc., that any one of the sensations A, when impressed alone, shall be able to excite in the mind b, c, etc., the ideas of the rest. Sensations may be said to be associated together, when their impressions are either made precisely at the same instant of time, or in the contiguous successive instants.
>
> —(1749/1971, p. 65)

Hartley drew inspiration from Newton's theory of gravitation in the development of his neurophysiological theory of association. To explain "action at a distance," Newton had postulated the ether, which Hartley described as a "very subtle and elastic fluid . . . diffused through the pores of gross bodies, as well as through the open spaces that are void of gross matter" (1749/1971, p. 13). Vibrations in the ether were held to be the vehicle for the propagation of the effects of gravitation, electricity, magnetism, and "animal sensation and motion" (1749/1971, p. 13). Hartley claimed that sense impressions are instantiated as vibrations in the "white medullary substance" of the brain, generated by "external objects impressed upon the senses" (1749/1971, p. 11). Like earlier empiricists, he treated sensory ideas as weaker or fainter versions of sense impressions: "sensations, by being often repeated, leave certain vestiges, types or images of themselves" (1749/1971, p. 57). He consequently claimed that ideas are instantiated as fainter vibrational traces, or **vibratiuncles** (miniature vibrations) in the brain:

> Sensory vibrations, by being often repeated, beget, in the medullary substance of the brain, a disposition to diminutive vibrations, which may also be called vibratiuncles and miniatures, corresponding to themselves respectively.
>
> —(1749/1971, p. 58)

Hartley claimed that association by temporal contiguity is grounded in neural connections between sensations and ideas. For example, repeated conjunctions of sensations of color with those of taste and smell establish neural connections between the vibratiuncles corresponding to their ideas, so that when the vibrations corresponding to the sensations of color are activated via sensory stimulation, they reactivate the weaker vibrations corresponding to the associated ideas of taste and smell (1749/1971, p. 67). The neural connections are established when originally distinct vibrations fuse into a single vibration:

> Since the vibrations A and B are impressed together, they must, from the diffusion necessary to vibratory motions, run into one vibration; and consequently, after a number of impressions sufficiently repeated, will leave a trace, or miniature, of themselves, as one vibration, which will recur every now and then, from slight causes. Much later, therefore, may the part b of the compound miniature a + b recur, when the part A of the compound original vibration A + B is impressed.
>
> —(1749/1971, p. 70)

Hartley extended this form of neurophysiologically grounded associationist psychology to include associations of ideas and behavior, via the repeated conjunction of ideas and "motory vibrations":

> The motory vibratiuncles will also cohere to ideal ones by association. Common ideas may therefore excite motory vibratiuncles, and consequently be able to contract the muscles.
>
> —(1749/1971, p. 102)

He also claimed that motory vibrations can be associated with each other, which enabled him to offer an explanation of skilled behavior, like playing the piano, in terms of the coordination of motor responses.

Hartley also employed the principle of association to explain learned behavior and habit formation. He distinguished between voluntary behavior, brought under the control of ideas (or "affections") through association, and automatic (involuntary) behavior, the product of sensory-motor associations unmediated by conscious thought. He treated many automatic behaviors as reflexive behaviors based upon vibratory connections in the spinal cord rather than the brain, although he also noted how certain skilled behavior that is originally consciously controlled, such as serving a tennis ball, becomes "secondary automatic" or habitual with practice. Conversely, he claimed that through ideomotor association we are able to gain voluntary control over some reflexive behavior, such as "swallowing, breathing, coughing and expelling the urine and faeces" (1749/1971, p. 108).

In developing his account of how originally reflexive behavior can come under the control of ideas via repeated temporal contiguity, Hartley provided an early account of classical conditioning. He noted how a child's reflexive muscular response to a toy can become conditioned to the mere sight of a toy:

> The fingers of young children bend upon almost every impression which is made upon the palm of the hand, thus performing the action of grasping, in the original automatic manner. After a sufficient repetition of the motory vibrations which concur with this action, their vibratiuncles are generated, and associated strongly with other vibrations and vibratiuncles, the most common of which, I suppose, are those excited by the sight of a favorite play thing which the child uses to grasp, and hold in its hand. He ought, therefore, according to the doctrine of association, to perform and repeat the action of grasping, upon having such a play thing presented to his sight. But it is a known fact, that children do this.
>
> —(1749/1971, pp. 104–105)

Hartley also developed an account of motivation through association that later came to be known as instrumental (or operant) conditioning. He identified pleasure and pain with moderate and excessive vibration respectively, pain being nothing more than pleasure "carried beyond its due limit," and held that all ideas and behavior are "attended to some degree by pleasure and pain" (1749/1971, p. 9). He followed the Reverend John Gay (1699–1745), who claimed that human behavior is regulated by associations of behavior with pleasure and pain, including imaginary pleasure and pain. Given that humans seek pleasure and avoid pain, they tend to pursue behavior that has come to be associated with pleasure and avoid behavior that has come to be associated with pain. Gay's views were published anonymously in 1731 in an essay titled "Dissertation on the Fundamental Principle of Virtue." Hartley claimed that Gay's "Dissertation" was the stimulus for his own work, and he reaffirmed Gay's contention that the association of behavior with pleasure and pain is the fundamental principle of morality, a view later developed as utilitarian theory by Jeremy Bentham (1748–1832) and John Stuart Mill (1806–1873).

Hartley differed from earlier empiricists in one critical respect. Although he followed them in treating complex ideas as compounded out of simpler atomistic elements, he maintained that the formation of complex ideas is more akin to chemical fusion than mechanical association. According to Hartley, the simple sensory ideas that compose complex ideas fuse into unitary ideas (as associated vibrations fuse into single vibrations), which bear little relation to the simple ideas from which they are generated:

> If the number of simple ideas which compose the complex one be very great, it may happen, that the complex idea shall not appear to bear any relation to its compounding parts, nor to the external senses upon which the original sensations, which gave birth to the corresponding ideas, were impressed.
>
> —(1749/1971, p. 402)

Consequently, in our perception or thought of an apple, for example, we are not aware of the sensational elements of color, texture, smell, and taste from which it is generated.

Hartley's *Observations* had little immediate impact (partly because of his rather turgid prose), although it was an important influence on James Mill (1773–1836) and his son John Stuart Mill, who went on to develop their own versions of associationist psychology and utilitarian theory. It had a greater impact when Hartley's views were championed by the English chemist and political radical Joseph Priestley (1733–1844), who produced an edited reprint of Hartley's *Observations* in 1775 titled *Hartley's Theory of the Human Mind, on the Principle of the Association of Ideas*. Priestley's advocacy of a materialist psychology based upon the principles of association attracted the same degree of odium as La Mettrie's *Man Machine,* and Priestley was driven out of England as La Mettrie had formerly been driven out of France and Holland. This was somewhat ironic, since Priestley had cut most of Hartley's (already outdated) discussion of neural vibrations from the reprint. It was also unfair to Hartley, who affirmed the existence of an immaterial soul and saw his own work as an exercise in natural theology, demonstrating the benevolence of God through the study of nature, including human nature.

Yet the distance between Hartley and La Mettrie was not great. Hartley also affirmed the strong continuity between human and animal psychology and behavior that La Mettrie had championed (Boakes, 1984). Although Hartley was committed to the existence of an immaterial soul that survives the destruction of the material body, it was an impoverished sort of thing, stripped of the essential

Cartesian property of thought. Hartley claimed that since the soul depends upon the brain and body for all its cognitive and affective operations, it is "reduced to a state of inactivity by the decomposition of the gross body" (1749/1971, p. 402) and remains in a "dormant" state until reincarnated at the Resurrection.

Priestley's advocacy of Hartley's theories had one significant consequence. Erasmus Darwin (1731–1802), the grandfather of Charles Darwin and a friend of Priestley's, generalized Hartley's neurophysiologically based associative account of how habits are acquired during the lifetime of individuals to provide an account of the maintenance of habits over generations of a species and developed an early account of the evolution of species in *Zoonomia: Or the Laws of Organic Life* (1794–1796). Darwin was a physician and, like Priestley, an uncompromising materialist. He stressed that associations are wholly determined by neurophysiology and dismissed appeals to the action of immaterial souls as "ghost stories."

Sensationalists and Ideologues in France

Sensationalists such as Étienne Bonnot de Condillac (1715–1780) and Claude Helvetius (1715–1771) developed the empiricist psychology of Locke, Berkeley, and Hume in France. Condillac was a great admirer of Locke: He translated Locke's *Essay Concerning Human Understanding* into French and developed his theories in *Essay on the Origin of Human Knowledge: A Supplement to Mr. Locke's Essay on the Human Understanding* (1746) and *Treatise on the Sensations* (1754). Condillac provided a stripped-down version of Locke's psychology: He held that all our ideas and mental faculties (which even Locke had supposed were innate) could be accounted for in terms of sensation, or sensation "transformed." He claimed that mental faculties are products of the intrinsic pleasure and pain of sensation, which stimulates the development of attention, comparison, imagination, memory, and reflection (based upon the employment of words as signs for ideas derived from sensation). Condillac famously illustrated these claims by imagining a statue possessing the single modality of smell, which he held to be the simplest form of sensation. This enabled him to claim that mental capacities are not grounded in the integration of different sensory modalities, such as an Aristotelian "common sense," and to distinguish the distinctive contribution of the different sensory modalities. For example, Condillac claimed that ideas of external objects are derived from the sense of touch.

Many rejected Condillac's theory as materialistic, notably Victor Cousin (1792–1867), the French critic of Locke, although it was more developmental than reductionist. Condillac was a former Catholic priest who railed against religious dogma, but affirmed the existence of the immaterial soul. He claimed that sensation enables the soul to attain knowledge, a view also promoted by the Swiss religious apologist Charles Bonnet (1720–1793). Like Locke, Condillac's interest in the development of ideas led him to focus on the educational implications of his theories, which he developed in *Logic* in 1780.

Claude Helvetius also promoted the developmental, educational, and political implications of psychological empiricism. He published *Essays on the Mind* in 1758; his *Treatise on Man, His Intellectual Faculties and His Education* was published posthumously in 1772. A radical and optimistic environmentalist, Helvetius reasoned that if all knowledge comes from experience, and behavior is motivated through association with consequent pleasure or pain, then virtually anything could be inculcated through the social manipulation of experience through education and legislation: science, morality, even genius. According to Helvetius, the primary impediment to progress through education and legislation is religious dogma. Yet like Hobbes, he maintained that the unbridled pursuit of pleasure and avoidance of pain would lead to selfish and destructive behavior. This could be constrained only through social approbation and directed education and laws that ensured, through the sanction of punishment, that the interests of individuals included the interests of others. Consequently Helvetius claimed that society, education, and law are the foundation of human character and virtue.

Although many criticized their theories, notably the clergy (the faculty of the Sorbonne condemned and burned Helvetius's *Essays on the Mind*), Condillac and Helvetius exerted a powerful influence in the decades before and immediately after the French Revolution. Their theories were embraced by the contributors to the multi-volumed ***Encyclopédie***, the Bible of the French Enlightenment that aimed to provide a comprehensive treatment of the various branches of human knowledge. They were also adopted by **idéologues** such as Antoine-Louis-Claude, comte Destutt de Tracy (1754–1836) and Pierre Jean George Cabanis (1757–1808), who played a significant role in reshaping French higher education and the legal and medical profession in the early days of the French Republic. Both served as supervisors of general education in the period between the Terror and the rise of Napoleon, who promptly banned their work. Their vision of a socially applied psychology provided a powerful inspiration for later scientific psychologists and social and political theorists in Europe and America, and their optimistic philosophy exerted an immediate influence on liberal theorists such as Thomas Jefferson (1743–1826), the author of the Declaration of Independence and the third American president (Robinson, 2003).

De Tracy, who claimed that both the development and application of human knowledge depends upon ideas, coined the term *ideology*. De Tracy held that "custom" is the source of human misery, but also the best hope for human progress through social and educational redirection. Cabanis provided a neurophysiological foundation for the psychology of Condillac and Helvetius in *Studies on the Physical and Moral Nature of Man* in 1799. A physician and admirer of La Mettrie, Cabanis held that the brain secretes thought as the stomach secretes gastric juices,

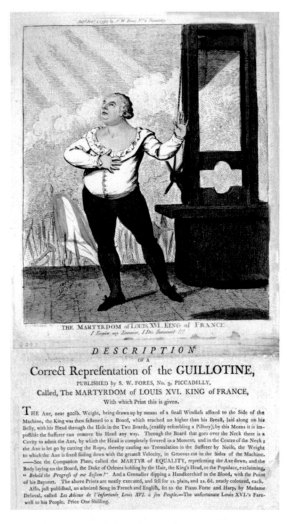

DESCRIPTION
OF A
Correct Representation of the **GUILLOTINE**,
PUBLISHED by S. W. FORES, No. 3, PICCADILLY,
Called, The MARTYRDOM of LOUIS XVI. KING of FRANCE,
With which Print this is given.

The guillotine: the empirical basis of Cabanis's theory that the brain is the seat of consciousness and that many sensory-motor reflexes are governed by the spinal cord.

which naturally drew down familiar charges of materialism and threats to morality and religion. Based upon his study of decapitated victims of the guillotine, Cabanis claimed that while the brain serves the central ego, the seat of consciousness, will, and rationality, many sensory-motor reflexes are governed by the spinal cord (a claim that had been advanced earlier by Hales and Whytt). He also claimed that the study of abnormality and sociality, in addition to development and physiology, is central to a proper theoretical understanding of human psychology and behavior—a programmatic statement, but one that clearly anticipated the later development of scientific psychology.

CRITICAL RESPONSES TO NEWTONIAN PSYCHOLOGY

Not all theorists embraced the notion of a scientific psychology based upon the principles of Newtonian science, especially as interpreted by British empiricists and French sensationalists and ideologues. Scottish realist philosophers such as Thomas Reid (1710–1796) and Dugald Stewart (1753–1828) developed a form of "common sense" psychology based upon the direct perception of material bodies and their properties and maintained that scientific, moral, and religious knowledge is grounded in innate powers or faculties bestowed upon humanity by a benevolent God. German rationalist philosophers such as Gottfried Leibniz (1646–1716) and Immanuel Kant (1724–1804) also claimed that certain ideas and forms of knowledge are innate and questioned the empiricist view that perception is based upon the association of sensory elements. More radical critics such as Giambattista Vico (1668–1744) rejected the common assumption that human sciences such as psychology should be modeled upon natural sciences such as physics and questioned whether psychology should be based upon Newtonian principles such as the universality of explanation and ontological invariance. Romantics such as Jean-Jacques Rousseau (1712–1778), Johann Wolfgang von Goethe (1749–1832), Arthur Schopenhauer (1788–1860), Friedrich Nietzsche (1844–1900), and Georg Wilhelm Hegel (1770–1831) rejected the general Enlightenment attempt to confine human spontaneity and creativity within the limits of reason and science.

Realism and Common Sense

Thomas Reid mounted one of the most sustained critiques of psychological atomism and associationist psychology, since he believed that such doctrines promoted a fatal combination of materialism, determinism, skepticism, and atheism. Reid was born and raised in Aberdeen, Scotland, where he served a short time as a Presbyterian minister before taking up a position as professor of moral philosophy at King's College, Aberdeen, in 1751. He became professor of moral philosophy at the University of Glasgow in 1764. Reid established what came to be known as the Scottish school of "common sense" psychology with the publication of *Enquiry into The Human Mind on the Principles of Common Sense* in 1764, followed by *Essays on the Intellectual Powers of Man* in 1785, and *Essays on the Active Powers of Man* in 1788.

Reid denied the fundamental tenets of psychological atomism endorsed by Locke, Berkeley, and Hume and recognized the fundamental problem of any psychology based upon the Lockean "way of ideas": Our perception and knowledge of physical bodies with shape, size, and motion cannot be accounted for in terms of the mere aggregation or association of atomistic sense-impressions. This had led Locke and Hume to treat perception and knowledge of physical bodies as a doubtful inference, and Berkeley to embrace idealism by claiming that our ideas about physical bodies refer to nothing but the association of atomistic sense-impressions. In contrast, Reid advocated a form of **direct realism**: He claimed that we directly perceive physical bodies and their properties without the mediation of atomistic sense impressions.

Reid distinguished between physical stimulation, sensation, and perception: between, for example, the physical stimulation of the retina, the sensation of color, and the perception of an apple. He maintained that sensation cannot be explained in terms of physical stimuli and that the intentional perception of physical bodies such as apples cannot be explained in terms of nonintentional states such as sensations of color, smell, and taste. Consequently, Reid vehemently rejected the form of associationist psychology grounded in neurophysiology propounded by Hartley, whose *Observations* Reid described as a "fallacious tract," and he denied the possibility of a science of psychology modeled upon the mechanistic program of Galileo and Newton.

Reid claimed that the active power to directly perceive physical bodies and their properties, such as their shape, size, distance, and motion, is part of the constitutional "common sense" of humanity. These are the set of common powers provided by a benevolent God, which are ideally suited to their purpose:

> When I perceive a tree before me, my faculty of seeing gives me not only a notion or simple apprehension of a tree, but a belief of its existence, and of its figure, distance and magnitude; and this judgment or belief is not got by comparing ideas, it is included in the very nature of the perception. . . .
>
> Such original and natural judgments are, therefore, a part of the furniture which Nature hath given to the human understanding. They are the inspiration of the Almighty, no less than our notions or simple apprehensions. They serve to direct us in the common affairs of life, where our reasoning faculty would leave us in the dark. They are part of our constitution; and all the discoveries of our reason are grounded upon them. They make up what is called *the common sense of mankind*.
>
> —(1764/1975, p. 188)

According to Reid, God ensures that perception generally accords with physical reality. There is no need to explain perception in mechanistic, atomistic, and associative terms and no possibility of doing so. Reid described a range of innate faculties that supposedly ground our mental powers, including our moral and religious sensibilities, whose reliability is guaranteed by their divine endowment. In this fashion he defended the common judgments of mankind against materialism, determinism, skepticism, and atheism and developed a purely descriptive psychology that documented innate human powers and faculties. His claim about the common cognitive, moral, and religious faculties of humankind became the foundational tenet of Scottish **common sense psychology**.

Reid's students and disciples, Dugald Stewart, Thomas Brown (1778–1820), and William Hamilton (1788–1856), reaffirmed his theory of innate faculties and denial of a mechanistic science of psychology, but also continued to develop associationist psychology (albeit shorn of its mechanistic and materialist trappings). Stewart, one of Reid's students, and later professor of moral philosophy at the University of Edinburgh, promoted associationist psychology in *Elements of the Philosophy of the Human Mind* (1792), while insisting that association is not susceptible to scientific analysis. Thomas Brown, who succeeded Stewart at Edinburgh (and was Stewart's own student), abandoned Reid's direct realism, because he felt it was too materialistic, and employed Hume's analysis of causation as constant conjunction to critique the materialist psychology of Darwin's *Zoonomia*. He maintained that Darwin merely described the correlation between mind and matter, not their causal relation. Brown developed a number of secondary laws of association, or "suggestion," and postulated a "muscle sense" to account for our perception of the externality of material objects, in terms of associations linked to feelings of resistance. William Hamilton, professor of logic and metaphysics at

Edinburgh, reaffirmed the directness of perception, albeit "conditioned" by the nature of the perceiving subject, and continued to deny the relevance of mechanistic science to psychology.

Common sense psychology was enormously influential in Europe and America. It was developed in France through the energies of the Academician Victor Cousin, who ensured that common sense psychology displaced the theories of the sensationalists and idéologues in French higher education. It was especially influential in America, where it was carried by generations of Presbyterian ministers trained in the common sense psychology of the Scottish universities, many of whom became presidents of American universities. John Witherspoon (1723–1794), the president of the College of New Jersey, later Princeton University, introduced Scottish common sense psychology in his lectures on moral philosophy. Stewart's *Elements of the Philosophy of the Human Mind* (1792), along with Brown's collected *Lectures on the Philosophy of the Human Mind* (1820) and James Abercrombie's *Inquiries Concerning the Intellectual Powers and the Investigation of Truth* (1830), were standard textbooks at American colleges and universities in the 19th century.

Rationalist Reaction

Another form of critical reaction came from rationalist philosophers in Germany, who claimed that some ideas and forms of knowledge are innate and that the mind plays a much more active role in perception and cognition than empiricists recognized. They also maintained that many mental states and processes are unconscious and rejected the traditional treatment of ideas or concepts as images derived from sense impressions.

Leibniz and Apperception   Gottfried Wilhelm Leibniz was a polymath who made major contributions to logic, mathematics, jurisprudence, and history, in addition to philosophy and psychology. He developed the differential and integral calculus independently of Newton and possibly before him. He also developed the notion of a universal logical language that forms the theoretical basis of modern computing devices. Leibniz entered the University of Leipzig at age 15 and presented his thesis for the degree of doctor of law at age 20. He traveled widely in Europe, where he met or corresponded with most of the major figures of his day. He became librarian to the Duke of Brunswick at Hanover, a position he held until his death.

Leibniz's first work and major psychological thesis was *New Essays on the Understanding*, a response to Locke's essay completed in 1704 but not published until 1765. This was because Locke died in 1704, and Leibniz delayed publication out of respect. Whereas Condillac had complained that Locke granted too many innate capacities to the human mind, Leibniz complained that he granted too few. In particular, Leibniz complained that Locke had neglected our abstract knowledge of mathematics and science, based upon our innate ideas of number, space, time, substance, and causality. In a prescient metaphor, he conceived of these ideas as analogous to the outline of a statue of Hercules marked out in the veins of a block of marble, both of which require development to become manifest:

> Hercules would be innate in it, in a way, even though labor would be required to expose the veins and to polish them into clarity, removing everything that prevents their being seen. This is how ideas and truths are innate in us—as inclinations, dispositions, tendencies, or natural potentialities.
>
> —(1765/1981, p. 46)

Leibniz's theoretical system is strange and intricate and distributed over a number of works. However, two aspects of his complicated system came to play a major role in the later development of psychology. Leibniz maintained that there are sensory impressions that are perceptually registered but so faintly that they do not enter consciousness, which he called **petites perceptions**. Sometimes the combined intensity of these petites perceptions is sufficient to generate perceptual awareness, or **apperception**. As an illustrative example, he noted how the perceived sound of a crashing ocean wave is composed of individually indistinguishable sounds produced by individual droplets of water. According to Leibniz, apperception is not a product of the passive aggregation of sensory elements, but of the active organization of sensory elements into a unified perceptual whole—an account that exerted a major influence on later theorists, notably the Gestalt psychologists. Leibniz also introduced the notion of a **sensory threshold**, below which sensory impressions do not register in consciousness (such as the sound produced by an individual droplet of water). This notion, anathema to empiricists such as Locke, Berkeley, and Hume, had a powerful influence on later theorists such as Johann Friedrich Herbart (1776–1841) and Moritz Drobisch (1802–1896) and became a central feature of the psychophysics of Gustav Fechner (1801–1887).

Kant and the Categories   Immanuel Kant was one of the greatest philosophers of the modern period. He was born in Königsberg, Prussia, and educated at the University of Königsberg, where he taught until his retirement at the age of 73. Kant's life was a paradigm of mundane order. He never married and left Königsberg only once (to visit a friend in a town 40 miles away): the townsfolk were said to set their watches according to the legendary punctuality of his daily walks. His early works were devoted primarily to physics and astronomy: He predicted the existence of the planet Neptune, later discovered by Herschel. However, in his middle age he developed what came to be known as his "critical philosophy," for which he became so famous that he had to keep changing restaurants to avoid the crowds of admirers that came to watch him eat lunch.

Kant's theories cannot be easily fitted into the traditional categories of "rationalism" or "empiricism," and his mature critical philosophy was, by his own account, an attempt to create "a Copernican revolution in thought." In the *Critique of Pure Reason*, published in 1781, Kant argued that the form (although not the specific content) of our knowledge of the external world is based upon a number of innate principles, or **categories**, of thought. For Kant, space and time represent the innate form of our sensory experience, which the mind actively organizes—through apperception—to form empirical concepts regulated by innate categories of substance, causality, unity, plurality, necessity, possibility, and the like.

Kant recognized the central problem of empiricist psychological accounts of our perception and knowledge of material bodies causally related in space and time. Our ideas or concepts of material substance and causality, for example, do not appear to be derived from sensory experience or constructed from atomistic ideas derived from sensory experience. The idea of material substance, for example, does not appear to be derived from the mere association of sensory impressions or ideas: Rather, it purports to represent an enduring particular with sensible properties. For this reason, according to Kant, empiricist treatments of our concepts of material substance and causality in terms of the "constancy and coherence" and "constant conjunction" of sensory impressions are hopelessly inadequate. With some justice Kant credited Hume as having woken him from his "dogmatic slumbers."

Since Kant held that the forms of sensibility and categorical concepts structure the form of our knowledge, he claimed that we have **synthetic a priori knowledge** of the fundamental principles of Newtonian physical science: We have forms of knowledge of the natural world that are not based upon experience. For example, Kant claimed that we can know a priori that throughout all change the quantum in nature remains constant, that every event has a cause, and that for every action there is an equal and opposite reaction. Although he maintained that such principles ground scientific disciplines, he insisted that particular causal laws can be determined only by observation and experiment. He also maintained that synthetic a priori knowledge is only knowledge of things in the external world *as they appear to our senses*, bound by the spatial and temporal forms of our sensibility, and not knowledge of things *as they are in themselves*. For this reason, Kant characterized his critical philosophy as **transcendental idealism**—transcendental because it described the conditions of the possibility of experience.

Kant was one the few theorists of the period to distinguish between sense perception and cognition, while stressing the necessary contribution of both to our knowledge of the world. As he famously put it, "thoughts without content are empty; intuitions [sense impressions] without concepts are blind" (1781/1973, p. 92). In contrast to Descartes, Locke, Berkeley, Hume, and Hartley, Kant denied that our empirical concepts of apples, trees, and tables are images of our sensory experience of them. Rather, our empirical concepts are cognitive schema for objects in space and time, which enable us both to re-identify instances of material substances such as apples, trees, and tables, and to form images of them.

Kant is famous for his supposed denial of the possibility of a science of psychology. In the *Metaphysical Foundations of Natural Science* he claimed that "empirical psychology [must] be removed from the rank of a natural science so called" (1783/1891, p. 8), because it could not be quantified and because self-observation would alter the objects of any putative science of "inner sense." Kant did deny the possibility of a scientific psychology based upon the introspective analysis of the association of sensations and ideas. This was because he maintained that such a psychology would be restricted to the description of correlation in a single temporal dimension and would not constitute a scientific psychological analogue of dynamical physics, which requires the four dimensions of space and time (motion being defined as change of position in three-dimensional space over time).

However, it is a misrepresentation to characterize Kant as having denied the possibility of a science of psychology altogether. He acknowledged that it is possible to provide quantitative measures of the intensity of sensation (in the *Anticipations of Perception* section of the *Critique of Pure Reason*), as later developed in Fechner's psychophysics (see also Sturm, 2006). He also recognized the potential of social and developmental psychology, which he detailed in his *Anthropology From a Pragmatic Point of View* (1797/1996). This work, which contains a marvelous warning about how introspective overindulgence can lead to madness, was representative of a radically different conception of psychological science.

Something Completely Different

From the time of the scientific revolution to the present day, it has been common to characterize psychology and other human sciences as the inferior relatives of the natural sciences, which they can at best approximate. Proponents of psychological science from Hume to Watson have argued that psychology can become an objective scientific discipline only by emulating the methods, explanatory modes, and principles of the natural sciences and that forms of psychological knowledge can at best merely approximate those of natural scientific knowledge.

Vico and Human Science   In stark contrast, Giambattista Vico argued that the objects of psychology and other human sciences are better known than the objects of natural science. Born in Naples, Vico taught rhetoric at the University of Naples. In the *New Science* (1725, reprinted in 1730 and 1744), he followed Aristotle in claiming that the governing principles of any entity or process are best known to its creator. Consequently, Vico argued that we know the forms of thought, emotion, and behavior that are the created products of our social being better than we know the world of nature, which can be known only by God: "since God made it, He alone knows." We have direct knowledge of our own internal psychological states through introspection and empathetic insight into the psychologies of other peoples, whereas we have only indirect knowledge of the fundamental properties of material substances through our theoretical representations or models of them.

Vico also rejected standard Newtonian assumptions of invariance and universality. He believed that many of the fundamental principles of human psychology and behavior are developed products of human culture and history and possibly as diverse as them. He recognized the problem this created for our understanding of the psychology of persons living in other cultures and at different historical periods. How can we understand their "web of belief" in terms of our own culturally and historically specific web of belief? Vico suggested we could make some inroads to understanding by considering the varied attitudes and practices of different communities relating to what appear to be the few cultural and historical invariants of human life, namely birth, sex, and death (1725/1984, pp. 332–333).

Although neglected in his own day, Vico's distinctive contribution marked the beginning of a tradition of social and developmental psychology that took seriously the possibility that the explanatory principles of human psychology and behavior vary cross-culturally and transhistorically. Vico's basic principles were restated by Johann Gottfried Herder (1744–1803) in his *Ideas Towards a Philosophy of History* (1784–1791). They were represented in Kant's *Anthropology From a Pragmatic Point of View* (1797) and John Stuart Mill's ethological "science of character," which Mill maintained was a necessary supplement to associationist psychology (Mill, 1843/1973–1974). They were also developed in Wundt's *Volkerpsychologie* (1900–1920), which Wundt treated as a complement to experimental psychology.

These theorists maintained that a distinctive feature of psychology and other human sciences is an understanding of the *meaning* of human thought and behavior. Later critics opposed to 19th-century forms of psychology grounded in empiricist and positivist conceptions of science developed this feature as the basis of a principled distinction between natural and human sciences. According to the German philosopher and historian Wilhelm Dilthey (1833–1911), the goal of the natural sciences (*Naturwissenschaften*) is mechanistic causal explanation (*erklären*), whereas the goal of human sciences (*Geisteswissenschaften*) is interpretive understanding (*verstehen*).

Romanticism

These reactions to a Newtonian science of psychology were paralleled by a repudiation of the Enlightenment ideals of reason and science by the **romantic** movement, represented by theorists such as Jean-Jacques Rousseau, Johann Wolfgang von Goethe, Arthur Schopenhauer, and Friedrich Nietzsche. Rousseau argued, first in the *Prize Essay for the Dijon Academy* in 1749 and later in *The Social Contract* (1762/1997), that human nature has been corrupted by reason and science. According to Rousseau, human beings in their natural state are "noble savages." They are naturally inclined to develop into free, fulfilled social beings, but these spontaneous impulses are corrupted by civilization. Consequently the ideal form of education is one in which the child's natural inclinations are encouraged and nurtured, a form of education Rousseau detailed (albeit in an idealized fashion) in *Emile* (1762/1979).

Rousseau commended the spontaneity of emotion over the sterility and artificiality of reason and science. Goethe, while not opposed to science, claimed that there are limits to the rational scientific approach to human nature. He suggested that certain human attributes, such as creativity and the capacity for self-transformation through a passionate approach to life, transcend scientific understanding. Schopenhauer focused on the irrational aspects of the human will, which he maintained is driven by fundamental needs that are continually frustrated. Nietzsche hymned the irrational, passionate, and impulsive side of human nature. Freud later developed his account of the conflict between the emotional and impulsive, and the rational and repressive, aspects of human nature.

Although romantics repudiated Enlightenment faith in reason and science, they shared the Enlightenment vision of human history as progressive and purposive, albeit conceived as a form of spiritual journey—thus the common theme of quests, journeys, and pilgrimages in romantic art. This conception reached its apotheosis in the psychological, social, and political theory of the German philosopher Georg Wilhelm Hegel (1770–1831). Hegel represented human history as a progress toward freedom, in which the human mind develops through all possible forms of experience to attain knowledge of the self and the world as it is in itself, or the Absolute. Thus Hegel's philosophy is often characterized as Absolute idealism.

In discussing the possible forms of experience, mentality, and consciousness, Hegel recognized the social dimensions of mind, the orientation of the thought and emotion of individuals to the represented thought and emotion of other individuals in a social group. He claimed that an individual's own feelings of self-respect are grounded in the represented respect of others. Unfortunately, Hegel elevated this account of the intersubjectivity of social thought and emotion into an ontological doctrine about the **social mind** (or spirit) of social groups, states, and nations, conceived of as an emergent form of mentality irreducible to the mentality of the members of social groups, states, and nations. Hegel's mystical conception of the state had disastrous consequences for later German history, by promoting unquestioning obedience to the authority of the state. His notion of social and political progress in history as a form of dialectical resolution of "contradictions" within historical epochs was the inspiration for the dialectical materialism of Karl Marx (1818–1883), the founder of revolutionary communism.

TOWARD A SCIENCE OF PSYCHOLOGY

These reactions to Newtonian psychology impeded but did not prevent the development of scientific psychology, which was instituted as an autonomous academic discipline in Germany and America at the end of the 19th century. Nonetheless, scientific psychology did not develop directly from David Hartley's neurophysiologically grounded form of associationist psychology, which was largely ignored in his own time and condemned when Priestley promoted it as materialist psychology. Although associationist psychology continued to develop in Britain and France, it was taught in British, French, and American universities only as an aspect of Scottish common sense psychology, which repudiated the materialistic and mechanistic basis of Hartley's theory.

The 19th century saw great advances in neuroanatomy, physiology, and evolutionary theory, which powerfully shaped the development of scientific psychology in the late 19th and early 20th centuries. Yet the emergence of institutionalized academic psychology in Germany and America in the 1880s was scarcely a triumph of materialism. Like associationist psychologists, many 19th-century physiologists and evolutionary theorists were careful to avoid or downplay questions about the material basis of mind. Some remained committed to interactive dualism, while others avowed a neutral parallelism and refused to speculate about the nature of the correlation between mental and material brain states.

DISCUSSION QUESTIONS

1. Is it reasonable to anticipate that some day psychologists will develop a universal theory that will unify the various subtheories and branches of psychology, in the fashion that Newton's gravitational theory unified the various laws of physical motion?

2. Why do you think that Locke was so convinced that consciousness is inseparable from thought? Can you be happy or miserable without being conscious that you are?

3. According to Berkeley, all concepts or ideas are derived from experience, but we can neither see nor touch distance. Is there any way to account for our ability to judge distance without having to postulate innate concepts of distance?

4. Try Hume's experiment of trying to "catch yourself" in introspection? Do you encounter nothing but perceptions, memories, feelings, and the like?

5. Do you agree with Condillac that it would be possible for a cognitive being to have only one sensory modality? Would this be sufficient (in principle) for the development of all cognitive faculties?

6. In what sense may we be said to collectively make our own psychology? Does Vico's account apply to all areas of psychology? To any areas?

GLOSSARY

apperception Term employed by Leibniz and Kant to describe the active organization of sensory elements in perception.

categories According to Kant, the innate concepts that organize and structure perception and knowledge.

Common sense psychology The form of psychology based upon the direct realism of Thomas Reid, according to which perception and knowledge are grounded in common and innate powers or faculties.

corpuscularian hypothesis The hypothesis that the properties and behavior of complex material bodies can be explained in terms of the properties and behavior of the corpuscles (or atoms) that compose them.

direct realism The view that we directly perceive physical bodies and their properties, without the mediation of atomistic sense impressions.

Encyclopédie A set of books produced in France in the 18th century under the direction of Denis Diderot that aimed to provide a comprehensive treatment of the various branches of human knowledge.

empiricist/positivist conception of scientific explanation The conception of scientific explanation as nothing more than the description of observational correlation.

epistemological empiricism The view that all knowledge derives from experience.

Enlightenment The period of European thought in the 17th and 18th centuries in which confidence in reason and experience came to displace faith in religion and traditional authority.

idealism The view that only immaterial minds and their ideas exist.

idéologues French empiricists dedicated to human progress through the application of psychology to social reform and education.

matters of fact and existence According to Hume, propositions rendered true or false by experience.

petites perceptions Sensory elements that register in perception but that are too faint to enter consciousness.

psychological atomism The view that mental states can be individuated independently of each other, and that complex ideas or concepts are compounded out of distinct simple ideas or concepts.

relations of ideas According to Hume, propositions rendered true or false by conceptual relations between ideas.

romanticism Eighteenth-century movement that repudiated the Enlightenment ideals of reason and science and celebrated human emotionality, spontaneity, and creativity.

sensationalism The French versions of empiricist psychology developed by Condillac and Helvetius.

sensory threshold The level below which sensory impressions do not register in consciousness.

social mind Conception of social thought and emotion as emergent forms of mentality of social groups, states, and nations that are irreducible to the mentality of their members.

synthetic a priori knowledge According to Kant, knowledge about the natural world that is not based upon experience.

theoretical unification View that science progresses through the theoretical unification of independently established scientific laws.

transcendental idealism Kant's account of synthetic a priori knowledge, based upon his analysis of the conditions of the possibility of experience.

vibratiuncles According to Hartley, neural vibrations that form the material basis of ideas.

REFERENCES

Berkeley, G. (1975). *An essay towards a new theory of vision*. In M. R. Ayers (Ed.), *Philosophical works*. Totowa, NJ: Rowman & Littlefield. (Original work published 1709)

Berkeley, G. (1975). *A treatise concerning the principles of human understanding*. In M. R. Ayers (Ed.), *Philosophical works*. Totowa, NJ: Rowman & Littlefield. (Original work published 1710)

Berkeley, G. (1975). *On motion*. In M. R. Ayers (Ed.), *Philosophical works*. Totowa, NJ: Rowman & Littlefield. (Original work published 1721)

Berkeley, G. (1975). *Three dialogues between Hylas and Philonous*. In M. R. Ayers (Ed.), *Philosophical works*. Totowa, NJ: Rowman & Littlefield. (Original work published 1713)

Boakes, R. (1984). *From Darwin to behaviorism: Psychology and the minds of animals*. Cambridge: Cambridge University Press.

Condillac, E. B. de. (1930). *Treatise on the sensations* (G. Carr, Trans.). Los Angeles: University of Southern California School of Philosophy. (Original work published 1754)

Condillac, E. B. de. (2001). *Essay on the origin of human knowledge: A supplement to Mr. Locke's essay on the human understanding* (H. Aarsleff, Trans.). New York: Cambridge University Press. (Original work published 1746)

Geach, P. (1975). Teleological explanation. In S. Körner (Ed.), *Explanation*. Oxford: Blackwell.

Hacking, I. (1975). *The emergence of probability: A philosophical study of early ideas about probability, induction and statistical inference*. New York: Cambridge University Press.

Hartley, D. (1971). *Observations on man: His frame, his duty, and his expectations*. Vols. 1–2. New York: Garland. (Original work published 1749)

Hull, C. L. (1937). Mind, mechanism and adaptive behavior. *Psychological Review, 44*, 1–32.

Hume, D. (1973). *Treatise on human nature* (L. A. Selby-Bigge, Ed.). Oxford: Clarendon Press. (Original work published 1739)

Hume, D. (1975). *An enquiry concerning human understanding*. In L. A. Selby-Bigge (Ed.), *Enquiries concerning human understanding, and concerning the principles of morals*. Oxford: Clarendon Press. (Original work published 1748)

Hume, D. (1975). *An enquiry concerning the principles of morals*. In L. A. Selby-Bigge (Ed.), *Enquiries concerning human understanding, and concerning the principles of morals*. Oxford: Clarendon Press. (Original work published 1751)

Kant, I. (1891). *Metaphysical foundations of natural science* (E. B. Bax, Trans.; 2nd Rev. ed.). London: George Bell. (Original work published 1783)

Kant, I. (1973). *Critique of pure reason* (N. K. Smith, Trans.). New York: Macmillan. (Original work published 1781)

Kant, I. (1996). *Anthropology from a pragmatic point of view* (V. L. Dowdell, Trans.). Carbondale: Southern Illinois University Press. (Original work published 1797)

Kimble, G. A. (1995). Discussant's remarks: From chaos to coherence in psychology. *International Newsletter of Uninomic Psychology, 15*, 34–38.

Leibniz, W. L. (1981). *New essays on the understanding* (P. Remnant & J. Bennett, Trans.). New York: Cambridge University Press. (Original work published 1765)

Leon, J. C. (1999). *Science and philosophy in the West*. Upper Saddle River, NJ: Prentice-Hall.

Locke, J. (1975). *Essay concerning human understanding* (P. H. Niddich, Ed.). Oxford: Clarendon Press. (Original work published 1690)

Locke, J. (1988). *Two treatises on government* (P. Laslett, Ed.). New York: Cambridge University Press. (Original work published 1689)

Locke, J. (1989). *Some thoughts concerning education* (J. W. Yolton & J. S. Yolton, Eds.). New York: Oxford University Press. (Original work published 1693)

Mill, J. S. (1973–1974). *A system of logic, ratiocinative and inductive; being a connected view of the principles of evidence, and the methods of scientific investigation*

(J. M. Robson, Ed.). Toronto: University of Toronto Press. (Original work published 1843)

Newton, I. (1952). *Opticks; or, A treatise of the reflections, refractions, inflections & colours of light.* New York: Dover. (Original work published 1704)

Newton, I. (1969). *Mathematical principles of natural philosophy* (F. Cajori, Trans.). New York: Greenwood Press. (Original work published 1687)

Reid, T. (1975). *Essays on the active powers of man.* In K. Lehrer & R. E. Beanblossom (Eds.), *Thomas Reid's inquiry and essays.* Indianapolis: Bobbs-Merrill. (Original work published 1788)

Reid, T. (1975). *Essays on the intellectual powers of man.* In K. Lehrer & R. E. Beanblossom (Eds.), *Thomas Reid's inquiry and essays.* Indianapolis: Bobbs-Merrill. (Original work published 1785)

Reid, T. (1975). *Inquiry into the human mind on the principles of common sense.* In K. Lehrer & R. E. Beanblossom (Eds.), *Thomas Reid's inquiry and essays.* Indianapolis: Bobbs-Merrill. (Original work published 1764)

Robinson, D. N. (2003). Jefferson and Adams on the mind-body problem. *History of Psychology, 6,* 227–238.

Rousseau, J-J. (1979). *Emile* (A. Bloom, Trans.). New York: Basic Books. (Original work published 1762)

Rousseau, J-J. (1997). *The social contract.* In V. Gourevitch (Ed. & Trans.), *The social contract and other later political writings.* New York: Cambridge University Press. (Original work published 1762)

Spence, J. T. (1987). Centrifugal versus centripetal trends in psychology: Will the center hold? *American Psychologist, 42,* 1052–1054.

Sturm, T. (2006). Is there a problem with mathematical psychology in the eighteenth century? A fresh look at Kant's old argument. *Journal of the History of the Behavioral Sciences, 42,* 353–377.

Vico, G. (1984). *The new science.* In *The new science of Giambattista Vico.* Ithaca: Cornell University Press. (Original work published 1725)

Wilkes, K. V. (1988). *Real people.* Oxford: Clarendon Press.

Wolpe, J. (1969). *The practice of behavioral therapy.* New York: Pergamon Press.

CHAPTER 6

Physiology and Psychology

T HE 19TH CENTURY WAS A TIME OF GREAT CHANGE IN EUROPE AND America. Agricultural reforms ensured a steady food supply, and improvements in public hygiene decreased fatalities due to contagious diseases such as cholera. The population of Europe increased from about 140 to 420 million people between 1750 and 1900, with many congregated in the new urban centers. The dramatic expansion of industry led to a general increase in wealth, although the insecurities of the capitalist state (with periods of boom followed by periods of economic downturn) led some to question a system in which most of the wealth was owned by a privileged few and to look to alternative political systems such as socialism and communism. New developments in transportation and communication saw the spread of modern road networks, railways, canals, ocean lines, and telegraph and postal systems (Jansz, 2004).

The 19th century witnessed the growth and increasing political strength of the middle class, whose long struggle to attain voting rights eventually bore fruit, although throughout most of the 19th century real political control remained in the hands of the conservative aristocracy. In the reactionary period following the Napoleonic wars in Europe, which ended with Napoleon's defeat at the battle of Waterloo in 1815, naturalistic approaches to psychology were repressed through censorship and the secret police. Nobody who promoted such views could hold a professorship in Europe and America in the early half of the century, and in the years immediately following 1815, advocacy of such views was punishable by imprisonment in some parts of Europe (Reed, 1997).

Joseph Priestley (1733–1804) was hounded out of Britain for his promotion of Hartley's associationist psychology as materialist psychology. Erasmus Darwin (1731–1802), the grandfather of Charles Darwin (1809–1882), who developed an early naturalistic evolutionary theory in *Zoonomia* (1794–1796), found his work suppressed. One of Darwin's followers, the British surgeon William Lawrence (1783–1867), published his theory that insanity is a neurophysiological disorder in *Lectures on Physiology, Zoology and the Natural History of Man* (1819). The medical establishment forced him to withdraw his book, and he lost his lectureship at the Royal College of Surgeons (Reed, 1997).

After the (failed) European revolutions of 1848, a new alliance of the conservative aristocracy and the middle class implemented a variety of reforms and ceased to depend upon traditional Christianity as the foundation of the social order. Although religion remained a conservative force in politics and education, the 19th century saw the emergence and general acceptance of more secularized systems of thought. While naturalistic treatments of physiology and psychology still stimulated vigorous reaction from the clergy, many came to see the development of science as independent of religion. Many 19th-century physiologists and psychologists avoided conflict with organized religion by maintaining that their theories had no implications for theology, since they held that questions about God are beyond the realm of scientific knowledge.

In the late 18th century, the work of Antoine Lavoisier (1743–1794) and John Dalton (1766–1844) had set chemistry upon a sound experimental footing. This stimulated 19th century physiologists to explore the physics and chemistry of organic structures and processes, including the structure and function of the nervous system. The 19th century witnessed major advances in neuroanatomy and physiology, which played a significant role in shaping the development of scientific psychology in Britain, Germany, and America.

POSITIVISM

Auguste Comte (1798–1857) introduced the term **positivism** to describe his view that the highest form of human knowledge is knowledge of the correlation of observables. In his **law of three stages**, he claimed that societies pass through three stages of cognitive development that represent different attitudes toward the explanation of natural events. In the **theological stage**, natural events are explained in terms of anthropomorphized forces; for example, lightning storms are explained in terms of the anger of the gods. In the **metaphysical stage**, natural events are explained in terms of depersonalized forces; for example, planetary motions are explained in terms of gravitational forces. In the **positive stage**, natural events are explained in terms of the description of observable correlation, which can be employed to predict the course of nature.

Comte believed that the natural sciences had developed systems of positive knowledge and that a similar approach should be applied to the science of society. A science of sociology (the term was coined by Comte) would ideally establish a system of laws describing regularities in human behavior. According to Comte, these laws could be employed to create a perfect society based upon scientific sociology, in contrast to the misery and chaos that were the natural outcome of social systems grounded in metaphysical speculation and religious superstition. He believed that a social and political system based upon scientific sociology would eventually displace traditional religion and politics.

Comte was greatly affected by the political upheavals following the French Revolution. He became secretary to the social theorist Henri Saint-Simon (1760–1825) in 1817 and supported himself in later years by private teaching and public lectures. He produced the six-volume *Cours de Philosophie Positive* during the years 1830 to 1842 and the four-volume *La Systeme de Politique Positive* during the years 1851 to 1854. His early work attracted many supporters, but he alienated many of them when he developed a new scientific religion based upon positivist principles. He set himself up as its pope, with his mistress substituting for the Virgin Mary (Reed, 1997).

The form of positivism that many 19th-century theorists embraced was the dogmatic empiricism advocated by Berkeley and Hume, shorn of their philosophical idealism and skepticism. According to this atheoretical form of empiricism, scientific theories and causal explanations are restricted to the description of the correlation of observables, which enable us to predict and control nature. In this view, we have no knowledge of real efficient causes or final causes, such as the nature of gravity or purposive design in nature. In *Auguste Comte and Positivism* (1866), John Stuart Mill characterized the basic principles of Comte's positive philosophy in the following dogmatic empiricist fashion:

> The constant resemblances which link phaenomena together, and the constant sequences which unite them as antecedent and consequent, are termed their laws. The laws of phaenomena are all we know respecting them. Their essential nature, and their ultimate causes, either efficient or final, are unknown and inscrutable to us.
>
> —(1866/1961, p. 6)

Although Comte endorsed dogmatic empiricism, his positivist system differed from British empiricism and associationist psychology in two respects. First, he treated the publicly observable properties of physical objects as the subject matter of scientific knowledge, rather than the privately introspectable sensations and ideas favored by British empiricists and associationist psychologists. Comte was contemptuous of introspection as a scientific method and denied the possibility of a psychology based upon it.

Second, Comte placed sociology at the pinnacle of his presumed hierarchy of scientific disciplines, with physics at the base and biology in between. However, he left no room for psychology as an autonomous science of consciousness or behavior, located between sociology and biology. For Comte, the whole content of psychological knowledge was exhausted by sociology, which studies behavior in its social context, and phrenology, the branch of biology devoted to the correlation of functionally characterized behavior (such as aggressive or amative behavior) with discrete psychological faculties located in specific regions of the brain.

Later positivists, such as Ernst Mach (1838–1916) in *The Analysis of Sensations* (1886) and Richard Avenarius (1843–1896) in *Critique of Pure Experience*

Positivism

Sociological

Auguste Compte (1798-1857)

- 3 Stages — 1) Theological; 2) Metaphysical; 3) Positive or scientific
- rejected introspection
- rejected Psychology

so → Sociology

↑ Biology + its branch Phrenology

Physics.

Psychological

Ernst Mach (1838-1916)

Richard Avenarius (1843-1896)

OK to correlate introspective sensory states.

(So- Both Watson + Titchener can be counted positive scientists)

Logical Positivism

Vienna Circle ~ (1924)

Operationism

Percy Bridgman (1892-1961)

Positivism

(1888–1890), followed earlier British empiricists in maintaining that the correlation of private sensory experience constitutes the observational subject matter of scientific knowledge. Thus, all positivists maintained that the correlation of observables is the subject matter of scientific knowledge, but differed as to whether publicly observable properties of physical objects or privately introspectable sensory experience constituted the observational subject matter of scientific knowledge. For this reason one can characterize both the experimental science of consciousness developed by Edward B. Titchener (1867–1927) at the end of the 19th century and the behaviorist psychology developed by John B. Watson in the early 20th century as systems of positivist science. The former was restricted to the description of the correlation of private mental states, and the latter to the description of the correlation of publicly observable stimuli and behavior.

Throughout the 19th century a great many scientific theorists avowed some form of positivism, including such figures as John Stuart Mill, William James (1842–1910), Thomas Huxley (1825–1895), Franz Brentano (1838–1917), Emil du Bois-Reymond (1818–1896), Sigmund Freud, and Edmund Husserl (1859–1938). Yet often this amounted to little more than a commitment to methodological empiricism, the view that scientific theories must be based upon observation. Many avowed positivists freely speculated about unobservable states and processes, including unconscious mental states and processes.

While this no doubt caused some confusion, it served a useful purpose in the development of 19th-century science, including physiology and psychology. For whatever they took to be the observational foundation of science, and however strict or loose their approach to theories about unobservable states and processes, most positivists and empiricists were committed to the principle that knowledge of real efficient and final causes (such as the nature of gravity, the human will, and the purpose of God's creation) is beyond the realm of science. This principle was occasionally employed to disparage religion, but more often than not it was advocated as a means of peaceful rapprochement with theologians, many of who came to agree that the realms of science and religion should be treated as distinct.

Thus, for example, when the evolutionary psychologist Herbert Spencer (1820–1903) was accused of promoting atheism in his *Principles of Psychology* (1855), he responded by withdrawing from the realm of religious debate:

> Not only have I nowhere expressed any such conclusion, but I affirm that no such conclusion is deducible from the general tenor of the book. I hold, in common, with most who have studied the matter to the bottom, that the existence of a Deity can neither be proved or disproved.
>
> —(Cited in Reed, 1997, p. 159)

The positivist and dogmatic empiricist claim that causal knowledge amounts to nothing more than knowledge of observable correlation also provided physiologists and psychologists with a convenient parallelist defense against charges of materialism, by enabling them to maintain that they were merely studying the physiological correlates of mental states, without speculating about the relation between them. While detailing the neurophysiological substrate of mentality in the "cortical grey matter of the brain," the 19th-century British neurophysiologist John Hughlings Jackson (1835–1911) claimed

> We cannot understand how any conceivable arrangement of any sort of matter can give us mental states of any kind. . . . I do not concern myself with mental states at all, except indirectly in seeking their anatomical substrata. I do not trouble myself about the mode of connection between mind and matter. It is enough to assume a parallelism.
>
> —(1931, 1, p. 52)

ASSOCIATIONIST PSYCHOLOGY

The tradition of associationist psychology initiated by Hume and Hartley in the early 18th century continued apace in the late 18th century and into the 19th. It was developed by a variety of British theorists, such as Abraham Tucker (1705–1774), who tried to derive principles of morality from associationist laws; Archibald Alison (1757–1839), who tried to account for aesthetic feelings in terms of association; Thomas Brown, who developed a number of "secondary" laws of association or "suggestion"; and George Henry Lewes (1817–1878), who extended association to accommodate logical reasoning, by developing "laws of thought" based upon a "logic of signs." In France the work of the sensationalists and ideologists was extended by M. F. P. G. Maine de Biran (1766–1824), Pierre Maurice Mervoyer (1805–c. 1866), and Hippolyte Adolphe Taine (1828–1893). James Mill (1773–1836), John Stuart Mill, Alexander Bain (1818–1903), and Herbert Spencer (whose contribution is considered in chapter 7) introduced the most significant modifications of associationist psychology.

James Mill: Points of Consciousness

James Mill, the Scottish philosopher and economist, was a close friend of Jeremy Bentham (1748–1832), the founder of **utilitarianism**. According to utilitarian theory, moral, social and political questions should be determined by the principle of utility: The right course of action in any situation is the one that maximizes human happiness and minimizes human misery. Mill was an early 19th-century radical who advocated utilitarian positions on government, jurisprudence, and education. Like Bentham, he supported a variety of interventionist social programs such as state education, health care, and poor relief, which he believed were justified in terms of their contribution to human happiness and the alleviation of human misery.

Mill published *A History of British India* in 1818, which provided him with entry to a successful career in the East India Company. His contribution to associationist psychology was his *Analysis of the Phenomena of the Human Mind* (1829). In this work he characterized the sensory elements out of which ideas and associations are supposed to be formed as atomistic **points of consciousness**. Mill added little to the basic principles of associationist psychology developed by Hume and Hartley and claimed that the main purpose of his work was to document further evidence for the principles of association. However, he did claim that the principle of similarity is not a fundamental law of association, since he believed that it could be derived from the principle of contiguity.

Mill's interest in associationist psychology was secondary to his political and educational projects, and his main concern was to adapt associationist psychology to utilitarian social goals. He maintained, for example, that a major task of education is to facilitate the association of individual happiness with benevolent social behavior.

John Stuart Mill: Mental Chemistry and Unconscious Inference

John Stuart Mill was lucky to survive his father's intensive private education, based upon associationist psychology and utilitarian principles. The young Mill was introduced to Greek at the age of 3, to Latin and mathematics at age 6, to philosophy at age 8 and logic at age 12. In his teenage years he studied economics and politics and prepared for a career as a lawyer, but eventually followed his father into the East India Company. A nervous breakdown at age 20 forced him to reevaluate his personal and political orientation.

Mill developed his own version of the utilitarian "greatest happiness" principle in *Utilitarianism* (1863). His moral and political views were tempered by his association with Harriet Taylor (1807–1858), who was married with two children (and another on the way) at the time they began their relationship. Mill scandalized many of his colleagues by practicing (with the approval of Taylor's husband) one of those "experiments in living" that he advocated in *On Liberty* (1859). After the death of Taylor's husband, the couple married. Taylor's influence inspired Mill's pioneering feminist tract *The Subjection of Women* (1869), which he dedicated to her, as well as his unsuccessful attempt to introduce legislation on female suffrage.

In 1843 Mill published *A System of Logic*, in which he described the methods of comparative causal analysis known as the methods of agreement, difference, and concomitant variation, now commonly characterized as Mill's methods. He claimed that these methods provide not only a means of generating hypotheses, a logic of discovery, but also a means of evaluating hypotheses, a logic of justification. Mill agreed with Whewell and Herschel that scientific hypotheses need not be generated inductively (on the basis of systematic observations), but may be the product of creative inspiration. However, he insisted that scientific hypotheses, however generated, could be verified only by observations made in accord with the methods of agreement, difference, and concomitant variation.

Mill was an early supporter of Comte's positivist philosophy and arranged for his *Cours de Philosophie Positive* to be translated into English. However, his own endorsement of positivism amounted to little more than an endorsement of methodological empiricism. He championed the view that science is ultimately grounded in the correlation of observables, but he did not feel obliged to restrict science to the mere description of observational correlation. He was quite prepared to advance hypotheses about unobservable states and processes, including unconscious mental states and processes.

Psychological Science   In *A System of Logic*, Mill characterized psychological and social sciences, which he called "moral sciences," as a "blot on the face of science." He maintained that "the backward state of the moral sciences can only be remedied by applying to them the methods of physical science, duly extended and generalized" (1843/1973–1974, p. 833), by which he meant his own methods of agreement, difference, and concomitant variation.

For Mill, a scientific discipline of psychology based upon the methods of agreement, difference, and concomitant variation could establish a system of associationist laws:

> The subject, then, of psychology, is the uniformities of succession, the laws, whether ultimate or derivative, according to which one mental state succeeds another; is caused by, or at least, is caused to follow, another.
>
> —(1843/1973–1974, p. 852)

However, Mill was realistic about the predictive possibilities of such a science. Although he thought it possible to determine the fundamental laws of association, he believed that practical prediction in psychology is limited by the difficulties of anticipating all the factors involved in human thought and behavior (1843/1973–1974, p. 554). For this reason, Mill maintained that psychology is bound to remain an inexact science, at least outside of controlled experimental situations. He also denied the standard Newtonian assumption about the universality of causal explanation and maintained that many psychological phenomena have a plurality of causes. He avoided speculation about the neurophysiological basis of mental states and processes, referring such matters to his friend and colleague Alexander Bain (Bain, 1855, 1859). Mill also championed the scientific study of character, which he called **ethology**. He conceived of character as a set of social capacities and propensities, which he suggested could be derived from the fundamental laws of association. However, he also deferred this task to Bain, who made a brave attempt in *On the Study of Character, Including an Estimate of Phrenology* (1861), probably the least successful of Bain's works.

Mill's primary contributions to associationist psychology were his *System of Logic,* his 1865 *Examination of Sir William Hamilton's Philosophy,* and his edited edition of James Mill's *Analysis of the Phenomena of the Human Mind* (1869). Mill reiterated the basic principles of associationist psychology detailed by his father, although he reintroduced the principle of similarity as a fundamental rather than a derived law.

Mill also questioned the universality of the aggregative account of concept formation common to most forms of associationist psychology. He claimed that the properties of complex ideas or concepts are often more closely analogous to the emergent properties of chemical bonding than the additive properties of mechanical combination and represented some associative processes as a form of **mental chemistry**:

> The laws of the phenomena of mind are sometimes analogous to mechanical, but sometimes also to chemical laws. . . . Our idea of an orange really *consists* of the simple ideas of a certain color, a certain form, a certain taste and smell, &c., because we can by interrogating our consciousness, perceive all these elements in the idea. But we cannot perceive, in so apparently simple a feeling as our perception of the shape of an object by the eye, all that multitude of ideas derived from other senses, without which it is well ascertained that no such visual perception would ever have existence. . . . These therefore are cases of mental chemistry: in which it is proper to say that the simple ideas generate, rather than that they compose, the complex ones.
>
> —(1843/1973–1974, pp. 853–854)

Unconscious Inference Although Mill's notion of mental chemistry was not developed for this purpose, he employed something very close to it in his response to the challenge posed by Samuel Bailey's (1791–1870) critique of Berkeley's theory of distance perception (Bailey, 1842, 1843). According to Berkeley's theory (Berkeley, 1709), our perceptual judgments about distance are based upon learned associations between visual and tactile sensations. Mill defended Berkeley against Bailey, but in the course of so doing was forced to revise the basic assumptions of associationist psychology.

Bailey raised the following objection to Berkeley's account: If (as Berkeley had admitted) neither visual nor tactile sensations alone can convey information about distance or "outness," then no mere association of such sensations can convey such information either. Bailey, a follower of Reid, claimed that we directly perceive distance visually. In response, Mill claimed that our perceptual judgments about distance involve a form of **ampliative inference** that goes beyond

Mill unconscious → Helmholtz inference

the information presented in visual and tactile sensation and accused Bailey of failing to distinguish between information derived from sensation and information derived from inference.

Bailey responded that we have no introspective awareness of any such inferential process:

> I cannot recognize in my experience such a process as the sensation of color suggesting an external thing. I directly and immediately see the colored external object.
>
> —(1855–1863, 2, p. 35)

He further claimed that we have no introspective awareness of the associated visual and tactual sensations from which judgments about distance are supposedly inferred:

> When I see an object under ordinary circumstances, I am not conscious of any affection in the organ of sight. I am conscious of perceiving the object at some distance but not of any sensation in the eye itself.
>
> —(1855–1863, 2, p. 40)

Mill granted both these points. However, he maintained that the visual perception of distance involves a form of unconscious inference or "unconscious cerebration" (Carpenter, 1874), based upon the association of visual and tactile sensations. Mill was the first to explicitly postulate a **rational unconscious**, governed by norms of rationality and logical inference (Reed, 1997). According to Mill, this unconscious inference is so automatic we naturally mistake it for a form of direct perception (1865, p. 166). Mill's account of perception influenced many later psychologists, notably Helmholtz and Wundt.

Mill was successful in defending Berkeley's account of distance perception, and Bailey's critique was quickly dismissed (Pastore, 1965). However, in defending Berkeley, Mill transformed associationist psychology almost beyond recognition, by sacrificing two fundamental principles of dogmatic British empiricism. In the first place, he abandoned the notion that scientific theories should be restricted to objects of conscious experience, by postulating that distance perception involves unconscious inference (Berkeley had rejected Descartes' theory of distance perception in terms of geometrical computations precisely because he had no conscious awareness of such computations). In the second place, Mill abandoned the notion that we have direct introspective access to all our mental states. He acknowledged that we do not have introspective access to the elemental visual and tactile sensations upon which our perceptual inferences are supposedly based. He noted that associated visual and tactile sensations become so integrated within perceptual judgment that the original sensations become "dim, confused, and difficult to be recalled" (1865, p. 180). Accordingly, later psychologists who developed Mill's account of perception as a form of unconscious inference from sensational elements increasingly relied upon physiological rather than introspective psychological data in support of their theories (Reed, 1997).

Alexander Bain: Psychology and Physiology

The last great British empiricist and associationist psychologist was Alexander Bain (1818–1903). His two-volume survey of contemporary associationist psychology and physiology, *The Senses and the Intellect* (1855) and *The Emotions and the Will* (1859), was the standard British text in psychology during the latter half of the 19th century and represented the first modern textbook of psychology.

Bain was the largely self-educated son of a poor weaver. He attended Marischal College, Aberdeen, where he attained top academic honors, and later traveled to London, where he befriended John Stuart Mill. The two met regularly to discuss their evolving ideas on philosophy and psychology, and Mill was so impressed by Bain that he asked him to read the proofs of *A System of Logic*. Mill in turn supported his protégé by persuading his own publisher to produce Bain's *The Senses and the Intellect*. When it lost money, Mill guaranteed the reluctant publisher 100 pounds sterling against losses on the second volume, *The Emotions and the Will*. Mill's praise for Bain's work in essays and reviews undoubtedly contributed to the eventual success of Bain's volumes. According to Mill, Bain was the first to achieve a substantive integration of psychology and physiology, based upon contemporary research in the physical sciences (Mill, 1859/1867).

Despite his best efforts, Bain originally failed to attain a university position and seemed fated to spend his years teaching geography at a finishing school for young women in London. He supplemented his meager income with royalties from articles in popular magazines such as the *Westminster Review* (on topics such as sympathy and toys) and from editorial work on the physiology of the nervous system. However, with the eventual success of his "big book," he was offered the Chair of Logic at Marischal College, Aberdeen, in 1860, where he remained until his retirement in 1876. That same year he founded the journal *Mind: A Quarterly Review of Psychology and Philosophy* with George Croom Robertson (1842–1892), who became the first editor. The first issues of the journal were devoted to the question of whether psychology could be a genuine science: The founding editorial hoped that the publication of the journal would enable its readers "to procure a decision on . . . the scientific standing of psychology" (Robertson, 1876, p. 3). Over time the focus shifted to purely philosophical questions, and *Mind* eventually became the premier British journal in philosophy, although reference to psychology in the subtitle was not dropped until 1974 (Neary, 2001).

The Senses and the Intellect and *The Emotions and the Will* were the first texts to integrate associationist psychology and the important developments of 19th-century physiology. They set the standard for later psychology texts, whose authors felt obliged to include some account of the structure and function of the nervous system. Although Bain maintained the traditional empiricist and asso-ciationist commitment to introspection, he acknowledged that "consciousness is not indispensable to the operations of intellect" (1855, p. 316). He also recognized the innate basis of many features of human and animal psychology and behavior, such as emotions and instincts.

In many respects Bain's texts were transitional. They looked backward to tradi-tional associationist psychology and the recent history of physiology and forward to theories of evolution and late-19th-century advances in neurophysiology. Bain updated these texts through four editions, but they were frequently outdated by the time the latest edition was published. Bain's own psychological and physiological positions were largely secondhand. His psychological theories were not based upon extensive introspective or behavioral observation, and he did no clinical or physio-logical work. *The Senses and the Intellect* (1855) was published the same year as Herbert Spencer's *Principles of Psychology,* and *The Emotions and the Will* (1859) the same year as Charles Darwin's *On The Origin of Species.* Yet although Bain included sections on their theories of biological and mental evolution in later editions of his work, he made little attempt to integrate associationist psychology with evolutionary theory.

Bain advanced a fairly standard account of the association of ideas and behav-ior in terms of contiguity with repetition:

> Actions, sensations, and states of feeling, occurring together or in close succession, tend to grow together, or cohere in such a way that, when any one of them is afterwards presented to the mind, the others are apt to be brought up in idea.
>
> —(1855, p. 318)

He followed John Stuart Mill in reintroducing similarity as a fundamental principle of association, which he believed was necessary to explain higher mental processes, notably those involved in analogical reasoning. Although he endorsed the basic principles of psychological and meaning empiricism, Bain was careful to point out that these principles are less restrictive than commonly supposed. He granted that our ideas are derived from sensory experience, but noted that it does not follow that we must have prior sensory experience of complex entities in order to form ideas or concepts of them. Bain emphasized the creative combinatory and devel-opmental possibilities of ideation. He claimed that we are able to form meaningful ideas of possibly nonexistent entities via novel combinations of simple ideas, such as our idea of a "golden mountain," and via analogical extensions of complex ideas, such as our theoretical notion of "light waves" (Bain, 1855, p. 571).

Voluntary Behavior   Bain's most fertile development of associationist psychology was his account of voluntary behavior, which he treated as a form of learned behavior based upon association. Unlike involuntary reflexive behavior, voluntary behavior is often generated *independently* of the stimulation of external sensory receptors.

Behavior can be generated independently of sensory stimulation, according to Bain, because nervous energy stored within the organism may be spontaneously discharged to motor nerves without antecedent stimulation ("where no stimulus from without is present as a cause"):

> There is in the constitution a store of nervous energy, accumulated during the nutrition and repose of the system, and proceeding into action with, or without, the application of outward stimulants.
>
> —(1859, p. 328)

According to Bain, such spontaneously generated behavior is converted into directed or purposive voluntary behavior when it becomes associated with the experience of pleasure and pain, as in the case of a newborn lamb progressively coordinating originally spontaneous movements until they develop into purposive movements toward its mother's teat (1855, pp. 404–405).

This account of behavioral learning, according to which behaviors followed by success, satisfaction, or pleasure tend to be repeated, later became known as the **Spencer-Bain principle** (Boakes, 1984). Earlier versions of Bain's account of voluntary behavior are to be found in Hartley, Erasmus Darwin, and the German physiologist Johannes Müller (1801–1858), from whom Bain may have derived his account (Müller is cited extensively in Bain's discussion of voluntary behavior). Both Müller and Bain stressed that the associative processes that transform spontaneous activity into voluntary behavior are generally unconscious, since they operate in lower animals and neonates as well as in adult humans.

Bain's distinction between involuntary (reflexive) and voluntary behavior also anticipated later distinctions between responsive (stimulus determined) and operant (consequence determined) forms of conditioning, and Bain recognized instances of both. He cited a number of stimulus-determined associative reflexes that Pavlov later characterized as conditioned reflexes:

> The mere idea of a nauseous taste can excite the reality even to the point of vomiting. The sight of a person about to pass a sharp instrument over glass excites the well-known sensation in the teeth. The sight of food makes the saliva begin to flow.
>
> —(1868, p. 90)

BAIN prefigured "Conditioning"

CEREBRAL LOCALIZATION

The 19th century saw great advances in neuroanatomy, especially during the 50-year period between Franz Joseph Gall's *On the Functions of the Brain* (Gall & Spurzheim, 1822–1825/1835) and David Ferrier's *The Functions of the Brain* (1876). This period also saw a marked shift of emphasis from correlational to controlled experimental studies of neurophysiological functions, a pattern later repeated in the development of comparative psychology and scientific psychology in general.

Despite advances in the neurophysiological location of psychological functions, the 19th century did not represent a progressive triumph of materialism and the reductive physiological explanation of human and animal psychology and behavior. On the contrary, many of the pioneers of neurophysiological localization either championed a form of substance dualism or maintained a neutral parallelism, which enabled them to avoid familiar charges of materialism, atheism, and fatalism. In the early part of the century at least, even those who abandoned substance dualism maintained a form of **neurophysiological dualism**, which preserved the rational autonomy of the human intellect and will championed by traditional substance dualists such as Descartes. Many early theorists held that the cognitive functions of the cerebral cortex are categorically distinct from the sensory-motor functions of the lower brain and spinal cord.

In the early 19th century the English physiologist Marshall Hall (1790–1857) established that there are numerous connections between sensory and motor nerves in the spinal cord and introduced the notion of a **reflex arc**: a system comprising a sensory nerve, interconnecting nervous tissue in the spinal cord, and a motor nerve (Boakes, 1984). Hall distinguished between the "excitory-motor" system, which he located in the lower brain and spinal cord (the "true spinal" system), and the "sensory-volitional" system, which he located in the cerebral cortex. According to Hall, the reflexive excitory-motor system accounts for automatic, instinctual, and emotional behavior, whereas the sensory-volitional system accounts for rational, learned, and purposive behavior.

Franz Joseph Gall: Phrenology

Franz Joseph Gall (1758–1828), a Viennese physician and anatomist, developed what became known as **phrenology**, the doctrine that the degree of development of psychological faculties is a function of the size of the area of the brain in which they are localized, which can be determined by measurements of the contours of the skull, or **cranioscopy**. Gall tried to map the functions of the brain by establishing correlations between behavioral manifestations of psychological faculties and protrusions and indentations of the skull, supposedly caused by the development or underdevelopment of the associated "separate organs" of the brain. According to Gall, a developed faculty of acquisitiveness, for example, is reflected in a protrusion just above and in front of the left ear; an underdeveloped faculty of acquisitiveness is marked by an indentation in the same place. Human behavior can be explained and predicted by reference to the degree of development of the contours, or "bumps," on the skull.

Gall's theory was reputedly inspired by his childhood observation that classmates who excelled in rote memory had "large prominent eyes" and his belief that such correlation was not accidental (Young, 1990). His medical training led him to the conclusion that "the difference in the form of heads is occasioned by the difference in the form of the brains" (Gall & Spurzheim, 1822–1825/1835, 1, p. 59). Gall claimed that moral and intellectual faculties are innately determined, in contrast to the optimistic environmentalism of French sensationalists such as Condillac and idéologues such as de Tracy. He argued that individual differences in psychological faculties and propensities among humans, and between humans and animals, cannot be explained in terms of environment and learning history, but must be explained in terms of biological endowment.

Such postulated limits on human intellectual and moral perfectibility led to inevitable charges of materialism, atheism, and fatalism, although Gall declined to take any position on the mind-body problem. He was forced to leave Vienna and move to Paris when the Catholic Church and the Austrian authorities condemned his works. They were placed on the Index of Prohibited Books, and Gall was denied a Christian burial when he died in 1828. However, his doctrine attracted many followers, notably Johann Casper Spurzheim (1776–1832), who collaborated with Gall on the publication of *The Anatomy and Physiology of the Nervous System* (in four volumes between 1810 and 1819, closely followed by popular editions of the same text). It was Spurzheim who coined the term *phrenology,* which Gall never used (Clarke & Jacyna, 1987).

Empirical and Biological Psychology   The scientific community originally treated Gall's work with respect. He was a skilled neuroanatomist whose dissection techniques were much admired, since they represented a significant improvement over traditional "mutilative" techniques. Gall was largely responsible for developing the surgical methods that enabled experimental physiologists to leave discrete convolutions of the brain intact (O'Donnell, 1985). However, his specific claims about the neural localization of particular psychological faculties and propensities were undermined by later research (which, ironically, employed the very same surgical methods that Gall had pioneered). Gall and his followers were also overly enthusiastic in their appeal to positive instances of correlation between protrusions of the skull and behavioral manifestations of psychological faculties and uncritically dismissive of negative instances in which no correlation was found. Their attempts to explain away negative instances by appealing to brain disease or damage or by withdrawing original attributions of a developed faculty (when Descartes' skull was found to lack the relevant protrusion for rationality, they concluded that Descartes had not been as great a thinker as had been previously supposed) led to the justified dismissal of phrenology as a pseudoscience, on a par with palmistry and astrology.

This was unfortunate, since Gall's attempt to develop an empirical biological psychology presaged a number of later developments in physiology and psychology. Although medieval "inner sense" theorists had speculated about the ventrical location of psychological faculties such as cognition and memory, Gall was the first to attempt to empirically identify the neural location of specific faculties. His localization of psychological faculties was based upon his study of the skulls of normal and abnormal adults, children, and the elderly, and his comparative analysis of the psychological faculties of different species of animals and men (even if he relied too much on anecdotal reports and was too cavalier in his dismissal of negative findings). Gall was arguably the first empirical physiological psychologist, even though later experimental researchers came to disparage his naturalistic correlational methods.

Gall maintained that the "fundamental, primitive faculties" of animals and humans should be established empirically. He was critical of the types of faculties postulated by empiricists and sensationalists, who focused almost exclusively on epistemological faculties such as perception, cognition, and memory. In contrast, Gall focused on adaptive and socially oriented faculties such as the "carnivorous instinct," the "maternal instinct," and the "disposition to murder," in addition to traditional cognitive and moral faculties (Young, 1990).

Gall insisted that anyone concerned with the objective study of the neurophysiological basis of psychological functions "should have a clearly defined conception of what he is looking for" (1822–1825/1835, 3, p. 160). According to Gall, psychological functions can be established only via the comparative study of the behavioral repertoires of normal adult humans, children, animals, and the insane. He insisted that only after empirical categories of psychological functionality have been established are neurophysiologists in the position to systematically correlate psychological functions with neurophysiological locations. Unfortunately, Gall's prescription was neglected by later generations of neurophysiologists and, to the detriment of his own legacy, often enough by Gall himself, who adopted many of the traditional categories of Scottish common sense psychology, such as self-preservation, duty, love, and imitation, not to mention "the instinct for property owning and stocking up on food."

Gall identified 27 fundamental faculties, atomistically conceived as distinct and independent. Gall claimed that animals share 15 of these with humans (Young, 1990), but did not endorse strong continuity between human and animal psychology and behavior: He maintained that there are 12 human faculties that animals do not have to any degree. Gall worked in a pre-evolutionary period and believed in a fixed natural hierarchy. However, his comparative studies of psychological faculties in different species, his emphasis on behavior and its adaptive function, and his stress on variation between and within species presaged later developments in comparative, functional, and differential psychology, although his commitment to the pseudoscience of phrenology relegated his own legacy to the intellectual dustbin of history.

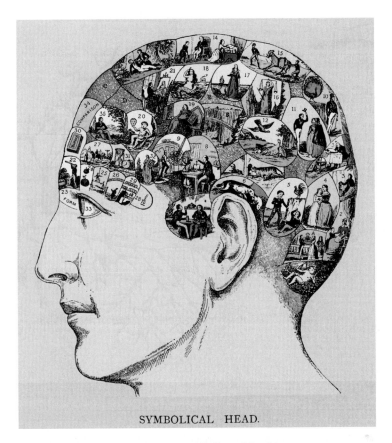

SYMBOLICAL HEAD.

Phrenological head representing psychological faculties.

While empirically discredited, Gall's psychology, with its emphasis on indi-vidual differences, anticipated the forms of functional and behaviorist psychol-ogy that dominated American psychology in the early half of the 20th century. William McDougall (1871–1938) employed Gall's methods of behavioral analysis of psychological functions in his influential 1908 work on instinct, *Introduction to Social Psychology*. Like Comte and later behaviorist psychologists, Gall was opposed to introspective psychology. He believed that introspective methods distorted psychological investigation in much the same way as traditional dissection tech-niques distorted neurophysiological investigation and that they posed a major threat to the development of an objective psychological science.

After Gall died in 1828, Spurzheim and his Scottish disciple George Combe (1788–1858) promoted phrenology in Europe and America. Sales of Combe's 1827 text *Essay on the Constitution of Man and Its Relation to External Objects* reached six figures, and Spurzheim toured America to great acclaim in 1832 (Walsh, 1972). Combe's American lectures of 1838–1840 were attended by physicians, ministers, educators, asylum superintendents, and college professors, who saw phrenology as a source of potentially useful knowledge (O'Donnell, 1985).

Phrenological societies and consulting offices were founded in major European and American cities. In the hands of American entrepreneurs such as Orson Fowler (1809–1887), Lorenzo Fowler (1811–1896), and Samuel Wells (1820–1875), who developed elaborately labeled busts and manuals for self-analysis, phrenology became big business. It eventually took on the status of a cult rather than a scientific discipline, which explains why it survived long after empirical demonstrations of its inadequacy and retained adherents even in the late 20th century (Leek, 1970).

Applied Phrenology   Phrenology was especially popular in America in the years prior to the Civil War, when itinerant phrenologists gave public lectures and demonstrations in churches and town halls and did private "delineations" to paying clients. The *Annals of Phrenology* began publication in 1833; the *American Phrenological Journal and Miscellany* began publication in 1838 and ran until 1911. Phrenologists offered vocational guidance to paying clients, and in some places potential employers required phrenological analyses. Sizer (1882) claimed that those with highly developed faculties of acquisitiveness and secretiveness were especially suited to be merchants and bankers (cited in Sokal, 2001), and railway companies considered using phrenologists to select competent trainmen in order to reduce accidents (O'Donnell, 1985). Phrenologists also offered child-rearing advice and marriage counseling. They advised prospective husbands and wives to marry those with underdeveloped faculties that matched their own developed faculties (and vice versa). Many flocked to the New York parlors of Fowler and Wells to receive swift diagnoses of their vocational aptitudes and marriage prospects (O'Donnell, 1985).

In their practical applications, American phrenologists went considerably beyond Gall's original theory. In contrast to Gall's commitment to the innate biological determination of human psychological faculties, American phrenologists stressed their plasticity and counseled their clients to cultivate or constrain them. The popular reception and real if limited efficacy of phrenological counseling is probably best explained in terms of placebo effects and the commonsensical nature of the advice offered, which was rarely based upon the specifics of phrenological theory. In this respect, the practice of early American phrenologists anticipated that of early-20th-century American applied psychologists, whose pioneering explorations in educational, industrial, and clinical psychology were often based more on common sense and practical experience than on the theoretical systems of scientific psychology (Bakan, 1966). Whatever their actual degree of success, the professional practice of American phrenologists nourished public expectations for a scientifically objective but socially useful form of psychology of the type later promoted by American functional and behaviorist psychologists (O'Donnell, 1985).

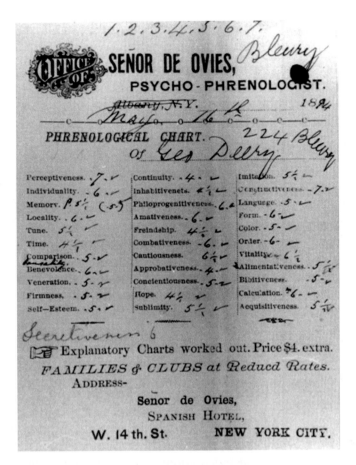

Phrenology examination chart: New York City, 1894.

Pierre Flourens: Experimental Physiology

The French surgeon Marie-Jean-Pierre Flourens (1794–1867) undertook the first systematic critique of phrenology in *An Examination of Phrenology* (1843) and *On Phrenology* (1863). Flourens established that many of Gall's localizations of psychological faculties were inaccurate and undermined the foundation of phrenology by demonstrating that the skull does not reflect the contours of the brain. In contrast to Gall, Flourens was a respected figure of the French scientific establishment. He received the Montyon prize in experimental physiology in 1824 and 1825 and shortly after was elected to the French Academy of Sciences (an honor refused to Gall). Flourens's pioneering experimental studies of the nervous system were documented in *Experimental Research on the Properties and Functions of the Nervous System in Vertebrates* (1824). He became professor of comparative physiology at the Collège de France in 1832 and received the ribbon of the Legion of Honor the same year (Young, 1990).

Experimental Ablation Flourens's experimental studies were a continuation of the program of neural localization initiated by Albrecht von Haller (1708–1777). Von Haller, who set the agenda for modern physiology in *Elements of Physiology* (1757–1765), pioneered the use of experimentation on live animals to identify physiological functions. Flourens extended this methodology to the exploration of the vertebrate nervous system and perfected the experimental method of **ablation**. This involves the systematic removal of neural tissue from live animals and careful observation of their consequent behavior in order to determine the function of the extirpated part of the nervous system. Although Flourens was not the first to employ the method of ablation, his meticulous surgical treatments set the standard for future research (later supplemented by electrical and chemical stimulation and electronic recording and graphing). Physiologists came to treat experimental intervention as the mark of a scientific approach to neural localization and rejected the correlational methods of Gall and his followers.

Flourens was the first to employ ablation to determine the functions of neural structures. His enduring achievement was to establish the cerebellum as the center for the control of motor behavior and the medula oblongata as the center for the control of vital functions such as respiration and heartbeat. He also extended von Haller's work on the **irritability**, or "excitability," of nerves, conceived of as the ability to transmit excitation that results in muscle contraction or sensation. On the basis of a series of experimental studies, Flourens concluded that irritability is not a universal property of the nervous system, since he found no evidence of it in the cerebral cortex.

As a means of localization of neural functions, Flourens's controlled ablative studies were in many respects superior to Gall's naturalistic correlations between behavior and protrusions and indentations of the skull. Yet he uncritically dismissed Gall's novel attempt to empirically establish a classification of psychological functions based upon distinctive behavioral repertoires (Young, 1990). Gall complained with some justification that the work of "mutilators" such as Flourens had little value, since it was not based upon empirical knowledge of "fundamental powers."

The Functional Unity of the Cerebral Cortex Although his stated aim was to "ascertain experimentally . . . which parts of the nervous system are used exclusively for sensation, which for [muscle] contraction, which for perception, etc." (1842, p. 3), Flourens was a very limited champion of neural localization. For his opposition to Gall went beyond disagreement about the neural location of particular psychological faculties and the advocacy of experimental over correlational methods. Flourens claimed that the cerebral cortex is the center of perception, will, and intelligence, but denied that these traditional faculties (and associated faculties of reasoning, memory, and judgment) are located in specific regions of the cerebral cortex. His denial was partly based upon the apparent lack of irritability of the cerebral cortex but also upon his conviction that the cognitive functions of the cerebral cortex are unitary. According to Flourens, the diverse functions of the lower nervous system, including the sensory-motor system localized in the lower brain and spinal cord, are presided over by the unitary cognitive functions of the cerebral cortex.

Flourens's claim that the integrated functions of perception, will, and intelligence are subserved by the "whole mass" of the cerebral hemispheres anticipated later doctrines of mass action and equipotentiality (Lashley, 1929). However, Flourens's primary ground for this claim was his commitment to substance dualism. According to Flourens, the unified cognitive functions of the cerebral cortex are the expression of the unified powers of the immaterial soul. This constituted his fundamental objection to Gall's project of neural localization: Gall had denied the unity or "indivisibility" of the immaterial soul that Descartes had affirmed. Like Descartes, to whom he dedicated his *Examination of Phrenology,* Flourens believed that the denial of the unity of the immaterial soul would lead to materialism, atheism, and fatalism.

François Magendie: The Bell-Magendie Law

The French physician François Magendie (1783–1855) abandoned his anatomical studies and surgery to focus on experimental physiology in 1813. He developed the first course on physiology as an autonomous discipline and founded the *Journal de Physiologie Expérimentale (Journal of Experimental Physiology)* in 1821. Magendie sought to establish physiology as a natural science in much the same fashion that Galileo and Newton had previously established physics and astronomy as natural sciences. He described this as the aim of his physiological textbook, *An Elementary Treatise on Human Physiology* (1838/1843), in which he championed experimentation as the basis of physiological and medical knowledge. Magendie was also a powerful member of the French scientific establishment, whose work inspired later generations of experimental physiologists, notably Claude Bernard (1813–1878) and Louis Pasteur (1822–1895), who were instrumental in establishing the supremacy of experimental over correlational methods in physiology.

Sensory and Motor Nerves Magendie's major contribution to experimental physiology was his demonstration of the location of distinct sensory and motor nerves in the spinal cord. Hartley had distinguished between sensory and motor nerve pathways, and von Haller and Whytt had located sensory-motor reflexes in the spinal cord; but Magendie was the first to demonstrate the separate locations of sensory and motor nerves in the posterior and anterior roots of the peripheral nerves in the spinal cord (respectively). Magendie exposed the spinal cord of a six-week-old puppy and found that severance of the anterior roots eliminated motor movements but left sensitivity intact and that severance of the posterior roots eliminated sensitivity but left motor movements intact. He concluded that

> the anterior and posterior roots of the nerves which arise from the spinal cord have different functions, that the posterior roots seem to be particularly destined for sensibility, while the anterior roots seem to be especially connected with movement.
>
> —(1822/1944, pp 101–102)

This was not an original discovery. The British physician and anatomist Charles Bell (1774–1842) had reported a similar result in 1811. He had exposed the spinal cord of stunned rabbits and noted how stimulation of the anterior roots produces convulsive movements, but stimulation of the posterior roots does not (Boakes, 1984). Bell believed he had identified the posterior and anterior roots as the vehicles of sensibility and movement, but his report was only circulated privately among friends. Knowledge of Bell's work led to a dispute about who deserved credit for the discovery of what later became known as the **Bell-Magendie law**. Flourens gave primary credit to Bell, possibly because of his own friction with Magendie, who was unpopular with his colleagues because of his vanity, jealousy, and fiery temper (Young, 1990). Bell was the first to attribute sensory and motor functions to the posterior and anterior spinal roots, but Magendie was the first to provide complete experimental confirmation of the different functions.

Cognition and Sensory-Motor Function   Magendie hoped to extend his experimental methods to the exploration of the higher cognitive functions of the cerebral cortex, but did little to illuminate their nature. He followed Flourens in categorically distinguishing the cognitive functions of the cerebral cortex from the sensory-motor functions of the lower brain and spinal cord. He avowed that cognitive functions could be studied as "the result of the action of the brain," but also held that they may be "dependent upon the soul" (1838/1843, p. 146). He was able to maintain this position because he endorsed a neutral parallelism and adopted a positivist attitude to the study of the physiological correlates of mental states. He claimed that science can only describe the correlation between mental and physiological states, but cannot causally explain the relation between them.

Johannes Müller, who conducted a parallel series of experiments on frogs, confirmed the Bell-Magendie law. Like Magendie, he agreed with Flourens that the cerebral cortex is not irritable and that the unitary cognitive functions are not localized to specific regions of the cortex. According to Müller, the various cognitive functions of the cerebral cortex (such as perception, thought, and memory) are merely "different modes of action of the same power" (1833–1840/1838, 1842, p. 1345).

Müller characterized the relation between the higher cognitive functions of the cerebral cortex and the sensory-motor functions of the lower brain and spinal cord in terms of a famous metaphor. He claimed that the will acts upon the lower brain centers like a musician playing on the keyboard of a pianoforte:

> The fibres of all the motor, cerebral and spinal nerves may be imagined as spread out in the medula oblongata, and exposed to the influence of the will like the keys of a pianoforte.
>
> —(1833–1840/1838, 1842, p. 934)

Physiologists in the first half of the 19th century generally accepted this characterization. It represented a form of neurophysiological dualism that preserved the autonomy of human thought, rationality, and will avowed by traditional dualists such as Descartes.

Pierre-Paul Broca: Aphasia

The French physician Pierre-Paul Broca (1824–1880) is often credited as the first person to have identified a specific neural location associated with a distinctive psychological function. Broca localized the "faculty of articulate language" to the superior region of the left frontal lobe, now known as **Broca's area,** based upon an autopsy performed upon his patient "Tan," who died within a week of admission to Broca's surgery (Broca, 1861/1960). Tan (whose real name was Leborgne) had lost his speech 21 years earlier and had been a patient at La Bicêtre Hospital in Paris.

Broca was neither the first person to study aphasia, nor the first to relate it to brain damage. Speculation about speech pathology and its neural origin goes back to the ancient Greeks, and Gall was the first to offer a "complete description of aphasia due to a wound in the brain" (Head, 1926, I, 9, cited in Young, 1990, p. 135). However, Broca gathered his evidence at a time when the scientific community was prepared to take it seriously. He presented his results in the course of an academic controversy over whether the cognitive functions of the cerebral cortex are unitary, as Flourens had maintained, or discrete, as Gall had maintained. Broca was secretary to the newly founded *Société d'Anthropologie,* where the debate had recently focused on the functions of a primitive skull presented by one of the members.

On the basis of the case of Tan and other autopsies, Broca claimed that he had isolated an autonomous faculty of language, which could be eliminated without damage to other intellectual faculties (such as memory and intelligence) and thus refuted Flourens's contention that the cerebral cortex acts "as a whole." However, some were cautious about Broca's evidence based upon "facts furnished by the experiments of disease in man" (Ferrier, 1876/1886, p. 270), especially since some of Broca's patients suffered from extensive brain damage and atrophy (Young, 1990).

Although Broca located the faculty of articulate language in the cerebral cortex, he followed Flourens and Magendie in maintaining that the functions of the cerebral cortex are essentially cognitive. He maintained the traditional distinction between the higher intellectual functions, attributed to the cerebral cortex, and the lower sensory-motor functions, attributed to the lower brain and spinal cord.

Gustav Fritsch and Eduard Hitzig: The Excitability of the Cerebral Cortex

Much of the early-19th-century debate about the cerebral localization of psychological functions took place in France, but it later shifted to Germany and Britain. The traditional distinction between the cognitive functions of the cerebral cortex and the sensory-motor functions of the lower brain and spinal cord had been supported by the experimentally demonstrated excitability of the nerves of the lower brain and spinal cord and the generally acknowledged inexcitability of the cerebral cortex. The work of Gustav Fritsch (1839–1927) and Eduard Hitzig (1838–1907) undermined this traditional distinction.

In a series of studies conducted on dogs and rabbits on a dressing table in a small Berlin house, Fritsch and Hitzig demonstrated that the cerebral cortex responds to electrical stimulation and that one region of the cortex is responsible for muscular contractions. They published their results in a paper titled "On the Electrical Excitability of the Cerebrum" (1870), whose significance was immediately recognized by the scientific community.

Like Broca, they rejected Flourens's view that the cerebral cortex acts "as a whole." However, they shared his commitment to dualism and maintained that the immaterial soul acts through the different regions of the cerebral cortex with their localized functions:

> It further appears, from the sum of all our experiments that the soul is not, as Flourens and others after him had thought, a function of the whole of the hemispheres, the expression of which one might destroy by mechanical means in the whole, but not in its various parts, but that on the contrary, certainly some psychological functions and perhaps all of them, in order to enter matter or originate from it need certain circumscribed centers of the cortex.
>
> —(1870, p. 96)

Their experiments were quickly replicated, initially by David Ferrier (1843–1928) in Britain (Ferrier, 1873) and by Leonardo Bianchi (1848–1927) in Italy (Bianchi, 1895). Ferrier, who was chair of forensic medicine at Kings College, London, mapped the motor cortex via a series of experiments on dogs, cats, rabbits, and guinea pigs. His 1876 book *The Functions of the Brain* (1876) represented the triumph of neural localization and initiated a program of research in England, Germany, France, and

Italy directed to the detailed mapping of the discrete functional centers of the cerebral cortex. Experimental explorations of the cortex, facilitated by improved techniques of ablation and stimulation, led to the identification of localized areas for different motor movements and the identification of the sensory centers for vision, hearing, touch, and other sensory modalities. This "new phrenology" had one immediate practical benefit: It greatly advanced the prospects of effective neural surgery by establishing targeted sites for the removal of suspected tumors or swelling (Young, 1990).

These pioneering experiments were also replicated on Mary Rafferty, an Irish domestic servant who was admitted to the Good Samaritan Hospital in Cincinnati in 1874 with a cancerous ulcer on the side of her head that exposed her brain through a 2-inch hole in her skull. One of her attending physicians, Robert Bartholow (1831–1904) of the Medical College of Ohio in Cincinnati, decided to exploit this opportunity to replicate the studies of Fritsch and Hitzig and Ferrier. He passed an electric current through needles inserted into her brain, which produced convulsive movements analogous to those of laboratory animals. In a paper titled "Experimental Investigations Into the Functions of the Human Brain" (1874), Bartholow described the effects on electrical neural stimulation on his unfortunate patient:

> When the needle entered the brain substance, she complained of acute pain in the neck. In order to develop a more decided reaction, the strength of the current was increased by drawing out the wooden cylinder one inch. When communication was made with the needles, her countenance exhibited great distress, and she began to cry. Very soon, the left hand was extended as if in the act of taking hold of some object in front of her; the arm presently was agitated with clonic spasm; her eyes became fixed with pupils widely dilated; her lips were blue, and she frothed at the mouth; her breathing became stertorous; she lost consciousness and was violently convulsed on the left side. The convulsion lasted five minutes, and was succeeded by a coma. She returned to consciousness in twenty minutes from the beginning of the attack, and complained of some weakness and vertigo.
>
> —(1874, pp. 310–311)

After the experiments, Mary began to complain of headaches and died a few days later; her death was certified as due to cancer.

The American Medical Association condemned Bartholow, although he insisted that he had performed the experiment with Mary's consent and maintained that it did not cause her death. He was forced to resign his professorship at the Medical College of Ohio, but went on to have a distinguished career as professor of medicine and dean of Jefferson Medical College in Philadelphia (Lederer, 1995). Bartholow published a number of successful books on medicine and therapeutics. He became a fellow of the College of Physicians of Philadelphia and a member of the American Philosophical Society. He was later elected president of the American Neurological Association.

The Sensory-Motor Theory of the Nervous System

The cerebral localization of centers for sensation and movement promoted the development of the **sensory-motor theory** of the nervous system, according to which the whole nervous system is a reflexive sensory-motor system, whose every component can be characterized as having a sensory or motor function (Danziger, 1982). On this theory, the higher cognitive functions of the cerebral cortex are strongly continuous with the lower sensory-motor functions of the lower brain and spinal cord: They are merely more complex elaborations of the reflexive sensory-motor functions to be found in humans and animals.

Thomas Laycock (1812–1876), professor of medicine at the University of Edinburgh, was one of the first to maintain that the principles that govern the reflexive system of the lower brain and spinal cord should be extended to the cerebral cortex:

> The brain, although the organ of consciousness, is subject to the laws of reflex action, and . . . , in this respect, it does not differ from the other ganglia of the nervous system. . . . The ganglia within the cranium, being a continuation of the spinal cord, must necessarily be regulated as to their reaction on external agencies by laws identical to those governing the functions of the spinal ganglia and their analogues in the lower animals.
>
> —(1845, p. 298)

John Hughlings Jackson, a former student of Laycock, treated sensation and movement as the basic elements of human psychology and claimed that they are instantiated in the cerebral cortex as "nervous arrangements representing impressions and movements" (1931, 1, p. 42). He argued that reflexive sensory-motor functions previously attributed exclusively to the lower brain and spinal cord should be attributed to the cerebral cortex, since he maintained that reflexive "sensori-motor processes are the physical side of, or . . . form the anatomical substrata of, mental states" (1931, 1, p. 49).

Jackson supported his sensory-motor theory with clinical autopsies of aphasics and epileptics, which revealed various forms of disease of or damage to the cerebral cortex. He claimed that all mental disorders caused by disease of or damage to the cerebral cortex, such as aphasia, epilepsy, and delirium are due to "lack, or to disorderly development, of sensori-motor processes" (1931, 1, p. 26). In contrast to Broca, who had claimed that aphasia is a cognitive disorder, Jackson maintained that it is a motor disorder, a defect of "articulatory movements" (Young,

1990). David Ferrier, who sought the "artificial reproduction of the clinical experiments produced by disease" (1873, p. 30), managed to create the convulsions of epilepsy by direct stimulation of the brain.

The identification of cortical centers for sensory and motor processes did not mandate the extension of reflexive sensory-motor forms of explanation to the cognitive operations of the cerebral cortex or the strong continuity of cognitive and sensory-motor functions presupposed by the sensory-motor theory of the nervous system. The location of sensory and motor centers in the cortex was consistent with the existence of distinct cognitive centers. Fritsch and Hitzig claimed that the anterior frontal regions of the cortex are responsible for abstract thought and play a minimal role in sensory-motor function, and Ferrier maintained that they are responsible for focused attention. Although the mechanistic explanation of all animal and human behavior undermined Descartes' account of voluntary behavior in terms of the free action of an immaterial soul, it was consistent with Bain and Muller's nonreflexive explanation of voluntary behavior as learned behavior generated independently of sensory stimulation.

However, many 19th-century physiologists embraced the reflexive sensory-motor theory of the nervous system and recognized the challenge it posed to traditional conceptions of mind, consciousness, and behavior. As George Croom Robertson, the editor of Bain's journal *Mind,* put it, 19th-century neurophysiology established a body of experimental results "to be reckoned with, by psychologists as well as physiologists" (Robertson, 1877, p. 92). Many 19th-century physiologists and medical psychologists extended reflexive explanation to cover the cognitive operations of the cerebral cortex, such as perception, memory, decision making, problem solving, and purposive behavior and focused their research on unconscious and automatic forms of cognition and behavior, such as hypnotic suggestion and somnambulism. For example, Laycock advanced reflexive explanations (albeit largely speculative) of complex, purposive but automatic behavior such as hysteria, impulsive insanity, and bizarre religious behavior in terms of cerebral reflexes (Danziger, 1982).

Ideomotor Behavior   William Carpenter (1813–1885), professor of physiology at University College, London, was the author of the influential textbook *Principles of Human Physiology* (1855), which helped to establish physiology as an autonomous discipline in Britain. He followed Hartley and Bain in maintaining that the laws of association connect ideas with behavior as well as with other ideas. According to Carpenter, ideas associated with behavior, or ideas of behavior, can come to generate behavior as a consequence of association. He identified a class of automatic but apparently purposive behavior mediated by ideas that he called **ideomotor behavior** (Carpenter, 1874) and appealed to association to explain the efficacy of hypnoses and other forms of suggestion, in which ideas automatically produce behavior without the agent willing the behavior or being conscious of the connection between the idea and behavior. Carpenter also introduced the notion of **unconscious cerebration** (which Mill employed in his account of unconscious inference in perception) to explain involuntary attention, unconscious problem solving, and dreams and hallucinations (Danziger, 1982). His theory of suggestibility provided the plot of Wilkie Collins's *The Moonstone*, the first British detective novel (Reed, 1997).

Although he claimed that some human behavior is a product of "self-regulation" by the will, Carpenter insisted that the action of the will is entirely dependent upon the reflexive mechanisms governing ideomotor behavior. For Carpenter, the will never initiates behavior directly, but can act only by "direction of the attention" (1874, p. 25), by focusing on ideas that automatically generate behavior. Attention strengthens certain ideas at the expense of others, and enables individuals to determine which automatic behavior comes into play. In contrast, inattention or misdirected attention (to imagined debauchery, for example) can result in bad habits and dissolution. In his own medical practice Carpenter recommended that peculiar mix of moral exhortation and directive rote learning characteristic of Victorian morality. He urged his patients to focus their attention on pledges to avoid strong drink, drugs, and prostitution and to ingrain good conduct through repetition of socially accepted behaviors until they became habitual (or "secondary automatic," as Hartley had put it).

Epiphenomenalism   One commonly represented consequence of the sensory-motor theory of the nervous system was the view that mentality and consciousness are merely epiphenomenal by-products of the reflexive mechanisms of the nervous system and play no role in the generation of behavior. Many theorists committed to the sensory-motor theory come to conceive of mentality and consciousness as "coincident" or "collateral" properties of those neurophysiological states that are responsible for the reception of sensory stimulation and the generation of behavior (Danziger, 1982).

The biologist Thomas Huxley championed this conception of mentality and consciousness in his address to the 1874 meeting of the British Association in Belfast, titled "On the Hypotheses That Animals Are Automata, and Its History." Huxley claimed that Descartes had been wrong to deny consciousness to animals, since the areas of the cerebral cortex established as the centers of consciousness in humans could be re-identified in animals such as apes and dogs, but maintained that 19th-century advances in neurophysiology supported Descartes' treatment of animals as automata. He claimed that the attribution of consciousness to animals is not inconsistent with their treatment as automata, because their consciousness is causally impotent with respect to their behavior:

> The consciousness of brutes would appear to be related to the mechanism of their
> body simply as a collateral product of its working, and to be as completely without any

power of modifying that working as the steam-whistle which accompanies the work of a locomotive engine is without influence on its machinery. Their volition, if they have any, is an emotion indicative of physical changes, not the causes of such changes.

—(1874, p. 575)

Huxley maintained that the same was true of humans, who, like animals, he characterized as **conscious automata**:

The argumentation which applies to brutes holds equally good for men; and, therefore . . . all states of consciousness in us, as in them, are immediately caused by changes in the brain substance. . . . it follows that our mental conditions are simply the symbols in consciousness of the changes which take place automatically in the organism; and that, to take an extreme illustration, the feeling we call volition is not a voluntary act, but the symbol of that state of the brain which is the immediate cause of the act.

—(1874, p. 577)

This doctrine came to be known as **epiphenomenalism**, although Huxley never used the term, which was originally employed to characterize symptoms of a disease that play no causal role in the progress of the disease. William James was the first to use the term to characterize Huxley's "conscious automaton-theory" (James, 1890, p. 129).

In defense of his claims about the causal impotency of mentality and consciousness, Huxley cited cases of animals and humans that engage in coordinated and purposive behavior despite decortication or temporary lack of consciousness due to brain damage. He noted that frogs with their cortex removed will continue to engage in such behavior, despite their presumed lack of consciousness: They will use their legs and feet to try to remove chemical irritants applied to their bodies (a phenomenon documented by Hales and Whytt in the 18th century). Huxley also described the case of a French army sergeant with a head wound, who suffered temporary periods of loss of consciousness, during which he would continue to eat, drink, smoke, and walk in the garden, while seemingly insensitive to pain and visual stimulation.

Yet at most these cases demonstrated only that animals and humans are able to engage in purposive behavior in the absence of consciousness, not that animal and human consciousness is impotent when it is present, far less that this is the case with respect to mentality per se (conscious or unconscious). As Huxley himself noted, a frog with a cortex responds to sights and sounds that the decorticated frog ignores, and the sergeant normally refused the quinine or vinegar that he happily drank during his periods of unconsciousness. Indeed, in a reference that would have delighted Descartes, Huxley noted that the sergeant was normally truthful and honest, but was a liar and a cheat during his unconscious lapses (1874, p. 572).

Epiphenomenalism was not mandated by either materialism or the sensory-motor theory of the nervous system, and neither La Mettrie nor Carpenter embraced the doctrine. Many psychologists continued to insist on the causal role of mentality and consciousness in the generation and control of behavior, although epiphenomenalism later found its most forceful expression in early American behaviorist psychology.

Control and Inhibition As the 19th century developed, neurophysiologists came to conceive of reflexive behavior in increasingly complex terms, as integrated adaptive reactions rather than isolated neuromuscular responses. Although the neurophysiological dualism of higher autonomous and lower reflexive processes was abandoned, the sensory-motor theory of the nervous system still retained elements of the traditional conception. The notion of distinct functional systems was replaced by the notion of a hierarchy of increasingly more complex reflexive systems, in which higher cerebral reflexes regulate the reflexes of the lower brain and spinal cord. Neurophysiologists also came to acknowledge that many reflexive behaviors are initiated centrally rather than peripherally, as the notion of the control of behavior by an immaterial will or autonomous cognitive center was replaced by the notion of control through cerebral inhibition. Ferrier treated reflexive cortical inhibition as the basis of a redefined notion of "voluntary" behavior:

> The primordial elements of . . . volitional acts . . . are capable of being reduced in ultimate physiological analysis to reaction between the centers of sensation and those of motion.
>
> But besides the power to act in response to feelings and desires, there is also the power to inhibit and restrain action, notwithstanding the tendency of feelings and desires to manifest themselves in active motor outbursts.
>
> —(1876, p. 282)

Whytt had demonstrated the enhancement of reflexes following decortication, and the liberating effects of drugs and alcohol on the cerebral cortex were well known. It became natural to offer explanations of epilepsy, aphasia, somnambulism, suggestibility, alcoholism, and insanity in terms of the breakdown of inhibitory cortical control of lower reflexive responses, through disease, damage, or the influence of chemical agents such as drugs or alcohol.

EXPERIMENTAL PHYSIOLOGY IN GERMANY

Given the major contributions to psychology by Hume, Hartley, Mill, and Bain, and to neurophysiology by Jackson, Carpenter, and Ferrier, one might have expected that institutional scientific psychology would have naturally developed in Britain at the end of the 19th century. After all, Bain's *Senses and the Intellect* (1855) pre-dated Wundt's *Principles of Physiological Psychology* (1873–1874) by 18 years, and his journal *Mind* (1876–) predated Wundt's journal *Philosophical Studies* (1881–) by five years.

However, academic psychology developed much later in Britain than in the rest of Europe and America. In 1877 James Ward and John Venn tried to get psychology introduced as an academic discipline at the University of Cambridge, but the University Senate rejected their proposal. Ward did manage to get a grant of 50 pounds for psychological equipment in 1891 and secured a lectureship in experimental psychology and physiology of the senses in 1897. But psychology never really developed as an autonomous discipline in Britain until after the First World War, and many universities remained unreceptive until after the Second World War (Hearnshaw, 1964).

This was due in part to the inherent conservatism of the British universities, whose primary mission for centuries had been the preparation of young men for the ministry, and to the reactionary philosophical and religious establishment. Yet the major reason was the lack of financial support for scientific research. It was not until the 1920s that the public funding of British universities began in earnest, with the founding of the University Grants Committee.

In contrast, German universities had a strong research tradition, which could be traced back to their early exploitation of the invention of printing. They were reorganized during the Napoleonic period by Wilhelm von Humboldt (1767–1835), then head of the newly created section of culture and education of the Prussian Ministry of the Interior. Humboldt believed that university professors should excel in both teaching and research, which he held to be mutually enhancing, and set about creating the institutional conditions necessary to support this ideal. Nineteenth-century German universities were committed to the principles of *Lehrfreiheit* and *Lernfreiheit*: the freedom of professors to teach what they like and the freedom of students to study what they like (Dobson & Bruce, 1972).

The Prussian and later the unified German state provided substantial financial support for the development of German universities, which insured a well-paid professoriate and liberal grants for laboratories, books, and equipment. The epitome of the new German university was the University of Berlin, founded by von Humboldt in 1810. As a new institution, it had no ties to tradition or religious authority and spearheaded the revolution in German university education in the 19th century.

The tradition of state-supported excellence in teaching and research established at German universities was enormously influential. The system of professional institutes, chairs, and research seminars provided the model for the modern university. It encouraged the creation of specialized disciplines, including newly emerging ones such as physiology and psychology, and promoted the treatment of the doctoral degree as the qualification for university teaching. The rapid growth of German universities in the 19th century, whose expansion was seen as a prerequisite of the modern industrial state, largely accounts for the many distinguished achievements of German science in the 19th century, including experimental physiology.

Johannes Müller: Experimental Physiology

The major figure in the development of 19th-century German experimental physiology was Johannes Müller (1801–1858). He received his doctorate from the University of Bonn in 1822 and was appointed chair in physiology at the University of Berlin in 1833. A highly productive scholar, Müller did much to establish experimental physiology as an autonomous scientific discipline in Germany and Europe. His two-volume *Handbook of Human Physiology* (1833–1840) became the internationally recognized sourcebook of contemporary research in physiology and neuroanatomy for generations of researchers, replacing von Haller's earlier compendium.

Müller made many important contributions to experimental physiology. He replicated Hall's studies of the reflex arc and Magendie's experimental discrimination of sensory and motor nerves in the spinal cord. He developed an integrated hierarchical theory of the functions of the nervous system and developed an early account of "trial-and-error" learning based upon spontaneous nervous activity, which was probably the source of Bain's account of voluntary behavior.

Following a speculation by Bell, Müller demonstrated that there are five types of sensory nerves, each with its own "specific energy," which give rise to distinctive sensations of color, smell, taste, sound, and touch. Müller believed that he was investigating the physiological basis of the Kantian categories and claimed that the distinctive properties of our sensations of color, smell, taste, sound, and touch are determined by our nervous system, although he was never sure whether specific nerves or the areas of the brain to which they project are responsible for them.

Perhaps Müller's greatest achievement was as a teacher. He inspired many distinguished students, such as Ernst W. von Brücke (1819–1892), Emil du Bois-Reymond (1818–1896), Carl F. W. Ludwig (1816–1895), Hermann von Helmholtz (1821–1894), and Theodor A. H. Schwann (1810–1882), who made significant contributions to experimental physiology and physiological psychology. A workaholic prone to depression, Müller is believed to have taken his own life when he grew fearful of his declining powers (Young, 1990).

Vitalism and the Berlin Physical Society Müller was in an important sense the inheritor of the mechanistic approach to animal and human psychology and behavior initiated by Descartes. And like Descartes, Müller was a champion of **vitalism**. Descartes had taken the revolutionary step of separating the principles of life and mind that had been equated by ancient and medieval theorists. He had maintained that vital processes such as respiration and digestion are a mechanical product of organized matter, rather than a product of the action of the rational soul.

Yet by the 19th century vitalism had developed into the view that physiological processes are the product of an emergent vital force *distinct* from the physical and chemical forces of attraction and repulsion. This was the view held by Xavier Bichat (1771–1802), who claimed that vital processes are not reducible to the laws of physics and chemistry, and the chemist Justus von Liebig (1803–1873), who treated vital force as "a peculiar property, which is possessed by certain material bodies and becomes sensible when their elementary particles are combined in a certain arrangement or form" (quoted in Lowry, 1982, pp. 71–72).

In the early 19th century, it was common to appeal to vital force to explain how physical-chemical forces binding the constituents of food are overcome in the process of digestion:

> The vital force causes a decomposition of the constituents of food, and destroys the force of attraction which is continually exerted between their molecules; it alters the direction of the chemical forces in such wise, that the elements of the constituents of food arrange themselves in another form. . . . It causes the new compounds to assume forms altogether different from those which are a result of the attraction of particles when acting freely, that is, without resistance. . . . The phenomenon of growth, or increase in the mass, presupposes that the acting vital force is more powerful than the resistance which the chemical force opposes to the decomposition or transformation of the elements of the food.
>
> —(quoted in Lowry, 1982, p. 71)

As Johann F. Blumenbach (1752–1840) stressed, vital force was postulated, like gravitational force, on the basis of its observed effects. So long as there remained physiological processes that could not be reductively explained in terms of the known forces of physics and chemistry, it was reasonable to postulate such a force.

This was the form of vitalism that Müller championed. However, his students would have none of it. In 1842, Brücke and du Bois-Reymond reported a solemn oath, sealed in blood, which they had taken with Ludwig and Helmholtz, to the effect that: "no other forces than the common physical-chemical ones are active in the organism" (du Bois-Reymond, 1842/1997, p. 19). They founded the **Berlin Physical Society** in 1845, dedicated to the reductive explanation of physiological processes. They all went on to hold major chairs at German universities.

Their commitment to reductive explanation was empirically validated by Ludwig's account of the formation of urine, the first detailed explanation of a physiological process in terms of a well-understood physical-chemical process (Boakes, 1984). The daunting complexity of most other physiological processes precluded the systematic reduction of the physiological to the physical-chemical in the 19th century (Cranefield, 1957), but the commitment of Müller's students to reductive explanation inspired them to make substantive contributions to the study of nervous transmission and reflexive behavior.

Yet it would be wrong to suppose that vitalism impeded the development of experimental physiology. Müller and fellow vitalists such as Claude Bernard (1813–1878) and Louis Pasteur (1822–1895) were gifted experimentalists who made substantive contributions to 19th-century physiology, just as dualists such as Flourens and Fritsch and Hitzig made significant contributions to the neural localization of psychological capacities. However, Müller's commitment to vitalism may partly explain the reluctance of many theorists to embrace his account of voluntary behavior, based upon the spontaneous activity of the nervous system.

Emil du Bois-Reymond: Electrophysiology

Electrical phenomena were the subject of great interest in the 18th and 19th century. Benjamin Franklin's (1706–1790) dramatic experiments with static electricity and his explanation of lightning were enthusiastically received in Europe and America. Popular demonstrations of the ability of the human body to serve as an electrical conductor led many to speculate about the role of electricity in physiology and psychology. One of the most popular scientific texts in mid-19th-century America was the Reverend John Bovee Dods's 1850 book *Electrical Psychology*, and electrotherapy was a common form of medical treatment in the late 19th century (Reed, 1997). William James recommended it for his sister Alice and himself.

In the early 18th century, Hales had speculated that electricity might be the elusive force behind nervous action, the "vis nervosa" about which Whytt had admitted ignorance. In the late 18th century Luigi Galvani (1737–1798) claimed to have demonstrated the electrical nature of nervous activity by producing contractions in the leg muscles of frogs, which he connected to different metallic elements. His nephew Giovanni Aldini engaged in more dramatic demonstrations by electrically inducing spasmodic muscular responses in the severed heads of criminals (Boakes, 1984).

Alessandro Volta (1745–1827) disputed Galvani's results. He claimed that Galvani had only identified a form of "metallic electricity" based upon the potential (or voltage) difference between two metals. The ensuing controversy was remarkably productive for the development of electrical theory and electrophysiology. During the following decades, more sophisticated technical devices for the electrical stimulation of living tissue were created, and finely calibrated instruments such as galvanometers enabled physiologists to measure very small amounts of electricity (Boakes, 1984).

Galvani and Volta were both vitalists, who believed that they were measuring the relation between electrical energy and vital force (Reed, 1997). Müller rejected the notion that the "vis nervosa" is electrical in nature, but his student du Bois-Reymond provided experimental evidence for the electrical basis of neural transmission. Du Bois-Reymond, who took over Müller's chair in physiology at

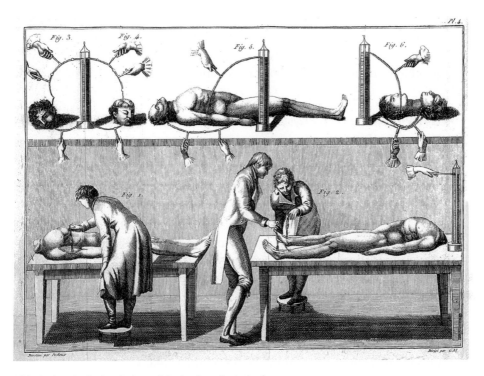

Aldini: electrical stimulation of the brains of criminals.

the University of Berlin, demonstrated that the nervous system conducts rather than generates electricity (as Galvani and Volta had maintained) and that every nervous tissue (and not merely muscular tissue) contains an electromotive force or "resting potential" (Boakes, 1984). His pioneering experimental studies were published in *Animal Electricity* (1848–1849).

Just how the nervous system conducted electricity remained a mystery, since it seemed a poor candidate for a conductive device. It was well known that a metal wire could conduct electricity as long as it was insulated, but the nervous system seemed to lack insulation, and its wet tissues appeared to guarantee the immediate dissipation of any electrical charge. The modern understanding of electrical transmission along individual cells—or neurons—only came about with the development of the cell theory, originally advanced by Theodor Schwann, another of Müller's students, and established by the Spanish physiologist Ramon y Cajal (1852–1934) toward the end of the 19th century (Boakes, 1984).

The notion that neural transmission is a form of electrical conduction had one theoretical virtue. Transmission of electrical current in an insulated conductor is very fast (close to the speed of light), which would explain the speed of executed human decisions. Our decision to wave to a friend, for example, is almost instantaneously followed by our arm rising, despite transmitted signals having to travel the length of nervous tissue linking the brain and arm muscles (Boakes, 1984). Müller, who rejected the electrical theory of nervous conduction, maintained that it was too fast to be measured, a claim that was quickly falsified by the experimental work of yet another of his students, Hermann von Helmholtz.

Hermann von Helmholtz: Physiological Psychology

Hermann von Helmholtz (1821–1894) made major contributions to physics as well as physiology and physiological psychology. An army surgeon who was honorably relieved of his duties so he could devote himself full-time to his scientific research, Helmholtz taught at the universities of Berlin, Königsberg, Bonn, and Heidelberg. In a famous paper produced in 1847, he advanced the principle of the conservation of energy, according to which the total quantity of energy remains constant throughout any qualitative change. The principle was held to be universal in scope, applying to physical, chemical, physiological, and—by implication—psychological systems. According to it, the physical world, including living beings and their psychologies, constitutes a closed system. To postulate a psychic or vital force that is categorically distinct from physical energy would be to violate the principle of "closed physical causality" and threaten the possibility of a law-governed science of physiology (O'Donnell, 1985).

This did not pose as much a threat to psychic or vital force as might be supposed, given the recognition of the exchangeability of physical forces, such as the conversion of heat to mechanical energy. Psychic force came to be conceived as a special form of physical or electrical force. For Helmholtz and his colleagues, this suggested that conscious experience could be identified with the transformation of energy traveling through the nervous system. The nervous system came to be represented primarily as a conductor of electrical energy, received via stimulation of sensory receptors and discharged through motor behavior, analogous to the recently developed telegraph (Lenoir, 1994).

Helmholtz was the first to measure the speed of neural conduction. He estimated it at around 25–45 meters per second in frogs and around 30–35 meters per second in humans. He demonstrated that the speed of neural conduction varies with distance from the central nervous system and that it is too slow to be purely electrical in nature. It was later determined to be electrochemical in nature, largely through the work of Thomas R. Elliott (1877–1961), Henry Dale (1875–1968), and Otto Loewi (1873–1961).

Perception as Unconscious Inference   Helmholtz also focused his attention on the problem that had concerned Berkeley 150 years earlier. Helmholtz, like Müller and many of his contemporaries, postulated a system of **punctiform sensations** (analogous to the atomistic sense impressions of the British empiricists) as the basis of complex perception. Individual receptors (in the retina, for example, in the case of vision) were held to carry sensory excitation along discrete neural pathways to individual projection areas in the brain. Yet it was recognized that we do not have punctiform sensations of distance, shape, size, causality, motion, and the like, and that our perception of these properties is more than the mere aggregation or association of punctiform sensations. Helmholtz claimed that our perception of these properties is based upon an unconscious *cognitive* inference.

Like Berkeley, Helmholtz insisted that distance perception is a product of empirical learning, but recognized that learning alone cannot explain how puncti-form sensations get transformed into unified perceptions of the distance of physi-cal bodies. According to Helmholtz, we have innate ideas of distance, shape, size, causality, motion, and the like that we correlate with sensory experience to yield cognitive judgments about physical bodies and their properties based upon infer-ence (Turner, 1977, 1982):

> If a connection is to be formed between the idea of a body of certain figure and cer-
> tain position, and our sensations of sense, then we first have to have the idea of such
> bodies. Just as with the eye, so it is also with the other senses; we never perceive the
> objects of the external world directly, on the contrary, we only perceive the effects of
> these objects on our nervous apparatuses, and it always has been like that from the
> first moment of our life. Now, in which way have we passed over for the first time
> from the world of sensations of our nerves to the world of reality? Obviously only
> through an inference.
>
> —(1855, p. 40, trans. Pastore, 1974)

Although our "perception" of distance, shape, size, causality, motion, and the like is really a cognitive judgment based upon inference from repeated sensory experience, it appears as a form of direct perception because it is unconscious and instantaneous. Helmholtz's theory anticipated the general form of many theories in late-20th-century cognitive psychology.

Helmholtz also developed a trichromatic theory of color vision (based upon the three primary colors), now known as the Young-Helmholtz theory of color vision, since it was developed independently by Thomas Young (1773–1829) in 1802. He also made important contributions to acoustics. His *Treatise on Physiolog-ical Optics* was published in 1856–1866 and his *On the Sensation of Tone* in 1862.

Ivan Sechenov: Inhibition

Theories of reflex behavior from Descartes to Müller had presupposed that reflexive behavior is grounded in the *excitation* of the nervous system, with energy from stim-ulated sensory receptors being conducted through the nervous system to generate

Ivan Sechenov and frogs.

motor responses. In 1845 the German physiologist Edouard Weber (1806–1871) of the University of Leipzig made a major discovery that eventually transformed theories of neurophysiological function. Weber demonstrated that stimulation of the vagus nerve (which runs from the brain to various internal organs) leads to a *reduction* in heart rate: this was the first experimental demonstration of increased activity in one part of the nervous system leading to *decreased* activity in another part. Weber demonstrated that the nervous system functions to *inhibit* as well as stimulate behavior (Boakes, 1984).

The significance of **inhibition** was not immediately appreciated. Edouard F. W. Pflüger (1829–1910), yet another of Müller's students, demonstrated that neural stimulation can inhibit activity in the intestine of a frog. Pflüger did not attach any special significance to neural inhibition. However, his experimental report was carefully studied by Ivan Mikhailovich Sechenov (1829–1905), a Russian student newly arrived at the University of Berlin.

Ivan Sechenov, the founder of Russian reflexology, studied with Müller, du Bois-Reymond, Ludwig, and Helmholtz. He later become professor of physiology at the Military-Medical Academy of the University of St. Petersburg and published *Reflexes of the Brain* in 1863. On the basis of experiments conducted on frogs, Sechenov demonstrated that stimulation of certain regions of the brain (for example, regions of the thalamus) depresses normal reflex activity, such as a frog's automatic withdrawal of its leg when placed in diluted acid. Sechenov was aware that many automatic reactions, such as sneezing and coughing, can be voluntarily suppressed, and he theorized that voluntary behavior is reflexive behavior that has come under the control of inhibitory stimuli. According to Sechenov, there are neural mechanisms that serve both to inhibit and to enhance reflexive behavior and that become associated with behavior through established habits. What is commonly conceived of as a strong will is simply the product of successfully learned inhibition or enhancement of reflexive behavior, such as the ability to refrain from alcohol or to increase one's speed in a competitive race.

Sechenov's account of voluntary behavior was thoroughly mechanistic: He treated all behavior as a function of innate and learned reflexes and learned inhibition and enhancement. He rejected Müller's account of voluntary behavior as a product of the spontaneous activity of the brain, because he associated the notion of spontaneous activity with vitalism. Sechenov claimed that all behavior is a causal product of sensory stimulation, since otherwise energy sufficient to produce behavior would have to come from some source outside the nervous system, such as an immaterial soul or vital force. He rejected explanations of behavior in terms of internal mental states such as thought and desire, because he believed that these are merely links in a causal chain running from sensory stimulation to (reflexive) behavior:

> Thought is generally believed to be the cause of behavior . . . but this is the greatest of falsehoods; the initial cause of all behavior always lies, not in thought, but in external sensory stimulation, without which no thought is possible.
>
> —(1863/1965, p. 322)

Yet Sechenov was no epiphenomenalist. He did not deny that behavior is a causal product of thought and desire. Rather, he maintained that thought and desire are merely the **proximate** or immediate causes of behavior, which are themselves fully determined by external sensory stimulation. He suggested that contemplative thought is a reflex in which the final behavioral outcome is suppressed through learned inhibition (Smith, 1992):

> Now, a psychical act . . . cannot appear in consciousness without an external sensory stimulation. Consequently, our thoughts are also subject to this law; therefore, in a thought, we have the beginning of a reflex, and its continuation; only the end of a reflex (i.e. the movement) is apparently absent.
>   *A thought is the first two thirds of a psychical reflex.*
>
> —(Sechenov, 1863/1965, pp. 320–321)

Sechenov's extreme position on this matter may have been a consequence of his independent commitment to an extreme environmentalism. He was a political radical who hoped that psychology would enable humans to realize their true potential and surmount the repressive constraints of traditional societies, such as the Tzarist Russia to which he returned. He was not driven to this position by his rejection of vitalism, because there is no intrinsic connection between Müller's account of voluntary behavior as the product of spontaneous neural activity and vitalist theories of physiological function. Both Bain in the 19th century and B. F. Skinner in the 20th century developed nonreflexive accounts of learned behavior that did not presuppose any commitment to vitalism. They developed accounts of learned behavior as originally spontaneous (Bain) or random (Skinner) behavior that is transformed into directed behavior through association with pleasure or reinforcement, *independently* of sensory stimulation.

Sechenov also may have been influenced by the popular conception of the central nervous system as a conductive device, analogous to the telegraph, through which electrical energy generated by the stimulation of sensory receptors is transformed into behavioral responses. This conception of the nervous system certainly shaped the German tradition of research on **psychophysics**, the study of the relation between the objective intensity of physical stimuli and subjective sensational experience.

Gustav Fechner: Psychophysics

The German physicist Gustav Theodor Fechner (1801–1887) provided the initial link between the experimental physiology of the 19th century and the experimental psychology of the late 19th and early 20th centuries. He earned a medical degree at the University of Leipzig in 1822, but his main interests lay in physics and mathematics. He became professor of physics at the University of Leipzig, where he did significant research on the measurement of electric current. Fechner used direct sunlight as a stimulus for his studies of visual after-images, with himself as experimental subject. He injured his eyes so badly that he was forced to resign his position at the university, although he returned a few years later.

Fechner believed that mental and physical states and processes are qualitatively different but quantitatively identical. Although they appear different, they are ultimately one and the same. After a number of years of depression and physical illness following his optical injury, Fechner made a dramatic recovery when he suddenly realized how he could establish the identity of the mental and the physical. He could make the "relative increase of bodily energy the measure of the increase of the corresponding mental intensity" (1860/1966, p. 3).

Assuming their identity, and Helmholtz's conservation of energy principle, Fechner reasoned that mental and physical processes must be functionally related. He also assumed they must be governed by laws of proportional variation rather than simple covariation, given the fact of resistance in any electrical system, including the nervous system. In a series of experiments, he set out to determine the mathematical laws governing this functional relationship. He systematically varied the intensity of (auditory, visual, tactual, and thermal) stimuli, and measured the intensity of sensational responses by means of **just noticeable differences** between the perceived intensity of sensations. Fechner concluded that the perceived intensity of a sensation is a logarithmic function of the physical intensity of a stimulus. This relationship is expressed in the formula now known as **Fechner's law**: $S = k \log R$ (where R represents the physical intensity of a stimulus, S the perceived intensity of a sensation, and k is a constant). Fechner's law was

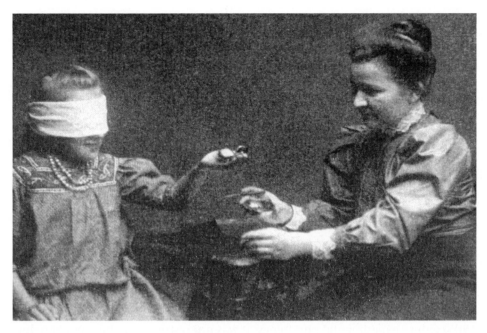

Psychophysics experiment: weight estimation.

a mathematical transformation of the ratio between the intensity of a physical stimulus and the perceived intensity of sensation established by his colleague, Ernst Weber (1795–1878), sometimes known as Weber's law.

Fechner's studies of the relationship between the intensity of physical stimuli and the perceived intensity of sensational responses were published in *Elements of Psychophysics* in 1860. William James dismissed his "dreadful" contribution as amounting to "nothing." However, many were convinced that Fechner had refuted Kant's claim that psychology could not attain the status of a genuine science, since he had established quantified psychophysical laws based upon experiments in which manipulated differences in the physical intensity of stimuli were correlated with subjects' introspective reports of sensational differences.

Because of his pioneering psychophysical studies, Fechner is often represented as having established the physical basis of mentality by demonstrating the functional dependence of the mental on the physical. There is some irony in this, since Fechner himself believed he had demonstrated the opposite: He believed that he had demonstrated the mentality of the physical and the existence of a "world-soul" (Reed, 1997). Under the pen name of Dr. Mises, he railed against the materialism of his age.

Boring (1957) called Fechner the founder of scientific psychology, but this is an exaggeration. Although Fechner did extend the experimental methods of physiology to psychology by developing psychophysics, his own experimental work was restricted to psychophysics, and he played no significant role in the institutional development of scientific psychology. However, Fechner's development of psychophysics was the first step in the evolution of a form of physiological psychology distinct from experimental physiology. The experimental studies of late-19th-century physiology were generally restricted to the electrophysiology of the nervous system, the physiology of the sensory organs, and the integration of motor reflexes. Although it was relatively easy to map the motor cortex of animals, it was much harder to map their sensory cortex, since differences in the sensory responses of animals are difficult to determine empirically. In order to develop the sensory-motor theory of the nervous system, the experimental method had to be extended to the introspective study of the nature of sensation, the historical domain of human psychology.

PHYSIOLOGICAL PSYCHOLOGY AND OBJECTIVE PSYCHOLOGY

Although German scientific psychology grew out of the achievements of 19th-century experimental physiology, it was not restricted to the types of reductive physiological explanation of psychological processes favored by the members of the Berlin Physical Society or to the psychophysical studies pioneered by Fechner. Wilhem Wundt, who founded scientific psychology in Germany in the late 19th century, insisted on the autonomy of psychological explanation with respect to physiological explanation. He called his form of experimental psychology **physiological psychology** because it was based upon the experimental methods of physiology, not because it was based upon the explanatory concepts of physiology.

In contrast, Sechenov advocated an **objective psychology** that was based not only upon the experimental methods of physiology but also upon its explanatory concepts. Sechenov's *Reflexes of the Brain* was originally titled *An Attempt to Bring Physiological Bases Into Mental Processes*. In his later article *Who Must Investigate the Problems of Psychology and How* (1871/1973), he maintained that progress in psychology could be achieved only by developing reflexive physiological theories of human and animal behavior.

Sechenov was committed to the strong continuity of human and animal psychology. He consequently maintained that the study of human psychology is best approached through the study of animal psychology, in which the basic reflexive components of human psychology are revealed in their elemental form:

> It is clear then that the psychical phenomena of animals, and not those of man, should be used as the primary material for studying psychical phenomena.
>
> —(1871/1973, p. 339)

This principle, which became the foundation of 20th-century behaviorist psychology, received powerful support from 19th-century developments in evolutionary theory.

DISCUSSION QUESTIONS

1. Try to make a case for Comte's claim that all of psychology is exhausted by sociology and biology. Do you find this convincing?

2. Mill thought that psychology was bound to remain an inexact science, and of limited predictive utility, because of the difficulty of anticipating the complex conditions of human behavior. Is psychology really different from other sciences in this respect?

3. Suppose (with Dr. Molyneux in the 18th century) that a man born blind, who learned to navigate his surroundings, gained his sight through an operation in later years. What would Berkeley predict with respect to his ability to perceive distance? What would Bailey predict? What would Mill predict?

4. According to Bain and Müller, voluntary behavior is a form of learned behavior that organisms originally generate spontaneously, that is, independently of sensory stimulation. Why do you think that early psychologists dismissed this account as unscientific? Is it unscientific?

5. Gall maintained that the 27 fundamental psychological capacities he had identified and located in various regions of the brain were distinct and independent. Would it have created any special problems for neural localization if he had conceived of these capacities relationally rather than atomistically?

6. Consider the relations between reflexive, purposive, conscious, and voluntary behavior. Can reflexive behavior be unconscious but purposive? Can behavior be reflexive and conscious? Can voluntary behavior be reflexive? Does voluntary behavior have to be conscious?

GLOSSARY

ablation Experimental method in physiology involving the systematic removal of neural tissue from live animals, in order to determine the function of the extirpated part of the nervous system.

ampliative inference Inference that goes beyond the information given. According to John Stuart Mill, distance perception involves an inference that goes beyond the information provided by sensation.

Bell-Magendie law The anatomical separation of sensory and motor nerves in the spinal cord, first identified by Charles Bell and experimentally confirmed by François Magendie.

Berlin Physical Society Society founded in 1845 by students of Müller opposed to vitalism, who maintained that all physiological processes can be reductively explained in terms of known physical-chemical processes.

Broca's area Superior region of the left frontal lobe of the cerebral cortex, which Broca identified as the location of the "faculty of articulate language."

conscious automata Term used by Thomas Huxley to describe humans and animals, in accord with his view that mentality and consciousness are merely epiphenomenal by-products of the reflexive mechanisms of the nervous system and play no role in the generation of animal or human behavior.

cranioscopy Phrenological identification of psychological faculties via the measurement of the contours of the skull.

epiphenomenalism Theory that mentality and consciousness are by-products of the reflexive neurophysiological states that mediate sensory-motor connections and are not causes of behavior.

ethology According to John Stuart Mill, the science of character. Mill believed that the social capacities and propensities that constitute human character could be derived from the fundamental laws of associationist psychology.

Fechner's law $S = \text{k} \log R$ (where R represents the physical intensity of a stimulus, S the perceived intensity of a sensation, and k is a constant).

ideomotor behavior Term introduced by William Carpenter to describe automatic but apparently purposive behavior that is mediated by ideas, based upon the prior association of ideas and behavior.

inhibition The ability of the nervous system to inhibit as well as stimulate activity; the ability of neural stimuli to inhibit normal reflex activity.

irritability The ability of nerves to transmit excitation resulting in muscle contraction or sensation. In the early 19th century, it was commonly believed that the cerebral cortex is not irritable or "excitable."

just noticeable difference In psychophysics, the subjective unit of measurement of the perceived difference in the intensity of a sensation.

law of three stages Comte's theory that societies pass through three stages of cognitive development—the theological, the metaphysical, and the positive—which represent fundamentally different attitudes to the explanation of natural events.

mental chemistry Term employed by John Stuart Mill to describe those association processes that are more closely analogous to chemical bonding than of mechanical combination.

metaphysical stage Second in Comte's law of three stages, in which natural events are explained in terms of depersonalized forces.

neurophysiological dualism Early-19th-century view that the cognitive functions of the cerebral cortex are categorically distinct from the sensory-motor functions of the lower brain and spinal cord.

objective psychology Sechenov's form of psychology based upon the explanatory concepts of physiology.

phrenology Theory developed by Franz Joseph Gall and Johann Casper Spurzheim, according to which the degree of development of psychological faculties is a function of the size of the area of the brain in which they are localized, which is reflected by protrusions and indentations of the skull.

physiological psychology Wundt's form of experimental psychology based upon the experimental methods of physiology, but not committed to the reductive physiological explanation of psychological processes.

points of consciousness Term introduced by James Mill to describe the discrete sensational elements of complex ideas and associations.

positive stage Last in Comte's law of three stages, in which natural events are explained in terms of the description of observable correlation.

positivism Comte's view that the highest form of human knowledge is knowledge of the correlation of observables.

proximate cause Immediate or precipitating cause.

psychophysics Study of the functional relationship between the physical intensity of stimuli and the perceived intensity of sensation.

punctiform sensations Discrete sensations (and associated neural excitations) that many 19th-century physiologists postulated as the atomistic basis of complex perception.

rational unconscious Unconscious inference governed by norms of rationality and logical inference, first postulated by John Stuart Mill in his explanation of complex perception.

reflex arc Term introduced by the English physiologist Marshall Hall to describe an elementary reflex system comprising a sensory nerve, interconnecting nervous tissue in the spinal cord, and a motor nerve.

sensory-motor theory Theory of the nervous system as a reflexive sensory-motor system whose every component can be characterized as having a sensory or motor function.

Spencer-Bain principle Theory that behavior followed by success, satisfaction, or pleasure tends to be repeated.

theological stage First in Comte's law of three stages, in which natural events are explained in terms of anthropomorphized forces.

unconscious cerebration Term introduced by William Carpenter to describe unconscious thought processes and employed by John Stuart Mill to describe unconscious inference in perception.

utilitarianism Theory that the right course of action in any situation is the one that maximizes human happiness and minimizes human misery.

vitalism Originally the view that vital processes such as respiration and digestion are a mechanical product of organized matter, rather than a product of the action of the rational soul. By the late 18th and 19th centuries it had developed into the view that physiological processes are the product of an emergent vital force *distinct* from physical and chemical forces of attraction and repulsion.

REFERENCES

Avenarius, R. (1888–1890). *Kritik der reinen Erfahrung* [*Critique of pure experience*] (Vols. 1–2). Leipzig: Fues (R. Reisland).

Bailey, S. (1842). *Review of Berkeley's theory of vision: Designed to show the unsoundness of that celebrated speculation.* London: Ridgeway.

Bailey, S. (1843). *Letter to a philosopher in reply to some recent attempts to vindicate Berkeley's theory of vision.* London: Ridgeway.

Bailey, S. (1855–1863). *Letters on the philosophy of the human mind* (Vols. 1–3). London: Longmans, Brown, Green, Longmans.

Bain, A. (1855). *The senses and the intellect.* London: Parker.

Bain, A. (1859). *The emotions and the will.* London: Parker.

Bain, A. (1861). *On the study of character, including an estimate of phrenology.* London: Parker.

Bain, A. (1868). *Mental science.* New York: Appleton.

Bakan, D. (1966). The influence of phrenology on American psychology. *Journal of the History of the Behavioral Sciences, 2,* 200–220.

Bartholow, R. (1874). Experimental investigations into the functions of the human brain. *American Journal of the Medical Sciences, 67,* 305–313.

Berkeley, G. (1975). *An essay towards a new theory of vision.* In M. R. Ayers (Ed.), *Philosophical works.* Totowa, NJ: Rowman & Littlefield. (Original work published 1709)

Bianchi, L. (1895). The functions of the frontal lobes. *Brain, 18,* 497–530.

Boakes, R. (1984). *From Darwin to behaviorism: Psychology and the minds of animals.* Cambridge: Cambridge University Press.

Boring, E. G. (1957). *A history of experimental psychology.* New York: Appleton-Century-Crofts.

Broca, P. P. (1960). Remarks on the seat of the faculty of articulate language, followed by an observation of aphemia. In *Some papers on the cerebral cortex* (G. von Bonin, Trans.). Springfield: Thomas. (Original work published 1861)

Carpenter, W. B. (1855). *Principles of human physiology* (5th ed.). London: Churchill.

Carpenter, W. B. (1874). *Principles of mental physiology with their applications to the training and discipline of the mind and the study of its morbid conditions* (7th ed.). London: King.

Clarke, E., & Jacyna, L. S. (1987). *Nineteenth-century origins of neuroscientific concepts.* Berkeley: University of California Press.

Cranefield, P. F. (1957). The organic physics of 1847 and the biophysics of today. *Journal of the History of Medicine, 12,* 407–423.

Danziger, K. (1982). Mid-nineteenth-century British psycho-physiology: A neglected chapter in the history of psychology. In W. Woodward & S. Ach (Eds.), *The problematic science: Psychology in nineteenth century thought.* New York: Praeger.

Darwin, E. (1794–1796). *Zoonomia: Or, the laws of organic life.* 2 vols. London: J. Johnson.

Dobson, V., & Bruce, D. (1972). The German university and the development of experimental psychology. *Journal of the History of the Behavioral Sciences, 8,* 204–207.

du Bois-Reymond, E. (1852). *Animal electricity* (H. B. Jones, Ed.). London: Churchill. (Original work published 1848–1849)

du Bois-Reymond, E. (1927). *Zwei grosse Naturforscher des 19 Jahrhunderts: Ein Briefwechsel zwischen Emil du Bois-Reymond und Karl Ludwig [Two major scientists of the 19th century: Emil du Bois-Reymond and Karl Ludwig].* Leipzig: Barth. (Original work published 1842)

Fechner, G. T. (1966). *Elements of psychophysics.* (H. E. Adler, Trans.) New York: Holt, Rinehart & Winston. (Original work published 1860)

Ferrier, D. (1873). Experimental researches in cerebral physiology and pathology. *West Riding Lunatic Asylum Medical Reports, 3,* 30–96.

Ferrier, D. (1886). *The functions of the brain* (2nd. ed.). London: Smith, Elder. (Original work published 1876)

Flourens, M-J. P. (1842). *Researches expérimentales sur les propriétés et les fonctions du systeme nerveux dans les animaux vertébrés [Experimental research on the properties and functions of the nervous system in vertebrates]* (2nd ed.). Paris: Ballière. (Original work published 1824)

Flourens, M-J. P. (1843). *Examen de la phrénologie [An examination of phrenology].* Paris: Paulin.

Flourens, M-J. P. (1863). *De la phrénologie [On phrenology].* Paris: Paulin.

Fritsch, G., & Hitzig, E. (1960). On the electrical excitability of the cerebrum. In G. von Bonin (Trans.), *Some papers on the cerebral cortex.* Springfield, IL: Thomas. (Original work published 1870)

Gall, F. J., & Spurzheim, J. C. (1810–1819). *The anatomy and physiology of the nervous system in general and of the brain in particular, with observations on the possibility of discovering the number of intellectual and moral dispositions of men and animals through the configurations of their heads* (Vols. 1–4). Boston: Marsh, Capen & Lyon.

Gall, F. J., & Spurzheim, J. C. (1835). *On the functions of the brain and each of its parts* (W. Lewis Jr., Trans.; Vols. 1–6). Boston: Marsh, Capen & Lyon. (Original work published 1822–1825)

Haller, A. von. (1803). *Elementa Physiologiae [Elements of physiology]* (Vols. 1–8). Troy, NY: Penniman. (Original work published 1757–1765)

Head, H. (1926). *Aphasia and kindred disorders of speech* (Vols. 1–2). Cambridge: Cambridge University Press.

Hearnshaw, L. J. (1964). *A brief history of British psychology*. London: Routledge & Kegan Paul.

Helmholtz, H. von. (1855) *Ueber das Sehen des Menschen [About seeing in humans]*. Leipzig: Voss.

Helmholtz, H. von. (1856–1866). *Handbuch der physiologischen Optik [Treatise on physiological optics]*. Hamburg: Voss.

Helmholtz, H. von. (1862). *Die Lehre von den Tonempfindungen [On the sensation of tone]*. Germany: Vieweg.

Jackson, J. H. (1931). *Selected writings of Hughlings Jackson* (J. Taylor, Ed.; Vols. 1–2). London: Hodder & Stoughton.

James, W. (1890). *The principles of psychology* (Vols. 1–2). New York: Holt.

Jansz, J. (2004). Psychology and society: An overview. In J. Jansz & P. van Drunen (Eds.), *A social history of psychology*. Oxford: Blackwell.

Lashley, K. S. (1929). *Brain mechanisms and intelligence*. Chicago: University of Chicago Press.

Laycock, T. (1845). On the reflex functions of the brain. *British and Foreign Medical Review, 19*, 298–311.

Lederer, S. E. (1995). *Subjected to science: Human experimentation in America before the Second World War*. Baltimore, MD: Johns Hopkins University Press.

Leek, S. (1970). *Phrenology*. New York: Collier Books.

Lenoir, T. (1994). Helmholtz and the materialities of communication. *Osiris, 9*, 185–207.

Lowry, R. (1982). *The evolution of psychological theory* (2nd ed.). Hawthorne, NY: Aldine de Gruyter.

Mach, E. (1959). *The analysis of sensations*. New York: Dover. (Original work published 1886)

Magendie, F. (1843). *An elementary treatise on human physiology* (J. Revere, Trans; 5th ed.) New York: Harper. (Original work published 1838)

Magendie, F. (1944). Experiments on the functions of the roots of the spinal nerves. In J. M. D. Olmsted, *Francois Magendie—pioneer in experimental method in medicine in XIX century France*. New York: Schuman. (Original work published 1822)

McDougall, W. (1908). *Introduction to social psychology*. New York: John Luce.

Mill, J. (1829). *Analysis of the phenomena of the human mind* (Vols. 1–2). London: Baldwin & Craddock.

Mill, J. (1869). *Analysis of the phenomena of the human mind* (J. S. Mill, Ed.; Vols. 1–2). London: Longmans, Green, Reader, and Dyer.

Mill, J. S. (1865). *Dissertations and discussions* (Vol. 2). Boston: Spencer.

Mill, J. S. (1867). Bain's psychology. In *Dissertations and discussions* (Vol. 2). London: Longmans. (Original work published 1859)

Mill, J. S. (1961). *Auguste Comte and positivism*. Ann Arbor: University of Michigan Press. (Original work published 1866)

Mill, J. S. (1973–1974). *A system of logic, ratiocinative and inductive; being a connected view of the principles of evidence, and the methods of scientific investigation* (J. M. Robson, Ed.). Toronto: University of Toronto Press. (Original work published 1843)

Mill, J. S. (1979). *An examination of Sir William Hamilton's philosophy and of the principal philosophical questions discussed in his writings* (J. M. Robson, Ed.). Toronto: University of Toronto Press. (Original work published 1865)

Müller, J. (1838–1842). *Handbook of human physiology* (W. Baly, Trans.; Vols. 1–2). London: Taylor & Walton. (Original work published 1833–1840)

Neary, F. (2001). A question of "peculiar importance": George Croom Robertson, *Mind*, and the changing relationship between British psychology and philosophy. In G. C. Bunn, A. D. Love, & G. D. Richards (Eds.), *Psychology in Britain: Historical essays and personal reflections*. Leicester: British Psychological Society.

O'Donnell, J. M. (1985). *The origins of behaviorism: American psychology, 1870–1920*. New York: New York University Press.

Pastore, N. (1965). Samuel Bailey's critique of Berkeley's theory of vision. *Journal of the History of the Behavioral Sciences, 1,* 321–337.

Pastore, N. (1974). Reevaluation of Boring on Kantian influence, nineteenth century nativism, Gestalt psychology and Helmholtz. *Journal of the History of the Behavioral Sciences, 10,* 375–390.

Reed, E. S. (1997). *From soul to mind*. New Haven: Yale University Press.

Robertson, G. C. (1876). Prefatory words. *Mind, 1,* 1–6.

Robertson, G. C. (1877). Critical notice of "The Functions of the Brain," by David Ferrier. *Mind, 2,* 92–98.

Sechenov, I. (1965). *Reflexes of the brain* (G. Gibbons, Ed.; S. Belsky, Trans.). Cambridge, MA: MIT Press. (Original work published 1863)

Sechenov, I. (1973). Who must investigate the problems of psychology and how. *In I. M. Sechenov: Biographical sketch and essays*. New York: Arno Press. (Original work published 1871)

Sizer, N. (1882). *Forty years in phrenology: Embracing recollections of history, anecdote and experience*. New York: Fowler & Wells.

Smith, R. (1992). *Inhibition: History and meaning in the sciences of mind and brain*. Berkeley: University of California Press.

Sokal, M. M. (2001). Practical phrenology as psychological counseling in the 19th century United States. In C. D. Green, M. Shore, & T. Teo (Eds.), *The transformation of psychology: Influences of 19th century philosophy, technology, and natural science.* Washington, DC: American Psychological Association.

Spencer, H. (1855). *Principles of psychology.* London: Longmans.

Turner, R. S. (1977). Hermann von Helmholtz and the empiricist vision. *Journal of the History of the Behavioral Sciences, 13,* 48–58.

Turner, R. S. (1982). Helmholtz, sensory physiology, and the disciplinary development of German psychology. In W. Woodward & S. Asch (Eds.), *The problematic science: Psychology in nineteenth century thought.* New York: Praeger.

Walsh, A. A. (1972). The American tour of Dr. Spurzheim. *Journal of the History of Medicine and Allied Sciences, 27,* 187–205.

Wundt, W. (1873–1874). *Grundzüge der physiologischen Psychologie* [*Principles of physiological psychology*]. Leipzig: Englemann.

Young, R. M. (1990). *Mind, brain and adaptation in the nineteenth century.* New York: Oxford University Press.

CHAPTER 7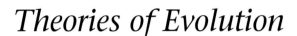

Theories of Evolution

THEORIES OF EVOLUTION DOMINATED INTELLECTUAL DEBATE IN Europe and America in the latter half of the 19th century, especially after the publication of Charles Darwin's *On the Origin of Species by Means of Natural Selection* (1859). Although religious authorities resisted, natural scientists and the educated public generally embraced theories of evolution: Such theories often represented human progress—or, at least, white, male, and Western human progress—as a triumph of the "survival of the fittest."

Early Greek thinkers such as Empedocles had advanced theories of the evolution of biological species. However, most scholars during the medieval period had accepted the Aristotelian account of an immutable and hierarchical natural order, or "scala naturae." Such an account not only sustained the popular conception of a purposive natural order created by a benevolent God, but also conveniently supported the notion of an immutable social hierarchy governed by kings, bishops, and the aristocracy. This account was generally accepted until the late 18th century and—by a good many theorists—beyond. The Enlightenment theories of social development and change advanced by Helvetius and Adam Ferguson (1723–1816) presupposed a fixed human nature, and Gall's phrenology presupposed a more or less fixed hierarchy of neurological function (Young, 1990).

Nineteenth-century evolutionary theorists abandoned the notion of an immutable "great chain of being" (Lovejoy, 1936) and developed explanations of the accepted fact of species change. They generally represented evolution as a process of progressive development toward a hierarchical natural order. Jean-Baptiste Lamarck (1744–1829) and Herbert Spencer (1820–1903) advanced theories that replaced the extrinsic teleology of a divinely created natural order with the intrinsic teleology of progressive development toward a natural order. Charles Darwin (1809–1882) was the exception. His rigorously materialist theory of evolution by natural selection treated evolution as a purely mechanistic process with no extrinsic or intrinsic purpose.

EARLY EVOLUTIONARY THEORIES

Theories of organic evolution began to resurface in the late 18th century (earlier anticipations are to be found in Leibniz and Kant). The English physician Erasmus Darwin (1731–1802), the grandfather of Charles Darwin, advanced a theory of the evolution of animal traits in *Zoonomia* (1794–1796), later popularized in his poem *The Temple of Nature* (1803). His theory was an extension of Hartley's associationist psychology. Darwin generalized traditional empiricist explanations of the development of individual psychology to the evolutionary development of species by claiming that learned associations and habits engender modifications of the nervous system that are passed on to future generations of a species. Darwin was a committed materialist, who dismissed the notion of an autonomous mental realm as a "ghost story." According to Darwin's **fluid materialism**, the electrical nature of the nervous system is the basis of life and mind. Darwin's work was published in the decades following the excesses of the French Revolution and attracted the same degree of odium as La Mettrie's *Man Machine*.

Jean-Baptiste Lamarck: The Inheritance of Acquired Characteristics

The evolutionary theory of the French naturalist Jean-Baptiste Lamarck (1744–1829) received a similar reception. Like Darwin and La Mettrie, Lamarck stressed the material continuity of animal species and treated humankind as the most complex form of animal life. He treated evolution as a natural progression from simpler to more complex forms of biological organization, as a consequence of the adaptation of individual organisms to their environments. According to Lamarck, organisms possess an innate drive to perfect themselves and strive to adapt to their environments. According to his principle of the **inheritance of acquired characteristics**, useful modifications that are made to existing organs through increased use or that are developed in response to environmental pressures during the lifetime of an organism tend to be inherited by future offspring (Lamarck, 1809).

To take a familiar example, if some giraffes extend their necks in their effort to reach the leaves on the highest branches of trees, such modifications would tend to be inherited by their offspring, which would account for the characteristically long necks of giraffes. Lamarck believed that the inheritance of such adaptive modifications explained the "transmutation" of species over time, in a linear progression from lower and simpler to higher and more complex organisms.

The principle of the inheritance of acquired characteristics played a significant role in late-19th-century theories of evolution, including Darwin's theory of evolution by natural selection, but few embraced Lamarck's own theory. This was largely because of its association with republican and socialist political movements. Political radicals treated his theory as a naturalistic justification for theories of social progress through active "development from below," particularly through the emancipation of the working class (Hawkins, 1997). Lamarck died in poverty and disrepute (Boakes, 1984).

A distinctive feature of Lamarck's theory was his teleological assumption of the progressive development of species. A similar assumption about the progressive development of species was made in Robert Chalmers's (1802–1871) anonymously published *Vestiges of the Natural History of Creation* (1844), which linked the development of species to embryonic development. Chalmers, an Edinburgh publisher, maintained that evolution is simply an extension of the growth process, which progresses toward a hierarchical ordering of organic life-forms predetermined by the Creator. At each progressive step, the embryos of a species develop a little further before they mature, increasing the general level of complexity of the species. Despite the fact that Chalmers's theory linked evolutionary development to a divine plan unfolding independently of the adaptation of individual organisms to their environment, *Vestiges* created a sensation when it was published and was subject to a barrage of criticism by both theologians and scientists (Secord, 2001).

Throughout the 19th century many scholars, including many theologians, came to accept the fact of species change, based upon the fossil record. If few rushed to embrace particular theories of evolution, this was because the (rather limited) fossil record was consistent with a variety of different theories of evolution, and the time required for evolutionary change appeared to massively exceed the generally accepted age of Earth, estimated by theologians and naturalists as not more than a few thousand years. Thus, for many, a major impediment to the acceptance of theories of evolution was removed with the publication of *Principles of Geology* (1830–1838) by the English geologist Charles Lyell (1797–1875). Lyell claimed that the forces of geological change are uniform and gradual and operate over extremely long periods of time. He estimated the age of Earth at around 100 million years.

Another work that influenced many evolutionary theorists, notably Herbert Spencer, Charles Darwin, and Alfred Russel Wallace (1823–1913), was *An Essay on the Principle of Population as It Affects the Future Improvement of Society* (1798), by the English political economist Thomas Malthus (1766–1834). He claimed that populations increase geometrically while their food supply increases only arithmetically. When populations outgrow their food supply (as they invariably do), this creates a **struggle for existence**. Spencer, Darwin, and Wallace claimed that in this struggle, only the fittest organisms—that is, those best adapted to their environments—survive and reproduce.

HERBERT SPENCER: EVOLUTION AS A COSMIC PRINCIPLE

Herbert Spencer was the popularizing prophet of evolutionary theory in the 19th century. He developed an account of the evolution of species based upon the inheritance of acquired characteristics and the survival of the fittest, a phrase he coined that was later adopted by Darwin and Wallace (the co-creator of the theory of evolution by natural selection). It was Spencer who gave the term *evolution* its modern meaning as a description of organic change and established its common association with the notion of progressive change (Bowler, 1975).

Spencer was born in Derby, England. He received only informal and intermittent schooling from his father and uncle, although it seems to have provided him with a critical attitude toward traditional beliefs and a voracious appetite for independent study. He was largely self-taught in biology, physiology, psychology, and philosophy. Spencer worked for some years as an engineer during the railway boom in England in the 1840s, but later moved to London, where he worked as subeditor at the *Economist* and as a freelance journalist. He developed a circle of friends that included Thomas Huxley and George Henry Lewes (1817–1878), the author of the hugely popular *Physiology of Common Life* (1859–1860) and *Biographical History of Philosophy* (1845–1846), who is usually only remembered today for his support of the literary career of his wife Mary Anne Evans (the novelist George Eliot).

Spencer developed an early interest in phrenology, having attended a lecture by Spurzheim as a child. He later became skeptical and turned his attention to philosophy and psychology. His interest in evolution was stimulated by discussions of the "development question" with Lewes (Spencer, 1908). Spencer defended a Lamarckian account of evolution in terms of the inheritance of acquired adaptive characteristics against the embryonic developmental account offered in *Vestiges*. He claimed to have become convinced of the truth of Lamarckian theory as a result of reading Lyell's critique of it in *Principles of Geology*.

Spencer's Theory of Evolution

Spencer conceived of evolution as a cosmic force governed by the principle of the conservation of energy, or the "persistence of force." His theory of evolution was based upon the theory of embryonic development as a process of increased specialization advanced by the German zoologist Karl Ernst von Baer (1792–1876). According to Spencer, the application of persistent force to material bodies leads to their progressive individuation. All forms of evolution involve progressive change from disorganized homogeneity to organized heterogeneity, via the differentiation and integration of the components of physical, chemical, biological, psychological, and social systems.

By this account, disorganized nebular masses evolved into planets and solar systems, material bodies evolved into increasingly more complex organic and living bodies, and primitive hunting and gathering societies evolved into complex industrial societies. The nervous system evolved from the simple forms of primitive organisms to the complex and integrated forms of the mammalian brain.

Spencer explained the evolution of species in terms of the inheritance of acquired adaptations to the environment and the elimination of the poorly adapted through the "survival of the fittest" in the Malthusian struggle for existence:

> The average vigor of any race would be diminished did the diseased and feeble habitually survive and propagate; . . . the destruction of such, through failure to fulfill some of the conditions of life, leaves behind those who are able to fulfill the conditions of life, and thus keeps up the average fitness to the conditions of life.
>
> —(1864–1867, 1, p. 531)

Only those organisms that are "well-endowed" through successful adaptation tend to survive and propagate, which ensures the progressive development of species. According to Spencer, this progressive development will continue until humanity attains a perfect congruity of faculties and environmental conditions, guaranteeing individual fulfillment, general happiness, and social harmony:

> Finally all excess and all deficiency must disappear; that is, all unfitness must disappear; that is, all imperfection must disappear.
>
> Thus the ultimate development of the ideal man is logically certain. . . . Humanity must in the end become completely adapted to its conditions. . . .
>
> Progress, therefore, is not an accident but a necessity.
>
> —(1851, pp. 64–65)

Spencer, like Lamarck, was committed to a progressive developmental account of evolution based upon the inheritance of acquired characteristics, although the two positions are conceptually independent. The author of *Vestiges* had made a case for the progressive development of species independently of individual environmental adaptation, and Darwin accepted the inheritance of acquired characteristics but denied that evolution is a progressive developmental process.

After the publication of Darwin's *Origin of Species*, Spencer incorporated the mechanism of natural selection within his general theory of evolution (and was somewhat chagrined that he had not thought of the idea himself). However, he never really embraced Darwin's most radical idea that the adaptation of species to environmental conditions occurs through natural selection operating on minor chance variations in the characteristics of organisms. Although he accepted the mechanism of natural selection, he claimed that it operated mainly on lower and simpler vegetative and animal species and that the evolution of higher and more complex animal species is governed by the inheritance of acquired adaptive characteristics:

> Natural selection, or survival of the fittest, is almost exclusively operative throughout the vegetal world or throughout the lower animal world, characterized by relative passivity. But with the ascent to higher types of animals, its effects are in increasing

degrees involved with those produced by inheritance of acquired characters; until, in animals of complex structures, inheritance of acquired characters becomes an important, if not the chief, cause of evolution.

—(1893, p. 45)

Spencer's theory, like Lamarck's, presupposed a model of **soft heredity**, according to which the mechanism of inheritance through biological reproduction can be influenced by the life history of organisms: Each new generation of developing offspring somehow "remembers" the experience of its parents and more distant ancestors (Bowler, 1989). Such a model allowed for the adaptive learning experiences of organisms to be "impressed" upon the embryonic development of their offspring.

Consequently, Spencer rejected the theory of the germ-plasm advocated by the biologist August Weismann (1834–1914), since it presupposed a model of **hard heredity**, according to which the mechanism of inheritance through biological reproduction is independent of the life history of organisms. According to Weissman (1893a), the germ-plasm is transmitted to offspring and controls embryonic development, but changes to adult organisms do not affect their germ-plasm, which is isolated in their reproductive cells. By this account, the adaptive characteristics that organisms develop in response to their environment during their lifetime cannot be transmitted to their offspring.

Social Darwinism

Social Darwinism is the application of theories of evolution based upon the survival of the fittest to theories of social change and political practice. The term is misleading because it was Spencer who coined the phrase "survival of the fittest" and because Darwin had little to say about social change and carefully avoided political controversy. The exact definition of the term remains a matter of debate, complicated by the fact that it is most often used as a term of abuse (Bannister, 1979). Many have been accused of being social Darwinists, but few have admitted to it (Bowler, 1989).

Spencer's own **laissez-faire** version of the doctrine is probably the best known and certainly the most influential. He maintained that social progress is best assured by leaving biological, psychological, and social evolution to take its natural course. Individuals should be left to fend for themselves in changing environments and suffer the consequences if they fail. He opposed any form of state intervention to relieve the plight of "inferior" creatures afflicted by poverty, unemployment, disease, or insanity, because it would impede the natural progression of evolutionary change:

There cannot be more good done than that of letting social progress go on unhindered; yet an immensity of mischief may be done in the way of disturbing, and distorting and repressing, by policies carried out in pursuit of erroneous conceptions.

—(1876, pp. 401–402)

Spencer protested vigorously against poor relief, state education and medicine, and even government banking and postal systems. He maintained that the struggle for existence must be left to work out its course without "the artificial preservation of those who are least able to take care of themselves" (1874, p. 343) and that publicly funded welfare schemes merely preserve those organisms that are unfit to survive. For Spencer, this protest amounted to something close to a moral crusade. As he starkly put it, all organisms, from the simple amoeba to the most complex industrial society (which Spencer conceived as a complex organism), get what is due to them from evolution:

> If they are sufficiently complete to live, they *do* live, and it is well they should live. If they are not sufficiently complete to live, they die, and it is best that they should die.
>
> —(1851, p. 380)

Spencer, who described his form of social Darwinism as "true" liberalism, mounted a sustained attack on utilitarian justifications of legislation and state intervention designed to ensure the greatest amount of happiness for the greatest number of people. He argued that utilitarian theory could not account for individual and racial differences, which Spencer claimed were a natural consequence of the "adaptation of constitution to conditions" (1851, p. 61). He maintained that general happiness could be achieved only by allowing individuals and societies to develop naturally, enabling superior individuals to attain true happiness through the exercise of their faculties, including their developed moral sense (which he rather idealistically supposed would lead men to recognize their mutual interdependence in society).

Spencer's commitment to a progressive developmental theory of evolution based upon the inheritance of acquired characteristics did not mandate his distinctive form of social Darwinism. Lamarck's theory was also a progressive developmental theory based upon the inheritance of acquired characteristics, yet Lamarck had suggested that "lower" or "inferior" organisms could improve their place in the hierarchy of nature through their directed effort (which is why his theory appealed to political radicals opposed to established social hierarchies).

Indeed, this was how many interpreted the struggle for existence that was believed to provide the engine of progress in the 19th century. Competition was seen as a stimulus that encouraged everyone to become fitter (Bowler, 1989). Many of Spencer's own followers represented his social Darwinism as a secularized form of the **Protestant work ethic**: Everyone has a chance to rise in society as long as they make the effort to adapt to changing circumstances, and only those who make the effort deserve to benefit (Moore, 1985). This moralistic position toward the poor and the unemployed was also shared by interventionist utilitarian theorists such as John Stuart Mill, who was concerned about the effects of misdirected charity upon the idle and degenerate. He believed it protected them from "the disagreeable consequences of their own acts" (1869, p. 304) and prevented them from learning from their own experience (Hawkins, 1997). Spencer's condemnation of the "dissolute and idle" urban underclass was an attitude common to many in the Victorian era (Himmelfarb, 1984).

Progressive developmental theories of evolution based upon the struggle for existence and the inheritance of acquired characteristics were also sometimes employed to support interventionist social programs. Advocates of so-called **reform Darwinism** argued that governments should introduce programs designed to create social conditions that would encourage individuals to improve themselves (Stocking, 1962, 1968), notably through improved public health and education (Bowler, 1989).

Spencer's own commitment to laissez-faire social Darwinism predated his commitment to evolution. He wrote an essay against poor relief when he was 16 (Hawkins, 1997), and in the 1840s served as an editor of the *Economist*, a periodical famous for its advocacy of laissez-faire economics.

Evolutionary Psychology

Spencer's major contribution to psychology was his integration of associationist psychology and evolutionary theory. For Spencer, the evolution of mind represented yet another example of the progression from undifferentiated homogeneity to organized heterogeneity, reflected in a mammalian nervous system that manifested increasingly complex modes of reaction to external stimuli, from basic reflexes and instincts to memory and reasoning.

Spencer's associationist psychology was largely based upon his reading of Mill and Bain. He treated the principle of association by contiguity as the basis of intelligence in humans and animals:

> Hence the growth of intelligence at large depends upon the law, that when any two psychical states occur in immediate succession, an effect is produced such that if the first subsequently recurs there is a certain tendency for the second to follow it.
>
> —(1855, p. 530)

Spencer was one of the earliest theorists to develop a general account of intelligence, which he held to be a function of the quantity and quality of adaptive associations made by organisms (Guilford, 1967). Since he claimed that these are a function of neurophysiological complexity, he maintained that intelligence is a function of brain size.

For Spencer, the principle of association by contiguity was the fundamental principle underlying adaptation, which he characterized in terms of the adjustment of internal (mental) relations to external (environmental) relations:

> The broadest and most complete definition of life will be—The continuous adjustment of internal relations to external relations.
>
> —(1855, p. 374)

Spencer was committed to strong continuity between human and animal psychology and behavior: He maintained that the differences between them are differences in degree rather than kind. Spencer claimed that humans and animals differ only in terms of the complexity of their associative capacities and that the higher cognitive capacities of humans are complex elaborations of their lower or more basic associative capacities, which are also to be found in animals. For Spencer, there was no fundamental difference between reflexive behavior, instinct, memory, and rationality: They were merely increasingly complex forms of association by contiguity.

Spencer's integration of associationist psychology and evolutionary theory enabled him to accommodate instincts within associationist psychology. Earlier theorists had found it difficult to account for instinctual behavior in terms of individual associative learning, but Spencer accommodated instincts by treating them as originally learned adaptive associations that are realized as modifications of nervous constitution and inherited by future generations. He maintained that "reflex and instinctive sequences" are "determined by the experiences of the race of organisms forming its ancestry" and established by "infinite repetition in countless successive generations" (1855, p. 526).

Spencer maintained that memory and reasoning are just more complex forms of association through which inner relations are adapted to outer relations, including Kantian forms of cognition representing relations of causality, space, and time, which he treated as adaptive associations inherited as anticipatory structures of cognition:

> Finally, on rising up the human faculties, regarded as organized results of this intercourse between the organism and the environment, there was reached the conclusion that the so called forms of thought are the outcome of the process of perpetually adjusting inner relations to outer relations; fixed relations in the environment producing fixed relations in the mind.
>
> —(1908, p. 547)

Spencer's account of strong continuity between reflexes, instincts, memory, and reasoning in terms of the principle of association by contiguity exerted a powerful influence on later neurophysiologists and psychologists. His account inspired Hughlings Jackson and Ferrier to develop the reflexive sensory-motor theory of the nervous system and anticipated later attempts by American functional and behaviorist psychologists to explain all forms of human psychology as more complex forms of animal psychology, governed by basic laws of stimulus-response learning identified via the experimental analysis of the behavior of animals.

In developing his account of how "complex reflexes" are inherited as modifications of the nervous system (1855, p. 540), Spencer described the forms of "anticipatory learning" that Pavlov later characterized as conditioned reflexes. He also followed Bain in extending the principle of association by contiguity to associations between behavior and its consequences, anticipating later theories of instrumental conditioning. According to what became known as the Spencer-Bain principle (Boakes, 1984), behaviors that are followed by success, satisfaction, or pleasure tend to be repeated:

> On the recurrence of the circumstances, these muscular movements that were followed by success are likely to be repeated; what was at first an accidental combination of motions will now be a combination having considerable probability.
>
> —(1870, p. 545)

Spencer's Impact

The first edition of Spencer's *Principles of Psychology* (1855) attracted little attention, and the later edition (Spencer, 1870) owed much of its success to the publicity surrounding the publication of Darwin's *Origin of Species*. However, the series of books that Spencer published under the rubric of his "systematic philosophy" eventually became best sellers in Europe and America (they sold hundreds of thousands of copies). *First Principles* (1862) was followed by *Principles of Biology* (1864–1867), *Principles of Sociology* (1876), and *Principles of Ethics* (1892), along with the revised *Principles of Psychology* (1870).

Spencer's theories appealed to businessmen and industrialists, who rationalized their ruthless financial practices in terms of the survival of the fittest. John D. Rockefeller and Andrew Carnegie justified their aggressive capitalism as the "working out of a law of nature and a law of God" (Rockefeller, cited in Hofstadter, 1955, p. 45). When Spencer visited America in 1882, Carnegie met him at the dockside. Spencer's national tour was a spectacular success and culminated with a public banquet in New York attended by notable industrialists and financiers of the day. However, Spencer's theories also appealed to the middle-class citizenry of his age, in particular the legions of clerks, bankers, and associated bureaucrats required in the new capitalist economy, who represented themselves as essential cogs in the great evolutionary wheel of industrial and social progress.

Spencer's theories were taught at British and American universities, and William James used his *Principles of Psychology* as a text for the first psychology courses he taught at Harvard, although he complained of Spencer's "hurdy-gurdy monotony." While Spencer was held in generally high regard by his contemporaries, members of the intellectual elite such as Mill, Huxley, and Darwin distanced themselves from him. Thomas Carlyle (1795–1881), who was not at all impressed, called Spencer a "perfect vacuum." His reputation went into rapid decline at the end of the 19th century.

CHARLES DARWIN: EVOLUTION BY NATURAL SELECTION

Charles Darwin's theory of evolution by natural selection was one of the most significant intellectual accomplishments of the 19th century, matching in significance Newton's theory of gravitation in the 17th century. It was significant for the same reason. Darwin's theory represented a triumph of mechanistic explanation over final causal or teleological explanation, in this instance in the realm of biology. Lamarck and Spencer were committed to intrinsic teleology within evolutionary development. Lamarck attributed to individuals an innate drive to perfect themselves through environmental adaptation, and Spencer represented progress as the necessary outcome of evolution. Darwin, by contrast, avoided any suggestion of purpose, perfection, or progress in his rigorously materialist and mechanistic account of the "descent of species." Like his grandfather Erasmus, Charles Darwin had no time for "ghost stories." Moreover, his theory of evolution by natural selection was based upon a wealth of accumulated empirical evidence, unlike the speculative theories of Lamarck and Spencer.

Charles Darwin was born in Shrewsbury, England. His father, Robert Darwin, was a wealthy physician, and his mother, Susannah Wedgwood, was the daughter of Josiah Wedgwood (who founded the Wedgwood pottery firm). Darwin did so poorly at school that his father began to despair that he would ever amount to anything. His university career was similarly less than stellar. He began studying medicine at the University of Edinburgh at the age of 16, but could not stomach watching operations. Two years later he transferred to the University of Cambridge to pursue a degree in theology (on his father's advice), although the prospect of a career as a country clergyman proved no more inspiring than a career in medicine. He graduated with a poor third-class B.A. degree in 1831 (about the equivalent of a 2.0 GPA by contemporary U.S. standards).

Despite his academic underachievement, Darwin was a born naturalist. From his early childhood days he was an avid collector and cataloguer of rocks, shells, and plants. In his autobiography, he claimed that he derived his main pleasure during his days at Cambridge from collecting beetles (Darwin, 1892/1958), which he often stored in his mouth when his hands were busy (Clark, 1986). At Cambridge Darwin made friends with the clergyman and botanist John Stevens Henslow (1796–1861), whom he accompanied on many field trips. Henslow provided Darwin with the opportunity that transformed his life and scientific biology—to travel on H.M.S. *Beagle* on its five-year scientific circumnavigation of the globe.

The Voyage of the *Beagle*

It is commonly supposed that Darwin was engaged as the *Beagle*'s naturalist, but this was not the case. The *Beagle* already had an official naturalist, Robert McKormick, who also served as the ship's surgeon, a not uncommon arrangement in the British navy at that time (Gruber, 1969). Darwin was engaged as an unpaid gentleman companion to Robert Fitzroy, the ship's captain (although Darwin's uncle had to pay £2,000 for the privilege). The previous captain of the *Beagle* had shot himself after three years at sea, and Fitzroy was concerned about his own mental stability. Fitzroy advertised among his aristocratic friends for a gentleman companion, ideally a naturalist, to share his dinner table and conversation. Henslow sponsored Darwin for the position, and on December 27, 1831, the *Beagle* set sail from Plymouth with the 23-year-old Darwin on board. The official naturalist, Robert McKormick, quit the ship in disgust in Rio in 1832, in protest against the privileges afforded the aristocratic gentleman-naturalist on board.

The *Beagle*'s scientific exploration lasted from 1831 to 1836. The primary mission of the voyage was to survey the coastlines of New Zealand, Australia, and South America. Darwin was able to study and collect biological specimens offshore at many of the landfalls made by the *Beagle,* including the Galápagos Islands (about 600 miles off South America). He became increasingly intrigued by the multitude of species he encountered and their differences in different environments, such as the varieties of tortoises and finches he discovered on the islands of the Galápagos. Throughout the voyage he collected a mass of biogeographical evidence for species change, although he had no idea of the mechanism responsible for it.

One of the books that Darwin took with him on the *Beagle* was Lyell's *Principles of Geology*, which undermined theological and naturalist estimates of the age of the earth at around 3,000 years. Lyell's geological estimate put the age of the earth at about 100 million years, sufficient to support a theory of evolution that postulated small and gradual changes over huge expanses of time, as Darwin's theory later did.

The Theory of Evolution by Natural Selection

On his return to England, Darwin began to develop a theory to account for the evolution of species, or the "descent with modification" of species. According to Darwin (1892/1958), there were two sources of his theory of evolution by natural selection. The first was the established practice of artificial selection by agricultural breeders, who developed desirable characteristics in their animals (such as high quality of fleece in sheep and large body mass in cattle) through selective breeding. Darwin noted how occasionally a harsh winter or drought obliged to produce the outcome desired by breeders, by weeding out the weaker stock. The second was Malthus's *Essay on the Principle of Population*. Darwin recognized that the competition for limited food resources that Malthus described would *naturally* ensure that variations in inheritable characteristics that were conducive to the survival of a species would tend to be passed on to future generations, whereas those that were not would not.

Darwin came to believe that the **natural selection** of variations in inheritable characteristics could explain the transformation of species over generations:

> In October 1838, that is, fifteen months after I had begun my systematic enquiry, I happened to read for amusement Malthus on *Population*, and being well-prepared to appreciate the struggle for existence which everywhere goes on from long continued observation of the habits of animals and plants, it at once struck me that under these circumstances favorable variations would tend to be preserved and unfavorable ones tend to be destroyed. The result of this would be the formation of new species.
>
> —(1892/1958, pp. 42–43)

This was the insight that was published in 1859 as the theory of natural selection in *On the Origin of Species by Means of Natural Selection, or the Preservation of Favored Races in the Struggle for Life*:

> As many more individuals of each species are born than can possibly survive; and as, consequently, there is a frequently recurring struggle for existence, it follows that any being, if it vary however slightly in any manner profitable to itself, under the complex and sometimes varying conditions of life, will have a better chance of surviving, and thus be *naturally selected*. From the strong principles of inheritance, any selected variety will tend to propagate its new and modified form.
>
> —(1859, p. 5)

According to Darwin's theory, organisms exhibit chance variations in their characteristics. They produce more offspring than can possibly survive in given environments, creating a struggle for existence. Those chance variations in characteristics that are conducive to the survival of an organism in a given environment are naturally selected, since organisms possessed of these characteristics tend to survive and reproduce, whereas organisms lacking such characteristics tend to die off and fail to reproduce.

In contrast to Lamarck's theory in terms of the inheritance of acquired characteristics, Darwin's theory of evolution by natural selection suggested that those giraffes that happened to have longer necks that enabled them to reach the leaves on the higher trees tended to survive and reproduce, whereas those with shorter necks tended to perish. The natural selection of minor variations in characteristics accounted for the gradual transformation of species over long periods of time.

Darwin's theory of species change through natural selection required that chance variations in characteristics conducive to the survival of an organism would be inherited by future generations of the organism. His own reproductive theory was based upon the "blending" of adult characteristics, according to which offspring inherit half of the "particles" that pass though the adult parents to their reproductive organs (Darwin, 1868/1896). Darwin's **blending theory** allowed for a hard theory of heredity, according to which inherited variations are independent of the adaptive adjustments made by individual organisms to their environment during their lifetimes, but also allowed for a soft theory of heredity based upon the inheritance of acquired characteristics (via the modification of reproductive particles). Darwin accepted the inheritance of acquired characteristics, although he tended to downplay its role in evolution (except in the case of human evolution), and always insisted that acquired characteristics are themselves subject to natural selection.

The most significant feature of Darwin's theory of evolution by natural selection was his suggestion that natural selection operating on chance variations in characteristics is in principle *sufficient* to explain the adaptation of species to their environments and the transmutation of species over time. In this account, there is no need to postulate any innate drive to perfection or inevitable progression. As Aristotle had recognized in his discussion of Empedocles' theory of evolution, such a process of natural selection operating on chance variations in characteristics could produce adapted species that would appear, but *only appear*, to be purposively designed.

There is no vestige of purpose, perfection, or progress in Darwin's theory. According to Darwin, evolution is an ongoing mechanistic process, with natural selection operating on chance variations in organisms in changing environments to produce constantly changing species. He claimed that the process of evolution was best represented as an "irregularly branching" tree, and cautioned against the use of terms such as *higher* and *lower* in comparing different species adapted to different environments (Boakes, 1984).

Although he eliminated intrinsic and extrinsic teleology from biological evolution, Darwin did not reject the intrinsic teleology of purposive animal and human behavior. In the case of humans in particular, he insisted that their developed intelligence enables them to consciously and purposively adapt themselves to their environments:

> [Man] has great power of adapting his habits to new conditions of life. He invents weapons, tools, and various stratagems, by which he procures food and defends himself. When he migrates into a colder climate he uses clothes, builds sheds, and makes fires; and, by the aid of fire cooks foods otherwise indigestible. He aids his fellow-men in many ways, and anticipates future events. Even at a remote period he practiced some division of labor.
>
> —(1871, p. 158)

The main conclusion of the argument of Darwin's *Origin of Species* was his denial of the independent creation of a fixed natural hierarchy of species and his

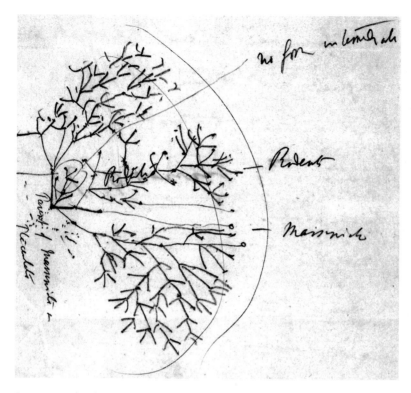

Darwin notebook: evolution as an irregularly branching tree.

claim that present species are descendants of a smaller number of earlier species modified through natural selection:

> I am fully convinced that species are not immutable; but that those belonging to what are called the same genera are lineal descendants of some other and generally extinct species, in the same manner as the acknowledged varieties of any one species are the descendants of that species. Furthermore, I am convinced that natural selection has been the most important, but not the exclusive means of modification.
>
> —(1859, p. 6)

Darwin's Delay

Darwin started work on his theory of evolution by natural selection almost as soon as he returned to England in 1836. He began a notebook on the "transmutation" of species in 1837, and probably came to develop his theory around 1840. He sketched versions of it in 1842 and 1844 to be published in the event of his premature death. Yet he did not publish his theory until 20 years after the voyage of the *Beagle*.

His delay was caused in part by the time spent on his return to England organizing and cataloguing his collection of specimens, accumulated during the voyage of the *Beagle* and forwarded to him by his numerous worldwide correspondents. Darwin published his *Journal of Researches Into the Natural History and Geology of the Countries Visited During the Voyage of the H.M.S. Beagle* in 1839 and spent much of the next decade writing a book on the taxonomy and natural history of barnacles. Another reason for his delay was the more or less constant ill health that he suffered, which restricted him to only a few hours of work each day.

Yet a major reason for his delay may have been his genuine reluctance to publish, given his justified fears of the reaction he anticipated would follow the publication of his theory. Such fears may provide a psychosomatic explanation of Darwin's later ill health (Colp, 1977), although it is also possible that he may have suffered from a tropical disease contracted on his travels (Adler, 1959). During the decades following the voyage of the *Beagle*, Darwin established and consolidated his scientific reputation. He was elected a fellow of the Royal Society in 1839 and a corresponding member of many international scientific societies. Yet he was in no rush to present a rigorously materialistic and mechanistic theory that was bound to provoke a hostile reaction among theologians, the general public, and many naturalists. Indeed, Darwin might never have published his theory in his own lifetime had he not received a copy of a paper from a fellow English naturalist, Alfred Russel Wallace, titled "On the Tendency of Varieties to Depart Indefinitely from the Original Type."

Wallace had spent years gathering biological specimens in the Amazon jungle, but had lost his collection at sea when his ship caught fire and sank on the return voyage to England in 1852 (he was rescued after 10 days in a leaky lifeboat). He renewed his research on the "question of questions" in the Malay Archipelago shortly afterward. During a bout of tropical fever, Wallace suddenly realized that natural selection could serve as the mechanism for evolutionary change and wrote his paper within a few days (Magner, 1994). Darwin immediately recognized that Wallace's theory (which also acknowledged the influence of Malthus) was almost identical to his own. Darwin's first inclination was to cede intellectual priority to Wallace. However, he was persuaded by his friends to have Wallace's paper and a hastily prepared statement of his own theory read at the July 1858 meeting of the Linnean Society. Neither Darwin nor Wallace was present, and the papers were read into the minutes of the society by its president.

The Reception of Darwin's Theory

These initial statements of what became known as the theory of evolution by natural selection aroused little immediate interest, and they were not noted as particularly significant in the Linnean Society's annual report. The publication of Darwin's *On the Origin of Species by Means of Natural Selection* the following year was a different matter. Darwin's work and reputation were well known, and the publication of his theory was eagerly anticipated (the first print run of 1,250 copies is reputed to have sold on the first day of publication). It immediately became the object of religious and scientific controversy. Wallace graciously ceded priority to Darwin and characterized the theory of evolution by natural selection as "Darwinism" (Magner, 1994).

A famous instance of this controversy was the Oxford meeting of the British Association in 1860, at which Thomas Huxley, who came to be known as "Darwin's bulldog," vigorously championed Darwin's theory against the objections to the "monkey-theory" advanced by Bishop Samuel ("Soapy") Wilberforce. In the course of his critique of Darwin's theory, Wilberforce insultingly inquired of Huxley whether he was descended from an ape on his grandmother or grandfather's side. Huxley responded that he would "rather have a miserable ape for a grandfather" than a man capable of abusing his intellect and resorting to ridicule in serious scientific debate (Bibby, 1959, p. 69). Darwin wrote to Huxley in congratulation:

> How durst you attack a live bishop in that fashion? I am quite ashamed of you! Have you no respect for fine lawn sleeves? By jove, you seem to have done it well.
>
> —(cited in Bibby, 1959, p. 70)

However, the Oxford meeting of the British Association was not as dramatic as it was later portrayed (Richards, 1987). Contrary to legend, the now Admiral Fitzroy did not wander around muttering "the book, the book," while holding a Bible above his head, but merely took his turn at the lectern. Yet, for Fitzroy, a staunch believer in the literal biblical account of creation, Darwin turned out to have been an unfortunate choice of gentleman companion to alleviate his suicidal tendencies. Fitzroy blamed himself for indirectly contributing to the development of Darwin's blasphemous theory, and five years later in 1865 he cut his own throat. In that same year Gregor Mendel (1822–1884) identified dominant and recessive factors in heredity, the foundation of the modern theory of genetics and the later neo-Darwinian theory of evolution.

In the United States, Darwin's theory was vigorously attacked by the prominent Harvard biologist Louis Agassiz (1817–1873) in the late 19th century and remained controversial in the 20th century. William Jennings Bryan (1860–1925) and Clarence Darrow (1857–1938) clashed during the Scopes "monkey-trial" in Tennessee in 1925, in which John Thomas Scopes, a high school teacher, was prosecuted and found guilty of the crime of teaching the theory of evolution by natural selection in high school. The Supreme Court struck down state laws banning the teaching of evolution in public schools in 1968, but the controversy continues (Magner, 1994). Even at the beginning of the 21st century, only about

50 percent of Americans believe that humans evolved over millions of years from earlier life forms (according to a 2007 Gallup poll).

Darwin was careful to avoid religious controversy and described himself as an agnostic. Although others were quick to identify *Origin of Species* as a materialist and atheist tract (both theological critics and communist sympathizers such as Karl Marx), Darwin played down these implications (and remained friends with Bishop Wilberforce). Although he denied the literal biblical account of creation and the fixity of species, these positions had already been abandoned or questioned by many scientists and a good number of theologians who accepted the evidence for species change.

Darwin did not deny the existence of a benevolent and intelligent Creator, only a divine role in the descent of species, and talked of the "several powers" that were "originally breathed into a few forms or into one" (1859, p. 490). But he was not hesitant to respond when others suggested a divine role in evolution. The American botanist Asa Gay (1810–1888), who was one of Darwin's foremost American supporters, suggested that God might have controlled variations in the characteristics of plants and animals to ensure certain desirable evolutionary outcomes. Darwin (1868/1896) responded that such a hypothesis was inconsistent with the evidence from plant and animal variation, a point that Gay eventually conceded (Reed, 1997).

However, the controversy generated by Darwin's theory was not restricted to its theological implications. It was almost immediately beset by a number of internal problems, and some of the most critical reviews of his work came from fellow scientists. The effects of natural selection operating on the minor variations in characteristics that Darwin postulated required a vast amount of time for the evolution of complex organisms, of the order of 100 million years. Yet calculations based upon the theory of thermodynamics made by the distinguished Victorian physicist William Thompson, Lord Kelvin (1824–1907) in the 1860s, put the age of the earth at only about 30 million years, later revised downward to about 20 million years. This was far too short a period for the operation of Darwinian evolution by natural selection (although later calculations based upon the theory of radioactivity made at the beginning of the 20th century yielded much higher estimates).

Fleeming Jenkin (1833–1885), a Scottish engineer, argued that species could not evolve through the natural selection of minor variations in characteristics given Darwin's "blending" theory of reproduction (Jenkin, 1867). Favorable variations would be eliminated through dilution within a few generations, as a consequence of organisms possessed of such variations interbreeding with organisms that were not. Jenkin's objection was not fatal, since as Wallace pointed out, Darwin could have accommodated it by postulating a greater range of variation than he originally allowed (Bowler, 1989). However, Darwin's blending theory of reproduction was dismissed as implausible by many biologists.

It was also inconsistent with Weismann's theory of the germ-plasm. Darwin did not endorse Weismann's theory, but its very appearance inclined many biologists to oppose the theory of evolution by natural selection. This was because they recognized that Weismann's hard theory of heredity undermined the still-favored conception of evolution as a progressive developmental process based upon the inheritance of acquired characteristics and entailed that natural selection is the *only* viable mechanism for evolution.

Many biologists continued to endorse progressive developmental theories, including neo-Lamarckian theories based upon the inheritance of acquired characteristics. Ernst Haeckel (1834–1919), the foremost German "advocate" of Darwinian theory, treated the individual development of the embryo as the model for the progressive development of species (as had earlier developmental theorists such as Robert Chalmers). Haeckel's **recapitulation theory**, according to which **ontogeny** (the growth of individual organisms) recapitulates **phylogeny** (the evolutionary history of a species), was based upon a teleological conception of evolution that represented humankind—or at least those white European races identified as the highest forms of humankind—as the pinnacle of evolutionary progress (Haeckel, 1876).

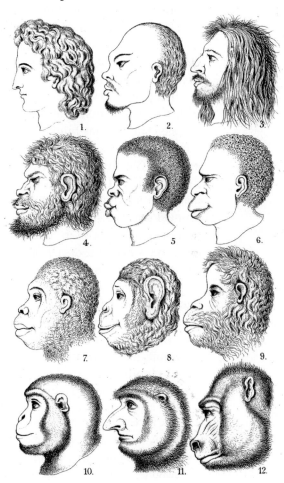

Darwin resisted such a conception (although he endorsed the theory of recapitulation), given his vision of evolution as an irregularly branching tree. Yet he failed to convince most of his fellow scientists as well as his theological critics. The late 19th century saw the "eclipse of Darwinism" (Bowler, 1983), and by the end of the century Darwin's theory was dismissed as a historical curiosity (Boakes, 1984). Most theorists continued to hold progressive developmental theories of evolution based upon the inheritance of acquired characteristics. It was only when experimental biologists turned their attention to the postulated biological mechanisms for the inheritance of acquired characteristics at the turn of the century and found them wanting that the climate began to shift again in favor of Darwin's theory of natural selection (Bowler, 1989).

Haeckel's representation of the white European race as the pinnacle of human evolutionary progress.

The Descent of Man

Darwin had studiously avoided discussion of the evolution of humans in *The Origin of Species*, although others (such as Bishop Wilberforce) had been quick to make the connection between apes and men. *The Origin of Species* contained only a single sentence addressed to the question, which promised that the theory of natural selection would throw light upon the evolution of the human species. Darwin was eventually forced to address the issue in *The Descent of Man* (1871), after Huxley drew attention to similarities between the brains of apes and humans in *Evidence as to Man's Place in Nature* (1863), and Wallace published two papers in which he denied that natural selection could account for the emergence of distinctive human characteristics.

In "The Origin of Human Races and the Antiquity of Man Deduced From 'The Theory Of Natural Selection'" (1864), Wallace claimed that although natural selection could account for the origin of the human species, the human brain had developed to such a degree that humans were able to surmount the mechanism of natural selection. According to Wallace, their superior intelligence, manifested by their ability to create fire, clothing, tools, and shelter and to form cooperative social arrangements, enabled humans to survive changes in climate and habitat. He claimed that human evolution had come to be based upon the cultural accumulation of knowledge rather than natural selection (Boakes, 1984). In "Geographical Climates and the Origin of Species" (1869), Wallace argued that many of the distinctive characteristics of humans, such as their capacity for language, logic, mathematics, music, and art, confer no advantage in the struggle for existence. He claimed that these characteristics could not have been developed through evolution by natural selection. They are so advanced of the needs of humans that they could have been produced only by the intervention of a higher (divine) intelligence (Boakes, 1984).

This proved too much for Darwin, who once again was moved by Wallace to publish his own theory. In *The Descent of Man and Selection in Relation to Sex* (1871), he argued that humans, like animals, are descended from simpler ancestral organisms through natural selection. He consequently maintained that there is strong continuity between human and animal psychology and behavior. According to Darwin, human forms of psychology and behavior are elaborations of the forms of psychology and behavior to be found in animals:

> The difference in mind between man and the higher animals, great as it is, is certainly one of degree and not of kind. We have seen that the senses and intuitions, the various emotions and faculties, such as love, memory, attention, curiosity, imitation, reason, &c., of which man boasts, may be found in an incipient, or even sometimes in a well-developed condition, in the lower animals.
>
> —(1871, p. 105)

Darwin held that differences between human and animal psychology and behavior are a product of their different degrees of intelligence. The distinctive characteristics of humans, such as their capacity for language, are a by-product of their superior intelligence, but are strongly continuous with evolutionary precursors in the animal kingdom, such as birdsong and the calls of chimpanzees. Darwin did not believe that humans are descended from apes (although he was popularly represented as having done so by his critics) but did claim that primates and humans are descended from a common ancestor.

Yet in order to explain the vastly superior levels of intelligence to be found in humans as opposed to even the highest primates, and the apparent irrelevance of many distinctive human characteristics to survival, Darwin was forced to downplay the role that natural selection played in human evolution. He suggested that there could be rapid leaps in evolutionary development generated by the inheritance of characteristics acquired in special environments that encourage their exercise, such as human social groupings. He also appealed to sexual selection in the explanation of distinctive human capacities that appear to have no survival value, likening the artistic productions of humans to the magnificent but apparently useless plumage of the male peacock (Boakes, 1984).

The *Times* of London predictably responded to the publication of *The Descent of Man* with an editorial claiming that the acceptance of Darwin's views about the origin of humanity would lead to the collapse of morality, echoing Descartes' fears about the consequences of explaining human behavior in mechanistic terms. Yet despite the controversy generated by his theories, Darwin was generally venerated as a distinguished scientist and model of Victorian propriety. When he died in 1882, he was honored by the nation with a burial in Westminster Abbey (where he is interred close to Isaac Newton).

Darwin's commitment to strong continuity between human and animal psychology may have been partly based upon his belief that nature does not move by leaps ("natura non facit saltum"):

> As natural selection acts solely by accumulating slight, successive, favorable variations, it can produce no great or sudden modifications; it can act only by short and slow steps.
>
> —(1859, p. 471)

Since evolution by natural selection operates on minor modifications to heritable characteristics over long periods of time, the evolutionary development of a species can be represented as a continuous series of variations of the original characteristics of ancestral organisms. For Darwin this meant that evolutionary antecedents of human characteristics such as language could be identified in related animal species and early human development, such as birdsong and the babbling of infants.

Yet continuous gradation within the process of evolution by natural selection does not entail strong continuity between human and animal psychology and behavior, any more than the continuous gradation between the states of molecules transformed from a liquid to a gas entails the identity of the properties of liquids and gases. In any case, Darwin abandoned continuous gradation within human evolution when he appealed to rapid leaps in the development of human characteristics to explain the large differences in intelligence between humans and even the highest primates.

Darwin recognized that strong continuity between human and animal psychology and behavior did not follow from the theory of evolution by natural selection. He acknowledged that it was possible that "certain powers, such as self-consciousness, abstraction, &c, are peculiar to man" (1871, p. 105) and tried to provide independent evidence for precursors of human language and rationality in the animal kingdom. Yet the evidence Darwin provided was rather weak. Much of it was anecdotal and intuitive and far less rigorous than the detailed fieldwork and experimental studies reported in *The Origin of Species* and *The Variation of Animals and Plants Under Domestication* (1868/1896). His characterization of the calls of chimpanzees as primitive forms of language was based upon reports by foreign correspondents, and he simply assumed that most people would agree that "animals possess some power of reasoning," since they "may constantly be seen to pause, deliberate and resolve" (1871, p. 46).

In affirming strong continuity between human and animal psychology and behavior, Darwin affirmed more than was required for a defense of the theory of evolution by natural selection in relation to man. All that was required for the demonstration of a common ancestry with animals was the re-identification in animals of *some* aspects of human psychology and behavior, such as associative learning and instinctual behavior. It was not necessary to demonstrate attenuated forms of human language and rationality in animals. As one of Darwin's eulogists remarked:

> [Mr Darwin] was so anxious to show that the moral life of man is but an evolution from the moral life of the lower animals, that he tried to explain that evolution in a false sense, as if the higher phrase involves nothing that is not found in the lower phrase.
>
> —(Hutton, 1882/1894, p. 145)

Darwinism, Racism, and Sexism

Many 19th-century theorists saw Darwin's account of evolution by natural selection as a justification of their racist views about the intellectual and social underdevelopment of non-Caucasian races. Haeckel represented Caucasians as the apex of human development, just as he represented the human race as the apex of evolutionary progress:

> The immense superiority that the white race has won over the other races in the struggle for existence is due to Natural Selection, the key to all advance in culture, to all so-called history, as it is the key to the origin of species in the kingdom of the living. That superiority will, without doubt become more and more marked in the future, so that still fewer races of man will be able, as time advances, to contend with the white in the struggle for existence.
>
> —(1883, p. 85)

Imperialists appealed to Darwin's theory in their justification of foreign wars of conquest and colonial expansion.

Yet such views were no more consequences of Darwin's theory of evolution than Spencer's laissez-faire form of social Darwinism. Darwin repudiated the idea that the level of intellectual and social development of other races was fixed by natural selection. Although he was horrified by the appearance and behavior of the natives of Tierra del Fuego that were taken aboard the *Beagle*, he was also impressed by their ability to learn Spanish and English and to adopt European habits and manners (Boakes, 1984). Despite his own advocacy of laissez-faire social Darwinism, Spencer repudiated the imperialism of Victorian Britain (Hawkins, 1997).

Late-19th- and early-20th-century theorists generally appealed to Darwin's theory in support of their *independently* held views on race and imperialism. As Stephen Jay Gould (1980) has noted, one implication of Haeckel's recapitulation theory was that "lower races" would manifest the infantile traits of the superior white race: Adult negroes, for example, would manifest the traits of white children. D. G. Brighton claimed that

> The adult who retains the more numerous fetal, infantile traits . . . is unquestionably inferior to him whose development has progressed beyond them. Measured by these criteria, the European or white race stands at the head of the list, the African or negro at its foot.
>
> —(1890, cited in Gould, 1980, p. 214)

Racist supporters of Haeckel's theory found multiple evidences of juvenile traits in the art and superstitious behavior of negroes and other "primitive" races. When the development of genetics undermined the theory of recapitulation and evolutionary theorists argued that humans evolved by retaining the juvenile traits of their ancestors, a process known as **neoteny**, racists simply reversed their position. They maintained the superiority of the white race by appeal to the greater retention of juvenile traits by the white race and quickly discovered multiple evidences of juvenile traits in the "child-like vivacity" of Europeans.

Gould (1980) also noted that supporters of neoteny tended to play down one implication of the theory: Since women are more childlike in their anatomy than men, they are superior to men in terms of evolutionary development. Yet late-19th-century and early-20th-century theorists continued to maintain the constitutional inferiority of women. E. H. Clark, professor of physiology at Harvard, claimed that menstruation exerts such a strain on female physiology that the demands of academic study would pose a danger to female health (Birke, 1986). Granville Stanley Hall (1844–1944), who founded the first laboratory and PhD program in psychology in America at Johns Hopkins University, was opposed to the admission of women to tertiary education, because he maintained that it would interfere with their biologically determined childbearing function (Shields, 1975). Hugo Münsterberg (1863–1916), who took over from William James as director of the Harvard laboratory and psychology program, argued that women should be disbarred from juries and denied the vote because of their constitutional irrationality (Hale, 1980).

Early women psychologists challenged these positions. Helen Bradford Thompson (1874–1947), later Helen Woolley, conducted the first systematic empirical study of sensory-motor and perceptual-cognitive differences between men and women at the University of Chicago and concluded that most differences between men and women are the product of social development (Thompson, 1903). She complained that most of the previous research on sex differences was based upon "personal bias, prejudice and sentimental rot and drivel" (Woolley, 1910). Leta Stetter Hollingworth (1886–1939), who received her doctorate in psychology from Columbia University in 1916, also challenged hereditarian assumptions about the intellectual inferiority of women. In her dissertation research at Columbia, she found that menstruation does not diminish the mental capacities of women (Hollingworth, 1914). Like Thompson-Woolley, she complained that common beliefs about the intellectual inferiority of women were social myths unsupported by evidence (Hollingworth, 1940).

Neo-Darwinism

The fortunes of Darwin's theory revived in the 20th century. However, the version that is generally accepted today is not Darwin's original theory, but **neo-Darwinian theory**. George J. Romanes (1848–1894) coined the term to characterize any theory of evolution that represents the mechanism of natural selection as *sufficient* to account for the evolution of species. This was the position adopted by Wallace (1858) and Weissman (1893b), but not by Darwin himself. Although Darwin did maintain that natural selection is in principle sufficient to account for the evolution of species, he also claimed that the inheritance of acquired characteristics plays a role (especially in human evolution). Wallace and Weissman, who were committed to a hard theory of heredity, denied the inheritance of acquired characteristics.

Twentieth-century neo-Darwinian theory is the synthesis of Darwin's theory of natural selection and the modern theory of genetics, which is a hard theory of heredity that precludes the inheritance of acquired characteristics. According to this theory, the mechanisms of variation and inheritance are independent of any adaptive responses made by organisms to their environment during their lifetimes.

The modern theory of genetics is based upon the work of Gregor Mendel (1822–1884), who identified dominant and recessive "factors" in 1866. Mendel sent a paper documenting his results to Darwin, who apparently never read it (Hearnshaw, 1987). He spent most of his life at a monastery in Brno in Moravia (now part of the Czech Republic), where he conducted his now famous researches on honeybees and peas. His results were published in the local *Proceedings of the Natural History Society* in 1866, but remained largely unread until his work was rediscovered in the late 1890s. However, the synthesis of genetic theory and the theory of evolution by natural selection did not occur until the 1930s, after experimental biologists eliminated support for soft theories of heredity that allowed for the inheritance of acquired characteristics.

Darwin's Influence on Psychology

Given the doubtful status of Darwin's theory at the end of the 19th century, one has to be careful in assessing Darwin's impact on the development of scientific psychology. Although most psychologists accepted the fact of evolution, not all of them accepted the theory of natural selection. Although early American psychologists were undoubtedly inspired by Darwin's naturalistic treatment of human and animal psychology and behavior, including his contributions to comparative and developmental psychology (Darwin, 1872/1998, 1877), few of them developed forms of evolutionary psychology based upon his theory of natural selection.

Early American functional psychologists often claimed that their psychology was grounded in Darwinian theory. For example, James Rowland Angell, the leader of the movement, claimed that functional psychologists were disposed to the view that human and animal psychology and behavior was "susceptible of explanation in an evolutionary manner" (1909, p. 152). However, functional psychologists focused on the intelligent adaptation of organisms to their environments rather than the evolutionary significance of psychological or behavioral characteristics developed through natural selection (Sohn, 1976). Early American psychologists did not generally embrace systematic explanations of psychological traits and behavior in terms of their survival value (a notable exception was Warren [1918, 1925]). American psychologists only developed these forms of explanation in the late 20th century (Richards, 1987), with the advent of sociobiology (Dawkins, 1978; Wilson, 1975) and evolutionary psychology (Buss, 1999).

Functional and behaviorist psychologists did advance **selectionist theories** of individual learning, according to which behavior is selected by its consequences for the organism, and often suggested that these were modeled upon Darwin's theory of evolution by natural selection. Yet such theories of individual learning were conceptually independent of Darwin's theory and predated the development of 19th-century theories of evolution. Gay, Whytt, and Hartley advanced selectionist theories of animal and human learning in the 18th century, and Hartley's theory of individual learning provided the model for Erasmus Darwin's theory of the evolution of species in *Zoonomia* (1794–1796). Müller and Bain developed their accounts of "trial-and-error" learning in advance of the publication of Darwin's theory of evolution by natural selection.

However, there are two important respects in which the development of scientific psychology in America may be said to be distinctively Darwinian in orientation. First, many functional and behaviorist psychologists accepted Darwin's commitment to strong continuity between human and animal psychology and behavior and appealed to strong continuity as justification for their generalization of experimentally identified principles of animal learning and behavior to human learning and behavior.

Second, many American psychologists embraced a distinctive implication of Darwin's theory of the evolution of species by natural selection: that evolution does not ensure human perfection or progress. Darwin claimed that evolution is a process driven by blind mechanistic variation and natural selection: It holds no guarantee of perfection or progress. Unlike Spencer, Darwin did not maintain that human evolution left to develop by itself would naturally ensure the best outcome for the human race, especially when the best outcome was defined in terms of the happiness, fulfillment, and moral worth of individuals and social communities: "We must remember that progress is no invariable rule" (1871, p. 177). According to Darwin, evolution by natural selection does not even ensure the survival of the human race, never mind its highest development.

Accordingly, American psychologists were not generally inclined to adopt the laissez-faire approach to the problems of human psychology and society that Spencer advocated. On the contrary, in the spirit of Francis Bacon, they earnestly believed that the fruits of their new scientific discipline could and should be applied to the alleviation of human suffering and the general improvement of the human condition. They almost immediately set about applying the theoretical principles of their new science in the fields of education, industry, and psychological therapy.

FRANCIS GALTON: INDIVIDUAL DIFFERENCES AND EUGENICS

Francis Galton (1822–1911), Darwin's half-cousin, was born near Birmingham, England, and came from a prosperous family (his father was a successful banker). Although a precocious child who could read by the age of 3 and write by the age of 4, Galton's scholastic record (like Darwin's) was extremely poor. At the age of 16 he was sent to study medicine at Birmingham General Hospital and continued his medical studies at King's College, London. He later transferred to Cambridge University, where he studied mathematics (on Darwin's advice) and received his degree in 1843. However, he abandoned his prospects for a medical career when he came into a large inheritance on the death of his father, which allowed him to pursue his own interests without the encumbrance of salaried employment or business commitments.

Galton had many interests, insatiable curiosity, and a passion for measurement. He pursued an early career as an explorer. From 1845 to 1846 he traveled throughout Egypt, Sudan, and Syria, hoping to discover the source of the Nile and shoot a hippopotamus upon its banks (Boakes, 1984). He explored a large portion of South-West Africa (now Namibia) in 1850, and the published accounts of his travels gained him the Gold Medal of the Royal Geographic Society in 1853. He was elected president of the Royal Geographic Society in 1856 and a fellow of the Royal Society in 1860.

Galton pioneered the scientific study of weather (he introduced the terms "anticyclone," "high," "low," and "front") and the employment of fingerprints in criminal investigation. He invented the teletype printer and did experiments on blood transfusion with different colored rabbits to test Darwin's "blending" theory of reproduction (they provided no support for it). He created a "beauty map" of Britain based upon the number of women of superior appearance he encountered in different towns.

Galton studied boredom, which he measured by degrees of fidgeting; paranoia, which he self-induced and self-observed over a number of days; and the power of prayer, which he judged not to be efficacious. He studied association, imagery, and memory and pioneered the use of questionnaires and word-association tests in *Inquiries Into Human Faculty and Its Development* (1883). He developed measures of sensory acuity, such as the Galton whistle, an instrument that produces high-pitched whistles of different frequency. He was knighted in 1909 and died in 1919.

Individual Differences

Galton's main contribution to psychology was his pioneering study of individual differences, inspired by Darwin's treatment of the chance variation of inherited characteristics in *Origin of Species*. In 1884, Galton set up an **anthropometric laboratory** at the International Health Exhibition in London and collected 12 months of data on about 10,000 people. In 1888, he created a similar laboratory in the Science Galleries of South Kensington Museum, which provided data on around 7,000 people. For a small fee, subjects were tested on a variety of physical

Galton's anthropometric laboratory in Kensington.

and sensory acuity measures: head size, physical strength, visual and auditory acuity, and reaction time. Since Galton claimed that sensory acuity is significantly correlated with intelligence (and that he had demonstrated the correlation), he claimed that sensory acuity is a measure of intelligence. Because he maintained that sensory acuity is largely inherited, he also maintained that intelligence is largely inherited.

Galton was the first person to systematically apply statistics to the study of psychological characteristics. In *Sur L'Homme* (1835/1969), Adolphe Quetelet (1796–1874) had demonstrated that the Gaussian normal probability curve describes the distribution of many biological and social factors, such as body weight, height, and examination grades. Galton maintained that many psychological characteristics, including human intelligence, are similarly distributed. He introduced the median and percentile as measures of central tendency and invented the correlation coefficient to explore the relation between test (and retest) scores accumulated at his anthropometric laboratories (Galton, 1888).

In *Natural Inheritance* (1889), Galton identified the phenomenon of regression toward the mean: the tendency of extreme values of inherited characteristics (such as the size of peas or human intelligence) to move toward the mean value in future generations. Karl Pearson (1857–1936), Galton's protégé at the University of London, developed this work, and in 1896 devised the measure now known as the Pearson product-moment coefficient of correlation. Pearson called it *r* in honor of Galton's discovery of regression toward the mean (*r* being the first letter in *regression*).

Nature and Nurture

Galton rejected the inheritance of acquired characteristics and Darwin's blending theory of reproduction. He embraced a theory of hard heredity analogous to the germ theory developed by Weissman, although he did little empirical research on biological reproduction. Instead, Galton employed his newly developed statistical tools to demonstrate that human characteristics such as intelligence are largely determined by heredity.

In *Hereditary Genius* (1869), *English Men of Science* (1874), and *Natural Inheritance* (1889), Galton claimed that "man's natural abilities are derived by inheritance, under exactly the same limitations as are the form and physical features" (1869, p. 45). He was the first person to discuss the relative contribution of heredity and environment to the determination of human characteristics and popularized the distinction between nature and nurture in *English Men of Science* (1874). He also pioneered the use of twin studies (comparing identical with fraternal twins, raised together and apart) as a means of estimating the respective contributions of heredity and environment (Galton, 1883).

Although his statistical analyses of kinship relations were impressive, the empirical data on which they were based were rather doubtful. Galton's studies of family relations between eminent professional men such as judges and scientists ignored social factors such as wealth and privilege, and his studies of stature, eye color, and artistic propensity were based upon "family records" submitted anonymously by correspondents as entries in a prize-winning competition (Boakes, 1984).

Given his commitment to the hereditarian determination of most human characteristics, Galton was dismissive of utilitarian environmentalists (such as Mill and Sechenov) who optimistically supposed that all human beings are capable of achieving the same levels of intellectual and moral development, given similar education, training, and experience:

> I have no patience with the hypothesis . . . that babies are born pretty much alike, and that the sole agencies in creating differences between boy and boy, and man and man, are steady application and moral effort. It is in the most unqualified manner that I object to pretensions of natural equality.
>
> —(1869, p. 12)

Although praised by Darwin, Galton's work was dismissed by many of his contemporaries, who remained committed to the inheritance of acquired characteristics and the possibilities of education and training. However, Galton initiated the modern debate between hereditarians and environmentalists, and the tide began to turn in favor of hereditarians at the turn of the century.

Eugenics

Like Darwin, Galton recognized that natural selection operating on chance variations in human characteristics does not ensure the evolution of socially desirable characteristics. In "Gregariousness in Cattle and Men" (1872), Galton claimed that gregariousness had been naturally selected because of its survival value in the distant past, but was now an impediment to social progress:

> The hereditary taint due to the primaeval barbarism of our race, and maintained by later influences, will have to be bred out of it before our descendants can rise to the position of members of a free and intelligent society.
>
> —(1872, p. 237)

He suggested that society and government should adopt the practice of "artificial selection" that had served as the original model for Darwin's theory of evolution by natural selection. Just as farmers employ selective breeding to promote the development of desirable characteristics (for farmers) in domestic animals, civilized societies ought to promote the development of socially desirable characteristics in humans through selective breeding.

Galton coined the term **eugenics** (from the Greek for "well-born") for this form of artificial selection designed to improve "the productivity of the best stock" (1901, p. 663). He claimed that his intelligence tests (based upon measures of sensory acuity) could be employed to select the most intelligent for the purposes of breeding:

> Consequently, as it is easy, notwithstanding these limitations, to obtain by careful selection a permanent breed of dogs or horses gifted with peculiar powers of running, or of doing anything else, so it would be quite practicable to produce a highly-gifted race of men by judicious marriages during several consecutive generations.
>
> —(1869, p. 45)

Galton proposed that "highly-gifted" people should be encouraged to breed early and regularly and should be financially supported by the government. He founded the Eugenics Education Society in 1907 and *Eugenics Review* in 1909. He established research fellowships and later a chair in eugenics at University College, London (with money bequeathed in his will). The first holder was Galton's protégé Karl Pearson, formerly a professor of mathematics. Galton and Pearson established University College, London, as an institutional base for the

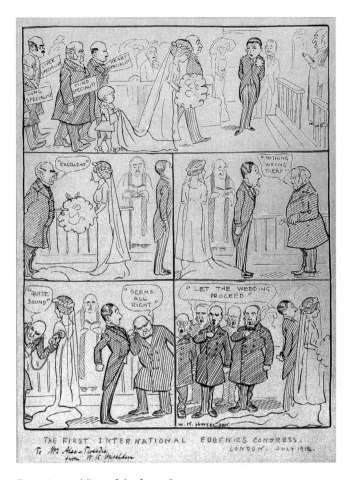

Eugenics wedding of the future?

study of statistics, heredity, and eugenics (Boakes, 1984) and launched the journal *Biometrika* (later *Biometrics*) in 1901. After Galton's death in 1911, Pearson and Charles Spearman (1863–1945) continued to promote the cause of eugenics, as did Cyril Burt (1883–1971) and Hans Eysenck (1916–1997) later in the century.

Galton's original concern was with positive eugenics, which encouraged the breeding of the "well-born" through financial incentives. However, eventually Galton and Pearson turned their attention to negative eugenics, which discouraged the breeding of the "ill-born" through institutionalization and sterilization, in response to public concerns about the overbreeding of "idiots and imbeciles."

Darwin had expressed similar concerns in *The Descent of Man*:

With savages, the weak in body and mind are soon eliminated; and those that survive commonly exhibit a vigorous state of health. We civilized men, on the other hand, do our utmost to check the process of elimination; we build asylums for the imbecile, the maimed and the sick; we institute poor-laws; and our medical men exert their utmost skill to save the life of every one to the last moment. There is reason to believe that vaccination has preserved thousands, who from a weak constitution would formerly have succumbed to small-pox. Thus the weak members of civilized society propagate their kind. No one who has attended to the breeding of domestic animals will doubt that this must be highly injurious to the race of man. It is surprising how soon a want of care, or care wrongly directed, leads to the degeneration of the domestic race; but excepting in the case of man himself, hardly anyone is so ignorant as to allow his worst animals to breed.

—(1871, p. 168)

The English biologist Edwin R. Lankester (1847–1929) avowed that according to Darwin's theory of natural selection, humans "are as likely to degenerate as progress" (1880, p. 60), a prediction that seemed to be confirmed by statistics demonstrating increases in crime, prostitution, alcoholism, tuberculosis, and "feeblemindedness" among the working class and urban poor (Soloway, 1990). Calls for negative eugenics programs were made by the physiologist John Berry Haycraft (1857–1922) in *Darwinism and Race Progress* (1895) and by the Oxford idealist philosopher Francis Herbert Bradley (1846–1924), who advocated the "social amputation" of the unfit (Bradley, 1894).

Pearson drew attention to the poor levels of health and education among recruits in the British Army during the Boer War (1899–1902), in which a nation of farmers held the mighty British Empire to a stalemate for three years. He claimed that such reduced levels of "national efficiency" posed a threat to national survival (Pearson, 1901). Galton and Pearson recommended the institutionalization and sterilization of the "unfit" to reverse this downward trend. The British Mental Deficiency Act, which required the institutionalization of the mentally retarded, was passed in 1913 (Bowler, 1989).

Similar concerns were expressed in Europe and America. The German Race Hygiene Society was founded in 1905 and the French Eugenics Society in 1912. Charles Davenport (1866–1944), the author of *Eugenics: The Science of Human Improvement by Better Breeding* (1911), founded the Eugenics Records Office at Cold Spring Harbor, New York. Programs of institutionalization and sterilization were introduced in America in the 1920s and with a vengeance in Nazi Germany in the 1930s.

Many of these programs were driven by prevalent elitist, racist, and sexist attitudes rather than scientific evidence. For example, it was generally assumed that alcoholism was an inherited mental disorder rather than a social problem, although there was little evidence for it. The social prejudice of many eugenicists against the weak, the poor, and the unemployed is plain in the following tirade by Major Leonard Darwin (1850–1943), Charles Darwin's son and president of the

British Eugenics Society from 1911 to 1928, who claimed that the aim of negative eugenics is to discourage and decrease the breeding of

> the stupid, the careless, the inefficient, the intractable, the idle, the habitual drunkard, as well as those too feeble in body or health to do a good day's work.
>
> —(1928, p. 58, cited in Hawkins, 1997, p. 230)

However, negative eugenics was not mandated by the theory of evolution by natural selection, and Darwin himself rejected such social policies. He claimed that moral compassion is a product of the evolved human capacity for sympathy and that the benefits of "artificial selection" did not justify the intrinsic evil of neglecting or eliminating the weak and the helpless:

> The aid which we feel impelled to give to the helpless is mainly an incidental result of the instinct of sympathy, which was originally acquired as part of the social instincts. . . . Nor could we check our sympathy, even if so urged by hard reason, without deterioration in the noblest part of our nature . . . if we were intentionally to neglect the weak and helpless, it could only be for a contingent benefit, with a certain and great present evil. Hence we must bear without complaining the undoubtedly bad effects of the weak surviving and propagating their kind.
>
> —(1871, pp. 168–169)

MENTAL EVOLUTION AND COMPARATIVE PSYCHOLOGY

The publication of Darwin's *The Descent of Man* (1871) stimulated intense debate about mental evolution in the late 19th century. It also promoted the development of the discipline of comparative psychology, the study of the relation between the psychology and behavior of humans and animals (and humans of different races and cultures). Darwin himself made a significant contribution to the emergent discipline. In *The Expression of Emotions in Man and Animals* (1872/1998), he tried to demonstrate the strong continuity and universality of emotional expression in humans and animals, based upon his own observations (including observations of his infant son) and correspondent reports of the behavior of wild and domestic animals, as well as photographs of actors and the insane.

From the beginning, comparative psychology was linked to developmental psychology via Haeckel's (1876) theory of recapitulation, according to which the development of the individual organism recapitulates the development of the species. As the evolutionary antecedents of human psychology and behavior were held to illuminate their nature, so too were their developmental antecedents. For example, complex human emotions were treated as elaborations of simpler emotions from

Darwin's representation of strong continuity of emotions in humans and animals.

which they were held to have developed, both phylogenetically in humans and animals and ontogenetically in human infants. Darwin also contributed to the fledgling discipline of developmental psychology with the publication of his "Biological Sketch of an Infant" in Bain's journal *Mind* in 1877. This "child diary" described the early development of Darwin's own son, William Erasmus Darwin.

A central focus of early comparative and developmental psychology was the question of the degree to which human and animal behavior is determined by instinct. Studies were often designed to investigate whether the early behavioral responses of animals and humans are modifiable by experiential learning.

Spalding on Instinct

Douglas Alexander Spalding (1840–1877) was a (London-born) Scottish roofer whom Alexander Bain took under his wing. Bain arranged for Spalding to attend his lectures at Marischal College, Aberdeen, without having to pay for tuition. Spalding later moved to London, where he qualified as a barrister and worked as a lawyer and teacher. He traveled in Europe in the hope of relieving his tuberculosis (which he had contracted in London), where he met John Stuart Mill, who was living in retirement in Avignon. The two men became close friends, and Mill later arranged for Spalding to serve as tutor to the sons of Lord and Lady Amberley at their country house Ravenscroft in Wales (the youngest of whom was Bertrand Russell, the future philosopher).

The Amberleys were a progressive and liberal couple; Lady Amberley, who was an early champion of female emancipation and birth control, took Spalding into her bed for his sexual education. Lady Amberley and her daughter died of diphtheria in 1874; when Lord Amberley died two years later, he designated Spalding as legal guardian of his two remaining sons. Lord Amberley's father, Lord Russell, the former prime minister, went to court and broke the will, on the grounds of Spalding's acknowledged atheism and materialism. Spalding was probably the original source of Thomas Huxley's theory of "conscious automata" (Gray, 1968). He died in France of tuberculosis in 1877.

While at Ravenscroft, Spalding conducted a variety of experiments on animal behavior, with Lady Amberley and her children serving as eager research assistants (Boakes, 1984), in which he varied the conditions under which newborn chicks develop (Spalding, 1872, 1873). Working with fertilized chicken eggs, he removed parts of the shell and placed hoods over the eyes of the chicks, to deprive them of visual stimulation:

> The conditions under which the little victims of human curiosity were first permitted to see the light were then carefully prepared.
>
> —(1873, p. 283)

Spalding's method of "sensory isolation" also involved inserting wax in the ears of the chicks to deprive them of auditory stimulation. His studies indicated that some responses are instinctual, such as pecking behavior toward insects and directed responses to the calls of the mother hen, whereas other responses are modifiable by experience, such as the chicks' initial tendency to peck at their own excrement (Boakes, 1984).

He also found that certain "imperfect instincts" such as maternal attachment require a critical learning period. According to Spalding, animals "forget" these instincts if they are never practiced: For example, chicks raised for 10 days without exposure to the sounds of other chicks do not subsequently orient themselves to their mother's call. Spalding also identified the form of learning Konrad Lorenz (1935) later characterized as *imprinting*: He noted that newborn chicks would follow the first moving object they experienced, whether it be the mother hen, a dog, or Spalding himself. Mill and Darwin praised Spalding's animal studies, and William James (1890) acknowledged "Mr. Spalding's wonderful article on instinct" in his *Principles of Psychology* (Reed, 1997).

George John Romanes: Animal Intelligence

George John Romanes (1848–1894) abandoned his original enthusiasm for religion after reading Darwin's *Origin of Species* and *Descent of Man* and developed an interest in the theory of mental evolution. The two men formed a close friendship after Romanes visited the aging naturalist at his home in 1874. Darwin informally designated Romanes as his successor in the emerging field of comparative psychology by bequeathing his notebooks on animal behavior to his young disciple. Romanes studied physiology at Cambridge University; but, as in the case of Darwin and Galton, his private income allowed him to devote his time to his scientific pursuits without having to worry about a profession or business. He built a private laboratory in his native Edinburgh, where he served for a period as a part-time lecturer at Edinburgh University. His experimental studies of reflexive behavior in jellyfish established his scientific reputation, and Romanes was elected to the Royal Society at the age of 31 (Boakes, 1984).

As his own interest in mental evolution developed, Romanes assembled an extensive collection of reports of animal behavior. Many of these were solicited by advertisements in the London *Times*. Others were gleaned from scientific and popular journals or communicated to him through his extensive network of international correspondents. These reports became the basis of his first book on *Animal Intelligence*, published in 1882, which was restricted to the documentation of evidence for mental evolution in animals and men. Romanes later developed his own theories of mental evolution in *Mental Evolution in Animals* (1884a) and *Mental Evolution in Man* (1885).

Like Darwin, Romanes was committed to strong continuity between the psychology and behavior of humans and animals. He claimed that there is "psychological, no less than physiological continuity extending throughout the length and breadth of the animal kingdom" (1882/1977, p. 113). Despite his reverence for Darwin, Romanes ignored his caution against talking of "higher" and "lower" species and represented humankind as the pinnacle of an evolved natural hierarchy. In his own version of the theory of recapitulation, Romanes claimed that the mental capacities of human babies develop through stages equivalent to those of insect larvae around 3 months, to those of reptiles at around 4 months, and to those of dogs at around 15 months (Boakes, 1984).

Romanes's Methodology   Romanes's own theories of mental evolution were quickly forgotten by later generations of comparative psychologists. His primary influence on the history of psychology was entirely negative, through the vigorous rejection of his methodology and data by animal and behaviorist psychologists. He was roundly condemned for his use of **introspection by analogy**, his attempt to understand animal mentality on the basis of analogies with human mentality accessible to introspection, and for his use of **anecdotal data**, based upon secondhand reports of animal behavior. Romanes was also condemned for his **anthropomorphism**: his ascription of human mental capacities such as abstract reasoning to animals.

Like earlier theorists such as John Stuart Mill (1865), Romanes claimed that we have direct and certain introspective knowledge of our own mental states, but have only indirect and uncertain knowledge of the mental states of other people and animals through inference from their observed behavior, based upon analogies with our own mental states and behavior. For example, although we can introspect our own pain when we step on a sharp stone and automatically withdraw our foot and scream, we can only infer that other people or animals are in pain when we observe them behaving in similar ways in similar circumstances:

> For if we contemplate our own mind, we have an immediate cognizance of a certain flow of thoughts or feelings. . . . But if we contemplate mind in other persons or organisms, we have no such immediate cognizance of their thoughts or feelings. In such cases we can only *infer* the existence and nature of thoughts and feelings from the activities of the organisms which appear to exhibit them. . . . Starting from what I know subjectively of the operations of my own individual mind, and the activities which in my own organism they prompt, I proceed by analogy to infer from the observable activities of other organisms what are the mental operations that underderlie them.
>
> —(1882/1977, pp. 1–2)

There was nothing inherently unscientific about Romanes's ascription of mentality and consciousness to animals on the basis of analogical inference. A great many theoretical inferences in science are based upon postulated analogies with the properties of observable entities. The wave theory of light was based upon a postulated analogy between the properties of light and the properties of ocean waves, and the Bohr theory of the atom was based upon a postulated analogy between the properties of atoms and planetary systems. The scientific adequacy of such theories does not depend upon their conjectural origin, but on the quality of observational and experimental evidence garnered in support of them.

Unfortunately the quality of the evidence garnered by Romanes in support of his attributions of mentality and consciousness to animals was rather poor. Most of it was based upon anecdotal reports of animal behavior, gleaned from responses to his newspaper solicitations or from overseas correspondents—although in this respect his *Animal Intelligence* was no different from Darwin's *Descent of Man,* and Romanes did include John Lubbock's (1834–1913) early experimental studies of ant behavior (Lubbock, 1882). These reports documented isolated instances of animal behavior that were apparently conscious and intelligent, but were doubtfully representative of the behavior of the relevant species. As Edward L. Thorndike (1874–1949), one of the pioneers of American experimental animal psychology, later complained, such anecdotal reports of animal behavior are generally unrepresentative because they describe unusual or surprising behavior:

> Dogs get lost hundreds of times and no one ever notices it or sends an account of it to a scientific magazine. But let one find his way from Brooklyn to Yonkers and the fact immediately becomes a circulating anecdote. Thousands of cats on thousands of occasions sit helplessly yowling, and no one takes thought of it or writes to his friend, the professor; but let one cat claw at the knob of a door supposedly as a signal to be

let out, and straightway this cat becomes the representative of the cat-mind in all the books. . . . In short, the anecdotes give really the *abnormal* or *supernormal* psychology of animals.

—(1911, pp. 24–25)

Thorndike and later behaviorist psychologists maintained than the scientific study of animal behavior should be based upon controlled experimental studies of animal behavior.

Romanes recognized the methodological weaknesses of anecdotal reports, which is why he tried to assemble such a wide range of naturalistic reports of animal behavior in *Animal Behavior.* Ironically, his main reason for assembling these reports was to improve upon the "works of anecdote mongers," by including only observations reported by "trustworthy" authorities. Unfortunately, his criteria for trustworthy authority tended to be more social than scientific. He included many reports of animal behavior because they were supported by "competent" judges such as bishops, major-generals, and well-bred young ladies.

Although he was an accomplished experimental physiologist, Romanes did not develop a program of experimental research on animal behavior and in fact conducted few empirical studies. He followed Darwin's suggestion that he procure a monkey for study, but entrusted its care to his sister (Boakes, 1984). He seems to have supposed that experimental studies are unnecessary in comparative psychology, since the direct introspection of mental states provides the basis of inferential knowledge in both human and animal psychology:

In the science of psychology nearly all of the considerable advances which have been made, have been made, not by experiment, but by observing mental phenomena and reasoning from these phenomena.

—(1884a, p. 12)

This claim did not recommend Romanes to later behaviorist psychologists, who rejected the introspective analysis of mental states and focused on the experimental study of animal and human behavior. However, their rejection of introspection and anecdotal evidence did not justify their almost exclusive commitment to experimentation. Although Romanes was wrong to base his theories of mental evolution on anecdotal reports, he was not wrong to base his theories on naturalistic as opposed to experimental studies of animal behavior. Naturalistic observations in open systems (not subject to experimental control) are commonplace in many sciences, and the only type of observational evidence available in many venerated physical sciences such as geology and astronomy. They have also been the staple diet of students of animal behavior from Aristotle to Niko Tinbergen (1907–1988) and Konrad Lorenz (1903–1989), who received the Nobel Prize in biology in 1973 for their **ethological** studies of the behavior of animals in their natural environment.

Although there was nothing inherently unscientific about Romanes's attribution of human forms of mentality and consciousness to animals, many of his attributions of mentality and consciousness to animals were excessively anthropomorphic. He ascribed complex human emotions such as hypocrisy to dogs and abstract knowledge of mathematical principles to monkeys. He solemnly reported the following instance of the trial of a crow, communicated to him by Major-General Sir George Le Grand Jacob, who made the observation during his service in India:

> Soon a gathering of crows from all quarters took place, until the roof of the guard house was blackened by them. Thereupon a prodigious clatter ensued; it was plain that a "palaver" [discussion] was going forward. . . . After much cawing and clamour, the whole group suddenly rose into the air, and kept circling round a half-dozen of their fellows, one of whom had been clearly told off for punishment, for the five repeatedly attacked it in quick succession, allowing no opportunity for their victim to escape, which he was clearly trying to do, until they cast him fluttering on the ground about thirty yards from my chair.
>
> —(1882/1977, pp. 324–325)

Although there is nothing inherently unscientific about a comparative psychology in which forms of human psychology and behavior are attributed to animals by analogical inference, based upon naturalistic observations of animal behavior, Romanes's excessive anthropomorphism and reliance on anecdotal data gave this form of comparative psychology a negative reputation that it took almost 100 years to recover from. With the rejection of Romanes's theoretical analogies and naturalistic observations, the scientific psychological study of animal mentality and consciousness did not revive until the 1970s (Griffin, 1976), in the wake of the general "cognitive revolution" in psychology.

Conwy Lloyd Morgan: Morgan's Canon and Emergent Evolution

Darwin had informally designated Romanes as his successor in the developing field of comparative psychology. Romanes did the same for Conwy Lloyd Morgan (1852–1936), whom he appointed as his literary executor. He considered Morgan to be an astute observer of animal behavior. Romanes had expressed some skepticism in *Animal Intelligence* about reports of scorpions being prone to suicide and was impressed by Morgan's report (1883) of some (rather cruel) experiments in which he had demonstrated that scorpions could not be induced to commit suicide even under conditions of extreme stress (Boakes, 1984). Morgan acknowledged Romanes's role in the early development of comparative psychology in his 1890 book *Animal Life and Intelligence*. Yet in contrast to Romanes, who revered Darwin and his work, Morgan adopted an increasingly critical attitude to Romanes's theories and methods.

Morgan originally trained as a mining engineer at the London School of Mines (later the Imperial College of Science and Technology). Thomas Huxley, who was a lecturer there at the time, persuaded him to study animal behavior instead. In 1884, after years of travel and part-time employment, Morgan secured the position of professor of geology and zoology at Bristol College, which later became the University of Bristol. Although he had hoped to establish a research institute and chair in comparative psychology, he was unsuccessful in his efforts, even when he was appointed vice-chancellor of the University of Bristol. He visited the United States in 1896 and lectured in Boston, Chicago, and New York. His first book was *Animal Life and Intelligence* (1890). It was followed by *Introduction to Comparative Psychology* (1894), *Habit and Instinct* (1896), which was based upon his American lectures, and *Animal Behavior* (1900). Morgan was elected a fellow of the Royal Society in 1899.

Morgan's Canon   Morgan is famous in the history of psychology for his formulation of the methodological principle that has come to be known as Morgan's canon. According to this principle, psychologists should eschew explanations of animal behavior in terms of complex cognitive states when simpler explanations will suffice, such as in terms of instincts or learned habits. In *Introduction to Comparative Psychology* Morgan claimed that

> In no case may we interpret an action as the outcome of the exercise of a higher psychical faculty, if it can be interpreted as the outcome of the exercise of one which stands lower in the psychological scale.
>
> —(1894/1977, p. 53)

Formally considered, Morgan's canon was simply a restatement of the scientific principle of simplicity, sometimes known as "Occam's razor": When two or more competing theories are equivalent in terms of their explanatory and predictive success (when they can accommodate the same range of empirical data), the simplest theory should be preferred over the more complex. In the case of comparative psychology, simpler explanations of animal behavior in terms of reflexes, instincts, or learned habits should be preferred over more complex explanations in terms of the comprehension of abstract mechanical principles, when they accommodate the same range of animal behavior. Wundt expressed a similar principle (the "law of parsimony") in his *Lectures on Human and Animal Psychology*, which only allowed "recourse to be had to complex principles of explanation when the simplest ones have proved inadequate" (1863/1894, p. 350).

Morgan believed that "a very large percentage of the activities of animals can be fairly explained as due to intelligent adaptation through association founded on sense-experience" (1894/1977, p. 358). For example, Romanes had explained the ability of cats and dogs to open gate and door latches in terms of their rational comprehension of mechanical principles (1884a, p. 193), but Morgan suggested that such behavior could be adequately explained as forms of "trial and error learning with accidental success"—as instances of the Spencer-Bain principle.

To illustrate his point, Morgan recounted how his fox terrier Toby had learned to open the latch on his courtyard gate:

> I watched from the first the development of the habit. The facts are as follows: I may premise that the gate is of iron, and has iron bars running vertically with interspaces of five or six inches between. On either side is a wall or low parapet, on which are similar vertical rails. The latch of the gate is at a level of about a foot above that of the top of a low wall. When it is lifted the gate swings open by its own weight. The gate separates a small garden, of only a few square yards area, from the road. When the dog is put out of the front door he naturally wants to get out into the road, where there is often much to interest him; cats to be worried; other dogs with whom to establish a sniffing acquaintance, and so forth. . . . He ran up and down the low wall, and put his head out between the iron bars, now here, now there, now elsewhere, anxiously gazing into the road. This he did for quite three or four minutes. At length it so happened that he put his head beneath the latch, which, as I have said, is at a convenient height for his doing so, being about a foot above the level of the wall. The latch was thus lifted. He withdrew his head, and began to look out elsewhere, when he found that the gate was swinging open, and out he bolted. After that, whenever I took him out, I shut the gate in his face, and waited till he opened it for himself and joined me. I did not give him any assistance in any way, but just waited and watched, sometimes taking him back and making him open it again. Gradually he went, after fewer pokings of his head in the wrong place, to the one opening at which the latch was lifted. But it was nearly three weeks

Trial-and-error learning. Lloyd Morgan's fox terrier Toby opening the gate.

from my first noticing his actions from the window before he went at once and with precision to the right place and put his head without any ineffectual fumbling beneath the latch. Even now he always lifts it with the back of his head and not with his muzzle which would be easier for him.

—(1894/1977, pp. 289–290)

Morgan granted that a casual observer of the dog's behavior might reasonably suppose that the dog had "clearly perceived how the end in view was to be gained and the most appropriate means for effecting his purpose" (1894/1977, p. 288). However, he claimed that upon learning how the "clever trick originated," any critical observer would agree that it was unnecessary to attribute rational comprehension of mechanical principles to explain the dog's behavior.

Morgan was especially skeptical of explanations of animal behavior in terms of their perception of "particular relations among phenomena" or as exercises of "conceptual thought," since he believed that animals were incapable of perceiving relations or engaging in conceptual thought. However, Morgan never claimed that it is scientifically illegitimate to offer explanations of animal behavior in terms of complex mentality or consciousness and freely admitted that

there is a small . . . outstanding percentage of cases, the explanation of which seems to involve the attribution to animals of powers of perception and rational thought.

—(1894/1977, p. 358)

He certainly did not believe that explanations of animal behavior in terms of "intelligent adaptation through association founded on sense-experience" should be preferred over explanations in terms of more complex cognitive states just because the former explanations are simpler, since he insisted that "the simplicity of an explanation is no necessary criterion of its truth" (1894/1977, p. 54). As he noted, the theory of the divine creation of species is simpler than the theory of the evolution of species by natural selection but is not preferred by biologists for that reason. Morgan insisted that a more complex cognitive explanation is to be preferred over a simpler explanation in terms of instincts or habits precisely when the evidence warrants such an explanation:

The canon by no means excludes the interpretation of a particular activity in terms of the higher processes, if we already have independent evidence of the occurrence of these higher processes in the animal under observation.

—(1903, p. 59)

Morgan kept an open mind about such matters, merely insisting that questions about levels of cognition and consciousness attributable to animals should be determined by empirical investigation. He was skeptical of many of the attributions of animal cognition and consciousness advanced by Romanes in *Animal Intelligence* and insisted that hypotheses about animal mentality and consciousness should be based upon the careful observation of animal behavior, ideally under controlled experimental conditions. He claimed that they should be evaluated "not by any number of anecdotes . . . but by carefully conducted experimental observations . . . carried out as far as possible under nicely controlled conditions" (1894/1977, p. 359).

However, Morgan did not reject naturalistic observation and was sensitive to the potential distortion of animal behavior created by experimental manipulation and control. Although he agreed with Thorndike's explanation of "trial and error" learning in terms of the "law of effect" (Thorndike, 1911), he was highly critical of the artificial experimental studies on which it was based, in which animals learned to escape from specially constructed "puzzle-boxes" (Morgan, 1898).

Morgan was also critical of Romanes's excessive anthropomorphism. Yet he did not object to the anthropomorphic interpretation of animal behavior per se (Costall, 1993), since he believed this was an integral feature of comparative psychology:

> Our psychological interpretations are invariably anthropomorphic. All we can hope to do is to reduce our anthropomorphic conclusions to their simplest expression.
>
> —(1900, p. 48)

Morgan introduced his canon to bring some measure of scientific objectivity to the theoretical attribution of mentality and consciousness to animals, but never intended it as a prohibition against such attributions. However, it did present a challenge to later animal psychologists to develop explanations of animal behavior without reference to mentality or consciousness. Thorndike and Pavlov took up this challenge in the early part of the 20th century (although neither were responding directly to Morgan): They offered explanations of animal behavior that did not appeal to cognition or consciousness (or at least did not appear to) and that were based upon controlled experimental studies of animal behavior. These served as exemplars of theory and method for later generations of behaviorist psychologists.

The conceptual link between Morgan's cautious approach to the attribution of mentality and consciousness to animals and the restrictive approach of later behaviorist psychologists may be demonstrated by considering Romanes's response to Morgan's original doubts about the scientific legitimacy of ascribing mentality and consciousness to animals as opposed to humans. Morgan had questioned whether an objective comparative psychology was possible. He believed that inferences to the mental states of other people on the basis of their behavior were legitimate because they could be confirmed by their verbal reports: For example, other people could affirm the pain or means-end reasoning ascribed to them on the basis of their behavior. However, since this is not possible with respect to animals, Morgan originally believed that inferences about the mental states of animals were illegitimate and that comparative psychology was restricted to the study of physiology and behavior (Morgan, 1884).

Romanes objected that acceptance of the verbal reports of other people is just another form of inference on the basis of observed behavior: "it is for me nothing more than my own interpretation of a meaning by the observable activities of an organism" (1884a, p. 379). He complained that Morgan could not consistently endorse inferences about the mental states of other humans but not animals, given obvious similarities in their adaptive and intelligent behavior. According to Romanes, inferences about human and animal mentality and consciousness stand or fall together. For, as he presciently noted, any doubts about the legitimacy of explanations of animal behavior in terms of mentality and consciousness based upon inferences from their behavior could be generalized to explanations of human behavior in these terms:

> In whatever measure [Morgan] is *on principle* a skeptic touching the inferences which this science [of comparative psychology] is able to draw as to the existence and nature of animal psychology, in that measure I think he ought in consistency also to be a skeptic with reference to the same points in the science of human psychology.
>
> —(1884b, cited in Costall, 1993, p. 119)

This was precisely the skeptical conclusion drawn by the behaviorist John B. Watson in the early decades of the 20th century: There is no need to appeal to cognition or consciousness in the explanation of either animal or human behavior. This conclusion was certainly in accord with the letter of Morgan's canon, since Morgan agreed that the canon applied to the explanation of both animal and human behavior. Just as Morgan had argued that most or all animal behavior could be explained in terms of "intelligent adaptation through association founded on sense-experience," so too it could be argued that most or all human behavior could also be explained in these terms.

Later behaviorist psychology was based upon the restrictive employment of Morgan's canon, initially as a prohibition against explanations of animal behavior in terms of cognition and consciousness and later as a prohibition against the explanation of human behavior in these terms. There is, however, considerable irony in this historical development, since part of the point of Morgan's canon was to preclude precisely the sorts of generalization of explanations of animal behavior to human behavior that became the hallmark of behaviorist psychology.

Emergent Evolution   Attributions of human forms of mentality and consciousness to animals by comparative psychologists were generally based upon the assumption of strong continuity between human and animal psychology and behavior. Romanes, like Darwin, maintained that evolutionary precursors of the psychology and behavior of humans, such as attenuated forms of the perception of relations, abstract reasoning, and language, could be found in animals. Yet Morgan's canon was based upon the assumption that there may be strong *discontinuity* between human and animal psychology and behavior. According to Morgan, certain forms of human psychology and behavior, such as abstract thought or behavior based upon means-ends reasoning, may not be identifiable *in any form or to any degree* in animals, since no animal may have reached the level of evolutionary development required for the emergence of these psychological and behavioral capacities. Although Morgan constantly stressed that theoretical disputes about animal mentality and consciousness should be determined by empirical and experimental research, and had no problem attributing consciousness to animals, he believed that animals are incapable of even attenuated forms of abstract thought and behavior based upon means-end reasoning. He denied that "any animals have reached that stage of mental evolution at which they are even incipiently rational" (1894/1977, p. 377).

Morgan pointed out that this (tentative) conclusion was entirely consistent with his canon:

> It is clear that any animal may be at a state where certain higher faculties have not yet been evolved from their lower precursors; and hence we are logically bound not to assume the existence of these higher faculties until good reasons have been shown for such existence.
>
> —(1894/1977, p. 59)

Morgan's own skeptical doubts about the explanation of animal behavior in terms of human capacities such as abstract thought and means-end reasoning were predicated on the assumption that *humans have these capacities but animals do not.* He claimed that if the evidence did not support the attribution of even attenuated forms of abstract thought or means-end reasoning to animals, then we should abandon the assumption of strong continuity and recognize that there may be a "radical difference" between the psychology and behavior of humans and animals:

> Are there apparent breaches of continuity in mental development? I am disposed to answer that such apparent breaches there are. The step from mere sentience to consentience probably involved such a breach or new departure in the development curve. The step from consentience, or sense-experience, to reflection and thought certainly involves, in my judgement such a new departure. . . .
>
> If the dividing line between sense-experience and reflection is to be drawn between the lower animals and man, then we may say that there is a breach of

continuity of development at this stage of evolution analogous to the breach of continuity between the organic and inorganic stages of development.

—(1894/1977, pp. 354–355)

Morgan claimed that some human capacities, such as the perception of relations and abstract thought, are not to be found in animals, even in incipient or attenuated form. He did not deny that such capacities are products of evolution, but maintained that animals had not reached a stage of evolutionary development in which these capacities had emerged.

Morgan's view that distinctive human capacities such as the perception of relations and abstract thought are forms of psychology that emerge at more complex levels of biological organization and development, which came to be known as **emergent evolutionism**, was the evolutionary analogue of Mill's principle of mental chemistry. There was nothing especially radical about Morgan's view, which, as he correctly maintained (and Darwin had earlier acknowledged) was entirely consistent with the theory of evolution by natural selection.

While he acknowledged continuities in reflexive behavior, instinct, and habit learning between humans and animals, Morgan believed it was premature to assume that animals had reached a stage of evolution in which capacities such as the perception of relations and abstract thought had emerged. For Morgan, this meant that although some forms of explanation in terms of associative processes could be applied to both animal and human behavior, some forms of explanation in terms of cognition and consciousness could be applied only to human behavior. Some human behavior but no animal behavior could be explained in terms of the perception of relations and abstract thought.

This is precisely what was denied by later generations of animal and behaviorist psychologists, who remained committed to the principle of strong continuity. Yet while later biologists and animal psychologists embraced the principle of strong continuity advocated by Romanes and Darwin, they *reversed* the explanatory direction of comparative psychology. Instead of following Romanes and Darwin in trying to explain animal psychology and behavior as attenuated approximations of the highest forms of human cognition and consciousness, later biologists and animal and behaviorist psychologists followed Spencer in explaining all human psychology and behavior in terms of the elaboration of basic associative and reflexive processes to be found at even the lowest levels of animal life.

Jacques Loeb (1859–1924), professor of biology at the University of Chicago, who taught Watson biology and physiology, tried to account for all forms of psychology and behavior in terms of basic associative processes. He maintained that the higher cognitive capacities of humans and animals are elaborations of associative memory, which is itself an elaboration of more basic associative mechanisms underlying reflexes and tropisms (the automatic, mechanical orientation of plants and animals to light and gravity). It was this type of associative theory that was generalized to the explanation of all human behavior by later behaviorist psychologists, on the basis of experimental studies of the behavior of cats, dogs, rats, and pigeons.

STIMULUS-RESPONSE PSYCHOLOGY

This was the legacy for early-20th-century psychology of the debates about mental evolution within the emerging discipline of comparative psychology. Although the theory of evolution by natural selection did not mandate commitment to strong continuity between human and animal psychology and behavior, this was the position adopted by most 20th-century functionalist and behaviorist psychologists.

This commitment was reinforced by the common commitment to the strong continuity between higher cognitive and lower sensory-motor reflexive processes presupposed by the sensory-motor theory of the nervous system. When every cognitive function was held to be sensory-motor in nature, it was natural to presume that human cognitive functions were merely elaborations of the basic sensory-motor functions to be found in animals.

This reinforcement was not accidental or unidirectional. Spencer's commitment to the strong continuity of the sensory-motor theory of the nervous system shaped his distinctive conception of evolutionary psychology, with its increasingly more complex levels of association. And neurophysiologists such as John Hughlings Jackson (who was directly influenced by Spencer) embraced the sensory-motor theory of the nervous system because of their commitment to the theory of evolution:

> If the doctrine of evolution be true, all nervous centers must be of sensory-motor constitution. *A priori*, it seems reasonable to suppose that, if the highest centers have the same composition as the lower, being, like the lower made up of cells and fibres, they have also the same constitution.
>
> —(Jackson, 1931, 2, p. 63)

These two commitments provided the conceptual foundation for the forms of stimulus-response psychology based upon principles of associative learning that dominated American psychology in the first half of the 20th century. Morgan's reasonable position that some but not all human behavior could be explained in terms of the principles of animal psychology was uniformly rejected by behaviorist psychologists and only resurrected in American psychology after the cognitive revolution of the 1950s. It was, however, the position adopted by Wilhelm Wundt, who founded the discipline of scientific psychology in Germany in the late 19th century.

DISCUSSION QUESTIONS

1. Lamarck and Spencer replaced the extrinsic teleology of a divinely created natural order with the intrinsic teleology of progressive evolutionary development toward a natural order. Is an intrinsic teleological account any more plausible than an extrinsic teleological account?

2. Spencer believed that his form of laissez-faire social Darwinism followed from his theory of evolution based upon the inheritance of acquired characteristics and natural selection. Others, including Darwin, disputed this. Do the principles of the inheritance of acquired characteristics and natural selection have any implications for social policy?

3. Is there really no vestige of purpose, perfection, or progress in Darwin's theory of evolution by natural selection? Is there really no justification for talking about human beings as higher than earthworms?

4. Wallace claimed that distinctively human characteristics such as capacities for mathematics, music, and art could not be explained as a product of natural selection, since they confer no advantage in the struggle for existence. Can such characteristics be explained in terms of the theory of natural selection?

5. Modern genetics and medical science offer far greater possibilities for positive and negative eugenics than could have been envisioned in Galton's time. Have the moral issues remained the same? What would Darwin have thought?

6. Morgan claimed that certain human capacities such as the perception of relations and abstract reasoning are strongly discontinuous with the capacities of other animals. Do you think his position was consistent with the theory of evolution by natural selection and with what was known about the nervous system at the end of the 19th century? Do you think there are human cognitive capacities that cannot be attributed to animals in even incipient form?

GLOSSARY

anecdotal data Data based upon secondhand reports.

anthropometric laboratory Galton's laboratory for the measurement of human characteristics such as sensory acuity and reaction time.

anthropomorphism Ascription of human mental capacities such as abstract reasoning to animals.

blending theory Darwin's theory of reproduction, according to which offspring inherit half of the particles that pass through the adult parents to their reproductive organs.

emergent evolutionism Theory that human capacities such as the perception of relations and abstract thought are distinctive forms of human psychology that emerge at more complex levels of biological organization and development.

ethology Study of the behavior of animals in their natural environment.

eugenics Galton's term (from Greek for "well-born") for programs of artificial selection that encourage or promote the breeding of the "highly gifted" and discourage or prevent the breeding of "idiots and imbeciles."

fluid materialism Theory that the electrical nature of the nervous system is the basis of life and mind.

hard heredity Theory of heredity according to which the mechanism of inheritance through biological reproduction is independent of the life history of organisms.

inheritance of acquired characteristics Doctrine that useful modifications that are made to existing organs through increased use or that are developed in response to environmental pressures during the lifetime of an organism tend to be inherited by future offspring.

introspection by analogy The attempt to understand animal mentality on the basis of analogies with human mentality accessible to introspection.

laissez-faire In economic theory, the doctrine (from French for "leave to do") that governments should not intervene in the market. In Spencer's theory of evolution, the doctrine that government should not intervene to alleviate the condition of the poor, sick, and unemployed and that societal progress is best assured by leaving biological, psychological, and social evolution to take its natural course.

natural selection The selection of variations in inheritable characteristics that are conducive to the survival of a species through the struggle for existence.

neo-Darwinian theory Theory of evolution that represents the mechanism of natural selection as sufficient to account for the evolution of species.

neoteny Theory that humans evolved by retaining the juvenile traits of their ancestors.

ontogeny The growth of individual organisms.

phylogeny The evolutionary history of a species.

Protestant work ethic Doctrine that everyone has a chance to rise in society as long as they make the effort to adapt to changing circumstances and that only those who make the effort deserve to benefit.

recapitulation theory Ernst Haeckel's theory that ontogeny recapitulates phylogeny.

reform Darwinism Doctrine that governments should introduce programs designed to create social conditions that encourage individuals to improve themselves (such as improved public health and education).

selectionist theory Theory of individual learning according to which behavior is selected via its consequences for the organism.

social Darwinism The application of theories of evolution based upon the survival of the fittest to theories of social change and political practice.

soft heredity Theory of heredity according to which the mechanism of inheritance through biological reproduction can be influenced by the life history of organisms.

struggle for existence Phrase coined by Spencer to describe competition between members of a population for limited food resources.

REFERENCES

Adler, S. (1959). Darwin's illness. *Nature, 184,* 1102–1103.

Angell, J. R. (1909). The influence of Darwin on psychology. *Psychological Review, 16,* 152–169.

Bannister, R. C. (1979). *Social Darwinism: Science and myth in Anglo-American thought.* Philadelphia: Temple University Press.

Bibby, C. (1959). *T. H. Huxley: Scientist, humanist and educator.* London: Watts.

Birke, L. (1986). *Women, feminism, and biology.* New York: Methuen.

Boakes, R. (1984). *From Darwin to behaviorism: Psychology and the minds of animals.* Cambridge: Cambridge University Press.

Bowler, P. J. (1975). The changing meaning of evolution. *Journal of the History of Ideas, 36,* 106–109.

Bowler, P. J. (1983). *The eclipse of Darwinism: Anti-Darwinian evolution theories in the decades around 1900.* Baltimore: Johns Hopkins University Press.

Bowler, P. J. (1989). *The Mendelian revolution: The emergence of hereditarian concepts in modern science and society.* London: Athlone Press.

Bradley, F. H. (1894). Some remarks on punishment. *International Journal of Ethics, 4,* 269–84.

Buss, D. M. (1999). *Evolutionary psychology: The new science of the mind.* Boston: Allyn & Bacon.

Chalmers, R. (1844). *Vestiges of the natural history of creation.* London: Churchill.

Clark, R. W. (1986). *The survival of Charles Darwin.* New York: Avon.

Colp, R., Jr. (1977). *To be an invalid: The illness of Charles Darwin.* Chicago: University of Chicago Press.

Costall, A. (1993). How Lloyd Morgan's canon backfired. *Journal of the History of the Behavioral Sciences, 29,* 113–122.

Darwin, C. (1859). *On the origin of species by means of natural selection.* London: John Murray.

Darwin, C. (1871). *The descent of man and selection in relation to sex.* London: John Murray.

Darwin, C. (1877). Biographical sketch of an infant. *Mind, 2,* 258–294.

Darwin, C. (1896). *Variation of animals and plants under domestication* (Vols. 1–2). New York: Appleton. (Original work published 1868)

Darwin, C. (1958). *The autobiography of Charles Darwin and selected letters* (F. Darwin, Ed.). New York: Dover. (Original work published 1892)

Darwin, C. (1998). *The expression of the emotions in man and animals.* New York: Oxford University Press. (Original work published 1872)

Darwin, E. (1794–1796). *Zoonomia: Or, the laws of organic life* (Vols. 1–2). London: Johnson.

Darwin, L. (1928). *What is eugenics?* London: Murray.

Davenport, C. (1911). *Eugenics: The science of human improvement by better breeding.*

Dawkins, R. (1978). *The selfish gene.* Oxford: Oxford University Press.

Galton, F. (1869). *Hereditary genius.* London: Macmillan.

Galton, F. (1872). Gregariousness in cattle and men. *Macmillan's Magazine, 23,* 357.

Galton, F. (1874). *English men of science: Their nature and nurture.* London: Macmillan.

Galton, F. (1883). *Inquiries into human faculty and its development.* London: Macmillan.

Galton, F. (1888). Co-relations and their measurement: Chiefly from anthropometric data. *Proceedings of the Royal Society, 45,* 135–145.

Galton, F. (1889). *Natural inheritance.* London: Macmillan.

Galton, F. (1901). The possible improvement of the human breed under the existing conditions of law and sentiment. *Nature, 64,* 659–665.

Gould, S. J. (1980). *Ever since Darwin.* New York: Penguin.

Gray, P. H. (1968). Prerequisite to an analysis of behaviorism: The conscious automaton theory from Spalding to William James. *Journal of the History of the Behavioral Sciences, 4,* 365–376.

Griffin, D. R. (1976). *The question of animal awareness: Evolutionary continuity of mental experience.* New York: Rockefeller University Press.

Gruber, J. W. (1969). Who was the Beagle's naturalist? *British Journal of the History of Science, 4,* 266–282.

Guilford, J. P. (1967). *The nature of human intelligence.* New York: McGraw-Hill.

Haeckel, E. (1876). *The history of creation* (Vols. 1–2). New York: Appleton.

Haeckel, E. (1883). *The pedigree of man and other essays.* London: Freethought.

Hale, M. (1980). *Human science and order: Hugo Münsterberg and the origins of applied psychology.* Philadelphia, PA: Temple University Press.

Hawkins, M. (1997). *Social Darwinism in European and American thought, 1860–1945.* Cambridge: Cambridge University Press.

Haycraft, J. B. (1895). *Darwinism and race progress.* London: Swan Sonnenschein.

Hearnshaw, L. S. (1987). *The shaping of modern psychology.* London: Routledge.

Himmelfarb, G. (1984). *The idea of poverty: England in the early industrial age.* London: Faber & Faber.

Hofstadter, R. (1955). *Social Darwinism in American thought.* Boston: Beacon Press.

Hollingworth, L. S. (1914). *Functional periodicity.* Contributions to Education, No. 69. New York: Columbia University Press.

Hollingworth, L. S. (1940). *Public addresses.* Lancaster, PA: Science Press.

Hutton, R. H. (1894). Charles Darwin. In R. H. Hutton (Ed.), *Criticisms of contemporary thought and thinkers: Selected papers from the Spectator* (Vol. 2). London: Macmillan. (Original work published 1882)

Huxley, T. (1863). *Evidence as to man's place in nature.* London: Williams & Norgate.

Jackson, H. (1931). *Selected writings of Hughlings Jackson* (J. Taylor, Ed.; Vols. 1–2). London: Hodder & Stoughton.

James, W. (1890). *Principles of psychology.* New York: Holt.

Jenkin, F. (1867). The origin of species. *North British Review, 46,* 277–318.

Lamarck, J-B. (1809). *Philosophie zoologique* (H. Eliot, Trans.). London: Macmillan.

Lankester, E. R. (1880) *Degeneration: A chapter in Darwinism.* London: Macmillan.

Lorenz, K. (1935). Der Kumpan in der Umwelt des Vegels. *Journal of Ornithology, 83,* 137–213.

Lovejoy, A. O. (1936). *The great chain of being.* Harvard: Harvard University Press.

Lubbock, J. (1882). *Ants, bees and wasps: A record of observations on the habits of social hymenoptera.* London: Kegan Paul, Trench.

Lyell, C. (1969). *Principles of geology, being an attempt to explain the former changes of the earth's surface by reference to causes now in operation.* New York: Johnson Reprint. (Original work published 1830–1838)

Magner, L. S. (1994). *A history of the life sciences.* New York: Marcel Dekker.

Malthus, T. (1914). *An essay on the principle of population as it affects the future improvement of society.* New York: Dutton. (Original work published 1798)

Mendel, G. (1866). Experiments in plant hybridization. *Proceedings of the Natural History Society of Brno, 4,* 3–47.

Mill, J. S. (1979). *An examination of Sir William Hamilton's philosophy and of the principal philosophical questions discussed in his writings* (J. M. Robson, Ed.). Toronto: University of Toronto Press. (Original work published 1865)

Mill, J. S. (1985). *The subjection of women.* London: Dent. (Original work published 1869)

Moore, J. R. (1985). Herbert Spencer's henchmen: The evolution of Protestant liberals in late-nineteenth-century America. In J. Durant (Ed.), *Darwinism and divinity.* Oxford: Blackwell.

Morgan, C. L. (1883). Suicide of scorpions. *Nature, 27,* 313–314.

Morgan, C. L. (1884). On instinct. *Nature, 29,* 370–374.

Morgan, C. L. (1890). *Animal life and intelligence.* London: Edward Arnold.

Morgan, C. L. (1896). *Habit and instinct.* London: Edward Arnold.

Morgan, C. L. (1898). Review of *Animal Intelligence* by E. L. Thorndike. *Nature, 58,* 249–250.

Morgan, C. L. (1900). *Animal behavior.* London: Edward Arnold.

Morgan, C. L. (1903). *Introduction to comparative psychology* (2nd ed.). London: Walter Scott.

Morgan, C. L. (1977). *Introduction to comparative psychology*. In D. N. Robinson (Ed.), *Significant contributions to the history of psychology, 1750–1920*. Series D: *Comparative psychology*. Vol. 2. Washington, DC: University Publications of America. (Original work published 1894)

Pearson, K. (1901). *National life from the standpoint of science*. London: Black.

Quetelet, L. A. (1969). *A treatise on man and the development of his faculties*. A reproduction of the English translation of 1842. Gainesville, FL: Scholars' Facsimiles & Reprints. (Original work published 1835)

Reed, E. S. (1997). *From soul to mind*. New Haven, CT: Yale University Press.

Richards, R. J. (1987). *Darwin and the emergence of evolutionary theories of mind and behavior*. Chicago: University of Chicago Press.

Romanes, G. J. (1884a). *Mental evolution in animals*. New York: Appleton.

Romanes, G. J. (1884b). Mr. Lloyd Morgan on instinct. *Nature, 29,* 379–381.

Romanes, G. J. (1885). *Mental evolution in man*. New York: Appleton.

Romanes, G. J. (1977). *Animal intelligence*. In D. N. Robinson (Ed.), *Significant contributions to the history of psychology, 1750–1920*. Series A: *Orientations*. Vol. 7. Washington, DC: University Publications of America. (Original work published 1882)

Secord, J. A. (2001). *Victorian sensation: The extraordinary publication, reception and secret authorship of vestiges of the natural history of creation*. Chicago: University of Chicago Press.

Shields, S. A. (1975). Functionalism, Darwinism, and the psychology of women: A study in social myth. *American Psychologist, 30,* 739–754.

Sohn, D. (1976). Two concepts of adaptation: Darwin and psychology's. *Journal of the History of the Behavioral Sciences, 12,* 367–375.

Soloway, R. (1990). *Demography and degeneration*. Chapel Hill: University of North Carolina Press.

Spalding, D. A. (1872). On instinct. *Nature, 6,* 485–486.

Spalding, D. A. (1873). Instinct. With original observations on young animals. *Macmillan's Magazine, 27,* 282–293.

Spencer, H. (1851). *Social statics, or, the conditions essential to human happiness*. London: John Chapman.

Spencer, H. (1855). *Principles of psychology*. London: Longmans.

Spencer, H. (1864–1867). *The principles of biology* (Vols. 1–2). London: Williams & Norgate.

Spencer, H. (1870). *Principles of psychology* (2nd ed.). London: Longmans.

Spencer, H. (1873). *The study of sociology*. London: Kegan Paul.

Spencer, H. (1876). *The principles of sociology*. London: Williams & Norgate.

Spencer, H. (1893). *The inadequacy of natural selection*. London: Williams & Norgate.

Spencer, H. (1908). *The life and letters of Herbert Spencer* (David Duncan, Ed.). London: Williams & Norgate.

Stocking, G. W., Jr. (1962). Lamarckianism in American social science. *Journal of the History of Ideas, 23,* 239–256.

Stocking, G. W., Jr. (1968). *Race, culture and evolution.* New York: Free Press.

Thompson, H. B. (1903). *The mental traits of sex.* Chicago: University of Chicago Press.

Thorndike, E. B. (1911). *Animal intelligence.* New York: Macmillan.

Wallace, A. R. (1858). On the tendency of varieties to depart indefinitely from the original type. *Proceedings of the Linnean Society, 3,* 53–63.

Wallace, A. R. (1864). The origin of human races and the antiquity of man deduced from "the theory of natural selection." *Anthropological Review, 2,* 158–187.

Wallace, A. R. (1869). Geological climates and the origin of species. *Quarterly Review, 126,* 359–394.

Warren, H. C. (1918). Mechanism vs. vitalism in the domain of psychology. *Philosophical Review, 27,* 597–605.

Warren, H. C. (1925) Mechanism and teleology in psychology. *Psychological Review, 32,* 266–285.

Weissman, A. (1893a). *The germ plasm: A theory of heredity.* New York: Scribner's.

Weissman, A. (1893b). The all-sufficiency of natural selection. *Contemporary Review, 64,* 309–338, 596–610.

Wilson, E. (1975). *Sociobiology: The new synthesis.* Cambridge, MA: Harvard University Press.

Woolley, H. T. (1910). A review of recent literature on the psychology of sex. *Psychological Bulletin, 7,* 335–342.

Wundt, W. (1894). *Lectures on human and animal psychology* (J. E. Crighton & E. B. Titchener, Trans.). New York: Macmillan. (Original work published 1863)

Young, R. M. (1990). *Mind, brain and adaptation in the nineteenth century.* New York: Oxford University Press.

CHAPTER 8

Psychology in Germany

T HE ACADEMIC DISCIPLINE OF SCIENTIFIC PSYCHOLOGY WAS FOUNDED
institutionally in Germany at the end of the 19th century. It was a natural
outgrowth of the progressive German university system, which was hospitable to
the development of new disciplines such as linguistics and psychology. Wilhelm
Wundt (1832–1920), who founded scientific psychology in Germany in 1879, the
year he set up his experimental laboratory at the University of Leipzig, characterized the new discipline as *physiological psychology*. This was not because he believed
that psychological states and processes must be reductively explained in terms of
physiological states and processes, but because he believed that scientific psychology should appropriate the experimental methods that had proved so successful
in the development of 19th-century German physiology.

Wundt's new experimental program attracted many foreign students, including many Americans, who sought to attain professional qualifications in the new
discipline. Having mastered the elements of the new psychology and the structure
of the German university system, they returned home to create their own laboratories and PhD programs in psychology.

Wundt's distinctive form of scientific psychology was eventually displaced
within Germany as rival programs were created at other German universities. As
the 20th century advanced, German psychology, which faced increasing opposition from the philosophical community, developed into precisely the type of
applied discipline that Wundt feared it would become. In a sense Wundt's fate was
like that of the sorcerer's apprentice. In creating a form of scientific psychology
based upon laboratory science, he unleashed powerful forces that he was unable to
control—forces that, over a few generations, radically transformed the discipline
(Danziger, 1990, p. 34).

PSYCHOLOGY IN GERMANY BEFORE WUNDT

Psychology had been recognized as a distinctive field of inquiry long before the
creation of Wundt's laboratory, and academic philosophers in various countries
had offered courses in the subject. For example, psychology was offered as a course

295

Wilhelm Wundt (center) with colleagues and students in the Leipzig laboratory.

at Marischal College, Aberdeen, in 1755 under the title "pneumology" (Robinson, 1986). Christian Wolff (1679–1754), professor of mathematics at the University of Halle, popularized the use of the term *psychology* in Europe in the 18th century. He distinguished between rational psychology, concerned with rationally demonstrable principles about the human soul (such as its simplicity), and empirical psychology, concerned with the empirical description and measurement of psychological faculties such as sensation, memory, and intellect (Wolff, 1732, 1734). However, Kant rejected the notion that there could be rationally demonstrable knowledge of human psychology analogous to that of logic and mathematics and famously denied that empirical psychology could attain the status of a genuine science of quantified dynamical laws.

Johann Friedrich Herbart: Dynamic Psychology

Johann Friedrich Herbart (1776–1841), who succeeded Kant as professor of philosophy at the University of Königsberg in 1809, tried to prove him wrong. He developed an elaborate quantified dynamical theory of the "movement" of ideas in *A Textbook of Psychology* (1816) and *Psychology as a Science Based Upon Experience, Metaphysics, and Mathematics* (1824–1825).

Herbart advanced an associationist psychology based upon a postulated system of ideas possessed of attractive and repulsive forces, which strive to attain dynamic equilibrium. He claimed that ideas are attracted to consciousness via effort and are repelled from consciousness when they conflict with ideas that constitute the current **apperceptive mass** of consciousness: the constellation of connected elementary mental representations that constitute the current object of apperception or focused attention.

Herbart claimed that his theory provided an account of the apparent spontaneity of thought, in the fashion that Newton's gravitational theory provided an account of the apparent "wandering" motion of the planets. In both cases, apparently irregular behavior was shown to be a determinate consequence of fixed mathematical laws. According to Herbart, ideas are never lost completely, but are merely repressed below a **threshold of consciousness**. The repressed ideas can sum their weaker energies to gain sufficient strength to force their way into consciousness, displacing the original apperceptive mass. In this fashion certain ideas "pop" into one's mind apparently unheralded, and certain thoughts keep recurring against one's will.

Herbart's psychological theory had all the trappings of a scientific theory. It was presented as a series of mathematical equations, such as the following equation governing the threshold of consciousness:

> Among the many, and for the most part, very complicated laws underlying the movements of concepts, the following is the simplest:
>
> While the arrested portion of the concept sinks, the sinking part is at every moment proportional to the part unsuppressed.
>
> By this it is possible to calculate the whole course of the sinking even to the statical point.
>
> Mathematically, the above law may be expressed: $\sigma = S (1 - e^{-t})$ in which S = the aggregate amount suppressed, t = the time elapsed during the encounter, σ = the suppressed portion of all the concepts in the time indicated by t.
>
> —(1816/1891, p. 395)

Unfortunately, Herbart did not specify empirical measures for his central constructs, so his theory was virtually impossible to evaluate empirically. Yet it served as a rich source of theoretical psychological concepts, such as the repression of ideas and cognitive equilibrium, which were later exploited by Freud and the social psychologist Leon Festinger (1919–1989). Although he maintained that psychology could become a dynamical and mathematical science like Newtonian physics, Herbart denied the possibility of an experimental psychology (since he claimed that ideas could not be individually isolated from the dynamical systems in which they occur) and an introspective psychology (since he claimed that many ideas are unconscious).

Herbart's follower, Moritz Wilhelm Drobisch (1802–1896), added an important new element to his theory in *Experimental Psychology According to the Method of*

Natural Science (1842). Drobisch noted that the continued operation of perception and memory ensures that any system of ideas will remain in a state of disequilibrium. Organisms experience a state of disequilibrium as unpleasant and are motivated to regain a state of equilibrium. This notion of **homeostatic motivation,** according to which organisms are motivated to eliminate states of disequilibrium that are experienced as unpleasant or painful, played a central role in the later theories of Freud and the behaviorist psychologist Clark L. Hull (1884–1952).

Herbart applied his abstract mathematical theory of ideas to the field of education. He claimed that novel ideas introduced to students should be consistent with and related to the apperceptive mass of previously mastered ideas. He held that learning occurs when new representational elements are associated with the apperceptive mass through **assimilation** (in which case the new representational element is integrated with the apperceptive mass) or **accommodation** (in which case the apperceptive mass is adjusted to incorporate the new representational element). Herbart is often treated as the founder of educational psychology and anticipator of Piaget's theory of cognitive development (which was based upon the concepts of assimilation and accommodation).

Herbart's theory was the dominant force in psychology in Germany when Wundt developed his program of physiological psychology in the late 19th century (Titchener, 1925), and the University of Leipzig was the center of Herbartian psychology (with Drobisch as its head) when Wundt took up his position there as professor of philosophy in 1875.

WILHELM WUNDT: PHYSIOLOGICAL PSYCHOLOGY

Wilhelm Maximilian Wundt was born in the village of Neckarau in the German principality of Baden, the fourth child of a Lutheran minister, Maximilian Wundt, and his wife, Marie Frederike. He came from a distinguished family that included university presidents and professors, scientists, physicians, government administrators, and theologians. After a poor academic start (he hated school, failed his classes, and was thought by his teachers to be ill-suited for any demanding professional career), Wundt excelled as a medical student at the University of Heidelberg and received his medical degree (with honors) in 1855.

Despite his academic success, Wundt had no interest in pursuing a professional career in medicine. He attributed his lack of interest to personal doubts about his own competence (Wundt, 1920, p. 99) and recounted an anecdote about his early days as a medical intern, when he was so tired that he accidentally gave a patient iodine instead of a narcotic (narrated in Diamond, 1980, p. 21). His interests turned to physiology, and he studied with Müller and du Bois-Reymond at the University of Berlin in 1856. He received his second doctoral degree in physiology in 1857 and returned to the University of Heidelberg as a lecturer that same year. Wundt's first course on experimental physiology was conducted in his mother's apartment. It attracted only four students, which was a financial as well as a professional disappointment, since in those days a lecturer's salary was funded from student fees. In 1858, he was appointed as an assistant to Helmholtz, the new head of the Institute of Physiology at the University of Heidelberg, where he served until 1864.

The assistantship turned out to be somewhat of a disappointment for Wundt. It required him to teach introductory courses on physiology and laboratory methods to medical students, and Wundt had little opportunity to work with Helmholtz on his research. However, he developed his first course on "psychology as a natural science" in 1862 (Bringmann et al., 1975) and published *Contributions Toward a Theory of Sense Perception* in 1862 and *Lectures on Human and Animal Psychology* in 1863. Wundt continued Helmholtz's measurement of neural transmission and calculated the time taken for the transmission of nerve impulses from the sense organs through the nervous system to the musculature. He identified a temporal remainder not accounted for by simple transmission, which he attributed to mental processes such as choice and volition (Blumenthal, 1985a). This type of theoretical inference about mental processes on the basis of reaction-time measurements became characteristic of Wundt's later experimental research in psychology.

Wundt resigned his position at the University of Heidelberg in 1864, supporting himself and his private psychological "institute" from his book royalties. He had created his own apparatus for measuring reaction time some years earlier and began to assemble a collection of laboratory instruments, such as chronoscopes, for measuring time intervals; kymographs, for making graphical records; and tachistoscopes, for the very brief presentation of visual stimuli. He returned to the University of Heidelberg from 1871 to 1874, using his private laboratory to support the courses in experimental physiology he was required to teach at the university (Bringmann, Bringmann, & Cottrell, 1976).

In 1873 and 1874 Wundt published the first edition of his two-volume *Principles of Physiological Psychology*. This work, which perhaps deserves to be classified as the first real textbook of experimental psychology, was revised and expanded in 1880, 1887, and 1893 and published as three-volume editions in 1902–1903 and 1908–1911. It constituted Wundt's self-conscious attempt to mark out physiological psychology as "a new domain of science," independent of but related to physiology and philosophy. Although about two thirds of the work was devoted to the physiology of the nervous system and sense organs, it was an instant international success and was favorably reviewed by leading academics such as William James.

After he failed to secure Helmholtz's vacated chair at the University of Heidelberg (when Helmholtz moved to the University of Berlin), Wundt took up the position of professor of inductive philosophy at the University of Zurich from 1874 to 1875. In 1875, he accepted a chair in philosophy at the University of

Leipzig, the largest university in Germany at the time, where he founded the Institute of Experimental Psychology in 1879. He remained there until his retirement in 1917.

Wundt supervised 186 dissertations at Leipzig between 1876 and 1917, of which 116 were psychological (the other 70 were philosophical or historical). He was by all accounts a popular teacher of a popular subject and was an indefatigable worker (Robinson, 1987). He published many works in both psychology and philosophy, including the 10-volume *Völkerpsychologie* (1900–1920). He died in 1920 shortly after publishing his autobiography (Wundt, 1920).

The Leipzig Laboratory

Wundt's new scientific discipline began modestly enough. The first course he taught at Leipzig was on physiological psychology. Some of the demonstrations and practicals relating to the course were conducted in a storeroom provided by the university in the summer of 1876. The room (promised to Wundt in 1875) was located in an unpretentious structure called the *Konvikt* building, which convicts had erected to serve as a cafeteria for poor students. As Wundt's courses in physiological psychology became more and more popular, his "psychological laboratory" came to occupy more and more rooms in the building.

Convict Building, Leipzig University (location of Wundt's first laboratory).

The year 1879 is conventionally designated as the one in which psychology was founded in Germany as an institutional scientific discipline, because it was in the winter semester of that year that students attending Wundt's Monday evening seminar began to develop their experimental projects in the Konvikt rooms; these later became the subjects of their PhD dissertations and academic publications in psychology:

> From the Fall of 1879 on, individual students began to occupy themselves in this room in the refectory building with experimental projects.
>
> —(Wundt, 1909, p. 118, cited in Bringmann, Voss, & Ungerer, 1997, p. 128)

One of these students was Max Friedrich (1856–1887), the first student in Wundt's new "practical seminar" and the first to be awarded a PhD in psychology at Leipzig (Tinker, 1932). Friedrich began his study "On the Duration of Apperception During Simple and Complex Ideas" in the winter of 1879–1880. Another was G. Stanley Hall (1844–1924), the first American student to visit Wundt's Leipzig laboratory. Both Hall and Wundt served as subjects in Friedrich's experiments (along with Friedrich himself).

Wundt managed to improve his situation when the University of Breslau made him a lucrative job offer in 1883. The Leipzig administration was anxious to retain him, and Wundt was able to set conditions for remaining. The university increased his salary and authorized funds for the expansion and improvement of the Konvikt building facilities. Wundt's "Institute for Experimental Psychology" was officially listed in the university catalogue and provided with a regular annual budget. The laboratory continued to expand and in 1893 moved to a well-equipped 11-room facility in a classroom building. In 1897, 18 years after its founding, the now famous Institute of Psychology moved to specially designed rooms on the top floor of a brand-new building. By this time Wundt's new science of experimental psychology and associated PhD program were well established, attracting students and visitors from all over the world. His program demonstrated that a systematic scientific psychology, sustained by a social collective of teachers and students engaged in a common research agenda, was indeed a "practical possibility" (Danziger, 1980, p. 106).

Wundt was most active as an experimentalist during his early years at Heidelberg. He took a lively and controlling interest in the work of the Leipzig laboratory in the 1870s and 1880s, but at the end of this period delegated the day-to-day direction of the laboratory to a variety of assistants, such as James McKeen Cattell (1860–1944), Oswald Külpe (1862–1915), and Wilhelm Wirth (1876–1952), who became co-director of the laboratory in 1904 (Schröder, 1997). Wundt remained a critical observer of and commentator on experimental work until the early 1890s, when he withdrew from laboratory work altogether. He became increasingly preoccupied with the development of the theoretical components of his psychology, although from time to time he published polemical defenses of his own conception of psychological experimentation (Wundt, 1907) and scientific psychology (Wundt, 1913).

In 1881 Wundt established *Philosophical Studies* (*Philosophische Studien*), the first journal dedicated exclusively to psychological research and the first to regularly publish experimental studies in psychology. He edited *Philosophical Studies* until 1902, when he relinquished the editorship to Wilhelm Wirth. The journal was retitled *Psychological Studies* (*Psychologische Studien*) in 1906. In the early years the journal mainly reported the experimental output of the Leipzig laboratory; one of the first reports published was Friedrich's PhD dissertation study on apperception.

Physiological Psychology

Herbart was the first to develop a theoretical system of quantified dynamical laws in psychology, but denied that mental states and processes could be investigated experimentally. Fechner was the first to develop quantified psychophysical laws based upon rigorous experiments, but did not extend experimentation to the exploration of purely mental states and processes. Wundt was the first to apply the experimental methods of physiology to those mental states and processes (such as thought, emotion, and the will) that were formerly the exclusive domain of philosophers and to establish the institutional resources necessary to develop the academic discipline of scientific psychology, such as a funded laboratory, PhD program, textbook, and journal.

Wundt's experimental psychology developed out of the German tradition of experimental physiology, but he insisted that his experimental psychology was distinct from it. He affirmed the reality of "psychic causality" and the autonomy of psychological explanation. Wundt acknowledged that "the facts of consciousness always presuppose, as their physiological substrate, complex nerve processes" (1902–1903/1904, p. 321), but denied that psychological principles could be reductively explained in terms of physiological principles. He consequently rejected the idea that the goal of physiological psychology was to "derive or explain the phenomena of the mental from those of physical life" (1902–1903/1904, p. 2).

Experimental Methods

Wundt promoted an experimental psychology of **immediate experience**, in contrast to **mediate experience**, which he treated as the subject matter of natural science. As Wundt put it, natural science deals with theoretically interpreted experience of the "outer" world, whereas psychology deals with "the facts of immediate experience in relation to the perceiving subject himself" (Mischel, 1970, p. 5). Wundt believed that he could make the study of conscious experience an exact science by rigorously controlling experimental conditions. His experimental program was based upon the assumption that rigorously controlled physical stimuli reliably generate the same sensational and perceptual responses in trained experimental observers, and he treated inter- and intrasubject replicability of results as the primary measure of the scientific objectivity of his experiments.

Wundt rejected the traditional philosophical conception of introspection as a form of "inner perception" (*innere Wahrnehmung*), which he condemned in the first issue of *Philosophical Studies*. He claimed that "there is . . . no such thing as an 'inner sense' which can be regarded as an organ of introspection" (1897/1902, p. 2). In contrast to "pure" or "armchair" self-observation, in which subjects simply describe or interpret their experience, he advocated the method of **experimental self-observation** (*experimentelle Selbstbeobachtung*), in which trained subjects provide concurrent commentaries on their conscious experience under rigorously controlled experimental conditions, which he hoped would avoid the distorting effects of intellectual reflection and reconstructive memory (Blumenthal, 1985a).

However, only a very small proportion of the work done in Wundt's laboratory involved the direct reporting of experience based upon experimental self-observation. Of the 180 experimental reports of studies conducted in Wundt's laboratory between 1883 and 1903 surveyed by Danziger (1979), only four contained introspective reports. Many of the experimental studies produced in Wundt's laboratory and published in *Philosophical Studies* were studies of sensation and perception, in which subjects made judgments about the quality or intensity of sensations, discriminated color differences and contrasts, estimated spatial positions and temporal intervals, or made determinations of simultaneity and succession (Danziger, 1990). Many were developments of Fechner's psychophysical studies, in which changes in physical stimuli were correlated with the perceived intensity of visual, tactile, and auditory sensations.

Other experiments employed measures of reaction time and were developments of the **complication experiments** pioneered by the Dutch physiologist Franciscus Cornelius Donders (1818–1889), in which the time taken for components of a complex task is calculated by subtraction of the measured time taken for other components of the task. Donders had used reaction times to simple and complex stimuli to measure the time taken to perform a variety of mental tasks. By subtracting simple reaction time for a response to a single stimulus from the time taken to discriminate a predesignated stimulus from a variety of presented stimuli, he estimated the time taken to perform the mental process of discrimination. By subtracting discrimination and simple reaction time from the time taken to choose a predesignated reaction to presented stimuli, he estimated choice reaction time (Donders, 1868). This experimental technique for measuring the duration of postulated mental processes became known as **mental chronometry** and was a common feature of the Leipzig laboratory program until the turn of the century.

Wundt and his students created more complex stimuli, requiring subjects to respond to visual stimuli of a specific color, intensity, or duration, for example, and more complex responses, requiring subjects to make concurrent responses to visual and auditory stimuli, for example, by locating the position of a pendulum when a certain sound is heard. In this fashion, Wundt hoped to measure the time taken by mental mediating processes and to determine the nature of processes such as attention, judgment, memory, and inference (O'Donnell, 1985).

Wundt had conducted experiments of this sort since the early 1860s, using his own specially designed "thought meter"—a pendulum clock hooked up to bells and a calibrated scale (Wundt, 1862b). He used this instrument to determine the time it takes to shift attention from one "thought" or perceived stimulus, such as the ringing of a bell, to another, such as the position of a moving pointer (supposedly one tenth of a second), and the maximum number of "thoughts" or stimuli that could be attended to at one time (supposedly only one). The complication experiments conducted in Wundt's laboratory went beyond the exploration of basic perceptual processes to the study of selective attention. James McKeen Cattell, one of Wundt's American students, conducted a series of experiments on the identification of letters. He determined that reaction time for the naming of letters decreases as more letters are presented and that reading (aloud) times for connected letters and words are shorter than those for unconnected letters and words. His work was published in *Philosophical Studies* in 1885.

Apart from the occasional use of experimental self-observation, the types of studies conducted in the Leipzig laboratory did not differ radically from many of those in physiological laboratories. "Psychological" topics such as sensation and perception had formed part of the theoretical and experimental repertoire of physiologists since von Haller and Müller, and (despite his avowals to the contrary) to a significant degree Wundt simply appropriated that area of experimental physiology concerned with psychological dependent variables.

Wundt's Psychology

Like most other German scientists, Wundt accepted the evolution of species, although his own position was closer to Lamarck's and Spencer's than to Darwin's. He endorsed the inheritance of acquired characteristics and conceived of individual and species development as intrinsically teleological—as a goal-directed process of differentiation. He agreed with Morgan that all animal psychology and behavior "can be accounted for by the simple laws of association" (Wundt, 1863/1894, p. 350), but (also like Morgan) denied that all human psychology and behavior could be explained in this fashion. Although he acknowledged that humans do passively associate ideas and behavior in accord with familiar principles of similarity, contiguity, and repetition, he maintained that the "elements" of human consciousness and cognition are not compounded in the aggregative fashion of associationist psychology, but are formed into integrated and unified configurations through the voluntary action of the will. He consequently denied that there is strong continuity between human cognitive processes and the associative processes common to humans and animals.

Wundt employed the term **apperception** to designate the creative and selective attentional processes that he believed are responsible for the configuration of conscious mental states. He claimed that apperception was the evolutionary advance in mental development that distinguished humans from animals and made possible the development of complex cultural forms of human mentality such as language, myth, and custom. Wundt held that the distinctive property of apperception is "creative synthesis" (*schöpferische Synthese*) and maintained that all other human psychological processes, such as perception, thought, and memory, are controlled by this central process, which he located in the frontal lobes of the brain (Blumenthal, 1975). According to Wundt, sensory elements are passively apprehended in the field of consciousness, but only some of these elements become the focus of attention in the selective configuration of mental states. Because of this emphasis on the voluntary, selective, and creative nature of the central control process of apperception, Wundt characterized his theoretical psychology as **voluntaristic psychology** (Wundt, 1896).

The two basic elements of Wundt's theoretical system were sensations and feelings (with volition conceived of as a form of feeling); he held that they admitted of two fundamental properties, quality and quantity. Wundt analyzed feelings as varying along three dimensions: pleasant versus unpleasant, high versus low arousal, and concentrated versus relaxed attention. His Leipzig students devoted much time to the exploration of his **tri-dimensional theory of feeling**, but eventually abandoned it as unworkable, although later researchers (employing factor analysis) claimed to have identified affective dimensions similar to Wundt's (Osgood, Suci, & Tannenbaum, 1957; Schosberg, 1954).

Wundt (1912/1973, p. 44) consistently maintained that

> The whole task of psychology can be summed up in these two problems: (1) what are the elements of consciousness? (2) what combinations do these elements undergo, and what laws govern these combinations?

However, he did not conceive of this task in terms of the determination of laws of the association of independent conscious elements, although later critics complained about the "elementalism" of his program. Wundt always stressed that consciousness is a *process* composed of constituent processes and that the "elements" of consciousness are intrinsic components of complex configurations, which can be identified or inferred only via experimental analysis and abstraction.

According to Wundt's **principle of psychical resultants** (also known as the *principle of creative synthesis*), the attributes of psychological configurations that are the product of apperception are distinct from the mere aggregation of the attributes of the elements from which they are configured. This principle was held to apply to quantities (e.g., the perceived intensity of a sensory stimulus) as well as qualities (e.g., the perception of spatial relations). According to Wundt, psychological configurations, such as the perception of a musical chord or understanding of a sentence, have emergent properties that cannot be reduced to the mere aggregation of elemental properties:

> Every psychological compound shows attributes which may indeed be understood from the attributes of its elements after these elements have once been presented, but which are by no means to be looked upon as the mere sum of the attributes of these elements.
>
> —(1897/1902, p. 321)

Wundt originally followed Mill and Helmholtz in accounting for the emergent properties of psychological configurations in terms of unconscious cognitive inference, but later came to treat them as a product of the creative "fusion" of the elements of consciousness. He also claimed that this creative fusion accounts for the integration of motor movements in goal-directed behavior.

Wundt did not merely claim with Mill and Helmholtz that complex ideas have emergent properties that cannot be reduced to the properties of their sensational components, in the fashion that the properties of molecular compounds such as water cannot be reduced to the properties of their atomic components, such as hydrogen and oxygen. He rejected Mill's account of the formation of complex ideas as a form of mental chemistry, because he claimed that Mill had neglected the "special creative character of psychic synthesis" (1902, cited in Blumenthal, 1975). Wundt maintained that the "elements" of psychological configurations cannot be identified and isolated independently of their configuration, unlike atomic elements such as hydrogen and oxygen, which can be identified and isolated independently of molecular compounds such as water.

Wundt held that the "elements" of consciousness are relational rather than atomistic. According to Wundt's **principle of psychical relations**, the nature and identity of the elements of psychological configurations are determined by their relational location within psychological configurations:

> Every single psychical content receives its significance from the relations in which it stands to other psychical contents.
>
> —(1897/1902, p. 323)

In the production of psychological configurations, the significance of the elements attended to derives from their apperceived relation to other elements in the psychological configuration. For example, Wundt claimed that words do not have meaning in isolation, but only via their role in configured sentences (1900, p. 37). This relational conception of the "elements" of perception and cognition later became the foundational principle of the Berlin school of Gestalt psychology represented by Max Wertheimer (1880–1943), Wolfgang Köhler (1887–1967), and Kurt Koffka (1886–1941).

Many of Wundt's experimental studies of apperception were precursors of contemporary research in cognitive psychology on attention span and short-term memory (Blumenthal, 1985a; Leahey, 1979). Wundt had originally thought it possible to attend to only one thought or stimulus at a time, but experimental studies in the Leipzig laboratory established that about six or seven items could be simultaneously attended to. These experimental studies, which were developed by Wilhelm Wirth in *The Experimental Analysis of the Phenomena of Consciousness* (1908), anticipated George Miller's (1956) classic study of the restriction of short-term memory capacity to about seven units. Wundt's studies also anticipated Miller's finding that the "chunking" of these "elements" into larger meaningful units can increase the capacity of short-term memory (by forming letters into words or numbers into ordered sequences, for example).

Wundt claimed that apperception plays a critical role in the perception of space and time, the operation of imagination and reasoning, and linguistic processing. He explained linguistic performance in terms of the transformation of thought configurations into symbolic representations in language. According to Wundt, a speaker apperceives a configured idea and selects a sequence of linguistic symbols to express it; a listener analyzes the speaker's linguistic production in an attempt to apperceive the original configured idea of the speaker. The process of communication can go astray via the failure of the speaker to properly express the original configured idea, or of the listener to reconstruct it. Wundt noted that the original configured idea can be expressed by the speaker (or reconstructed by the listener) in a variety of different linguistic forms, which he thought explained how we can often remember the meaning of a verbal communication (or of a piece of prose or poetry) after we have forgotten the specific sentences used to express its meaning (Wundt, 1900). Wundt's account of linguistic processing anticipated later developments in psycholinguists and the transformational grammar of Noam Chomsky (1928–); he invented the tree diagrams representing sentence structure later employed by many linguists, including Chomsky (1957).

Wundt also suggested that disruption of the attentional mechanisms of apperception might be the source of some psychological disorders—a suggestion developed by his student and friend Emil Kraepelin (1856–1926), one of the pioneers of German scientific psychiatry.

Völkerpsychologie

By the early 1900s Wundt had lost interest in laboratory work, although he never abandoned his commitment to experimental psychology and defended it vigorously against philosophical critics in his 1913 book *Psychology Struggling for Survival*. He stopped serving as editor of *Philosophical Studies* in 1902 and turned over the everyday operations of the Institute of Psychology to Wilhelm Wirth in 1908. He devoted most of his remaining years to his 10-volume *Völkerpsychologie* (1900–1920), variously translated as "social psychology," "cultural psychology," or "folk psychology," a comparative-historical study of the "mental products" of social communities, such as language, myth, and custom.

The idea of a psychology grounded in social community had been suggested by Herbart and developed by Humboldt. Moritz Lazarus (1824–1903) first articulated the idea of a special discipline devoted to the comparative and historical study of the mental products of social communities in a paper titled "On the Concept and Possibility of a *Völkerpsychologie*" in 1851 (Jahoda, 1997). Lazarus founded the journal *Zeitschrift für Völkerpsychologie und Sprachwissenschaft* with Hajm Steinthal (1823–1899) in 1860. However, the notion of a comparative and developmental psychology grounded in cultural and historical differences in social community has a much longer history. Wundt's own project represented the continuation of a tradition that can be traced back to Vico and Herder and that found partial expression in Kant's anthropology and Mill's ethology.

Many historians of psychology have claimed that Wundt denied the possibility of studying "higher" psychological states and processes experimentally and have asserted that Wundt believed these could be studied only by the naturalistic comparative-historical methods of *Völkerpsychologie* (Farr, 1996; Shook, 1995). Yet this is a misrepresentation of Wundt's position. He did lose interest in laboratory work at Leipzig, but did not turn to the naturalistic observational methods of *Völkerpsychologie* in reaction to the problems of laboratory experimentation directed toward "higher" psychological states and processes. Wundt became interested in *Völkerpsychologie* very early his career. He offered his first course on the subject (entitled *Anthropologie*) in 1859, during his second year of teaching at Heidelberg (Leary, 1979) and detailed the project of *Völkerpsychologie* in his *Lectures on Animal and Human Psychology* in 1863. He claimed that naturalistic comparative-historical observation, the method of Darwin, is the best method for studying processes of development, whether biological, psychological, or social.

Wundt supervised experimental projects on "higher" psychological processes such as thought and memory in the Leipzig laboratory—for example, Harry K. Wolfe's "Studies on the Memory of Tones" and Edward W. Scripture's "Thinking and Feeling" (Benjamin et al., 1992). Apperception, which Wundt held to be the central control process governing all other human psychological processes (Blumenthal, 1975), was a major focus of the *Völkerpsychologie*, but was also the subject of experimental research in the Leipzig laboratory: The very first experimental study conducted in Wundt's laboratory was Friedrich's study of apperception.

Wundt saw the naturalistic observational methods of *Völkerpsychologie* as a *complement* to those of experimental psychology:

> Psychological analysis of the most general mental products, such as language, mythological ideas, and laws of custom, is to be regarded as an aid to the understanding of all the more complicated psychical processes.
>
> —(1897/1902, p. 10)

According to Wundt, experimental psychology can never be a science of pure observation, because unlike physical sciences that deal with "relatively permanent objects of nature" that are independent of human consciousness, it is restricted to the study of fleeting psychological "processes" that are dependent upon human consciousness. This was the reason Wundt insisted upon rigorous control in the experimental investigation of conscious psychological processes. However, he claimed that the mental products of social communities that form the subject matter of *Völkerpsychologie* are sufficiently akin to the "relatively permanent objects of nature" to admit of something analogous to pure observation, "inasmuch as they possess . . . attributes of relative permanence, and independence of the observer" (1897/1902, p. 22).

Wundt maintained that social-psychological facts about language, myth, and custom could serve as observational grounds for inferences about psychological processes:

> The origin and development of these products depend in every case on general psychological conditions which may be inferred from their objective attributes. Psychological analysis can, consequently, explain the psychical processes operative in their formation and development.
>
> —(1897/1902, p. 23)

He claimed that differences in psychological processes could be inferred from differences in the linguistic, mythical, and cultural products of social communities. For example, he suggested that differences in psychological motives could be inferred from the different types of word orderings of sentences in different languages (1912/1970, p. 28).

Wundt held that psychological processes and products could be investigated by both laboratory experimentation *and* the naturalistic comparative-historical methods of *Völkerpsychologie*. When he claimed that the subject matter of *Völkerpsychologie* is "unapproachable by means of experiment in the common acceptance of the term" (1897, p. 23), he meant that the historical development of social forms of language, myth, and custom cannot be investigated via experimental self-observation, since

> individual consciousness is wholly incapable of giving us a history of the development of human thought, for it is conditioned by an earlier history concerning which it cannot of itself give us any knowledge.
>
> —(1916, p. 3)

Wundt's attitude toward experimentation in relation to *Volkerpsychologie* was analogous to his attitude toward experimentation in child and animal psychology. He never denied that experimental methods of intervention and manipulation could be employed in these fields of psychology, but claimed that experimental *introspection* was of limited utility:

> Results of experiment are here matters of objective observation only, and the experimental method accordingly loses the peculiar significance which it possesses as an instrument of introspection.
>
> —(1902–1903, p. 5)

Wundt's 10 volumes of *Völkerpsychologie* constituted a rather disappointing compilation of largely anecdotal ethnographic accounts of myths, rituals, religions, and customs, which provided doubtful evidential support for his theoretical speculations about social and cognitive development (Jahoda, 1997). The most interesting are the first two volumes devoted to language, which were also the most successful. Wundt rejected the Herbartian conception of language as a set of linguistic elements compounded according to principles of association (Paul, 1880) and maintained that language is creatively generated in accord with abstract rules governing the production of sentences (Blumenthal, 1970; Mischel, 1970). Despite its limitations, Wundt's *Völkerpsychologie* indicated the potential of comparative historical studies of the social foundations of thought and language, of the type later developed by Lev Vygotsky (1896–1934) and his colleagues in Russia (Cole, 1996).

Wundt's Legacy

Wundt had many students but few intellectual disciples and is not generally remembered for his substantive contributions to theoretical or experimental psychology—there are no enduring psychological laws or principles named after him. His main achievement was the establishment of a research community of psychologists working on a common set of experimental problems, who disseminated their results through PhD dissertations and journal publications (Danziger, 1990).

Wundt established the viability of scientific psychology and trained a generation of PhD certified professional psychologists who set about reproducing their own research communities as they instituted laboratories in Europe and America, although their own research programs and practical agendas often differed radically from Wundt's own vision of scientific psychology.

Wundt established psychology as an academic discipline in Germany in the face of vigorous opposition from the philosophers of his day, who claimed that too much self-observation would drive young people to insanity. Although he insisted that scientific psychology was distinct from physiology, it was never his intention to establish psychology as an academic discipline independent of philosophy. Wundt's chair in Leipzig was in philosophy, and he carried out his teaching and supervisory duties in philosophy as enthusiastically as he did those in psychology, publishing works on logic, ethics, metaphysics, and philosophy of science along with his psychological output. He considered scientific psychology to be intimately related to philosophy and hoped that it would transform and reinvigorate late-19th-century German philosophy. He considered psychology to be "both a part of the science of philosophy and an empirical Geisteswissenschaft": "its value for both philosophy and the empirical special sciences resides in its being the main negotiator between them" (1913, p. 32).

This commitment did not save him from the criticisms of philosophers like Wilhelm Windelband (1848–1915), who complained that

> For a time it was thought in Germany that one was close to being qualified for a philosophical chair as soon as one had learned to press electric buttons in a methodological way, and as soon as one could numerically prove by means of well-ordered and tabulated series of experiments that some people get ideas more quickly than others.
>
> —(quoted in Kusch, 1995, p. 171)

Wundt made a heroic (if unsuccessful) effort to integrate the principles of experimental psychology and *Völkerpsychologie* and conceived of psychology as a **propaedeutic science** (Blumenthal, 1985a) that provided the foundation of both the natural and social or human sciences. However, later psychologists followed Dilthey in maintaining that the natural and social or human sciences are fundamentally different, and they opted for the natural scientific version of scientific psychology, with its promise of technological application.

Wundt's lasting achievement was the establishment of psychology as an autonomous scientific discipline. He trained generations of German and foreign students in the new science; they went on to found their own laboratories and psychology programs in Germany, the Americas, India, Russia, and Asia. Wundt's Indian students produced a large commemorative volume in 1932, the centenary of Wundt's birth, and his Russian and Japanese students constructed replicas of Wundt's Leipzig laboratory in Moscow in 1912 and in Tokyo in 1920 (Blumenthal, 1975).

After Wundt's death in 1920, some of his former students, such as Felix Krueger (1874–1948), Friedrich Sander (1880–1971), and Wilhelm Wirth continued to develop his configurational psychology at Leipzig and reinstituted *Psychological Studies* (which ceased publication after Wundt's retirement in 1919) as *New Psychological Studies* (Blumenthal, 1975). They later became known as the Leipzig school of Gestalt psychology, although the more famous Berlin school of Gestalt psychology represented by Wertheimer, Köhler, and Koffka eclipsed their work.

Along the way Wundt's substantive achievements in cognitive psychology and his project for a comparative historical *Völkerpsychologie* were forgotten. This was because they were neglected by the Americans who studied under Wundt and who returned home to shape the development of the form of scientific psychology that eventually came to establish a virtual global hegemony. As American psychology expanded dramatically in the early 20th century, German psychology was emaciated by the economic depression of the 1920s. Leipzig University could not afford to purchase Wundt's last works for the university library, and a Japanese consortium purchased his personal library (Miyakawa, 1981). Many of Wundt's students were removed from their positions in Germany, Italy, and Russia by hostile Fascist and Marxist regimes (Blumenthal, 1985b).

Wundt's American Students

Most of Wundt's American students came to the Leipzig laboratory in search of academic qualifications that they could not get back home (only a few Ivy League institutions offered the PhD degree in the late 19th century, and fewer still in psychology) and the prestige and earning potential of a German degree. They returned with only the experimental skeleton and institutional structure of the new psychology. Two exceptions were G. Stanley Hall and Charles Judd (1873–1946). Hall persuaded Franz Boas (1858–1942) to visit Wundt in Leipzig and to offer a course on *Völkerpsychologie* when he returned to Clark University. Boas moved to Columbia University, where he founded the school of "cultural anthropology" that came to include such distinguished figures as Margaret Mead (1901–1978) and Ruth Benedict (1887–1948). Judd made a valiant attempt to promote an "institutional" form of social psychology based upon Wundt's *Völkerpsychologie* (Judd, 1926), but with little success. Eventually he abandoned the project and turned to educational psychology.

For those Americans who did not study with Wundt, their exposure to Wundt's psychology was generally filtered through the translations and expositions of his work produced by Edward B. Titchener (1867–1927), who interpreted his psychology in terms of the atomistic and associationist psychology of British empiricism, to which it bore little resemblance (Blumenthal, 1975; Leahey, 1981). Wundt's spirited defense of Germany in the First World War did little to promote his theoretical system, but by that time the distinctive features of his psychology had already been lost to most Americans.

Still, Wundt's influence on the development of scientific psychology in America should not be underestimated. Thirty-three Americans completed their doctoral degrees under his supervision. Ten years after the founding of Wundt's laboratory in Leipzig, there were over 40 American laboratories, about a dozen of which were founded by his students (Benjamin et al., 1992). Wundt's American students included Frank Angell (1857–1939), who founded laboratory programs at Cornell University and Stanford University; James McKeen Cattell, who founded laboratory programs at the University of Pennsylvania and Columbia University; Walter Dill Scott (1869–1955), who founded the laboratory program at Northwestern University and was a pioneer of industrial psychology; and Lightner Witmer (1867–1956), who took over the laboratory at Pennsylvania (founded by Cattell) and instituted the first psychological clinic. Other laboratory programs were founded by Harry Kirke Wolfe (1858–1918) at the University of Nebraska; Edward Wheeler Scripture (1864–1945) at Yale University; Edward Aloysius Pace (1861–1938) at the Catholic University of America; and George Stratton (1865–1957) at the University of California at Berkeley.

GERMAN PSYCHOLOGY BEYOND LEIPZIG

Wundt's Leipzig program remained a dominant force in German psychology for many years, but was not the only laboratory-based psychology program developed in Germany at the end of the 19th and early 20th centuries. A number of other German universities created institutes of psychology, whose programs came to rival and eventually supersede Wundt's own version of physiological psychology.

Hermann Ebbinghaus: On Memory

Hermann Ebbinghaus (1850–1909) originally trained in philosophy at the University of Bonn. He traveled throughout Europe for a number of years, working as a part-time teacher and private tutor. He is reputed to have developed an interest in experimental psychology after reading a copy of Fechner's *Elements of Psychophysics* (1860), which he bought in a secondhand bookstore in Paris. The story may be apocryphal, but Ebbinghaus committed himself to the task of studying memory experimentally as Fechner had earlier committed himself to the task of studying sensation experimentally. He returned to Germany in 1880, where he served as an untenured instructor at the University of Berlin. He began a series of experimental studies on memory, defined as "learning, retention, association and reproduction" (1885, p. v), with himself as the single experimental subject.

To avoid the contamination of learning and memory by previous associations and meaningful relations, Ebbinghaus created lists of meaningless syllables (based upon consonant-vowel-consonant combinations) and used randomly selected combinations of these syllables as his stimulus material. On each learning trial, he looked at each syllable on a list for a fraction of a second, as measured by a metronome. He repeated this process every 15 seconds until he attained mastery of the list—when he was able to recall each syllable on a list without error. Ebbinghaus established that the number of repetitions required to learn a list increases with the length of a list: A list with 7 syllables requires only 1 repetition, a list with 16 requires 30 repetitions, and a list with 36 requires 55 repetitions. He demonstrated that memory deteriorates rapidly in the first few hours and days after learning, and much more slowly thereafter: over 50 percent of the material is forgotten in the 1st hour, and over 60 percent in the 1st day, with around 20 percent retained between the 2nd and the 30th day. Ebbinghaus also established that the time taken to relearn lists after initial exposure decreases as the number of original repetitions increases, demonstrating the importance of overlearning.

Twelve years after graduating from the University of Bonn, Ebbinghaus published *On Memory* (1885), which he dedicated to Fechner. This book described an elegant set of studies directed to specific hypotheses, in the scientific tradition of Gilbert's *On Magnetism* (1600) and Newton's *Opticks* (1704), and became an instant classic of experimental reportage. William James, who had little good to say about the work of most of the pioneers of German psychology, called Ebbinghaus one of Germany's "best men." As a result of the success of his book, Ebbinghaus was appointed professor extraordinarius at the University of Berlin.

On Memory stood the test of time better than most of Wundt's publications and initiated a long tradition of research on memory (Postman, 1968). However, Ebbinghaus did not continue his memory research at Berlin. His own interests turned to sensory and perceptual psychology, possibly because of the influence of Helmholtz, who held a chair in physics at the university at the time. Ebbinghaus founded an Institute of Experimental Psychology at the University of Berlin, but played only a minor role in the institutional development of German psychology. He published little else of note and devoted much of his energy to the editorship of the *Journal of Psychology and the Physiology of the Sense-Organs,* which he founded (with Arthur Konig) in 1890 as an alternative to Wundt's *Philosophical Studies.*

Possibly as a consequence of his lack of research output, he was not promoted to the chair in philosophy at the University of Berlin, which was given to Carl Stumpf (1848–1936) in 1894. Ebbinghaus spent the later years of his career at the universities of Breslau and Halle, where he published two extremely popular textbooks of psychology, *Principles of Psychology* (1897) and An *Elementary Textbook of Psychology* (1902), which ran into several editions. He also pioneered the use of completion tests for assessing the intelligence of children after a Breslau education committee asked him to advise them on the most effective way of structuring the school day with a view to promoting productive learning. Alfred Binet (1857–1911) employed some of these tests in his intelligence scales, and they were later incorporated in the Stanford-Binet intelligence test.

Georg Elias Müller: The Experimentalist

Georg Elias Müller (1850–1934) was a native of Saxony who originally studied philosophy and history at the University of Leipzig. After service in the infantry during the Franco-Prussian war (1870–1871), he returned to Leipzig to study with Moritz Drobisch. Throughout his academic career, Müller followed Drobisch in defending Herbart's form of associationist psychology. On Drobisch's recommendation, he went to study at the University of Göttingen with Rudolf Hermann Lotze (1817–1881), who held the chair in philosophy formerly held by Herbart. After producing a thesis on attention under Lotze's supervision in 1873, Müller returned to the University of Leipzig, where he met Fechner and developed an interest in psychophysics.

In 1878 he published *Fundamentals of Psychophysics,* a critical evaluation of Fechner's *Elements of Psychophysics* (1860/1866). Fechner's own detailed response to his critique, *Revision of the Main Points of Psychophysics* (1882), established Müller's reputation, and shortly afterward he was appointed to the chair of philosophy at the University of Göttingen (when Lotze moved to the University of Berlin), where he remained until his retirement in 1921. Müller immediately set about founding a laboratory and PhD program in psychology, although he did not secure dedicated laboratory space until 1887 and (modest) funding until 1891 (Blumenthal, 1985b).

Müller was a dedicated experimentalist, whose lifelong commitment to methodological rigor, quantification, and instrumentation was possibly more representative of the spirit of modern scientific psychology than Wundt's own version (Müller had no interest in philosophy or *Völkerpsychologie*), which led William James to describe his contribution as "brutal." Müller's form of physiological psychology was also far more physiological than Wundt's. He was a reductive explanatory materialist, who insisted that scientific psychological theories must be grounded in physiological theories; his own psychological theories were based upon physiological theories of cortical blood supply and neural excitation (Blumenthal, 1985b).

Although he was not an innovative theorist, Müller was an enormously productive scholar, who developed the work of earlier theorists such as Ebbinghaus, Fechner, and Helmholtz (Behrens, 1978). He extended Fechner's program of psychophysics, making Göttingen a major center for psychophysical research. He introduced a number of methodological and statistical innovations and produced masterful studies of the psychophysics of lifted weights (Müller & Martin, 1889; Müller & Schumann, 1889).

Müller also developed the program of memory research that Ebbinghaus had initiated and established the research tradition of verbal learning (Blumenthal, 1985b). He and his student Friedrich Schumann (1863–1940), a PhD in physics who became Müller's first laboratory assistant in 1881, invented the memory drum (Müller & Schumann, 1893), which was for many years the standard instrument for the study of verbal learning and memory (Behrens, 1997). He also developed an early interference theory of memory with another of his students, Alfons Pilzecker (Müller & Pilzecker, 1900). Müller's extensive experimental studies of recall and recognition were summarized in his three-volume *Analysis of the Processes of Memory and Mental Representation* (1911–1913). He also developed and modified Ewald Hering's (1834–1918) "opponent-process" theory of visual perception and Wundt's theory of spatial localization.

Müller recognized the critical role of configurational properties (*Gestaltsqualitäten*) in the organization of perception, thought, and memory, but rejected Wundt's theory of creative synthesis. He based his own structural theory (*Komplextheorie*) upon traditional Herbartian principles of association (Behrens, 1997) and treated configurational properties as complex by-products of association (Blumenthal, 1985b). He was highly critical of the form of Gestalt psychology developed by Wertheimer, Köhler, and Koffka, which he dismissed as unoriginal and methodologically unsound in *Structure Theory and Gestalt Psychology* (1923). However, a number of Müller's students went on to develop their own versions of Gestalt psychology, such as Erich R. Jaensch (1883–1940), David Katz (1884–1953), Albert Michotte (1881–1965), and Edgar Rubin (1886–1951).

Müller played almost as influential a role as Wundt in the early development of experimental psychology in Germany and in establishing the 20th-century research traditions that grew out of it. However, he is rarely remembered in introductory texts and histories of psychology, although his work was extensively cited in Titchener's 1905 *Experimental Psychology*, second only to Wundt and Fechner (Behrens, 1997), and in Robert S. Woodworth's 1938 *Experimental Psychology*, second only to Wundt and more frequently than Ebbinghaus, Köhler, Pavlov, Thorndike, and Titchener (Blumenthal, 1985b). Few of Müller's works were published in or translated into English. He played a significant role in the creation of the German Society of Experimental Psychology in 1904 but was uninterested in developments in psychology outside Germany and contributed little to them.

Müller had less influence than Wundt on the institutional development of American psychology and had fewer American students. However, he had some very interesting ones, including a number of American women. Christine Ladd-Franklin (1847–1930), one of the first graduates of Vassar College, worked briefly with Müller on color perception in 1891. She also studied with Helmholtz and developed her own version of the "opponent-process" theory of color vision. Before she visited Müller in Germany, she fulfilled all the requirements for a graduate degree (in mathematics) at Johns Hopkins, but the university would not grant her one because in its early years it denied degrees to women. She never managed to attain a full-time academic position (her marriage to Fabian Franklin, a Hopkins mathematician, precluded her from consideration for the few academic positions that were open to women in her day). Hopkins finally awarded her a degree in 1926, 44 years after she completed her studies and 4 years before she died (Scarborough & Furumoto, 1987). In later years she became a militant feminist.

Lillien Martin (1851–1943), another graduate of Vassar College, was a student of Müller's from 1894 to 1898. They published a joint study on the psychophysics of lifted weights that became a classic (Müller & Martin, 1899). She completed all the courses required for a degree, but never received one because the University of Göttingen prohibited women from graduating. When Martin returned to the United States, she got a job in the department of psychology at Stanford University. She continued to work on perception (and aesthetics) and became chair of the department in 1915 (Scarborough & Furumoto, 1987). After her retirement in 1916, she continued to travel and lecture on psychological topics, including (appropriately enough) aging. She died at the age of 91, after a brief dizzy spell.

Eleanor Gamble (1868–1933), who completed her PhD with Edward B. Titchener at Cornell on the psychophysics of smell, received a postdoctoral research grant to study with Müller in 1906. On her return, she became director of the Wellesley psychological laboratory, where she supervised psychological research for the next 25 years. Gilbert Haven Jones (1883–1966), an African American from Fort Mott, South Carolina, earned a doctoral degree in philosophy at the University of Jena in 1901, and studied with Müller for a few years before returning to the United States. He was appointed professor of philosophy and education at St. Augustine College in North Carolina, where he became the first African American with a doctoral degree to teach psychology. William McDougall (1871–1938), the "purposive" behaviorist and early pioneer of American social psychology, also studied with Müller, and Oswald Külpe (1862–1915), the founder of the Würzburg school of psychology, received his first degree at Göttingen.

Franz Brentano: Intentionality

Franz Brentano (1838–1917), the son of an Italian merchant immigrant to Germany, began training for the priesthood at the age of 17. He studied philosophy at the universities of Berlin and Munich, where he developed a lifelong interest in the philosophy of Aristotle. Brentano received his PhD from the University of Tübingen in 1862 for a dissertation on Aristotle and was ordained as a priest shortly afterward. He obtained a position at the University of Würzburg, where he proved to be a popular teacher of philosophy. Finding himself on the wrong side of the debate about the pope's infallibility, Brentano resigned from the priesthood and his academic position in 1873 (he felt obligated to since he had originally been appointed as a priest).

During the next few years Brentano worked on what became his magnum opus, *Psychology From an Empirical Standpoint,* which was published in 1874 (the same year as the second volume of Wundt's *Principles of Physiological Psychology*). He secured an academic appointment as professor of philosophy at the University of Vienna, where he remained for the next 20 years, retiring from the university in 1894. He was forced to resign his official position at the university in 1880 when he renounced the Catholic Church and married. He taught as an unpaid instructor (albeit a very popular one) in his later years (Baumgartner & Baumgartner, 1991).

Following Aristotle and Aquinas, Brentano treated *intentionality* as the distinctive "mark of the mental." According to Brentano, mental states such as thoughts, memories, and emotions are intentionally directed upon objects of thought, memory, and emotion. For example, my thought that the Empire State Building is the tallest building in New York is *about* the Empire State Building, and my anger at Sarah for having borrowed my laptop without asking is directed *at* Sarah. As Brentano put it,

> Every mental phenomenon is characterized by what the Scholastics of the Middle Ages called the intentional. . . . Every mental phenomenon includes something as object within itself, although they do not all do so in the same way. In presentation something is presented, in judgment something is affirmed or denied, in love loved, in hate hated, in desire desired, and so on.
>
> —(1874/1995, p. 88)

Because of his focus on the intentionality of acts of perception, judgment, and desire, Brentano is often characterized as a proponent of **act psychology**, in contrast to Wundt's supposed **psychology of contents**, concerned with the elemental contents of consciousness. However, Wundt placed at least as much emphasis on mental acts as he did on mental contents and always insisted that experimental psychology was directed to the exploration of mental *processes*.

Like Wundt, Brentano was firmly committed to the utility of experimental methods in physiological psychology, which he employed in his own empirical research on color vision. He petitioned the University of Vienna for funding for a psychological laboratory, but with less success than Wundt at Leipzig. However, Brentano was less enthusiastic than Wundt about the potential of physiological psychology. Like Müller, he was an explanatory reductive materialist, who believed that causal explanatory understanding of psychological processes was dependent upon causal explanatory understanding of the physiological processes that ground them

> Psychology . . . will never fulfill its task without the inclusion of physio-chemical processes and the identification of anatomic structures.
>
> —(Brentano, 1982/1995, p. 3)

Since he believed that physiology had few established causal explanatory principles at its disposal in the late 19th century, and fewer still of relevance to the causal explanation of the "succession of psychic phenomena," he thought the immediate prospects for an explanatory scientific psychology were poor. His classification of mental acts and their properties in *Psychology From an Empirical Standpoint* (1874/1995) was entirely descriptive.

Although he did not develop a substantive research program in experimental psychology, Brentano had some important and influential students. At the University of Würzburg they included Carl Stumpf (1848–1936), who was preferred over Ebbinghaus and Müller for the chair in philosophy at the University of Berlin. At the University of Vienna, they included Edmund Husserl (1859–1938), the founder of phenomenological philosophy and psychology; Christian von Ehrenfels (1859–1932), one of the founders of Gestalt psychology; and Sigmund Freud, the founder of psychoanalysis.

Carl Stumpf: The Berlin Institute of Experimental Psychology

Carl Stumpf discovered philosophy as a student of Brentano's at the University of Würzburg and completed his PhD at the University of Göttingen under Lotze's supervision in 1868. For a few years he studied for the ministry, but abandoned this projected vocation in 1870 over the issue of papal infallibility. He accepted a position as instructor in philosophy at the University of Göttingen (on Lotze's recommendation), where he worked with Weber and Fechner. He took over Brentano's position at the University of Würzburg when Brentano resigned in 1873. That same year Stumpf published a book on the psychology of visual perception that anticipated many of the themes of Gestalt psychology. In 1883 he published the first volume of his major work *The Psychology of Tone* (the second was published in 1890). An accomplished musician, Stumpf maintained a lifelong interest in the theory, practice, and psychology of music.

After holding positions at the universities of Prague, Halle, and Munich, Stumpf was appointed to the chair of philosophy at the University of Berlin in 1894, with an adjunct appointment as director of the Institute of Experimental Psychology (founded by Ebbinghaus). He did little empirical research and was skeptical of the potential of experimentation in psychology. Stumpf claimed that his own very limited training in experimental techniques was based upon a single course in chemistry, during which he narrowly avoided burning down the chemistry building (Stumpf, 1930), and allegedly boasted that he could carry all the laboratory apparatus he needed in a cigar box under his arm (O'Donnell, 1985).

However, Stumpf was an excellent organizer and administrator who quickly expanded the Institute of Experimental Psychology, focusing initially on space

Clever Hans.

perception and audition. He hired Friedrich Schumann, Müller's former research assistant, who began a 10-year program of research on time perception and the emergence of configurational properties in spatial perception and word recognition (Blumenthal, 1985b). As director, Stumpf instituted schools of medical, musical, military, and child psychology, as well as a center for the study of traditional music. Eventually the Berlin Institute of Experimental Psychology, which occupied the top floor of the former Imperial Palace in Berlin, came to rival Wundt's Leipzig Institute as the primary center for psychology in Germany.

Stumpf also promoted the development of industrial and other forms of applied psychology. Although he took little active part in applied research himself, he collaborated with one of his students Oskar Pfungst (1874–1933) in the investigation of the case of Clever Hans, a horse owned by Herr von Osten (1838–1909). The horse could apparently solve mathematical puzzles by tapping out answers when questioned by von Osten, a miraculous display that attracted daily crowds to von Osten's home in the northern suburbs of Berlin. Pfungst demonstrated that Clever Hans was incapable of performing his mathematical "solutions" when von Osten was not present and that the horse's "achievements" were responses to unconscious behavioral cues supplied by von Osten.

In 1896 Stumpf presided over the Third International Congress in Psychology, held at the University of Munich. In recognition of his achievements, and with the enthusiastic support of his friend William James, Stumpf was elected a fellow of the American Academy of Sciences and the American Psychological Association.

Stumpf was deeply critical of Wundt's psychology, which was roundly condemned at the Berlin Institute as too passive and elemental, albeit unjustly, given Wundt's emphasis on the active and constructive role of apperception in the creative synthesis of psychological configurations. Stumpf's hostility toward Wundt was a product of personal animosity and institutional rivalry, engendered by an acrimonious public dispute over the discrimination of tonal distances that reflected their radically different approach to empirical validation. Wundt's position was based upon controlled experimental studies employing naïve subjects, who were trained in introspective techniques but were not professional musicians, whereas Stumpf's position was based upon his own introspective experience, which he considered to be more sophisticated and consequently superior to that of musically untrained experimental subjects. Characteristically, James sided with his friend Stumpf against Wundt (Blumenthal, 1985b).

Although his own research had little direct influence, many of Stumpf's students had a major impact on subsequent developments in philosophy and psychology. Husserl was a student of Stumpf's from 1884 to 1886. The Gestalt psychologists Wertheimer, Köhler, and Koffka were all students of Stumpf's, as was Kurt Lewin (1890–1947), who later applied the principles of Gestalt psychology to social psychology (Lewin, 1948), and Max Meyer (1873–1967), who promoted the behaviorist program in psychology in the United States two years before Watson (Meyer, 1911).

Stumpf's last years in Berlin were not happy ones. During the First World War, he lost many of his American and Russian colleagues, and the student population of the Institute of Experimental Psychology was decimated. Wolfgang Köhler succeeded Stumpf as director of the Institute when he retired in 1921.

Oswald Külpe: The Würzburg School

Oswald Külpe (1862–1915) enrolled at the University of Leipzig in 1881, intending to study history and philosophy, but became interested in experimental psychology after attending some of Wundt's lectures. He moved to the University of Berlin from 1882 to 1883 to study history and to the University of Göttingen from 1883 to 1886, where he began a PhD on sensation with Müller. He returned to the University of Leipzig in 1886 and completed his degree under Wundt's supervision. From 1887 to 1894 he served as an instructor and assistant to Wundt at the Institute of Psychology. Külpe published *Outline of Psychology* in 1893, an elegant popularization of Wundtian psychology. He was appointed professor of philosophy and aesthetics at the University of Würzburg in 1894, where he developed the psychology laboratory instituted by Brentano and Stumpf; and with Karl Marbe (1869–1953), he founded the Institute of Psychology at the University of Würzburg. Külpe left Würzburg for the University of Bonn in 1909, and in 1913 he transferred to the University of Munich, where he died in 1915.

The Würzburg Institute Research at the Würzburg Institute of Psychology was directed primarily toward the experimental study of cognitive and volitional processes. The work of Külpe's associates, such as Narziss Ach (1871–1946), Karl Bühler (1879–1963), Karl Marbe, August Mayer (1874–1951), August Messer (1867–1937), Johannes Orth (1872–1949), Otto Selz (1881–1943), and Henry J. Watt (1879–1925), laid the foundations of 20th-century cognitive psychology. Distinguished students who worked at the institute included Wertheimer, Koffka, Richard Pauli (1886–1951), Charles Spearman (1863–1945), and Robert Sessions Woodworth (1869–1962). Although Külpe and his associates became engaged in a major controversy with Wundt concerning the experimental analysis of cognitive processes, the general program of the Würzburg Institute was broadly Wundtian in orientation (much more so, for example, than the rival programs of Müller at Göttingen and Stumpf at Berlin).

Experimental subjects (who included Külpe and his associates) were carefully trained in **systematic experimental self-observation** (Ach, 1905), often based upon the experimenter's active questioning or interrogation (*Ausfrage*) (Bühler, 1907/1964). Subjects were required to reflect upon and provide detailed verbal reports of any sensations or images they experienced prior to and during experimental tasks, which included free and controlled word association, choice reactions, puzzles, word problems, and psychophysical judgments. While short-lived, the work of the Würzburg psychologists marked an important transition from associationist to rule-governed theories of cognition.

Imageless Thoughts and Determining Tendencies The work of the Würzburg psychologists is important because they conducted a number of experimental studies that undermined two fundamental assumptions of associationist psychology. First, Mayer and Orth (1901), Marbe (1901), and Bühler (1907/1964) demonstrated the existence of **imageless thoughts**: "states of consciousness" and "forms of judgment" that were not associated with any sensations or images. While some of their subjects did report idiosyncratic sensations and images while forming associations or making judgments, others reported none at all. Subjects reported in experimental "protocols" that they had thoughts "without any trace of imagery." This result, reported around the same time by Binet in Paris (Binet, 1903) and Woodworth in New York (Woodworth, 1906), eventually proved fatal to the tradition of associationist psychology from Hume to Bain in which thoughts were conceived of as images derived from sense impressions.

Second, Külpe (1912/1964), Watt (1904), and Ach (1905) demonstrated that **determining tendencies**, or "directed thoughts," play a critical role in cognitive processing, different from (and often countervailing) associations based upon traditional principles of similarity and contiguity. They demonstrated that directive instructions override idiosyncratic associations based upon imagery when experimental instructions direct subjects to draw sentential inferences or explicate conceptual entailments, such as stating a subordinate or superordinate category. They claimed that such instructions establish a preparatory mental schema, or "set" (*Einstellung*), that directs cognitive processing. For example, in a free association task, when asked for a response to "farmer," subjects might say "tradesman." When directed to respond with a coordinate category, subjects might also say "tradesman." Yet when directed to respond with a superordinate category, subjects would generally say "occupation" (Selz, 1927/1964, p. 227). These studies suggested that traditional principles of association play only a minor role in cognitive processing and that semantic and syntactic connections between thoughts override "accidental" associations between images based upon similarity and contiguity.

As Külpe put it,

> The importance of the task and its effects on the structure and course of mental events could not be explained with the tools of association psychology. Rather, Ach was able to show that even associations of considerable strength could be overcome with a counteracting task. The force with which a determining tendency acts is not only greater than the familiar reproductive tendencies, it also derives from a different source and its effectiveness is not tied to associative relations.
>
> —(1912/1964, p. 216)

Since according to Külpe, determining tendencies play a role in all forms of thought, "the psychology of the task became an essential part of the modern investigation of thinking" (1912/1964, p. 216).

The Modern Investigation of Thinking Külpe and his colleagues not only demonstrated the limitations of associationist psychology, but also recognized the possibility of a cognitive psychology based upon the processing of thought contents in accord with rules that are *independent of image association*:

> The fact that thoughts are independent of the signs in which they are expressed, and that they have peculiar and fluid interrelations, uninfluenced by the laws of the association of images, demonstrated their autonomy as a special class of conscious contents.
>
> —(1912/1964, pp. 212–213)

Although most of the Würzburg psychologists still tended to talk in terms of *conscious* contents, they recognized that the form of consciousness involved in following a rule is quite different from the form of consciousness involved in awareness of a sensational image:

> But consciousness of a rule is not thinking *of* a rule, rather it is thinking a rule or according to a rule. The object of consciousness of a rule is not the rule, but rather the state of affairs, the object, that the rule describes, on which it is used.
>
> —(Bühler, 1907/1964, p. 163)

Bühler (1907/1964, 1908) and Selz (1922, 1927/1964) developed early forms of autonomous cognitive theory (independent of image association). Bühler was originally a student of Stumpf's at Berlin and served as an assistant to Külpe at Würzburg from 1907 to 1909. He stressed the critical role of rules in the processing of thought contents and was a pioneer of the so-called **rules and representations** approach of cognitive psychology, in which cognition is conceived of in terms of the rule-governed processing of symbolic representations (Bechtel, 1988).

Selz developed perhaps the closest approximation to contemporary cognitive theory. He received his PhD in philosophy from the University of Munich in 1909 (after having previously studied with Stumpf in Berlin). He did a postdoctoral thesis on the "laws of the ordered thought processes" under Külpe's supervision at the University of Bonn, after Külpe transferred there in 1909, and also worked with Bühler, who followed Külpe to Bonn in 1910. Selz became an instructor and junior professor at the University of Bonn from 1919 to 1921, and later professor of philosophy, psychology, and educational theory at the Commercial College of Mannheim. His theory of the role of anticipatory schema in problem solving (Selz, 1922, 1927/1964) represented the most sophisticated expression of the "modern investigation of thinking" promoted by the Würzburg psychologists (although Selz himself was never formally associated with the University of Würzburg) and anticipated later developments in cognitive psychology, particularly the computer simulation of problem solving.

The Controversy With Wundt The experimental program of the Würzburg school brought its members into conflict with Wundt, who wrote a famous critique of their experiments (Wundt, 1907). The work of the Würzburg psychologists came to be seen as a challenge to Wundt's supposed claim that "higher" cognitive processes cannot be studied experimentally, but must be explored via the naturalistic observational methods of *Völkerpsychologie*.

However, Wundt was not opposed to the Würzburg theories of cognition. His own theory of apperception precluded the equation of thoughts and sensational images, and he did not believe that human cognitive processes could be adequately explained in terms of associationist principles of similarity and contiguity. Wundt was fully supportive of the study of determining tendencies, which, he maintained, deserved "further application and development in the same direction" (1911, cited in Woodward, 1982, p. 449). The so-called **imageless-thought debate** caused a stir in America, but mainly because imageless thoughts created a problem for the form of structural psychology promoted at Cornell University by Edward B. Titchener, who interpreted Wundt's psychology in line with traditional British empiricism and associationist psychology. It was Müller, not Wundt, who defended associationist psychology against the Würzburg critiques (Müller, 1913/1964).

As noted earlier, research in Wundt's laboratory was not restricted to the study of elemental sensational processes; his students worked on apperception, memory, and other "higher" thought processes. Wundt's objections to the Würzburg experiments were not objections to the experimental study of "higher" thought processes per se, but were specific objections to the methodological practices of the Würzburg experimentalists, especially those of Ach and Bühler.

Wundt (1907) laid down four conditions of experimental adequacy: that the observer should be in a position to observe the process investigated and should be in a state of anticipatory attention; that experimental conditions should be varied and that experiments should be repeated. He admitted that these conditions were idealizations that are only approximated by experiments in natural science, but complained that all four conditions were violated by the Würzburg experiments. He claimed that they were "sham experiments which have the appearance of being systematic only because they take place in a psychological laboratory" and maintained that

> they have no scientific value because they fall short when judged by all the criteria which distinguish the self-observations of experimental psychology from those of ordinary life.
>
> —(1907, p. 329)

However, Wundt's complaints about the "reprehensible method" of the Würzburg psychologists were somewhat disingenuous. As a number of later commentators noted, Wundt's own experimental program of "trained and strained" self-observation could be faulted on his first two conditions of experimental adequacy, and the Würzburg psychologists routinely varied experimental conditions and repeated experiments (Humphrey, 1951; Woodworth, 1938). In his response to Wundt, Bühler (1908) made a reasonable case that the Würzburg experiments satisfied all four of Wundt's conditions (a view also endorsed by Humphrey and Woodworth), at least to the degree that they were satisfied by studies in his own experimental program.

Certainly Wundt was not averse to appealing to self-observation in support of his own theories of thought processes. In taking issue with the Würzburgers' interpretation of some of their experimental results, Wundt championed his own theoretical account of the transformation of mental configurations into sequential linguistic representations (a "higher" thought process if ever there was one), and cited as evidence his own "self-observations" of the process. Bühler (1908) expressed his surprise at Wundt's critique because he believed that he and his colleagues had followed Wundt's own methodological practice. Robert Woodworth, the American co-discoverer of "imageless-thoughts," was less charitable:

> He first demolishes the method of the thought experiment by his critique, and then proceeds to employ the same method himself and to reach the same results (as to

"imageless thought") which had been reached by the Külpe school and which had seemed so objectionable.

—(1938, p. 785)

However, there was a significant difference between the experimental studies conducted by the Würzburg psychologists and those conducted in Wundt's Leipzig laboratory. Most of the experimental studies conducted in Wundt's laboratory employed objective measures of psychological processes such as reaction time, with experimental introspection normally only (and rarely) used to provide supplementary information about such processes. In contrast, the Würzburg psychologists, like Titchener's students at Cornell, made introspective reports the primary measure of experimentally investigated thought processes.

There was another perceived weakness of the Würzburg experiments. The published reports of experiments conducted in Wundt's laboratory (and other early German and American laboratories) provided the identity of the subjects engaged in experimental self-observation and described their level of training. The published experimental reports of the Würzburg psychologists failed to include such information (Bazerman, 1987; Danziger, 1990). This was no small failing for Wundt, who regularly refused to allow students to participate in experiments because they were not sufficiently trained or properly "calibrated." Lightner Witmer, one of Wundt's American students, reported how Wundt refused to allow him to take part in reaction time experiments because he did not consider him properly calibrated as an observer: "In his opinion my sensory reaction to sound and touch was too short to be a true sensory reaction" (Witmer, letter to Boring, 1948, cited in O'Donnell, 1985, p. 35).

Other critics, such as Ebbinghaus (1902) and Müller (1911–1913), complained about the laxity of experimental controls and the danger of biasing subject responses through the use of subject interrogation, anticipating later concerns about experimenter expectancy effects (Rosenthal, 1966) and demand characteristics (Orne, 1962).

Gestalt Psychology

The best known and most influential school of psychology that developed in Germany in the years following the creation of Wundt's Leipzig program was the Gestalt school of psychology, founded by Max Wertheimer, Wolfgang Köhler, and Kurt Koffka. The basic principles of Gestalt psychology, which stressed the active and organized nature of perception, can be traced back to the work of theorists such as Kant, who claimed that the sensational elements of perception are actively organized in accord with the intuitive forms of space and time and conceptual categories such as substance and causality. The more immediate anticipators acknowledged by the Gestalt psychologists themselves were the physicist Ernst Mach (1838–1916) and the psychologist Christian von Ehrenfels (1859–1932).

Mach did empirical research on brightness perception and movement. In *Principles of a Theory of Movement Perception* (1875/1967), he claimed that the perception of movement is determined by a sensational element additional to visual sensation (according to Mach, the inner ear is the organ that perceives movement). In *Contributions to the Analysis of Sensations* (1886), Mach claimed to have identified sensations of "space-form" and "time-form" that are independent of visual sensation.

Christian von Ehrenfels, a student of Alexius Meinong's (1853–1920) at the Institute of Psychology at the University of Graz in Austria, introduced the notion of "form-qualities" (*Gestaltqualität*) in "On Gestalt Qualities" (1890), which he illustrated by reference to a perceived melody. The form-quality of a melody is not equivalent to the aggregate sum of its tonal elements: One may produce a different melody by rearranging of the same tonal elements in a different order, and one may produce the same melody by arranging different tonal elements (in a different key, for example) in the original order. According to Ehrenfels, the form-quality of a melody is something different from, or something "over and above," the sum of its sensational elements. The form-quality is not determined by the sensory elements (*Fundamente*), but by the structure or pattern of their relationship (*Grundlage*): It is an emergent configuration actively created by the organizational propensities of the mind.

However, the Gestalt psychologists went beyond Mach and Ehrenfels's stress on the emergent nature of form-qualities, which had also been recognized by Mill (as a product of cognitive inference) and Wundt (as a product of the fusion of sensational elements). They maintained not only that holistic form-qualities are underdetermined by sensational elements, but also that so-called sensational "elements" are artificial abstractions, whose nature and identity are determined by their *relational* location within a perceptual configuration (as Wundt had also claimed). The Gestalt psychologists were opposed to all forms of psychological atomism and associationist psychology: They denied that perception is a function of the combination of independent sensational elements and that perception is grounded in some form of association or cognitive inference.

The Phi Phenomenon   Max Wertheimer was born in Prague. He studied law at the University of Prague but became more interested in psychology when he attended lectures by Ehrenfels. He spent a few years at the University of Berlin with Stumpf, then worked with Külpe at the University of Würzburg on his doctoral degree, which he received in 1904. From 1904 to 1910 Wertheimer held positions at the universities of Prague, Vienna, and Berlin. He taught at the University of Frankfurt from 1910 to 1916 and, after 13 years at the University of Berlin, returned as full professor in 1929. In 1933 he emigrated to the United States, where he taught at the New School for Social Research. Wertheimer was one of a number of refugees from Nazi Germany who founded the "University in Exile" (later called the New School for Social Research) in New York, the first university in the United States devoted to adult education. He died in 1943.

According to Wertheimer's own account (Sarris, 1997), the discovery of the phi phenomenon was the fortuitous outcome of a train journey. He was on his way to a vacation on the German Rhine during the summer of 1910. Looking out of the carriage window, he was fascinated by the telephone poles and mountains that seemed to whiz by and began to wonder about the cause of this apparent motion. He abandoned his vacation and got off the train at Frankfurt. He rented a hotel room, where he contemplated images of a moving child and horse that he produced with the aid of a stroboscope he bought at a local toy store. The next day Wertheimer visited the University of Frankfurt, where he consulted Friedrich Schumann, the former assistant to Müller and colleague of Stumpf's, who was now working at the Institute of Psychology. Schumann had done extensive research on spatial perception (and had a PhD in physics), but could not provide an explanation of apparent motion. He offered Wertheimer the use of his laboratory, including the improved tachistoscope that he had developed. Schumann also introduced Wertheimer to two of his colleagues, Wolfgang Köhler and Kurt Koffka, assistants at the Institute of Psychology, who worked with Wertheimer and served as subjects in his motion-perception experiments. Köhler and Koffka, along with Wertheimer, are generally recognized as the joint founders of Gestalt psychology, or the **Berlin (or Berlin-Frankfurt) school of Gestalt psychology**.

In Wertheimer's original experiments, he projected flashes of light successively through two horizontal slits onto a screen. At a projection rate of about 50–60 milliseconds, a single line of light appeared to move from one position to another. At higher rates, two lines of light appeared simultaneously, and at lower rates they appeared individually in succession. Wertheimer called the impression of motion generated by alternative illumination at the middle projection range the **phi phenomenon.** He reported the results of these experiments in his 1912 paper "Experimental Studies in the Visual Perception of Motion." Vittorio Benussi (1878–1927), a student of Meinong's at the University of Graz, reported a similar phenomenon with respect to the sense of touch: When points on the skin are stimulated in rapid succession, they produce a subjective impression of apparent motion, as if the tactile stimulus moves in an arc through space (Benussi, 1914).

On the basis of these experiments, Wertheimer concluded, somewhat paradoxically, that apparent motion is *perceived.* What he meant was that our impression of both apparent and real motion is not the product of association or cognitive inference made on the basis of discrete sensational elements, as Berkeley, Mill, and Helmholtz had maintained. Wertheimer rejected the prevalent explanation of the perception of motion as an inference based upon eye movements. He demonstrated that subjects still perceive apparent motion when they are asked to visually fixate on a single central point and when the cycle of illumination is less than the minimal reaction time required for eye movements (Lowry, 1982).

Relational Elements   Wertheimer denied that visual stimuli on the retina give rise to punctiform visual sensations in the brain, which form the basis of a distinct process of association or inferential judgment. Rather, he maintained that retinal input is processed directly by the brain to generate the perception of motion, via what he called "a kind of physiological short circuit" (*Kurzschluss*) (1912/1925, p. 88). According to Wertheimer, excitations in the brain become integrated into a kind of "physiological whole-process" (*Gesamtprozess*) (1912/1925, p. 92).

This last point is important to stress, because it grounded the central thesis of the Gestalt psychologists: the denial of the existence of atomistic sensational elements (Ash, 1995). According to Wertheimer (and Köhler and Koffka), sensational elements are not autonomously determined by the external world and our sensory receptors, and perception is not a product of "senseless additive combining" (Lowry, 1982, p. 186). Although we can conceptually distinguish elements of perception, the nature and identity of such elements is relationally determined by their location within perceptual configurations or structures. One configuration of sensory input will generate a perception analyzable in terms of one set of elements; another configuration of the *same* sensory input will generate a quite different perception, analyzable in terms of a different set of elements. As Wertheimer put it,

> There are wholes, the behavior of which is not determined by that of their individual elements, but where the part-processes are themselves determined by the intrinsic nature of the whole.
>
> —(1925/1938, p. 2)

Probably the best phenomenological illustration of this claim is the old woman/young woman ambiguous figure. When the visual input is configured one way, a particular point on the visual image represents the end of the old woman's nose; when the visual input is configured another way, the same point represents the end of the young woman's chin. The identity of the point *as* the end of the old woman's nose or the young woman's chin is determined by its relational location within the perceptual configuration. As Wertheimer put it, "'Elements' . . . are determined as parts by the intrinsic conditions of their wholes and are to be understood 'as parts' relative to such wholes" (1922/1938, p. 14).

Good Form   Wertheimer, Köhler, and Koffka founded the journal *Psychological Research* (*Psychologisische Forschung*) in 1921 to publish experimental reports and theoretical articles relating to the new Gestalt psychology. According to the Gestalt psychologists, the elements of perception are actively organized into wholes according to various principles, such as continuity (elements grouped in lines tend

Ambiguous figures: vase/faces and old woman/young woman.

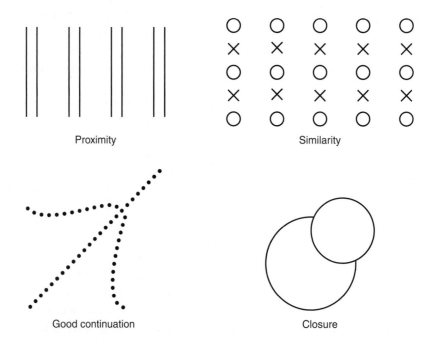

Good form: Gestalt principles of proximity, similarity, good continuation, and closure.

to be perceived as continuous), inclusiveness (elements tend to be perceived as the largest possible figure), similarity (similar elements tend to be grouped together), proximity (temporally or spatially adjacent elements tend to be grouped together), and closure (incomplete configurations tend to be completed). According to the **law of Prägnanz**, or law of good form, sensational input will be organized into a form that is as concise, ordered, and proportioned as is possible given the conditions.

Gestalt psychological theory worked best with respect to the explanation of perceptual illusions. These created a problem for standard empiricist accounts of perception, but were readily accommodated by Gestalt accounts in terms of alternative configurations of stimulus input, as in Koffka's account of our perceptual responses to the Necker cube (1935). Analogously, different perceptual responses to ambiguous figures, such as the familiar vase/faces and old woman/young woman figures, could be readily explained in terms of different perceptual configurations of sensory input, in terms of different figure-ground configurations, for example (Rubin, 1915/1921).

Koffka and Köhler   Kurt Koffka was born in Berlin and took his PhD with Stumpf in 1909. He served as an assistant at the universities of Würzburg and Frankfurt from 1909 to 1910 and as lecturer and later professor at the University of Giessen from 1911 to 1924. He visited the United States in 1924, where he served as a visiting professor at Cornell University and the University of Wisconsin. Eventually he accepted a permanent position at Smith College in Massachusetts. His 1922 *Psychological Bulletin* article introduced Gestalt psychology to many Americans, although it focused almost exclusively on perception. His 1935 book *Principles of Gestalt Psychology* was broader in scope, but the difficulty of the work limited its influence. Koffka also extended Gestalt principles to child development in *The Growth of the Mind: An Introduction to Child Psychology* in 1924.

Wolfgang Köhler was perhaps the most effective advocate of Gestalt psychology and became its informal spokesperson. He was born in Estonia and originally trained as a physicist with Max Plank (1858–1947). He took his PhD with Stumpf in 1909 and accepted a position at the University of Frankfurt that same year. In 1913 the Prussian Academy of Sciences invited him to serve as director of its anthropoid station in Tenerife. During his years there Köhler did pioneering research with primates, documented in *The Mentality of Apes* (1917), in which he extended the principles of Gestalt psychology to animal learning. In one series of studies, chimpanzees demonstrated their ability to stack boxes to reach hanging bananas and to manipulate sticks of different lengths to access bananas placed outside their enclosure. Köhler claimed that the chimpanzees' success in these tasks was a product of **insight learning**, a creative form of learning that involves perceptual restructuring of the problem situation, in contrast to the mechanical forms of "trial-and-error" learning that comparative and animal psychologists such as Morgan and Thorndike attributed to animals. In opposition to Morgan and later behaviorists, Köhler maintained

Insight learning: chimpanzee stacking boxes.

that chimpanzees engage in means-ends reasoning and that many animals are capable of perceiving relations (including animals of lower intelligence such as chickens). In what Köhler called **transposition learning**, animals respond to similarities in relationships between stimuli rather than similarities between stimuli themselves. For example, chimpanzees trained to choose a 15-cm over a 10-cm disk, and subsequently presented with 15-cm and 20-cm disks, choose the larger 20-cm disk: they make *relational* rather than stimulus-specific responses.

It has been suggested that Köhler's business in Tenerife was not entirely academic. He may have been involved in espionage during the First World War, sending out radio reports on the movement of British shipping (Ley, 1990), although the suggestion has been disputed by Harris (1991). Köhler returned to take up a position at the University of Göttingen in 1921. The following year he succeeded Stumpf to the chair in philosophy at the University of Berlin, with directorship of the Institute of Psychology, now one of the premier positions in the German psychological academy. Köhler visited the United States in the 1930s, where he served as a visiting professor at Clark, Harvard, and Chicago. His influential statement of the general principles of Gestalt psychology was published as *Gestalt Psychology* in 1929.

From his position of academic authority, Köhler bravely criticized the Nazis and defended the Jews (Henle, 1978a). He expected to be arrested at any time, although he never was. He resigned from the Berlin Institute of Psychology in 1934, but the authorities would not accept his resignation. Köhler visited Harvard in 1934, where he gave the William James Memorial Lecture and a series of public lectures and graduate seminars. He was considered for an appointment at Harvard, but Edwin G. Boring, the chair of the psychology department, opposed his candidacy. Boring wanted an accredited experimentalist and successfully lobbied in favor of the neurophysiologist Karl Lashley (1890–1958).

Köhler emigrated to the United States in 1935, when things became intolerable in Nazi Berlin (he refused to take the Nazi loyalty oath, and the authorities finally accepted his resignation). He secured a full-time position at Swarthmore College in Pennsylvania, where he remained until he retired in 1958. Köhler continued writing and conducting research at Princeton, Dartmouth, and MIT until he died in 1967. He published *The Place of Value in a World of Facts* in 1938 and

Dynamics in Psychology in 1940. Köhler received an APA Distinguished Scientific Contribution Award in 1956 and was elected president of the APA in 1959. Some found him aloof and ill-humored as a person, but not the graduate students at Clark University, whom he taught to tango during his visit there.

Gestalt Psychology and Field Theory Köhler also developed the fundamental neurophysiological theory of Gestalt psychology (modeled on recent advances in physical field theory), which received its formal statement in *Static and Stationary Physical Gestalts* in 1920. According to Köhler, the basic principles of Gestalt psychology are a function of the "inherent dynamical properties of the brain." Force fields in the brain tend to seek equilibrium and remain in stationary equilibrium until some external force disturbs them. When so disturbed, force fields become dynamic and strive to regain equilibrium.

Köhler reductively explained perception in terms of the principle of **psychoneural isomorphism**: Configured perceptual fields are structurally identical to configured neural fields, of which they are products. If sensational input generates a balanced neural field, perceptual output will correspond to sensational input. If sensational input generates an unbalanced neural field, the field will reconfigure itself and perceptual output will not correspond to sensational input: The neural elements corresponding to the sensory input will be *transformed* in the reconfiguration of the neural field to attain equilibrium. The law of Prägnanz was held to be a consequence of the reconfiguration of neural fields to attain equilibrium. Thus, in the case of space perception, for example, Köhler held that "experienced order in space is always structurally identical with functional order in the distribution of underlying brain processes" (1929, p. 61).

This neural theory was entirely speculative, and Köhler freely admitted that Gestalt psychologists were "not in the position to derive the respective physiological and phenomenal characteristics [of psychological processes] in individual cases" (1920, p. 259). The rare experimental studies of neural field theory proved negative. Lashley manipulated electrical fields on the surface of the brains of monkeys, but with no discernible effect on their performance on visual discrimination tasks (Lashley, Chow, & Semmes, 1951).

Wertheimer, Köhler, and Koffka extended the basic principles of Gestalt psychology beyond perception to provide explanations of reflexive behavior, the ego, adjustment, will, memory, thought, personality, and the social world. Karl Duncker (1903–1940) and Wertheimer developed Gestalt principles to provide a general theory of problem solving in *Psychology of Thinking* (Duncker, 1935/1945) and *Productive Thinking* (Wertheimer, 1945). Köhler extended Gestalt principles to the study of memory (Köhler & von Restorff, 1933) and Koffka to the study of child development (1924). Kurt Gottschaldt (1902–1901), who studied with Wertheimer and Köhler, taught at the University of Berlin from 1935 to 1962 and extended Gestalt principles to developmental psychology and personality theory (he was the only member of the Berlin school of Gestalt psychology who did not emigrate to America during the Nazi era).

Koffka articulated the basic justification for this extension in *Principles of Gestalt Psychology* (1935). He claimed that the law of Prägnanz applied to all psychological processes, since all psychological processes are a function of dynamic forces in the brain. According to Koffka, all psychological processes involve some form of tension displacement: Dynamic forces are brought into balance as the neural system reduces the tension caused by disequilibrium. On the psychological level, the tension created by some perceived problem, for example, motivates our attempts to resolve it, which involves cognitive scanning and imaginative rehearsal, as in the case of Wertheimer's account of productive thinking, Köhler's account of insight learning in primates, and Koffka's account of memory.

A good illustration of this principle was the study that Bluma Zeigarnik conducted on the memory of waiters. Zeigarnik studied with Kurt Lewin, who was a colleague of Köhler's and Koffka's at the Berlin Institute of Psychology in the 1920s. Lewin noted that Berlin waiters tended to remember the details of a client's bill while it remained unpaid, but immediately forgot them once the bill was paid. Zeigarnik explored Lewin's suggestion that the tension created by the lack of cognitive closure facilitates recall. Once payment is received, closure is achieved, dissipating tension and erasing memory. Zeigarnik found that interrupted and unfinished tasks tend to be remembered better and quicker than uninterrupted and completed tasks (Zeigarnik, 1927).

The Support for Gestalt Psychology   Many of the theoretical explanations offered by the Gestalt psychologists, including Wertheimer's original explanation of the phi phenomenon, were highly speculative and undersupported by experimental data. Wertheimer's experiments demonstrated the inadequacy of a specific account of the perception of motion based upon eye movements, but not the general inadequacy of accounts based upon association or cognitive inference (Lowry, 1982).

Müller, Bühler, Spearman, and members of the Leipzig school of Gestalt psychology were critical of the work of the Berlin Gestalt psychologists. Members of the **Graz school of Gestalt psychology**, located at the Institute of Psychology at the University of Graz, advanced an alternative account of the production of perceptual configurations. Stephan Witasek (1870–1915), a former student of Meinong's, claimed that different perceptual configurations are psychological products of preexisting sensational elements (Witasek, 1908). He and his associates Vittorio Benussi (1878–1927) and Alois Höfler (1853–1922) maintained that this explained how *different* perceptual configurations could be generated from the *same* sensory elements:

> Between the sensory impressions, which remain constant, and the perception of figures, which may differ from each other, an event X must take place, which,

depending on the form it takes, will lead to the perception of totally different objects from the same constant sensory stimulation.

—(Benussi, 1914, p. 400, cited in Fabian, 1997, p. 254)

The members of the Graz school agreed that perceptual wholes have properties that are not an aggregative function of the properties of their sensory elements and that the same sensory elements can result in different perceptual configurations. However, they denied that the creative psychological processes involved in perception transform the *identity* of the original sensory elements: They denied that the identity of sensory elements is determined by their relation to other elements in a configured whole.

On the face of it, this distinctive thesis of the Berlin school of Gestalt psychology was hard to defend. Recalling Ehrenfels's example of a melody, Wertheimer claimed that the identity of a tone derives from its role in a particular melody: "The flesh and blood of a tone depends from the start upon its role in the melody" (1925/1938, p. 5). Yet tones appear to exist and be identifiable *independently* of the melodies in which they often occur. Indeed, this is presupposed by the common Gestalt psychological claim, originally advanced by Ehrenfels, that the *same* tonal elements of one melody can be rearranged to form a *different* melody: The identity of the tonal elements remains the same, but the melody changes with the different configuration of the elements. Ironically, this atomistic assumption about the identity of sensory elements appears central to some of the explanations the Berlin Gestalt psychologists offered for a variety of perceptual phenomena, such as perceptual constancy, in which perceived objects remain the same shape and size despite changes in elemental sensory inputs (supposedly because of invariance in figure-ground ratios in perceptual and brain fields).

Even the old woman/young woman ambiguous figure doubtfully serves as an illustration of the transformation of sensory elements in perceptual configurations. Edgar Rubin, the former student of Muller's who created many of the ambiguous figures of Gestalt psychology, thought it demonstrated only that the same sensory elements could be "completed" in different ways to generate different perceptions (Rubin, 1915/1921). David Katz, another student of Müller's, probably provided the best empirical support for the claims about the relational identity of sensational elements championed by the Berlin school. Katz's (1911) research on "phenomenal modes of color" indicated that the phenomenal appearance of colors depends upon the context in which they are viewed, as "surface," "volumic," or "film" colors (Lowry, 1982).

The Legacy of Gestalt Psychology   The limited empirical support for Gestalt theories of perception cast doubt upon their extension to other psychological domains, and continued interest in Gestalt psychology has tended to remain restricted to perception. The theory of psychological isomorphism, which grounded the explanatory reduction of psychological configurations to neural configurations, was undermined by the failure of neural field theory. Köhler's own neurophysiological research at MIT did not provide any empirical support for the theory.

The Gestalt psychologists were dismissive of alternative explanations of the various perceptual, cognitive, and social psychological processes covered by their theories. They promoted Gestalt psychology with evangelical zeal, behaving like "intellectual missionaries, spreading a new gospel" (Sokal, 1984, p. 1257), and located the principles of Gestalt psychology within a general holistic philosophical worldview. These features partially account for the limited impact of Gestalt psychology on the development of American psychology.

While the Gestalt psychologists were accorded due respect by the American psychological community, they attracted few American disciples to continue their general theoretical program. One reason for their lack of impact was the fact that Wertheimer and Koffka died fairly young, and they all held positions at institutions without graduate programs in psychology (Wertheimer at the New School, Koffka at Smith College, and Köhler at Swarthmore College).

Although Gestalt psychology was opposed to the atomism of traditional associationist psychology and behaviorism, it was as thoroughly mechanistic as both. Some have come to associate Gestalt psychology with an emphasis on human agency and creativity and a holistic rejection of mechanistic and reductive approaches to the explanation of human behavior. "Gestalt therapy" has also been championed as a form of "self-discovery," as opposed to more directive forms of therapy (Perls, Hefferline, & Goodman, 1951). However, there is little support for such characterizations in the work of Wertheimer, Köhler, and Koffka, who all insisted that psychological processes are wholly determined by automatic neural processes. Although they made some theoretical contributions to psychotherapy (Knapp, 1986), Köhler explicitly repudiated the form of "Gestalt therapy" promoted by Fritz Perls (1893–1970) and his colleagues (Henle, 1978b).

APPLIED PSYCHOLOGY IN GERMANY

Despite their theoretical differences (and personal animosity), Wundt and Stumpf saw psychology as a natural development of philosophy. However, the majority of German philosophers and later psychologists did not share this view. Wilhelm Dilthey, Stumpf's philosophical colleague at the University of Berlin, claimed that natural scientific methods are inappropriate for the study of psychological states and processes and engaged in critical debates with Wundt, Stumpf, and Ebbinghaus about the legitimacy of experimental psychology.

Opposition to the appointment of psychologists to philosophy chairs in Germany reached such a pitch that in 1913 Wilhelm Windelband (1848–1915) was able to organize a petition by 107 philosophers in Germany, Austria, and

Switzerland, who protested against "the filling of chairs in philosophy with representatives of experimental psychology" (quoted in Ash, 1980, p. 407). Opposition from philosophers threatened to overwhelm psychology in Germany (Metzger, 1965), forcing Wundt to defend both experimental psychology and its integral relation to philosophy in *Psychology Struggling for Survival* (1913).

After the First World War, experimental psychologists were no longer appointed to chairs in philosophy, and traditional philosophers recaptured the chairs at the universities of Bonn and Wroclaw. New positions were introduced for psychologists during the 1920s and 1930s, but these were almost exclusively at technical universities and institutes (Kusch, 1995). German psychologists eventually followed the lead of their philosophical critics and organized their own petition in 1931 for the establishment of separate chairs of psychology at leading German universities.

Wundt had rejected what he called the "American model" of separate psychology departments and chairs, which he feared would lead to an overemphasis on applied over theoretical and experimental psychology. Yet this is precisely what happened in Germany in the years after Wundt's death. During the 1920s psychology in Germany became increasingly applied, and by 1925 publications in applied psychology outnumbered those in "pure" or general psychology by two to one (Osier & Wozniak, 1984, cited in Kusch, 1995, p. 124).

Psychotechnics: group training facility for streetcar drivers in Berlin.

Karl Marbe, who had studied with Wundt and Külpe, turned to the psychology of advertising and studied the psychology of accidents and industrial damage. He pioneered the development of **psychotechnics** by creating aptitude tests for train conductors, insurance agents, prison guards, dentists, and surgeons and played a major role in instituting the subdisciplines of school and forensic psychology.

While serving as an assistant at Wundt's Leipzig Institute, Ernst Meumann (1862–1915) directed work on educational psychology, which he called "experimental pedagogy." A progressive social and school reformer like John Dewey (1859–1952) and G. Stanley Hall in the United States, Meumann held posts in psychology and education at various universities, until he settled as director of the philosophical seminar and psychology laboratory at the Hamburg Colonial Institute. Wundt thought him an outstanding student, and they remained close friends, although Wundt withdrew his original support for Meumann's research, because of the limited number of publications that came out of it. Meumann's *Introductory Lectures on Experimental Pedagogy and Its Psychological Basis* (1907) became a required text for generations of education students in Germany and was well received in North and South America and Russia. Meumann founded *The Archives of Psychology* in 1903 and the *Journal of Experimental Education* (later the *Journal of Educational Psychology*) in 1911. His studies of what became known as "social facilitation" in the classroom were later developed by Floyd Allport (1890–1978), one of the founders of American social psychology (Allport, 1920, 1924).

William Stern (1871–1938), a former student of Ebbinghaus's, took over from Meumann at the Hamburg Colonial Institute in 1916 (after 19 years at the University of Breslau). He became director of the New Psychological Institute (which he helped to found) in 1919. Stern was committed to the application of psychological knowledge to industry, commerce, and education and founded the *Journal of*

Farm Kitchen: Picture used in William Stern's eyewitness research.

Applied Psychology in 1908 (with Otto Lipmann). He introduced the term **differential psychology** to characterize the study of individual differences, originally in the context of his own pioneering studies of eyewitness testimony (Stern, 1902). He also introduced the notion of a **mental quotient**, defined as a child's mental age (which he held to be determined by performance on the Binet-Simon test of intelligence) divided by its chronological age (Stern, 1914). Stern also pioneered the development of personality psychology and had a special influence on Gordon Allport (1897–1967), the Harvard social psychologist and founder of personality theory in America (Allport, 1937). With his wife Clara, Stern published some classic studies of child language and memory. His work was well received by American educators and psychologists, and he accepted a position at Duke University in 1934, where he died suddenly in 1938.

Karl Bühler, another of Külpe's students, founded the Psychological Institute at the University of Vienna (sometimes known as the Vienna School of Psychology) in 1922. It became known for its tradition of rigorous experimental research and application, particularly through its productive association with the Institute of Education. Karl was joined by his wife Charlotte Bühler (1893–1974) in 1923, the first female instructor in Germany at Dresden Technical University. Charlotte, who was known for her original research on teenagers (Bühler, 1918), established the Institute of Child Psychology. The Bühlers pioneered the use of naturalistic developmental studies at the Vienna Reception Center for Children, a children's shelter now known as the Charlotte Bühler home. Charlotte visited the United States on a Rockefeller Foundation Fellowship in 1924–1925 and managed to secure 10 years of funding for the Vienna Institute from the Foundation (Rollett, 1997).

Famous students of the Institute included Paul Lazarfeld (1901–1976), the social psychologist, methodologist, and statistician; Else Frenkel-Brunswik (1908–1958), wife of Egon Brunswik (1903–1955) and one of the coauthors of *The Authoritarian Personality* (Adorno et al., 1950); and Karl Popper (1902–1994), the future philosopher of science, whose PhD thesis on "The Genetic Theory of Intelligence" was examined by Bühler and Moritz Schlick (1882–1936), one of the founders of logical positivism. Karl Bühler was a visiting professor at Johns Hopkins and Stanford and received an invitation to join the faculty at Harvard in 1930, but unfortunately turned it down. When the Nazis annexed Austria in 1938, he was demoted, then discharged and imprisoned. The new director Gunther Ipsen (1889–1984) introduced "racial psychology" the following year.

By this time psychology in Germany, now increasingly applied, had been appropriated by the military. Many of the leading German psychologists had already fled to the United States (including Wertheimer, Köhler and Koffka, Lazarfeld, Frenkel-Brunswik, and William and Clara Stern), and others suffered at the hands of the Nazis. Otto Selz, Külpe's student and anticipator of 20th-century cognitive psychology, perished in the concentration camp at Auschwitz.

DISCUSSION QUESTIONS

1. Wundt believed that scientific psychology should be based upon the experimental methods but not the explanatory concepts of physiology. Sechenov believed that scientific psychology should be based upon the experimental methods and the explanatory concepts of physiology. Who do you think was right? Why?

2. Wundt characterized his configurational psychology as active and voluntary, in supposed contrast to passive associationist psychology. In a mechanistic psychology, is there any difference between active as opposed to passive perception and cognition?

3. According to Wundt's principle of psychical relations, psychological "elements" are relational in nature. Wundt's illustrative example was words, which he claimed have meaning only in the sentences in which they are configured. Was this a good example of a relational psychological element?

4. Is intentionality the mark of the mental, as Brentano maintained? Can you think of any mental states that are not intentional?

5. Did Wertheimer's experiments on the phi phenomenon demonstrate that perceptual "elements" are relational in nature? Did any Gestalt studies demonstrate this?

GLOSSARY

accommodation In Herbart's theory of learning, the process by which an apperceptive mass is adjusted to incorporate a new representational element.

act psychology Term used to characterize Brentano's psychology concerned with mental acts, as opposed to Wundt's supposed psychology of mental contents.

apperception In Herbart, focused attention. In Wundt, the creative and selective attentional process responsible for the configuration of conscious mental states.

apperceptive mass According to Herbart, the constellation of connected elementary mental representations that constitute the current object of apperception or focused attention.

assimilation In Herbart's theory of learning, the process by which a new representational element is integrated with an apperceptive mass.

Berlin (or Berlin-Frankfurt) school of Gestalt psychology Form of Gestalt psychology associated with Max Wertheimer, Wolfgang Köhler, and Kurt Koffka, who maintained that the nature and identity of perceptual "elements" is determined relationally by their position within perceptual configurations or structures.

complication experiment Form of reaction-time experiment in which the time taken for components of a complex task is calculated by subtraction of the measured time taken for other components of the task.

determining tendency Structure of task that determines cognitive processing independently of image association, experimentally identified by members of the Würzburg school.

differential psychology Term introduced by William Stern to describe the study of individual differences.

experimental self-observation Form of self-observation in which trained subjects provide concurrent commentaries on their conscious experience under rigorously controlled experimental conditions.

Graz school of Gestalt psychology Form of Gestalt psychology associated with psychologists at the University of Graz, who maintained that perceptual configurations are psychological products of preexisting sensational elements.

homeostatic motivation Theory of motivation according to which organisms are motivated to eliminate states of disequilibrium that are experienced as unpleasant or painful.

imageless thought Instances of thought not accompanied by sensations or images, experimentally identified by members of the Würzburg school.

imageless-thought debate The debate about the existence of imageless thoughts between members of the Würzburg school and Edward B. Titchener, the representative of structural psychology in the United States.

immediate experience The kind of experience that is not subject to theoretical interpretation. According to Wundt, the subject matter of psychology.

insight learning According to Köhler, a creative form of learning that involves perceptual restructuring of the problem situation.

law of Prägnanz In Gestalt psychology, law of good form.

mediate experience The kind of experience that is theoretically interpreted. According to Wundt, the subject matter of natural science.

mental chronometry Use of complication experiments to estimate the duration of postulated mental processes such as discrimination and choice.

mental quotient As defined by William Stern, a child's mental age divided by its chronological age.

modern investigation of thinking Form of cognitive psychology based upon the rule-governed processing of thought contents developed by members of the Würzburg school.

phi phenomenon Perception of apparent motion generated by projected light.

propaedeutic science A foundational science.

psychical resultants, principle of Formulated by Wundt, assertion that the attributes of psychological configurations that are the product of apperception are distinct from the mere aggregation of the attributes of the elements from which they are configured. Also known as the principle of creative synthesis.

psychical relations, principle of Formulated by Wundt, assertion that the nature and identity of the elements of psychological configurations is determined by their relational location within psychological configurations.

psychology of contents Term used to characterize Wundt's experimental analysis of the elements of consciousness, in contrast to Brentano's act psychology.

psychoneural isomorphism Theory that configured perceptual fields are the product of structurally identical neural fields.

psychotechnics Early German name for aptitude testing.

rules and representations The approach in cognitive psychology in which cognition is conceived of in terms of the rule-governed processing of symbolic representations.

systematic experimental self-observation Method of self-observation associated with the Würzburg school, in which untrained subjects were required to produce detailed verbal reports of sensations or images associated with experimental tasks, often based upon active questioning or interrogation by experimenters.

threshold of consciousness In Herbart, the level below which unconscious ideas are repressed.

transposition learning Form of learning identified by Köhler in which animals respond to similarities in relationships between stimuli rather than to similarities between stimuli themselves.

tri-dimensional theory of feeling Wundt's theory that feelings vary along three dimensions: pleasant versus unpleasant, high versus low arousal, and concentrated versus relaxed attention.

Völkerpsychologie Comparative-historical form of "folk" (or "cultural" or "social") psychology that Wundt considered to be an important supplement to experimental psychology.

voluntaristic psychology Wundt's theoretical psychology, so-called because of his emphasis on the voluntary, selective, and creative nature of the central control process of apperception.

REFERENCES

Ach, N. K. (1905). *Uber die Willenstätigkeit und das Denken* [*On the will and think-ing*]. Göttingen: Vandenhoeck & Ruprecht.

Adorno, T. W., Frenkel-Brunswik, E., Levinson, D. J., & Nevitt, Sanford, R. (1950). *The authoritarian personality*. New York: Harper & Row.

Allport, F. H. (1920). The influence of the group upon association and thought. *Journal of Experimental Psychology, 3,* 159–182.

Allport, F. H. (1924). *Social psychology*. Boston: Houghton Mifflin.

Allport, G. (1937). *Personality: A psychological interpretation*. New York: Holt.

Ash, M. G. (1980). Wilhelm Wundt and Oswald Külpe on the institutional status of psychology: An academic controversy in historical context. In W. G. Bringmann & R. D. Tweney (Eds.), *Wundt studies: A centennial collection*. Toronto: Hogrefe.

Ash, M. G. (1995). *Gestalt psychology in German culture 1890–1967*. Cambridge: Cambridge University Press.

Baumgartner, E., & Baumgartner, W. (1991). Brentano: Psychology from an empirical standpoint. In W. G. Bringmann, H. E. Lück, R. Miller, & C. E. Early (Eds.), *A pictorial history of psychology*. Carol Stream, IL: Quintessence.

Bazerman, C. (1987). Codifying the social scientific style: The APA publication manual as a behavioristic rhetoric. In J. Nelson, A. Megill, & D. N. McClowsky (Eds.), *The rhetoric of the human sciences*. Madison: University of Wisconsin Press.

Bechtel, W. (1988). Connectionism and rules and representation systems: Are they compatible? *Philosophical Psychology, 1,* 5–16.

Behrens, P. J. (1978). Bibliography of the works of G. E. Müller. *JSAS Catalog of Selected Documents in Psychology, 8*(28), Ms. No. 1669.

Behrens, P. J. (1997). G. E. Müller: The third pillar of experimental psychology. In W. G. Bringmann, H. E. Lück, R. Miller, & C. E. Early (Eds.), *A pictorial history of psychology*. Carol Stream, IL: Quintessence.

Benjamin, L. T., Jr., Durkin, M., Link, M., Verstal, M., & Acord, J. (1992). Wundt's American doctoral students. *American Psychologist, 47,* 123–131.

Benussi, V. (1914). Gesetze der inadäquaten Gestaltauffassung [Laws of the inade-quate understanding of form]. *Archiv für die gesamte Psychologie, 32,* 396–419.

Binet, A. (1903). *L'étude expérimentale de l'intelligence* [*Experimental studies of intelli-gence*]. Paris: Schleichter.

Blumenthal, A. L. (Ed.). (1970). *Language and psychology: Historical aspects of psy-cholinguistics*. New York: Wiley.

Blumenthal, A. L. (1975). A reappraisal of Wilhelm Wundt. *American Psychologist, 30,* 1081–1088.

Blumenthal, A. L. (1985a). Wilhelm Wundt: Psychology as the propaedeutic sci-ence. In C. E. Buxton (Ed.), *Points of view in the modern history of psychology*. New York: Academic Press.

Blumenthal, A. L. (1985b). Shaping a tradition: Experimentalism begins. In C. E. Buxton (Ed.), *Points of view in the modern history of psychology*. New York: Academic Press.

Brentano, F. (1995). *Descriptive psychology* (Benito Müller, Trans. & Ed.). London: Routledge. (Original work published 1982)

Brentano, F. (1995). *Psychology from an empirical standpoint*. London: Routledge. (Original work published 1874)

Bringmann, W. G., Balance, W. D. G., & Evans, R. (1975). Wilhelm Wundt, 1832–1920: A brief biographical sketch. *Journal of the History of the Behavioral Sciences, 11,* 287–297.

Bringmann, W. G., Bringmann, N. J., & Cottrell, D. (1976). Helmholtz und Wundt an der Heidelburger Universität [Helmholtz and Wundt at the University of Heidelberg]. *Heidelberger Jahrbücher, 20,* 79–88.

Bringmann, W. G., Voss, U., & Ungerer, G. A. (1997). Wundt's laboratories. In W. G. Bringmann, H. E. Lück, R. Miller, & C. E. Early (Eds.), *A pictorial history of psychology*. Carol Stream, IL: Quintessence.

Bühler, C. (1918). *The mental life of teenagers*. Vienna.

Bühler, K. (1908). Antwort auf die von. W. Wundt erhobenen Einwände gegen die Methode der Selbstbeobachtung an experimentell erzeugten Erlebnissen [Response to Wundt's objections to the method of experimental self-observation]. *Archiv fur des Gesamte Psychologie, 12,* 93–122.

Bühler, K. (1964). Tatsachen und Probleme zu einer Psychologie der Denkvorgänge [Facts and problems regarding a psychology of thought processes]. Translated G. Mandler & J. M. Mandler (Eds.), *Thinking: From association to Gestalt*. New York: Wiley. (Original work published 1907)

Chomsky, N. (1957). *Syntactic structures*. The Hague: Mouton.

Cole, M. (1996). *Cultural psychology: The once and future discipline*. Cambridge, MA: Harvard University Press.

Danziger, K. (1979). The positivist repudiation of Wundt. *Journal of the History of the Behavioral Sciences, 15,* 205–230.

Danziger, K. (1980). Wundt and the two traditions of psychology. In R. W. Rieber (Ed.), *Wilhelm Wundt and the making of scientific psychology*. New York: Plenum.

Danziger, K. (1990). *Constructing the subject*. Cambridge: Cambridge University Press.

Diamond, S. (1980). Wundt before Leipzig. In R. W. Rieber (Ed.), *Wilhelm Wundt and the making of scientific psychology*. New York: Plenum.

Donders, F. C. (1868). Over de snelheid van psychische processen [On the speed of mental proceses]. *Tweede Reeks, 2,* 92–120.

Drobisch, M. W. (1842). *Empirische Psychologie nach naturwissenschaftlicher Methode [Empirical psychology according to the methods of natural science]*. Hamburg: Voss.

Duncker, K. (1945). On problem solving (L. S. Lees, Trans.). *Psychological Monographs, 58*(5, Whole No. 270). (Original work published 1935).

Ebbinghaus, H. (1885). *Über das Gedächtnis [On memory]*. Leipzig: Duncker & Humblot.

Ebbinghaus, H. (1897). *Grundzüge der Psychologie [Principles of psychology]* (Vols. 1–2). Leipzig: Feit.

Ebbinghaus, H. (1908). An *elementary textbook of psychology* (M. Myer, Trans.). Boston: Heath. (Originally published 1902)

Ehrenfels, C. von. (1890). Über Gestaltqualitäten [On Gestalt qualities]. *Vierteljahresschrift für wissenschaftliche Philosophie, 14*, 242–292.

Fabian, R. (1997). The Graz school of Gestalt psychology. In W. G. Bringmann, H. E. Lück, R. Miller, & C. E. Early (Eds.), *A pictorial history of psychology*. Carol Stream, IL: Quintessence.

Farr, R. M. (1996). *The roots of modern social psychology 1872–1954*. Oxford: Blackwell.

Fechner, G. T. (1882). *Revision der Hauptpuncte der Psychophysik [Revision of the main points of psychophysics]*. Leipzig: Breitkopf, Härtel.

Fechner, G. T. (1966). *Elements of psychophysics* (H. E. Adler, Trans.). New York: Holt, Rinehart & Winston. (Original work published 1860)

Harris, B. (1991). A review of Ronald Ley's *A whisper of espionage. Contemporary Psychology, 36*, 727.

Henle, M. (1978a). One man against the Nazis—Wolfgang Köhler. *American Psychologist, 33*, 939–944.

Henle, M. (1978b). Gestalt psychology and Gestalt therapy. *Journal of the History of the Behavioral Sciences, 14*, 23–32.

Herbart, J. F. (1891). *A textbook in psychology: An attempt to found the science of psychology on experience, metaphysics, and mathematics* (M. K. Smith, Trans.). New York: Appleton. (Original work published 1816).

Herbart, J. F. (1968). *Psychology as a science based upon experience, metaphysics, and mathematics*. Amsterdam: Bonset. (Original work published 1824–1825). Selection reprinted from B. Rand (Ed.). (1912). *The classical psychologists*. New York: Houghton Mifflin.

Humphrey, G. (1951). *Thinking: An introduction to its experimental psychology*. New York: Wiley.

Jahoda, G. (1997). Wilhelm Wundt's "Völkerpsychologie." In W. G. Bringmann, H. E. Lück, R. Miller, & C. E. Early (Eds.), *A pictorial history of psychology*. Carol Stream, IL: Quintessence.

Judd, C. H. (1926). *The psychology of social institutions*. New York: Macmillan.

Katz, D. (1911). Die Erscheinungsweisen der Farben und ihre Beeinflussung durch die individuelle Erfahrung [The modes of appearance of colors]. *Zeitschrift für Psychologie, 7*.

Knapp, T. J. (1986). Ralph Franklin Hefferline: The Gestalt therapist among the Skinnerians or the Skinnerian among the Gestalt therapists? *Journal of the History of the Behavioral Sciences, 22*, 49–60.

Koffka, K. (1922). Perception: An introduction to gestalt theory. *Psychological Bulletin, 19,* 531–585.

Koffka, K. (1924). *The growth of the mind: An introduction to child psychology* (R. M. Ogden, Trans.). New York: Harcourt, Brace.

Koffka, K. (1935). *Principles of Gestalt psychology.* New York: Harcourt, Brace.

Köhler, W. (1920). *Die physischen Gestalten in Ruhe und im stationären Zustand.* [*Static and stationary physical Gestalts*]. Braunschweig: Vieweg.

Köhler, W. (1925). *The mentality of apes.* London: Routledge & Kegan Paul. (Original work published 1917)

Köhler, W. (1929). *Gestalt psychology: An introduction to new concepts in modern psychology.* New York: Liveright.

Köhler, W. (1938). *The place of value in a world of facts.* New York: Liveright.

Köhler, W. (1940). *Dynamics in psychology.* New York: Liveright.

Köhler, W., & von Restorff, H. (1933). Analyse von Vorgängen im Spurenfeld [Analysis of processes in trace fields]. *Psychologische Forschung, 18 & 21.*

Külpe, O. (1895). *Outline of psychology* (E. B. Titchener, Trans.). New York: Macmillan. (Original work published 1893)

Külpe, O. (1964). The modern psychology of thinking. In G. Mandler & J. M. Mandler (Eds. & Trans.), *Thinking: From association to Gestalt.* New York: Wiley. (Original work published 1912 in German)

Kusch, M. (1995). *Psychologism.* New York: Routledge.

Lashley, K. S., Chow, K. L., & Semmes, J. (1951). An examination of the electrical field theory of cerebral integration. *Psychological Review, 40,* 175–188.

Leahey, T. H. (1979). Something old, something new: Attention in Wundt and modern cognitive psychology. *Journal of the History of the Behavioral Sciences, 15,* 242–252.

Leahey, T. H. (1981). The mistaken mirror: On Wundt's and Titchener's psychologies. *Journal of the History of the Behavioral Sciences, 17,* 273–282.

Leary, D. E. (1979) Wundt and after: Psychology's shifting relations with the natural sciences, social sciences and philosophy. *Journal of the History of the Behavioral Sciences, 15,* 231–241.

Lewin, K. (1948). *Resolving social conflicts: Selected papers on group dynamics.* New York: Harper.

Ley, R. (1990). *A whisper of espionage.* Garden City Park, NY: Avery.

Lowry, R. (1982). *The evolution of psychological theory* (2nd ed.). New York: Aldine de Gruyter.

Mach, E. (1886). *Beiträge zur Analyse der Empfindungen.* [*Contributions to the analysis of sensations.*] Jena: G. Fischer.

Mach, E. (1967). *Grundlinien der Lehre von den Bewegungsempofindungen.* [*Principles of a theory of movement perception*]. Amsterdam: E. J. Bonset. (Original work published 1875)

Marbe, K. (1901). *Experimentell-psychologische Untersuchung über das Urteil* [*Experimental-psychological analysis of judgment*]. Leipzig: Engelmann.

Mayer, A., & Orth, J. (1901). Zur Qualitativen Untersuchung der Assoziationen [About the qualitative analysis of sensations]. *Zeitschrift fur Psychologie, 26,* 1–13.

Metzger, W. (1965). The historical background to national trends in psychology: German psychology. *Journal of the History of the Behavioral Sciences, 1,* 109–115.

Meumann, E. (1907). Vorlesungen zur Einführung in die experimentelle Pädagogik und ihre psychologischen Grundlagen (Vols. 1–2) [*Introductory lectures on pedagogy and its psychological basis*]. Leipzig: Engleman.

Meyer, M. (1911). *The fundamental laws of human behavior.* Boston: Badger.

Miller, G. E. (1956). The magical number seven, plus or minus two: Some limits on our capacity for information processing. *Psychological Review, 63,* 81–97.

Mischel, T. (1970). Wundt and the conceptual foundations of psychology. *Philosophical and Phenomenological Research, 31,* 1–26.

Miyakawa, T. (1981). The Tohoku University Wundtian collection. *Journal of the History of the Behavioral Sciences, 17,* 299.

Müller, G. E. (1878). *Zur Grundlegung der Psychophysik* [*Fundamentals of psychophysics*]. Berlin: T. Grieben.

Müller, G. E. (1911–1913). *Zur Analyse der Gedächtnistätigkeit und des Vorstellungsverlaufes* [*Analysis of the processes of memory and mental representation*]. Leipzig: Barth.

Müller, G. E. (1923). Komplextheorie und Gestalttheorie: Ein Beitrag zur Wahrnehmungspsychologie [*Structure theory and gestalt theory: A contribution to the psychology of perception*]. Göttingen: Vandenhoeck, Ruprecht.

Müller, G. E. (1964). In defense of association psychology. In G. Mandler & J. M. Mandler (Eds.), *Thinking: From association to Gestalt.* New York: Wiley. (Original work published 1913 in German)

Müller, G. E., & Martin, L. J. (1899). *Zur Analyse de Unterschiedsempfindlichkeit.* [*An analysis of sensitivity to difference*]. Leipzig: Barth.

Müller, G. E., & Pilzecker, A. (1900). Experimentelle Beiträge zur Lehre vom Gedächtnisses [Experimental contributions to the theory of memory]. *Zeitschrift für Psychologie, 1*(Suppl.).

Müller, G. E., & Schumann, F. (1889). Ueber die psychologischen Grundlagen der Vergleichung gehobener Gewichte [On the psychological basis of lifted weight comparisons]. *Archiv fuer die gesamte Physiologie, 45,* 37–112.

Müller, G. E., & Schumann, F. (1893). Experimentelle Beiträge zur Untersuchungen des Gedächtnisses [Experimental contributions to the investigation of memory]. *Zeitschrift für Psychologie und Physiologie der Sinnesorgane, 6,* 81–190, 257–339.

O'Donnell, J. M. (1985). *The origins of behaviorism: American psychology, 1870–1920.* New York: New York University Press.

Orne, M. T. (1962). On the social psychology of the psychology experiment: With particular reference to demand characteristics and their implications. *American Psychologist, 17,* 776–783.

Osgood, C. E., Suci, G., & Tannenbaum, P. (1957). *The measurement of meaning.* Urbana: University of Illinois Press.

Osier, D. V., & Wozniak, R. H. (1984). *A centenary of serial publications in psychology, 1850–1950: An international bibliography.* Millwood, NY: Kraus International.

Paul, H. (1880). *Principien der Sprachgeschichte* [*Principles of the history of language*]. Halle: Niemeyer.

Perls, F., Hefferline, R. F., & Goodman, P. (1951). *Gestalt therapy.* New York: Dell.

Postman, L. (1968). Hermann Ebbinghaus. *American Psychologist, 23,* 149–157.

Robinson, D. N. (1986). The Scottish enlightenment and its mixed bequest. *Journal of the History of the Behavioral Sciences, 22,* 171–177.

Robinson, D. K. (1987). *Wilhelm Wundt and the establishment of experimental psychology, 1875–1914: The context of a new field of scientific research.* Doctoral dissertation, University of California, Berkeley.

Rollett, B. A. (1997). The Vienna school of developmental psychology. In W. G. Bringmann, H. E. Lück, R. Miller & C. E. Early (Eds.), *A pictorial history of psychology.* Carol Stream, IL: Quintessence.

Rosenthal, R. (1966). *Experimenter effects in behavioral research.* New York: Appleton-Century-Crofts.

Rubin, E. J. (1921). *Visuell wahrgenommene Figuren* [*Visually perceived figures*]. *Studien in psychologischer Analyse* (Pt. 1). Copenhagen: Gyldendal. (Original work published 1915)

Sarris, V. (1997). Gestalt psychology at Frankfurt University. In W. G. Bringmann, H. E. Lück, R. Miller, & C. E. Early (Eds.), *A pictorial history of psychology.* Carol Stream, IL: Quintessence.

Scarborough, E., & Furumoto, L. (1987). *Untold lives: The first generation of American women psychologists.* New York: Columbia University Press.

Schosberg, H. (1954). Three dimensions of emotion. *Psychological Review, 61,* 81–88.

Schröder, C. (1997). Wilhelm Wirth and the Psychological Seminar of Leipzig. In W. G. Bringmann, H. E. Lück, R. Miller & C. E. Early (Eds.), *A pictorial history of psychology.* Carol Stream, IL: Quintessence.

Selz, O. (1922). *Zur Psychologie des Produktiven Denkens und des Irrtums* [*About the psychology of productive thinking and error*]. Bonn: Cohen.

Selz, O. (1964). The revision of the fundamental conceptions of intellectual processes. In G. Mandler & J. M. Mandler (Eds.), *Thinking: From association to Gestalt.* New York: Wiley. (Original work published 1927)

Shook, J. R. (1995). Wilhelm Wundt's contribution to John Dewey's functional psychology. *Journal of the History of the Behavioral Sciences, 31,* 347–369.

Sokal, M. M. (1984). The Gestalt psychologists in behaviorist America. *American Historical Review, 89,* 1240–1263.

Stern, W. (1902). Zur Psychologie der Aussage [On the psychology of testimony]. *Zeitschrift für die gesamte Strefrechtswissenschaft, 22,* 315–370.

Stern, W. (1914). *The psychological methods of testing intelligence.* Baltimore: Warwick & York.

Stumpf, C. (1883). *Tonpsychologie* [*The psychology of tone*] (Vol. 1). Leipzig: Hitzel.

Stumpf, C. (1890). *Tonpsychologie* [*The psychology of tone*] (Vol. 2). Leipzig: Hitzel.

Stumpf, C. (1930). Autobiography. In C. Murchison (Ed.), *A history of psychology in autobiography* (Vol. 1). Worcester, MA: Clark University.

Tinker, M. A. (1932). Wundt's doctorate students and their theses, 1875–1920. *American Journal of Psychology, 44,* 630–637.

Titchener, E. B. (1925) Experimental psychology: A retrospect. *American Journal of Psychology, 36,* 313–323.

Watt, H. J. (1904). *Experimentelle Beiträge zu einer Psychologie des Denkens* [*Experimental contributions to the psychology of thinking*]. Leipzig: Engelmann.

Wertheimer, M. (1912). Experimentelle Studien über das Sehen von Bewegung [Experimental studies on the visual perception of motion]. *Zeitschrift für Psychologie, 61,* 161–265). Reprinted in *Drei Abhandlungen zur Gestalttheorie.* Erlangen: Verlag der philosophischen Akademie (1925).

Wertheimer, M. (1938). Gestalt theory. In W. D. Ellis (Ed.), *A sourcebook in Gestalt psychology.* London: Routledge & Kegan Paul. (Original work published 1925)

Wertheimer, M. (1938). The general theoretical situation. In W. D. Ellis (Ed.), *A sourcebook in Gestalt psychology.* London: Routledge & Kegan Paul. (Original work published 1922)

Wertheimer, M. (1945). *Productive thinking.* New York: Harper & Row.

Wirth, W. (1908). *Die experimentelle Analyse der Bewusstseinsphanomene* [*The experimental analysis of the phenomena of consciousness*]. Brunswick: Vieweg.

Witasek, S. (1908). *Grundlinien der Psychologie* [Principles of psychology]. Leipzig: Dürr.

Wolff, C. (1732). *Psychologia empirica* [*Empirical psychology*]. Frankfurt: Renger.

Wolff, C. (1734). *Psychologia rationalis* [*Rational psychology*]. Frankfurt: Renger.

Woodward, W. R. (1982). Wundt's program for the new psychology: Vicissitudes of experiment, theory, and system. In W. R. Woodward & M. G. Ash (Eds.), *The problematic science: Psychology in nineteenth-century thought.* New York: Praeger.

Woodworth, R. S. (1906). Imageless thought. *Journal of Philosophy, Psychology and Scientific Methods, 3,* 701–708.

Woodworth, R. S. (1938). *Experimental psychology.* New York: Holt.

Wundt, W. (1862a) *Beiträge zur Theorie der Sinneswahrnehmung* [*Contributions toward a theory of sense perception*]. Leipzig: Winter.

Wundt, W. (1862b) Die Geschwindigkeit des Gedankens [The speed of thought]. *Gartenlaube,* 263–265.

Wundt, W. (1873–1874). *Grundzüge der physiologischen Psychologie* [*Principles of physiological psychology*]. Leipzig: Englemann.

Wundt, W. (1894). *Lectures on human and animal psychology* (J. E. Crighton & E. B. Titchener, Trans.). New York: Macmillan. (Original work published 1863)

Wundt, W. (1896). Ueber die Definition der Psychologie [About the definition of psychology]. *Philosophische Studien, 12,* 1–66.

Wundt, W. (1900). *Völkerpsychologie* (Vol. 1). Leipzig: Engelmann.

Wundt, W. (1900–1920). *Völkerpsychologie* (Vols. 1–10). Leipzig: Engelmann.

Wundt, W. (1902). *Outlines of psychology* (C. H. Judd, Trans.). Leipzig: Engelmann. (Original work published 1897)

Wundt, W. (1904). *Principles of physiological psychology* (E. B. Titchener, Trans.). (5th ed.). New York: Macmillan. (Original work published 1902–1903)

Wundt, W. (1907). Über Ausfrageexperimente und über die Methoden zur Psychologie des Denkens [About interrogative experiments and the methods regarding the psychology of thinking]. *Psychologische Studien, 3,* 301–360.

Wundt, W. (1909). Das Institut für Experimentelle Psychology [The Institute of Experimental Psychology]. In Rektor und Senat (Eds.), *Festschrift zur Feisser des 500-jährigen-Bestehens der Universität Leipzig* (Vol. 4). Leipzig: Hirzel.

Wundt, W. (1913). *Die Psychologie im Kampf ums Dasein.* [*Psychology struggling for survival*]. Leipzig: Engelmann.

Wundt, W. (1916). *Elements of folk psychology* (Edward Leroy Schaub, Trans.). New York: Macmillan.

Wundt, W. (1920). *Erlebtes und Erkanntes.* Stuttgart: Kröner.

Wundt, W. (1970). The psychology of the sentence. In A. L. Blumenthal (Ed. & Trans.), *Language and psychology: Historical aspects of psycholinguistics.* New York: Wiley. (Original work published 1912)

Wundt, W. (1973). *An introduction to psychology.* New York: Arno Press. (Original work published 1912)

Zeigarnik, B. (1927). Über Behalten von erledigten und unerledigten Handlungen [About memory for executed and non-executed actions]. *Psychologische Forschung, 9,* 1–95.

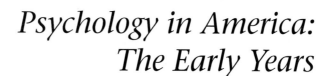

CHAPTER 9

Psychology in America: The Early Years

PSYCHOLOGY FIRST BECAME AN ACADEMIC SCIENTIFIC DISCIPLINE IN Germany because Germany developed the modern university system that enabled Wundt and his colleagues to create an experimental psychology grounded upon the earlier success of experimental physiology. However, psychology developed faster institutionally in America than it did in Germany (Ash, 1980; Danziger, 1979). By the end of the 19th century, American psychology had an active professional organization, the American Psychological Association, founded in 1892; journals devoted to general, experimental and applied psychology, such as the *American Journal of Psychology, Pedagogical Seminary, Psychological Review, Psychological Index,* and *Psychological Monographs*; and a substantial academic presence within the American university system. By 1892, America had more and better laboratories than Germany. Formal research laboratories were established at the University of Chicago, Clark University, Columbia University, Cornell, Harvard, Pennsylvania, Wisconsin, and Yale; and demonstration facilities for teaching and training were available at Brown, Catholic University of America, Indiana, Kansas, Michigan, Nebraska, Illinois, Iowa, and Wellesley (Hale, 1980; O'Donnell, 1985). By 1904, there were 49 laboratories, 169 members of the APA, and 62 institutions offering three or more courses in psychology; in addition, psychology ranked fourth in the sciences with respect to the number of PhDs awarded (Camfield, 1973; Miner, 1904). By 1913, the year that Watson published his behaviorist manifesto "Psychology as the Behaviorist Views It," America had surpassed Germany in research publications (Cattell, 1917).

Much the same was true of the academic institutionalization of other social sciences in the early 20th century. Émile Durkheim (1858–1917) introduced sociology in France at the end of the 19th century, but it made slow progress, and by 1930 there were only three chairs in sociology. Yet by 1910 there were about 50 full-time professors of sociology in America, and the subject was taught at around 400 colleges (Smith, 1997).

In contrast to the often reactionary response to attempts to introduce psychology in Britain and Europe, in America it was generally accepted by the public, government, and university administrators as a legitimate intellectual and practical pursuit, with much to offer the academy and society at large. Psychological questions were matters of common interest in the increasingly secular, industrial, and urban American culture, as evidenced by the popular appeal of phrenology and mesmerism. In 1850 the Reverend John Bovee Dods (1795–1872) gave a series of lectures on "electrical psychology" in the Hall of Representatives in Washington, DC, at the invitation of state senators such as Sam Houston, Henry Clay, and Daniel Webster. His published version of these lectures, *Electrical Psychology* (1850), became a national best seller (Reed, 1997). The democratic culture and progressive social values of late-19th-century America made it fertile ground for the development of the new social sciences, including psychology. And American psychologists were not hesitant in the promotion of their new discipline, as they strove for public and administrative support.

American psychology was originally based upon the German model of laboratory research, but those Americans who trained with Wundt adapted the new science to their own idiosyncratic interests, as well as local institutional and social demands. Most psychology departments were established in conjunction with laboratories and conducted practical teaching demonstrations of experiments in psychophysics, reaction time, and sensory and perceptual processes throughout the early decades of the 20th century. However, American psychologists did not restrict themselves to research in physiological psychology, but directed their scientific interests to a wide range of topics in applied psychology, such as education and industry. Indeed, perhaps the most distinctive feature of early American psychology was its eclecticism, which promoted the early growth of scientific approaches to social and psychological problems that eventually developed into full-blown subdisciplines of psychology, such as educational, industrial, clinical, social, developmental, forensic, and personality psychology.

PSYCHOLOGY AND THE DEVELOPMENT OF THE AMERICAN UNIVERSITY

Prior to the U.S. Civil War, colleges of higher education were largely devoted to the training of ministers and the intellectual elite. They were also rather small affairs. Although already nearly 200 years old, Harvard had fewer than 20 faculty in the 1850s. Much emphasis was placed upon the classics, mathematics, and logic as a means of fostering mental discipline. The educational goal of most early-19th-century colleges was to organize natural, moral, and religious knowledge into a coherent system.

Moral philosophy (or "moral science") was based upon the Scottish common sense psychology of Reid and Stewart and was taught to seniors as the capstone of their liberal education. It affirmed the reliability of perception and intuition in the pursuit of natural, moral, and religious knowledge and maintained the traditional dualist distinction between immaterial mind and material body. Scottish Presbyterian émigrés such as James McCosh (1811–1894), the president of Princeton, and Noah Porter (1811–1892), the president of Yale, promoted this form of moral philosophy in America. McCosh was the author of *The Scottish Philosophy* (1875) and *Psychology: The Cognitive Powers* (1886); Porter's *The Human Intellect: With an Introduction Upon Psychology and the Soul* (1868) was based upon Dugald Stewart's *Elements of the Philosophy of the Human Mind* (1792).

Moral philosophy was not antagonistic to science. On the contrary, moral philosophers committed to Scottish common sense psychology were philosophical realists who argued that the immaterial mind can have genuine knowledge of the material world through veridical perception and the employment of scientific methods. The sciences themselves expanded considerably within the American educational system in the middle decades of the 19th century, when colleges upgraded their teaching in mathematics, physics, and astronomy and added subjects like chemistry, geology, and biology. By the late 19th century, scientific training, including the laboratory methods of the new scientific psychology, came to be accepted as a legitimate alternative to the classics as a means of instilling mental discipline (O'Donnell, 1985).

The Morrill Act of 1862 promoted the development of state universities by awarding land and grants to state-founded institutions of research and instruction, especially in new technological areas such as mining, agriculture, and industry (although some state universities predated the act, such as the precursors of the universities of Georgia, Iowa, Michigan, and North Carolina). Competition for resources and prestige between these state institutions, which were usually governed by boards of local businessmen and politicians, led to their inevitable expansion, including the offering of a wider range of academic subjects.

Some of the major American universities founded in the late 19th century were effectively the creation of American business, and the emerging social scientific disciplines were to an almost unhealthy degree the creatures of American capitalism (Manicas, 1987). Cornell University, which opened in 1865, was founded by a huge financial bequest from the businessman Ezra Cornell (1807–1874), who insisted on control of administrative matters at the university. Andrew D. White (1832–1918), the first president of Cornell, was a crusading advocate of secular and scientific approaches to education. He vigorously opposed the historical influence of religion on the universities and published *A History of the Warfare of Science With Theology in Christendom* in 1896. He introduced a new "liberal arts" curriculum that was no longer restricted to the classics and other formal disciplines, but included natural and social sciences (including psychology), literature, art, and history.

Charles Eliot (1834–1926), appointed president of Harvard in 1869, became a champion of academic professionalism. While he continued to promote the virtues of a general liberal education, he also recognized the need for academic specialization attuned to the demands of an industrial society. He expanded the curriculum and introduced the then novel idea of an elective system of course offerings in place of the older and more rigid system of required courses. When philosophy suffered as a result, Eliot allowed William James to introduce a course on the new physiological psychology. By 1878 Eliot had doubled the instructional staff, recruiting faculty on the basis of their specialized qualifications rather than (as previously) their character and alumni status. As the academic market became more competitive, Eliot increased faculty salaries and welcomed curricular innovations such as James's course in psychology as a means of increasing enrollment to fund expansion (O'Donnell, 1985).

Academic competition accelerated as a consequence of the founding of Johns Hopkins University in 1876, the first exclusively graduate school in America, at the bequest of the Baltimore financier Johns Hopkins. On the instructions of the businessmen-trustees, Daniel Coit Gilman (1831–1908), the first president of Hopkins, tried to create from scratch a national center of research and graduate education oriented to science and modeled upon the ideals of the German university. Gilman attracted faculty to the new university by introducing lighter teaching loads and financial support for research (including the provision of research assistants). He attracted graduate students by introducing graduate fellowships, and between 1876 and 1880 graduate enrollments at Harvard, Yale, and Cornell dropped precipitously. The older universities were forced to compete by refurbishing their graduate programs, creating the "precondition for the American development of psychology as a research science and an academic profession" (O'Donnell, 1985, p. 115). In 1884 G. Stanley Hall (1844–1924) created the first laboratory and PhD program in psychology in America at Johns Hopkins, although he virtually dismantled the program when he accepted the presidency of Clark University in 1888, taking his staff, students, journal, and laboratory apparatus with him.

Perhaps the most famous academic product of American capitalism was the University of Chicago, founded by John D. Rockefeller in 1890. Designed to bring prestige to the new metropolis and address its pressing social problems (such as urban growth, labor conflicts, and crime, themselves arguably the product of runaway capitalism), Chicago used its financial muscle to raid other universities for talent and quickly became a recognized center of excellence in a variety of disciplines, including psychology. Distinguished psychologists associated with the university included John Dewey (1859–1952), James Rowland Angell (1869–1949), John B. Watson, Harvey Carr (1873–1954), George Herbert Mead (1863–1931), Helen Woolley (1874–1947), Walter V. Bingham (1880–1952), and Walter S. Hunter (1889–1956).

Around this time a number of colleges for women were also founded. Vassar College, founded in 1861, provided the intellectual stimulus for a number of early American women psychologists, such as Lillien Martin and Margaret Washburn

(1871–1939). Martin, a former teacher, studied with Müller. Washburn studied with James McKeen Cattell and Edward B. Titchener and was the first woman to attain a PhD degree in psychology (at Cornell). She returned to a teaching position at Vassar, where she had a long and distinguished career, being elected president of the APA in 1921 and to the American Academy of Sciences in 1931 (Bolles, 1993).

The new private universities began to incorporate the German model of research disciplines and PhD certification of university teachers, as the older ones scrambled to revise their goals and curricula in response to the new conditions and the new state colleges and universities developed and expanded their own. This created ideal conditions for institutional investment in a new discipline like psychology, identified as one of the successful 19th-century products of the German university system.

This academic expansion, especially in new disciplines such as psychology, created a critical demand for qualified PhDs. This was a demand that the nascent American system was initially unable to satisfy, since few colleges outside the Ivy League were able to grant the PhD degree. It was for this reason that many aspiring American educators in the new social scientific disciplines went to Europe for professional certification. Early American psychologists were attracted to Wundt's program largely because of the professional qualification it offered and the advantages it provided them in securing positions and advancement at the more prestigious academic institutions back home. James Mark Baldwin (1861–1934), who founded laboratories at Princeton and Toronto, frankly admitted that he spent time in Leipzig only "to secure a distinct advantage in the professional race at home" (Baldwin, 1926, 1, p. 35). Much the same was true of many of the institutional founders of other social sciences in America at the end of the 19th century. Albion Small (1854–1826), one of the founders of sociology at the University of Chicago, studied at the Universities of Berlin and Leipzig, and Franz Boas (1858–1942), the founder of anthropology at Columbia University, studied at the Universities of Heidelberg, Bonn, and Keil (Manicas, 1987).

American psychologists who returned from Leipzig and other German universities reproduced the institutional structures of the German university, notably the laboratories and research seminars associated with the new scientific disciplines (Veysey, 1965). Yet few American psychologists were imbued with the German commitment to scientific research for its own sake, and fewer still pursued research careers devoted to the experimental programs pursued in German laboratories. During the early decades of American psychology, graduate students were trained in traditional laboratory techniques, but more as a means of instilling a spirit of scientific rigor than as a preparation for research careers in physiological psychology (O'Donnell, 1985). Laboratory training served as the mark of scientific authority and status for academic psychologists, distinguishing "expert" from amateur psychologists such as traditional moral philosophers, physiologists, physicians, mesmerists, and spiritualists.

American psychologists regularly invoked the laboratory-based nature of their fledgling discipline as they strove to secure the autonomy and advancement of their discipline in the years prior to the First World War, citing experimental rigor as the basis of the objectivity of their new science (O'Donnell, 1985). However, some did question the identification of psychology with laboratory science. Joseph Jastrow (1863–1944), the first person to gain a PhD in psychology in America (at Johns Hopkins), warned against equating scientific psychology with experimentalism (Jastrow, 1887). William James, the first to introduce courses on the new physiological psychology, soon became skeptical of the utility of "brass instrument" psychology and championed a more practical and applied approach. Yet, with few exceptions, American psychologists simply adjusted their own laboratory-inspired scientific attitudes to whatever topics happened to interest them or to whatever opportunities for research happened to arise in their varied careers.

Although American psychologists returned with only the academic and experimental skeleton of German psychology, they set about reproducing it with such speed and efficiency that American psychology quickly overcame German psychology. By the turn of the century, dozens of laboratories and psychology programs were established at both Ivy League and state universities, many by Wundt's former students. Laboratories and programs in psychology were also established at smaller private colleges, including women's colleges. Mary Calkins founded a laboratory at Wellesley College in 1891, and Lillie Williams founded a laboratory at the State Normal School at Trenton in New Jersey in 1892 (Bolles, 1983).

By 1917, there were 307 members of the APA (84 percent with a PhD), 74 laboratories, and 35 separate departments of psychology, with psychology represented in 122 institutions (Camfield, 1973, based upon Cattell, 1917). The number of American psychologists listed in the British publication *Who's Who in Science* that year equaled the combined number in Germany, France, and Britain. By 1929, there were around 1,000 psychologists in America, representing over 300 institutions—outnumbering the total number of academic psychologists in Europe, if not the rest of the world (Cattell, 1929).

The Success of Psychology

There were a number of reasons for the success of psychology as an academic discipline in America. While aspiring psychologists in Germany and Britain had to battle reactionary philosophers and conservative administrators, American philosophers generally welcomed the **new psychology**, as experimental psychology was called, and the pragmatically oriented businessmen and politicians who directed American universities were hospitable to the new discipline and persuaded of its great social promise (albeit much exaggerated by its promoters).

The new psychology was not generally perceived as a threat to the traditional form of moral philosophy based upon Scottish common sense psychology. What was perceived as a threat was the materialism and mechanism of Darwin's theory of evolution by natural selection and the reflexive sensory-motor theory of the nervous system. Like most scientists, moral philosophers accepted the fact of evolution, but were opposed to Darwin's claim that evolution could be explained as the mechanical outcome of biological variation and natural selection, without reference to divine purpose and design. They condemned his treatment of human psychology and behavior as strongly continuous with that of animals, since, like Descartes, they saw the denial of the distinctiveness of human rationality as a threat to freedom and moral responsibility. They also followed the proponents of the sensory-motor theory of the nervous system in supposing that the theory implied that cognition and consciousness are merely epiphenomenal by-products of the reflexive neurophysiological processes directly responsible for all animal and human behavior.

Traditional moral philosophers embraced Wundt's physiological psychology as an intellectual bastion against materialism and epiphenomenalism, since Wundt claimed that psychological principles could not be reduced to physiological principles and insisted upon the voluntary nature of "psychic causality." American moral philosophers were quite happy to subject consciousness to the experimental control of the laboratory, because they saw it as an affirmation of the reality and autonomy of consciousness against the materialist reductionism of evolutionary theory and experimental physiology.

James McCosh, a major interpreter of Scottish common sense psychology, who defined psychology as the "science of the soul" (1886, p. 1), introduced courses on the new psychology at Princeton. George Trumbull Ladd (1842–1921), who took over the teaching of psychology at Yale from Noah Porter, introduced the new psychology and promoted it in *Elements of Physiological Psychology* (1887), a work that combined Wundt's physiological psychology with traditional elements of Scottish common sense psychology. Ladd maintained that Wundt's physiological psychology, which transcended its physiological origins, had rescued mind from the materialism and epiphenomenalism of the physiologists, who denied "the reality, unity and possibility of a permanent existence of the human mind" and reduced it to "a stream of mechanically associated 'epiphenomena,' thrown off from the molecular machinery of the cerebral hemispheres" (1895, p. x).

Academic administrators recognized the threat posed to traditional moral philosophy by developments in experimental physiology. The overseers of Harvard University, for example, complained that the philosophical neglect of "the physical side of mental phenomena has had the natural effect of exaggerating the importance of materialist views" (O'Donnell, 1985, p. 62). This led Princeton's McCosh to proclaim that moral philosophers ("metaphysicians") should engage the implications of experimental physiology:

> The metaphysician must enter the physiological field. He must, if he can, conduct researches; he must at least master the ascertained facts. He must not give up the study of the nervous system and brain to those who cannot comprehend anything beyond what can be made patent to the senses or disclosed to the microscope.
>
> —(McCosh, 1875/1980, p. 458)

Consequently, pioneers of the new psychology in America such as William James and G. Stanley Hall had little difficulty in representing the new psychology to the presidents and trustees of Harvard and Johns Hopkins as antithetical to crude materialism and mechanism (Leary, 1987).

Philosophy and Psychology

Some philosophers resisted the development of scientific psychology. Frances Bowen, the Alford Professor of moral philosophy at Harvard, vigorously but ineffectively protested the listing of James's 1877 course on "Physiological Psychology" in the department of philosophy (Leary, 1987). However, many others supported the development of psychology as a scientific discipline, and philosophers such as James, Dewey, and Hall played a major role in establishing psychology as an autonomous scientific discipline. Eventually American psychologists came to resent the constraining influence of philosophy and campaigned for autonomous chairs and departments of psychology, but in the early years philosophers and psychologists saw the new psychology as a means of revitalizing traditional philosophy.

In a very real sense it did. The autonomous academic disciplines of philosophy and psychology emerged at around the same time at the end of the 19th century. American academic psychology developed institutionally by sundering its connections with philosophy, but the disciplinary identity of late-19th- and early-20th-century academic philosophy was itself developed in reaction to the emerging discipline of scientific psychology. Anglo-American **analytic philosophy**, based upon the logic of Gottlob Frege (1848–1925) and Bertrand Russell (1872–1970), and Continental **phenomenological philosophy**, based upon the phenomenology of Brentano and Husserl, were developed in reaction to **psychologism**, the theory that logical and conceptual relations can be treated as naturalistic psychological "laws of thought." This was the theory advanced by John Stuart Mill and John Venn (1834–1923) and accepted by many practitioners of the new psychology. In contrast, analytic philosophy defined itself as a discipline concerned with the conceptual analysis of abstract systems of thought (based upon the new forms of symbolic logic developed by Frege and Russell), and phenomenological philosophy defined itself as a discipline concerned with the abstract essence of thought. Thus both psychology and philosophy, which shared a common prehistory, developed in the 20th century as autonomous academic disciplines with the emergence of the new psychology originally developed within philosophy departments at the end of the 19th century (Reed, 1997). The other distinctive form of 20th-century philosophy, American **pragmatist philosophy**, was an offshoot of evolutionary theory and American functionalist psychology (O'Donnell, 1985).

Philosophy certainly developed from psychology at the level of professional associations. The American Psychological Association was founded in 1892, 10 years before the American Philosophical Association. In the early years, many philosophers joined the APA and presented papers at the annual convention. This eventually created a problem, since at the 1896 and 1898 meetings (at Harvard and Columbia) there were more papers on philosophical topics than on psychological ones. This led to some minor friction, leading to calls for the creation of a separate philosophical association, originally conceived of as a division of the American Psychological Association. The problem was resolved when philosophers meeting in Kansas City formed the Western Philosophical Association in January 1900. Philosophers on the East Coast followed by creating the Eastern Philosophical Association in 1901. The two associations later amalgamated, and the American Philosophical Association now includes Eastern, Central, and Western divisions (Sokal, 1992). The American Psychological and Philosophical Associations continued to meet together for a number of years, a practice nowadays maintained only by the Southern Society of Philosophy and Psychology.

From the point of view of traditional moral philosophy, the acceptance of the new psychology was a mixed blessing. It proved to be a Trojan horse bearing the progenitors of later forms of materialism and epiphenomenalism. Laboratory-based physiological psychology gave way to a functional psychology avowedly inspired by evolutionary theory and eventually to a behaviorist psychology that equated consciousness with the outdated notion of an immaterial soul.

Applied Psychology

The pragmatically oriented presidents and boards of trustees of American universities were much more enthusiastic about the prospects of psychology than were their European counterparts. And if they had any doubts, American psychologists were extremely skillful in presenting the new psychology not only as compatible with religion and traditional moral philosophy, but also as a great benefit to society.

If American psychologists did not generally deliver on their grandiose visions of the potential of psychology to improve education, industry, and mental health, they were masterful in their promotion of the social utility of the discipline. Indeed, it might be fairly said that the promotion of psychology as a discipline was their greatest applied psychological achievement. From the very beginning, James, Hall, Dewey, and Cattell presented psychology as offering an applied scientific approach to human psychological and behavioral problems—as a discipline of immediate practical relevance to educators, businessmen, medical practitioners, advertisers, and penal administrators.

From the early years, American psychology entered into a fertile developmental relationship with American education. As primary and secondary education expanded dramatically in the later decades of the 19th century and early decades of the 20th century, American psychologists established their intellectual authority with respect to the training of the new generation of teachers and the progressive reform of education. Psychologists came to be revered by educators as representing the scientific hope and promise of their discipline. Although psychology had perhaps little of concrete value to offer the educators, the early focus on education powerfully shaped the course of the later development of psychology, including the intensive focus on theories of learning in the first half of the 20th century (Leary, 1987).

The rhetorical emphasis on the potential of psychology to alleviate human suffering and improve the human condition through scientifically informed social intervention was entirely concordant with the evangelical goals of Scottish common sense moral philosophers (Fuchs, 2000). Many of the early pioneers of American psychology inherited the crusading mantle of traditional moral philosophers, and it is probably no accident that many originally considered careers in the ministry. James considered such a career, and Ladd, Hall, Walter D. Scott, and Watson originally trained for the ministry.

The earliest and originally most influential centers of scientific psychology were at Harvard, Johns Hopkins, Clark, Cornell, Chicago, and Columbia. Yet in the early decades of American psychology, literally hundreds of psychologists were working on just about every aspect of psychology at American universities and colleges, where Wundt was taught along with Bain, Spencer, Darwin, Galton, and Morgan, and James, Ladd, and Dewey. While the 20th-century history of American psychology can be fairly represented in terms of a historical progression from experimental psychology to a more eclectic functional psychology and from the varieties of behaviorism to the cognitive revolution, one does well to remember that these movements represented only the major orienting currents of the discipline at particular points in time and not the complex undercurrents and subdisciplinary developments upon which they supervened.

JAMES AND MÜNSTERBERG AT HARVARD

William James

William James holds a peculiar position in the history of American psychology. He anticipated many of the later developments of scientific psychology, but did not found any distinctive school and had few theoretical disciples. Yet he scores consistently high in surveys of influential figures in the development of

American psychology. Cattell's 1903 poll of leading psychologists ranked him first in influence, and later polls invariably place him in the top 10. Although present day psychologists admire the encyclopedic breadth of his interests, many of his contemporaries found him too eclectic and strongly disapproved of his interests in spiritualism and free will.

James himself was ambivalent about psychology. Originally enthusiastic about the prospects for a scientific psychology, he hated laboratory work and was not much impressed by the work of German pioneers such as Fechner, Wundt, and Müller. He was respectfully critical of Wundt, but cruelly dismissive of most of the others. He described Fechner's psychophysics as destined to amount to "nothing" and Müller's experimental work as "brutal." In later years James became disillusioned with what he called the "nasty little subject," but worked conscientiously throughout his life to promote its development. He founded a demonstration laboratory at Harvard and encouraged interested students to pursue a career in the new psychology, correctly predicting that departments of philosophy would soon have "a number of vacant places calling for their peculiar capacity" (1876, p. 179).

While he championed psychology as a laboratory science capable of safeguarding traditional moral philosophy and religion from the materialism and epiphenomenalism of reductive physiology, he came to disparage "the new prism, pendulum and chronograph-philosophers." From the beginning he emphasized that psychology was a positivist science concerned with "practical prediction and control," with much of value to offer to society:

> We live surrounded by an enormous body of persons who are most definitely interested in the control of states of mind, and incessantly craving for a sort of psychological science that will teach them how to act. What every educator, every jail-warden, every doctor, every clergyman, every asylum-superintendent, asks of psychology is practical rules. Such men care little or nothing about the ultimate philosophical grounds of mental phenomena, but they do care immensely about improving the ideas, dispositions and conduct of the particular individuals in their charge.
>
> —(1892a, p. 151)

James was born in Astor House, an opulent New York hotel, into a wealthy and cultured family. He had three brothers (one of whom was the novelist Henry James) and one sister. He was educated in Europe and America, in a stimulating social and intellectual environment that included personal acquaintance with many of the leading intellectuals of his day, such as Ralph Waldo Emerson, Henry David Thoreau, Thomas Carlyle, and John Stuart Mill. His father encouraged him to be a scientist, although James originally explored a career in art and studied with William Hunt in Newport, Rhode Island. He abandoned art in 1861 to study chemistry and physiology at Harvard (as others went off to the Civil War), switching to medicine in 1864. He found he had little interest or native aptitude for any of these subjects, and a zoological expedition to the Amazon in 1865 convinced him he had none for biology either. James contracted smallpox, and his health, never good, deteriorated on his return to Harvard. He suffered backache, poor eyesight, insomnia, and depression (which may have been psychosomatic in origin, at least according to James).

A compulsive traveler all his life, he took himself off to Germany in 1867, hoping that he might relieve his back pain by taking mineral baths at local spas. There he visited Fechner, Helmholtz, du Bois-Reymond, and Wundt, and came to believe that "perhaps the time has come for psychology to begin to be a science" (1920, 1, p. 118). Returning to America, James completed his medical degree in 1869 and immediately resolved never to practice medicine. His health deteriorated further, and he became depressed and suicidal. In characteristic fashion, James claimed to have cured his depression by convincing himself of his own free will, through his act of coming to believe in free will. His first act of free will was "to believe in free will" (1920, 1, p. 147).

James was offered the post of instructor in physiology at Harvard medical school in 1872. In 1875 he managed to persuade Charles Eliot, the president of Harvard, to let him introduce a course on "The Relations Between Physiology and Psychology." That same year he managed to get money from Harvard to set up a laboratory for experimental demonstrations. "Laboratory" is probably somewhat of an exaggeration, since as Hall later pointed out, it included no more than "a metronome, a device for whirling a frog, a horopter chart, and one or two bits of apparatus" stored in a stairwell closet (Hall, 1923, p. 218).

James's course was a great success, and in 1876 he was promoted to the rank of assistant professor of philosophy. He became professor of philosophy in 1885. In 1878 James married Alice Gibbons, whom his father had chosen as his wife (Allen, 1967). This introduced some stability in his life (they had five children), although it did nothing to reduce his recurrent wanderlust. That same year James contracted with Henry Holt to write a book on psychology, which became the *Principles of Psychology*, published in two volumes in 1890. *Psychology: A Briefer Course* was published two years later (1892b).

The *Principles* was also a great success. It was widely read in America and Europe, and by the educated public as well as psychologists. For many years it was the standard psychology textbook in most American and many European universities. However, not all of James's psychological peers approved of it. Wundt dismissed it as "literature . . . not psychology," and Edward B. Titchener, the founder of structural psychology in America, condemned it. Later functional and behaviorist psychologists were less than enthusiastic about James's commitment to introspection, free will, and spiritualism, not to mention his definition of psychology as "the science of mental life" (1890, 1, p. 1).

James seems to have lost interest in psychology after the publication of *Principles*. He arranged for Hugo Münsterberg (1863–1916), a former student of Wundt's, to take over his psychology courses and the laboratory at Harvard in 1892 and devoted most of his later years to philosophy (and further travel). However, he continued to fight to maintain Harvard's prominence in psychology (O'Donnell, 1985). He raised over $4,000 (more than $90,000 in today's dollars) to purchase laboratory equipment to match the facilities of the newly founded Clark University, since, as he put it to Münsterberg: "We are the best university in America, and we must lead in psychology" (1892c, p. 68). He retired in 1907 and died in 1910 (on returning from a final trip to Europe).

In many ways, James resembled his German friend and colleague Carl Stumpf. Both were skeptical of the pretensions of the new psychology and had little personal taste for laboratory work, but both successfully championed the development of psychology as an experimental and applied discipline in their respective institutions and countries.

The Metaphysical Society In the early 1870s at Harvard, James organized the informal meetings of the **Metaphysical Society**, devoted to the philosophical problems of the day, such as the nature of knowledge, meaning, and truth; the relation between science and religion; and the role of the new psychology in relation to the older common sense psychology of Reid and Stewart. The group included James, the philosophers Chauncey Wright (1830–1875) and Charles Sanders Peirce (1839–1914), and the legal theorist Oliver Wendell Holmes (1809–1894), who later served as chief justice of the Supreme Court. One significant outcome of these meetings was the development of the philosophical view known as **pragmatism**: the view that the adequacy of any theoretical system should be judged by its practical utility. The name derives from Kant's characterization of uncertain beliefs with practical value as pragmatic beliefs (Kant, 1788). Since the members of the society did not think there were (or could be) any certain theoretical beliefs, they held that all theoretical beliefs are pragmatic beliefs: that is, beliefs that are only justifiable by their practical consequences.

They differed concerning the relevant consequences, however. Wright expounded a theory of the selection of beliefs via their practical consequences for an individual during his or her lifetime: a cognitive version of the Spencer-Bain principle. Peirce developed a **pragmatist theory of meaning**, according to which the content of a belief or proposition is specified in terms of its empirical consequences. Pierce also avowed a form of instrumentalism, insofar as he claimed that scientific theories should be evaluated only by their empirical consequences, rather than by reference to their supposed correspondence with theoretical reality.

Although Peirce was the first to develop pragmatism, which he originally called pragmaticism (1905/1982), he was a poor promoter of it during his lifetime. An 1859 Harvard graduate, he never managed to secure a full-time academic job (although he lectured at Johns Hopkins from 1879 to 1884), and worked for most of his life with the U.S. Coast and Geodesic Survey. James was the one who successfully promoted pragmatism in *The Will to Believe* (1897), *Pragmatism* (1907), and *The Meaning of Truth* (1909). He also developed a **pragmatist theory of truth**, according to which a belief or proposition is true if it "works satisfactorily in the widest sense of the word." James really did mean "in the widest sense of the word," because he held that a belief or proposition should be accepted as true if it satisfies our feelings or produces a beneficial effect, such as a religious belief or a belief that mineral baths relieve backache.

Most American psychologists embraced pragmatism in the broad sense that theories should be judged by their practical utility, although few were committed to the specifics of the pragmatist theories of meaning and truth, and most rejected James's idea that the truth of a theory could be warranted by the satisfaction derived from believing it.

James's Psychology   James was highly critical of Wundt's experimental analysis of the elemental contents of consciousness and laid much greater stress on the continuity of consciousness. He famously talked of a "stream of consciousness" rather than a "chain" or "train" of conscious states and stressed the selectivity and functionality of consciousness. Yet he criticized a caricature of Wundt, who also recognized these features.

James affirmed the standard account of the association of ideas in terms of similarity and continuity, which he treated as a consequence of elementary laws of neural excitation and succession (although he added secondary principles of association such as vividness and congruity in emotional tone). He followed Hartley, Spencer, Bain, and Morgan in extending associationist principles to the formation of behavioral habits. While he famously held that acquired behavioral habits form the "great fly-wheel of society," he also followed Darwin in maintaining that much of human and animal behavior is governed by instinct.

James developed an account of emotion that came to be known as the **James-Lange theory of emotion**, published by James in 1884 and independently by the Danish physiologist Carl Georg Lange (1834–1900) in 1885. According to this theory, emotion is not the cause of physiological arousal and behavior, as is commonly supposed, but rather our experience of physiological arousal and behavior. Thus he suggested that we should say that "we feel sorry because we cry, angry because we strike, afraid because we tremble, and not that we cry, strike or tremble because we are sorry, angry or fearful" (1884, p. 190). By this account, our fear of the bear, for example, does not cause us to run away, but is simply our experience of physiological and behavioral responses to our perception of the bear. James's treatment of emotion as epiphenomenal was a consequence of his commitment to the reflexive sensory-motor theory of the nervous system, which he accepted and defended at length in the *Principles*. Yet although he treated instincts, habits, and emotions as reactive and automatic, he was reluctant to accept that consciousness and cognition were merely "impotent, paralytic spectators" of reflexive sensory-motor sequences. He retained a causal role for consciousness and cognition in the generation of behavior by embracing a version of Carpenter's ideomotor theory, according to which selective attention to ideas can determine which automatic ideomotor sequences are activated. James also developed some interesting theoretical distinctions between different aspects of the empirical self, such as the material, social, and spiritual selves.

James's Influence   James functioned as a kind of father figure in the development of American psychology, as an intellectual conduit who reflected 19th-century developments in experimental physiology and evolutionary theory and the pragmatic and functional approaches to psychology that came to dominate in future decades. The demonstration laboratory he instituted at Harvard in conjunction with his first course in psychology in 1875 predated Wundt's, but was not used for serious research until much later—the first functional American laboratory was created by G. Stanley Hall at Johns Hopkins in 1884 (Hulse & Green, 1986). Scientific psychology would probably have developed in America at the time it did and in the fashion it did even if James had never introduced psychology courses or a demonstration laboratory at Harvard, but his early commitment to the new discipline helped to promote its development, and many individuals were inspired to follow a career in psychology after reading James's *Principles*.

James also had a number of students who went on to play a significant role in the early development of American psychology, even if they did not develop it in a particularly Jamesian direction, such as G. Stanley Hall, who founded the first PhD program in psychology in America at Johns Hopkins; James Rowland Angell (1869–1949), who played a major role in the development of functional psychology at the University of Chicago; Edward L. Thorndike (1874–1949), who established the "law of effect" at Columbia University; and Robert Sessions Woodworth (1869–1962), who promoted a form of functional psychology at Columbia.

Mary Calkins (1863–1930), the first female president of the APA, was also a student of James's. A Wellesley graduate, she took courses with James, although Harvard refused to formally admit her, despite the support of James and Josiah Royce (1855–1916). She later worked with Hugo Münsterberg on associative memory and defended her dissertation before Münsterberg, James, and Royce, who claimed it was the best PhD thesis that they had ever examined. All this was to no avail, since Harvard refused to award the degree. Calkins worked for most of her life at Wellesley College (where she founded a laboratory) and received numerous awards and honorary degrees. She was elected president of the APA in 1905 and president of the American Philosophical Association in 1918. She never received a Harvard degree and turned down an honorary degree from Radcliffe College in 1902 because she saw it as acceptance of "second best" for women.

Hugo Münsterberg

Hugo Münsterberg accepted the position of director of the Harvard psychological laboratory in 1892. He was one of Wundt's earliest students and research assistants, attaining his degree at Leipzig in 1885 at the age of 22 (followed by a medical degree at Heidelberg in 1887). He took up a teaching position at the University of Freiburg, where he founded a psychology laboratory (at his own expense) and published a number of papers on perception, learning, memory, and attention. Münsterberg disagreed with Wundt on a number of theoretical and methodological issues. He claimed that our apparent consciousness of will is not consciousness of an autonomous act of will that determines behavior, but of an automatic sensational response to our physical anticipation of behavior, based upon muscular feedback. He consequently denied that we have introspective access to acts of will. Wundt refused to accept his work in this area and made him change his dissertation topic to "The Doctrine of Natural Adaptation."

Münsterberg published his theory of the will as *Voluntary Action* in 1888. Wundt and Titchener condemned it but James praised it, which is perhaps not surprising, since Münsterberg's epiphenomenalist treatment of the will matched James's epiphenomenalist treatment of emotion. James met Münsterberg at the

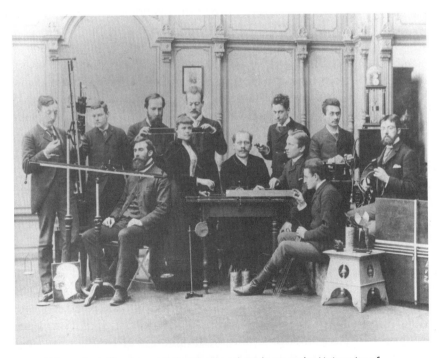

Hugo Münsterberg (center, seated at desk) and students at the University of Freiburg in 1891.

First International Congress in Psychology in Paris in 1889 and cited his writings in *Principles*. James's encouragement (and a personal visit) induced Münsterberg to take up a three-year appointment in 1892. He did not adapt easily to America, and it took some pressure and persuasion to secure his acceptance of a full-time appointment at Harvard in 1897. Wundt consoled him with the thought that, after all, "America is not the end of the world" (quoted in Hale, 1980, p. 55).

Despite the fact that he had to learn English from scratch, Münsterberg became as popular a lecturer as James. He was elected president of the APA and head of Harvard's philosophy department in 1899 and president of the American Philosophical Association in 1907. To a significant degree, he satisfied James's ambition of making the Harvard laboratory the best in America. The archetypal German professor, Münsterberg developed a quintessentially American orientation to psychology as he pursued his academic career at Harvard. Originally hired to develop German experimental psychology, his own interests quickly turned to the practical applications of psychology, and he left the everyday running of the Harvard laboratory to his students Edwin B. Holt (1873–1946) and Robert M. Yerkes (1876–1956).

Popular and Applied Psychology   Münsterberg turned out to be a greater promoter of American psychology than most of Wundt's American students and was probably the greatest popularizer of psychology before Watson. He wrote more than 20 books, popular expositions as well as academic texts, and numerous magazine articles on topics such as mental health, education, advertising, and jury trials. James had championed the practical value of psychology, but remained staunchly theoretical and committed to what Münsterberg called "psychic hocus-pocus" such as spiritualism. It was Münsterberg who developed applied fields of psychology such as psychotherapy, forensic psychology, and industrial psychology.

One of the early pioneers of psychotherapy, Münsterberg offered his services free of charge at the Harvard laboratory. He treated people suffering from a variety of disorders, including phobias, obsessions, alcoholism, and sexual problems, based upon his own largely speculative theories and explicitly suggestive therapies. He rejected Freud's theories, although he did acknowledge the sexual etiology of some psychological disorders. He employed hypnosis for a while, until one of his female clients threatened him with a gun, causing the president of Harvard to ban the use of the practice. Münsterberg's book *Psychotherapy* (1909) defined the new field for some years, until his work was eclipsed by Lightner Witmer (1867–1956), the founder of clinical psychology in America.

Münsterberg was also a pioneer in the development of forensic psychology. He demonstrated the variability and unreliability of eyewitness testimony, including the frequently biased and distorted nature of perception and memory. *On the Witness Stand* (1908) was a popular best seller, reprinted in many editions. He questioned the utility of conventional methods of police interrogation based upon physical force and intimidation and developed physiological tests of veracity—based upon pulse and respiration rates and electrical skin resistance—that were precursors of modern "lie-detector" machines. Münsterberg employed some of these tests in the sensational public trial of Harry Orchard, who confessed to a number of murders but accused the president of the Western Federation of Miners of having ordered them. Based upon the results of what one newspaper called the "lying machine" of "Professor Monsterwork," Münsterberg declared that Orchard's testimony was truthful, although the jury acquitted the union boss. While his work was popular with the public, the legal profession scorned it (Wigmore, 1909), and a number of psychologists joined in the critical chorus (including Titchener, 1914). Thus he pioneered but probably also impeded the development of forensic psychology.

Münsterberg was also one of the founders of industrial psychology. He conducted studies of personnel selection, task-oriented aptitude testing, work efficiency, motivation, marketing, sales, and advertising. He published *Vocation and Learning* in 1912 and *Psychology and Industrial Efficiency* in 1913, and his advice was sought by businessmen and government officials. He promoted his views in popular magazine articles and in a movie that played in commercial theatres.

Münsterberg was a colorful and controversial character. His public stance against prohibition, and the financial support he received for it from Adolphus Busch, the German brewer, raised a few eyebrows. Although he supported the PhD candidacy of Mary Calkins at Harvard, he was against graduate education for women and was generally opposed to women pursuing any professional career, including elementary school teaching. He believed that women lacked the capacity for logical reasoning and maintained that they should be barred from juries (and denied the vote). His views were based upon comparative experimental studies of judgments made by men and women in isolation and after participation in group discussion (Münsterberg, 1913b). These studies were precursors of the **social facilitation** studies later conducted by the social psychologist Floyd Allport (Allport, 1920), which explored the influence of social groups on judgment and behavior. Allport studied with Münsterberg, who introduced him to the earlier German work in this area (Meumann, 1907) and suggested it as a dissertation topic.

Münsterberg's controversial public pronouncements and vigorous popular presentations of psychology alienated many of his academic colleagues, including the more staid faculty members at Harvard. Lightner Witmer claimed that Münsterberg's self-promotion of his therapeutic success cheapened the profession, and Jacques Loeb called him a "journalistic money-making hack" (Loeb, 1916, cited in O'Donnell, 1985).

Münsterberg developed some influential connections in industry, government, and the arts (including the movie industry). He was friends with Andrew Carnegie and dined with presidents Roosevelt and Taft at the White House. However, none of these connections shielded him from the public odium that followed his support of Germany's position before and during the First World War. He was vilified by the press and suspected of being a spy. One Harvard alumnus offered the university $10 million to fire him (which to its credit it did not). At the height of his unpopularity, he made his way through the winter snow to an early morning class at Harvard in 1916 and collapsed from a fatal stroke the moment he entered the lecture hall.

The painting of the philosophy department at Harvard in the early 20th century that hangs in Emerson Hall includes James, Royce, and George Herbert Palmer, but not Münsterberg—although the photograph on which it was based does. In the painting there is an empty chair in the place where Münsterberg stood. According to one story, Münsterberg was painted out after his death (Roback, 1952, p. 208). According to another, he requested to be removed for "aesthetic reasons," because he was not placed in the center of the painting (Kuklick, 1977).

LADD AND SCRIPTURE AT YALE

The introduction of the new psychology did not proceed quite as smoothly at Yale, where the former Congregationalist minister George Trumbull Ladd (1842–1921) promoted it. Ladd was professor of mental and moral philosophy at Bowdoin College in Maine from 1879 to 1881, during which time he published a number of popular articles advocating the relevance of empirical research in physiology and evolutionary biology to traditional philosophy and theology. To Noah Porter, Yale's president and professor of moral philosophy and metaphysics, he seemed the ideal person to mediate between the old and new traditions in philosophy and psychology (O'Donnell, 1985). Although Ladd had no training in physiology or laboratory experimentation, he began teaching physiological psychology at Yale in 1884. After years of research on physiology and psychology, he published *Elements of Physiological Psychology* in 1887. Ladd's text, like James's later *Principles* that eclipsed it, provided a philosophical justification for the new psychology, as well as a detailed survey of contemporary research, including experimental studies from Wundt's Leipzig laboratory. Yet although *Elements* acknowledged Wundt's contribution, it remained heavily influenced by Scottish common sense psychology, and the later edition (Ladd & Woodworth, 1911) contained only token references to Wundt.

Trouble began when Ladd arranged for the appointment of Edward Wheeler Scripture (1864–1945) as director of the Yale laboratory in 1892. Scripture studied with Ebbinghaus in Berlin and enrolled in Wundt's program in 1888. He completed his PhD degree in 1891 with a dissertation on "Thinking and Feeling." Scripture was a committed and prolific experimentalist, who initiated the annual *Studies from the Yale Psychological Laboratory* (which ran from 1892 to 1902), albeit largely based upon his own work on sensory tone. When the laboratory attracted few students, he turned his Leipzig-inspired commitment to precise measurement to industrial research (mainly time-motion studies) and clinical explorations of speech disorders.

Scripture was unwilling to accept Ladd's subordination of psychology to philosophy and criticized the speculative theories of philosophers such as James and Ladd in his popular text *Thinking, Feeling, Doing* (1895). He claimed that the new experimental psychology owed nothing to traditional philosophy, which represented an impediment to the development of the new academic discipline:

> And what about philosophy, the science of sciences? Alas! Philosophy is still in the Middle Ages. One by one the other sciences have freed themselves; the lingering clutch of philosophy on psychology is the last hope of respectability.

> —(1895, p. x)

He repeated his strident call for the separation of the new psychology from philosophy in *The New Psychology* in 1897. Ladd was so outraged by Scripture's criticism of philosophy and his own work that he demanded that a university committee investigate the conflict within the department. The committee failed to resolve the problem, Scripture was fired, and Ladd was forced to resign. Charles Hubbard Judd (1873–1946), another student of Wundt's, who had been appointed as an instructor in psychology in 1902, took over as director of the Yale program, which took years to recover (Rieber, 1980). Scripture abandoned American psychology and traveled to Britain, where he founded a laboratory in speech neurology in London's West End Hospital for Nervous Diseases in 1912 (O'Donnell, 1985).

HALL AT JOHNS HOPKINS AND CLARK

Granville Stanley Hall was a farm boy from Ashfield, Massachusetts, who made good on his ambition to make his mark in the world. His career was distinguished by a number of psychological firsts. He was the first person to gain a PhD in philosophy at Harvard with a dissertation on a psychological topic (the muscular perception of space). He was the first to create a laboratory and PhD program in psychology in America at Johns Hopkins in 1883. He was one of Wundt's first American students: Although he did not study for a degree with Wundt, he attended some of his lectures and served as a subject in Max Friedrich's laboratory research on apperception in the fall of 1879. He founded the *American Journal of Psychology* in 1887, the first American psychology journal. He founded the American Psychological Association in 1892 and served as its first president. He became the first president of the newly founded Clark University in 1888.

Hall attended Williams College in Massachusetts, where he studied Scottish common sense psychology. Mark Hopkins, professor of moral philosophy and rhetoric and president of Williams, introduced him to the challenges posed to traditional philosophy by experimental physiology and evolutionary theory. After graduating in 1867, Hall prepared for a career in the ministry at Union Theological Seminary in New York City. He spent much of his time exploring the multifarious delights the city had to offer, such as its theaters, law courts, and zoos. His theological studies suffered, and he came to recognize that he was perhaps not best-suited to the ministry. After he gave his trial sermon at Union, he was summoned to the president's office for the usual critique: Instead of evaluating his sermon, the president fell down on his knees and prayed that Hall might be saved (Hall, 1923).

The Union College faculty encouraged students to study philosophy in Germany (O'Donnell, 1985), so Hall interrupted his studies to travel there in 1869. He took courses in philosophy at the universities of Bonn and Berlin, but also enjoyed the beer halls and other less academic delights of Europe, such as its theaters and zoos. Lack of funds prevented Hall from pursuing a doctoral degree in Germany, so he returned to America, where he completed his degree at Union Theological Seminary in 1870 (although he was never ordained). He worked as a private tutor for a Jewish family in New York City for two years and tried preaching for about three months before accepting a temporary position as Bellows Professor of mental philosophy and English literature at Antioch College in Ohio in 1872 (O'Donnell, 1985). He taught there until 1876, during which time he read Wundt's *Principles of Physiological Psychology*. His passion turned to psychology, which he saw as a "safe route to a permanent philosophical position." He took a leave of absence from Antioch to become an instructor of English at Harvard, where he enrolled as a graduate student with James. Despite his own heavy teaching load, he managed to find some time for physiological research and submitted his dissertation "On the Muscular Perception of Space" in 1878.

After receiving his degree, Hall returned to Germany, where he studied physiology with du Bois-Reymond at the University of Berlin and attended Helmholtz's lectures on physics. He moved to the University of Leipzig in 1879, where he took classes with Ludwig, Fechner, and Wundt. He only took philosophy classes with Wundt, but worked in the Leipzig laboratory during the fall of 1879. He later claimed that he was "on the whole disappointed with Wundt" (Hall, 1923). He returned to the United States in 1880, in debt and with a new wife, but no job prospects.

Johns Hopkins and the New Psychology

Hall recognized early in his career that the new psychology offered the best route for professional advancement in philosophy. He also recognized that the application of psychology to education was an effective means of promoting the fledgling discipline and advancing his own career within it. He secured an appointment as university lecturer at Harvard, where he gave a popular series of public talks on education in 1881. Their success led Daniel Gilman, the president of Johns Hopkins, to invite Hall to take up an appointment as a part-time lecturer in philosophy and pedagogy at the new university in 1882. Like James with Harvard's Eliot, Hall managed to persuade Gilman that the new psychology could serve as a bulwark against materialism and mechanism and as a buttress for traditional religion. According to Gilman, Hall assured him that the "new psychology, which brings simply a new method and a new standpoint to philosophy, is . . . Christian to its root and center" (Gilman, 1885, p. 48, cited in O'Donnell, 1985, p. 119). Given his religious background and training in physiological psychology (albeit much exaggerated by Hall), Gilman considered him an ideal person to smooth relations between the science-oriented university and the religious establishment and to develop the practical applications of psychology.

Hall was a great success at Hopkins and was elevated to a full professorship in psychology and pedagogy in 1884. He created the first fully functional psychological laboratory in America, reproducing the system of seminars and doctoral certification characteristic of German programs. Joseph Jastrow, the first person to attain a PhD in psychology in America at Hopkins, conducted the first experiments (on perception) in the new laboratory with Peirce (Peirce & Jastrow, 1884) in 1883–1884 (Kihlstrom, 2004).

Hall did not restrict psychology to Wundt's physiological psychology. In his inaugural lecture at Hopkins, he characterized the new psychology as comprising comparative psychology (based upon evolutionary theory), experimental psychology (based upon physiological psychology), and historical psychology (patterned after Wundt's *Völkerpsychologie*). He also staked out his claim that the new psychology provided the scientific basis of education:

> Those who devote themselves to the work of education as a profession are strongly recommended to give their chief time and labor to grounding themselves in Philosophy and Psychology, which constitute the scientific basis of their profession. Pedagogy is a field of applied psychology, and if the latter is known the application is not hard to make.
>
> —(1885, p. 248)

His students originally published their experimental studies in Bain's journal *Mind*, but later published in the *American Journal of Psychology*, which Hall founded in 1887 as the first American journal devoted to theoretical and empirical reports in psychology. Jastrow wrote the set of conventions for reporting psychology experiments that later evolved into the "APA style" (Jastrow, 1890). Like many editors of early American journals in psychology, Hall owned the *American Journal of Psychology* and financed it out of his own private income (he sold it to Titchener in 1920). Hall's other doctoral students at Hopkins included John Dewey, Edmund Clark

Sanford (1859–1924), William H. Burnham (1855–1941), and the neurophysiologist Henry Herbert Donaldson (1857–1938).

Clark and Genetic Psychology

In 1888 Hall was invited to join the newly founded Clark University in Worcester, Massachusetts, as its first president, with an academic position as professor of psychology. After a glorious year spent studying the operation of European universities and military academies, Greek archeological sites, brothels, beer halls, circuses, and the inevitable zoos, Hall returned to model Clark as a smaller version of Hopkins (according to the wishes of Jonas Clark, the mining equipment magnate whose endowment established the university). He created five departments—of physics, chemistry, biology, mathematics, and psychology—devoted to graduate studies (although Clark, like Hopkins, was eventually forced to introduce undergraduate programs to maintain the financial viability of the university). Hall left the day-to-day running of the psychology programs to two former students who transferred with him to Clark. E. C. Sanford headed the laboratory and psychology program, and W. H. Burnham headed the program in educational psychology.

While he continued to employ the rhetoric of experimental science in his promotion of psychology as a scientific discipline and profession, by the mid-1890s Hall shifted the direction of research at Clark to **genetic psychology.** According to Hall, whereas experimental psychology was based upon the method of physics and physiology and focused upon measured responses to manipulated sensory stimulation, genetic psychology was based upon the method of evolutionary biology and focused on the development of individual organisms, especially the (extended) development of human children. Hall made genetic psychology the foundation of his developmental and educational psychology.

Hoping to develop a broader institutional base for his work in education (and to secure a share in increased government funding for secondary education, teacher training colleges, and schools of education), Hall formed an alliance with the National Education Association (NEA). In 1891 he founded *Pedagogical Seminary* (later the *Journal of Genetic Psychology*), devoted to the study of child development, and that same year announced the need for scientific pedagogy to an enthusiastic audience at the Toronto meeting of the NEA. Hall became a leader in the emerging child-study movement and instituted a very successful summer school for professional educators in 1892 (which was repeated every year until 1903). He persuaded the NEA that the new psychology constituted the scientific basis of child study; in 1904 it organized a Committee on Psychological Enquiry and its own department of child study. Child study congresses sprang up all over the country, and Hall created the Child Study Institute at Clark in 1910.

Studies of child development at Clark were based upon standard anthropometric measures of sensory acuity and reaction time (originally developed by Galton) and questionnaires constructed by Hall and his colleagues, which anticipated the later work of Jean Piaget and Lawrence Kohlberg (1927–1987). The projected goal of this genetic psychological research was to establish the course of normal child development so that teaching practices could be suitably adapted to it and to explore the degree to which learning could be facilitated by educational intervention. Hall believed that many differences in children's abilities were innately determined: He was a committed eugenicist who bequeathed a quarter of a million dollars (equivalent to about $3 million today) in his will for a chair in eugenics at Clark (Rosenzweig, 1984). However, he also believed that child and adult behavior is often the product of adaptive adjustment to the environment.

Most psychologists trained in laboratory techniques were skeptical of the use of questionnaires, and experimental child research at Clark came to grief when Hall's colleague Franz Boas created a public outcry by loosening children's clothes in 1891 (as part of a study of classroom conditions for learning). Animal psychology, which Hall had introduced as an integral component of genetic psychology, provided a convenient solution to both problems. Animal psychology maintained the commitment to objective experimental research while avoiding any suggestion of moral impropriety (although Hall had to defend his animal psychologists against anti-vivisectionist protestors).

Linus Kline (b. 1866), a psychology instructor at Clark, who published *Suggestions Towards a Laboratory Course in Comparative Psychology* in 1899, introduced rats into his laboratory courses in comparative psychology. Adolf Meyer (1866–1950), a physician from Switzerland who took up an appointment at Worcester Hospital for the Insane, and whom Hall invited to teach courses in abnormal psychology at Clark, introduced the albino rat to America. Laboratory rats had many virtues for researchers: They were easy to house and cheap to maintain (unlike cats, dogs, and monkeys) and were much closer to humans than the amoebae and insects that were the focus of early biological studies of animal behavior (Logan, 1999). Kline and his graduate student Willard S. Small (1870–1943) conducted a series of experimental studies of associative learning, in which rats had to burrow through sawdust or gnaw through a door-latch to attain a food reward (Small, 1900). Small also studied maze learning in rats, by constructing a miniature replica of the maze at Hampton Court Palace in London (Small, 1901). These studies, and the work of other Clark students such as Andrew J. Kinnaman (who studied discrimination and intelligence in monkeys), set the stage for the later distinctive focus of animal and human psychology on the problem of learning, although animal psychology at Clark was discontinued at the turn of the century (Boakes, 1984).

The American Psychological Association

Hall recognized the need for a professional organization for psychologists, both to promote relations with other professional organizations (such as the National

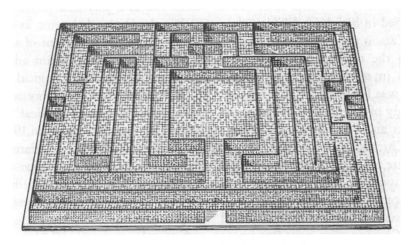

Willard S. Small's replica of Hampton Court maze for the study of learning in rats.

Education Association) and the general public and to fulfill his own personal goal of leadership of the psychological community. In the summer of 1892 Hall invited 26 American psychologists to Clark to form a psychological association. These included prominent philosopher-psychologists such as James and Ladd, but also heads of laboratories and asylums (and 14 of his former students and colleagues at Clark). Only a dozen of the invitees were able to attend the first organizational meeting held in Hall's office on July 8, 1892, where the American Psychological Association was founded, with Hall elected as its first president. Those present heard that many absent invitees had agreed to join (including Dewey, James, Scripture, Witmer, and Harry K. Wolfe), and they elected additional members such as Münsterberg and Titchener. They also agreed to hold their first meeting at the University of Pennsylvania in December 1892, where Hall delivered the first presidential address on the "History and Prospects of Experimental Psychology in America."

From the beginning the APA was inclusive in its membership policy, at least in terms of religion and gender. The charter members included two Jews, Jastrow and Münsterberg, and one Catholic, Edward A. Pace. Two women, Mary Calkins and Christine Ladd-Franklin, were elected members in 1893 (Sokal, 1992). However, the APA was less inclusive in terms of professional qualifications. Despite the common rejection of experimentalism and general advocacy of the practical application of psychology, for many decades membership was restricted to academic psychologists with established publication records. The stated professional aim of the APA was to promote "the advancement of psychology as a science," although exactly what that amounted to remained the focus of intensive debate in the following decades.

2 *Proceedings of the American Psychological Association.*

ciation in Philadelphia, at the University of Pennsylvania, on Tuesday,
December 27, 1892, at 10 A.M.

Professor Jastrow was appointed secretary to provide a programme
for that meeting. He invites all members to submit to him at Madison, Wisconsin, titles of papers with brief abstracts and estimates of
time required for presentation.

The original members who were either present at this meeting or
sent letters of approval and accepted membership are the following:

Angell, Frank, Leland Stanford, Jr., University,
Baldwin, J. Mark, Toronto University,
Bryan, W. L., Indiana University,
Burnham, W. H., Clark University,
Cattell, J. McK., Columbia College,
Cowles, Edward, McLean Asylum,
Delabarre, E. B., Brown University,
Dewey, John, University of Michigan,
Fullerton, G. S., University of Pennsylvania,
Gilman, B. I., Clark University,
Griffin, E. H., Johns Hopkins University,
Hall, G. Stanley, Clark University,
Hume, J. G., Toronto University,
Hyslop, J. H., Columbia College,
James, William, Harvard University,
Jastrow, Joseph, University of Wisconsin,
Krohn, W. O., Clark University,
Ladd, G. T., Yale University,
Nichols, Herbert, Harvard University,
Noyes, William, McLean Asylum,
Patrick, G. T. W., University of Iowa,
Royce, Josiah, Harvard University,
Sanford, E. C., Clark University,
Scripture, E. W., Yale University,
Witmer, Lightner, University of Pennsylvania,
Wolfe, H. K., University of Nebraska.

The following additional members were elected:

Mills, T. Wesley, McGill College, Montreal,
Münsterberg, Hugo, Harvard University,
Ormond, A. T., Princeton College,
Pace, Edward, Catholic University, Washington,
Titchener, E. B., Cornell University.

Professor Jastrow asked the co-operation of all members for the
Section of Psychology at the World's Fair, and invited correspondence
upon the matter.

List of original members of the American Psychological
Association.

Adolescence and Sex

Hall's own developmental research was focused on adolescence, which he defined
as ages 15–25. He maintained that adolescence is a critical period of developmental transition, during which humans rely on instincts as they abandon the habits
of childhood and begin to embrace those of adulthood. In 1904 he published the
two-volume *Adolescence: Its Psychology and Its Relations to Physiology, Anthropology,
Sociology, Sex, Crime, Religion, and Education.* Although the work was a best seller
(reprinted in many editions), it was not well received by the academic psychological

community, who complained of its emphasis on sex. They were equally shocked by Hall's weekly lectures on sex at Clark (they were officially restricted to a male audience, but he was forced to abandon them because of female gatecrashers and eavesdroppers) and by his revolutionary proposal that sex education be provided in schools. Hall thought that sex played an important role in child development and adolescence, although he did not embrace Freud's psychosexual theories.

Like Münsterberg, Hall was a great popularizer, writing articles on psychology for periodicals such as *Ladies' Home Journal* and *Appleton's Magazine*, usually offering practical advice on dealing with children and adolescents. Although he abandoned his career in the ministry, he maintained an interest in religion, albeit now oriented to the psychology of religion. He created the (short-lived) *Journal of Religious Psychology* in 1904 and in 1917 published a book with the doubtful title *Jesus, the Christ, in the Light of Psychology,* which was not well received.

Despite his free discussion of sexual matters and promotion of sex education, Hall was opposed to coeducation. Since he believed that adolescence is a time of sexual catharsis for men and of preparation for motherhood for women, he thought their institutional physical proximity was a recipe for disaster. Nevertheless, Hall's program at Clark was more hospitable to women and minorities than most other psychology programs of the day. Mary Calkins worked with Edward C. Sanford at Clark in 1890 (although the university did not officially admit women until 1900). Although he endorsed Haeckel's recapitulation theory, which placed blacks at a less developed evolutionary stage, Hall was personally committed to their education. Francis Cecil Sumner (1895–1954), later chair of the psychology department at Howard University, became the first black to be awarded a PhD in psychology in 1920, and Clark graduated more black PhDs than any other institution in the early 20th century.

However, progress in psychology remained slow for blacks. The number of PhDs in psychology increased by only about one per year, reaching a total of 32 by 1950 (Guthrie, 1988). Things were not much better for the first generation of women psychologists, who were forced to choose between family or career (Bolles, 1993; Scarborough & Furumoto, 1987). Prior to the dramatic expansion of professional psychology after the Second World War, those blacks who managed to make a career in psychology found their career trajectories generally restricted to colleges of education (Guthrie, 1988), and women found themselves professionally directed to practical studies of child development (Cahan, 2005).

Hall was influential in shaping the careers of the first generation of American PhDs in psychology: by 1898, he had supervised 30 of the 54 psychology PhDs thus far awarded (R. I. Watson, 1978). Clark produced many graduates committed to Hall's scientifically grounded but practically oriented approach to psychology, and he succeeded in his ambition in establishing the Clark program as one of the top psychology programs, rivaling Harvard in terms of the quality of its faculty and students.

Group photo of psychologists attending Freud's lectures at Clark University.
Front row, left to right: Franz Boas (first), Edward B. Titchener (second), William James (third), William Stern (fourth), G. Stanley Hall (sixth), Sigmund Freud (seventh), Carl G. Jung (eighth), Adolf Meyer (ninth), H. S. Jennings (tenth).
Second row, left to right: C. F. Seashore (first), Joseph Jastrow (second), James M. Cattell (third), Ernst Jones (sixth), A. A. Brill (seventh). Third row, left to right: Sandor Ferenczi (seventh). Fourth row, left to right: E. B. Holt (third), H. H. Goddard (tenth).

Hall invited both Freud and Wundt to be guest speakers at the 20th anniversary of the founding of Clark in 1909. Both declined, citing prior lecturing commitments (and Freud citing the insufficiency of the stipend). However, by changing the date of the anniversary celebrations, and by increasing the honorarium, Hall managed to attract Freud and Jung to give a series of lectures. This was an intellectual coup, for there was widespread interest as well as widespread suspicion of psychoanalysis at the time; and the conference attracted many of the major American psychologists of the day (including James, dying of angina pectoris, who made a great impression on Freud).

Old Age

A powerfully built man (he was over 6 feet tall), full of energy and enthusiasm for all matters psychological, Hall was a personally and intellectually dominating force in the formative years of American psychology. While many of his colleagues and students found him difficult to get along with, and as enthusiastic in promoting himself as in promoting psychology, most appreciated and respected his multivaried contributions to the discipline.

In his academic career and professional service, Hall achieved his own adolescent ambition to make something of his life. However, his private life and presidency at Clark were not without their heartbreaks and setbacks. Personal tragedy struck in 1890 when his wife and child were killed in an accident, and Hall was stricken with diphtheria. In the early 1890s Clark was attacked in the press over (unfounded) reports of cruel animal experiments. Financial problems caused by Jonas Clark's limited endowment of the university led to (unsuccessful) calls for Hall's resignation by the faculty. He soldiered on, despite his bitterness over president William Rainey Harper's raid of Clark faculty and students for the newly instituted University of Chicago in 1892 (the majority of faculty and about half the student body accepted the generous financial inducements to transfer). Hall resigned as president of Clark in 1919, at the age of 75.

In 1922, at the apt age of 78, Hall published *Senescence: The Last Half of Life*, anticipating the later development of life-span psychology. He published two autobiographies, *Recreations of a Psychologist* in 1920 and *Life and Confessions of a Psychologist* in 1923. In his old age he was critical of the manner in which he saw psychology developing, particularly its fragmentation into schools such as structuralism, functionalism, and behaviorism. In 1924 he was elected to the presidency of the APA for a second time (the second person to receive such an honor after James), but he died later that same year before he could complete his term.

APPLYING THE WUNDTIAN SKELETON: CATTELL, WITMER, SCOTT, AND WOLFE

James, Münsterberg, Ladd, and Hall served as sorts of father (or grandfather) figures of American psychology and occupied the promotional foreground in their lifetimes. Other early American pioneers, many of them students of Wundt's, worked on the establishment of the professional and institutional structure of American psychology and the specialist subdisciplines such as clinical and industrial psychology. While they did not embrace the theoretical details of Wundt's experimental psychology or his *Völkerpsychologie*, they adapted his commitment to scientific objectivity and experiment to their range of distinctively applied interests.

James McKeen Cattell: Mental Testing

James McKeen Cattell (1860–1944) was one of Wundt's first Leipzig students and his first full-time American student. He graduated from Lafayette College (which he entered at the age of 15) in Easton, Pennsylvania, in 1880. His father, a Presbyterian clergyman, was professor of Greek and Latin and later president of Lafayette College. His mother came from a wealthy family, and Cattell used an inheritance from his grandfather to fund a trip to Europe in 1880. Originally interested in literature, he studied German at the University of Göttingen and studied briefly with Wundt at Leipzig. He did not take part in laboratory work and began preparation of a thesis on the philosophy of Rudolf Hermann Lotze.

An essay on this topic gained Cattell a fellowship at Johns Hopkins in 1882. Under Hall's supervision, he worked on the measurement of the time taken to name colors and objects. Despite his academic promise, Cattell lost the fellowship. This may have been a result of his constant bickering with the president of the university or his youthful experimentation with mental stimulants such as alcohol, nicotine, hashish, and morphine (Sokal, 1981). Hall may also have blocked the renewal of the fellowship because he perceived Cattell as a potential rival (O'Donnell, 1985).

Cattell returned to Leipzig in 1883, with accumulated data, a research design, and plans for the construction of apparatus to complete the experiments he had conducted at Johns Hopkins. He became Wundt's first research assistant, based upon his own recommendation (Boring, 1957). Cattell continued his research on the time taken to perform "cerebral operations," a study well suited to Wundt's own program of mental chronometry. His research on reaction time for the naming of letters was published in Wundt's journal *Philosophical Studies* in 1885; a shorter version titled "On the Time It Takes to See and Name Objects" appeared in the British journal *Mind* in 1886.

Cattell recognized the instrumental value of a Leipzig degree (and of laboratory experience and publications) as a professional credential. However, he did not think much of the quality of the laboratory work at Leipzig, "the work done in it is decidedly amateurish" (Jan. 1885, p. 156, in Sokal, 1981) or of Wundt himself: "Wundt himself is scarcely a great man" (Nov. 1885, p. 193, in Sokal, 1981). Cattell described himself as an "apparatus man," with no interest in theory or philosophy. However, the brash young American and distinguished German professor appear to have got on surprisingly well (and much better than Wundt and Titchener, his professed American disciple). As Cattell wrote to his parents, "Wundt seems to like me and appreciate my phenomenal genius."

Wundt characterized Cattell as representing the "typically American" (*ganz Amerikanisch*) attitude of independence and self-confidence. Wundt allowed him to study individual differences in reaction time, a decidedly Galtonian rather than Wundtian research topic. Cattell studied the psychometrics of attention and individual differences in the effects of fatigue and practice. He created a "gravity chronometer," which enabled stimulus words to be presented at controlled intervals and even managed to convince Wundt to consider the idea of different "styles" of responding.

This was quite remarkable, give the later controversy between James Mark Baldwin and Edward B. Titchener over "type" versus "practice" theories of reaction time (Baldwin, 1895, 1896; Titchener, 1895a, 1895b, 1896a). Wundt, like Titchener, maintained that differences in fatigue and practice are subjective biases to be eliminated or attenuated through experimental control, whereas Cattell, like Baldwin, maintained that such individual differences are a legitimate object of experimental investigation. Cattell's "Psychometric Investigations" was the first American dissertation completed in the Leipzig program (Benjamin et al., 1992), and he gained his PhD in 1886. He may also be said to have contributed to Wundt's own published output by introducing him to the typewriter.

After Leipzig, Cattell traveled to England, where he worked with Francis Galton (with whom he had corresponded for some years) and completed the first year of a two-year fellowship at the University of Cambridge. He was hugely impressed with Galton's work and began to apply the techniques he had developed at Leipzig to anthropometric measurement, which reinforced and refined his interest in individual differences (O'Donnell, 1985). He also supported Galton's program of positive eugenics and offered each of his seven children $1,000 as a positive incentive to marry college professors.

When the Seybery chair in philosophy was created by bequest at the University of Pennsylvania, Cattell's father persuaded president William Pepper that his son would be the ideal person for the position. Pepper may have been swayed by the father's insistence that salary was not an issue, since Cattell was appointed to the chair in 1887 at an annual salary of $300 (a paltry sum even in those days, equivalent to about $6,500 in today's dollars). When his title was changed to professor of psychology the following year, Cattell boasted that he was the first person promoted to a full professorship in psychology in America.

At the University of Pennsylvania, Cattell initiated a program of mental testing based upon a variety of psychophysical measures, such as grip strength, speed of movement, skin sensitivity, and sensory and motor reaction time. He described these measures in a paper published in *Mind* in 1890, in which he coined the term **mental test**:

> Psychology cannot attain the certainty and exactness of the physical sciences, unless it rests on a foundation of experiment and measurement. A step in this direction could be made by applying a series of mental tests and measurements to a large number of individuals. The results would be of considerable scientific value in discovering the constancy of mental processes, their interdependence, and their variation under different circumstances.
>
> —(1890, p. 373)

Cattell continued his program of mental testing when he moved to a more lucrative post at Columbia University in 1891, subjecting hundred of students to batteries of tests in the hope that psychology might "be applied in useful ways" (1904, p. 185). He assumed that his various tests were measures of intelligence and thus useful indicators of academic performance. However, this assumption was seriously undermined when one of his own students, Clark Wissler (1870–1947), attempted to validate it by exploring the correlation between test scores and course grades (employing Galtonian measures of correlation, including Pearson's newly developed correlation coefficient). To Cattell's consternation, Wissler found almost zero correlation (Wissler, 1901). This marked the effective end of the Galtonian program of anthropometric testing in America (although Joseph Jastrow continued it at Michigan for a few years after).

Cattell developed the psychology program at Columbia with great success in the early 20th century. He hired a distinguished faculty, which included former students such as Edward L. Thorndike and Robert S. Woodworth. Columbia became one of the leading programs in psychology, and produced the largest number of PhDs in the early decades of the 20th century (surpassing Harvard, Hopkins, and Clark). Cattell was elected fourth president of the APA in 1895.

His other main contribution to the fledging science of psychology was in his role as editor and publisher. In 1894 Cattell and Baldwin launched *Psychological Review*, which quickly became the premier theoretical journal in psychology and the organ of the APA, publishing its proceedings, news, and presidential addresses. *Psychological Review* was followed by *Psychological Index* (which listed publications in psychology) and *Psychological Monographs* (which published lengthy and specially commissioned experimental and technical reports) in 1895.

Cattell sold his interest in *Psychological Review* to Baldwin in 1904 (after a bitter quarrel) and began to devote more attention to general scientific publications. He owned and edited *Popular Science Monthly, American Men of Science, School and Society, American Naturalist,* and *Science* (which he edited for 50 years). He was the first psychologist admitted to the National Academy of Sciences (in 1901) and served as president of the American Association for the Advancement of Science (which he helped to form) in 1924.

Although his students remembered him with warmth and affection, he gained a reputation as a brash and prickly personality (Sokal, 1971), especially in his relations with college administrators, for whom he reserved a special contempt. A staunch defender of academic freedom and tenure against "academic servitude," he (along with John Dewey) played a major role in the founding of the American Association of University Professors. Eventually the administrators prevailed, and in 1917 the president of Columbia dismissed Cattell from the university for his pacifism (he had defended his son's distribution of anticonscription literature in an open letter to the United States Congress written on Columbia stationary). Cattell sued Columbia and was awarded substantial damages, but he never again held an academic position. He continued to edit and publish, and he founded the highly successful Psychological Corporation in 1921, which began to market psychological expertise to the business community (and continues to do so to this day). Cattell died in 1944.

Lightner Witmer: Clinical Psychology

Lightner Witmer graduated from the Wharton School of Business at the University of Pennsylvania in 1888. After he entered law school, he took a psychology class with Cattell, who persuaded him to take up psychology instead and arranged for Witmer to be his assistant. Cattell urged Witmer to complete his studies of individual differences in reaction time with Wundt in Leipzig. The university promised him a salary hike if he obtained a doctoral degree from Wundt's laboratory, which he did in 1892. Although it served his professional interest, Witmer's Leipzig experience was not happy. Wundt refused to allow him to work with untrained subjects and even refused to allow him to serve as an experimental subject himself, because he did not consider him properly "calibrated."

On his return to the United States, Witmer took over Cattell's position at Pennsylvania (on his recommendation) after Cattell moved to Columbia. Although Witmer later claimed that he got nothing from Germany but a doctoral degree and did not consider that he owed much to Wundt (Witmer, letter to Boring, 1948, cited in O'Donnell, 1985, p. 35), he built up the psychology department and laboratory at Pennsylvania along conventional lines. He began a program of laboratory research based upon his reaction-time studies and published an experimental text titled *Analytic Psychology* in 1902. However, his interests turned increasingly to applied psychology as the years progressed. In 1894 he taught an evening course on child psychology for teachers, which developed into a regular Saturday morning program, and he became interested in learning disabilities and the behavioral problems of schoolchildren. One of his students, Margaret McGuire, an English teacher in the Philadelphia public school system, introduced him to an apparently intelligent 14-year-old pupil with spelling difficulties (Routh & Reisman, 2003). He identified a vision problem that was partially resolved by eyeglasses, and the pupil made some improvement with tutoring (although the case was probably more complex, since the pupil may also have been dyslexic [McReynolds, 1997]). This stimulated Witmer to initiate an informal program of educational intervention, working in conjunction with the teachers and families of the children he treated.

His modest success with largely improvised methods motivated him to institute the Psychological Clinic at the University of Pennsylvania in 1896 and to urge his colleagues at the APA to adopt the "clinical" method (Witmer, 1897). The Philadelphia philanthropist Mary L. Crozer provided funding for *Psychological Clinic: A Journal for the Study and Treatment of Mental Retardation*

University of Pennsylvania Psychological Clinic (staff members Helen Backus, Karl G. Miller, and Alićе Jones).

and Deviation, which Witmer founded in 1907 and edited for the next 30 years. In the lead article, he coined the term **clinical psychology** to describe a new diagnostic branch of applied psychology: The term "clinical" referenced the clinical method of medicine from which the diagnostic method was appropriated. In describing the development of clinical psychology from his work with pupils with learning difficulties, Witmer claimed that the ultimate value of psychological science lay in its practical utility:

> There is no valid distinction between a pure science and an applied science. . . . The pure and the applied sciences advance in a single front. What retards the progress of one, retards the progress of the other; what fosters one, fosters the other. But in the final analysis the progress of psychology, as of every other science, will be determined by the value and amount of its contributions to the advancement of the human race.
>
> —(1907, p. 4)

Consequently, he maintained that the success or failure of remedial treatment was the best test of the adequacy of a clinical diagnosis.

Witmer's own clinical program was largely based upon the remedial training of children, or what would nowadays be described as "school psychology," but he stressed that the clinical method extended beyond the treatment of "mentally and morally retarded children" to the treatment of adults:

> The methods of clinical psychology are necessarily invoked wherever the status of an individual mind is determined by observation and experiment, and pedagogical treatment applied to effect a change, *i.e.,* the development of such an individual mind. Whether the subject be a child or an adult, the examination and treatment may be conducted and their results expressed in the terms of the clinical method.
>
> —(1907, p. 9)

Witmer relied upon the help and advice of teachers, social workers, and physicians affiliated with the Psychological Clinic. By 1909 it was staffed by Witmer as director, an assistant director, five trained psychology PhD examiners, a social worker, and three assistant social workers (Routh & Reisman, 2003). The success of his program of clinical intervention and training led to the creation of psychological clinics and training programs at other universities, with new courses introduced in clinical psychology. The Iowa Psychological Clinic and the Clark University Psychological Clinic were founded in 1913, and by 1920 there were psychology clinics at 19 universities (Routh & Reisman, 2003). The expanded Psychological Clinic at Pennsylvania became a major center for the training of clinical psychologists, who went on to staff institutions across the country. Many of these institutions also followed Witmer's initiative in creating residential homes for the treatment of educational and other psychological disorders.

One of Witmer's students was Edwin Twitmyer (1873–1943), a pioneer in speech pathology. Twitmyer worked at the Pennsylvania Psychological Clinic and later became director of the speech clinic. In his doctoral dissertation, he described the classical conditioning of the patellar (knee-jerk) reflex, which he identified independently of Pavlov's work (Twitmyer, 1902/1974).

Witmer was generally skeptical of mental tests and condemned much of the mental testing movement as bad science (although he later became interested in gifted children and defined intelligence as the ability to solve new problems). He devised two psychological tests that came to be widely used as diagnostic tools, the Witmer Formboard and the Witmer Cylinders. While committed to applied psychology, he continued to respect the rigor of the laboratory methods that he had been taught at Leipzig and insisted that applied research should be held to the same critical standards as laboratory research. He roundly condemned James's psychic research and dismissed Münsterberg's psychotherapy as quackery. He was an early advocate of the creation of a society of "serious" experimental psychologists as an alternative to the mongrel membership of the APA, a goal later realized through Titchener's creation of the society known as the Experimentalists.

Unlike later behaviorists who claimed that the results of laboratory experiments on animals such as rats and pigeons could be directly applied to human problems in everyday settings, Witmer maintained that clinical psychology must be based upon case studies of individual persons with particular psychological problems. Indeed, this was the main reason for calling his form of applied psychology "clinical" psychology, because it was based upon the method of case histories associated with clinical medicine (although he had little enthusiasm for the work of Freud, which was also based upon case histories):

> I have borrowed the word "clinical" from medicine, because it is the best term I can find to indicate the character of the method which I deem necessary for this work. . . . Clinical psychology . . . is a protest against a psychology that derives psychological

and pedagogical principles from philosophical speculations and against a psychology that applies the results of laboratory experimentation directly to children in the school room.

—(Witmer, 1907, p. 8)

Although his own theory and practice was directed to school and vocational psychology, Witmer played a significant role in establishing the legitimacy of psychological (as opposed to psychiatric or medical) treatments of psychological disorders (McReynolds, 1996); nonetheless, most American clinical psychologists did not devote their attention to psychological therapy until after the Second World War. Witmer remained at the University of Pennsylvania until his retirement in 1937. Before his death in 1956, he was the last surviving charter member of the APA.

Walter Dill Scott: Industrial Psychology

Walter Dill Scott (1869–1955) originally planned for a career as a missionary and gained a divinity degree from McCormick Theological Seminary in Chicago. When he later developed an interest in psychology, he traveled to Leipzig in 1898 to study with Wundt. He received his degree in 1900 with a dissertation on the psychology of impulse. On returning to the United States, he was appointed lecturer in psychology and pedagogy at Northwestern University, where he instituted a psychology laboratory. However, he did little research himself and did not publish any experimental studies. His interests quickly turned to the business applications of psychology, especially advertising.

Scott published *The Theory of Advertising* in 1903, based mainly upon articles written for *Mahin's Magazine* (founded by John Mahin, the head of a Chicago advertising agency), and a spate of articles in periodicals such as *The Woman's Herald*, *Atlantic Monthly*, *Business World,* and *Advertising World*. These were speculative discussions about the association of ideas, suggestion, and individual differences in mental imagery, perception, and attention, which reflected the current "state of knowledge" in these areas (Ferguson, 1962, cited in Benjamin, 1997), although some were based upon research done for businesses on particular problems. Scott published *The Psychology of Public Speaking* in 1906, followed by *Increasing Human Efficiency in Business* and *Influencing Men of Business* in 1911.

Scott is generally recognized as the founder of American industrial psychology (Benjamin, 1997), although Münsterberg was a notable precursor. Borrowing from the work of Galton and Cattell, he created a series of mental tests designed to assess business skills, which he later developed as director of the Bureau of Salesmanship Research at the Carnegie Institute of Technology. He also created rating scales for employee selection, which he adapted for officer selection when

Hawthorne experiment.

he became head of the Committee on the Classification of Personnel in the Army (CCPA) during the First World War (von Mayrhauser, 1989). Scott was awarded the Distinguished Service Medal for his army work in 1919 and was elected president of the APA that same year. He started the Scott Company in 1919 (with former members of the CCPA); it offered counseling services to business. Scott became president of Northwestern University in 1920 and served for 19 years as one of its most successful administrators.

Industrial psychology expanded dramatically after the First World War, especially in the realm of personnel selection and evaluation, but also through studies of industrial efficiency. The most famous of those were conducted at the Hawthorne, Illinois, plant of the Western General Electric Company during the 1920s and 1930s. These studies indicated that changes in lighting and temperature improved efficiency, although investigators later noted that almost any environmental change produced the same effect, as a function of the apparent interest researchers (and by inference managers) were taking in workers' progress (Mayo, 1933). What came to be known as the "Hawthorne effect" was later questioned empirically and criticized for its promotion of the interests of managers over workers (Bramel & Friend, 1981).

Harry Kirke Wolfe: Scientific Pedagogy

Harry Kirke Wolfe (1858–1918), whose parents were schoolteachers, developed a program of research on education conceived of as an aid to "scientific pedagogy." A native of Nebraska, Wolfe studied memory with Ebbinghaus and took his PhD with Wundt in Leipzig in 1886 with a dissertation on tonal memory (Wolfe, 1886). After a few years as a teacher in California, he was appointed chair of the department of philosophy at the University of Nebraska in 1899, where he instituted a psychology laboratory. Nebraska was one of the land grant universities, and in contrast to Hall at Johns Hopkins, Wolfe failed to secure institutional funding for psychology texts and equipment, because he failed to convince the university of the applied value of experimental psychology. Wolfe adapted the scientific rigor of Wundt's laboratory to the development of tests of memory, imagination, attention, reasoning, and moral development for use in educational assessment (Benjamin, 1991).

Although Wolfe promoted the value of the new psychology to education as vigorously as Hall, his own lack of training in pedagogy inclined the university authorities to doubt his competence to pronounce on matters of education, and he was dismissed from the university in 1897. After serving as superintendent of the South Omaha Public School System and principal of Lincoln High School (both in Nebraska), he returned to the University of Nebraska in 1906 as professor of educational psychology (O'Donnell, 1985).

EDWARD B. TITCHENER AND STRUCTURAL PSYCHOLOGY

Edward Bradford Titchener was born in Chichester, England. His academic excellence secured him scholarships at Malvern College (an English public school) and Brasenose College, Oxford. He studied philosophy and classics at Oxford, but became a research assistant in physiology in his final year. He developed an interest in the work of Darwin and Huxley and did some physiological studies, which he published in 10 papers in *Nature* between 1889 and 1891 (Tweney, 1997). During this period he read Wundt's *Principles of Physiological Psychology*, which stimulated his interest in psychology.

Titchener translated the third edition of Wundt's *Principles* into English. Shortly afterward, Wundt produced the fourth edition, which Titchener also duly translated, only to discover that Wundt had produced the fifth edition! Although he later came to represent himself as the champion of Wundtian psychology in America, there is some question about the adequacy of Titchener's translations (Blumenthal, 1979), which he claimed rendered "literal" rather than "verbal" translations of Wundt (Creighton & Titchener, 1894). Unlike Charles Judd's later translations (e.g., Wundt, 1897/1902), Titchener's translations were not approved by Wundt.

Recognizing that he could not satisfy his new interest in psychology at Oxford or any other British university, Titchener traveled to Leipzig to study with Wundt after completing his degree in 1890 (at the age of 23). He worked with Wundt for two years and attained his doctorate in 1892. Wundt had a huge influence upon Titchener, although they were not close, and Titchener actually saw little of him during his years at Leipzig. He made friends with Oswald Külpe and Frank Angell, an American student who established the psychology laboratory at Cornell in 1891. When Angell accepted a position at Stanford University in 1892, he recommended Titchener as his replacement. Although Titchener was also offered a job at Oxford (where he had been working as a lecturer in biology), he recognized that psychology had no immediate future in Britain and accepted Cornell's offer.

On arrival at Cornell, Titchener immediately set about creating what was to become the largest doctoral program in psychology in America during the early decades of the 20th century. He transformed the original 4-room laboratory into a 26-room laboratory. Between 1893 and 1900 he published *An Outline of Psychology* (1896b), 62 papers, and translations of Wundt and Külpe. For these energetic efforts he was promoted to full professor in 1896. He published *A Primer of Psychology* in 1898, and the magisterial four-volume *Experimental Psychology: A Manual of Laboratory Practice* from 1901 to 1905 (which comprised two manuals for students and two for instructors).

Experimental Psychology became the standard manual for experimental psychology courses in America for the next 20 years (Watson used it in his laboratory courses at Chicago), and it was translated into most European languages and Russian. Although these manuals were eventually superseded, they played a major role in promoting the development of experimental psychology in America and instilling a respect for scientific rigor that came to be shared by even the most virulent critics of Titchener's own experimental program. After 1905, Titchener devoted most of his time to running the psychology program and laboratory and published little research under his own name (Tweney, 1987).

Edwin G. Boring, one of Titchener's students and author of *A History of Experimental Psychology*, described him as the "Englishman who represented the German psychological tradition in America" (Boring, 1957, p. 410). However, he might better be described as the Englishman who presented himself as the representative of the Wundtian tradition in America, albeit successfully for most of the 20th century—until the original Wundt was "rediscovered" in the 1970s (Blumenthal, 1975, 1979; Leahey, 1979, 1981). Titchener modeled the psychology program at Cornell upon Wundt's experimental program in Leipzig, and his own lifestyle upon Wundt's. A popular and effective lecturer, Titchener built the reputation of the psychology program upon his elaborate laboratory demonstrations and the rigorous training he required of his students. He presided over the program in an authoritarian fashion that bordered on the dictatorial, prescribing legitimate projects for PhD dissertations and determining who should work on them (in this latter respect he was probably more rigid than Wundt). He always lectured in his Oxford gown, which he claimed gave him the right to be dogmatic.

While he was harsh and unrelenting with students who crossed him, he was supportive of those who treated him with the deference he considered his due. He inspired affection and loyalty among his students, who volunteered to wash his car and even took to smoking cigars because they believed that Titchener thought this was an essential habit of a good psychologist (Dallenbach, 1967). He also helped to advance the careers of many female psychologists: During his tenure at Cornell about a third of the PhDs who graduated from the program were women. Although this was Cornell's own policy, Titchener seems to have followed it willingly. He was not miserly in crediting the work of his female graduate students or reluctant to recommend them for academic positions.

Margaret Floyd Washburn (1871–1939), a graduate of Vassar College, was Titchener's first graduate student. She was also the first student to receive a PhD in psychology at Cornell and the first woman to receive a PhD in psychology. She had studied with Cattell at Columbia, but transferred to Cornell (on Cattell's advice) because Columbia did not formally admit women. Washburn's dissertation was on visual and tactile sensation and was later published in Wundt's journal *Philosophical Studies*. She was the second female president of the APA and the second American woman (and first female psychologist) to be elected to the American Academy of Sciences. After teaching at a variety of institutions, she returned to Vassar in 1903, where she set up a psychology laboratory. She remained active in teaching and research until she died in 1939. She published *The Animal Mind: A Text-book of Comparative Psychology* in 1908 (based upon a course she taught at Cornell in 1901) and *Movement and Mental Imagery* in 1916.

Throughout his lifetime Titchener was associated with the *American Journal of Psychology*, founded by Hall in 1887. He served as associate editor from 1895 to 1920, and as editor from 1920 to 1925 (after which his students Karl Dallenbach and Margaret Washburn took over the journal). Most of his own work was published in this journal, because he refused to publish in journals such as *Psychological Review* and *Psychological Bulletin* after he fell out with their editors, Cattell and Baldwin.

Structural Psychology

Like Wundt, Titchener conceived of experimental psychology as the study of immediate experience and maintained that its subject matter, unlike that of the natural sciences, is dependent upon consciousness. However, his program of experimental psychology owed more to the British empiricist tradition of associationist psychology than it did to Wundt's voluntaristic psychology (as Titchener acknowledged in the original preface to *An Outline of Psychology*, 1896b). Titchener's aim was to identify the atomistic constituents of conscious experience and determine the correlational laws of their combination. His positivistic science was restrictively descriptive, and he eschewed Wundt's appeal to explanatory constructs such as apperception. Titchener called his psychology "descriptive psychology" for the same positivist reasons that B. F. Skinner later called his form of behaviorism "descriptive behaviorism."

Titchener claimed that the primary goal of experimental psychology (at least for the foreseeable future) was to describe the basic structure of the mind: the conscious elements of mind and their modes of combination. For this reason, he characterized his form of psychology as **structural psychology** and distinguished it from **functional psychology**, which he claimed was primarily concerned with the functions of consciousness (Titchener, 1898b, 1899).

The experimental focus of Titchener's program was on conscious elements, defined as the simplest components of consciousness available to introspection that are incapable of further discrimination or analysis. According to Titchener, the experimental psychologist dissects mental experience until he "is left with certain mental processes which resist analysis, which are absolutely simple in nature, which cannot be reduced, even in part, to other processes" (1910, pp. 37–38). He identified these elements as sensations such as sights, smells, and tastes (the elements of perception), images (the elements of ideas), and affections (the elements of emotions).

In addition to Wundt's fundamental properties of quality and quantity (intensity), Titchener added clarity and duration, and extension or extensity (in the case of vision and touch). He claimed that affections have quality, quantity, and duration, but not clarity (since they dissipate when we try to focus attention on them). He rejected Wundt's tridimensional theory of emotion and claimed that the dimensions of high/low arousal and concentrated/relaxed attention are nothing more than combinations of sensation and the affective dimension of pleasant/unpleasant.

Most of the experimental studies conducted in the Cornell laboratory focused on the identification of sensational elements. Titchener claimed to have documented more than 44,435 of these in his 1896 *Outline of Psychology* (which makes good nighttime reading for insomniacs), the majority of which were visual (32,820, with 11,600 auditory). Although the focus of these studies was the introspective analysis of ordinary sensations, some were directed toward more exotic targets and required more invasive forms of experimental intervention. Some experimental subjects reported on sensational and affective elements of urination and defecation (and sex, in the case of married students), while others reported on sensational and affective responses to hot and iced water ingested through a rubber tube they were required to swallow.[1]

---

[1]According to Cora Friedline, one of Titchener's graduate students, who recalled these experiments at a talk she gave in 1960 at Randolph-Macon College in Virginia (reported in Schultz & Schultz, 1992, p. 122).

Titchener accounted for the organization of sensory elements into complex perceptual wholes (such as the perception of an apple) by appeal to traditional principles of association, the "laws of connection of the elementary sensory processes," and combinatory laws of color contrast and tonal fusion. Wundt had supposed that these principles account only for passive forms of perception and cognition and appealed to the principles of psychical resultants and relations to account for more complex psychological processes. Titchener maintained that the principles of association account for all psychological processes and analyzed Wundt's active attentional processes in terms of differential degrees of clarity among mental elements (analogously, he interpreted feelings of concentration as sensations of muscular responses that accompany vivid sensations).

Inspection and Introspection

If Titchener's theoretical program was more restricted than Wundt's, his conception of introspection as an experimental method was broader, although no less rigorous in practice. He repeated Wundt's mantra of repetition, isolation, and variation as the essence of experimentation: "an experiment is an observation that can be repeated, isolated and varied" (1910, p. 20). However, he relied more heavily on introspective reports than Wundt, who favored objective measures such as reaction time. Titchener's subjects were specially trained to avoid what he called **stimulus error** (1912, p. 488): They were trained to report only the pure contents of experience, not the (theoretically interpreted) meaning of the sensory array or the purported real-world object of the experience. For example, in reporting their immediate sensory experience of an apple, subjects were required to describe colors, tastes, smells, and the like, but not their theoretically mediated experience: the meaning of the complex or its purported real-world object (the apple).

Like Wundt, Titchener claimed that the processes of introspection and **inspection** (the observation of independent physical objects in the external world) are fundamentally identical, differing only with respect to their objects: The objects of introspection are dependent upon consciousness, whereas those of inspection are not. Consequently he claimed that "in general the method of psychology is much the same as the method of physics" (1910, p. 25). Also like Wundt, Titchener maintained that the validity of introspection as a scientific method, like the validity of inspection, is dependent upon intersubjective agreement among observers about observed properties, whether these be the private objects of introspection or the public objects of inspection. It was the perceived failure to attain intersubjective agreement among introspecting subjects that led to the demise of Titchener's brand of experimental psychology.

Titchener followed Külpe in calling his method of introspection "systematic experimental introspection." Although he maintained that there is an "essential likeness" between introspection and inspection, Titchener also acknowledged an important difference that had been the focus of earlier critics of introspection such as Kant and Comte. Attempts to introspect mental processes, unlike attempts to inspect physical ones (with the possible exception of quantum mechanical processes), tend to interfere with the mental processes themselves.

> Here, however, there seems to be a difference between introspection and inspection. The observer who is watching the course of a chemical reaction, or the movements of some microscopical creature, can jot down from moment to moment the different phases of the observed phenomenon. But if you try to report the changes in consciousness, while these changes are in progress, you interfere with consciousness; your translation of the mental experience into words introduces new factors into that experience itself.
>
> —(1910, pp. 21–22)

However, Titchener did not think that this difference constituted an insurmountable impediment to experimental introspection. He suggested that one way of alleviating the problem was to delay reporting on mental processes until after their completion, so that in many cases introspection became a form of retrospection or "postmortem" examination. He also maintained that experienced experimental subjects could overcome problems of interference:

> The practised observer gets into an introspective habit, has the introspective attitude ingrained in his system; so that it is possible for him, not only to take mental notes while the observation is in progress, without interfering with consciousness, but even to jot down written notes, as the histologist does while his eye is still held to the ocular of the microscope.
>
> —(1910, p. 23)

He conceived of the training of experimental subjects as analogous to the calibration of scientific instruments. He claimed that once experimental subjects ("reagents") were properly trained in "hard introspective labor," they found that accurate introspection became a largely mechanical process.

Gestalt psychologists criticized Titchener's structural psychology for its artificiality and complained that conscious experience cannot be decomposed into isolatable elements. Yet Titchener (like Wundt) was well aware that conscious experience is not a mere aggregation of static elements, but an ongoing process. With James, Titchener recognized that consciousness is like a stream: "our subject-matter is a stream, a perpetual flux, and not a collection of unchanging objects"

(1910, p. 16). He also noted the (Heraclitean) methodological problem this gener-ated for experimental psychology: "In strictness, we can never observe the same consciousness over; the stream of mind flows on, never to return" (1910, p. 19). However, he claimed that subjects can observe sufficiently similar experiential sequences through experimental repetition:

> Practically, we can observe a particular consciousness as often as we wish, since men-tal processes group themselves in the same way, show the same pattern of arrange-ment, whenever the organism is placed under the same circumstances.
>
> —(1910, p. 19)

He also suggested a means of dealing with the problem, by segmenting sequences of a conscious process (a method that harked back to Aristotle's studies of the embryology of the chick):

> For we must remember . . . that the observations in question may be repeated. There is, then, no reason why the observer to whom the word is called out, or in whom the emotion is set up, should not report at once upon the first stage of his experience: upon the immediate effect of the word, upon the beginnings of the emotive process. It is true that this report interrupts the observation. But, after the first stage has been accurately described, further observations may be taken, and second, third and fol-lowing stages similarly described; so that presently a complete report upon the whole experience is obtained. There is, in theory, some danger that the stages become artifi-cially separated. . . . In practice, however, this danger has proved to be very small; and we may always have recourse to retrospection, and compare our partial results with our memory of the unbroken experience.
>
> —(1910, pp. 22–23)

Völkerpsychologie and Applied Psychology

Because of Titchener's vigorous promotion of an experimental science of con-sciousness, he is often represented as being antipathetic to applied psychology, such as educational and clinical psychology, and to developmental and social psy-chology, including the form of comparative-historical psychology represented by Wundt's *Völkerpsychologie*. Yet on numerous occasions Titchener acknowledged their legitimacy. With respect to *Völkerpsychologie*, for example, he affirmed the value of a branch of psychology devoted to the study of the cultural products of different social groups, such as language, myth, and custom (1910, p. 28).

Historians have generally portrayed Titchener as a dismissive critic of Wundt's *Völkerpsychologie*, based upon a number of negative comments he made in his obituary on Wundt (Titchener, 1921). Yet he maintained an active interest in the project of *Völkerpsychologie* and was an astute commentator on the methodological problems of any form of comparative psychology that dealt with different social and cultural communities. He was critical of the psychological findings of the Torres Strait expedition, which explored cultural differences in sensory acuity, but was supportive of its intellectual goal (Titchener, 1916). If he was not enthusiastic about the development of *Volkerpsychologie*, it was because he thought it premature until the experimental analysis of consciousness was sufficiently advanced:

> The functional psychology of the social mind is, as might be expected, in a very rudimentary condition . . . we must have an experimental psychology of the individual mind, before there can be any great progress.
>
> —(1898b, p. 455)

This was also Titchener's attitude to other branches of psychology, including forms of applied psychology, such as educational and clinical psychology. When he distinguished structural from functional psychology, his aim was not to disparage functional psychology, but to establish the conceptual and developmental priority of structural psychology. He maintained that structural psychology had the best chance of instilling the intellectual rigor that was necessary for psychology to develop as a proper science:

> The morphological study of mind serves, as no other method of study can, to enforce and sustain the thesis that psychology is a science, and not a province of metaphysics.
>
> —(1898b, p. 454)

Titchener followed Wundt in characterizing Meumann's "experimental pedagogy" as "educational technology," but never impugned its utility. He recognized the value of abnormal psychology and followed Albert Binet in treating pathological cases as forms of "natural experiment" (1898b, p. 465). He was less charitable toward the work of Münsterberg, whom he accused of "trading science for technology," and programs of mental testing, which he dismissed as "second-rate and cheap" (Titchener, 1914). Yet he was not alone in his critical attitude toward them, which was shared by applied psychologists such as Lightner Witmer and John B. Watson.

Titchener maintained that the experimental analysis of consciousness represented the hard core of scientific psychology and thought that the development of other branches was premature until the scientific core had been firmly established. He also feared (like Wundt, and with similar justification and premonition) that this scientific core was in danger of being diluted and displaced by applied psychology or "technology" (1898b, p. 454).

1916 Princeton Meeting of Experimentalists (Edward B. Titchener in foreground, second from left).

The Experimentalists

Titchener was a charter member of the APA, but never attended its meetings, even when they were held at Cornell. He resigned from the organization in 1904, ostensibly because of its failure to act on a charge of plagiarism made against Edward W. Scripture, relating to the unacknowledged use of his translation of Wundt's *Principles* in Scripture's *Thinking, Feeling, and Doing* (1895). That same year, Titchener founded his own group, which came to be known as the **Experimentalists** (reconstituted in 1929 as the "Society of Experimental Psychologists"). Titchener ran this group—from 1904 to 1927—in the same authoritarian fashion as he ran his PhD program and determined the legitimate topics and attendance. This led to the public humiliation of Gordon Allport (1897–1967), the social psychologist and personality theorist, when the Experimentalists met at Clark University in 1922. Allport, who was a graduate student at Harvard at the time, presented a three-minute paper on personality traits. This was met with a blank silence, "punctuated by a glare of disapproval from Titchener" (Allport, 1967, p. 9), after which the group pointedly continued their discussion of sensory perception.

Titchener ran the group like a gentleman's club, inviting only the top people from the top laboratories. Robert Woodworth of Columbia was blacklisted for not having behaved like a gentleman. Unable to attend, he had improperly posted his personal invitation on the Columbia psychology department notice board with the comment "Who wants to go?" (Boring, 1938). Women were excluded during Titchener's lifetime, and female faculty and students from Bryn Mawr College were "promptly turned out" when they tried to attend the 1907 meeting at the University of Pennsylvania (Titchener, letter to Münsterberg, 1908, quoted in Furumoto, 1988). In later years they hid under the tables and listened at the doors. Christine Ladd-Franklin (1847–1930), the Vassar graduate who studied with Helmholtz and Müller, waged a long campaign to have women admitted. When Titchener tried to defend his exclusion of women by appeal to the need for critical discussion and cigar smoking, she responded that she was as critical as any man and enjoyed cigars as much as any man.

Titchener dominated the Experimentalists during his lifetime. However, the invited membership was fairly eclectic and included comparative, behaviorist, and clinical psychologists such as Robert M. Yerkes, John B. Watson, and Lightner Witmer. Although few accepted Titchener's own brand of structural psychology, many early American psychologists felt the need for a more scientifically and experimentally oriented alternative to the APA. In 1898, Witmer proposed the idea of an experimental society that would "exclude half-breeds and extremists" (Hall, quoted in Furumoto, 1988, p. 96). Titchener opposed it because of potential conflict with the APA, but the type of society he described in the form letter advertising the Experimentalists in 1904 was almost identical to that originally suggested by Witmer.

Imageless Thought

Titchener's program of structural psychology came to methodological grief over the debate about "imageless thought." As noted earlier, a number of researchers at the University of Würzburg claimed to have detected thoughts that were not accompanied by images (Kulpe, 1912/1964). Binet in Paris and Woodworth in New York reported similar results at around the same time (Binet, 1903; Woodworth, 1906). Wundt had responded critically to the Würzburg studies (Wundt, 1907), but his critique was focused on the method of "systematic experimental introspection" and not on the results obtained (with which he in fact agreed). Wundt was equally critical of Titchener's own method of "systematic experimental introspection" (Wundt, 1900), even though Titchener insisted upon the rigorous training of experimental subjects (which the Würzburg psychologists did not).

Titchener took issue with the Würzburg results as well as the experimental procedures, which he condemned as sloppy. Between 1907 and 1915 he repeated the Würzburg experiments with his own students at Cornell. He claimed that in all cases subtle sensations and images could be identified by "properly trained observers" in controlled experiments (Clark, 1911). Woodworth, who had spent a summer working with Külpe at the University of Bonn in 1912, defended imageless thought in his presidential address to the 1914 meeting of the APA at Yale. At that same meeting, John Baird tried to support Titchener by arranging a public demonstration of the effectiveness of systematic experimental introspection. Unfortunately, it was a public relations disaster, which succeeded only in boring the audience to tears (Boring, 1953).

Wundt and Titchener had stressed the fundamental identity of inspection and introspection. They maintained that the scientific objectivity of inspection of the properties of physical objects (their size and acceleration, for example) is grounded in intersubjective agreement among observers, which is a necessary condition for any empirical science. Wundt and Titchener held that the introspective study of immediate experience could be objective because they believed that intersubjective agreement could be attained via laboratory control and repetition. Yet the imageless-thought debate raised serious doubts about this, since the Würzburg and Cornell labs produced consistently different results.

Titchener treated the ability to report images for thoughts as the criterion of a "properly trained observer" and dismissed the recalcitrant results of other laboratories as due to subject naiveté or insufficient training. In this, he may have been influenced by his own experience as a student of Wundt's. Witmer recounted how Wundt had made Titchener "do over again an investigation . . . because the results obtained by Titchener were not as he, Wundt, had anticipated" (Witmer, letter to Boring, 1948, quoted in O'Donnell, 1985, p. 35). Titchener's attitude naturally led to the suggestion that the "reagents" in his laboratory were subject to a form of experimenter bias (Müller, 1911–13). Ogden (1911) attributed the different results of the Cornell and Würzburg laboratories to "unconscious bias" due to the different forms of training that subjects received in them. He also suggested that if Wundt's critique of the form of "systematic experimental introspection" employed by Külpe and the other Würzburg researchers was sound, it could be generalized to all methods of introspection, including those employed by Wundt and Titchener (Humphrey, 1951; Woodworth, 1938). Consequently, many psychologists concluded that the imageless-thought debate was incapable of empirical resolution by appeal to introspective reports.

The Eclipse of Structural Psychology

Yet in a sense the imageless-thought debate was a side show. Cornell remained a bastion of structural psychology during Titchener's lifetime, and his laboratory texts continued to be employed to instill respect for scientific rigor in psychology students. However, Titchener became increasingly isolated in the first two decades of the 20th century. Critics such as Cattell (1904), Thorndike (1905), Judd (1907), Pillsbury (1911), Dunlap (1912), and Dodge (1912) raised doubts about the utility of introspective methods, so that by the time Watson launched his famous attack on introspection in "Psychology as the Behaviorist Views It" (1913), he was preaching to a largely converted audience. Moreover, the theoretical and methodological debate about introspection lagged behind experimental practice. By 1898, only about *2 percent* of the published experimental studies in psychology in America employed introspection, and only about half employed adult human subjects (Bruner & Allport, 1940, cited in O'Donnell, 1985).

In later years Titchener became somewhat of a recluse. Although a legendary figure at Cornell, some of his colleagues never met him. After 1909, he lectured only on Monday evenings and worked mostly from home, with his wife screening his telephone calls. He conducted a musical group from home on Sunday evenings. He spoke half a dozen languages, including Arabic and Chinese, in order to authenticate his extensive coin collection. He died of a brain tumor in 1927 at the age of 60 (his pickled brain remains on display at Cornell).

When Titchener died, structural psychology died with him. The Experimentalists continued to meet, although they no longer restricted their research topics, or their membership to men. Madison Bentley (1870–1955), a loyal Titchener supporter and founding member of the Experimentalists, took over the chairmanship of the Cornell department. Within a few years, he had transformed it by introducing new specialties such as educational and clinical psychology.

SCIENTIFIC AND APPLIED PSYCHOLOGY

The American students who studied with Wundt returned to America impressed by the scientific rigor of Wundt's experimental laboratory, but developed their own vision of the discipline as they strove to develop more applied and socially relevant forms of psychology. This reorientation was manifest in the development of the APA. The founding meeting held at Clark University on July 8, 1892, had a distinctly Wundtian flavor. Many of the experimental papers that the Clark faculty and visitors presented were on topics in physiological psychology. Yet the first annual meeting of the APA at the University of Pennsylvania in December 1892 reflected the growing eclecticism and applied orientation of American psychology. Cattell and Witmer gave papers critical of psychophysics and mental chronometry. William Brian discussed the use of psychological tests in Indiana schools. Herbert Nichols reported experiments on hospital patients undergoing physiological examination of pain. Joseph Jastrow described the laboratory demonstrations he planned to set up for the psychology exhibit at the Chicago World's Fair in 1893 (Sokal, 1992).

As the century developed, the APA continued to grow, although it went through a lean period when the philosophers broke away to found their own professional

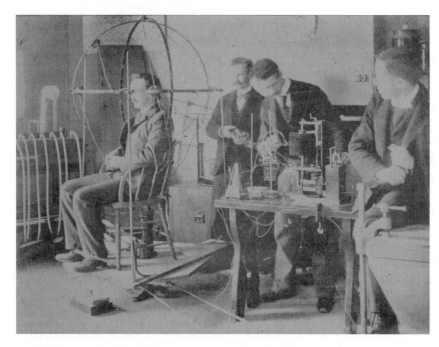

Experiment on influence of dizziness on localization of sounds, presented by Joseph Jastrow at the Chicago World's Fair (1893).

association. It also suffered temporarily as a result of Titchener's formation of the Experimentalists. The 12th annual meeting of the APA in 1902 was held in a school hall in Princeton and was poorly attended. There were only 12 papers delivered, in contrast to 26 the previous year (Furumoto, 1988). By 1910 the membership had expanded from the original 31 charter members to 228, and to 1,113 by 1930 (Fernberger, 1932). Yet many of the 1930 membership were from the new class of nonvoting associate members, founded in 1926 to accommodate psychologists without academic institutional affiliations (Pickren & Fowler, 2003).

DISCUSSION QUESTIONS

1. The academic disciplines of sociology and anthropology were founded in America at around the same time as psychology, yet psychology was much more successful with respect to its institutional development than sociology and anthropology. Why do you think this was the case? Why was the emerging American university system so hospitable to psychology?

2. Why do you think that William James remains such a popular figure in psychology despite his limited contribution to it?

3. When he defined clinical psychology, Witmer claimed that it was a diagnostic branch of applied psychology based upon case histories. Is it still today? Should it be?

4. Harry Kirke Wolfe was fired from the University of Nebraska because educators objected to having someone pronounce on education who had never received training in pedagogy. Is it reasonable to require that educational psychologists receive teacher training? Should industrial psychologists have experience in industry?

5. Is introspection fundamentally the same as inspection, as Titchener claimed? Or are they fundamentally different? If intersubjective agreement cannot be attained over the issue of imageless thought, does that mean that introspection should be completely abandoned in psychology?

GLOSSARY

analytic philosophy Form of 20th-century Anglo-American philosophy based upon the conceptual analysis of abstract systems of thought.

clinical psychology Term coined by Lightner Witmer to describe a "diagnostic" branch of applied psychology based upon the case study method of medicine.

Experimentalists Group of experimental psychologists founded by Titchener in 1904 as a more scientifically rigorous alternative to the APA.

functional psychology According to Titchener, the form of psychology concerned with the functions of consciousness.

genetic psychology Form of developmental psychology based upon the method of evolutionary biology.

inspection The observation of independent physical objects in the external world.

James-Lange theory of emotion Theory that emotion is not the cause of physiological arousal and behavior but the experience of physiological arousal and behavior.

mental test Term coined by Cattell to describe psychophysical measures.

Metaphysical Society Harvard society founded in the 1870s devoted to the discussion of philosophical problems of the day.

new psychology Term employed by early American psychologists to characterize experimental psychology.

phenomenological philosophy Form of 20th-century Continental European philosophy concerned with the abstract essence of thought.

pragmatism View that the adequacy of any theoretical system should be judged by its practical utility.

pragmatist theory of meaning (Peirce) View that the content of a belief or proposition is specified in terms of its empirical consequences.

pragmatist theory of truth (James) View that a belief or proposition is true if it works to our satisfaction.

pragmatist philosophy Form of 20th-century American philosophy that was an offshoot of evolutionary theory and American functionalist psychology.

psychologism Theory that logic and conceptual relations can be treated as naturalistic psychological "laws of thought."

social facilitation Influence of social groups on judgment and behavior.

stimulus error According to Titchener, the error of confusing the pure contents of experience with the meaning of the sensory array or the real-world object of experience.

structural psychology According to Titchener, the form of psychology that aims to describe the basic structure of the mind: the conscious elements of mind and their modes of combination.

REFERENCES

Allen, G. W. (1967). *William James: A biography.* New York: Viking.

Allport, F. H. (1920). The influence of the group upon association and thought. *Journal of Experimental Psychology, 3,* 159–182.

Allport, G. W. (1967). Autobiography. In E. G. Boring & G. Lindzey (Eds.), *A history of psychology in autobiography* (Vol. 5). New York: Appleton-Century-Crofts.

Ash, M. G. (1980). Experimental psychology in Germany before 1914: Aspects of an academic identity problem. *Psychological Research, 42,* 75–86.

Baldwin, J. M. (1895). Types of reaction. *Psychological Review, 2,* 259–273.

Baldwin, J. M. (1896). The "type-theory" of reaction. *Mind, 5,* 81–90.

Baldwin, J. M. (1926). *Between two wars, 1861–1921.* London: Stratford.

Benjamin, L. T., Jr. (1991). *Harry Kirke Wolfe: Pioneer in psychology.* Lincoln: University of Nebraska Press.

Benjamin, L. T., Jr. (1997). Wilhelm Wundt: The American connection. In W. G. Bringmann, H. E. Lück, R. Miller, & C. E. Early (Eds.), *A pictorial history of psychology.* Chicago: Quintessence.

Benjamin, L. T., Jr., Durkin, M., Link, M., Vesta, M., & Accord, J. (1992). Wundt's American doctoral students. *American Psychologist, 47,* 123–131.

Binet, A. (1903). *L'étude expérimentale de l'intelligence* [Experimental studies of intelligence]. Paris: Schleichter.

Blumenthal, A. L. (1975). A reappraisal of Wilhelm Wundt. *American Psychologist, 30,* 1081–1088.

Blumenthal, A. L. (1979). The founding father we never knew. *Contemporary Psychology*, *24*, 547–550.

Boakes, R. (1984). *From Darwin to behaviorism: Psychology and the minds of animals.* Cambridge: Cambridge University Press.

Bolles, R. C. (1993). *The story of psychology: A thematic history.* Belmont, CA: Wadsworth.

Boring, E. G. (1938). The Society of Experimental Psychologists: 1904–1938. *American Journal of Psychology*, *51*, 410–423.

Boring, E. G. (1953). A history of introspection. *Psychological Bulletin*, *50*, 169–189.

Boring, E. G. (1957). *A history of experimental psychology* (2nd ed.). New York: Appleton-Century-Crofts.

Bramel, D, & Friend, R. (1981). Hawthorne, the myth of the docile worker, and class bias in American psychology. *American Psychologist*, *36*, 867–878.

Bruner, J. S., & Allport, G. W. (1940). Fifty years of change in American psychology. *Psychological Review*, *37*, 757–776.

Cahan, E. (2005). *Science, practice, and gender roles in early child psychology.* Paper presented at the 37th Annual Meeting of *Cheiron*, University of California at Berkeley, June 23–26.

Camfield, T. M. (1973). The professionalization of American psychology, 1870–1917. *Journal for the History of the Behavioral Sciences*, *9*, 66–75.

Cattell, J. M. (1885). Über die Zeit der Erkennung und Benennung von Scriftzeichen, Bilden und Farben [About the time of recognition, and the naming of written signs, pictures and colors]. *Philosophische Studien*, *2*, 635–650.

Cattell, J. M. (1886). On the time it takes to see and name objects. *Mind*, *11*, 63–65.

Cattell, J. M. (1890). Mental tests and measurements. *Mind*, *15*, 373–381.

Cattell, J. M. (1903). Statistics of American psychologists. *American Journal of Psychology*, *14*, 310–328.

Cattell, J. M. (1904). The conceptions and methods of psychology. *Popular Science Monthly*, *66*, 176–186.

Cattell, J. M. (1917). Our psychological association and research. *Science*, *45*, 275–284.

Cattell, J. M. (1929). Psychology in America. *Science*, *70*, 335–347.

Clark., H. M. (1911). Conscious attitudes. *American Journal of Psychology*, *22*, 214–249.

Creighton, J. E., & Titchener, E. B. (1894). Translator's preface to W. Wundt, *Lectures on animal and human psychology.* New York: Macmillan.

Dallenbach, K. (1967) Autobiography. In E. G. Boring & G. Lindzey (Eds.), *A history of psychology in autobiography* (Vol. 5). New York: Appleton-Century-Crofts.

Danziger, K. (1979). The social origins of modern psychology. In A. R. Buss (Ed.), *Psychology in social context.* New York: Irvington.

Dodge, R. (1912). The theory and limitations of introspection. *American Journal of Psychology, 23,* 214–229.

Dods, J. B. (1850). *Electrical psychology* (2nd ed.). New York: Fowler & Wells.

Dunlap, K. (1912). The case against introspection. *Psychological Review, 19,* 404–413.

Ferguson, L. (1962). *The heritage of industrial psychology: Walter Dill Scott, first industrial psychologist.* Privately printed.

Fernberger, S. W. (1932). The American Psychological Association, a historical summary, 1892–1930. *Psychological Bulletin, 29,* 1–89.

Fuchs, A. H. (2000). Contributions of American moral philosophers to psychology in the United States. *History of Psychology, 3,* 3–19.

Furumoto, L. (1988). Shared knowledge: The Experimentalists, 1904–1929. In J. G. Morawski (Ed.), *The rise of experimentation in American psychology.* New Haven, CT: Yale University Press.

Gilman, D. C. (1885). Annual address to the university. *Johns Hopkins Circular, 4,* 48–49.

Guthrie, R. V. (1988). *Even the rat was white* (2nd ed.). Boston: Allyn & Bacon.

Hale, M. (1980). *Human science and order: Hugo Münsterberg and the origins of applied psychology.* Philadelphia, PA: Temple University Press.

Hall, G. S. (1885). The new psychology. *Andover Review, 3,* 120–135, 239–248.

Hall, G. S. (1904). *Adolescence: Its psychology and its relations to physiology, anthropology, sociology, sex, crime, religion and education.* New York: Appleton.

Hall, G. S. (1917). *Jesus, the Christ, in the light of psychology.* Garden City, NY: Doubleday.

Hall, G. S. (1920). *Recreations of a psychologist.* New York: Appleton.

Hall, G. S. (1922). *Senescence: The last half of life.* New York: Appleton.

Hall, G. S. (1923). *Life and confessions of a psychologist.* New York: Appleton.

Hulse, S. H., & Green, B. F. (Eds.). (1986). *One hundred years of psychological research in America: G. Stanley Hall and the American tradition.* Baltimore, MD: Johns Hopkins University Press.

Humphrey, G. (1951). *Thinking: An introduction to its experimental psychology.* New York: Wiley.

James, W. (1876). The teaching of philosophy in our colleges. *Nation, 23,*178–179.

James, W. (1884). What is an emotion? *Mind, 9,* 188–205.

James, W. (1890). *The principles of psychology* (Vols. 1–2). New York: Holt.

James, W. (1892a). A plea for psychology as a "natural science." *Philosophical Review, 1,* 146–153.

James, W. (1892b). *Psychology: A briefer course.* New York: Holt.

James, W. (1893). Letter to Hugo Münsterberg, February 21. In L. T. Benjamin, *A history of psychology in letters.* Malden, MA: Blackwell, 2006.

James, W. (1897). *The will to believe, and other essays in popular philosophy.* New York: Longmans.

James, W. (1907). *Pragmatism.* New York: Longmans.

James, W. (1909). *The meaning of truth*. New York: Longmans.

James, W. (1920). Letter to Thomas W. Ward (November, 1867). In H. James (Ed.), *Letters of William James* (Vols. 1–2). Boston: Atlantic Monthly Press.

Jastrow, J. (1887). Physiological psychology. *The Christian Union*, October 27.

Jastrow, J. (1890). Minor contributions. Studies from the laboratory of experimental psychology of the University of Wisconsin. *American Journal of Psychology*, *3*, 43–58.

Judd, C. H. (1907). *Psychology: General introduction*. Boston: Ginn.

Kant, I. (1993). *Critique of practical reason* (L. W. Beck, Trans.). New York: Macmillan. (Original work published 1788)

Kihlstrom, J. F. (2004, November). Joseph Jastrow and his duck—or is it a rabbit? Letter to the editor submitted to *Trends in the Cognitive Sciences*.

Kline, L. W. (1899). Suggestions towards a laboratory course in comparative psychology. *American Journal of Psychology*, *10*, 399–430.

Kuklick, B. (1977). *The rise of American philosophy: Cambridge, Massachusetts, 1860–1930*. New Haven, CT: Yale University Press.

Külpe, O. (1964). The modern psychology of thinking. In G. Mandler & J. M. Mandler (Eds.), *Thinking: From association to Gestalt*. New York: Wiley. (Original work published 1912)

Ladd, G. T. (1887). *Elements of physiological psychology*. New York: Scribner's.

Ladd, G. T. (1895). *Philosophy of mind: An essay in the metaphysics of psychology*. New York: Scribner's.

Ladd, G. T., & Woodworth, R. S. (1911). *Elements of physiological psychology* (Rev. ed). New York: Scribner's.

Leahey, T. H. (1979). Something old, something new: Attention in Wundt and modern cognitive psychology. *Journal of the History of the Behavioral Sciences*, *15*, 242–252.

Leahey, T. H. (1981). The mistaken mirror: On Wundt's and Titchener's psychologies. *Journal of the History of the Behavioral Sciences*, *17*, 273–282.

Leary, D (1987). Telling likely stories: The rhetoric of the new psychology, 1880–1920. *Journal of the History of the Behavioral Sciences*, *23*, 315–331.

Logan, C. (1999). The altered rationale for the choice of a standard animal in experimental psychology: Henry H. Donaldson, Adolf Meyer, and "the" albino rat. *History of Psychology*, *2*, 3–24.

Manicas, P. T. (1987). *A history and philosophy of the social sciences*. Oxford: Blackwell.

Mayo, E. (1933). *The human problems of an industrial civilization*. Cambridge, MA: Harvard University Press.

McCosh, J. M. (1886). *Psychology: The cognitive powers*. New York: Scribner's.

McCosh, J. M. (1980). *The Scottish philosophy*. New York: ASM Press. (Original work published 1875)

McReynolds, P. (1996). Lightner Witmer: A centennial tribute. *American Psychologist*, *51*, 237–240.

McReynolds, P. (1997). *Lightner Witmer: His life and times*. Washington, DC: American Psychological Association.

Meumann, E. (1907). *Introductory lectures on pedagogy and its physiological basis*. Leipzig: W. Engelmann.

Miner, B. C. (1904). The changing attitude of universities towards psychology. *Science, 20,* 299–307.

Müller, G. E. (1911–1913). *Analysis of the processes of memory and mental representation*. Leipzig: Edelmann.

Münsterberg, H. (1888). *Voluntary action*. Freiburg, Germany: Mohr.

Münsterberg, H. (1908). *On the witness stand*. New York: Clark Boardman.

Münsterberg, H. (1909). *Psychotherapy*. New York: Moffat, Yard.

Münsterberg, H. (1912). *Vocation and learning*. St. Louis: People's University.

Münsterberg, H. (1913a). *Psychology and industrial efficiency*. New York: Houghton Mifflin.

Münsterberg, H. (1913b). The mind of the juryman. With a side-light on women as jurors. *Century Illustrated Monthly Magazine, 86,* 711–716.

O'Donnell, J. M. (1985). *The origins of behaviorism: American psychology, 1870–1920*. New York: New York University Press.

Ogden, R. M. (1911). Imageless thought. *Psychological Bulletin, 8,* 183–197.

Peirce, C. S. (1982). What pragmaticism is. In H. S. Thayer (Ed.), *Pragmatism: The classic writings*. Indianapolis: Hackett. (Original work published 1905)

Peirce, C. S., & Jastrow, J. (1884). On small differences in sensation. *Proceedings of the National Academy of Sciences, 3,* 75–83.

Pickren, W. E., & Fowler, R. D. (2003). Professional organizations. In D. K. Freedheim (Ed.), *Handbook of psychology: Volume 1. History of psychology*. Hoboken, NJ: Wiley.

Pillsbury, W. B. (1911). *Essentials of psychology*. New York: Macmillan.

Reed, E. S. (1997). *From soul to mind*. New Haven: Yale University Press.

Rieber, R. W. (1980). Wundt and the Americans: From flirtation to abandonment. In R. W. Rieber (Ed.), *Wilhelm Wundt and the making of American psychology*. New York: Plenum.

Roback, A. A. (1952). *History of American psychology*. New York: Library Publishers.

Routh, D. K., & Reisman, J. M. (2003). Clinical psychology. In D. K. Freedheim (Ed.), *Handbook of psychology: Vol. 1. History of psychology*. Hoboken, NJ: Wiley.

Rozenzweig, S. (1984). Hail to Hall. *APA Monitor* (March), 5–6.

Scarborough, E., & Furumoto, L. (1987). *Untold lives: The first generation of American women psychologists*. New York: Columbia University Press.

Schultz, D. P., & Schultz, S. E. (1992). *A history of modern psychology*. New York: Harcourt Brace Jovanovich.

Scott, W. D. (1903). *The theory of advertising: A simple exposition of the principles of psychology in their relation to successful advertising*. Boston: Small, Maynard.

Scott, W. D. (1906). *The psychology of public speaking.* New York: Noble & Noble.

Scott, W. D. (1911a). *Increasing human efficiency in business.* New York: Macmillan.

Scott, W. D. (1911b). *Influencing men of business.* New York: Ronald Press.

Scripture, E. W. (1895). *Thinking, feeling, and doing.* New York: Putnam.

Scripture, E. W. (1897). *The new psychology.* New York: Scribner's.

Small, W. S. (1900). An experimental study of the mental processes of the white rat: I. *American Journal of Psychology, 11,* 133–64.

Small, W. S. (1901). An experimental study of the mental processes of the white rat: II. *American Journal of Psychology, 12,* 206–239.

Smith, R. (1997). *Norton history of the human sciences.* New York: Norton.

Sokal, M. M. (1971). The unpublished biography of James McKeen Cattell. *American Psychologist, 26,* 626–635.

Sokal, M. M. (1981). *An education in psychology: James McKeen Cattell's journal and letters from Germany and England, 1880–1888.* Cambridge, MA: MIT Press.

Sokal, M. M. (1992). Origins and early years of the American Psychological Association, 1890–1906. *American Psychologist, 47,* 111–122.

Thorndike, E. L. (1905). *The elements of psychology.* New York: Macmillan.

Titchener, E. B. (1895a). Simple reactions. *Mind, 4,* 74–81.

Titchener, E. B. (1895b). The "'type-theory'" of simple reaction. *Mind, 4,* 506–514.

Titchener, E. B. (1896a). The "'type-theory'" of simple reaction. *Mind, 5,* 236–241.

Titchener, E. B. (1896b). *An outline of psychology.* New York: Macmillan.

Titchener, E. B. (1898a). *A primer of psychology.* New York: Macmillan.

Titchener, E. B. (1898b). The postulates of a structural psychology. *Philosophical Review, 7,* 449–465.

Titchener, E. B. (1899). Structural and functional psychology. *Philosophical Review, 8,* 290–299.

Titchener, E. B. (1901–1905). *Experimental psychology: A manual of laboratory practice* (Vols. 1–2). New York: Macmillan.

Titchener, E. B. (1910). *A textbook of psychology.* New York: Macmillan.

Titchener, E. B. (1912). The schema of introspection. *American Journal of Psychology, 23,* 485–508.

Titchener, E. B. (1914). Psychology: Science or technology? *Popular Science Monthly, 39,* 51.

Titchener, E. B. (1916). On ethnological tests of sensation and perception. *Proceedings of the American Philosophical Society, 55,* 204–236.

Titchener, E. B. (1921). Wilhelm Wundt. *American Journal of Psychology, 32,* 161–178.

Tweney, R. D. (1987). Programmatic research in experimental psychology: E. B. Titchener's laboratory investigations, 1891–1927. In M. G. Ash & W. R. Woodward (Eds.), *Psychology in twentieth-century thought and society.* Cambridge: Cambridge University Press.

Tweney, R. D. (1997). Edward Bradford Titchener (1867–1927). In W. G. Bring-mann, H. E. Lück, R. Miller, & C. E. Early (Eds.), *A pictorial history of psychology*. Chicago: Quintessence.

Twitmyer, E. B. (1974). A study of the knee jerk. *Journal of Experimental Psychology, 103,* 1047–1066. (Original work published 1902 as doctoral dissertation, University of Pennsylvania)

Veysey, L. (1965). *The emergence of the American university*. Chicago: University of Chicago Press.

von Mayrhauser, R. T. (1989). Making psychology functional: Walter Dill Scott and applied psychology testing in World War I. *Journal of the History of the Behavioral Sciences, 25,* 60–72.

Washburn, M. F. (1908). *The animal mind: A text-book of comparative psychology*. New York: Macmillan.

Washburn, M. F. (1916). *Movement and mental imagery: Outline of a motor theory of consciousness*. Boston: Houghton Mifflin.

Watson, J. B. (1913). Psychology as the behaviorist views it. *Psychological Review, 20,* 158–177.

Watson, R. I. (1978). *The great psychologists from Aristotle to Freud* (4th ed.). New York: Lippincott.

White, A. D. (1960). *A history of the warfare of science with theology in Christendom*. New York: Dover. (Original work published 1896)

Wigmore, J. (1909). Professor Münsterberg and the psychology of testimony: Being a report of the case of Cokestone vs. Münsterberg. *Illinois Law Review, 3,* 412–413.

Wissler, C. (1901). The correlation of mental and physical tests. *Psychological Review Monograph Supplements, 3,* No 6.

Witmer, L. (1897). The organization of practical work in psychology. *Psychological Review, 4,* 116.

Witmer, L. (1902). *Analytical psychology: A practical manual for schools and normal colleges*. Boston: Ginn.

Witmer, L. (1907). Clinical psychology. *The Psychological Clinic, 1,* 1–9.

Wolfe, H. K. (1886). Untersuchungen über das Tongedächtniss [Studies on the memory of tone]. *Philosophische Studien, 3,* 534–571.

Woodworth, R. S. (1938). *Experimental psychology*. New York: Holt.

Woodworth, R. S. (1906). Imageless thought. *Journal of Philosophy, Psychology and Scientific Methods, 3,* 701–708.

Wundt, W. (1900). Bumerkungen zur Theorie der Gefühle [Remarks on the theory of feeling]. *Philosophische Studien, 15,* 149–182.

Wundt, W. (1902). *Outlines of psychology* (C. H. Judd, Trans.). Leipzig: Engelmann. (Original work published 1897)

Wundt, W. (1907). Über Ausfrageexperimente und über die Methoden zur Psychologie des Denkens [About interrogative experiments and the methods regarding the psychology of thinking]. *Psychologische Studien, 3,* 301–360.

Functionalism, Behaviorism, and Mental Testing

I N THE EARLY DECADES OF THE 20TH CENTURY, WUNDT'S STUDENTS AND the indigenous pioneers of American psychology continued to promote and develop their varied conceptions of scientific psychology. Cattell claimed in his 1895 presidential address to the APA that the "wide range of individual interests" of American psychologists demonstrated their "adjustment in a complex environment" (1896, p. 134). Yet these different interests also proved to be forces of division in the following decades, sometimes characterized as the period of the competing "schools" of psychology (Murchison, 1930; Woodworth, 1931).

Titchener's form of structural psychology remained an intellectual force in the first two decades of the 20th century, but became increasingly isolated at Cornell and was eventually displaced by functionalist and behaviorist psychology. As the 20th century developed, psychology in America distanced itself from its philosophical roots, including the notion that scientific psychology should be grounded in the introspective analysis of consciousness. Many psychologists had abandoned introspective methods by the time John B. Watson issued his behaviorist "manifesto" in 1913 (Watson, 1913a). This was partly because of the "imageless thought" debate, but also because they had little use for introspection in their applied educational, industrial, and clinical work. Psychology in America also distanced itself from its roots in German physiological psychology. Although courses and demonstration practicals in laboratory methods continued to be employed in the PhD certification of American psychologists as bona fide practitioners of scientific psychology, the "brass instruments" of the new psychology were increasingly appropriated and adapted by educational, industrial, and clinical psychologists as part of their battery of mental and physical aptitude tests.

Many psychologists who came to embrace Watson's (1913a) call for a behavioral science of prediction and control did so because it suited their already well developed applied interests, not because they were convinced by Watson's arguments or rhetoric. These interests were frequently a product of the various institutional and social pressures and opportunities that promoted the development of applied psychology in the first two decades of the 20th century. Indeed, Watson's own goal of developing a behaviorist psychology had as much to do with his own professional career interests and institutional realities as his avowed arguments against introspection and in favor of a positivistic science of behavior.

THE TURN TO APPLIED PSYCHOLOGY

There were a variety of reasons why early-20th-century American psychologists turned to applied psychology, beyond their own personal interests and inclinations. One simple reason, familiar to contemporary students of psychology, was the shortage of academic jobs in teaching and research that were available to newly minted PhDs. By the end of the 19th and early 20th centuries, the supply of PhD certified psychologists exceeded the demand of academic departments of psychology, and new graduates were obliged to seek positions in education, industry, and clinical work if they wished to continue to have a career in psychology. Most of Hall's Clark graduates—including most of those in animal psychology—secured positions in education, as professors of pedagogy, educational testers, or heads of normal schools. Henry Herbert Goddard (1866–1957), a student of Hall's, was one of the first psychologists appointed to a full-time nonacademic position: He became director of psychological research at the Vineland Training School for Feebleminded Girls and Boys in New Jersey in 1906 (O'Donnell, 1985).

Another reason was the public and professional demand for psychological services, evidenced by the early positive public reception of phrenology and mesmerism and stimulated by the applied rhetoric of the early promoters of scientific psychology, such as James, Münsterberg, Hall, and Cattell. In the 1850s railroad companies had considered using phrenologists to select trainmen in the hope of reducing accidents. In 1896 William Lowe Bryan (1860–1955), a student of Hall's, who founded the laboratory and psychology program at the University of Indiana, was commissioned by the Union and Wabash Railway to study habit formation in telegraphy (Bryan & Harter, 1897). In the early 20th century Münsterberg took on the problem of selecting competent trainmen when he was approached by urban electric railway companies seeking to avoid costly lawsuits (O'Donnell, 1985). The early decades of the 20th century witnessed an ever-increasing demand for mental tests in education and industry.

A third reason was the flight from teaching overload. Assistant professors and instructors in psychology (who were often situated in philosophy departments) were required to teach a wide variety of courses. For example, Raymond Dodge (1871–1942), who later became an applied psychologist at Yale, was required to teach courses in psychology, logic, history of philosophy, ethics, history of English literature, pedagogy, and aesthetics at Ursinus College in Pennsylvania (O'Donnell, 1985). Harry Levi Hollingworth (1880–1956), who taught every available course at Columbia, Teachers College, and Barnard in order to feed himself, claimed that he "became an applied psychologist in order to earn a living" (cited in O'Donnell, 1985, p. 225). James R. Angell recalled how he had to supplement his meager salary "by teaching in the summer, by teaching university extension courses, by lecturing before clubs, and by teaching at local institutions in the late afternoons, at night, or on Saturdays" (Angell, 1936, p. 15, cited in O'Donnell, 1985, p. 223). Watson's own formulation of behaviorism was motivated by his need to select a popular theme that could be the focus of a text-book written "largely for money." As Watson admitted to his friend Robert Yerkes (1876–1956), "I am in debt and I've got to get out" (letter to Yerkes, 1909, cited in O'Donnell, 1985, p. 226).

A final reason was the growth of state-supported public universities in the West, whose development differed in significant respects from the private universities and liberal arts colleges in the East where psychology first flourished (Bolles, 1983). At western public universities, academic concerns about curriculum and research were subordinated to more practical ideals of efficiency, expertise, and service (Rudolph, 1962). By the end of the first decade of the 20th century, more than a third of American psychologists were employed in these universities, most of them engaged in some form of applied (and usually educational) psychology. Not surprisingly, many of these, such as Max Meyer at the University of Missouri, Joseph Jastrow at the University of Wisconsin, and Paul Weiss (1879–1931) at Ohio State University, were early anticipators and supporters of Watson's behaviorism (O'Donnell, 1985).

FUNCTIONAL PSYCHOLOGY

The "school" of **functional psychology**, which was associated with the University of Chicago and Columbia University in the early decades of the 20th century, was unusual in a number of respects. In a very real sense it was the intellectual creation of Titchener, who distinguished between his own form of structural psychology, concerned with the experimental analysis of consciousness, and functional psychology, concerned with the functions of consciousness (Titchener, 1898, 1899). James Rowland Angell and Harvey Carr (1873–1954), the acknowledged leaders of the movement, insisted that functional psychology was not committed to any distinctive theoretical or methodological position. Angell claimed that functional psychology merely aimed to broaden the scope of psychology beyond Titchener's structuralism (Angell, 1907), and Carr maintained that it was equivalent to American psychology, defined by its dual emphasis on scientific rigor and practical application (Carr, 1925). Although functional psychology was officially defined in contrast to Titchener's experimental analysis of consciousness, which purported to represent the Wundtian tradition in America, functional psychology was itself remarkably

Wundtian in orientation, given its emphasis on the active, creative, and purposive role of consciousness in the generation and control of adaptive behavior.

Historians of psychology often represent functional psychology as grounded in Darwin's theory of evolution by natural selection, as did functional psychologists themselves (Angell, 1907, 1909). Yet functional psychology owed little to the hereditarian determinism of Darwin's theory. Functional psychologists did not develop systematic explanations of human and animal psychology and behavior in terms of the survival value of inherited psychological and behavioral traits. Although they recognized the survival value of consciousness as a product of evolution, they focused on the conscious and purposive adaptation of individual organisms to their environment during their lifetimes, rather than on the natural selection of psychological traits and behavior in the evolution of human and animal species. Darwin had recognized that man has "great power of adapting his habits to new conditions of life" (1871, p. 158), but insisted that this power was itself a product of natural selection and constrained by inherited instincts (Sohn, 1976). In contrast, functional psychologists laid much greater emphasis on the *plasticity* of human psychology and behavior, to the point that they sometimes came close to denying a significant role to instincts—as did later behaviorists such as Kuo (1921) and Watson (1924/1930). They suggested that humans had evolved to such a degree that they were able to surmount the constraints of natural selection—at least with the aid of scientific psychology. As earlier proponents of the new psychology had seen the experimental analysis of consciousness as an affirmation of the reality and autonomy of consciousness, functional psychologists saw individual adaptation and learning as an affirmation of the reality and efficacy of consciousness and purpose in human behavior and development.

Baldwin and Titchener on Reaction Time

The origins of the distinction between structural and functional psychology can be traced to the dispute between Titchener and James Mark Baldwin (1861–1934) over the measurement of sensory and motor reaction times. Baldwin had been a student of McCosh's at Princeton. He met Cattell when he visited Wundt's laboratory in 1885, and they later founded the journal *Psychological Review* (in 1894). After returning to Princeton to complete his degree, Baldwin accepted the chair of logic and metaphysics at the University of Toronto in 1889, where he set up the first Canadian laboratory the following year. He produced two introductory psychology texts, *Senses and Intellect* in 1889 and *Feeling and Will* in 1891, which might have been very successful had they not been eclipsed by James's *Principles* in 1890. However, they were sufficient to establish his reputation and gain him the Stuart chair in psychology at Princeton, where he set up another laboratory in 1893 and conducted the series of experimental studies on reaction time that brought him into conflict with Titchener.

Wundt's studies of reaction time employing trained experimental subjects in the Leipzig laboratory had indicated that sensory reaction times are longer than motor reaction times. Titchener had replicated this result with trained experimental subjects in the Cornell laboratory. Baldwin, working with untrained subjects at Princeton, found that motor reaction times are often longer than sensory reaction times and that there are significant individual differences in both sensory and motor reaction times. Baldwin claimed that these differences in reaction times were a product of differences in practice and attention.

The ensuing dispute between Titchener and Baldwin over **type** versus **practice theories of reaction time** (Baldwin, 1895a, 1896; Titchener, 1895a, 1895b, 1896) was expressive of a fundamental disagreement between them concerning the subject matter and methods of psychology. For Titchener, scientific psychology was directed to the study of the universal dimensions of the normal adult human mind via the introspective reports of trained subjects, based upon the method of controlled experimentation in physics and physiology. Baldwin maintained that scientific psychology was as much concerned with the study of individual differences in human psychology and behavior, based upon the naturalistic observational methods of developmental biology and comparative psychology.

Titchener dismissed Baldwin's results as unscientific because Baldwin employed untrained subjects. Baldwin responded that Titchener's results were experimental artifacts and criticized as objectionably circular Titchener's treatment of a subject's ability to attain anticipated results as a criterion of introspective competence. Titchener was incensed and consequently refused to publish in *Psychological Review* while Baldwin edited it.

Yet by the turn of the century most psychologists had come to reject Wundt and Titchener's view that experiments in psychology must employ trained psychologists. As Cattell put it,

> It is usually no more necessary for the subject to be a psychologist than it is for the vivisected frog to be a physiologist.
>
> —(1904, p. 180)

Individual Differences   Baldwin's claim that individual differences in human psychology and behavior were a legitimate subject of psychological study was repeated by later functional psychologists. Since Darwin's theory of evolution by natural selection was based upon postulated individual differences in inherited characteristics, functional psychology is often represented as a development of Darwin's theory, on a par with Galton's (1889) anthropometric studies of individual differences.

Yet although Baldwin and later functional psychologists made variability the key to understanding evolution and development, they focused on the variability of the *conscious and purposive adaptation of individual organisms to their environment*, rather than the random variation of inherited characteristics subject to mechanistic natural selection that was the focus of Darwin's theory of evolution and Galton's anthropometric studies.

Baldwin acknowledged the existence of evolved human (and animal) instincts, but championed the role of plasticity in the conscious and purposive adaptation of individuals to the environment. He claimed that "social heredity" through imitation was the source of distinctive human capacities such as language and morality. He consequently laid great stress on the social development of mentality, consciousness, and behavior, which he documented in *Mental Development in the Child and the Race* in 1895, *Social and Ethical Interpretations in Mental Development* in 1897, and *The Individual and Society* in 1911, works that anticipated the later social developmental theories of Charles Horton Cooley (1864–1929) and George Herbert Mead (1863–1931). While he recognized that consciousness, plasticity, and gregariousness (the basis of imitation) were themselves products of evolution, Baldwin claimed that intelligent and purposive adaptation had come to displace instinct and heredity in the higher animals:

> One of the most striking features . . . of the evolution of mammals is the progress made by the brain. It is the organ of increasing plasticity and "educability." Its evolution has been correlated with the decline of the instinctive and completely congenital functions. As we advance upward in the mammalian scale, we find decreasing instinctive endowment and increasing plasticity, accompanied by increasing mental capacity and educability.
>
> —(1909, p. 23)

He also claimed that "social heredity'" had replaced physical heredity in the transmission and development of distinctively human psychology and behavior:

> All the resources of "social transmission"—the handing down of intelligent acquisitions by parental instruction, imitation, gregarious life, etc.—come in directly to take the place of the physical inheritance of such adaptations.
>
> —(1902, p. 81)

While he maintained that his theory of "social heredity" was consistent with the theory of evolution by natural selection, Baldwin followed Wallace (1864) in claiming that humans had evolved to such a degree of conscious intelligence that they had freed themselves from the pressures of natural selection and surmounted instinctual constraints on behavior (1902, p. 144). In this fashion Baldwin provided a defense of human freedom against the hereditarian determinism of

Darwin's theory of evolution (O'Donnell, 1985), by claiming that thought and will had emancipated humans from the constraints of natural selection:

> Thinking and willing stand for the opposite of that fixity of structure and directness of action which characterize the life of instinct. . . . The intelligence secures the widest possible range of personal adjustments, and in doing so widens the sphere of organic selection, so that *the creature that thinks has a general screen from the action of natural selection.* . . . This means that with the growth of intelligence, creatures free themselves more and more from the direct action of natural selection.
>
> —(1902, p. 145)

Baldwin moved to Johns Hopkins in 1903 to revive the psychology program and laboratory (which had been decimated when Hall took his equipment, colleagues, and students to Clark University). By that time Baldwin had virtually abandoned laboratory work and focused upon the promotion of his genetic psychological theories of development. He had hoped to reorient the program to developmental studies of mental function rather than the experimental analysis of consciousness, but institutional and local community pressures to develop applied forms of psychology such as educational psychology frustrated his ambition. However, he managed to satisfy his own goals and institutional demands for educationally relevant research by persuading the university to establish a substantial animal laboratory. He hoped that animal psychology would provide experimental support for the prevalence of imitative learning.

Baldwin was the editor of the *Dictionary of Philosophy and Psychology* (1901). He founded the journal *Psychological Bulletin* in 1904 and published a *History of Psychology* in 1913. His professional psychological career in America came to an abrupt end when he was dismissed from Johns Hopkins after being discovered in a brothel in 1908. A man of independent means, he spent most of the rest of his life traveling, mainly in South America and Europe (he ended his career teaching at the Sorbonne in Paris). He published his autobiography, *Between Two Wars*, in 1926.

John Dewey: Purpose and Adaptation

Anticipations of the functionalist program can be found in James, Münsterberg, Hall, Cattell, and Baldwin. However, it is generally recognized that the movement that came to be known as functional psychology was developed by John Dewey and James Roland Angell and inaugurated institutionally when they came to the newly founded department of philosophy at the newly founded University of Chicago in 1894. The University of Chicago was a natural home for this distinctively American form of psychology, since it had been created with Rockefeller money to serve the social needs of the city as well as the intellectual needs of the nation.

John Dewey was born in Burlington, Vermont. As an undergraduate at the University of Vermont he became interested in philosophy and pursued his study of the subject independently while working as a high school teacher. He was accepted by Johns Hopkins as a graduate student in philosophy in 1882 (although he failed to win the competitive scholarship, which went to Cattell). While at Hopkins Dewey studied with Hall, but was probably more influenced by the philosopher George S. Morris (1840–1889), a neo-Kantian and neo-Hegelian idealist. After attaining his PhD in philosophy in 1884 (with a dissertation on Kant's philosophy), Dewey accepted a job teaching philosophy and psychology at the University of Michigan, where he remained for 10 years (except for one year at Minnesota). While at Michigan he published *Psychology* (1886a), arguably the first American textbook of scientific psychology. The work was a peculiar mix of Hegel and anticipations of functional psychology, which sold well for a few years until (like many early textbooks of psychology) it was eclipsed by James's *Principles*.

Dewey was invited to become chair of the newly established department of philosophy at the University of Chicago in 1894, which at that time included psychology and pedagogy. Although he became an important educational theorist, Dewey was not himself a great teacher: He lectured in a monotone that encouraged somnolence rather than creative thinking. His major achievement at the University of Chicago was the creation of an experimental (or laboratory) school in which new teaching practices could be explored. This innovation became a stimulus for the progressive movement in education, championed by Dewey himself, who devoted his 1899 presidential address to the APA, "Psychology and Social Practice," to the advocacy of progressive education (Dewey, 1900).

Dewey opposed the forms of rote learning then prevalent in schools and argued for a more flexible approach that exploited creative student learning through practice, which created some conflict with the education department at the University of Chicago. Dewey moved to Teachers College at Columbia University in 1904, where he remained until his retirement in 1930. In later years he focused on issues in philosophy and education, and his contributions to psychology were subsidiary to this end. He was active in the New York Teacher's Union, the American Association of University Professors (which he helped found with Cattell), and the American Civil Liberties Union. After his retirement in 1930, he sold vegetables on Long Island until he died at the age of 92.

Like Baldwin, Dewey laid great stress upon the plasticity of human psychology and behavior:

> There must be a constant growth, adjustment to new relations, intellectual and moral, and this requires plasticity, variability.
>
> —(Dewey, 1886b, p. 260)

Also like Baldwin, Dewey claimed that humans are capable of transcending the mechanistic constraints of evolution. Through his emphasis on the role of conscious purpose in adaptive responses to environmental change and his interventionist approach to education, Dewey championed the view that scientific psychology and pedagogy could develop strategies for surmounting human limitations and promoting positive psychological and social change (Dewey, 1900). Dewey's effective denial of instinctual constraints on human psychology and behavior is perhaps best illustrated by his famous claim that (with the exception of certain basic instincts, the subject matter of "biological psychology") "all psychology is . . . social psychology" (Dewey, 1917, p. 276). By this he meant that most psychological and behavioral capacities and liabilities are the product of social learning, which can be redirected through alternative forms of social learning through education and training.

The Reflex Arc Dewey's major psychological contribution to functional psychology was "The Reflex Arc Concept in Psychology" (1896), the paper that Titchener christened as the first explicit statement of the functionalist program. In this paper Dewey attacked the atomism and mechanism of prevalent conceptions of the reflex arc, which he argued ought to be conceived as a circuit rather than an arc. Dewey claimed that adaptive adjustments to the environment cannot be reduced to discrete stimulus-response sequences, any more than consciousness can be reduced to an aggregation of elemental sensational units. Using James's example of a child attracted to a flame, Dewey argued that the original stimulus is transformed by the child's adaptive behavior of withdrawing her hand from the flame when it is burned, so that the flame is consequently perceived as a source of pain rather than attraction (1896, p. 359).

Dewey maintained that psychologists needed to consider the significance of the adaptive response for the organism, since such behavior is always directed "to a given end" (1886b, p. 245). According to Dewey, the mechanistic reduction of adaptive behavior to discrete stimulus-response sequences ignores the purposive direction of behavior, within a continuous process of learning guided by consciousness:

> The fact is that stimulus and response are not distinctions of existence, but teleological distinctions, that is distinctions of function, or part played, with reference to reaching or maintaining an end.
>
> —(1896, p. 365)

Dewey's paper was as much an anticipatory critique of the atomism and mechanism of the behaviorist stimulus-response psychology that came to displace functional psychology as a critique of the artificiality and sterility of Titchener's structural psychology. While his complaints about the artificiality of reductive analysis applied to the experimental analysis of the elements of consciousness, these were acknowledged by both Wundt and Titchener. Ironically, this founding document of functional psychology, with its emphasis on psychic unity, the creative nature of cognition, and the critical role of consciousness in purposive adaptation seems to have been largely inspired by Wundt's voluntaristic psychology (see Shook, 1995, for a detailed defense of this view). Dewey also followed Wundt in maintaining the autonomy of "psychical" explanation with respect to physiological explanation, particularly with respect to what both held to be the irreducibly teleological component of psychological explanation.

Dewey recognized that Darwin's theory of evolution by natural selection had eliminated the extrinsic teleology of a divinely created and fixed natural order, but insisted that the intrinsic teleology of conscious and intelligent adaptive behavior was the primary engine of human psychological and social development. He rejected explanations of the purposiveness of human psychology and behavior in terms of naturally selected inherited characteristics because they made "the teleological an accidental product of the mechanical" (Dewey, 1886b, pp. 249–250). Consequently there was some point to Titchener's complaint that Dewey and later functional psychologists were in danger of returning psychology to the (Aristotelian) teleological conception of psychological functions that Darwin's mechanistic theory of evolution by natural selection had supposedly displaced (1898, p. 453).

Psychologists frequently rank Dewey's paper as one of the most influential in the history of psychology (Leahey, 1992). This is rather surprising, since Dewey's critique of atomism and mechanism seems to have had little impact on the behaviorist movement that came to displace functional psychology (Manicas, 1987).

James Rowland Angell: The Province of Functional Psychology

James Rowland Angell (1869–1949) took over from Dewey as head of the department of psychology at the University of Chicago when Dewey left for Teachers College in 1904 and came to be identified as the leader of the functionalist movement. During his tenure at Chicago he made the department of psychology the recognized center of functional psychology. He trained a generation of psychologists committed to the eclectic functionalist approach and provided a guiding statement of functionalist principles (Angell, 1904, 1907).

Like Dewey, Angell was born in Vermont. His father was president of the University of Vermont and later of the University of Michigan, where Angell studied psychology with Dewey as an undergraduate. He received his degree in 1890, staying on an extra year to complete an MA in philosophy in 1891. Inspired by James's *Principles*, Angell spent a year at Harvard and completed a second MA in psychology in 1892. On the advice of his brother Frank (who had studied at

Leipzig and set up the laboratory at Cornell University), he tried to work with Wundt, but found to his disappointment that the Leipzig program was fully booked. In an effort to gain the coveted German qualification, Angell traveled to Germany in 1892, where he attended some lectures by Ebbinghaus and enrolled in the graduate program at the University of Halle. He never completed his conditionally accepted dissertation on Kant (accepted on condition that he improve upon his German) because he ran out of funds. Angell returned to the United States in 1893 to take up an instructorship in philosophy and psychology at the University of Minnesota (and to get married). Although he later became president of Yale (where he founded the Institute of Human Relations, home to the neobehaviorist program of Clark L. Hull) and received many honorary degrees, Angell never completed his own doctoral degree.

The following year Dewey offered his former student a position at the University of Chicago. During his 25-year tenure at Chicago, Angell forged the PhD program in psychology into a major force in American psychology and produced the closest thing to a manifesto for functional psychology in his 1906 presidential address to the APA, "The Province of Functional Psychology." Angell claimed that functional psychology was not a distinctive school, but more of "a point of view, a program, an ambition" (1907, p. 61). He acknowledged the legitimacy of both the atomistic theory and introspective methodology of structural psychology, objecting only to its restrictive definition of psychology in terms of the experimental analysis of the elements of consciousness.

The Utilities of Consciousness　Angell claimed that functional psychology was concerned with mental operations or processes rather than mental elements or contents. According to Angell, the aim of the functional psychologist was to

> discern and portray the typical *operations* of consciousness under actual life conditions, as over against the attempt to analyze and describe its elementary and complex *contents*.
> —(1907, pp. 62–63)

Angell claimed that the primary focus of functional psychology was on the role of consciousness in the generation and control of adaptive behavior. For Angell, this naturally led the functional psychologist to take greater interest in recent developments in animal psychology, which he characterized as one of "the most pregnant [movements] with which we meet in our own generation," and to explore the possible contributions of functional psychology to applied disciplines such as "pedagogy and mental hygiene (1907, p. 69).

Yet unlike later behaviorists whose program was also in large part inspired by animal psychology, Angell maintained that the goal of functional psychology was to understand the "fundamental utilities" of consciousness, which he believed would contribute significantly to applied forms of psychology. He aligned functional psychology with the biological theories of Darwin and Spencer (and Aristotle), but extended talk about the utilities of consciousness way beyond the Darwinian notion of a characteristic naturally selected in accord with past survival value to a teleological conception in which conscious purpose played as significant a role in the generation and control of adaptive behavior as it did in Wundt's voluntaristic psychology and *Völkerpsychologie*.

When Angell left the University of Chicago in 1921 to become president of Yale (after a year as president of the Carnegie Corporation), he handed leadership of the functionalist movement over to Harvey A. Carr, along with the chairmanship of the psychology department. Carr maintained essentially the same position as Angell and claimed that functional psychology was so eclectic that it was equivalent to American psychology. He treated other avowed schools of psychology, such as structuralism, psychoanalysis, Gestalt psychology, and behaviorism as merely exaggerated and restrictive developments of one aspect of functional—or American—psychology (Carr, 1925). Carr stressed the importance of the study of adaptive behavior, supported mental testing, and promoted the development of educational, industrial, clinical, and other forms of applied psychology. However, he also defended traditional forms of physiological psychology and wrote a book on space perception in 1935. As in the case of Angell and Dewey, one of the striking features of Carr's statement of the functionalist program was how thoroughly Wundtian it was. He championed a teleological conception of adaptive behavior based upon conscious purpose and control and even embraced a form of *Völkerpsychologie*:

> The nature of mind may also be studied indirectly through its creations and products—industrial inventions, literature, art, religious customs and beliefs, ethical systems, political institutions, etc. This method might well be termed the social avenue of approach.
>
> —(1925, p. 10)

Carr acknowledged the scientific objectivity of both introspection and behavioral observation, whether naturalistic or experimental. However, during his tenure at Chicago the research emphasis shifted toward the experimental analysis of behavior, including animal behavior. Carr served as chair of the department of psychology between 1919 and 1938, during which time it awarded around 150 PhD degrees, ensuring that functional psychology had a significant influence on the consequent development of American psychology.

Edward L. Thorndike and Robert Sessions Woodworth (who were both former students of Cattell's) promoted functionalist forms of psychology at Columbia University, although neither identified themselves as functionalist psychologists, and Woodworth strenuously objected to being identified with any school of psychology. Woodworth published *Contemporary Schools of Psychology* in 1931, which included chapters on structural psychology, functional psychology, behaviorism, Gestalt psychology, and psychoanalysis, but refused to treat any as the definitive school of American psychology:

> Every school is good, though no one is good enough. No one of them has the full vision of the psychology of the future.
>
> —(1931, p. 255)

Social Engineering

Functional psychologists believed that they could exploit their knowledge of human adaptability to improve education, training, personnel selection, and mental health and to relieve psychological and behavioral disorders that were products of individual maladjustment. Their pragmatic vision of the goal of psychology echoed James's plea for a science of "practical prediction and control" that would make a significant contribution to the improvement of the human condition. For James, control of human psychology and behavior through scientific psychology promised to be "an achievement compared with which the control of the rest of physical nature would appear comparatively insignificant" (1892, p. 148).

This vision of psychology as a science that could surmount the constraints of evolution by natural selection and improve the human condition was shared by later behaviorist psychologists and by eugenicists in the mental testing movement, who argued that many aspects of human psychology and behavior are determined by heredity. Behaviorists argued that scientific psychologists could and should improve the human condition by modifying human psychology and behavior through the manipulation and control of its environmental determinants. Eugenicists argued that scientific psychologists could and should improve the human condition by artificially selecting desirable psychological and social traits through positive and negative eugenic programs.

In this critical respect, functional psychologists and other early-20th-century American psychologists and social scientists did embrace one critical implication of Darwin's theory of evolution by natural selection: namely, that natural selection does not ensure human progress. Baldwin had developed his own evolutionary and developmental theories to counter Spencer's form of "laissez-faire" social Darwinism (O'Donnell, 1985), according to which evolution should be allowed to continue unhindered by artificial social intervention. Functional psychologists, behaviorist psychologists, and eugenicists were disinclined to let evolution develop unhindered and committed themselves to social interventionist programs based upon scientific psychology that were purposively directed to the improvement of the human condition.

However, it is not clear whether this was a consequence of their commitment to this implication of Darwin's theory or their independent pragmatist principles.

For in this respect functional psychologists, behaviorist psychologists, and eugenicists replicated the missionary zeal of early American moral philosophers, who likewise championed the social benefits of common sense and experimental psychology, but who were firmly committed to the purposive and progressive nature of divinely guided evolution (Fuchs, 2000).

BEHAVIORISM

In *Behaviorism at Fifty* (1963), B. F. Skinner observed that

> Behaviorism, with its emphasis on the last syllable, is not the scientific study of behavior but a philosophy of science concerned with the subject-matter and methods of psychology.

—(p. 951)

All behaviorists were committed to the view that observable behavior (as opposed to conscious experience) is the subject matter of scientific psychology, but they differed on a variety of substantive issues.

The development of American behaviorism may be usefully characterized in terms of three distinct but related phases. The first phase, often called **behaviorism**, was the position advocated by John B. Watson. Watson saw psychology as a positivist science restricted to the correlation of observable stimuli and responses and rejected mentalistic explanations of behavior. He was also (at least in his later years) a committed environmentalist who maintained that most human behavior can be modified through the manipulation of environmental conditions. The second phase, often called **neobehaviorism**, was represented by Edward C. Tolman (1886–1959) and Clark L. Hull (1884–1952). Tolman and Hull agreed that observable behavior is the subject matter of scientific psychology, but acknowledged the legitimacy of mentalistic explanations of behavior. The third phase, often called **radical behaviorism**, was represented by B. F. Skinner and his followers. Skinner, like Watson, saw psychology as a form of positivist science restricted to the correlation of observable stimuli and responses and rejected mentalistic explanations of behavior. Also like Watson, Skinner was a committed environmentalist who claimed that most human behavior can be modified via the manipulation of environmental conditions (contingencies of reinforcement).

Background to Behaviorism

Functional psychology represented the last remnant of the new psychology in America. Functional psychologists recognized the need for a socially useful psychology, but remained tied to the earlier philosophical tradition of James, Ladd, and Hall; and their emphasis on the conscious and purposive adaptation of behavior harked back to pre-Darwinian teleological conceptions of psychological functions.

Although functional psychologists such as Angell and Carr acknowledged the value of structural psychology and the reliability of introspection, the experimental analysis of consciousness was neglected in practice at the University of Chicago, as it came to be in most places (outside of Cornell) in the early decades of the 20th century. Moreover, while earlier studies of animal behavior at Chicago (and Clark and Harvard) were designed to throw light on the comparative psychology of different species, animal psychology came to focus almost exclusively on the experimental study of animal learning, conceived of as a way to study the fundamental laws governing all animal and human behavior. In this fashion the advocacy of animal psychology by functional psychologists eventually came to undermine their own position, as animal psychologists developed explanations of animal learning that made no appeal to consciousness or cognition. As the rigor of the experimental study of animal learning came to displace the rigor of the experimental study of human consciousness as the paradigm of scientific objectivity, the methods of the animal laboratory were generalized to the study of human behavior.

Early Forms of Behaviorism   The conceptual foundations of behaviorism were developed by the **new realist** philosophers, notably Edwin Bissell Holt (1873–1946) and Ralph Barton Perry (1876–1957) at Harvard and Edgar Arthur Singer (1873–1955) at the University of Pennsylvania (Mills, 1998). These philosophers maintained that consciousness and cognition are best explicated in terms of behavioral adjustments to the environment (Holt, 1914; Holt et al., 1910; Perry, 1904) to the point of the virtual equation of cognition and adaptive behavior in the work of Singer (1911, 1924) and Grace Mead Andrus de Laguna (1919).

Max Meyer advanced the earliest statement of the behaviorist position in *The Fundamental Laws of Human Learning* in 1911, followed by *The Psychology of the Other One* in 1921. Meyer, a former student of Stumpf's, accepted an appointment at the University of Missouri in 1900, where he remained for the rest of his career (Esper, 1966). He claimed that psychology could attain the status of a science of prediction and control only when the "facts and laws of introspective psychology have been correlated with—replaced by—facts of behavior and its laws" (1911, p. 241). Meyer also anticipated Watson's account of habit learning in terms of the recency and frequency of correlated stimuli and responses and his treatment of cognitive processes as motor responses. Meyer's work was largely neglected, possibly because his statement of behaviorism was tied to a very specific neurophysiological theory of stimulus-response learning. He also suffered the same type of academic fate as Watson: He was fired in 1930 for distributing questionnaire data on illicit sexual relations in his course on social psychology (O'Donnell, 1985).

Albert Paul Weiss's radically reductive version of behaviorism was also neglected (although Weiss, a modest and retiring man, made little attempt to publicize his views and died at an early age after an incapacitating illness). He trained as an under-graduate and postgraduate student at the University of Missouri, but spent the rest of his career at Ohio University. Weiss's comprehensive behaviorist approach accom-modated all forms of behavior, from muscle twitches to socially embedded forms of thought and behavior (Weiss, 1917, 1918, 1925). He held that traditional problems of consciousness and cognition had been resolved or dissolved by the new realist philosophy (Mills, 1998) and defended the autonomy and pragmatic rationale of behaviorist psychology:

> The success of behavior methods will not depend on how they treat the problem of consciousness; they will succeed or fail according as they do or do not further the general welfare of society.
>
> —(1918, p. 637)

William McDougall: Purposive Behaviorism   The Englishman William McDougall (1871–1938) advanced another early statement of behaviorism. In his *Introduction to Social Psychology* he claimed that

> psychologists must cease to be content with the sterile and narrow conception of their science as the science of consciousness, and must boldly assert its claim to be the positive science of the mind in all its aspects and modes of functioning, or as I would prefer to say, the positive science of conduct and behavior.
>
> —(1908, p. 15)

McDougall trained in medicine and physiology at the universities of Cambridge and London. He studied psychology with Müller at Göttingen and taught at the universities of London and Oxford before joining the philosophy faculty at Harvard (he accepted the position previously held by James and Münsterberg). McDougall developed a form of purposive behaviorism: He rejected introspective psychology but supported mentalistic explanations of behavior and maintained that many forms of purposive or goal-directed behavior are grounded in instinct. Although McDougall was well aware of the danger of "cheap and easy" explanations of behav-ior that merely postulate a corresponding instinct for every behavior to be explained (McDougall, 1908), his increasingly detailed theoretical inventory of instincts became the target of critics who depreciated the role of instinct in the explanation of human behavior (Dunlap, 1919; Kuo, 1921; Watson, 1924/1930).

McDougall was a prolific writer who made a significant contribution to the fledgling science of social psychology (1908, 1920), although his "group-mind" conception of social psychology was displaced by the individualist conception developed by Floyd Allport (1890–1971) and his followers (Allport, 1924, 1933). McDougall's behaviorism is particularly interesting because although he was committed to the view that scientific psychology is concerned with the explanation of behavior, he did not share the optimistic environmentalism of Watson and most other behaviorists. McDougall was a committed hereditarian who advocated positive and negative eugenic programs in *Is America Safe for Democracy?* (1921). His position demonstrated that commitment to a science devoted to the prediction and control of behavior did not entail commitment to environmentalism, although in practice most American behaviorists were environmentalists.

McDougall's defense of a Lamarckian account of evolution during the period in which it was critically assessed and rejected by experimental biologists, along with his advocacy of spiritualist research, generated a storm of protest among psychologists, who called for his dismissal from the APA. He was never a popular figure, although he was the declared victor in a famous debate with Watson about the nature and prospects of behaviorism (Watson & McDougall, 1929). McDougall resigned from his position at Harvard in 1926 and moved to Duke University in 1927, where he remained until his death in 1938. He was lampooned in the press for his support of Lamarckianism and spiritualist research, but did not deserve the vilification he received from his colleagues when he died. In announcing McDougall's death at the APA meeting in 1938, Knight Dunlap claimed that McDougall had done a great service to psychology by dying (Smith, 1989).

Animal Psychology

McDougall held that a science of behavior should be grounded in a comparative psychology based upon "the observation of the behavior of men and animals of all varieties under all possible conditions of health and disease" (1908, p. 15), and Watson and later behaviorists made the experimental study of animal behavior the foundation of their psychologies. Animal psychology had been developed at major psychological centers such as Clark, Chicago, Columbia, Hopkins, and Harvard, but was in a rather precarious position at the time Watson issued his behaviorist "manifesto" in 1913. Although animal psychology had become more rigorously objective and experimental and had developed a coherent research program directed to the study of animal learning, only a handful of psychologists devoted themselves to the study of animal behavior in the first decade of the 20th century. When Watson suggested to his friend Robert M. Yerkes that those interested in animal behavior should get together at the APA meeting in 1909, he listed only five other psychologists and two biologists (O'Donnell, 1985). In the first decade of the 20th century, animal and comparative psychology accounted for only about 4 percent of the experimental output of American psychology laboratories (Bruner & Allport, 1940).

There were a variety of reasons for this. Animal psychology, like comparative psychology in the tradition of Darwin, Romanes, and Morgan, was criticized by traditional philosophers and structural psychologists as largely irrelevant to human psychology, and institutions that supported animal psychology were subject to public criticism and campaigns by anti-vivisectionists. Most college administrators were reluctant to provide funds for the care and maintenance of cats, dogs, and raccoons (which were smelly, dirty and noisy), in addition to the chronoscopes and reaction timers of the traditional psychology laboratory.

Most PhD students who did dissertation research on topics in animal psychology ended up in education, and most doctoral students in psychology considered animal psychology a doubtful and precarious career choice. Both Watson and Yerkes were advised to redirect their research focus to issues in education, as Edward L. Thorndike later did with great success at Columbia. Animal psychology was seen as peripheral to human psychology and was the first to have its budgets cut and faculty retrenched in times of financial depression, as happened in the years following the financial crisis of 1907. For example, Lawrence Wooster Cole, who conducted influential research on passive and delayed learning in raccoons at the University of Oklahoma, was fired in 1908, as was Eliot P. Frost at Yale in 1912 (O'Donnell, 1985).

The career of Robert Mearns Yerkes provides a usefully illustrative example. Yerkes came to Harvard as a graduate student in zoology, but was persuaded by the philosopher Josiah Royce (1855–1916) to combine his interests in zoology and psychology into comparative psychology. He transferred to philosophy in 1899 and completed his degree in 1902. Münsterberg's special pleading secured him an instructorship rather than the lowly teaching fellowship he was originally offered at Harvard. Yet despite a series of publications on animal instinct and learning and an appeal by Royce to the president, Yerkes remained an instructor for the next six years. Increasingly isolated (he was disinvited from philosophy department meetings in 1906) and personally humiliated by the promotion of a mediocre Harvard alumnus philosopher from a wealthy Boston family, Yerkes asked Münsterberg to once again plead his case with the president. Münsterberg secured his promotion to assistant professor on the explicit condition that Yerkes emphasize "the more educational aspects of psychology" (letter to President C. W. Eliot of Harvard, 1908, cited in O'Donnell, 1985).

When Yerkes continued to doggedly pursue his own animal research without even a nod to educational psychology, Münsterberg withdrew his support and threatened to shut down the program in comparative psychology. Yerkes's position improved only when he accepted a position at Boston Psychopathic Hospital in 1913, where he worked with all-too-human subjects. When Yerkes was offered the position of state psychologist prior to the First World War, Harvard doubled his salary and gave him a half-time teaching schedule (at full pay).

Yerkes was joint author of the first general introduction to Pavlov's work on classical conditioning (Yerkes & Morgulis, 1909). He published an *Introduction to Psychology* in 1911, and that same year he and Watson founded the *Journal of Animal Behavior*. Yerkes developed a lifelong interest in primates while working with orangutans at a primate laboratory in California during a two-year sabbatical from Harvard. He developed his talent for organization and committee work as head of the Army Testing Project during the First World War, and after the war he promoted the development of professional psychological research through his service on various committees of the National Research Council. He returned to academic life as a research professor at Yale in 1924, and in 1929 realized his lifetime ambition when he managed to secure funding to establish the Yale laboratories of primate biology in Jacksonville, Florida (now the Yerkes laboratories). That same year he published his major work *The Great Apes: A Study of Anthropoid Life* (1929).

The Albino Rat　The perceived relevance of the experimental analysis of animal behavior for human psychology changed for the better as psychology became increasingly applied. Yet as it did so, animal psychologists abandoned the original conception of a genetic psychology based upon the comparative naturalistic observation of animal and human development and began to focus on the experimental study of the learning abilities of a limited number of animal species, most notably the domesticated albino variant of the Norwegian rat (*Rattus norvegicus var albinus*).

The Swiss psychiatrist Adolf Meyer (1866–1950), who became Massachusetts state pathologist at the Worcester Hospital for the Insane in 1896 (with an academic appointment at Clark University), introduced the albino rat to America. He established a breeding colony, although he did little research himself. However, he persuaded the developmental neurologist Henry Donaldson (1857–1938) of the rats' value in experimental neurology and supplied him with his first laboratory animals.

Donaldson had been a student of Hall's at Johns Hopkins in the 1880s. When Hall moved to Clark in 1889, he took Donaldson with him as an assistant professor of neurology. Donaldson was one of the many Clark faculty lured to the newly instituted University of Chicago in 1892, where he became head of the department of neurology. At Chicago Donaldson and his students began to use albino rats in their research, and he served as one of the advisors for John B. Watson's dissertation on neural development and learning in the albino rat (Watson, 1903). In 1906 Donaldson moved to the Wistar Institute, taking four pairs of rats with him. These formed the basis of the Institute's commercial breeding program, which became the main supplier of albino rats to neurology and animal psychology laboratories in America (Logan, 1999).

The albino rat had a number of advantages for research in neurology and psychology, including its slow rate of physiological, neural, and psychological maturation, which made it an ideal animal for the study of development and learning. Although Meyer and Donaldson had originally conceived of the experimental study of rat behavior as an integral component of the comparative study of species differences and diversity, with the commercial production of the albino rat the experimental study of rat behavior came to be seen as the means of attaining maximum generality in animal research. American psychologists treated the albino rat as a generic animal model that could be used to represent developmental and learning processes common to all vertebrates, including humans (Logan, 1999). In this fashion the assumption of strong continuity between human and animal psychology and behavior that underpinned the standard behaviorist generalization from animal to human behavior was built into the "industrial standard" production model of the albino rat.

Criteria of the Psychic   There was continued debate in the late 19th and early 20th centuries about the scientific legitimacy of theoretical attributions of consciousness and cognition to animals. Yerkes tried to resolve these doubts by developing objective criteria such as neurophysiological complexity and behavioral plasticity (Yerkes, 1905a). Like Romanes and Morgan before him, he acknowledged that questions about the scientific legitimacy of theoretical attributions of consciousness and cognition applied equally to humans and animals:

> Human psychology stands or falls with comparative psychology. If the study of the mental life of lower animals is not legitimate, no more is the study of human consciousness.

> —(1905b, p. 527)

Watson, in his capacity as review editor of animal psychology for the *Psychological Bulletin,* became increasingly dissatisfied with such attempts to develop "criteria of the psychic" (Yerkes, 1905a). He expressed his skepticism about the possibility of consistently applying such criteria in a paper he presented at the 1908 meeting of the Southern Society of Philosophy and Psychology at Johns Hopkins, titled "A Point of View in Comparative Psychology" (Watson, 1909), in which he argued that animal psychology should be restricted to the identification of observable stimulus-response sequences. Five years later, Watson extended this argument to human psychology when he advanced his behaviorist position in his Columbia lecture "Psychology as the Behaviorist Views It" (1913a). In promoting his position, Watson derived support from the work of Edward L. Thorndike in America and Ivan Pavlov in Russia, both of whom had taken up Morgan's implicit challenge to develop accounts of animal behavior without reference to consciousness and cognition and had suggested that these accounts could be generalized to the explanation of human behavior.

Edward L. Thorndike: The Law of Effect

When Conwy Lloyd Morgan delivered the Lowell Lectures at Harvard in 1896, Edward Lee Thorndike may have been inspired to take up his challenge to explain animal behavior without reference to consciousness and cognition. Thorndike was at Harvard at the time and may very well have been in the audience, although he never claimed to have attended the lectures and there is no evidence that he did (Stam & Kalmanovitch, 1988). However, it is clear that Thorndike knew of Morgan's work, and he acknowledged that his own animal experiments were a development of Morgan's studies of learning in chickens. Morgan had trained chickens to discriminate different types of corn through what he had called "trial-and-error" learning (Morgan, 1894/1977), a characterization that Thorndike later appropriated.

Thorndike was born in Williamsburg, Massachusetts, the son of a Methodist minister. From 1891 to 1895, he attended Wesleyan University, where he excelled academically and developed an interest in psychology after reading James's *Principles*. He attended Harvard, where he worked with and became friends with James, receiving his master's degree in 1897. Thorndike, who later confessed that he had had "no special interest in animals," worked with children on his original research project (Thorndike, 1936). However, the Harvard authorities refused to allow him to continue after Franz Boas conducted an anthropometric study that involved the loosening of children's clothes—creating a public outcry in Boston (O'Donnell, 1985). After consulting with James, Thorndike prepared to conduct a series of experiments on animal intelligence using chickens. When his landlady and the university refused to allow him space to conduct his experiments, James obliged by providing Thorndike with space in the basement of his house.

In 1897 Thorndike left Harvard for Columbia University. Cattell secured him a fellowship and encouraged him to continue his animal research. After difficulties with Thorndike's New York landlady, Cattell managed to secure some laboratory space at the university, where Thorndike conducted his famous studies of trial-and-error learning, based upon a series of experiments in which cats learned to escape from specially constructed "puzzle-boxes." His doctoral dissertation was accepted in 1898 and published that same year as *Animal Intelligence: An Experimental Study of the Associative Processes in Animals* (in the form of a monograph supplement in *Psychological Review*—it was republished in 1911 as an independent monograph). After a year teaching as an instructor in education at Case Western Reserve College for Women, Thorndike returned to New York as an instructor in genetic psychology at Teachers College, where he remained until his retirement in 1940.

The Law of Effect   Thorndike's experimental studies of trial-and-error learning were based upon Morgan's reported observation of how his dog Toby had managed to escape from his back yard. Toby had learned to lift the latch on the gate after repeated occasions in which originally accidental movements of the latch led to its opening and escape (Morgan, 1894/1977). Thorndike's cats were food-deprived and placed in slatted cages: They were required to open a latch (or series of latches) in order to escape and receive a food reward. Like Morgan's dog, the cats initially responded in a random fashion. They clawed and bit at the bars, sniffed around the cage, pushed their paws between the bars, and tried to squeeze between them. Eventually they hit upon the movement required to release the latch, which enabled them to escape and receive the food reward. On subsequent trials, the cats exhibited less and less random behavior until they learned the required behavior, which they would then produce whenever they were placed in the puzzle-box.

Thorndike measured the decreased time it took for animals to produce the required behavior and the decreased number of incorrect responses over the series of trials until learning was completed. His data indicated that the required response was learned incrementally, rather than through any spontaneous act of insight or reasoning. By varying the conditions, Thorndike also demonstrated

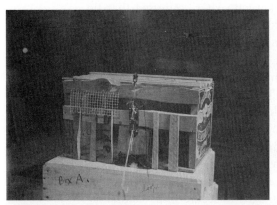
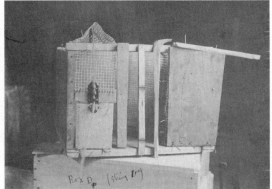
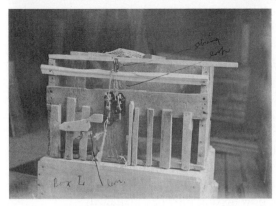

Thorndike's puzzle-boxes.

that learning was not a product of imitation, since the observation of successful responses by other cats did not decrease the time it took for a cat to learn the correct response.

Thorndike claimed that through this process of trial-and-error learning successful responses were "stamped in" and unsuccessful responses "stamped out":

> Gradually all the . . . nonsuccessful impulses will be stamped out and the particular impulse leading to the successful act will be stamped in by the resulting pleasure, until after many trials, the cat will, when put in a box, immediately claw the button or loop in a definite way.
>
> —(1911, p. 36)

Thorndike characterized his account of this process as the **law of effect**:

> Of several responses made to the same situation, those which are accompanied or closely followed by satisfaction to the animal will, other things being equal, be more firmly connected with the situation, so that, when it recurs, they will be more likely to recur; those which are accompanied or closely followed by discomfort to the animal will, other things being equal, have their connections with that situation weakened, so that, when it recurs, they will be less likely to occur. The greater the satisfaction or discomfort, the greater the strengthening or weakening of the bond.
>
> —(1911, p. 244)

Thorndike supplemented the law of effect with what he called the **law of exercise**:

> Any response to a situation will, other things being equal, be more strongly connected with the situation in proportion to the number of times it has been connected with that situation and to the average vigor and duration of the connections.
>
> —(1911, p. 244)

Connectionism Thorndike's theory of learning, which he characterized as **connectionism**, appealed to traditional principles of association based upon contiguity and repetition. However, he focused on associations between behavior and its consequences rather than associations between ideas (although the main principle of the law of effect had been recognized by Hartley, Spencer, and Bain). Indeed, part of the point of Thorndike's experiments was to demonstrate that animal learning did not involve any form of insight, reasoning, or association of ideas. As Thorndike put it, "The effective part of the association [is] a direct bond between the situation and the impulse" (1911, p. 109). He believed this bond or connection to be automatic and unconscious.

Thorndike rather rashly concluded from these experiments that all animal and human behavior could be explained in terms of the laws of effect and exercise and the law of instinct:

> The higher animals, including man, manifest no behavior beyond expectations from the laws of instinct, exercise and effect.
>
> —(1911, p. 274)

For such conclusions he was roundly criticized, largely on the basis of the artificiality of his experimental studies.

Köhler (1917/1925) complained that Thorndike's cats were effectively forced into trial-and-error learning. According to Köhler, the cats were precluded from employing insight or reasoning because they could not see how the escape mechanism worked. Despite the fact that he agreed with Thorndike's conclusions, Morgan suggested that

> The conditions of his experiments were perhaps not the most conducive to the discovery of rationality in animals if it exists. The sturdy and unconvinceable advocate of reasoning (properly so-called) in animals may say that to place a starving kitten in the cramped confinement of one of Mr. Thorndike's box-cages, would be more likely to make a cat swear than to lead it to act rationally.
>
> —(1898, p. 249)

The comparative psychologist Wesley Mills complained that the artificial and restricted nature of Thorndike's experimental setting precluded generalizations about normal animal and human behavior and famously remarked that one might as well "enclose a living man in a coffin, lower him, against his will, into the earth, and attempt to deduce normal psychology from his conduct" (Mills, 1899, p. 266).

Thorndike defended his theory and methods vigorously. He claimed that his manipulative experimental methods made his study scientifically superior to the previous "anecdotal tradition," of which he was openly contemptuous and dismissive (although he acknowledged Morgan's work and that of early experimental pioneers such as Spalding and Lubbock). Yet by the late 1920s he was forced to modify his theoretical position. He abandoned the law of exercise and the second half of the law of effect relating to the weakening of connections with "discomfort" (Thorndike, 1929).

Educational Psychology   Although he was offered a position at Columbia (and later Harvard), Thorndike remained at Teachers College for the rest of his career, devoting most of his later years to educational psychology (Thorndike, 1903a, 1913–1914). He was a prolific author of academic articles and books, which prompted Titchener to complain about Thorndike's tendency to "publish his lecture courses as soon as the lectures have been delivered" (1905, p. 522), as well as of texts and test instruments for educators (mainly on reading and arithmetic). The latter proved to be extremely lucrative, providing Thorndike with an income of around $70,000 per annum in the 1920s (more than $800,000 a year in today's dollars). He also ventured into the fields of industrial and social psychology, although with rather less success. Thorndike was the recipient of many awards and prizes, including honorary degrees. He was elected president of the APA in 1912, a member of the National Academy of Sciences in 1917, and president of the American Association for the Advancement of Science in 1934.

Although later behaviorists treated his research as exemplary, Thorndike himself was no behaviorist. He came to recognize the limitations of his account of learning with respect to distinctive human capacities such as language. He never denied the utility of introspection as a method of studying human consciousness or as a theoretical "window" into animal consciousness (Samelson, 1985). He was also a hereditarian who maintained that many human abilities and liabilities are innately determined. Thorndike published *Heredity, Correlation and Sex Differences in School Abilities* in 1903 and *Introduction to the Theory of Mental and Social Measurement* in 1904. He developed his own intelligence test, which was employed at Columbia and other educational institutions. He was also a committed eugenicist, who served with Henry H. Goddard and Robert M. Yerkes on the 1913 Committee on the Heredity of Feeblemindedness, which recommended the compulsory sterilization of "mental defectives."

Later behaviorists treated Thorndike's research as exemplary because he did not appeal to consciousness or cognition in his connectionist account of trial-and-error learning. However, Thorndike did make reference to mental states such as "satisfaction," "annoyance," and "discomfort" in his statement of the law of effect, and he insisted that it was a virtue of his experimental method that it provided information about the feelings of animals. He also made the same inferences about the mental states of animals as had Romanes and Morgan:

> For Thorndike, as for Morgan, detailed analysis of an animal's mental operations on the basis of objective inference was followed by descriptions of the animal's private experience on the basis of subjective inference.
>
> —(Mackenzie, 1977, p. 70)

For example, Thorndike suggested that

> One who has seen the phenomena so far described, who has watched the life of a cat or dog for a month or more under test conditions, gets, or fancies he gets, a fairly definite idea of what the intellectual life of a cat or dog feels like.
>
> —(1911, pp. 123–124)

Ivan Pavlov: Classical Conditioning

Ivan Petrovich Pavlov (1849–1936) was born in the town of Ryazan, south of Moscow, the eldest son of a family of seven. His father was a parish priest, and Pavlov originally studied for the priesthood at Ryazan Ecclesiastical Seminary. He later developed an interest in natural science and enrolled at the University of St. Petersburg in 1870. He took a degree in natural science in 1879 and a medical degree at the Imperial Medical-Military Academy of St. Petersburg in 1883. After a few years in minor positions, he was appointed professor of pharmacology at the Imperial Medical-Military Academy in 1890 and professor of physiology in 1895. In 1891 he became director of the Institute of Experimental Medicine of St. Petersburg, the home of his research for the next 40 years. He was elected to the Russian Academy of Sciences in 1907.

Conditioned Reflexes During the first decade of his career, Pavlov focused his research on the physiological study of the digestive system, which won him the Nobel Prize in 1904. In his Nobel address, he mentioned the problem of "psychic secretions" that was to occupy him for the next three decades. Pavlov reported that his laboratory dogs salivated in reflexive reaction not only to food stimuli (in the form of meat powder), but also to associated stimuli, such as the sight or sound of the experimenter. Pavlov and his students investigated the determinants of these **conditioned responses** (originally characterized as conditional responses, since they were conditional upon the original reflex),[1] which he described in *Conditioned Reflexes* (1928).

Pavlov distinguished between an unconditioned or innate reflex and a conditioned or learned reflex. In the case of an unconditioned reflex, an unconditioned stimulus (US), such as food powder placed in a dog's mouth, generates an unconditioned response (UR), such as salivation. In the case of a conditioned reflex, Pavlov and his students demonstrated that an originally neutral stimulus, such as the sound of a metronome, will function as a conditioned stimulus (CS) and elicit a conditioned response (CR), such as salivation, after repeated pairing of the originally neutral stimulus with the unconditioned stimulus. However, Pavlov never used a bell as a conditioned stimulus. The cultural myth that he did derives from the fact that the artist who transposed the illustration of his experimental set-up for an American translation of Pavlov's work substituted a bell for the original metronome.

Pavlov and his students also identified the phenomena of **extinction** (the attenuation of a conditioned response when a conditioned stimulus is no longer

---

[1]The Russian phrase *uslovnyi refleks* that Pavlov used can be translated as either "conditional reflex" or "conditioned reflex." Although the former is closer to Pavlov's original meaning (Todes, 1997), early English translations used the latter term, which has stuck.

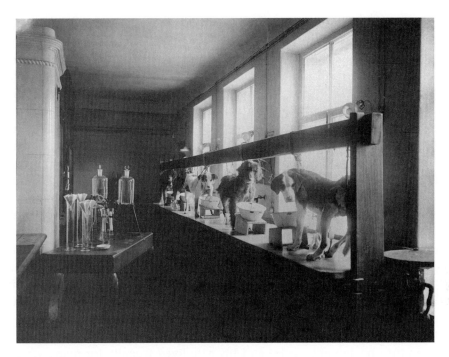

Pavlov's dogs.

paired with an unconditioned stimulus), **spontaneous recovery** (the tendency of a conditioned stimulus to elicit a conditioned response after some time has passed since extinction), and **disinhibition** (the tendency of any strong stimulus to elicit a conditioned response after extinction). Natalia R. Shenger-Krestovnikova, one of Pavlov's students, induced an "experimental neurosis" in dogs, by pairing food stimuli with presentations of a circle but not an ellipse. As presentations of ellipses were made progressively more circular, the dogs manifested violent and erratic behavior. For Pavlov, this provided some support for his conviction that most neuroses and psychoses are a product of the "derangement" of inhibitory reflexes in the brain (Boakes, 1984).

Like Thorndike's explanation of trial-and-error learning, Pavlov's explanation of conditioned responses appealed to traditional principles of contiguity and repetition. He maintained that his experiments on conditioned reflexes provided "a solid foundation for associationist psychology" (Simon, 1957, p. 18). Pavlov tried (unsuccessfully) to accommodate trial-and-error learning by treating it as a form of classical conditioning after the Polish physicians Jerzy Konorski and Stefan Miller claimed that his explanation of conditioned salivatory responses did not generalize to motor responses. Konorski and Miller maintained that classical conditioning and instrumental conditioning (trial-and-error learning) are two distinct forms of learning (Boakes, 1984).

Also like Thorndike, Pavlov eschewed appeals to consciousness and cognition in the explanation of animal learning. He claimed that all animal and human behavior could be explained in terms of "the influence of external stimuli" without reference to any "fantastic internal world." Pavlov's psychology was reductively materialistic and atomistic. For Pavlov, the ultimate explanation of all innate and learned responses was neurophysiological in nature, and all complex conditioned reflexes were additive functions of elementary reflexes. Pavlov was highly critical of the work of the Gestalt psychologists and dismissed their explanations of animal behavior in terms of insight and creative problem solving.

Like Sechenov, Pavlov promoted a form of objective psychology based upon the concepts as well as the methods of experimental physiology, although he credited Thorndike as the first objective psychologist. He was critical of Wundt's "new psychology," with its appeal to autonomous psychical processes. He was not opposed to the study of consciousness per se, but dismissed introspection as a method of investigation and claimed that consciousness could only be studied via "scientifically based methods." Pavlov also followed Sechenov in maintaining that all animal and human behavior is a product of innate or learned reflexes, both generative and inhibitory.

Pavlov was a dedicated experimentalist who poured all his financial resources into his laboratory. He and his wife lived frugally for many years in order to support it. She agreed to this so long as he agreed not to drink or smoke and to limit his social life. Pavlov was a perfectionist and disciplinarian in the laboratory and famously reprimanded a student who arrived late to the laboratory because he had been trying to avoiding street fighting during the Russian Revolution. By contrast, he was sentimental and impractical in his private life. He took one of his wife's shoes with him on an overseas trip and was robbed of $2,000 that protruded from his open briefcase while he waited for a train in Grand Central Station, New York. His wife often had to remind him to collect his wages. Unusually for his day, he accepted women and Jews as students in his laboratory (although he initially barred them), but would not tolerate explanations that appealed to consciousness—for such a sin a student could be fined (Boakes, 1984).

Pavlov lost his savings (including his Nobel Prize money) when the Bolsheviks liquidated assets after the revolution. His relations with Lenin and Stalin were often stormy, but he survived the revolution better than did most of his contemporaries (although at one point he contemplated transferring his laboratory to England or America). The Communist government generally valued and supported his work, and Lenin proclaimed him a hero of the revolution in 1921.

Bechterev and Motor Reflexes   Vladimir M. Bechterev (1857–1927), who graduated from the Imperial Medical-Military Academy of St. Petersburg in 1878, also developed an objective psychology based upon reflexes. He received his doctorate from the academy in 1881 and later studied with Wundt and du Bois-Reymond. Bechterev created the first Russian laboratory devoted to experimental psychology at the University of Kazan in 1885. He returned to the Imperial Medical-Military Academy in 1893 as professor of psychic and nervous diseases, but later left to found the Psychoneurological Institute with some of his colleagues. He published *Objective Psychology* in three volumes between 1907 and 1912 and *General Principles of Human Reflexology* in 1917. Bechterev maintained that the aim of objective psychology (or reflexology) was to "determine correlations between man and his environment, both physical, biological and, above all, social" (1917/1932, p. 33). Like Pavlov, he acknowledged that objective psychology had originally been developed by Americans such as Thorndike.

Bechterev was somewhat disparaging of Pavlov's own work. He claimed that Pavlov's "association reflexes" had been known for years. This was certainly true: They had been identified by Whytt in the 18th century and by Spencer and Bain in the 19th century (Rosenweig, 1959). Bechterev's own research focused upon conditioned motor responses associated with motor reflexes, such as the patellar (knee-jerk) reflex, and he was critical of Pavlov's "saliva method" (which focused upon conditioned physiological reflexes).

John B. Watson: Psychology as the Behaviorist Views It

John B. Watson was not the first to adopt the behaviorist position, but was undoubtedly its most forceful and successful advocate. He was born and raised in Greenville, South Carolina (the second of five children), the son of a drunken philanderer and a devoutly religious woman. His father abandoned the family in 1891 when Watson was 13, and Watson never forgave him for it (in later years his father sought him out, but Watson refused to see him). A troublemaker during his high school years, Watson was arrested for rioting and discharging a gun in public. Due to his own persuasive powers or his mother's Baptist connections, he managed to get himself accepted by Furman College in 1894 (at age 16), from which he graduated with a master's degree in 1899 (at the age of 21). At Furman he was taught philosophy and psychology by Gordon B. Moore, who had spent a recent sabbatical at the University of Chicago, and who introduced Watson to the work of Wundt, James, Titchener, and Angell. Watson supported himself through college by working in the chemistry laboratory and then taught for a year in a local Greenville school. He promised his mother that he would become a minister and avowed this as his vocation while attending Furman (Creelan, 1974). However, Watson abandoned any interest he may have had in a religious vocation after his mother's death in 1900, when he was accepted by the University of Chicago for graduate study in psychology.

Arriving in Chicago in 1900 with $50 in his pocket, Watson worked as a waiter, a janitor in the psychology laboratory, and a caretaker in the animal laboratory of the neurologist Henry H. Donaldson to support himself during his three years of graduate study. He studied experimental psychology with Angell and philosophy with Dewey, whom he claimed never to have understood. Watson studied neurology (as a minor) with Donaldson, who taught him basic research techniques, and biology and physiology with Jacques Loeb, the physiologist famous for his reductive account of animal psychology and behavior in terms of basic associative processes underlying reflexes and tropisms. Watson's dissertation project was a developmental study of the neurophysiological conditions of learning in albino rats, supervised by Angell and Donaldson.

Watson submitted his thesis on "Animal Education: The Psychical Development of the White Rat, Correlated With the Growth of Its Nervous System" in 1903, which gained him his doctorate at the age of 25. Watson was the first to receive a PhD in psychology at Chicago as well as the youngest person to receive a PhD at Chicago. He published his thesis as *Animal Education* that same year, and it was favorably reviewed in the main psychology journals. Watson was hired as an assistant and instructor at Chicago, where he taught courses on animal and human psychology. He used Titchener's laboratory manuals in his courses on experimental psychology, although he later confessed that he was uncomfortable working with human subjects (1936, p. 276). That same year he married Mary Ickes, one of his students, who bore him two children.

Watson set about developing the animal laboratory at the University of Chicago. He began a program of research with Harvey Carr on the role of sensation in maze learning in rats, concluding that kinesthetic (muscular) cues form the basis of learning (Carr & Watson, 1908; Watson, 1907). In 1907 Watson began field studies of the migratory instincts of noddy and sooty terns on the Tortugas Islands near Key West, which gives the lie to later complaints about his exclusive emphasis on laboratory experimentation. During this time he stumbled upon the form of learning later characterized as *imprinting* by Konrad Lorenz (1935), although he seems to have missed its significance. Watson noted,

> The birds have formed a great attachment to me. They will follow me all around the room. It is becoming more and more difficult to keep them in any box.
>
> —(1908, p. 240)

Watson later claimed that he came to form his behaviorist position during his years at Chicago, but got little encouragement from his colleagues, and that Angell warned him against trying to develop a psychology that excluded the study of consciousness (Watson, 1936). In 1907 Baldwin offered Watson an assistant professorship at Johns Hopkins, but Angell made a matching offer that was enough to persuade Watson to remain at Chicago. The following year Baldwin came back with an offer that Watson could scarcely refuse and Angell did not even try to match: a full professorship and a $1,000 increase in salary. Watson later claimed that he left Chicago with great reluctance and would have remained if Angell had made an offer of even an associate professorship (Watson, 1936). However he had become increasingly disenchanted with the lack of support for his animal research at Chicago and was well aware of the virtues of an academic position within the Eastern academic establishment (O'Donnell, 1985). He was also attracted to Hopkins by the presence of Herbert Spencer Jennings (1868–1947) in the department of biology. Watson considered Jennings one of the "big three" in animal psychology, along with himself and Yerkes.

Watson was thus elevated to a full professorship in psychology at Johns Hopkins at the age of 30. His position was further advanced when the Baltimore police found Baldwin in a "colored house of prostitution" in 1908. The university dismissed him when they discovered that despite this embarrassing episode, Baldwin had accepted a nomination to serve on the Baltimore School Board (Pauly, 1979). Baldwin handed over the chairmanship of the psychology department and the editorship of *Psychological Review* to Watson before leaving for South America. In the ensuing years Watson's career went from strength to strength. He was elected president of the APA and the Southern Society of Philosophy and Psychology in 1914.

Knight Dunlap (1875–1949), a student of Münsterberg's who came to Hopkins in 1906, encouraged Watson in his more radical views. He later claimed to have persuaded Watson of his behaviorist principles, and Watson acknowledged his influence. Dunlap's paper "The Case Against Introspection," published in *Psychological Review* in 1912, anticipated many of Watson's distinctive positions, although, like McDougall, Dunlap rejected introspection but accepted mentalistic explanations of behavior. Karl S. Lashley (1890–1958), who later went on to have a distinguished career in neurophysiology, enrolled as a graduate student in zoology at Hopkins in 1912 and worked with Watson on a variety of projects, including his field study of noddy and sooty terns (Watson & Lashley, 1915). He was an early supporter of Watson's behaviorism (Lashley, 1923), although his later research undermined the neurophysiological assumptions of Watson's theory of learning (Lashley, 1929).

In 1913 Cattell invited Watson to deliver a series of lectures on his "new psychology" at Columbia University. The first of these lectures, "Psychology as a Behaviorist Views It," was published in *Psychological Review* that year. It became known as the behaviorist "manifesto," although Watson himself never represented it as such—it was first called a "manifesto" by Woodworth in 1931. This was followed by a fuller statement of his behaviorist position in *Behavior: An Introduction to Comparative Psychology* in 1914.

Watson's Behaviorism   Watson initiated what was later called the "behaviorist revolution" by declaring that

> Psychology as the behaviorist views it is a purely objective experimental branch of natural science. Its theoretical goal is the prediction and control of behavior. Introspection forms no part of its methods, nor is the scientific value of its data dependent upon the readiness with which they lend themselves to interpretation in terms of consciousness.
>
> —(1913a, p. 158)

He maintained that psychology is a positivist science of prediction and control, based upon the description of behavior and its observable antecedents. Watson's advocacy of a behaviorist psychology was one of many early-20th-century appeals for an atheoretical or "behavioral" approach in the human and social sciences. Similar positivist positions were developed by Luther Lee Bernard (1919) in sociology, Charles E. Merriam (1921) in politics, and Wesley Claire Mitchell (1925) in economics (Mills, 1998). Aside from his rejection of introspection, Watson's basic positivist position was remarkably similar to Titchener's. Like Titchener, he advocated an experimental science based upon repeatable observations, but focused upon observations of behavior rather than the introspection of mental states.

Watson's behaviorism was grounded in his disenchantment with the debate about animal mind and the problems of introspective psychology. However, it was not mandated by them, and Watson's radical position went beyond anything licensed by Morgan's canon or the "imageless-thought" debate. His behaviorist program was not based upon any established contrast between the success of his own program of animal research and the failure of introspective psychology. Watson's own limited experimental research on maze learning in rats scarcely provided the foundation for a general psychology encompassing all forms of animal and human behavior. His behaviorism was in fact little more than a restatement of traditional empiricist and associationist principles transposed from the realm of privately introspectable mental states to publicly observable behavior. The familiar "principle of contiguity" grounded Watson's stimulus-response laws, and the "principle of frequency" served as his explanation of "habit formation."

By 1913, when Watson delivered his Columbia lecture, most psychologists had already moved beyond the experimental study of consciousness, and the work of functional and applied psychologists had established observable behavior as a legitimate subject of scientific psychology. Cattell, who had invited Watson to speak at Columbia, claimed in his 1904 address at the World's Fair in St. Louis:

> I am not convinced that psychology should be limited to the study of consciousness as such . . . the rather widespread notion that there is no psychology apart from introspection is refuted by the brute argument of accomplished fact. It seems to me that

most of the research work that has been done by me or in my laboratory is nearly as independent of introspection as work in physics or in zoology.

—(1904, pp. 179–180)

At the 1910 meeting of the APA, Angell had predicted that behavior would displace consciousness as the primary subject matter of scientific psychology, and at the 1912 meeting he cautioned that it was threatening to replace consciousness altogether (Angell, 1913). Psychology had already come to be defined in terms of behavior in textbooks such as Walter B. Pillsbury's (1872–1960) *Essentials of Psychology* (1911, p. 1–2) and McDougall's *The Science of Human Behavior* (1912).

However, although these psychologists rejected the introspective method, they still retained mentalistic explanations of behavior (McDougall, 1908) or treated observable behavior as the basis for inferences about human and animal consciousness and cognition (Pillsbury, 1911). Watson complained that Pillsbury "went back" on his definition and considered conventional topics such as mental imagery (which was not surprising, since Pillsbury was a former student of Titchener's). In contrast, Watson claimed that the time had come for psychology to develop as a "science of behavior" and "discard all reference to consciousness." According to Watson, psychology should abandon the terms "consciousness, mental states, mind, content, introspectively verifiable, imagery, and the like" (1913a, p. 166). He claimed that a science of behavior based upon the public observation of behavior could and should be developed in place of a science of consciousness based upon private introspection—a scientific psychology whose principles would be developed "in terms of stimulus and response, in terms of habit formation, habit integrations and the like" (1913a, p. 167).

Watson gave three main reasons for abandoning references to consciousness and cognition and focusing upon behavior. The first was that such references are redundant in animal psychology. Watson had come to the conclusion that speculation about the minds of animals had no theoretical or practical value in animal psychology:

> More than one student in behavior has attempted to frame criteria of the psychic—to devise a set of objective, structural and functional criteria which, when applied in the particular instance, will enable us to decide whether such and such responses are positively conscious, merely indicative of consciousness, or whether they are purely "physiological." Such problems as these can no longer satisfy behavior men. It would be better to give up the province altogether and admit frankly that the study of the behavior of animals has no justification, than to admit that our search is of such a "will o' the wisp" character. One can assume either the presence or the absence of consciousness anywhere in the phylogenetic scale without affecting the problems of behavior by one jot or one tittle; and without influencing in any way the mode of experimental attack upon them.
>
> —(1913a, p. 161)

He generalized this conclusion that one can study animal behavior without reference to consciousness or cognition to the study of human behavior:

> It is granted that the behavior of animals can be investigated without appeal to consciousness. . . . The position is taken here that the behavior of man and the behavior of animals must be considered on the same plane.

> —(1913a, p. 176)

Watson's second reason was the failure of structural psychology. He cited the lack of inter- and intrasubject agreement with respect to the method of "systematic experimental introspection" practiced by Titchener and his followers, including the so-called imageless-thought debate and the lack of agreement about theoretical definitions of conscious states. These were fair criticisms of structural psychology, but were insufficient grounds for the rejection of all theoretical references to consciousness and cognition in animal and human psychology.

Watson's third reason was the practical irrelevance of a psychology of consciousness. He noted that "experimental pedagogy, the psychology of drugs, the psychology of advertising, legal psychology, the psychology of tests, and psychopathology" had all managed to thrive while distancing themselves from the psychology of consciousness (1913a, p. 113). He maintained that psychology would attain substantive practical benefits by adopting a behaviorist approach:

> If psychology would follow the plan I suggest, the educator, the physician, the jurist and the business man could utilize our data in a practical way, as soon as we are able, experimentally, to obtain them.

> —(1913a, p. 168)

However, Watson's appeal to applied psychology was somewhat disingenuous, since he did not himself engage in any form of applied psychology until after he left academia. He steadfastly resisted attempts to persuade him to move into "experimental pedagogy" and had little time for "the psychology of tests." During the First World War he was almost court-martialed from the army because of a negative report he wrote questioning the validity of the personnel selection tests he was charged with supervising (Cohen, 1979).

Watson represented his advocacy of behaviorism as a generalization from his developed position in animal psychology. However, it was as much a plea for the legitimacy of animal psychology, independent of any bearing it might have on human psychology. In defense of a discipline of doubtful professional status, Watson argued that established laws governing the behavior of animals, from the lowly amoebae upward, "have value in and of themselves without reference to the behavior of man" (1913a, p. 177).

It was also somewhat misleading for Watson to represent his argument for a behaviorist human psychology as a generalization from animal psychology. This was because he claimed that humans have unique cognitive capacities that are based upon language, which animals lack. Watson maintained that

> it can readily be understood that the search for reasoning, imagery, etc., in animals must forever remain futile, since such processes are dependent upon language or upon a set of similarly functioning bodily habits put on after language habits.
>
> —(1914, p. 334)

In this fashion Watson reprised the Cartesian account of the fundamental difference between humans and animals in terms of cognition and language, based upon his conception of cognition as a form of "inner speech" located in the larynx:

> The fundamental difference between man and animal from our point of view lies in the fact that the human being can form [linguistic] habits in the throat.
>
> —(1914, p. 299)

In denying cognitive and linguistic capacities to animals, Watson denied strong continuity between human and animal psychology and behavior—"the continuity theory of the Darwinians" (1914, p. 321). However, he affirmed strong continuity with respect to the explanatory principles of habit learning (based upon contiguity, recency, and frequency), which he believed accounted for all forms of animal and human behavior. Watson maintained this position without contradiction because he treated all forms of cognition (including language) as motor responses subject to the laws of habit formation.

Cognition as Motor Response   Watson rejected theoretical references to consciousness and cognition as illegitimate in human psychology, but only insofar as they were interpreted and defined in terms of introspective analysis. He did not deny the existence of human consciousness or cognition per se. He identified thought with inner speech, specifically with movements of the larynx: "All natural thought goes on in terms of sensori-motor processes in the larynx" (1913a, p. 174). This identification led Watson to make the bold prediction that if someone "suddenly lost his laryngeal apparatus without any serious injury to the other bodily mechanisms," he would suffer a "serious limitation" in his ability to think (1914, p. 327). When this was falsified by documented cases of persons who continued to think after removal of their larynx, he modified his position to include other muscles involved in speech production. Watson believed that a method could be developed for observing thought by correlating overt speech with movements of the larynx, to obtain "a record similar in character to that of the phonogram" (1913b, p. 424), although he admitted that the ability to "study reflective processes by such methods" would be "about as far off as the day when we can tell by physicochemical methods the difference in the structure and arrangement of molecules between living protoplasm and inorganic substances" (1913a, p. 174).

Watson claimed that thoughts are usually unconscious, since the sensory-motor processes involved in speech production "rarely come into consciousness in any person who has not groped for imagery in the psychological laboratory" (1913a, p. 174). For Watson, the virtue of identifying thought with movements of the larynx and other muscles involved in speech production was that it made thought an *observable behavior* on a par with other observable behavior and thus subject to prediction and control. As he put it, if such "implicit behavior" could be "shown to consist of nothing but word movements," then the "behavior of the human being as a whole is as open to objective observation and control as the behavior of the lowest organism" (1913b, p. 424).

What was significant about Watson's account was not his specific physiological location of cognition and language, but his conception of cognition and language as *peripheral motor responses*. He denied that consciousness and cognition play any role in the explanation of human behavior because he maintained that consciousness and cognition are themselves behavioral responses rather than "inner causes" of behavior. His equation of thought with "inner speech" enabled him to conclude that "reflective processes" are "as mechanical as habit" (1913a, p. 174). Sechenov had also denied that consciousness and cognition are explanatory causes of behavior, but Watson's position was more radical. Sechenov had maintained that thought is only the proximate cause of behavior, which is itself determined by external environmental stimuli. Watson denied that thought is even the proximate cause of behavior. He maintained that thought is a behavioral response to environmental stimuli that plays no role in the generation of other forms of behavior: He treated thought as an epiphenomenal by-product of the habit mechanisms underlying stimulus-response laws. Watson thus repudiated the central thesis of functional psychology that consciousness and cognition play an "active role in the world of adjustment" (1913a, p. 166).

Watson denied that cognitive states are "centrally initiated" causes of behavior and consequently rejected the ideomotor theory of behavior (1913a, p. 174). He claimed that thoughts are motor responses that can be "integrated into systems which respond in serial order (associative mechanisms)" (1913a, p. 174). Assuming this to be the case, Watson maintained that there is "no theoretical limitation of the behavior method" (1913a, p. 174).

Conversely, in his second Columbia lecture, "Image and Affection in Behavior" (1913b), and in *Behavior: An Introduction to Comparative Psychology* (1914), Watson acknowledged that if cognition was a "centrally initiated process" that played a causal role in the generation of behavior, this would undermine his conception of a behaviorist psychology grounded in laws describing observable stimulus-response sequences. This was because Watson held that the brain and central nervous system are nothing more "than a mechanism for coordinating incoming and outgoing impulses" (1913b, p. 424). For Watson, the possibility of such "centrally initiated" cognitive processes represented the most serious "stumbling block" to the "free passage from structuralism to behaviorism." As he admitted,

> If thought goes on in terms of centrally aroused sensations, as is maintained by the majority of both structural and functional psychologists, we should have to admit that there is a serious limitation on the side of method in behaviorism.
>
> —(1913b, p. 421)

Watson recognized that many psychologists and some "psychologically inclined neurologists" were tempted to locate autonomous cognitive processes in the higher regions of the cerebral cortex, but claimed that this form of neurophysiological dualism was little more than a rearguard action to maintain the traditional conception of an autonomous rational soul:

> When the psychologist threw away the soul he compromised with his conscience by setting up a "mind" which was to remain always hidden and difficult of access. The transfer from periphery to cortex has been the incentive for driving psychology into vain and fruitless searches of the unknown and unknowable.
>
> —(1913b, p. 424)

The Reception of Watson's Behaviorism   Watson's Columbia lectures were well attended, but few rushed to embrace his theoretical position, and it took some time for his form of behaviorism to make inroads into American psychology (Samelson, 1981). Watson's extreme position was rejected by friends and critics alike, such as Calkins, Cattell, McDougall, Washburn, Woodworth, and Yerkes. The strongest criticism came from Angell, who described Watson's position as "scientifically unsound and philosophically essentially illiterate" (letter to Titchener, 1915, quoted in Larson & Sullivan, 1965, p. 342), although Angell refrained from making his views public out of respect for his former student. Titchener's own response was surprisingly muted. However, Titchener refused to acknowledge behaviorism as a form of scientific psychology and insisted that it was merely a technology: "Watson is asking us, in effect, to exchange a science for a technology" (1914, p. 14).

This seems to have been because Titchener valued the experimental rigor of Watson's animal studies but dismissed the theoretical rationale of behaviorism. As he put it in a letter to Watson in 1924, "It is quite true that the logic of the behaviorists is muddled. . . . The strength of the movement lies not in its fundamental logic but in its laboratory performance" (quoted in Larson & Sullivan,

1965, p. 348). Watson and Titchener formed a genuine friendship. Titchener was Watson's houseguest when Johns Hopkins hosted the 1910 meeting of the Experimentalists, and Watson talked of "introspectionists" such as Titchener as his "friendly enemies" (Watson, 1920, p. 97).

For most psychologists, and especially applied psychologists, the primary and enduring attraction of Watson's behaviorist vision was its technological promise of prediction and control (Samelson, 1981). Yet if the forms of applied psychology to which Watson appealed, such as "experimental pedagogy, the psychology of drugs, the psychology of advertising, legal psychology, the psychology of tests, and psychopathology" (1913a, p. 169) owed little or nothing to the experimental analysis of consciousness, they owed little or nothing to behaviorism either. Applied psychologists such as Scott, Witmer, and Wolfe endorsed Watson's appeal for a practically useful psychology, but eschewed his specific theories of behavioral learning.

Watson made some genuine converts, such as Walter Samuel Hunter (1889–1954), who published a number of works supportive of behaviorism (Hunter, 1922, 1925, 1928) and offered the first course on learning in American psychology (Mills, 1998). Within a decade of Watson's Columbia lecture, a number of texts appeared championing Watson's behaviorist position in general psychology (Dunlap, 1922; Smith & Guthrie, 1921), clinical psychology (Burnham, 1924), social psychology (Allport, 1924), and developmental psychology (Mateer, 1918). Yet many psychologists called themselves behaviorists merely as a convenient label for their own independent rejection of an experimental science of consciousness and commitment to applied psychological science. While the established academic "old guard" protested Watson's critical rhetoric, the "silent majority" of applied psychologists continued with their practical explorations in educational, industrial, and clinical psychology (O'Donnell, 1985).

Watson himself had supreme faith in the potential of behaviorism. He believed that a commitment to behaviorist principles would enable psychology to establish a system of laws such that "given the stimulus, psychology can predict what the response will be; or, on the other hand, given the response, it can specify the nature of the effective stimulus" (1919, p. 10).

Learning and Conditioning   Watson claimed that the principles of recency and frequency were sufficient to explain habit formation. He believed that this enabled him to eliminate all references to associations made by an organism:

> When the useless movements are eliminated the correct movements arise serially [on account of their greater frequency] without any chaining or linking in any material sense (bonds, connections, etc.). . . . Stated in other terms, we find no necessity for speaking of "associations."

—(1914, p. 260)

In later years, Watson abandoned this account of habit formation in favor of Pavlov's account of conditioned reflexes, beginning with his 1915 presidential address to the APA titled "The Place of the Conditioned Reflex in Psychology" (Watson, 1916).

Yerkes and Morgulis had introduced Pavlov's work to American psychologists in a paper they published in 1909. Watson also described it in some detail in *Behavior: An Introduction to Comparative Psychology* (1914), and he and his graduate students translated Bechterev's *Objective Psychology* (from the French version of 1913). However, Watson's sudden enthusiasm for conditioned reflexes was a little surprising, given the failure by Watson's colleagues to experimentally replicate either the Pavlovian salivatory reflex (Lashley, 1916) or the Bechterev finger-withdrawal reflex (Hamel, 1919). Watson based his presidential address upon a single study in which he generated conditioned heart rate and foot flexion reflexes in a dog through pairing of a signal with electric shock to its paw (Bolles, 1993). He had originally intended to present the results of experiments conducted in the summer and fall of 1915, in which he and Lashley had tried to record the "faint contractions of musculature" involved in subvocal thought. When this also proved a failure, Watson changed his topic to conditioned reflexes at the last minute.

Watson exploited the principles of classical conditioning to induce a conditioned fear of a white rat in an 11-month-old infant who came to be known as "little Albert." This experiment was based upon research on newborns that Watson had begun in 1916 at the Henry Phipps Psychiatric Clinic in Baltimore, directed by Adolf Meyer. Meyer, then professor of psychiatry at Johns Hopkins, approved of Watson's behaviorist approach and invited him to create a laboratory for the study of child development. As a result of this research, Watson came to believe that although there are a number of innate emotional responses, most are the product of conditioned learning. Working with Rosalie Rayner, one of his graduate students, Watson induced a conditioned fear of rats in Albert by repeatedly pairing the presentation of the white rat with a loud and frightening stimulus, created by smashing a metal rod against a pan lid (Watson & Rayner, 1920). Watson and Rayner intended to extinguish Albert's fear of rats, but he was removed from the institution before they were able to do so (Harris, 1979).

Life's Little Difficulties   By 1919, with the publication of *Psychology From the Point of View of a Behaviorist*, Watson was at the pinnacle of his academic career, and behaviorism was beginning to have a significant impact. However, his academic career came to an abrupt end the following year. He was publicly humiliated as a result of his affair with his graduate student, Rosalie Rayner. While visiting Rayner's parents, Watson's wife discovered love letters between Watson and Rayner, in which he had pledged that "every cell I have is yours." The press pilloried Watson during the sensational divorce trial that followed, in which the judge castigated Watson as "an expert in misbehavior." He was fired from Johns Hopkins in 1920,

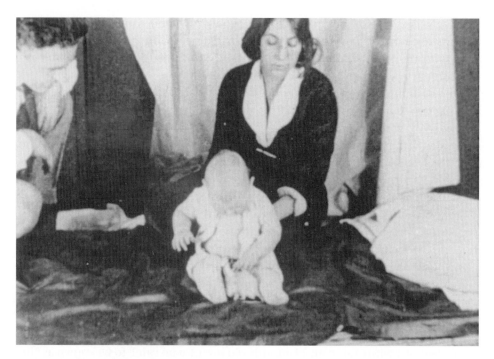

John B. Watson and Little Albert with white rat.

although not because of his affair or his divorce. Watson and Rayner had developed laboratory instruments to measure the physiology of the female orgasm. Meyer demanded that the university fire Watson as a "matter of principle," and Watson was terminated on the grounds of the "moral delinquency" of his orgasm research (Rodgers, 2001).

This made it very difficult for Watson to secure another academic position, and he never did (although he did secure a part-time position as a lecturer at the New School of Social Research in New York). Titchener was one of the few psychologists willing to defend him and to provide him with a letter of reference. Undeterred by what he later called one of "life's little difficulties," Watson turned to a career in advertising, in which he achieved even greater success than he had in academia. He developed strategies for predicting and controlling consumer behavior that were far more effective than any of his earlier forays into animal and human psychology. Watson started with J. Walter Thompson, rising to a vice-presidentship and salary of around $70,000 (over $800,000 today) by 1930, after which he transferred to William Esty & Co. from 1935 to 1945. He increased the sales of products such as Johnson's Baby Powder, Pond's Cold Cream, and Maxwell House Coffee and initiated marketing strategies such as demographic surveys and free samples. He invented the coffee break to sell coffee and introduced candy at supermarket checkouts to ambush mothers and their children.

Although he no longer held an academic position, Watson continued to publish articles and books, including *Behaviorism* in 1924. During the 1920s, mainstream psychology journals continued to publish discussions of his work, although references to it began to decline precipitously after 1935 (Todd, 1994). A Laura Spelman Foundation grant in 1923 enabled Watson to work with Mary Cover Jones on the elimination of conditioned fears (such as those induced in little Albert). Watson and Cover Jones eliminated a fear of rabbits from a child known as Peter (Jones, 1924) via "counterconditioning," by teaching the child to relax in progressive approximations to the fear-inducing stimulus—a technique later characterized as "systematic desensitization" (Wolpe, 1958, 1973).

Watson's Environmentalism   In his last major work, *Behaviorism* (1924/1930), Watson virtually denied the existence of inherited instincts, traits, and abilities (although he had earlier granted the instinctual basis of many forms of animal and human behavior [Watson, 1914]) and proclaimed that, given the resources, a behaviorist psychology could be employed to create any type of human being that society desired:

> Give me a dozen healthy infants, well-formed, and my own specified world to bring them up in and I'll guarantee to take any one at random and train him to become any type of specialist I might select—a doctor, lawyer, artist, merchant-chief and yes, even into beggarman and thief, regardless of his talents, penchants, tendencies, abilities, vocations and race of his ancestors.
>
> —(1924/1930, pp. 103–104)

Watson's extreme environmentalism was not mandated by his positivist commitment to the description, prediction, and control of observable behavior as the goal of scientific psychology. However, it was a view shared by many other behaviorists, especially those critical of McDougall's theory of instincts, such as Knight Dunlap (1919) and Luther Bernard (1921). Perhaps the most extreme environmental behaviorist was Zing-Yang Kuo (1898–1970), a student of Edward C. Tolman's at the University of California at Berkeley, who wrote a series of influential critiques of the concept of instinct (1921, 1924, 1930). Kuo conducted a series of experiments in which kittens were raised with rats and birds, but failed to display supposedly instinctive aggressive and predatory behavior. Kuo returned to China in 1923, where he is said to have introduced behaviorism (Hothersall, 1995), although recent research has cast doubt upon his commitment to it (Blowers, 1998).

Last Years   In 1928 Watson and Rosalie Rayner (now Rosalie Watson) published *The Psychological Care of Infant and Child*. This popular work, which was favorably reviewed by the philosopher Bertrand Russell (who particularly approved of

Watson's advocacy of sex education), sold over 100,000 copies in the first few months. They recommended an austere approach to child-raising, supposedly based upon behaviorist principles, in which overt love and affection were constrained:

> Never hug and kiss them, never let them sit on your lap. If you must, kiss them once on the forehead when they say good night. Shake hands with them in the morning.
>
> —(1928, p. 81)

Such practices were doubtfully effective with Watson's own children. His eldest son, James Watson, later described his father as "unresponsive, emotionally uncommunicative, unable to express and cope with any feelings or emotions of his own" (Hannush, 1987, p. 137). James attempted suicide, and his brother Billy, a psychiatrist and chronic alcoholic, committed suicide. Rosalie later expressed doubts about some of their parenting practices in an article in *Parents Magazine* titled "I Am the Mother of a Behaviorist's Sons" (R. R. Watson, 1930).

Aside from his academic publications and popular books, Watson also published regularly in fashionable magazines such as *Harper's*, *New Republic*, and *Cosmopolitan*. An articulate and persuasive publicist, Watson gave regular radio talks and newspaper interviews, and in later years he became somewhat of a celebrity. He built himself a mansion in Connecticut from the proceeds of his popular books and remuneration from his work in advertising. Watson was by all accounts a handsome and charming man and a snappy dresser who enjoyed the good life. He was also a hard drinker and incorrigible womanizer. Although McDougall officially won the debate with Watson known as "the battle of behaviorism" (Watson & McDougall, 1929), he wryly noted that Watson had secured all of the female votes.

While Watson surmounted many of "life's little difficulties," he never managed to cope with the death of his wife Rosalie in 1935 (from a fever contracted on an overseas trip). He had more or less abandoned psychology by then and in later years became somewhat of a recluse. He sold his mansion in Connecticut and drowned his sorrows in alcohol when he failed to consume them with his work in advertising.

Watson was awarded an APA citation in 1957 for his contribution to psychology, which stated that he had "initiated a revolution in psychological thought" (Karier, 1986, p. 148). At the age of 79, he traveled to the New York hotel where the convention ceremony was being held, but at the last moment could not bring himself to go in—his eldest son Billy went instead to acknowledge the honor (Buckley, 1989). Watson's legacy remained ambiguous for many psychologists, including neobehaviorists, who were reluctant to acknowledge him as an intellectual predecessor. It was hard to find someone willing to write Watson's obituary when he died the following year (according to Franz Samelson, cited in Mills, 1998).

On the farm: John B. Watson in retirement.

MENTAL TESTING, IMMIGRATION, AND STERILIZATION

Watson and later behaviorists extended their principles of learning based upon experimental studies of animal behavior to encompass all forms of animal and human behavior and treated them as the foundation of their technologies of prediction and control. This explanatory imperialism exposed them to later critiques of the scope of their theories by ethologists, animal psychologists, and cognitive psychologists. However, behaviorists were not the only ones who overreached themselves in the early decades of the 20th century. Other psychologists realized Wundt's and Titchener's fears in their attempt to transform psychology from a "science of trivialities" to a "science of human engineering" through programs of mental testing (Terman, 1924, p. 106).

Cattell's attempt to develop mental testing at Columbia based upon Galton's theory that sensory acuity is significantly correlated with intelligence came to grief when Wissler's studies indicated that there was no significant correlation between mental test scores and course grades (Wissler, 1901). However, mental testing did not die out with Cattell's anthropometric program. The British psychologist Charles Spearman (1863–1945), a former student of Wundt's, was highly critical of Wissler's results and claimed that his own research demonstrated a strong correlation between measures of sensory acuity and intelligence (Spearman, 1904). He maintained that the various tests he employed were measures of a common capacity that he called "general intelligence" (g). A dedicated Galtonian, Spearman claimed that this capacity is determined by inheritance. Many American psychologists accepted this view and developed programs of mental testing based mainly upon measures of intelligence, but also upon measures of attitude, aptitude, development, mental health, and personality.

The Binet-Simon Intelligence Test

Alfred Binet (1857–1911), director of the laboratory of physiological psychology at the Sorbonne and editor of the journal *L'Année Psychologique*, developed a series of tests designed to identify retarded but educable children in the French elementary school system, which had expanded dramatically in the late 19th century when primary education became compulsory. Binet first described these tests, which included measures of association, sentence completion (derived from Ebbinghaus), memory, and moral judgment in *Experimental Studies of Intelligence* in 1903.

With his research assistant, Theodore Simon (1873–1961), Binet published a series of papers in *L'Année Psychologique* in 1905 describing a new scale for measuring child intelligence (Binet & Simon, 1905a, 1905b, 1905c). This scale, which included 30 items ranked in order of difficulty, was administered to large numbers of schoolchildren between 1905 and 1908. The scale was revised in 1908, with 54 tests arranged according to appropriate age levels between 3 and 13, ensuring that most children would test according to age (so that an average 10-year-old would test at age 10). The Binet-Simon scale (revised again in 1911, just before Binet's death) was a great success in Europe and was translated into a variety of languages. It provided an objective measure of general intelligence that was easy to administer, although Binet and Simon stressed the limitations of their test.

Binet and Simon employed the term "mental level" rather than the later and more popular "mental age" (Stern, 1914) to characterize the appropriate age levels. This was because they held that their scale was a useful instrument for identifying children in need of special remedial education and not a measure of a fixed level of intelligence. They devised special programs of education by which they hoped to raise the mental level of retarded children.

However, such caution was thrown to the winds when Henry H. Goddard and Lewis M. Terman (1877–1956) imported the Binet-Simon scale to America. Goddard, an energetic and enthusiastic graduate of Clark University, became director of the research laboratory for the study of feeblemindedness at the Vineland Training School for Feeble-Minded Girls and Boys in New Jersey in 1906. He translated the 1908 Binet-Simon scale into English (with only minor revisions) and trained teachers at local schools to administer and score the test. He also translated the revised 1911 Binet-Simon scale (Goddard, 1911), which became the standard American intelligence test until Lewis Terman brought out his version in 1916.

Lewis M. Terman was a farm boy from Indiana who excelled at school and college and secured a fellowship at Clark University in 1903. He gained his PhD in 1905 with a bluntly titled dissertation on "Genius and Stupidity" (Terman, 1906). Terman moved to California for health reasons, and after a few years as principal of San Bernardino High School and as professor of pedagogy at Los Angeles State Normal College, he became professor of child study at Stanford University in 1910. There he remained for the rest of his career, serving as chair of the department of psychology for many years. Terman's 1916 revision of the Binet-Simon scale was more than a translation: It included 36 additional items and was calibrated in relation to a substantial standardization sample drawn from California schools. The Stanford-Binet scale, as it came to be known, was designed to ensure that the average child at any age between 5 and 16 would test at that age. Thus the average 10-year-old would test at the "mental age" of 10, and the average "intelligence quotient" (IQ) for any age would be 100. Terman defined the **intelligence quotient** (IQ) as Stern's "mental quotient" (the ratio of mental age to chronological age) multiplied by 100. The Stanford-Binet scale became the standard American intelligence test until it was itself revised in 1937.

Goddard and the Feebleminded

Goddard and Terman did not follow Binet and Simon in treating their scales as merely useful instruments for identifying children in need of remedial education. Rather, they treated them as objective measures of genetically determined levels of intelligence, to be employed in interventionist programs of social engineering. Goddard's study of a New England family, *The Kallikak Family: A Study in Feeblemindedness* (1912), purported to demonstrate the inheritance of intelligence and feeblemindedness. Goddard, who had read Galton and heard about Mendel's work while visiting Germany, believed that intelligence and feeblemindedness were inherited. He had learned from his experience at Vineland that the relatives of feebleminded persons (individuals with an IQ of less than 70) were often feebleminded themselves. When Goddard came across a girl of 22 who tested with a mental age of 9, whom he called Deborah Kallikak, he set about retracing her family tree.

According to Goddard and his researchers, Deborah's family tree could be traced back to one Martin Kallikak, a Revolutionary War soldier. Martin Kallikak had come from good Quaker stock and had married a maidenly Quaker girl who bore him seven children. The descendants of this "good" side of the family tree went on to become upstanding citizens, who served as lawyers, doctors, judges, teachers, and landed gentry. However, Martin had also dallied with a feebleminded

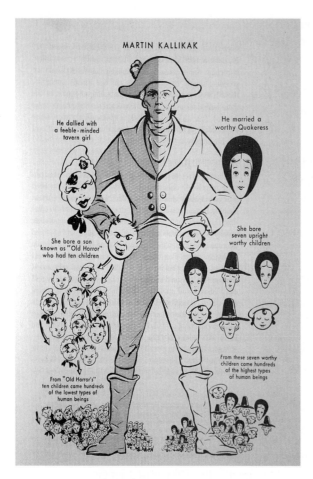

MARTIN KALLIKAK

He dallied with a feeble-minded tavern girl

He married a worthy Quakeress

She bore a son known as "Old Horror" who had ten children

She bore seven upright worthy children

From these seven worthy children come hundreds of the highest types of human beings

From "Old Horror's" ten children came hundreds of the lowest types of human beings

Representation of the "good" and "bad" descendants of Martin Kallikak.

serving wench while intoxicated. She had born him an illegitimate son, Martin Kallikak, Junior, who fathered seven children by his own marriage. The descendants of this "bad" side of the family tree went on to become immoral and sexually licentious horse thieves, prostitutes, brothel owners, and alcoholics—clear indicators of feeblemindedness (the original Martin Kallikak's own sexual licentiousness and intoxication was conveniently ignored).

Although Goddard called the study a "natural experiment," there was no attempt to control for environmental or social differences, and his conclusion that feeblemindedness is inherited was based upon the implausible assumption that it is determined by a recessive gene. Nonetheless, many accepted his conclusions, which were widely cited. Goddard's study served as a paradigm for a host of similar (but equally flawed) studies of the inheritance of intelligence and feeblemindedness and was seen as a scientifically reputable version of Richard Dugdale's (1877) earlier study of the Jukes, an upstate New York family with an ancestry of degeneracy and criminality. The phrase "Jukes and Kallikaks" was later employed to describe problem families of dubious heritage (Zenderland, 1998).

Goddard also managed to persuade immigration officers at Ellis Island that he was able to identify the feebleminded among the increasing numbers of eastern and southern Europeans of "poor stock" (in comparison to northern and western Europeans of "good stock") then immigrating to the United States. The inspectors were particularly impressed by Goddard's ability to identity the feebleminded by sight and then have his identification "objectively" confirmed by their low scores on the Binet-Simon test (although the translators who administered the test complained that they would not have been able to answer questions about the New York Giants when they first came to America). As immigration inspectors began to make use of Goddard's intelligence tests (and the intuitive judgments of Goddard's Vineland staff), they refused entry to increasing numbers of immigrants on grounds of feeblemindedness.

Intelligence testing at Ellis Island

The First World War and the Army Testing Project

The contribution of psychologists to the First World War enormously boosted the public profile of mental testing and American psychology. Titchener's Experimentalists were meeting at Harvard when America's entry to the war was announced on April 6, 1917. They convened a special session (from which Titchener excused himself) to discuss the proposed contribution of psychologists, which was chaired by Robert M. Yerkes, then president of the APA. Although he was primarily a comparative psychologist at Harvard, Yerkes also worked as a consulting psychologist at Boston State Psychopathic Hospital, where he developed the Yerkes-Bridges Point Scale of Intelligence (Yerkes, Bridges, & Hardwick, 1915).

A born organizer, Yerkes lost no time in following the Experimentalists' recommendation that he visit Canada to study the role that Canadian psychologists had played in the war (as a British Dominion, Canada had entered the war with the Allies in 1914). A few days later, he met with Carl C. Brigham of the Canadian Military Hospitals Commission. At the meeting of the APA Council in Philadelphia later that month, Yerkes formed a committee, which included him, Cattell, Hall, Thorndike, and Watson, to explore the ways that psychologists could contribute to the war effort.

One proposal was to develop forms of psychological examination to facilitate the selection of officers and the discharge of feebleminded recruits. Yerkes formed the Committee on Methods of Psychological Examining for Recruits, while Walter Dill Scott (who had a falling-out with Yerkes, whom Scott believed to be promoting his own interests) formed the Committee on the Classification of Personnel in the Army (CCPA). Yerkes's committee, which included Terman and Goddard, along with other educational, vocational, and medical testers, spent two weeks at Vineland creating intelligence tests for the army and running trials of these tests at local institutions and a few selected army bases. Recognizing that individual testing would be too time-consuming, they developed a number of group intelligence tests.

They submitted their proposal to test army recruits through the **National Research Council**, the national body founded in 1916 to administer government-funded natural science research projects. When the army approved what came to be known as the **Army Testing Project**, it created a division of psychology within the Sanitary Corps, which operated under the office of the Surgeon General (Scott's Committee on the Classification of Personnel operated under the office of the Adjutant General). The Army Testing Project eventually employed a team of over 400 army personnel who administered group intelligence tests to all army recruits: The Alpha test to literate soldiers, and the Beta (pictorial) test to those

Group intelligence testing of recruits in the First World War.

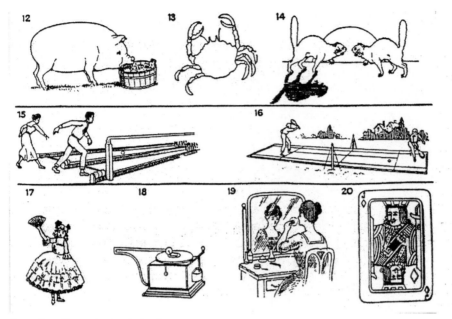

Army Beta Test: what's missing?

who could not read or could not read English. By the time the program ended in early 1919, they had tested close to 2 million soldiers.

Putting Psychology on the Map   The practical utility of such mass testing was doubtful. Aside from the discharge of a small percentage of soldiers on grounds of mental incompetence (high levels of intelligence were not really necessary for the slaughter of trench warfare), the army accepted few of the recommendations of Yerkes's committee and discontinued the Army Testing Project after the war ended (Samelson, 1977). Nonetheless, many recognized that large-scale mental testing could have increased efficiency in the army and reduced costs (O'Donnell, 1985). The Army Testing Project, and the acknowledged success of Scott's committee on personnel classification, served to promote the public perception of the utility of mental testing and the public reputation of psychologists, with publications like the *New York Times* and *Harper's* magazine lauding their "achievement." As Cattell remarked, the Army Testing Project "put psychology on the map of the United States, extending in some cases beyond these limits into fairyland" (1922, p. 5).

Many psychologists who worked on the various army committees found the experience exciting and stimulating—and more rewarding than traditional academic life. Yerkes himself regretted that the war did not last longer! (O'Donnell, 1985). The emotional satisfaction of having their professional contributions recognized inspired and encouraged many psychologists to extend their practical war experience to the resolution of peacetime problems. Yerkes and Angell

Psychology Magazine, 1928.

were appointed to the National Research Council, which sponsored the development of the **National Intelligence Test** for children (National Research Council, 1920). This was financed by a Rockefeller grant of $25 thousand and administered to over 7 million schoolchildren in the 1920s. Carl Brigham, the Canadian psychologist who later moved to Princeton, used the Army Alpha Test (which he had helped to develop) as the basis of the Scholastic Aptitude Test (SAT), which was first introduced as an admissions test for Princeton applicants.

Whatever the reality, the public believed that psychologists had developed a simple and effective means of measuring intelligence, and business and industry increased their demand for psychological testing services in order to promote their own efficiency and cost-cutting. The popularity of psychology increased dramatically in the 1920s, amidst the euphoria and general economic prosperity that followed victory in the First World War (Sokal, 1984). Promoters of the practical utility of psychology wrote articles for magazines such as *Harper's, Colliers,* and *Atlantic Monthly*; and Joseph Jastrow contributed a syndicated daily newspaper column titled "Keeping Mentally Fit" (Jastrow, 1928, cited in Benjamin & Bryant, 1997). In his column "Exploring the Mind," the journalist Albert Wiggam touted the potential of psychology as an instrument of personal and social change:

> Men and women never needed psychology as much as they need it today. You cannot achieve these things [effectiveness and happiness] in the fullest measure without the new knowledge of your own mind and the personality that the psychologists have given us.
>
> —(1928, p. 13)

The 1920s saw the publication of the first wave of self-help books, with newspapers and magazines offering extensive psychological advice on a variety of issues, such as marriage, adolescence, depression, and child rearing. The 1920s also saw the founding of the first popular psychology magazines (Benjamin & Bryant, 1997), such as *Psychology: Health, Happiness, Success* (founded 1923), *The Psychological Review of Reviews* (founded 1923), and *Industrial Psychology Monthly* (founded 1926). The public appetite for psychological knowledge and services provided new opportunities for educational, industrial, and clinical and counseling psychologists, but also for individuals with no psychological training who professed to psychological knowledge. Concerned with such developments, applied psychologists pressed the APA to develop a program of certification for psychologists, but with little success in the ensuing decades.

Immigration and Sterilization

Unfortunately, the new self-confidence of applied psychologists led them down a number of dangerous roads. One alarming finding of the Army Testing Project was that around half of the army recruits tested at or below the level of **moron**, defined by Goddard as between the mental age of 8 and 12 (with an IQ of between 50 and 70). Goddard claimed that the army test results demonstrated that "half the human race [is] little above the moron" (1919, p. 234). In his final report on the Army Testing Project, Yerkes concluded that "feeblemindedness . . . is of much greater frequency than had previously been supposed" (Yerkes, 1921, p. 789). This generated a moral panic among psychologists and the public at large and accelerated two developments that had begun before the war, based upon assumptions about the inheritance of intelligence and feeblemindedness: the demand for immigration quotas and sterilization programs.

A number of works painted bleak pictures of the consequences of allowing immigrants from eastern and southern Europe to contaminate the gene pool of the original Nordic (northern and western European) settlers. Carl Brigham argued in *A Study of American Intelligence* (1923, with a forward by Yerkes) that the average intelligence of recent immigrants was less than that of native-born Americans and that average intelligence had been decreasing significantly since 1900. Racist fears about the overbreeding of new immigrants (supposedly a sign of feeblemindedness in itself) and claims about the intellectual and moral superiority of the Nordic race were developed in Madison Grant's *The Passing of the Great Race* (1916). McDougall's *Is America Safe for Democracy?* (1921) contained specific recommendations for programs of positive and negative eugenics to reverse the perceived downtrend in levels of intelligence. Goddard's own *Human Efficiency and Levels of Intelligence* (1920) expressed dark thoughts about the future of democracy and argued that the average mental age of other races, including blacks, was much lower than the average mental age of (male) whites. He recommended that intelligence tests should be employed to disenfranchise those of low intelligence, as well as to determine the suitability of job applicants.

A few psychologists urged caution and warned about the dangers of jumping to conclusions on the basis of limited data (Boring, 1923). Watson and the anthropologist Franz Boas vigorously challenged hereditarian assumptions about intelligence. Perhaps the most pointed critic was the journalist Walter Lippmann (1889–1974), who in a series of articles in the *New Republic* (which he founded) poured scorn upon the idea that psychologists had developed objective measures of intelligence. He dismissed the claim that the average intelligence of adult Americans was little above the level of a moron as equivalent to the absurd claim that the average intelligence of adults was below the average intelligence of adults (Lippmann, 1922). According to Lippmann, those who lamented the Army Testing Project estimate of the average mental age of 13 (Yerkes, 1921) were comparing this estimate with the average mental age of 16 estimated by the Stanford-Binet revision of 1916 (based upon a sample of white adults), which only demonstrated the inconsistency of the different estimates of average intelligence (a point echoed by Freeman, 1922). Lippmann identified the intelligence testing movement for what he believed it to be—an "engine of cruelty" based upon the "pretentiousness" of psychologists and the "abuse of the scientific method" (Passmore, 1978).

To little avail. The Army Testing Project also indicated a progressive decline in the intelligence of foreign-born soldiers when northern and western Europeans were compared to southern and eastern Europeans. Yerkes, in his introduction to Brigham's *A Study of American Intelligence* (1923), echoed Galton's and Pearson's earlier concerns about British "national efficiency" by dramatizing "the menace of race deterioration" in America and "the evident relations of immigration to national progress and welfare" (Yerkes, 1923, pp. vii–viii, cited in Samelson, 1977, p. 278). Social and political concerns about the pollution of the "national stock" and Nordic gene pool by overbreeding hordes of Poles, Russians, Lithuanians, Jews, Irish, and other races led to the passing of the **National Origins Act** in 1924, which imposed quotas on each nationality based upon the 1890 census (before the post-1900 wave of eastern and southern European immigration).

Goddard and Terman served on the 1914 **Committee for the Heredity of Feeblemindedness**, which also included Thorndike, Yerkes, Walter B. Cannon, and Alexander Graham Bell. The committee recommended a negative eugenics program: the sterilization of mental defectives, along with other "defective classes" such as criminals and the insane. The first state law licensing the sterilization of the feebleminded was passed in Indiana in 1907, although it was eventually struck down by the state supreme court. However, other states followed the committee's recommendation and introduced **sterilization laws** in the decades that followed. By the end of the 1920s close to 30 states had such laws on their books, and by 1930 around 12,000 people had been compulsorily sterilized.

This was the natural consequence of an age and scientific psychology "saturated with the development of a pragmatic theory of life" (Buchner, 1911, p. 3), and it represented the institutional realization of the pragmatist vision of James's

Metaphysical Society at Harvard in the 1870s. Supreme Court Justice Oliver Wendell Holmes, one of the original members of the Metaphysical Society, wrote the majority decision in the case of **Buck vs. Bell** in 1927. The case challenged the right of the Commonwealth of Virginia to sterilize Carrie Buck, an 18-year-old inmate of the State Colony for Epileptics and Feeble-Minded. The commonwealth maintained that Carrie had a mental age of 9 years and that both her mother and 7-month-old daughter were feebleminded (Zenderland, 1998). Writing in favor of compulsory sterilization, Holmes claimed,

> It is better for all the world if instead of waiting to execute degenerate offspring for crime, or to let them starve for their imbecility, society can prevent those who are manifestly unfit from continuing their kind. . . . Three generations of imbeciles are enough.
>
> —(1927, p. 207)

The dangers of such overreaching science were fully recognized only when the Nazis followed McDougall's (1921) recommendations for increasing the Nordic stock by introducing weekend retreats for blond and blue-eyed SS officers to breed with blonde and blue-eyed fräulein and created extermination camps as a logical extension of their own massive sterilization program for defective classes, including criminals, gypsies, and Jews. In 1930 Carl Brigham rejected his earlier racist views as "without foundation" and described his *Study of American Intelligence* (1923) as "one of the most pretentious of these comparative racial studies" (cited in Samelson, 1977, p. 278). (Brigham also later repudiated the use of the SAT for educational testing and opposed the formation of the Educational Testing Service.) By this time many of the more grandiose claims about the practical applications of scientific psychology to education, industry, and clinical practice were being questioned by a more skeptical public and more cautious government agencies, and the public image of psychology did not revive until after the Second World War. However, the immigration and sterilization laws remained in effect for a long time afterward. The Commonwealth of Virginia repealed the last sterilization law as late as 1981 (a formal apology to the victims of the law was issued 20 years later).

Yet the voices were not stilled for long. During the 1940s the British government instituted a national program of intelligence testing in schools (the "11-plus" test) that streamed students into academic and trade classes on the basis of their performance. The program was created by Cyril Burt (1833–1971), a committed hereditarian who held the chair in psychology at University College, London, founded by Galton. Burt was knighted in 1946 for his services to psychology and education, but in the mid-1970s serious doubts (including accusations of fabrication and fraud) were cast on the authenticity of his twin studies, which were frequently cited in support of hereditarian accounts of intelligence (Kamin, 1974; Samelson, 1992).

In the late 1960s Arthur Jensen's (1969) promotion of the claim that the (largely) genetic basis of intelligence renders educational interventions (such as Head Start) ineffective created a fierce debate and campus protests. In the 1990s Charles Murray and Richard J. Herrnstein reopened the debate with their claims about the genetic determination of intelligence and its correlation to socioeconomic status in *The Bell Curve* (Murray & Herrnstein, 1994).

THE STATUS OF APPLIED PSYCHOLOGY

While most of the American pioneers of scientific psychology did not share Wundt's and Titchener's antipathy to applied psychology and developed programs devoted to educational, industrial, and clinical psychology, they remained reluctant to grant the status of "scientific psychologist" to those whose psychological work was purely applied. The APA, which was originally founded by academic psychologists committed to experimental research, was also disinclined to accept purely applied psychologists, such as those working as clinical or consulting psychologists in hospitals or in private practice or those employed in testing and personnel selection for public companies. Part of the motivation for the creation of Titchener's Experimentalists (supported by applied psychologists such as Witmer, who had the original idea) was to develop a society of professional scientific psychologists, to distinguish themselves from unqualified charlatans who merely professed to have psychological knowledge.

In 1915 consulting psychologists petitioned the APA to create a program for the certification of psychologists, in order to protect the public and to establish their own professional status as experts. The APA leadership declined to act, citing the primary commitment of the association to the advancement of psychology as a science (Benjamin et al., 2003). Despite the lauded contributions of applied psychologists during the First World War, by the end of the war the 300-odd membership of the APA was restricted to academics with research credentials (a PhD, academic position in psychology, and publications in mainstream psychology journals).

Dissatisfied with this situation, Leta S. Hollingworth, J. E. Wallace Wallin, and Rudolf Pinter formed the American Association of Clinical Psychologists (AACP) in 1917. The aim of the association was to create professional standards for clinicians and mental testers and to attain legal recognition of clinical psychologists as authorities in the fields of psychopathology and mental retardation. Of the original 45 members of the AACP, some were affiliated with universities, while others worked in applied settings such as hospitals or child guidance clinics. The AACP sponsored a symposium on professional issues at the 1918 meeting of the APA, but the association was short-lived. Robert Yerkes, then president of the APA, managed to persuade the clinicians that their interests would be better served by becoming a section of the APA. Yerkes was a member of both the APA and the AACP, but was deeply concerned about the dangers of a split between them.

In 1919 the AACP disbanded itself to become the Clinical Section of the APA, whose stated aim was to establish links between clinical psychology and other applied fields, to encourage research and publication, and to develop professional standards in clinical psychology (Napoli, 1981). A second APA section for consulting psychology was established in 1921, although requests for additional sections for industrial and educational psychology were denied (Routh & Reisman, 2003). The APA established a certification program of sorts in 1924, but merely issued certificates of professional acknowledgment that had no legal status. Few psychologists applied for them, and the program was abandoned in 1928 (Sokal, 1982). In 1925 the APA introduced a form of associate membership for applied psychologists who lacked academic credentials (such as employment in university departments and journal publications). This swelled the official membership of the APA but did little to advance the interests of applied psychologists, since the new associate membership did not carry voting rights.

Calls for a code of professional ethics and changes in graduate training to include applied experience and internships were largely ignored by the APA, although a committee of the Clinical Section of the APA was formed in 1931 to set standards for clinical training. Four years later the committee recommended that clinical psychologists should have a PhD and a year of practical experience (Report of Committee, 1935), although little was done to implement this recommendation (far less enforce it). Dissatisfied with the lack of support from the APA, the New York Association of Consulting Psychologists (founded in 1921), the largest of the state associations of applied psychologists, reorganized itself as the national Association of Consulting Psychologists (ACP) in 1930. The ACP pressed for legal standards and recognition and published a code of professional ethics in 1933. *The Journal of Consulting Psychology* was founded in 1937 as the official organ of the association.

The early 1930s saw the beginning of a development that later come to haunt the APA: The number of applied or "consulting" psychologists began to grow at a faster rate than the number of traditional academic or "scientific" psychologists. In 1938 the danger that Yerkes had foreseen came to pass. Dissatisfied with their influence within the APA, most of the members of the Clinical Division of the APA joined with members of the ACP to form the American Association for Applied Psychology (AAAP), which adopted the *Journal of Consulting Psychology* as its official organ. The Clinical Division of the APA and the ACP consequently disbanded themselves (although many AAAP members retained their APA membership). The AAAP originally comprised four sections, clinical, consulting, industrial, and educational, with their own officers, committees, and program at the annual meeting of the AAAP. Although the split was temporary, the tensions remained even after the AAAP disbanded when the APA was reformed and reconstituted in 1944 as a divisional federation (with a structure modeled upon the sectional organization of the AAAP).

DISCUSSION QUESTIONS

1. Did functional psychology owe anything to Darwin?

2. Woodworth dismissed the exclusive claims of the various schools of psychology and maintained that "every school is good, though no one is good enough." Woodworth cited the schools of structural psychology, functional psychology, behaviorism, Gestalt psychology, and psychoanalysis. Can all these schools be held to be good together? Are they consistent?

3. Were "centrally initiated" cognitive states such a threat to Watson's behaviorism as he supposed? Could he have accommodated them within his behaviorist system?

4. Although Binet and Simon stressed that their measures of child intelligence were merely useful instruments for identifying children who could benefit from remedial education, American translators and revisers of the Binet-Simon scale such as Goddard and Terman treated them as measures of genetically determined levels of intelligence. Why do you think this was the case? Do you think it had anything to do with their different national backgrounds?

5. Moral panic about the breeding of the feebleminded fueled racist fears and led to immigration restrictions and sterilization programs. Are eugenics programs too dangerous to be implemented in the present day? While the dangers of negative eugenics are obvious, what are the dangers of positive eugenics (e.g., government support for the families of individuals who score high on intelligence tests)?

GLOSSARY

Army Testing Project The group intelligence testing of around 2 million army recruits during the First World War.

behaviorism 1. Form of psychology that treats observable behavior as the subject matter of scientific psychology. 2. Form of behaviorism developed by John B. Watson, who saw psychology as a positivist science restricted to the correlation of observable stimuli and responses, and rejected mentalistic explanations of behavior.

***Buck vs. Bell* (1927)** Supreme Court case in which Carrie Buck's appeal against compulsory sterilization was denied.

Committee for the Heredity of Feeble-Mindedness Committee established in 1914 whose members recommended the compulsory sterilization of mental defectives.

conditioned response An originally innate reflexive response that has come to function as a conditioned response through the repeated pairing of the originally eliciting stimulus with a neutral stimulus, which then comes to function as a conditioned stimulus.

connectionism Term employed by Thorndike to describe his theory of trial-and-error learning, in terms of automatic connections between situations and responses.

disinhibition The tendency of any strong stimulus to elicit a conditioned response after some time has passed since extinction.

extinction The attenuation of a conditioned response when a conditioned stimulus is no longer paired with an unconditioned stimulus.

functional psychology Form of psychology concerned with the functions of consciousness for adaptive behavior and associated with approaches to psychology developed at the University of Chicago and Columbia University.

intelligence quotient Measure introduced by Lewis Terman, defined as Stern's mental quotient (the ratio of mental age to chronological age) multiplied by 100.

law of effect According to Thorndike, responses that lead to satisfaction for an animal are more likely to be repeated, and responses that lead to discomfort are less likely to be repeated.

law of exercise According to Thorndike, the strength of a connection between a response and situation increases as a function of the vigor and duration of the connection.

moron As defined by Henry Goddard, an adult with a mental age between 8 and 12 (with an IQ between 50 and 70).

National Origins Act Congressional act of 1924 that restricted U.S. immigration to nationality quotas based upon the 1890 census.

National Research Council National body formed in 1916 to administer government-funded natural science research projects.

National Intelligence Test Group test of intelligence sponsored by the National Research Council and administered to over 7 million children in the 1920s.

neobehaviorism Form of behaviorist psychology originally developed by Edward C. Tolman and Clark L. Hull, which treated observable behavior as the subject matter of scientific psychology, but recognized the legitimacy of mentalistic explanations of behavior.

new realism Philosophical theory that held that consciousness and cognition are best explicated in terms of behavioral adjustments to the environment.

practice theory of reaction time Theory of Baldwin and Cattell that motor reaction times are often longer than sensory reaction times and that there are significant individual differences in both sensory and motor reaction times that are a product of differences in practice and attention.

radical behaviorism Form of behaviorism developed by B. F. Skinner and his followers, which treated observable behavior as the subject matter of scientific psychology, but rejected mentalistic explanations of behavior.

spontaneous recovery The tendency of a conditioned stimulus to elicit a conditioned response after extinction.

sterilization laws State laws passed in the early decades of the 20th century licensing the compulsory sterilization of the feebleminded.

type theory of reaction time Theory of Wundt and Titchener that sensory reaction times are longer than motor reaction times.

REFERENCES

Allport, F. (1924). *Social psychology.* Boston: Houghton Mifflin.

Allport, F. H. (1933). *Institutional behavior.* Chapel Hill, NC: University of North Carolina Press.

Angell, J. R. (1904). *Psychology: An introduction to the structure and function of consciousness.* New York: Holt.

Angell, J. R. (1907). The province of functional psychology. *Psychological Review, 14,* 61–91.

Angell, J. R. (1909). The influence of Darwin on psychology. *Psychological Review, 16,* 152–169.

Angell, J. R. (1913). Behavior as a category of psychology. *Psychological Review, 20,* 255–270.

Angell, J. R. (1936). James Roland Angell. In C. Murchison (Ed.), *A history of psychology in autobiography.* New York: Russell & Russell.

Baldwin, J. M. (1889). *Handbook of psychology: Vol. 1. Senses and intellect.* New York: Holt.

Baldwin, J. M. (1891). *Handbook of psychology: Vol. 2. Feeling and will.* New York: Holt.

Baldwin, J. M. (1895a). Types of reaction. *Psychological Review, 2,* 259–273.

Baldwin, J. M. (1895b). *Mental development in the child and the race.* New York: Macmillan.

Baldwin, J. M. (1896). The "type-theory" of reaction. *Mind, 5,* 81–90.

Baldwin, J. M. (1897). *Social and ethical interpretations in mental development.* New York: Macmillan.

Baldwin, J. M. (1901). *Dictionary of philosophy and psychology.* New York: Macmillan.

Baldwin, J. M. (1902). *Development and evolution.* New York: Macmillan.

Baldwin, J. M. (1909). *Darwin and the humanities.* Baltimore: Review Publishing.

Baldwin, J. M. (1911). *The individual and society.* New York: Macmillan.

Baldwin, J. M. (1913). *History of psychology.* New York: Putnam.

Baldwin, J. M. (1926). *Between two wars, 1861–1921.* London: Stratford.

Bechterev, V. M. (1913). *La psychologie objective* [*Objective psychology*]. Paris: F. Alcan. (Original work published 1907–1912)

Bechterev, V. M. (1932). *General principles of human reflexology* (E. Murphy & W. Murphy, Trans.). New York: International. (Original work published 1917)

Benjamin, L. T., Jr., & Bryant, W. H. M. (1997). A history of popular psychology magazines in America. In W. G. Bringmann, H. E. Lück, R. Miller, & C. E. Early (Eds.), *A pictorial history of psychology.* Chicago: Quintessence.

Benjamin, L. T., Jr., DeLeon, P. H., Freedheim, D. K., & Vandenbos, G. R. (2003). Psychology as a profession. In D. K. Freedheim (Ed.), *Handbook of psychology: Vol. 1. History of psychology.* Hoboken, NJ: Wiley.

Bernard, L. L. (1919). The objective method in sociology. *American Journal of Sociology, 25,* 298–325.

Bernard, L. L. (1921). The use of instinct in the social sciences. *Psychological Review, 28,* 96–119.

Binet, A. (1903). *L'étude expérimentale de l'intelligence* [Experimental studies of intelligence]. Paris: Schleicher.

Binet, A., & Simon, T. (1905a). Sur la necessité d'etablir un diagnostic scientifique des états inférieurs de l'intelligence [On the necessity of establishing a scientific diagnosis of inferior states of intelligence]. *L'Année Psychologique, 11,* 163–190.

Binet, A., & Simon, T. (1905b). Méthodes nouvelles pour le diagnostic du niveau intellectuel des anormaux [New methods for the diagnosis of the intellectual level of the abnormal]. *L'Année Psychologique, 11,* 191–244.

Binet, A., & Simon, T. (1905c). Applications des méthodes nouvelles au diagnostic du niveau intellectuel chez des enfants normaux et abnormaux d'hospice et d'école primaire [Applications of new methods of the diagnosis of intellectual level with normal and abnormal infants in the hospital and primary school]. *L'Année Psychologique, 11,* 245–336.

Blowers, G. (1998). Was Z. Y. Kuo (Guo Renyuan) a radical behaviorist? *Proceedings of the 30th Annual Meeting of Cheiron* (The International Society for the History of Behavioral and Social Sciences), University of San Diego, June 18–21.

Boakes, R. (1984). *From Darwin to behaviorism: Psychology and the minds of animals.* Cambridge: Cambridge University Press.

Bolles, R. C. (1993). *The story of psychology: A thematic history.* Belmont, CA: Wadsworth.

Boring, E. G. (1923). Facts and fancies of immigration. *New Republic,* 245–246.

Brigham, C. C. (1923). *A study of American intelligence.* Princeton: Princeton University Press.

Bruner, J. S., & Allport, G. W. (1940). Fifty years of change in American psychology. *Psychological Review, 37,* 757–756.

Bryan, W. L., & Harter, N. (1897). Studies in the physiology and psychology of the telegraphic language. *Psychological Review, 4,* 27–53.

Buchner, E. F. (1911). Psychological progress in 1910. *Psychological Bulletin, 8,* 1–10.

Buckley, K. W. (1989). *Mechanical man: John Broadus Watson and the beginnings of behaviorism.* New York: Guilford Press.

Burnham, W. H. (1924). *The normal mind.* New York: Harper.

Carr, H. C. (1925). *Psychology: A study of mental activity.* New York: Longmans Green.

Carr, H. C. (1935). *An introduction to visual space perception.* New York: Longmans Green.

Carr, H. C., & Watson, J. B. (1908). Orientation in the white rat. *Journal of Comparative Neurology and Psychology, 18,* 27–44.

Cattell, J. M. (1896). Address of the president before the American Psychological Association, 1895. *Psychological Review, 3,* 134–158.

Cattell, J. M. (1904). The conceptions and methods of psychology. *Popular Science Monthly, 66,* 176–186.

Cattell, J. M. (1922). The first year of the Psychological Corporation. Report at Annual Meeting of the Psychological Corporation, December 1. Lewis M. Terman Papers, Stanford University Archives.

Cohen, J. (1979). *J. B. Watson: The founder of behaviorism.* London: Routledge & Kegan Paul.

Creelan, P. G. (1974). Watsonian behaviorism and the Calvinist conscience. *Journal of the History of the Behavioral Sciences, 10,* 183–189.

De Laguna, G. (1919). Emotion and perception from the behaviorist standpoint. *Psychological Review, 26,* 409–427.

Dewey, J. (1886a). *Psychology.* New York: Harper & Brothers.

Dewey, J. (1886b). Soul and body. *Bibliotheca Sacra, 43,* 239–263.

Dewey, J. (1896). The reflex arc concept in psychology. *Psychological Review, 3,* 357–370.

Dewey, J. (1900). Psychology and social practice. *Psychological Review, 7,* 105–124.

Dewey, J. (1917). The need for social psychology. *Psychological Review, 24,* 266–277.

Dugdale, R. (1877). *The Jukes: A study in crime, pauperism, disease and heredity.* New York: Putnam.

Dunlap, K. (1912). The case against introspection. *Psychological Review, 19,* 404–413.

Dunlap, K. (1919). Are there any instincts? *Journal of Abnormal and Social Psychology, 14,* 307–311.

Dunlap, K. (1922). *Elements of scientific psychology.* St. Louis: Mosby.

Esper, E. A. (1966). Max Meyer: The making of a scientific isolate. *Journal of the History of the Behavioral Sciences, 2,* 341–356.

Freeman, F. N. (1922). The mental age of adults. *Journal of Educational Research, 6,* 441–444.

Fuchs, A. H. (2000). Contributions of American mental philosophers to psychology in the United States. *History of Psychology, 3,* 3–19.

Galton, F. (1889). *Natural inheritance.* London: Macmillan.

Goddard, H. H. (1911). *The Binet-Simon measuring scale for intelligence.* Vineland, NJ: Training School.

Goddard, H. H. (1912). *The Kallikak family: A study in the heredity of feeblemindedness.* New York: Macmillan.

Goddard, H. H. (1919). *Psychology of the normal and subnormal.* New York: Dodd, Mead.

Goddard, H. H. (1920). *Human efficiency and levels of intelligence.* Princeton, NJ: Princeton University Press.

Grant, M. (1916). *The passing of the great race.* New York: Scribner's.

Hamel, I. A. (1919). A study and analysis of the conditioned reflex. *Psychological Monographs, 27* (Whole No. 118).

Hannush, M. J. (1987). John B. Watson remembered: An interview with James B. Watson. *Journal of the History of the Behavioral Sciences, 23,* 137–152.

Harris, B. (1979). Whatever happened to little Albert? *American Psychologist, 34,* 151–160.

Herrnstein, R., & Murray, C. (1994). *The bell curve.* New York: Free Press.

Hollingworth, H. (1940). *Years at Columbia.* Typescript autobiography. Hollingworth papers, Nebraska State Historical Society, Lincoln, Nebraska.

Holmes, O. W. (1927). *Buck vs Bell.* 274 US 200.

Holt, E. B. (1914). *The concept of consciousness.* New York: Macmillan.

Holt, E. B., Marvin, W. T., Montague, W. P., Perry, R. B., Pitkin, W. B., & Spaulding, E. G. (1910). The program and first platform of six realists. *Journal of Philosophy, Psychology and Scientific Methods, 7,* 393–401.

Hothersall, D. (1995). *History of psychology.* New York: McGraw-Hill.

Hunter, W. S. (1922). An open letter to the anti-behaviorists. *Journal of Philosophy, 19,* 307–308.

Hunter, W. S. (1925). General anthroponomy and its systematic problems. *American Journal of Psychology, 36,* 286–302.

Hunter, W. S. (1928). *Human behavior.* Chicago: University of Chicago Press.

James, W. (1892). A plea for psychology as a "natural science." *Philosophical Review, 1,* 146–153.

Jastrow, J. (1928). *Keeping mentally fit.* New York: Garden City Publishing.

Jensen, A. (1969). How much can we boost IQ and educational achievement? *Harvard Educational Review, 39,* 1–23.

Jones, M. C. (1924). A laboratory study of fear: The case of Peter. *Pedagogical Seminary, 31,* 308–315.

Kamin, L. J. (1974). *The science and politics of IQ.* Potomac, MD: Erlbaum.

Karier, C. J. (1986). *Scientists of the mind.* Urbana: University of Urbana Press.

Köhler, W. (1925). *The mentality of apes.* London: Routledge & Kegan Paul. (Original work published 1917)

Kuo, Z. Y. (1921). Giving up instincts in psychology. *Journal of Philosophy, 18,* 645–664.

Kuo, Z. Y. (1924). A psychology without heredity. *Psychological Review, 31,* 427–448.

Kuo, Z. Y. (1930). The genesis of the cat's responses to the rat. *Journal of Comparative Psychology, 11,* 1–35.

Larson, C. A., & Sullivan, J. J. (1965). Watson's relation to Titchener. *Journal of the History of the Behavioral Sciences, 1,* 338–354.

Lashley, K. S. (1916). The human salivary reflex and its use in psychology. *Psychological Review, 23,* 446–464.

Lashley, K. S. (1923). The behaviorist interpretation of consciousness. *Psychological Review, 30,* 232–272, 329–353.

Lashley, K. S. (1929). *Brain mechanisms and intelligence.* Chicago: University of Chicago Press.

Leahey, T. H. (1992). *A history of psychology: Main currents in psychological thought.* Englewood Cliffs, NJ: Prentice-Hall.

Lippmann, W. (1922). The mental age of Americans. *New Republic, 32,* 213–215.

Logan, C. (1999). The altered rationale for the choice of a standard animal in experimental psychology: Henry H. Donaldson, Adolf Meyer, and "the" albino rat. *History of Psychology, 2,* 3–24.

Lorenz, K. (1935). Der Kumpan in der Umwelt des Vogels. *Journal of Ornithology, 83,* 137–213, 289–413.

Mackenzie, B. D. (1977). *Behaviourism and the limits of scientific method.* London: Routledge & Kegan Paul.

Manicas, P. T. (1987). *A history and philosophy of the social sciences.* Oxford: Blackwell.

Mateer, F. (1918). *Child behavior: A critical and experimental study of children by the method of conditioned reflexes.* Boston: Badger.

McDougall, W. (1908). *Introduction to social psychology.* London: Methuen.

McDougall, W. (1912). *The science of human behavior.* New York: Macmillan.

McDougall, W. (1920). *The group mind.* New York: Putnam.

McDougall, W. (1921). *Is America safe for democracy?* New York: Scribner's.

Merriam, C. E. (1921). The present state of the study of politics. *American Political Science Review, 15,* 183–184.

Meyer M. (1911). *The fundamental laws of human behavior.* Boston: Badger.

Meyer, M. (1921). *The psychology of the other-one.* Columbia: Missouri Book Company.

Mills, J. A. (1998). *Control: A history of behavioral psychology.* New York: New York University Press.

Mills, W. (1899). The nature of animal intelligence. *Psychological Review, 6,* 262–274.

Mitchell, W. C. (1925). Quantitative analysis in economic theory. *American Economic Review, 15,* 1–12.

Morgan, C. L. (1898). Review of *Animal intelligence* by E. L. Thorndike. *Nature, 58,* 249–250.

Morgan, C. L. (1977). *Introduction to comparative psychology.* In D. N. Robinson (Ed.), *Significant contributions to the history of psychology,* 1750–1920: Series D. *Comparative psychology.* Vol. 2. Washington, DC: University Publications of America. (Original work published 1894)

Murchison, C. (1930). *Psychologies of 1930.* Worcester, MA: Clark University Press.

Napoli, D. S. (1981). *Architects of adjustment: The history of the psychological profession in the United States.* Port Washington, NY: Kennikat Press.

National Research Council. (1920). *Fourth annual report.* Washington, DC: U.S. Government Printing Office.

O'Donnell, J. M. (1985). *The origins of behaviorism, American psychology, 1870–1920.* New York: New York University Press.

Passmore, N. (1978). The army intelligence tests and Walter Lippmann. *Journal of the History of the Behavioral Sciences, 14,* 316–327.

Pauly, P. J. (1979). Psychology at Johns Hopkins: Its rise and fall and rise and fall and . . . *Johns Hopkins Magazine, 30,* 36–41.

Pavlov, I. (1928). *Conditioned reflexes* (Vol. 1; W. H. Gantt & G. Volborth, Trans.). New York: International.

Perry, R. B. (1904). Conceptions and misconceptions of consciousness. *Psychological Review, 11,* 282–296.

Pillsbury, W. B. (1911). *Essentials of psychology.* New York: Macmillan.

Report of Committee of Clinical Section of the APA. (1935). *Psychological Clinic, 23,* 1–140.

Rodgers, J. E. (2001). *Sex: A natural history.* New York: Times Books.

Rosenweig, M. R. (1959). Salivary conditioning before Pavlov. *American Journal of Psychology, 72,* 628–633.

Routh, D. K., & Reisman, J. M. (2003). Clinical psychology. In D. K. Freedheim (Ed.), *Handbook of psychology: Vol. 1. History of psychology.* Hoboken, NJ: Wiley.

Rudolph, F. (1962). *The American college and university.* New York: Knopf.

Samelson, F. (1977). World War I intelligence testing and the development of psychology. *Journal of the History of the Behavioral Sciences, 13,* 274–282.

Samelson, F. (1981). Struggle for scientific authority: The reception of Watson's behaviorism, 1913–1920. *Journal of the History of the Behavioral Sciences, 17,* 399–425.

Samelson, F. (1985). Organizing for the kingdom of behavior: Academic battles and organizational policies in the twenties. *Journal of the History of the Behavioral Sciences, 21,* 33–47.

Samelson, F. (1992). Rescuing the reputation of Sir Cyril. *Journal of the History of the Behavioral Sciences, 28,* 221–233.

Shook, J. R. (1995). Wilhelm Wundt's contribution to John Dewey's functional psychology. *Journal of the History of the Behavioral Sciences, 31,* 347–369.

Simon, B. (1957). *Psychology in the Soviet Union.* London: Routledge & Kegan Paul.

Singer, E. A. (1911). Mind as observable object. *Journal of Philosophy, 8,* 180–186.

Singer, E. A. (1924). *Mind as behavior and studies in idealism.* Columbus, OH: Adams.

Skinner, B. F. (1963). Behaviorism at fifty. *Science, 140,* 951–958.

Smith, M. B. (1989). Comment on the case of William McDougall. *American Psychologist, 44,* 13–18.

Smith, S., & Guthrie, E. (1921). *Chapters in general psychology.* Seattle: University of Washington Press.

Sohn, D. (1976). Two concepts of adaptation: Darwin and psychology's. *Journal of the History of the Behavioral Sciences, 12,* 367–375.

Sokal, M. M. (1982). James McKeen Cattell and the failure of anthropometric mental testing, 1890–1901. In W. R. Woodward & M. G. Ash (Eds.), *The problematic science: Psychology in 19th century thought.* New York: Praeger.

Sokal, M. M. (1984). James McKeen Cattell and American psychology in the 1920s. In J. Brozek (Ed.), *Explorations in the history of psychology in the United States.* Lewisburg, PA: Bucknell University Press.

Spearman, C. (1904). "General intelligence," objectively determined and measured. *American Journal of Psychology, 15,* 201–293.

Stam, H., & Kalmanovitch, T. (1988). E. L. Thorndike and the origins of animal psychology. *American Psychologist, 53,* 1135–1144.

Stern, W. (1914). *The psychological methods of testing intelligence.* Baltimore: Warwick & York.

Terman, L. M. (1906). Genius and stupidity. *Pedagogical Seminary, 13,* 307–373.

Terman, L. M. (1916). *The measurement of intelligence.* New York: Houghton Mifflin.

Terman, L. M. (1924). The mental test as a psychological method. *Psychological Review, 31,* 93–117.

Thorndike, E. B. (1898). Animal intelligence: An experimental study of the associative processes in animals. *Psychological Review, Monograph Supplement, 2*(8).

Thorndike, E. B. (1903a). *Educational psychology.* New York: Teachers College.

Thorndike, E. B. (1903b). *Heredity, correlation and sex differences in school abilities.* New York: Macmillan.

Thorndike, E. B. (1904). *An introduction to the theory of mental and social measurements.* New York: Science Press.

Thorndike, E. B. (1911). *Animal intelligence.* New York: Hafner.

Thorndike, E. B. (1913–1914). *Educational psychology* (Vols. 1–3). New York: Teachers College.

Thorndike, E. B. (1929). *Human learning.* New York: Appleton.

Thorndike, E. L. (1936). Edward Lee Thorndike. In C. A. Murchison (Ed.), *A history of psychology in autobiography* (Vol. 3). Worcester, MA. : Clark University Press.

Titchener, E. B. (1895a). Simple reactions. *Mind, 4,* 74–81.

Titchener, E. B. (1895b). The "type-theory" of simple reaction. *Mind, 4,* 506–514.

Titchener, E. B. (1896). The "type-theory" of simple reaction. *Mind, 5,* 236–241.

Titchener, E. B. (1898). The postulates of a structural psychology. *Philosophical Review, 7,* 449–465.

Titchener, E. B. (1899). Structural and functional psychology. *Philosophical Review, 8,* 290–299.

Titchener, E. B. (1905). Review of E. B. Thorndike, *Elements of Psychology. Mind, 20,* 552–554.

Titchener, E. B. (1914). On "Psychology as the behaviorist views it." *Proceedings of the American Philosophical Society, 53,* 1–17.

Todd, J. (1994). What psychology has to say about John B. Watson. In J. Todd & E. K. Morris (Eds.), *Modern perspectives on John B. Watson and classical behaviorism.* Westport, CT: Greenwood Press.

Todes, D. P. (1997). From the machine to the ghost within: Pavlov's transition from digestive physiology to conditional reflexes. *American Psychologist, 52,* 947–955.

Wallace, A. R. (1864). The origin of human races and the antiquity of man deduced from "the theory of natural selection." *Anthropological Review, 2,* 158–187.

Watson, J. B. (1903). *Animal education.* PhD dissertation, University of Chicago.

Watson, J. B. (1907). Kinaesthetic and organic sensations: Their role in the reactions of the white rat to the maze. *Psychological Review, Monograph Supplements, 8*(33).

Watson, J. B. (1908). The behavior of noddy and sooty terns. *Publications of the Carnegie Institution, 2,* 187–255.

Watson, J. B. (1909). A point of view in comparative psychology. *Psychological Bulletin, 6,* 57–58.

Watson, J. B. (1913a). Psychology as the behaviorist views it. *Psychological Review, 20,* 158–177.

Watson, J. B. (1913b). Image and affection in behavior. *Journal of Philosophy, Psychology and Scientific Methods, 10,* 421–428.

Watson, J. B. (1914). *Behavior: An introduction to comparative psychology.* New York: Holt.

Watson, J. B. (1916). The place of the conditioned reflex in psychology. *Psychological Review, 23,* 89–116.

Watson, J. B. (1919). *Psychology from the standpoint of a behaviorist.* Philadelphia: Lippincott.

Watson, J. B. (1920). Is thinking merely the action of language mechanisms? *British Journal of Psychology, 11,* 87–104.

Watson, J. B. (1930). *Behaviorism* (2nd ed.). New York: Norton. (Original work published 1924)

Watson, J. B. (1936). John Broadus Watson. In C. Murchison (Ed.), *A history of psychology in autobiography.* New York: Russell & Russell.

Watson, J. B., & Lashley, K. S. (1915). *Homing and related activities of birds* (Vol. 7). Washington, DC: Carnegie Institution, Department of Marine Biology.

Watson, J. B., & McDougall, W. (1929). *The battle of behaviorism.* New York: Norton.

Watson, J. B., & Rayner, R. (1920). Conditioned emotional reactions. *Journal of Experimental Psychology, 3,* 1–14.

Watson, J. B., & Watson, R. R. (1928). *The psychological care of infant and child.* New York: Norton.

Watson, R. R. (1930). I am the mother of a behaviorist's sons. *Parents Magazine,* Dec., 16–18.

Weiss, A. P. (1917). Relation between functional and behavior psychology. *Psychological Review, 24,* 353–368.

Weiss, A. P. (1918). Conscious behavior. *Journal of Philosophy, Psychology and Scientific Methods, 15,* 631–641.

Weiss, A. P. (1925). *A theoretical basis of human behavior.* Columbus, OH: Adams.

Wiggam, A. E. (1928). *Exploring your mind with the psychologists.* New York: Bobbs-Merrill.

Wissler, C. (1901). The correlation of mental and physical tests. *Psychological Review Monograph Supplements, 3*(6).

Wolpe, J. (1958). *Psychotherapy by reciprocal inhibition.* Stanford, CA: Stanford University Press.

Wolpe, J. (1973). *The practice of behavior therapy* (2nd ed.). New York: Pergamon.

Woodworth, R. S. (1931). *Contemporary schools of psychology.* New York: Ronald Press.

Yerkes, R. M. (1905a). Animal psychology and the criterion of the psychic. *Journal of Philosophy, Psychology and Scientific Methods, 2,* 141–149.

Yerkes, R. M. (1905b). Review of E. Claparede, *La psychologie comparé est-ille légitime?* [Is comparative psychology legitimate?]. *Journal of Philosophy, Psychology and Scientific Methods, 2,* 527–528.

Yerkes, R. M. (1911). *Introduction to psychology.* New York: Henry Holt.

Yerkes, R. M. (Ed.). (1921). Psychological examining in the United States Army. *Memoirs of the National Academy of Sciences, 15,* 1–890.

Yerkes, R. M. (1923). Introduction to C. C. Brigham's *A study of American intelligence*. Princeton: Princeton University Press.

Yerkes, R. M., Bridges, J. W., & Hardwick, R. S. (1915). *A point scale for measuring mental ability*. Baltimore: Warwick & York.

Yerkes, R., M., & Morgulis, S. (1909). The method of Pavlov in animal psychology. *Psychological Bulletin, 6,* 257–273.

Yerkes, R. M., & Yerkes, A. W. (1929). *The great apes: A study of anthropoid life*. New Haven, CT: Yale University Press.

Zenderland, L. (1998). *Measuring minds: Henry Herbert Goddard and the origins of American intelligence testing*. Cambridge: Cambridge University Press.

CHAPTER 11

Neobehaviorism, Radical Behaviorism, and Problems of Behaviorism

WHILE MANY PSYCHOLOGISTS ACCEPTED WATSON'S RHETORIC OF prediction and control, few accepted the theoretical details of his behaviorist system, and in the 1930s and 1940s the neobehaviorism of Clark L. Hull (1884–1952) and Edward C. Tolman (1866–1959) superseded Watson's positivist brand of behaviorism. Hull and Tolman followed Watson in maintaining that scientific psychology should be directed to the explanation, prediction, and control of observable behavior rather than introspected mental states, and they rejected the form of structural psychology championed by Titchener and his followers. Yet in contrast to Watson, they recognized the legitimacy of theoretical explanations of observable behavior in terms of the internal states of organisms, including their mental states, on a par with theoretical explanations of the observable properties of physical elements in terms of their internal composition and structure (such as the explanation of the properties of carbon in terms of its molecular composition and structure).

The neobehaviorist attempt to more closely approximate the theoretical orientation of the natural sciences marked an advance over Watson's restriction of behaviorist psychology to the description of observable stimulus-response sequences. However, in their attempt to model behaviorist psychology upon the natural sciences, neobehaviorists did not look to the actual practice of natural sciences such as physics and chemistry, but adopted the equally restrictive logical positivist account of theory advanced by philosophers of science in the early decades of the 20th century. As Sigmund Koch put it,

> In pursuit of these ends, psychology did not go directly to physics, but turned instead for its directives to middlemen. These were, for the most part, philosophers of science (especially logical positivists) and a number of physical scientists who had been codifying a synoptic view of the nature of science and who, by the early

thirties, were actively exporting that view from their specialties in the scholarly community at large.

—(Koch, 1964, p. 10)

The logical positivist account of theory exercised a debilitating influence on the development of neobehaviorist theory. Burrhus F. Skinner (1904–1990) exploited the limitations of this account of theory and developed a **radical behaviorism** that eschewed theories about the internal states of organisms. Skinner returned to Watson's positivist conception of behaviorist psychology as restricted to the description, prediction, and control of observable behavior.

Neobehaviorism was the dominant orientation in American departments of psychology until after the end of the Second World War, when it was displaced by radical behaviorism. In the decades after the war, the theories of conditioned learning that provided the theoretical foundation for all forms of behaviorism came under increasing criticism, preparing the way for the cognitive revolution of the 1950s and 1960s. The decades following the Second World War also witnessed a major transformation of the institutional structure of scientific and professional psychology.

NEOBEHAVIORISM

Watson's brand of behaviorism was an expression of his commitment to a positivist science restricted to the description, prediction, and control of observable behavior:

> The behaviorist asks: Why don't we make what we can *observe* the real field of psychology? Let us limit ourselves to things that can be observed, and formulate laws concerning only those things. Now what can we observe? Well, we can observe behavior—what the organism does or says.

—(1924, p. 6)

It was also an expression of his *inductivist* conception of the development of scientific theories, according to which the aim of science is to accumulate observational laws that can eventually be integrated by summative theories, in the fashion in which the various gas laws relating pressure, temperature, and volume (Boyle's law, Charles's law and Graham's law) were independently established and then integrated by the kinetic theory of gases. As Watson put it,

> You will find, then, the behaviorist working like any other scientist. . . . We collect our facts from observation. Now and then we select a group of facts and draw certain general conclusions about them. In a few years as new experimental data are gathered by better methods, even these tentative general conclusions have to

be modified. . . . Experimental technique, the accumulation of facts by that technique, occasional tentative consolidation of these facts into a theory or a hypothesis describe our procedure in science. Judged upon this basis, behaviorism is a true natural science.

—(1924, pp. 18–19)

In contrast, neobehaviorists such as Hull and Tolman embraced the *hypothetico-deductive* account of the development of scientific theories. According to this account, theories play more than a merely summative role. Theoretical postulates are introduced not only to accommodate previously established observational laws, but also to generate new observational predictions. Bohr's theory of the atom, for example, not only accommodated the known empirical laws governing spectral emissions, but also generated additional predictions about the spectral emissions of more complex elements and phenomena such as the Zeeman effect (the splitting of spectral lines in a magnetic field).

Thus Hull, for example, maintained that scientific psychology should proceed via the deduction of the empirical implications of postulated theoretical principles:

The typical procedure in science is to adopt a postulate tentatively, deduce one or more of its logical implications concerning observable phenomena, and then check the validity of the deductions by observation.

—(1943a, p. 15)

Similarly, if somewhat more picturesquely, Tolman famously proclaimed,

I in my future work, intend to go ahead imagining how, if I were a rat, I would behave.

—(1938, p. 24)

This was not intended as a return to speculative anthropomorphism, but as a heuristic for generating hypotheses about the cognitive states of animals, which could then be tested via their empirical implications.

The logical positivists developed the hypothetico-deductive account of scientific method into a general account of theoretical explanation in science. They conceived of explanation as the deduction of empirical laws (or theorems) from theoretical postulates (or axioms), modeled upon the deductive systems of Euclid and Newton. This account "held forth an ideal of rigorous theory and seemed to define a route towards its achievement":

In barest outline, it asserts theory to be a hypothetic-deductive system. Laws or hypotheses believed fundamental are asserted as postulates, and the consequences of these (theorems) are deduced by strict logical and mathematical rules. The theorems are then to be tested by experiment. Positive results increase the probability of a hypothesis; negative results call them into question.

—(Koch, 1962, p. 401)

Thus the difference between the behaviorism of Watson and the neobehaviorism of Hull and Tolman was essentially the difference between original positivism (or dogmatic empiricism) and logical positivism.

Logical Positivism

A group of philosophers, scientists, mathematicians, and social scientists who met in Vienna in the 1920s and early 1930s formulated the set of doctrines known as **logical positivism**, which played an influential role in the development of neobehaviorism. Moritz Schlick (1882–1936) founded the group that came to be known as the Vienna Circle, whose members included Gustav Bergmann (1906–1987), Rudolf Carnap (1891–1970), Herbert Feigl (1902–1988), Otto Neurath (1882–1945), and Kurt Gödel (1906–1978). The logical positivists were influenced by earlier forms of empiricism and positivism and by more recent developments in logic and science, notably Russell and Whitehead's reduction of arithmetic to logic in *Principia Mathematica* (1910) and Einstein's theory of relativity.

The central doctrines of logical positivism were essentially linguistic restatements of the psychological and meaning empiricism of David Hume (whom the positivists admired). Hume had claimed that the only meaningful ideas and terms are those derived from experience, and the logical positivists advanced the **verification principle**, according to which the only meaningful factual propositions are those verifiable by observation. As Moritz Schlick put it, "the meaning of a proposition is its method of verification" (Schlick, 1936, p. 341). The logical positivists distinguished between formal and factual propositions, between propositions rendered true or false by internal relations of meaning or logic (such as "all triangles have three sides") and propositions rendered true or false by facts about the world (such as "all unsupported bodies fall to the ground"), which corresponded to Hume's distinction between "relations of ideas" and "matters of fact and existence." They also appropriated Hume's account of causality in terms of the constant conjunction (or correlation) of observables.

As Hume had employed the principle of meaning empiricism to dismiss metaphysical ideas or concepts as "mere sophistry and illusion," the logical positivists employed the verification principle to dismiss metaphysical, ethical, religious, and aesthetic propositions as literal nonsense, because they could not be empirically verified. However, they recognized that many of the theoretical propositions of science, such as propositions about electrons and gravitational fields, were also incapable of direct empirical verification, but they were reluctant to dismiss them as nonsense. To accommodate theoretical propositions about unobservable entities such as electrons and gravitational fields, the logical positivists claimed that it is legitimate to introduce theoretical propositions so long as they are defined in terms of observables, via **correspondence rules** or **operational definitions** relating theoretical propositions to propositions about observables.

In the early version of logical positivism known as **sensationalism,** observational propositions were held to describe the properties of private sense experience, such as the intensity of colors or apparent differences in weight. In the later version of logical positivism known as **physicalism,** observational propositions were held to describe the publicly observable properties of physical objects, such as readings on spectrometers or the motion of bodies. Neobehaviorists such as Hull and Tolman embraced this later version of logical positivism, which became known as **scientific empiricism** (or logical empiricism). They treated theoretical references to consciousness and cognition in psychology as analogous to theoretical references to electrons and gravitational fields in natural science, as theoretical postulates related to publicly observable behavior:

> They are to behavior as electrons, waves, or whatever it may be are to the happenings in inorganic matter.
>
> —(Tolman, 1932, p. 414)

S. S. Stevens, in "The Operational Definition of Psychological Concepts," maintained that a theoretical proposition "has meaning . . . if, and only if, the criteria of its applicability or truth consist of concrete operations that can be performed" (1935, pp. 517–518). Scientific empiricists treated theoretical postulates relating to the internal states of organisms as **intervening variables,** defined in terms of relations between observable independent variables such as environmental or physiological stimuli and observable dependent variables such as behavioral responses (Bergmann & Spence, 1941; Carnap, 1936, 1937; Pratt, 1939). This conception of psychological theories held powerful sway during the heyday of neobehaviorism, from the 1930s to the 1950s, and remained influential for many subsequent decades.

The concept of an intervening variable was ambiguous, since it could be interpreted as either a **logically** or a **causally** intervening variable. According to the former interpretation, an intervening variable is merely a logical device for integrating descriptions of observable stimuli and behavioral responses. By the latter interpretation, an intervening variable represents an internal state of an organism that causally mediates between observable stimuli and behavioral responses. (Of course every causally intervening variable is also a logically intervening variable, but not every logically intervening variable need be treated as a causally intervening variable.) The logical interpretation of intervening variables was an expression of the instrumentalist conception of scientific theories, according to which theoretical postulates are merely logical devices for integrating observational laws, whereas the causal interpretation was an expression of the realist conception of scientific theories, according to which theoretical postulates are potentially true descriptions of entities such as electrons and cognitive states.

Many neobehaviorists embraced an instrumentalist conception of theory and maintained that intervening variables merely serve as "economical devices to order experimental variables in relation to the dependent variables":

> They are "shorthand" descriptions, and nothing more, of the influence on behavior of several independent variables. The only meaning possessed by these intervening variables is their relationship to both the independent and dependent variables.
>
> —(Kendler, 1952, p. 271)

Other neobehaviorists, notably Hull and Tolman, were committed realists who treated intervening variables as explanatory references to internal states that causally mediate between observed stimuli and behavior. However, they all insisted that intervening variables must be operationally defined in terms of observable stimuli and behavioral responses (even if they did not always practice their operational preaching).

The degree to which logical positivism influenced the development of Hull's and Tolman's original theoretical positions is a matter of dispute. Laurence D. Smith (1986) has argued that they developed their theoretical views independently of logical positivism and only later appealed to the scientific empiricist account as a convenient justification of their positions. However, their later metatheoretical and methodological pronouncements were clearly shaped by scientific empiricism (as Smith acknowledged), as was the theory and practice of later neobehaviorists such as Kenneth W. Spence (1907–1967) and Charles E. Osgood (1916–1991).

Operationism

The scientific empiricist account of the operational definition of scientific theories was supposedly based upon the **operationism** of Percy Bridgman (1882–1961), the Harvard physicist who won the Nobel Prize in physics in 1946 for his work on matter under high pressure. According to Bridgman (1927), any legitimate scientific concept must be linked to measurement procedures that can be employed to determine its empirical values. Such **operational measures** provide the empirical significance of a scientific concept or an operational definition of the concept. Bridgman claimed that since concepts such as "absolute simultaneity" and "absolute space" could not be operationally defined, they lacked empirical significance and were of no use in science.

However, Bridgman's concern was with the scientific utility of concepts, not their theoretical meaning—thus a concept such as absolute simultaneity might be perfectly meaningful but useless in science. Bridgman was critical of neobehaviorists who appropriated his operationism in support of their claim that theoretical propositions in psychology must be operationally defined in terms of observable stimuli and behavior (Koch, 1992), and in later years lamented that he had "created a Frankenstein" (cited in Green, 1992, p. 310).

Edward C. Tolman: Purposive Behaviorism

Edward Chance Tolman was born in Newton, Massachusetts, in 1886. Edward and his brother Richard earned undergraduate degrees in electrochemistry at MIT, where their father had been a member of the first graduating class. Richard went on to a distinguished career in chemistry. Edward became interested in philosophy and psychology after reading James's *Principles* during his last year at MIT.

Tolman enrolled at Harvard in 1911 with the aim of studying both philosophy and psychology, but quickly came to focus on psychology. He took philosophy courses with the new realists Holt and Perry, and psychology courses with Yerkes and Münsterberg. Tolman became interested in the behaviorist approach when Yerkes assigned Watson's 1914 text *Behavior* as required reading in his comparative psychology course. He spent the summer of 1912 in Germany, where he studied with Koffka. Although he never embraced Gestalt psychology, he remained interested in the Gestalt approach (he returned to Germany in 1923 to pursue his interest) and appropriated some of its concepts, such as the notion of a "sign-Gestalt." Tolman completed his PhD in 1915 with a thesis supervised by Münsterberg on the learning of meaningless syllables conjoined with pleasant and unpleasant odors. *Studies in Memory* was published in *Psychological Monographs* in 1917.

Upon graduation from Harvard, Tolman took up an appointment at Northwestern University. He was dismissed in 1918, for either his poor teaching or his pacifism. He wrote an essay on the subject just after the United States entered the First World War, and it remained a strong personal theme throughout his life. He later wrote a book exploring the motivation for war, entitled *Drives Towards War* (1942), although his pacifism did not prevent him from serving in the Office of Strategic Services during the Second World War.

Tolman joined the University of California at Berkeley, where he taught comparative psychology and set up a laboratory for animal research. He began to work with rats and formed such a genuine affection for the animals that he dedicated his 1932 book to them. As Tolman put it,

> Rats do not kill each other off in war; they do not invent engines of destruction . . .
> they do not go in for either class conflicts or race conflicts. . . . They are marvelous,
> pure and delightful.

—(1945, p. 166)

He remained at Berkeley for most of the rest of his career. He managed to avoid trouble with the university over his pacifism, but was suspended from 1950 to 1953 for refusing to take a loyalty oath (during which time he taught at Chicago and Harvard). Tolman took the university to court and won his case, and he later had the personal satisfaction of having the university acknowledge the moral validity of his position when he was awarded an honorary doctorate in 1959. He was elected president of the APA in 1937 and received its Distinguished Scientific Contribution Award in 1957. While Tolman may not have had as revolutionary an impact as Watson or as immediate an influence as Hull, his theoretical position has endured better than theirs. He claimed to have enjoyed his academic career from beginning to end. In commenting upon the guiding principles of his psychological research, he admitted that "In the end the only sure criterion is to have fun. And I have had fun" (1959, p. 159).

Purposive Behaviorism Tolman followed Watson in rejecting introspective psychology and maintaining that observable behavior is the subject matter of psychology, but he dismissed Watson's form of behaviorism as "muscle-twitchism." Tolman's own research was focused on purposive or goal-directed behavior in animals and humans. He called his version of behaviorism **purposive behaviorism** and titled his first book *Purposive Behavior in Animals and Men* (1932).

Like McDougall, who developed an earlier form of purposive behaviorism (McDougall, 1908), Tolman claimed that most animal and human behavior is intentionally directed toward goal or end states. As he put it, there is "something either *toward which* or *from which* the behavior is directed" (Tolman, 1925, p. 39). Like Aristotle, Tolman maintained that most animal and human behavior is intrinsically purposive or teleological. He insisted that the purposiveness or goal-directedness of behavior is "quite an objective and purely behaviorist affair":

> It is a descriptive feature immanent in the character of behavior qua behavior. It is not a mentalistic entity supposed to exist parallel to, and to run alongside of the behavior. It is *out there* in the behavior, of its descriptive warp and woof.
>
> —(1926, p. 355)

Tolman was influenced by the new realism of Holt and Perry, who maintained that consciousness and cognition should be explicated in terms of behavioral adjustments to the environment (Smith, 1986). Yet although he objected to inferences about mentality based upon introspective psychology (and to conceptions of purposive behavior as behavior accompanied by special introspective states), Tolman did not deny the independence of conscious mentality and behavior. He thought it was perfectly legitimate to postulate mental determinants of the purposive behavior of animals and humans (as McDougall had before him):

> For the behaviorist, "mental processes" are to be identified and defined in terms of the behaviors to which they lead. "Mental processes" are, for the behaviorist, naught but inferred determinants of behavior, which ultimately are deducible from behavior. Behavior and these inferred determinants are both objectively defined types of entity.
>
> —(Tolman, 1932, p. 3)

Accordingly, Tolman postulated a variety of cognitive determinants of behavior, such as "internal presentations," "representations," "expectations," "hypotheses," "sign-Gestalts," and "cognitive maps" and developed increasingly complex cognitive theories of animal learning in contrast to traditional stimulus-response accounts. He rejected the common conception of learning as the automatic connection of stimulus and response, based upon principles of contiguity, frequency, and reinforcement:

> Behavior (except in the case of the simplest reflexes) is not governed by simple one-to-one stimulus response connections. It is governed rather by more or less complicated sets of patterns of adjustment which get set up within the organism.
>
> —(Tolman, 1928, p. 526)

During his years at Berkeley, Tolman and his students developed a set of cognitive theories of learning based upon the experimental analysis of maze-learning behavior in rats. He claimed that animals learn "representations" rather than stimulus-response connections, often independently of motivation and reinforcement. On the basis of a famous series of experiments on **latent learning**, Tolman and Honzik (1930) maintained that rats are able to learn maze layouts in the absence of reinforcement. Tolman held that rats develop cognitive maps of their spatial environment based upon "confirmations" of their "expectancies": "in the course of learning something like a field map of the environment gets established in the rat's brain" (Tolman, 1948, p. 192).

Tolman's commitment to the cognitive determination of both animal and human behavior was a distinctive feature of his purposive behaviorism. It distinguished it from the forms of behaviorism advocated by most other behaviorists, including Watson, Hull, and Skinner, who all denied that cognition and consciousness play a role in the determination of animal and human behavior. Tolman rejected Lloyd Morgan's claim that all animal behavior could be explained in terms of association and never embraced the standard behaviorist attempt to accommodate all forms of animal and human behavior in terms of conditioned learning, based upon the experimental analysis of animal behavior. In his 1937 APA presidential address he claimed that much of "what is important in psychology" can be "investigated in essence through the continued experimental and theoretical analysis of rat behavior at a choice point in a maze," but doubted whether this was true for human social, moral, and linguistic behavior or "such matters as involve society and words" (Tolman, 1938, p. 34). Also unlike most other behaviorists, including Watson, Hull, and Skinner, Tolman was not an environmentalist. Like McDougall, he maintained that a significant portion of animal and human behavior is innately determined (Tolman, 1936/1951).

Intervening Variables and Hypothetical Constructs Tolman developed his basic theoretical position in the 1920s (Tolman, 1922, 1923, 1925, 1926, 1927), but refined it in the language of scientific empiricism in the 1930s. Moritz Schlick, the founder of the Vienna Circle of logical positivists, visited Berkeley in 1931, and in 1933–1934 Tolman spent his sabbatical in Vienna, where he met with some of the original members of the circle. As a result of his exposure to logical positivism, Tolman came to treat cognitive states as intervening variables, operationally defined in terms of external environmental or internal physiological stimulus variables (independent variables) and behavioral response variables (dependent variables):

> Mental processes, whether they be those of another or of ourselves, will figure only in the guise of objectively definable intervening variables. . . . the sole "cash-value" of mental processes lies, I shall assert, in their character as a set of intermediating functional processes which interconnect between the initiating causes of behavior, on the one hand, and the final resulting behavior, on the other. . . . Mental processes are but intervening variables between the five independent variables of (1) environmental stimuli, (2) physiological drive, (3) heredity, (4) previous training, and (5) maturity, on the one hand, and the final dependent variable, behavior, on the other.
>
> —(1936/1951, pp. 116–117)

Tolman also called his form of purposive behaviorism **operational behaviorism,** because of his commitment to an "operational psychology" grounded in the principles of scientific empiricism. He claimed that such a psychology "seeks to define its concepts in such a manner that they can be stated and tested in terms of concrete operations by independent observers":

> The behaviorism which I am going to present seeks, then, to use only concepts which are capable of such concrete operational verification.
>
> —(1936/1951, p. 89)

Although Tolman championed the scientific empiricist account of theories and insisted upon the empirical grounding of theoretical postulates, he did not embrace the instrumentalist conception of psychological theories. He was a committed realist who treated intervening variables as theoretical references to internal cognitive states that play an essential role in the causal explanation of animal and human behavior, and which are not reducible to mere descriptions of correlation between observable stimuli and responses.

The point may be put in terms of MacCorquodale and Meehl's (1948) later distinction between **hypothetical constructs** and intervening variables. They distinguished between intervening variables, for which "the statement of such a concept does not contain any words which are not reducible to the empirical laws," and hypothetical constructs, which are "not wholly reducible to the words in the empirical laws" (1948, p. 107). They claimed that hypothetical constructs, unlike intervening variables, contain **surplus meaning** that is not reducible to empirical laws. Tolman's theoretical cognitive postulates were hypothetical constructs rather than intervening variables, as he later acknowledged:

> To use MacCorquodale and Meehl's distinction, I would now abandon what they call pure "intervening variables" for what they call "hypothetical constructs."
>
> —(Tolman, 1949, p. 49)

However, Tolman did not restrict the surplus meaning of his theoretical cognitive constructs to an existential commitment to causally efficacious internal states of organisms, which MacCorquodale and Meehl granted was sufficient to distinguish a hypothetical construct from a pure intervening variable (according to this minimalist conception, a causally intervening variable counts as a hypothetical construct). Rather, he specified the meaning of his theoretical cognitive constructs *independently* of any operational definition in terms of observational stimuli and responses. Tolman specified his theoretical references to cognitive maps, for example, in terms of an organism's representation of its spatial environment, not in terms of its behavior in that environment. Given this theoretical specification, one could understand how rats represent their environment *without* knowing how they behave in that environment.

Clark L. Hull: A Newtonian Behavioral System

Hull came from a poor rural family in New York State. He worked on his parents' farm while attending local schools and survived a typhoid outbreak that took the lives of some of his schoolmates. He worked his way through Alma College, where he studied mining engineering. Hull often had to interrupt his school and college career to replenish his finances by taking on a variety of jobs, including teaching in his former high school, working as an apprentice mining engineer in Hibbing, Minnesota, and teaching at a normal school of education in Kentucky. A polio attack at the age of 24 ended his hopes of a mining career. Hull was left paralyzed in one leg and wore a heavy iron leg brace (which he designed himself) for the rest of his life. He switched to psychology as a career that combined his joint interests in theory and apparatus, as well as promising speedy promotion (Hull, 1952). He read James's *Principles* while working as a high school teacher and continued his studies at the University of Michigan, graduating in 1913. Hull took courses in experimental psychology and logic and turned his engineering skills to the development of a machine for processing logical syllogisms. When he had saved enough money, he attended the University of Wisconsin, where he gained his PhD in 1918 at the age of 34. (Hull also applied to but was rejected by Yale, where he later spent the bulk of his professional career as a psychologist.) He was invited to join the faculty at the University of Wisconsin, where he remained as an instructor until 1929 (Hull, 1952).

Hull was proud of his dissertation on concept formation, supervised by Joseph Jastrow, which he considered to be a genuine experimental study of thought, and was deeply disappointed when it failed to generate much critical attention after being published in *Psychological Monographs* in 1920. Reprising Hume's comment on his *Treatise,* Hull described his first work as "still-born." However, as in the case of Hume, his comment was both exaggerated and premature. His work was regularly cited after J. P. Dashiell drew attention to it in his 1928 textbook *Fundamentals of Objective Psychology* (Hilgard, 1987).

During his years at Wisconsin, Hull conducted experimental studies of hypnotism and the effects of tobacco on efficiency. His critical survey of current theory and research on aptitude testing (Hull, 1928) cemented his growing reputation. While working in this area, Hull created a mechanical device for computing correlations, to avoid the time and effort of paper and pencil calculations. His "correlation machine" is now housed in the Smithsonian Museum in Washington. Hull was originally interested in Gestalt psychology and was instrumental in persuading the university to invite Koffka as a visiting professor. However, Hull was not persuaded by his advocacy of Gestalt principles. He later claimed that Koffka's critique of Watson's behaviorism inspired him to improve behaviorism rather than embrace Gestalt psychology (Hull, 1952).

In 1929 Hull accepted an appointment as research professor at Yale University, where he headed a group of researchers at the Institute of Human Relations. Throughout the following two decades Hull and his colleagues and students developed a program of research devoted to the study of the basic principles of learning, based upon maze-running experiments with rats. Hull also continued his research on hypnosis at Yale and published *Hypnosis and Suggestibility: An Experimental Approach* in 1933. However, the university directed Hull to discontinue his research after a female subject brought a lawsuit claiming that hypnosis was responsible for her nervous breakdown.

Hull admired Pavlov's work on conditioned reflexes, which he read in 1927 when it first appeared in English translation. He began research on conditioned responses at Wisconsin and continued with it at Yale. At the time it was generally agreed that Watson and Pavlov had failed to integrate instrumental conditioning (trial-and-error learning) and classical conditioning (Boakes, 1984), and Tolman (1932) maintained that they were two distinct forms of learning. Hull developed a drive-reduction theory of reinforcement in which he attempted to accommodate both forms of conditioning under a single set of learning principles (by treating the unconditioned stimuli of classical conditioning as reinforcers):

> Pavlov's conditioned reactions and the stimulus-response "bonds" resulting from Thorndike's so-called "law of effect" are in reality special cases of the operation of a single set of principles.
>
> —(1937, p. 11)

Hull claimed that all learning is based upon the reduction of drives related to an organism's primary biological needs (such as food, drink, sexual gratification, temperature regulation, and relief from pain) and that reinforcement is equivalent to drive reduction or satisfaction. He theorized that the reaction potential of a response (sEr), the probability that a learned response will be emitted on any particular occasion, is a function of the habit strength (sHr) of the response, the number of times the response has been reinforced, and the level of drive (D). Hull extended his learning theory to accommodate complex behavior by appeal to secondary drives (and secondary reinforcement) that become associated (via classical conditioning) with the reduction of primary drives (primary reinforcement).

Hull developed his theoretical system in a series of papers in the 1930s, culminating in the publication of his *Principles of Behavior* in 1943. In this work, he formally presented his theory of learning as a set of theoretical axioms and derived empirical theorems. Hull modeled this presentation upon the system of Newton's *Principia*, a copy of which he had purchased while lecturing at Harvard in the summer of 1930; he required his graduate students to read and digest the work. Newton's gravitational theory was based upon a set of postulated axioms from which empirical laws about the motions of physical bodies were deduced, and Hull's theory of learning was based upon a set of postulated axioms from which empirical laws of observable behavior were deduced. Hull was not modest about the explanatory scope of his theory, based upon maze-running experiments on rats. In the *Preface* of his *Principles of Behavior*, he claimed that

> all behavior, individual and social, moral and immoral, normal and psychopathic, is generated from the same primary laws.
>
> —(1943a, p. v)

Unlike Tolman, Hull did not have fun. Throughout his life he was driven by the fear that he would die before completing his theoretical project, and his life ended in disappointment. He was forced to retract most of his earlier claims about the generality of his theory in *A Behavior System*, published in 1952, the year he died from a heart attack. He regretted that he had never been able to complete a planned work that would have extended his theory to accommodate human moral and social behavior, and it was left to Hull's students, notably Robert Sears, John Dollard, and Neil Miller, to complete this part of his theoretical project (Dollard & Miller, 1950; Sears, 1943). Hull's theory was enormously influential in the 1940s (Spence, 1952), and his achievements in psychology were widely acknowledged. He was elected president of the APA in 1936, and in 1945 he was awarded the Warren Medal by the Society of Experimental Psychologists (the institutional descendant of Titchener's Experimentalists).

Intervening Variables and Cognitive Constructs Like Tolman, Hull endorsed the principles of scientific empiricism, which he claimed had the potential of transforming psychology into a "full-blown natural science" (1943b, p. 273). He claimed that theoretical intervening variables such as "drive" and "habit strength" must be related to observable independent and dependent variables:

> It is evident that this equational mode of anchoring symbolic constructs to objectively observable and measurable antecedent and consequent conditions or phenomena is necessary, because otherwise their values would be indeterminate and the theory of which they constitute an essential part would be impossible of empirical verification.
>
> —(Hull, 1943b, p. 282)

Also like Tolman, Hull rejected the instrumentalist conception of scientific theories. He treated theoretical postulates realistically, as causally intervening variables or hypothetical constructs. Although he avowed that theoretical references to habits must be operationally defined in terms of observable stimuli and responses, he maintained that habits exist independently of their particular behavioral expression in stimulus situations (as dispositions of the nervous system):

> These symbols . . . represent entities or processes which, if existent, would account for certain events in the observable molar world. Examples of such postulated entities in the field of physical sciences are electrons, protons, positrons, etc. A closely parallel concept in the field of behavior familiar to everyone is that of *habit* as distinguished from habitual action. The habit presumably exists as an invisible condition of the nervous system quite as much when it is not mediating action as when habitual action is occurring; the habits upon which swimming is based are just as truly existent when a person is on the dance floor as when he is in the water.
>
> —(1943a, p. 21)

Similarly, he claimed that theoretical references to drives must be defined in terms of observable stimuli and responses, but maintained that they exist independently as internal states of an organism that causally mediate between environmental stimuli and behavioral responses.

Although he granted the existence of consciousness and cognition, Hull rejected most explanations of animal and human behavior in terms of them. He acknowledged that explanations in terms of consciousness are legitimate in principle, but held that there is no need to appeal to them in practice. In the abbreviated axiomatic theoretical system he presented in his 1936 APA presidential address (titled "Mind, Mechanism and Adaptive Behavior"), Hull claimed that theoretical references to consciousness are legitimate but unnecessary:

> What, then, shall we say about consciousness? Is its existence denied? By no means. But to recognize the existence of a phenomenon is not the same thing as insisting on its basic, i.e., logical priority. Instead of furnishing a means for the selection of problems, consciousness appears to be itself a problem needing solution. In the miniature theoretical system, no mention of consciousness was made for the simple reason that no theorem has been found as yet whose deduction would be facilitated in any way by including such a postulate. . . . There is, however, no reason at all for not using consciousness or experience as a postulate in a scientific theoretical system if it clearly satisfies the deductive criteria already laid down.
>
> —(1937, p. 30)

Hull doubted that theoretical references to consciousness would ever be needed to explain animal or human behavior:

> Considering the practically complete failure of all this effort to yield even a small scientific system of adaptive or moral behavior in which consciousness finds a position of logical priority as a postulate, one may, perhaps, be pardoned for entertaining a certain amount of pessimism regarding such an eventuality.
>
> —(1937, p. 31)

Hull also acknowledged the legitimacy of cognitive theoretical postulates and sometimes employed them in his own work (Hull, 1920, 1930), but he rejected Tolman's theories of "representations" and "cognitive maps." He believed that all behavior, including human moral and social behavior, could be explained in purely mechanistic terms. Hull and his colleagues and students at Yale tried to demonstrate that all apparently purposive behavior could be explained in terms of automatic principles of conditioning, without reference to cognitive states such as expectancies or cognitive maps. For example, Kenneth Spence maintained that the "systematic response patterns" that Tolman's student Ivan Krechevsky had explained by reference to postulated "hypotheses" (Krechevsky, 1932) were simply products of reinforcement history (Spence, 1936). This generated a number of theoretical disputes between Hull and Tolman and their followers, including the famous debate about whether rats running mazes learn cognitive maps or stimulus-response connections, the so-called **place versus response controversy** (Amundson, 1985).

There was also a fundamental difference between the theoretical cognitive constructs that Hull and Tolman employed. Hull agreed with Tolman that cognitive constructs are hypothetical constructs with surplus meaning that is not reducible to the mere description of correlations between observable stimuli and responses, but insisted that postulated cognitive states must be defined operationally as internal causal variables: as internal response-stimulus (r-s) connections that mediate between observable stimuli and responses. Tolman agreed that postulated cognitive states are internal causal variables that mediate between observable stimuli and responses and agreed on the need to relate cognitive constructs to observable stimuli and behavior. However, Tolman specified the meaning of his cognitive constructs (such as "cognitive map") independently of their relation to observable stimuli and responses. In consequence, Hull's avowedly "cognitive" theories lacked the autonomous cognitive content of Tolman's theories.

This is worth noting in relation to recent claims that Hull anticipated contemporary forms of computational cognitive psychology through his discussion of the possibility of a **psychic machine** (Leahey, 1992; Schultz & Schultz, 1992). Hull conceived of a psychic machine (Hull, 1937, p. 30) as operating on automatic principles of learning based upon stimulus-response connections (including internal r-s connections), not as operating on the "rules and representations" postulated by contemporary computational cognitive psychologists (Bechtel, 1988). Hull also employed the notion of a psychic machine as a methodological device analogous to Morgan's canon. He believed that the concept of a mechanized robot operating on automatic principles of conditioned learning served as a useful prophylactic against the theoretical attribution of cognitive states to animals, which helped to prevent such attribution from degenerating into "sheer anthropomorphism" (1943b, p. 287). He claimed that "one of the greatest obstacles to the attainment of a genuine theory of behavior is anthropomorphic subjectivism":

> One aid to the attainment of behavioral objectivity is to think in terms of the behavior of subhuman organisms, such as chimpanzees, monkeys, dogs, cats and albino rats. Unfortunately this form of prophylaxis against subjectivism all too often breaks down when a theorist begins thinking what he would do if he were a rat, a cat, or a chimpanzee; when that happens, all his knowledge of his own behavior, born of years of self-observation, at once begins to function in place of the objectively stated general rules or principles which are the proper substance of science.
>
> A device much employed by the author has proved itself to be a far more effective prophylaxis. This is to regard, from time to time, the behaving organism as a completely self-maintaining robot, constructed of materials as unlike ourselves as may be.
>
> —(1943a, p. 27)

The reference to "a theorist . . . thinking what he would do if he were a rat" was of course directed to Tolman. Like Watson before him, Hull was deeply suspicious of cognitive explanations of animal and human behavior.

While he acknowledged that cognitive states are internal states of organisms that play a causal role in the generation of behavior, Hull followed Watson in denying that they are "centrally initiated states." He claimed that cognitive states are **pure stimulus acts**—defined as internal response-stimulus (r-s) sequences— that causally mediate between environmental stimuli and behavioral responses and which are fully determined by external stimuli (Hull, 1930). Like Watson, Hull was a committed environmentalist, albeit for different reasons.

Hull's theories of conditioned learning had far greater initial impact than Tolman's cognitive theories, although it is questionable whether this was a product of their superior theoretical fertility or empirical support. While the economic depression of the 1930s led to a general reduction in university funding, Hull's program was the fortunate recipient of generous support from the Laura Spelman Rockefeller Memorial Fund. Beardsley Ruml (1894–1960), who had been a student of Angell's at Chicago, was the administrator of the fund. Ruml had followed Angell to the Carnegie Corporation, where he served as Angell's assistant prior to his appointment as administrator of the Rockefeller Fund. When Angell became president of Yale, he was highly successful in securing research grants from the Rockefeller Fund for the social sciences at Yale, including Hull's program at the Institute of Human Relations. This meant reduced faculty teaching loads, better equipment, and support for graduate students, all of which enabled Hull's program to thrive at a time when other universities (including Tolman's University of California at Berkeley) were cutting back on their research budgets and hiring, while increasing the workload of their remaining faculty (Boakes, 1984).

Hull's theories remained highly influential throughout the 1940s and 1950s. They were modified and extended by Kenneth Spence (1956, 1960) and his students at the University of Iowa and by former students and colleagues such as Carl Hovland (1912–1961) and O. Hobart Mowrer (1907–1982). Hull's form of neobehaviorism remained the dominant force in American departments of psychology until the advent of radical behaviorism and the cognitive revolution in the 1950s and 1960s.

Neobehaviorist Theory and Operational Definition

The neobehaviorist conception of theoretical postulates as operationally defined intervening variables (instrumentally or realistically construed) impeded the development of psychological theory. For although neobehaviorists reasonably insisted upon the empirical grounding of psychological theories (the requirement that psychological theories generate testable predictions about observable behavior), their commitment to the operational definition of theoretical meaning placed quite unnecessary restrictions on the content of psychological theories. The potentially fertile strategy of postulating internal states to explain observable behavior was transformed into a set of emaciating dogmas about the exhaustive operational definition of postulates in terms of observable stimuli and responses—a doubtful ideal that few neobehaviorists actually satisfied in practice (Estes et al., 1954).

What Is Learned? Nowhere is this more apparent than in Howard Kendler's (1952) supposed solution to the theoretical dispute between Hull and Tolman about "what is learned" by rats in mazes. Tolman claimed that rats develop a cognitive representation of the spatial layout of the maze (a cognitive map), whereas Hull claimed that rats learn differentially reinforced stimulus-response connections. Although both Tolman and Hull were committed realists who conceived of intervening variables as causally efficacious internal states, Kendler claimed that the debate about what is learned was a "pseudo issue," since theoretical postulates in psychology are

The tongues of men: Lewin, Tolman, and Hull, all having fun.

nothing more than economical summaries or "'shorthand' descriptions" of the observable stimulus-response sequences in terms of which they are operationally defined. Given that both theories were operationally defined in terms of (and purported to explain) the same observable behavior in the same stimulus situations, Kendler maintained there was no difference in the content of the two theories— they amounted to the same theory. He held that to suppose otherwise, to treat theoretical postulates as references to independently real entities or processes, was to commit "the fallacy of reification or hypostatization":

> The construct of learning, whether it be conceived in terms of modifications in cognitive maps or S-R connections, does not refer to an object, thing, or entity as is suggested by those who are concerned with the question of what is learned. These intervening variables possess no meaning over and above their stated relationships between the independent and dependent variables. The basic error underlying the problem of what is learned is the assumption that these intervening variables are

entities capable of being described and elaborated on, independently of their operational meaning.

—(1952, pp. 271–272)

If Kelman had been correct that Tolman's and Hull's theories were wholly specified in terms of the same relations between observable independent and dependent variables, this would have precluded the empirical development and evaluation of these theories, as it would with respect to any competing theories that shared the same empirical domain. The absurdity of this position is perhaps best illustrated by considering the equivalent suggestion to the effect that there was nothing at issue between the Copernican and Ptolemaic astronomical theories, or the wave and particle theories of light, just because they shared the same empirical domain (the same empirical predictions could be derived from both sets of theories).

Theoretical Meaning and Operational Measures The neobehaviorist error, inherited from scientific empiricist philosophy of science, was to confuse the reasonable demand for operational measures of postulated theoretical states and processes with the peculiar notion that the meaning of theoretical postulates must be specified in terms of such operational measures. The meaning of theoretical postulates in natural science is generally determined independently of operational definition. This explains why it is possible to understand Bohr's theory of the atom, for example, which postulates that electrons are held in orbit by a nucleus of protons and neutrons, without having any inkling of how changes in the energy level of electrons explain differences in the observed spectral emission lines for elements. For the same reason it is possible to understand Tolman's theoretical descriptions of cognitive maps without knowing how rats behave in mazes.

Of course, operational measures of theoretical constructs such as "electron" and "short-term memory" are important, but they do not determine their meaning, as evidenced by the fact that their meaning remains invariant when different operational measures are employed in different empirical or experimental contexts. Theoretical claims about electrons, for example, do not change their meaning between experiments in which the presence of electrons is demonstrated through spectography or tracks in a Wilson cloud chamber. Similarly, theoretical claims about short-term memory do not change their meaning when they are evaluated by experimental studies employing verbal as opposed to written measures.

The substantive differences in the contents of competing theories in natural and psychological science derive from their independent contents, which are not defined operationally. The substantive differences between the Copernican and Ptolemaic theories, and the wave and particle theories of light, were differences in "surplus" meaning. These generated the different predictions (about the stellar parallax and the speed of light in air and water) that eventually enabled disputes between these theories to be empirically adjudicated. The inconclusiveness of the original Tolman-Hull debate about "what is learned" is probably best explained in terms of the temporary ability of both theories to accommodate failed predictions via auxiliary hypothesis modification, which is the best explanation for the long periods of time during which the debates between the Copernican and Ptolemaic theories and the wave and particle theories of light were empirically undecidable, as Kendler (1981) later acknowledged.

Yet most neobehaviorists would have none of this. They insisted that surplus meaning has no place in psychological science and maintained that "operationally valid intervening variables . . . are the only kinds of constructs ultimately admissible in sound scientific theory" (Marx, 1951, p. 246). This placed quite unnecessary constraints on the development of psychological theory and created a critical conceptual dilemma for neobehaviorists. If the meaningful content of theoretical postulates really is exhaustively determined by the observational stimulus-response sequences in terms of which they are operationally defined, then why not simply dispense with theoretical constructs altogether and restrict psychological science to the description of observational stimulus-response sequences? As one scientific empiricist put it,

> If the terms and principles of a theory serve their purpose, that is, they establish definitive connections among observational phenomena, then they can be dispensed with, since any chain of laws and interpretative statements establishing such a connection should then be replaceable by a law that directly links observational antecedents to observational consequents.
>
> —(Hempel, 1965, p. 186)

The radical behaviorist B. F. Skinner grasped the nettle of this implication, often characterized as the **theoretician's dilemma**, and maintained that putative theoretical references to internal cognitive states are circular and unnecessary "explanatory fictions" (Skinner, 1953).

RADICAL BEHAVIORISM

Burrhus F. Skinner was born in 1904 in Susquehanna, Pennsylvania, into a middle-class family (his younger brother died at an early age). At high school, Skinner did poorly in science, but excelled in literature. He attended Hamilton College in Clinton, New York, where he gained a reputation as a trickster and prankster. After graduating with a BA in English literature, Skinner tried his hand as a writer. He lived in Paris and Greenwich Village and smoked a pipe, but he frittered his time away and produced nothing (although Robert Frost did comment favorably on some of his work at a summer writing school). He became depressed and considered himself a failure in love as well as in literature, having been rejected by half a dozen girls who took his fancy. Unlike many earlier psychologists, this disillusioned writer was not inspired by James's *Principles*, but by the work of Watson and Pavlov, which stimulated him to follow a career in psychology.

Skinner was accepted into the graduate program in psychology at Harvard in 1928 (where he eventually spent most of his career). He devoted himself to psychology and physiology during his years at Harvard, where he was influenced by Walter S. Hunter (1889–1954), who introduced Skinner to behaviorism in a course he taught on animal behavior (Skinner, 1967). Skinner heard Pavlov lecture at the 1929 International Congress in Psychology held at Harvard and obtained a signed photograph of his hero (which he hung over his desk). He earned his master's degree in 1930 and his PhD in 1931, and he continued at Harvard for five more years as a postgraduate fellow (of the Harvard Society of Fellows). He taught at the University of Minnesota from 1936 to 1945, during which time he published *The Behavior of Organisms* (1938). The book received mixed reviews and had little initial impact (the first print run of 800 copies took about 10 years to sell), being overshadowed by the anticipated publication of Hull's *Principles of Behavior*. Appleton-Century-Crofts was initially reluctant to publish the book, having already contracted for Hull's *Principles*, but was persuaded by an enthusiastic external review by Tolman and a publication grant from Harvard.

Operant Conditioning

Skinner's research focused upon what he called operant behavior, as opposed to Pavlovian respondent behavior. He defined **operant behavior** as behavior whose probability of recurrence is increased by reinforcement: an "emitted" behavior is positively or negatively reinforced via a food reward or removal of a painful stimulus. In contrast, he defined **respondent behavior** as behavior "elicited" by unconditioned and conditioned stimuli. According to Skinner, **operant conditioning** increases the probability of the recurrence of a behavior (in a stimulus situation) and the frequency of its recurrence, through reinforcement of the behavior. Thus a rat in a Skinner box (a box specially constructed to eliminate potentially interfering stimuli and to control the reinforcement of emitted behavior) will eventually depress a lever that delivers a food pellet into a tray, and the rat's rate of bar pressing will increase cumulatively once it begins to be reinforced. Skinner's *Behavior of Organisms* (1938) described the basic principles of operant conditioning, including reinforcement, extinction, spontaneous recovery, discrimination learning, and the effect of punishment on learning. This work demonstrated Skinner's ability to predict and control the behavior of laboratory rats and established his reputation as a rigorous experimentalist.

Skinner moved to Indiana University in 1945, where he served as chair of the department of psychology until 1948. He then returned to Harvard, where he remained (as professor emeritus from 1974) until his death in 1990 (at the age of 86 from leukemia). He published *Science and Human Behavior* in 1953, *Verbal Behavior* in 1957, and *About Behaviorism* in 1974. From the 1940s onward Skinner began to explore the influence of different **schedules of reinforcement** on learning, such as fixed and variable interval and ratio schedules (Ferster & Skinner, 1957), which he considered to be his most significant contribution to scientific psychology. He also investigated the **shaping** of behavior through the reinforcement of progressive approximations to a target behavior (Skinner, 1951), such as the pecking of piano keys by pigeons and vocalization by catatonic schizophrenics.

Skinner claimed that his account of operant conditioning was merely a refinement of Thorndike's "law of effect." However, Skinner abjured Thorndike's references to satisfaction and discomfort and rejected Hull's interpretation of reinforcement as drive reduction. He maintained that "the only defining characteristic of a reinforcing stimulus is that it reinforces" (1953, p. 72), ignoring the obvious circularity of the definition.

Explanatory Fictions

Skinner rejected the scientific empiricist and neobehaviorist account of psychological theories. He claimed that theories about unobservable states and processes, including theories about cognitive states and processes, are **explanatory fictions**: They are vacuous as explanations of relations between observable stimuli and responses and play no role in the development of novel predictions about behavior. According to the neobehaviorist account of the meaning of psychological theories, intervening variables must be operationally defined in terms of observable stimuli and responses. Skinner argued that if theoretical postulates such as "cognitive maps" or "habit strength" really were defined in terms of empirical laws relating observable stimuli and responses, then any avowed explanation of empirical laws in terms of "cognitive maps" or "habit strength" would be vacuously circular. According to Skinner, such an "explanation" would appeal to the very functional relationships that it purported to explain:

> To what extent is it helpful to be told, "He drinks because he is thirsty"? If to be thirsty means nothing more than to have a tendency to drink, this is mere redundancy.
>
> —(1953, p. 33)

For similar reasons, he maintained that there is no need to appeal to intervening variables in the "practical control of behavior":

> When an example of maladjusted behavior is explained by saying that the individual is "suffering from anxiety," we still have to be told the cause of the

anxiety. But the external conditions which are then invoked could have been directly related to the maladjusted behavior. Again, when we are told that a man stole a loaf of bread because "he was hungry," we still have to learn of the external conditions responsible for the "hunger." These conditions would have sufficed to explain the theft.

—(1953, p. 35)

Skinner also recognized that the notion that operationally defined intervening variables can generate novel empirical predictions is completely illusory. Since at any point in time, the content of postulated intervening variables is supposedly determined by the functional relationships between observable stimuli and responses in terms of which they are operationally defined, the only basis for the prediction of novel functional relationships *is our present knowledge of functional relationships between observable stimuli and responses*. Skinner claimed that the whole apparatus of intervening variables and operational definitions is redundant with respect to the explanation and prediction of observable behavior, which is ultimately based upon functional laws relating observable stimuli and behavior:

The objection to inner states is not that they do not exist, but that they are not relevant in a functional analysis. We cannot account for the behavior of any system while staying wholly inside it; eventually we must turn to forces operating on the organism from without. Unless there is a weak spot in our causal chain so that the second link is not causally determined by the first, or the third by the second, then the first and third links must be lawfully related. If we must always go back beyond the second link for prediction and control, we may avoid many tiresome and exhausting digressions by examining the third link as a function of the first.

—(1953, p. 35)

These were legitimate criticisms of the standard neobehaviorist account of theoretical meaning in terms of operationally defined intervening variables, but they did not extend to the "surplus meaning" of Tolman's theoretical constructs or those developed by later cognitive theorists.

Radical Behaviorism

Skinner's radical behaviorism marked a return to the positivist and inductivist form of behaviorism championed by Watson, with an emphasis on response reinforcement contingencies rather than stimulus-response connections.

Skinner maintained that behaviorist psychology should focus on the description of functional relationships between observable behavior and environmental stimuli, based upon the experimental analysis, control, and manipulation of environmental reinforcement:

> We can predict and control behavior, we can modify it, we can construct it according to specifications, and all without answering the explanatory questions which have driven investigators into the study of the inner man.
>
> —(Skinner, 1961, p. 254)

Skinner eschewed theory and rejected the hypothetico-deductive method advocated by Tolman and Hull. In "Are Theories of Learning Necessary?" (1950), he argued that significant experimentation in psychology does not need to be theory-guided, but can proceed via the inductive accumulation of functional laws relating observable stimuli and responses, or behavior and reinforcement.

Skinner characterized his behaviorism as **descriptive behaviorism** for the same positivist reasons that Titchener characterized his structural psychology as descriptive psychology. Skinner and Titchener rejected explanatory appeals to unobservable states and processes and equated causal explanation with the description of observable correlation. However, Skinner's frequent presentation of his radical behaviorist position as atheoretical was somewhat disingenuous, since his own research program was firmly grounded upon distinctive theoretical commitments, as he later admitted (Skinner, 1967).

Like Watson and Hull, Skinner acknowledged the existence of cognitive states, but denied that they are "centrally initiated." Like Hull (and Sechenov), Skinner maintained that cognitive states are merely internal links in fully determined causal chains relating behavior and environmental stimuli. He rejected the notion that the cognitive agent is the "true originator or initiator of action" (Skinner, 1974, p. 225) and, like most other behaviorists, was a committed environmentalist.

Skinner's theoretical commitment to the environmental determination of behavior led him to champion programs of social engineering based upon experimentally derived principles of behavior modification. Skinnerian principles of behavior modification came to be employed in a wide variety of industrial, educational, and clinical training programs, as well as commercial animal training services (such as Animal Behavior Enterprises, formed by Keller and Marian Breland, two former students of Skinner's). Managers employed reinforcement schedules to maximize production in factories, educators introduced teaching machines to schools and colleges, and clinicians employed token-economy programs to shape the behavior of patients in psychiatric hospitals (in which patients could trade tokens for reinforcers such as candy or cigarettes). Clinical psychologists adopted forms of behavior therapy based upon Skinnerian principles of behavior modification, which remain popular to this day.

Skinner's reprisal of Watson's entry into the realm of child rearing was less successful and brought him some notoriety. He designed an air-crib that allowed

Baby in a box: Yvonne and Debby Skinner.

parents to manipulate an infant's environment, based upon the same principles as the Skinner box. His eldest daughter Deborah was raised in this "baby-box" for the first two and a half years of her life. The device was described in an article titled "Baby In A Box," published in *Ladies' Home Journal* in 1945 and received extensive coverage in the media. While it aroused interest among some parents seeking relief from the more mundane tasks of child rearing (such as laundry—the crib was temperature controlled, so there was no need for heavy clothing or blankets), it also generated outrage from those who considered it a cruel practice, analogous to raising children like household pets. About 130 parents used Skinner's "air-crib," or "heir-conditioner," as he called it.

Rumors later abounded about how Deborah Skinner had been psychologically scarred by her isolation in the baby box and (like Watson's children) had become psychotic and suicidal in later life. These rumors proved to be mere wishful thinking on the part of Skinner's critics. Deborah had happy memories of her childhood, and after graduating with honors from Radcliffe College, embarked on a successful artistic career. Skinner's other daughter Julie was not raised in an "air-crib" but raised her own children in one.

In 1948 Skinner published *Walden Two,* a novel about a community run on principles of behavior modification. The book was a bizarre cross between Aldous

Huxley's *Brave New World* and Henry David Thoreau's utopian *Walden*. In 1971 Skinner published *Beyond Freedom and Dignity,* in which he dismissed the notion of human freedom as a superstition that impeded the application of the methods of science to the control of human behavior. The book became a best seller and made Skinner a household name. In television shows and newspaper articles, Skinner (like Watson before him) became something of an academic celebrity and (also like Watson before him) relished the controversy generated by his provocative remarks. When asked whether, if he had to choose, he would burn his books or his children, Skinner picked the latter, a response that generated predictable public outrage.

In the decades after the Second World War, Skinner's radical behaviorism became a distinctive movement within scientific psychology. The *Journal for the Experimental Analysis of Behavior* was founded in 1958 as a publication outlet for radical behaviorists (to avoid the statistical publication conditions of other psychology journals that Skinner and his followers rejected) and the *Journal of Applied Behavior Analysis* in 1968 (to cope with the increased volume of radical behaviorist submissions). Division 25 of the American Psychological Association was designated as the Division of the Experimental Analysis of Behavior. Radical behaviorists came to play an influential role in the development of many psychology departments, notably at Columbia University, where Fred Keller, a friend and fellow-student of Skinner's at Harvard, and his student William Nathan (Nat) Schoenfeld transformed the curriculum in accordance with radical behaviorist principles (Bolles, 1993). This was perhaps apt, since it was at Columbia that the "behaviorist revolution" began with Watson's 1913 lecture.

Skinner was the most famous 20th-century psychologist, both for his substantive scientific achievements and for his controversial public persona. He was awarded the Warren Medal by the Society of Experimental Psychologists in 1942, a Distinguished Scientific Contribution Award by the APA in 1958, and the Gold Medal of the American Psychological Foundation in 1971. He was never elected president of the APA, but served as president of the Midwest Psychological Association in 1948.

Skinner had no truck with the later cognitive revolution in psychology. He believed that it betrayed the principles of scientific psychology and marked a return to superstition and introspection. He accused cognitive psychologists of employing unscientific speculations about "internal processes" as the causes of behavior and of "emasculating the experimental analysis of behavior" (1985, p. 300).

Skinner remained active intellectually until his death in 1990. In 1983 (at the age of 78) he published *Enjoying Old Age* (with Margaret Vaughan), a behaviorist primer for remaining active and happy in old age, based upon his own practical experience. In 1990 he received a Lifetime Contribution to Psychology Award from the APA, in recognition of his "dynamic and far-reaching-impact on the discipline" (1990, p. 1205). Skinner accepted the Award Citation at the 1990 meeting of the APA in Boston, where he made his final public appearance, delivering a critical address titled "Can Psychology Be a Science of the Mind?" (published in *American Psychologist*, November 1990). He died a week later.

THE SECOND WORLD WAR AND THE PROFESSIONALIZATION OF ACADEMIC PSYCHOLOGY

Skinner's form of radical behaviorism displaced neobehaviorism in the decades following the Second World War, although it was later overshadowed by the cognitive revolution in psychology, which was stimulated by theoretical and technical developments during the war. The Second World War, which began in Europe when Germany invaded Poland in 1939 and which America entered after the Japanese bombed Pearl Harbor in 1941, also precipitated a major transformation of the structure of scientific and professional psychology.

The heady public optimism about the potential of psychology in the 1920s was replaced by general public skepticism in the 1930s, as economic prosperity gave way to economic depression. Newspaper and magazine coverage of psychology declined. The general disillusionment with the promised social contribution of psychology was aptly expressed in a *New York Times* editorial in 1934, which lamented the fact that psychology was strong on promises during the good times but weak on the delivery of solutions to real problems in times of hardship (Benjamin, 1986).

Psychological Contributions to the War Effort

Once again, the contribution psychologists made to the war effort did wonders for their public reputation. In contrast to the First World War, psychologists were well prepared for the Second World War. The APA and the American Association of Applied Psychologists (AAAP) organized planning committees prior to the outbreak of war. These committees held their first joint meeting in 1939 and merged in 1940 under government pressure for the integration of psychological services. Walter V. Bingham and Robert M. Yerkes, both veterans of psychological service in the First World War, worked vigorously to promote the military applications of psychology. Although they failed to persuade the army to adopt their comprehensive plan, American psychologists made significant contributions to the war effort, working through the office of the Emergency Committee of Psychology, which comprised representatives from the APA and AAAP, the Society for the Psychological Study of Social Issues (SPSSI), the Society of Experimental Psychologists (SEP), and Section I (Psychology) of the American Association for the Advancement of Science (AAAS).

As in the First World War, much of the psychological war effort was focused on personnel selection and aptitude testing, which was directed by Bingham, who became chairman of the Committee on Classification of Military Personnel (with the rank of colonel). However, psychologists also contributed to intelligence work and the evaluation of prisoners of war (Capshew, 1999). They worked with other social scientists and psychiatrists on studies of the attitudes, morale, and adjustment of combat troops (Stouffer, Lumsdane, et al., 1949; Stouffer, Suchman, et al., 1949), the psychological effects of saturation bombing on the enemy (U.S. Strategic Bombing Survey, 1946), French civilian reaction to the D-Day landings (Riley, 1947), and civilian morale and propaganda (Watson, 1942). Psychologists also played a major role in **human factors research**, which focused on the interaction between human operators and machines such as torpedoes and anti-aircraft guns, and radar and communication systems. This research promoted developments in information theory that stimulated the later cognitive revolution in psychology. Psychologists also exploited group dynamics to encourage wartime changes in food habits and the purchase of U.S. war bonds (Cartwright, 1949; Lewin, 1947), and they played a major role in the provision of psychotherapy and counseling for emotionally disturbed soldiers, since psychiatrists were overwhelmed by the sheer number of psychological casualties during the war (Benjamin et al., 2003).

The Reorganization of the APA

Government pressure for cooperation between scientific and professional psychologists during wartime led to the formation of the Office of Psychological Personnel (OPP), located in Washington, DC. Yerkes exploited the situation to try to repair the prewar split between the APA and the AAAP and organized a constitutional convention to plan for the postwar reconstruction of the APA. The American Psychological Association was reorganized and reconstituted in 1944 with 18 charter divisions, which represented the interests of applied psychologists such as clinical, consulting, industrial, and school psychologists, and the various scientific societies (such as the Society for the Psychological Study of Social Issues) and interest groups (such as the National Council of Women Psychologists). The divisional structure of the new APA was modeled upon the divisional structure of the AAAP, which disbanded that same year. According to the constitution of the new APA, the goal of the association was "to advance psychology as science, as a profession, and as a means of promoting human welfare" (Wolfle, 1946/1997, p. 721), in contrast to the goal of the original APA, which was restricted to "the advancement of psychology as a science." Applied psychologists demanded the reference to the "profession" of psychology, and the reference to "promoting human welfare" was added at the last minute at the insistence of the Society for the Psychological Study of Social Issues. The Executive Secretariat of the new APA was housed in the former offices of the OPP in Washington, and *American Psychologist* was instituted in 1946 as the new "professional journal" of the APA (Benjamin et al., 2003).

Postwar Expansion

Clinical, consulting, and industrial psychology (three of the four original sections of the AAAP) expanded dramatically after the war. Recognizing that there were too few psychiatrists to cope with the psychological needs of returning veterans, the government authorized the U.S. Public Health Service (USPHS) and the Veterans Administration (VA) to expand the pool of mental health professionals by creating and funding training programs in clinical psychology at major universities. The USPHS and the VA worked with the new APA to develop program evaluations, which led to accreditation programs in clinical psychology in 1946 and in counseling psychology in 1952 (Benjamin et al., 2003).

Industrial psychology also got a major boost from its perceived record of accomplishment in the war. Businesses increased their employment of psychological tests from around 14 percent in the prewar period to around 75 percent by 1950 (Napoli, 1981, p. 138, cited in Benjamin et al., 2003). As applied branches of psychology established their professional identity through the creation of specially tailored doctoral programs, so too did subdisciplines such as social and developmental psychology. Psychology became a popular subject once again, with newspapers, magazines (such as *Psychology Today*, founded in 1967), and a veritable avalanche of self-help books fueling the public demand for psychological advice and knowledge.

Neobehaviorists such as Carl Hovland contributed to the war effort through the study of mass communication (Hovland, Lumsdaine, & Sheffield, 1949), as did radical behaviorists such as Skinner and his students. Skinner worked with Keller and Marian Breland on Project Orcon, for which they trained pigeons as "missile guidance systems" or "organic control systems" (Skinner, 1960). The pigeons performed successfully in missile guidance simulations, but the military declined to adopt them. After the war, behaviorist theories of conditioned learning faced increasing problems, both theoretical and empirical, and were rejected by proponents of the emerging cognitive revolution in psychology. Radical behaviorists remained an active force in psychology, but became increasingly isolated in the fashion of Titchener's structural psychologists at the beginning of the 20th century (Krantz, 1972).

PROBLEMS OF BEHAVIORISM

By the end of the Second World War, many psychologists had come to question the behaviorist presumption that all or most of human psychology and behavior could be explained in terms of general theories of conditioning based upon the experimental study of rats and pigeons. They doubted that such theories could be extended to accommodate human moral, social, and linguistic behavior, as most behaviorists had maintained (with the notable exception of Tolman). Neobehaviorists themselves were forced to develop **mediational theories** that appealed to complex internal response-stimulus (r-s) sequences in order to accommodate linguistic behavior and symbolic meaning (N. Miller, 1959; Osgood, 1957).

In the 1950s and 1960s behaviorist theories based upon conditioning came under increasing attack, in terms of both the scope and basic principles of conditioning theory. Although none were perhaps sufficient to undermine the entire behaviorist program, these critiques prepared the way for the cognitive revolution in psychology.

Chomsky's Critique of Skinner

B. F. Skinner advanced the most detailed attempt to develop a behaviorist account of linguistic behavior in his 1957 book *Verbal Behavior.* In this work Skinner identified the referents of words (or, in his terminology, verbal operant responses, or "tacts") with discriminative stimuli in the environment that come to control the correct emission of verbal responses through reinforcement by the linguistic community. Skinner maintained that

> The basic processes and relations which give verbal behavior its special characteristics are now fairly well understood. . . . most of the experimental work responsible for the advance of the experimental analysis of behavior has been carried out on other species. . . . the results have proved to be surprisingly free of species restrictions. . . . recent work has shown that the methods can be extended to human behavior without serious modification.
>
> —(1957, p. 3)

Noam Chomsky (1928–) subjected Skinner's claim that the complexities of verbal behavior could be explained in terms of discriminative stimuli and reinforcement history to a devastating critique. In a famous review of Skinner's book in *Language* in 1959, Chomsky argued that Skinner's basic concepts of stimulus, response, and reinforcement could be objectively defined only in terms of rigorously controlled experiments and could not be extended to accommodate complex verbal behavior subject to "ill-defined factors of attention, set, volition and caprice" (1959, p. 30). He claimed that Skinner had failed miserably in his attempt to explain verbal behavior by reference to a "few external factors . . . isolated experimentally with lower organisms," without any appeal to the cognitive contribution of the speaker. Chomsky also suggested that

> The magnitude of the failure of this attempt to account for verbal behavior serves as a kind of measure of the importance of the factors omitted from consideration, and an indication of how little is actually known about this remarkably complex phenomenon.
>
> —(1959, p. 28)

Anticipating the form of explanation that would later become characteristic of cognitive psychology, Chomsky argued that human verbal behavior could only be explained in terms of representations of the rules governing the construction of sentences. According to Chomsky, our ability to recognize sentences cannot be explained in terms of behaviorist principles such as "stimulus generalization" or in terms of basic associationist principles (such as contiguity, frequency, and reinforcement), but must be explained in terms of the internal representation of the grammar of a language:

> We constantly read and hear new sequences of words, recognize them as sentences, and understand them. It is easy to show that the new events that we accept and understand as sentences are not related to those with which we are familiar by any simple notion of formal (or semantic or statistical) similarity or identity of grammatical frame. Talk of generalization in this case is entirely pointless and empty. It appears that we recognize a new item as a sentence not because it matches some familiar item in any simple way, but because it is generated by the grammar that each individual has somehow and in some form internalized. And we understand a new sentence, in part, because we are somehow capable of determining the process by which this sentence is derived in this grammar.
>
> —(1959, p. 56)

Chomsky stressed the extraordinary nature of the child's achievement in learning a language:

> The child who learns a language has in some sense constructed a grammar for himself on the basis of his observation of sentences and nonsentences (i.e. corrections by the linguistic community). Study of the actual observed ability of a speaker to distinguish sentences from non-sentences, detect ambiguities, etc., apparently forces us to the conclusion that this grammar is of an extremely complex and abstract character, and that the young child has succeeded in carrying out what from the formal point of view, at least, seems to be a remarkable type of theory construction. Furthermore, this task is accomplished in an astonishingly short time, to a large extent independently of intelligence, and in a comparable way by all children. Any theory of learning must cope with these facts.
>
> —(1959, p. 57)

These considerations led Chomsky to doubt that any behaviorist theory could account for the remarkable fact that all normal children acquire "essentially comparable grammars with remarkable rapidity" (1959, p. 57), based upon a very limited set of data (the so-called "poverty of the stimulus" argument). According to Chomsky, the child's ability to acquire grammar at such a rapid rate can be explained only by the postulation of some innate "'hypothesis-formulating' ability" (1959, p. 57), a suggestion Chomsky later developed in his theory of (innate) transformational grammar—a postulated system of rules governing the production of grammatically well-formed sentences (Chomsky, 1965, 1966, 1972).

Although linguistic phenomena such as reference might appear to be susceptible to a behaviorist analysis in terms of stimulus control, Chomsky maintained that no behaviorist theory could explain the *structure* of grammar or the productivity and creativity of language. And Chomsky's followers argued that not even reference could be explained in terms of stimulus control, since one of the distinctive features of language is that it is not "stimulus-bound":

> A striking feature of linguistic behavior is its freedom from the control of specifiable local stimuli or independently identifiable drive states. In typical situations, what is said may have no obvious correlation with conditions in the immediate locality of the speaker or with his recent history of deprivation or reward.
>
> —(Fodor, 1965, p. 73)

Chomsky's own linguistic theory underwent a multitude of transformations from *Aspects of a Theory of Syntax* in 1965 to *Language and the Problem of Knowledge* in 1988 and shaped the development of postwar linguistics to such a degree that it is not unreasonable to maintain that "the history of modern linguistics *is* the history of Chomsky's ideas and of the diverse reactions to them on the part of the community" (Gardner, 1985, p. 185, original emphasis). Although Chomsky influenced many individual psychologists and persuaded some (such as George Miller) to abandon behaviorism and embrace cognitive forms of psychological explanation, his own distinctive theoretical position had little direct impact upon the development of later theories in cognitive psychology. While all cognitive psychologists embraced Chomsky's **cognitivism**, his commitment to the legitimacy and utility of cognitive theoretical constructs, many were (and remain) reluctant to embrace the extreme nativism and formalism of his linguistic theory.

The Misbehavior of Organisms

While Chomsky's critique was powerful, it demonstrated the limits of behaviorist explanation with respect to only one distinctively human behavior—language. Other critiques pointed to the limits of behaviorist explanation with respect to animal behavior, the original foundation of the behaviorist program. Behaviorists had generally depreciated the role of instinct in animal and human behavior. European biologists and ethologists such as Konrad Lorenz (1903–1989) and Nikolaas (Niko) Tinbergen (1907–1988), who received the Nobel Prize in physiology and medicine in 1973 for their naturalistic studies of species-specific instinctual behavior (Lorenz, 1950; Tinbergen, 1951), criticized American "ratrunners" for their failure to study animals in their natural environment (ignoring Watson's early field studies of the behavior of noddy and sooty terns) and their neglect of instinctual constraints on learning—criticisms that were echoed by American psychologists such as Frank Beach (1950, 1960).

Psychologists within the behaviorist camp also developed similar criticisms. Keller and Marian Breland were former students and colleagues of Skinner's who founded a company called Animal Behavior Enterprises. They employed operant conditioning principles in training animals commercially for entertainment parks and television, but began to question some of the basic assumptions of conditioning theory. Their extensive practical experience in training animals taught them that it is extremely difficult for animals to learn certain forms of behavior: What they were eventually forced to recognize as instinctual behavior interfered with learning and came to displace learned behavior. The Brelands described numerous cases of animals that had been conditioned to a behavior but would then engage in a quite different behavior. They claimed that "it can easily be seen that these particular behaviors to which the animals drift are clear-cut examples of instinctive behaviors having to do with the natural food getting behaviors of the particular species" (1961, p. 683).

For example, although one could train raccoons and pigs to deposit wooden tokens into containers, they quickly reverted to instinctual "washing" and "rooting" behaviors. The Brelands described their attempt to teach a raccoon to drop a wooden "coin" into a "piggy bank":

> The raccoon really had problems (and so did we). Not only could he not let go of the coins, but he spent seconds, even minutes, rubbing them together (in a most miserly fashion), and dipping them into the container. He carried on this behavior to such an extent that the practical application we had in mind—a display featuring a raccoon putting money in a piggy bank—simply was not feasible. The rubbing behavior became worse and worse as time went on, in spite of nonreinforcement.
>
> —(1961, p. 682)

They claimed that the raccoon was demonstrating the form of "washing behavior" that it would normally employ in the removal of the exoskeleton of a crayfish, for example, and concluded that

> It seems obvious that these animals are trapped by strong instinctive behaviors, and clearly we have here a demonstration of the prepotency of such behavior patterns over those which have been conditioned.
>
> —(1961, p. 684)

The Brelands called this phenomenon **instinctual drift**:

> The general principle seems to be that wherever an animal has strong instinctive
> behaviors in the area of the conditioned response, after continued running the organ-
> ism will drift toward the instinctive behavior to the detriment of the conditioned
> behavior and even to the delay or preclusion of the reinforcement.
>
> —(1961, p. 684)

The Brelands presented a strong empirical case that there are significant evolutionary biological limits to animal learning. They claimed that their examples of
instinctual drift demonstrated the "clear and utter failure of conditioning theory"
(1961, p. 683) and maintained that animal behavior "cannot be adequately understood, predicted or controlled without knowledge of its instinctive patterns, evolutionary history, and ecological niche" (1961, p. 684). In a similar vein, Martin
Seligman (1970) later claimed that certain species are biologically prepared to
learn some behaviors and contraprepared to learn others.

Contiguity and Frequency

These critiques were damaging, but essentially maintained that behaviorist explanations of animal behavior, like behaviorist explanations of human behavior,
were more limited in scope than behaviorists had presumed. The Brelands did not
think their critique was fatal to behaviorism and suggested that it "should make
possible a worthwhile revision in behavior theory" (1961, p. 684). Other critiques
questioned the basic explanatory principles of behaviorist learning theories. Theories of classical and operant conditioning, like earlier associationist psychology
from Hume to Bain, had assumed that animal and human learning is based upon
the principles of contiguity and frequency. As Sigmund Koch put it,

> In effect they have given to us as the primary analytic concepts for the most ambi-
> tious science ever conceived a mildly camouflaged paradigm for Hume's analysis of
> causality.
>
> —(1964, p. 34)

These theories assumed that the strength of a connection between a conditioned
stimulus and response (in classical conditioning) or response and reinforcement
(in operant conditioning) was a function of the frequency with which a conditioned stimulus is paired (contiguously) with a unconditioned stimulus (in classical conditioning), or a response paired (contiguously) with reinforcement (in
operant conditioning), with the optimal temporal interval for pairing being of the
order of a fraction of a second.

John Garcia (1917–) challenged these assumptions in a now famous series of studies of conditioned taste aversion (Garcia & Koelling, 1966). Garcia worked for a spell at the Naval Radiation Defense Laboratory in San Francisco, after he failed the statistics course in the psychology department at the University of California at Berkeley (Bolles, 1993). In studying the effects of radiation on rats, he noticed that they would later refuse to drink saccharin if they were exposed to radiation (which made them sick) when they first tasted it. When he returned to Berkeley, Garcia made this the topic of his PhD dissertation. He discovered that rats that refuse to drink saccharin that has been paired with radiation sickness do so after a single trial, violating the principle of frequency, and after an interval of up to 12 hours between drinking saccharin and sickness, violating the principle of contiguity.

Garcia's work demonstrated forms of instinctual preparation and contrapreparation in animal learning, and he co-authored a paper on biological constraints on learning that was included in the 1972 Seligman and Hager collection *The Biological Boundaries of Learning* (Garcia, McGowan, & Green, 1972). However, it took some time for Garcia's work to be generally accepted. When he described the results of his experiments to a learning theorist at the University of California at Los Angeles, he was assured they were impossible (Bolles, 1993), and the mainstream journals rejected his original experimental report (Lubek & Apfelbaum, 1987). However, Garcia's work eventually precipitated a critical reappraisal of theories of conditioning, and he became a distinguished professor of psychology at UC Berkeley.

Garcia's studies indicated that contiguity and frequency are not necessary for conditioned learning. Other studies indicated that contiguity and frequency are not sufficient. Kamin's (1969) studies of "blocking" suggested that prior conditioning to one element of a compound stimulus (such as light in a light and noise complex) attenuates or blocks conditioning to the other element. These and related studies (such as Revusky, 1971) led Rescorla and Wagner (1972) to develop a cognitive explanation of conditioning in terms of discrepancies between anticipated and actual reinforcement, which cast doubt upon the presumed automatic nature of conditioning. As N. J. Mackintosh (1978, p. 54) put it,

> Simple associative learning is simple in name only. Animals do not automatically associate all events that happen to occur together. If they did, they would be at the mercy of every chance conjunction of events. In fact, they behave in an altogether more rational manner. By conditioning selectively to good predictors of reinforcement at the expense of poor predictors, and by taking their past experience into account, they succeed in attributing reinforcers to their most probable causes. It is time that psychologists abandoned their outmoded view of conditioning and recognized it as a complex and useful process whereby organisms build an accurate representation of their world.

Consciousness and Conditioning

If this were not bad enough, other researchers suggested that in order for some forms of conditioning to be effective, the link between response and reinforcement must be *consciously* represented. Studies of verbal conditioning had indicated that one could manipulate subjects' use of linguistic items (such as plural nouns) via social reinforcement without their awareness, a form of conditioning commonly known as the **Greenspoon effect** (Greenspoon, 1955). However, Dulany (1968) suggested that, in many of these studies, not only were subjects aware of the relevant response reinforcement connections, but also that such awareness was a necessary condition of successful conditioning. This also cast doubt upon the presumed automaticity of conditioning and undermined the confident denials by Thorndike, Watson, Hull, and Skinner that consciousness plays a role in learning.

Ironically, Skinner's own daughter had pointed this out to him at an early age. In his 1987 book, *Upon Further Reflection*, Skinner reminisced about how he had tried to condition his daughter's foot movements (when she was 3 years old) by rubbing her back:

> I waited until she lifted her foot slightly and then rubbed briefly. Almost immediately she lifted her foot again, and again I rubbed. Then she laughed. "What are you laughing at?" I said. "Every time I raise my foot you rub my back!"
>
> —(Skinner, 1987, p. 179)

The Neurophysiology of Learning

Finally, Karl Lashley (1890–1958), Watson's former colleague and one-time supporter of behaviorism (Lashley, 1923), raised critical doubts about the neurophysiological assumptions of traditional behaviorist **peripheralist theories of learning**, which maintained that connections between stimuli and responses are determined independently of "centrally initiated" cognitive cortical processes. Lashley, who held professorships at the universities of Minnesota, Chicago, and Harvard and was later director of the Yerkes Primate Laboratories in Florida, became famous for his work on the neuropsychology of learning in the 1920s. He maintained that there are no cognitive centers of the cerebral cortex governing intelligence and learning comparable to the established sensory and motor centers and that cognitive functions are distributed over the cortex (Lashley, 1929).

At the 1948 Hixon Symposium on "Cerebral Mechanisms in Behavior" held at the California Institute of Technology, he argued that standard behaviorist accounts of conditioned learning could not accommodate many forms of complex human and animal behavior:

> My principle thesis is that . . . input is never into a quiescent or static system, but always into a system which is always already excited and organized. In the intact organism, behavior is the result of interaction of this background of excitation with input from any designated stimulus. Only when we can state the general characteristics of this background of excitation, can we understand the effects of a given input.
>
> —(1951, p. 112)

Lashley claimed that traditional behaviorist explanations in terms of reflex arcs and chains of association or connection could not account for complex serially ordered behavior such as language. He focused on language because it "presents in a most striking form the integrative functions that are characteristic of the cerebral cortex and that reach their highest development in the human thought processes" (Lashley, 1951, p. 113). However, he insisted that these integrative functions, which cannot be explained "in terms of successions of external stimuli," are also to be found in many other forms of animal and human behavior:

> This is true not only of language, but of all skilled movements or successions of movement. In the gaits of a horse, trotting, pacing, and single footing involve essentially the same pattern of muscular contraction in the individual legs. The gait is imposed by some mechanism in addition to the direct relations of reciprocal innervation among the sensory-motor centers of the legs. The order in which the fingers of the musician fall on the keys or fingerboard is determined by the signature of the composition; this gives a *set* which is not inherent in the association of the individual movements.
>
> . . . Not only speech, but all skilled acts seem to involve the same problems of serial ordering, even down to the temporal coordination of muscular contractions in such a movement as reaching and grasping.
>
> —(1951, pp. 116, 121–122)

He maintained that many forms of human and animal behavior require explanation in terms of hierarchically organized cognitive control structures that determine complex sequences of serially ordered behavior, which are occasioned by environmental inputs but cannot be explained in terms of associations between environmental inputs and responses or reinforcement histories.

Lashley acknowledged that the forms of explanation he was advocating in terms of central cognitive control processes were analogous to the "determining tendencies" and "ordered thought-processes" postulated by early-20th-century

Würzburg theorists such as Külpe and Selz. In maintaining that cognitive processes in the cerebral cortex play a critical role in the determination of human and animal behavior, Lashley repudiated Watson's famous denial of the causal role of "centrally initiated processes" in the determination of behavior (and vindicated Müller and Bain's 19th-century commitment to "spontaneous" forms of behavior that are products of stored nervous energy in the cerebral cortex).

THE EVE OF THE COGNITIVE REVOLUTION

At the same 1948 Hixon Symposium where Lashley championed cognitive control structures, John von Neumann (1903–1957) and Warren McCulloch (1898–1969) drew parallels between the cognitive processing of information by the cerebral cortex and the newly developed electronic computer (McCulloch, 1951; von Neumann, 1951). Two years later, at the Dartmouth Conference on Learning, neobehaviorist theories of learning were condemned as inconsistent and beset by empirical anomalies (Estes et al., 1954). Six years later, at the 1956 Symposium on Information Theory at MIT, the cognitive revolution in psychology was launched, at least according to Jerome Bruner and George Miller, two of its undisputed leaders (Bruner, 1980; G. Miller, 1989).

Participants at the Hixon Symposium: Karl Lashley (front, second from left), John von Neumann (back, fifth from left), and Wolfgang Köhler (front, fourth from left).

DISCUSSION QUESTIONS

1. Do you agree with the logical positivists that the only things that can be meaningfully stated are those that can be empirically verified? Can you think of claims (including psychological claims) that might be true even if they cannot be empirically tested?

2. If a behavior is purposive—that is, intentionally directed toward a goal or end state—must it be explained in terms of cognition or consciousness? Is it legitimate to explain purposive behavior in terms of instincts or conditioned learning?

3. Tolman held that not all human and animal behavior could be explained in terms of conditioned learning. Did he accept or reject the principle of strong continuity with respect to human and animal psychology?

4. Was Skinner correct in claiming that behavior explained by appeal to anxiety or hunger is sufficiently explained by the external causes of anxiety or hunger? If so, does this mean that explanations of behavior in terms of anxiety or hunger have no independent substantive content?

5. Do you think Chomsky was correct in maintaining that theories of conditioning are incapable in principle of explaining children's acquisition of grammar, given the speed with which they learn grammar on the basis of impoverished data?

GLOSSARY

causally intervening variable A term referencing an internal state of an organism that causally mediates between observable stimuli and behavioral responses. The realist conception of an intervening variable.

cognitivism The view that cognitive theoretical constructs are legitimate and useful in psychological science.

correspondence rule See *operational definition.*

descriptive behaviorism Term employed by B. F. Skinner to describe his form of behaviorism, because he rejected explanatory appeals to unobservable states and processes.

explanatory fiction Term employed by B. F. Skinner to characterize theories about internal cognitive states and processes, which he claimed are vacuous as explanations of relations between observable stimuli and responses and play no role in the development of novel predictions about behavior.

Greenspoon effect The conditioning of verbal behavior through social reinforcement.

human factors research Type of research that focuses on the interaction between human operators and machines, such as torpedoes and anti-aircraft guns, and radar and communication systems.

hypothetical construct Theoretical construct whose meaning is not reducible to empirical laws.

instinctual drift Term employed by Keller and Marian Breland to describe the displacement of learned behavior by instinctual behavior.

intervening variable Theoretical postulate defined in terms of observable independent variables (such as environmental or physiological stimuli) and observable dependent variables (such as behavioral responses).

latent learning Term describing learning in the absence of reinforcement.

logical positivism Form of positivism developed by the Vienna Circle in the 1920s and 1930s, based upon the verification principle.

logically intervening variable A logical device for integrating descriptions of observable stimuli and behavioral responses. The instrumentalist conception of an intervening variable.

mediational theory Type of theory of complex internal response-stimulus (r-s) sequences introduced by neobehaviorists in order to accommodate linguistic behavior and symbolic meaning.

operational definition In logical positivism, the definition of the meaning of a theoretical proposition in terms of observables.

operational behaviorism Term employed by Edward C. Tolman to characterize his form of behaviorism, because of his avowed commitment to the operational definition of theoretical constructs.

operant behavior Emitted behavior whose probability of recurrence is increased by reinforcement.

operant conditioning Form of (instrumental) conditioning that was the focus of B. F. Skinner's research, based upon operant as opposed to respondent behavior.

operational measure Empirical measure of a concept.

operationism Position held by the physicist Percy Bridgman, who maintained that scientific concepts are useful only if there are operational measures of their values.

peripheralist theory of learning Theory of learning in which connections between stimuli and responses are held to be determined independently of "centrally initiated" cognitive cortical processes.

physicalism Version of logical positivism in which observational propositions were held to describe publicly observable properties of physical objects, such as readings on spectrometers or the motion of bodies.

place versus response controversy Famous debate between the followers of Tolman and Hull about whether rats running mazes learn cognitive maps or stimulus-response connections.

psychic machine Concept of a mechanized robot employed by Hull as a prophylactic against the cognitive interpretation of animal behavior.

pure stimulus act According to Hull, an internal response-stimulus (r-s) sequence that causally mediates between an environmental stimulus and a behavioral response.

purposive behaviorism Form of behaviorism developed by Edward C. Tolman that focused on purposive or goal-directed behavior.

radical behaviorism Form of behaviorism developed by B. F. Skinner based upon operant conditioning, which marked a return to the positivist and inductivist form of behaviorism developed by John B. Watson.

respondent behavior Behavior elicited by unconditioned or conditioned stimuli.

schedules of reinforcement The variety of fixed and variable interval and ratio schedules of reinforcement employed by B. F. Skinner in his study of conditioned learning.

scientific empiricism (logical empiricism) Later form of logical positivism based upon physicalism that neobehaviorists embraced.

sensationalism Version of logical positivism in which observational propositions were held to describe the properties of private sense experience, such as the intensity of colors or apparent differences in weight.

shaping Method of operant conditioning developed by B. F. Skinner in which a target behavior is produced through the reinforcement of progressive approximations to that behavior.

surplus meaning The meaning of theoretical postulates that is additional to or independent of operational definition in terms of empirical laws.

verification principle The logical positivist principle that the only meaningful factual propositions are those verifiable by observation.

theoretician's dilemma Conceptual dilemma created by insistence on the exhaustive operational definition of theoretical postulates, which implies their dispensability.

REFERENCES

Amundson, R. (1985). Psychology and epistemology: The place versus response controversy. *Cognition, 20,* 127–153.

APA Lifetime Award. (1990). Citation for Outstanding Lifetime Contribution to Psychology: Presented to B. F. Skinner. *American Psychologist, 45,* 1205.

Beach, F. A. (1950). The snark was a boojum. *American Psychologist, 5,* 115–124.

Beach, F. A. (1960). Experimental investigations of species-specific behavior. *American Psychologist, 15,* 1–18.

Bechtel, W. (1988). Connectionism and rules and representation systems: Are they compatible? *Philosophical Psychology, 1,* 5–16.

Benjamin, L. T. (1986). Why don't they understand us? A history of psychology's public image. *American Psychologist, 41,* 941–946.

Benjamin, L. T., Jr., DeLean, P. H., Freedheim, D. K., & Vandenbos, G. R. (2003). Psychology as a profession. In D. K. Freedheim (Ed.), *Handbook of psychology: Vol. 1. History of psychology.* Hoboken, NJ: Wiley.

Bergmann, G., & Spence, K. W. (1941). Operationism and theory in psychology. *Psychological Review, 48,* 1–14.

Boakes, R. (1984). *From Darwin to behaviorism: Psychology and the minds of animals.* Cambridge: Cambridge University Press.

Bolles, R. C. (1993). *The story of psychology: A thematic history.* Pacific Grove, CA: Brooks-Cole.

Breland, K., & Breland, M. (1961). The misbehavior of organisms. *American Psychologist, 16,* 681–684.

Bridgman, P. (1927). *The logic of modern physics.* New York: Macmillan.

Bruner, J. (1980). Jerome. S. Bruner. In G. Lindzey (Ed.), *A history of psychology in autobiography* (Vol. 7). San Francisco: Freeman.

Capshew, J. H. (1999). *Psychologists on the march: Science, practice, and professional identity in America, 1929--1969.* New York: Cambridge University Press.

Carnap, R. (1936). Testability and meaning. *Philosophy of Science, 3,* 419--447.

Carnap, R. (1937). Testability and meaning. *Philosophy of Science, 4,* 1–40.

Cartwright, D. (1949). Some principles of mass persuasion: Selected findings of research on the sale of U.S. War bonds. *Human Relations, 2,* 253–267.

Chomsky, N. (1959). Review of B. F. Skinner's *Verbal Behavior. Language, 35,* 26–58.

Chomsky, N. (1965). *Aspects of a theory of syntax.* Cambridge: MA: MIT Press.

Chomsky, N. (1966). *Cartesian linguistics.* New York: Harper & Row.

Chomsky, N. (1972). *Language and mind.* New York: Harcourt Brace Jovanovich.

Chomsky, N. (1988). *Language and the problem of knowledge.* Cambridge: MIT Press.

Dashiell, J. F. (1928). *Fundamentals of objective psychology.* Boston: Houghton Mifflin.

Dollard, J., & Miller, N. E. (1950). *Personality and psychotherapy.* New York: McGraw-Hill.

Dulany, D. E. (1968). Awareness, rules, and propositional control: A confrontation with S-R behavior theory. In T. R. Dixon & D. C. Horton (Eds.), *Verbal behavior and general behavior theory.* Englewood Cliffs, NJ: Prentice-Hall.

Estes, W. K., Koch, S., MacCorquodale, K., Meehl, P. E., Müller, C. G., Schoenfeld, W. N., & Verplanck, W. S. (Eds.). (1954). *Modern learning theory.* New York: Appleton-Century-Crofts.

Ferster, C. S., & Skinner, B. F. (1957). *Schedules of reinforcement.* New York: Appleton-Century-Crofts.

Fodor, J. A. (1965). Could meaning be an rm? *Journal of Verbal Learning and Verbal Behavior, 4,* 73–81.

Garcia, J., & Koelling, R. A. (1966). Relation of cue to consequence in avoidance learning. *Psychonomic Science, 4,* 123–124.

Garcia, J., McGowan, B. K., & Green, K. F. (1972). Constraints on conditioning. In M. E. P. Seligman & J. L. Hager (Eds.), *Biological boundaries of learning.* New York: Appleton-Century-Crofts.

Gardner, H. (1985). *The mind's new science: A history of the cognitive revolution.* New York: Basic Books.

Green, C. D. (1992). Of immortal mythological beasts: Operationism in psychology. *Theory and Psychology, 2,* 291–320.

Greenspoon, J. (1955). The reinforcing effect of two spoken sounds on the frequency of two behaviors. *American Journal of Psychology, 68,* 409–416.

Hempel, C. G. (1965). *Aspects of scientific explanation.* New York: Free Press.

Hilgard, E. R. (1987). *Psychology in America: A historical survey.* New York: Harcourt Brace Jovanovich.

Hovland, C. I., Lumsdaine, A. A., & Sheffield, F. D. (Eds.). (1949). *Experiments on mass communication.* Princeton, NJ: Princeton University Press.

Hull, C. L. (1920). Quantitative aspects of the evolution of concepts: An experimental approach. *Psychological Monographs, 28* (Whole No 123).

Hull, C. L. (1928). *Aptitude testing.* Yonkers-on Hudson, NY: World Books.

Hull, C. L. (1930). Knowledge and purpose as habit mechanisms. *Psychological Review, 36,* 511–525.

Hull, C. L. (1933). *Hypnosis and suggestibility: An experimental approach.* New York: Appleton-Century.

Hull, C. L. (1937). Mind, mechanism and adaptive behavior. *Psychological Review, 44,* 1–32.

Hull, C. L. (1943a). *Principles of behavior.* New York: Appleton-Century-Crofts.

Hull, C. L. (1943b). The problem of intervening variables in molar behavior theory. *Psychological Review, 50,* 273–288.

Hull, C. L. (1952). Clark Leonard Hull. In E. G. Boring (Ed.), *A history of psychology in autobiography* (Vol. 4). New York: Russell & Russell.

Kamin, L. J. (1969). Predictability, surprise, attention and conditioning. In B. A. Campbell & R. M. Church (Eds.), *Punishment and aversive behavior.* New York: Appleton.

Kendler, H. H. (1952). What is learned?—A theoretical blind alley. *Psychological Review, 59,* 269–277.

Kendler, H. H. (1981). *Psychology: A science in conflict.* Philadelphia: Temple University Press.

Koch, S. (1962). Behaviorism. *Encyclopedia Britannica.*

Koch, S. (1964). Psychology and emerging conceptions of science as unitary. In T. W. Wann (Ed.), *Behaviorism and phenomenology*. Chicago: University of Chicago Press.

Koch, S. (1992). Psychology's Bridgman vs Bridgman's Bridgman. *Theory and Psychology, 2,* 261–290.

Krantz, D. L. (1972). The mutual isolation of operant and non-operant psychology as a case study. *Journal of the History of the Behavioral Sciences, 8,* 86–102.

Krechevsky, I. (1932). Hypotheses in rats. *Psychological Review, 39,* 516–532.

Lashley, K. S. (1923). The behaviorist interpretation of consciousness. *Psychological Review, 30,* 232–272, 329–353.

Lashley, K. S. (1929). *Brain mechanisms and intelligence*. Chicago: Chicago University Press.

Lashley, K. S. (1951). The problem of serial order in behavior. In L. A. Jeffress (Ed.), *Cerebral mechanisms in behavior: The Hixon Symposium*. New York: Wiley.

Leahey, T. H. (1992). *A history of psychology* (3rd ed.). Englewood Cliffs, NJ: Prentice-Hall.

Lewin, K. (1947). Group decision and social change. In T. M. Newcomb & E. L. Hartley (Eds.), *Readings in social psychology*. New York: Holt.

Lorenz, K. (1950). Innate behaviour patterns. In *Symposia of the Society for Experimental Biology: No. 4. Physiological mechanisms in animal behaviour*. New York: Academic Press.

Lubek, I., & Apfelbaum, E. (1987). Neo-behaviorism and the Garcia effect: A social psychology of science approach to the history of a paradigm clash. In M. G. Ash & W. R. Woodward (Eds.), *Psychology in twentieth century thought and science*. Cambridge: Cambridge University Press.

MacCorquodale, K., & Meehl, P. E. (1948). On a distinction between hypothetical constructs and intervening variables. *Psychological Review, 55,* 95–107.

Mackintosh, N. J. (1978). Conditioning. In B. M. Foss (Ed.), *Psychology survey No 1*. London: Allen & Unwin.

Marx, M. H. (1951). Intervening variable or hypothetical construct? *Psychological Review, 58,* 235–247.

McCulloch, W. S. (1951). Why the mind is in the head. In L. A. Jeffress (Ed.), *Cerebral mechanisms in behavior: The Hixon Symposium*. New York: Wiley.

McDougall, W. (1908). *Introduction to social psychology*. London: Methuen.

Miller, G. A. (1989). George A. Miller. In G. Lindzey (Ed.), *A history of psychology in autobiography* (Vol. 8). Stanford: Stanford University Press.

Miller, N. E. (1959). Liberalization of basic S-R concepts. In S. Koch (Ed.), *Psychology: Study of a science* (Vol. 2). New York: McGraw-Hill.

Napoli, D. S. (1981). *Architects of adjustment: The history of the psychological profession in the United States*. Port Washington, NY: Kennikat Press.

Osgood, C. E. (1957). A behaviorist analysis of perception and language as cognitive phenomena. In H. E. Gruber (Ed.), *Contemporary approaches to cognition.* Cambridge, MA: Harvard University Press.

Pratt, C. C. (1939). *The logic of modern psychology.* New York: Macmillan.

Rescorla, R. A., & Wagner, A. R. (1972). A theory of Pavlovian conditioning: Variations in the effectiveness of reinforcement and nonreinforcement. In A. H. Black & W. F. Prokasy (Eds.), *Classical conditioning II: Current research and theory.* New York: Appleton-Century-Crofts.

Revuski, S. (1971). The role of interference in association over a delay. In W. K. Honig & P. H. R. James (Eds.), *Animal memory.* New York: Academic Press.

Riley, J. W., Jr. (1947). Opinion research in liberated Normandy. *American Sociological Review, 12,* 698–703.

Russell, B., & Whitehead, A. N. (1910). *Principia mathematica.* Cambridge: Cambridge University Press.

Schlick, M. (1936). Meaning and verification. *Philosophical Review, 45,* 339–-369.

Schultz, D. P., & Schultz, S. E. (1992). *A history of modern psychology.* (5th ed.). New York: Harcourt Brace Jovanovich.

Sears, R. R. (1943). *Survey of objective studies of psychoanalytic concepts.* Bulletin 51. New York: Social Science Research Council.

Seligman, M. E. P. (1970). On the generality of the laws of learning. *Psychological Review, 77,* 406–418.

Skinner, B. F. (1938). *The behavior of organisms.* New York: Appleton-Century-Crofts.

Skinner, B. F. (1945). Baby in a box. *Ladies' Home Journal.* October.

Skinner, B. F. (1948). *Walden two.* New York: Macmillan.

Skinner, B. F. (1950). Are theories of learning necessary? *Psychological Review, 57,* 193–216.

Skinner, B. F. (1951). How to teach animals. *Scientific American, 185,* 26–29.

Skinner, B. F. (1953). *Science and human behavior.* New York: Macmillan.

Skinner, B. F. (1957). *Verbal behavior.* Englewood Cliffs, NJ: Prentice-Hall.

Skinner, B. F. (1960). Pigeons in a pelican. *American Psychologist, 15,* 28–37.

Skinner, B. F. (1961). *Cumulative record.* New York: Appleton-Century-Crofts.

Skinner, B. F. (1967). B. F. Skinner. In Edwin G. Boring & Gardner Lindzey (Eds.), *A history of psychology in autobiography* (Vol. 5). New York: Appleton-Century-Crofts.

Skinner, B. F. (1971). *Beyond freedom and dignity.* New York: Knopf.

Skinner, B. F. (1974). *About behaviorism.* New York: Knopf.

Skinner, B. F. (1985). Cognitive science and behaviorism. *British Journal of Psychology, 76,* 291–301.

Skinner, B. F. (1987). *Upon further reflection.* Englewood Cliffs, NJ: Prentice-Hall.

Skinner, B. F. (1990). Can psychology be a science of the mind? *American Psychologist, 45,* 1206–1210.

Skinner, B. F., & Vaughan, M. E. (1983). *Enjoy old age: Living fully in your later years*. New York: Warner.

Smith, L. D. (1986). *Behaviorism and logical positivism: A revised account of the alliance*. Stanford, CA: Stanford University Press.

Spence, K. W. (1936). The nature of discrimination learning in animals. *Psychological Review, 43,* 427–449.

Spence, K. W. (1952). Clark Leonard Hull: 1884–1952. *American Journal of Psychology, 65,* 639–-646.

Spence, K. W. (1956). *Behavior theory and conditioning*. New Haven, CT: Yale University Press.

Spence, K. W. (1960). *Behavior theory and learning: Selected papers*. Englewood Cliffs, NJ: Prentice-Hall.

Stevens, S. S. (1935). The operational definition of psychological concepts. *Psychological Review, 42,* 517–527.

Stouffer, S. A., Lumsdane, A. A., Lumsdane, M. H., Williams, R. M., Smith, M. B., Janis, I. L., Star, S. A., & Cottrell, I. S. (Eds.). (1949). *The American soldier: Combat and its aftermath*. (Studies in Social Psychology in World War II, No 2). Princeton, NJ: Princeton University Press.

Stouffer, S. A., Suchman, E. A., De Vinney, L. C., Star, S. A., & Williams, R. B., Jr. (Eds.). (1949). *The American soldier: Adjustment during army life*. (Studies in Social Psychology in World War II, No 1). Princeton, NJ: Princeton University Press.

Tinbergen, N. (1951). *The study of instinct*. Oxford: Clarendon Press.

Tolman, E. C. (1917). Retroactive inhibition as affected by conditions of learning. *Psychological Monographs, 25* (Whole No. 107).

Tolman, E. C. (1922). A new formula for behaviorism. *Psychological Review, 29,* 44–53.

Tolman, E. C. (1923). A behaviorist account of the emotions. *Psychological Review, 30,* 217–277.

Tolman, E. C. (1925). Behaviorism and purpose. *Journal of Philosophy, 22,* 36–41.

Tolman, E. C. (1926). A behaviorist theory of ideas. *Psychological Review, 33,* 352–369.

Tolman, E. C. (1927). A behaviorist's definition of consciousness. *Psychological Review, 34,* 433–439.

Tolman, E. C. (1928). Purposive behavior. *Psychological Review, 35,* 524–530.

Tolman, E. C. (1932). *Purposive behavior in animals and men*. New York: Century.

Tolman, E. C. (1938). The determiners of behavior at a choice-point. *Psychological Review, 45,* 1–41.

Tolman, E. C. (1942). *Drives towards war*. New York: Appleton-Century-Crofts.

Tolman, E. C. (1945). A stimulus-expectancy need-cathexis psychology. *Science, 101,* 160–166.

Tolman, E. C. (1948). Cognitive maps in rats and men. *Psychological Review, 55,* 189–209.

Tolman, E. C. (1949). Discussion. *Journal of Personality, 18,* 48–50.

Tolman, E. C. (1951). Operational behaviorism and current trends in psychology. In *Collected papers in psychology.* Berkeley: University of California Press. (Original work published 1936)

Tolman, E. C. (1959). Principles of purposive behaviorism. In S. Koch (Ed.), *Psychology: A study of a science* (Vol. 2). New York: McGraw-Hill.

Tolman, E. C., & Honzik, C. H. (1930). Introduction and removal of reward, and maze performance in rats. *University of California Publications in Psychology, 4,* 257–273.

U.S. Strategic Bombing Survey. (1946). The effects of bombing upon German morale. Washington, DC: U.S. Government Printing Office.

von Neumann, J. (1951). The general and logical theory of automata. In L. A. Jeffress (Ed.), *Cerebral mechanisms in behavior: The Hixon Symposium.* New York: Wiley.

Watson, G. (Ed.). (1942). *Civilian morale.* Boston: Houghton Mifflin.

Watson, J. B. (1924). *Behaviorism.* New York: Norton.

Wolfle, D. (1997). The reorganized American Psychological Association. *American Psychologist, 52,* 721–724. (Original work published 1946)

CHAPTER 12

The Cognitive Revolution

T HE "COGNITIVE REVOLUTION" IN PSYCHOLOGY EMERGED FROM postwar developments in information theory and computer science. The development of the electronic computer created a new and technically proven model of the mind as a mechanical information processor, conceived of as operating on the same sorts of "rules and representations" employed by "intelligent" machines (Bechtel, 1988).

One of the peculiarities of the cognitive revolution was that many of its pioneers came to conceive of their own intellectual achievement in terms of Thomas Kuhn's (1970) analysis of the structure of scientific revolutions, according to which one general theoretical or methodological paradigm is replaced by a radically different paradigm, under the pressure of accumulating empirical anomalies (Lachman, Lachman, & Butterfield, 1979). Kuhn's influential *The Structure of Scientific Revolutions* was first published in 1962, as the new forms of cognitive psychology were being advanced and developed by Jerome Bruner (1915–), George Miller (1920–), Ulric Neisser (1928–), Allen Newell (1927–1992), and Herbert Simon (1915–2001). As James J. Jenkins (1923–) later remarked, during the early years of the cognitive revolution in psychology, "everyone toted around their little copy of Kuhn's *The Structure of Scientific Revolutions*" (Jenkins, quoted in Baars, 1986, p. 249).

Although there was no revolution in the strict Kuhnian sense, the development of cognitive theories from the 1950s and 1960s onward did mark a genuine discontinuity with behaviorist theories, including later "liberalized" neobehaviorist theories in terms of internal "mediating" r-s sequences (N. Miller, 1959; Osgood, 1957). Although the primary stimulus for the cognitive revolution came from without, the empirical problems faced by neobehaviorism in the 1950s and 1960s created an intellectual climate that left many psychologists predisposed to theoretical and methodical change. As Jenkins put it, "things were boiling over . . . a new day was coming" (Jenkins, quoted in Baars, 1986, p. 249).

INFORMATION THEORY

The primary stimulus for the growth of cognitive psychology came from outside academic psychology, notably from developments in logic, mathematics, and computer science, which were themselves a product of applied research on radar, message encoding, and missile guidance conducted during the Second World War.

Claude Shannon: Communication Theory

The wartime need to transmit maximum coded information in limited capacity channels promoted the development of information theory. Claude E. Shannon (1916–2001), an MIT engineering graduate who worked for Bell Laboratories, developed a mathematical theory of communication based upon the transmission of information from a "source" through a "channel" to a "destination." His goal was to identify the most efficient means of transmitting information via media such as telephone circuits and radio waves. Shannon measured information in terms of reduction in uncertainty and treated the **bit** (short for "binary unit") as the elemental unit of information: the amount of information required to determine between two equiprobable alternatives (Shannon, 1948). Shannon and Warren Weaver (1894–1978) developed statistical theories that described the relationships between variables in a communication system and the process of information flow though such a system (Shannon & Weaver, 1949). They were particularly concerned with the problem of loss of information as a signal is transformed in the course of transmission from source to destination, when it has to compete with background **noise**, defined as any random disturbance superimposed upon a signal (such as electrical noise caused by heat in electrical circuits).

George Miller, one of the pioneers of the cognitive revolution, introduced the statistical measures of information theory to psychology (Miller, 1953; Miller & Frick, 1949) and employed them in his analysis of language in *Language and Communication* (1951). Although information theory was first employed in psychology in the analysis of stimulus-response learning (Miller & Frick, 1949), units of information soon threatened to displace the stimulus-response connection as the primary focus of scientific psychology.

Shannon's binary analysis of units of information was based upon an assumed analogy between the binary values of symbolic logic (true/false) and switching circuits (on/off), which he described in his MIT master's thesis "A Symbolic Analysis of Relay and Switching Circuits" (1938). This analogy became the electrical engineering foundation for the later development of digital computers, or "logic machines."

Norbert Wiener: Cybernetics

Norbert Wiener (1894–1964), who had been a student of Bertrand Russell's at Cambridge, also made important contributions to information theory. During the war, he worked on guidance systems for torpedoes, which employed feedback from sound detectors to adjust their trajectory. He described the behavior of such mechanical but purposive devices in *Cybernetics* (1948). He defined **cybernetics** (derived from the Greek term for "steerman") as the scientific study of control and communication in animals and machines, which he analyzed in terms of the acquisition, use, retention, and transmission of information. Wiener characterized purposive behavior as the intelligent adjustment of behavior to environmental change, echoing earlier functionalist accounts (Angell, 1907), and complained that a major obstacle to the development of mechanical systems that could "mimic" purposive behavior in humans was the inadequacy of neobehaviorist theory.

In contrast to Hull, who tried to provide mechanistic explanations of the apparently purposive behavior of humans and animals, Wiener, in a paper that he co-authored with Arturo Rosenblueth and Julian Bigelow in 1943, maintained that the behavior of **servomechanisms** such as torpedoes is intrinsically purposeful:

> Some machines . . . are intrinsically purposeful. A torpedo with a target-seeking mechanism is an example. The term servomechanisms has been coined precisely to designate machines with intrinsic purposive behavior.
>
> —(Rosenblueth, Wiener, & Bigelow, 1943, p. 19)

He claimed that such machine behavior requires a teleological explanation in terms of regulation by **feedback**, defined as "signals from the goal that modify the activity of the object in the course of the behavior'" (Rosenblueth, Wiener, & Bigelow, 1943, pp. 19–20), and that this form of explanation applies to both living and mechanical systems:

> The behavior of some machines and some reactions of living organisms involve a continuous feed-back from the goal that modifies and guides the behaving object.
>
> —(Rosenblueth, Wiener, & Bigelow, 1943, p. 20)

Wiener maintained that the same information-theoretical principles of explanation apply to the restricted class of animal, human, and machine behavior that involves regulation by information feedback. In doing so, he made a major contribution to the development of the cognitive revolution. He legitimized the concepts of purposive behavior and teleological explanation for hard-nosed scientific skeptics by demonstrating their applicability to the behavior of inanimate machines, the paradigm of mechanistic explanation since Descartes. Wiener also championed the autonomy of cognitive psychological explanation with respect to neurophysiology and physiology, by arguing that the same principles of teleological explanation apply to the purposive behavior of different material systems, whether composed of cells or silicone. As he put it, "Information is information, not matter or energy" (1948, p. 132). In this respect Wiener returned to the Aristotelian functionalist conception of the relation between psychological capacities and their modes of material instantiation.

In documenting the various ways in which animals, humans, and machines can employ information feedback, Wiener introduced many of the concepts that were later to play a significant role in computer science and cognitive psychology, such as "working memory" and "executive function." He maintained that the ability of any mechanical system to engage in purposive behavior was based upon structural features suitable for the "acquisition, use, retention, and transmission of information" (1948, p. 161).

Between 1946 and 1953, the Macy Foundation funded twice-yearly conferences on cybernetics in New York, which were attended by neurophysiologists, logicians, statisticians, engineers, biologists, anthropologists, and social psychologists. Although interest in cybernetics declined in the 1950s, the meetings demonstrated the interdisciplinary appeal of cognitive theories based upon the flow of information, presaging the later interdisciplinary enterprise that became cognitive science.

Donald Broadbent: Information Processing

Psychologists originally employed information theory in the statistical description of information flow in communication systems, which reached a high-water mark with Wendell Garner's *Uncertainty and Structure as Psychological Concepts* in 1962. However, they soon developed theories of information processing to explain cognitive processes. One of the first to do so was the British psychologist Donald Broadbent (1926–1993), who used the language of information processing in his theory of selective attention for auditory messages. In "A Mechanical Model for Human Attention and Immediate Memory" (1957), Broadbent treated human short-term memory as a "limited capacity channel" and provided a theoretical account of attention in terms of the active processing of information rather than the passive reaction to stimuli. He developed this account in *Perception and Communication* (1958), in which he recommended that the behaviorist language of stimulus and response be replaced by the language of information theory. For Broadbent, this was not a mere linguistic convenience, since he held that "the performance of selective listeners seems to vary with information as defined by communication theory, rather than with amount of stimulation in the conventional sense" (1958, p. 15). He maintained that theories of attention needed to "distinguish between the arrival of a stimulus at the sense-organ and the use of the information it conveys" (1958, p. 59).

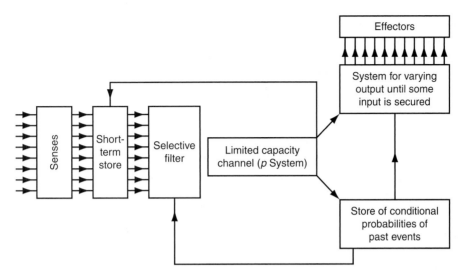

Information-processing system.

Broadbent, D. E. (1958). Perception and communication. Oxford: Pergamon Press.

Broadbent stressed that one of the virtues of the language of information processing was that it preserved the autonomy of cognitive psychological explanation by enabling theorists to describe cognitive psychological processes without committing themselves to the details of the material systems in which they were instantiated (be they humans, animals, or machines). Broadbent claimed that one of the weaknesses of Hebb's (1949) theory of pattern recognition was that it was tied to a very specific neurophysiological hypothesis, which made his theory hostage to falsification by recalcitrant neurophysiological data. Yet, as Broadbent pointed out, Hebb's theory might "well be true even though the elements are not physically what Hebb supposed them to be" (1958, p. 306). He noted that this was precisely the fate of Gestalt psychology, which was rejected by most psychologists because of its link to an untenable theory of neural fields: "Their unlikely physiology has produced neglect of their genuine psychological achievements" (1958, p. 306). Broadbent's own cognitive psychological theories were neutral with respect to neurophysiology and were designed to provide cognitive psychological explanations of "what happened inside a man which was not a mentalistic introspective language, which was not hypothetical neurophysiology, and which wasn't simply a description of the visible behavior" (in Cohen, 1977, p. 63). Like Wiener, Broadbent championed the Aristotelian functionalist conception of cognitive capacities and their modes of material instantiation.

Broadbent's own theoretical perspective had developed from wartime research on human vigilance, which focused on the performance of human operators of radar, calculating machines, and aircraft. Wartime concerns with the complex behavioral repertoires demanded of pilots and machine-gunners forced psychologists to recognize the inadequacy of neobehaviorist accounts of skilled performance in terms of habit hierarchies, which had been favored in prewar industrial psychology. They developed theories of skilled performance in terms of the flexible adjustment of behavior governed by central control structures (Bartlett, 1943; Craik, 1947), akin to those developed by Lashley and Wiener in their accounts of serially ordered and intrinsically purposive behavior. As Broadbent put it in *Perception and Communication,*

> The picture of skilled performance built up by modern researches is one of a complex interaction between man and environment. Continuously the skilled man must select the correct cues from the environment, take decisions upon them which may possibly involve prediction of the future, and initiate sequences of responses whose progress is controlled by feedback, either through the original decision-making mechanism, or through lower-order loops. The processes of filtering the information from the senses, of passing it through a limited capacity channel, and of storing it temporarily are only part of the total skilled performance.
>
> —(1958, pp. 295–296)

In the United States E. B. Hunt extended and developed Carl Hovland's information-theoretic analysis of concept learning (Hovland, 1952) into a full-blown theory of information processing in *Concept Learning: An Information Processing Problem* (Hunt, 1962), in which he treated concept learning as an active decision process operating on cognitive hypotheses. George Miller published a classic paper on the limited capacity of attention and memory as information channels titled "The Magical Number Seven, Plus or Minus Two: Some Limits on Our Capacity for Processing Information" (Miller, 1956). He demonstrated the limited capacity of sensory judgment, tachiscopic perception, and short-term memory and reprised in information-theoretical terms Wundt's earlier claim that the capacity of human attention is restricted to around seven units (Wundt, 1912).

Miller also demonstrated the limitations of the pure information-theoretical approach. Like Wundt, he noted that constraints on memory capacity can be surmounted by recoding information into meaningful "chunks" such as "mother" rather than the units "r" "h" "m" "t" "e" "o" (which can be rearranged to form the meaningful word "*mother*"):

> We must recognize the importance of grouping or organizing the input sequence into units or chunks. Since the memory span is a fixed number of chunks, we can increase the number of bits of information that it contains simply by building larger and larger chunks, each chunk containing more information than before.
>
> In the jargon of communication theory, this process would be called *recoding*.
>
> —(1956, p. 93)

Thus Miller, who had originally introduced information theory to psychology (Miller, 1951, 1953; Miller & Frick, 1949), was also instrumental in developing information-processing theory. He "set the agenda for the next phase of cognitive psychology in which information-processing concepts went beyond the confines of information theory" (Baddeley, 1994, p. 353).

Computers and Cognition

The most influential form of information-processing theory was the product of the creation of the electronic computer. The use of mechanical devices to perform mathematical operations goes back to the ancient Babylonians, and the idea of employing machines to process symbols was developed by Leibniz and Charles Babbage (1791–1871) in the 18th and 19th centuries. In the late 19th and early 20th centuries, George Boole (1815–1864), Gottlob Frege (1848–1925), and Bertrand Russell (1872–1970) developed the **new logic**, which considerably advanced the theoretical potential of symbol-processing machines. The significance of this logic was that it was truth-functional: Sentential operators such as "if . . . then" were defined in terms of primitive operators such as "and" and "not,"[1] which could be physically instantiated as on/off stitches in electrical circuits. Claude Shannon was the first to recognize the relation between the binary systems of symbolic logic and electronic circuitry and thus to explore the possibility of a "logic machine" (Shannon, 1938). McCulloch and Pitts (1943) developed a similar binary analysis of neural networks, whose operations they represented by the hypothetical firing or nonfiring of individual neurons.

Turing Machines In his attempt to answer the question of whether there could be a decision procedure for determining whether mathematical propositions are provable, the English mathematician Alan Turing (1912–1954) developed the abstract idea of a hypothetical machine, now known as a **Turing machine**, capable of performing elementary operations on symbols printed on a paper tape (Turing, 1936). He employed this notion to determine the computable numbers, defined as those printable by a Turing machine. Turing originally approached the question by conceiving of a human operator, or human "computer," who mechanically performed a "set of instructions" from a rulebook. By imagining a human replaced by a machine with a stored "set of instructions," Turing created the notion of a computer **program**.

Turing machines are defined by their "tables of instructions" or "programs," which specify their operations. Turing also conceived of a general-purpose machine, or **universal Turing machine**, capable of performing operations specified by the

---

[1]Thus "if p then q" could be defined as "not" (p and not q).

programs of a number of different Turing machines. In conceiving of a machine capable of performing a variety of tasks (such as computing numbers, drawing logical implications, and playing chess), Turing developed the principle of the modern computer (a decade before fast electronic calculating machines were produced).

Turing also explored an idea that was later to inspire American pioneers of cognitive psychology and cognitive science: that computing machines could be programmed to simulate human cognitive processes. One implication of Turing's theoretical analysis of computation was that any set of procedures specifiable in a binary code could be instantiated in a mechanical computer. Since Turing believed that the logical operations involved in human cognitive processing could be specified as a series of steps in binary code, he believed that a mechanical computer could simulate them. He had originally conceived of a Turing machine as a machine designed to perform tasks that could be performed by a human following a rulebook of instructions. As he later put it, "The idea behind digital computers may be explained by saying that these machines are intended to carry out any operations which could be done by a human computer" (1950, p. 436).

During the Second World War, Turing served with British Intelligence at Bletchley Park, where he and his colleagues used calculating machines to decipher German cipher codes, including the Enigma Code used by U-boats. At the end of the war he submitted his design for an "Automatic Computing Engine" (or for "building a brain," as he put it to a colleague) to the National Science Laboratory (Turing, 1946/1992). Although his ambitious scheme was formally accepted, it was never implemented (Hodges, 1992).

At the outbreak of the war, Turing converted his savings into silver bullion bars and buried them in the countryside surrounding Bletchley Park, but forgot where they were buried when he returned to retrieve them at the end of the war. A tormented homosexual trapped in a society in which homosexuality was still a criminal offense, he was forced to undergo treatment of his "unnatural" tendencies with injections of estrogen. Turing committed suicide in 1954 at the age of 42 by eating a cyanide-poisoned apple (Hodges, 1992).

ENIAC and EDVAC During the war, high-speed calculating machines were employed not only to decipher enemy codes, but also to handle the complex mathematical computations required for the operation of anti-aircraft guns and navigation systems. In engineering terms, the modern electronic computer was born when such devices became self-regulating: when machines operating on stored sets of instructions (programs) replaced human operators (Hunt, 1994).

The first fast electronic calculating machine or computer, called ENIAC (Electronic Numerical Integrator and Automatic Computer), was constructed at the University of Pennsylvania in 1948 (it was originally designed to calculate artillery tables). John von Neumann (1903–1957), the Princeton mathematician and polymath, was a consultant on the project. He was responsible for a number of practical and conceptual innovations in the development of **digital computers**, which perform operations on binary units of information.[2] Von Neumann distinguished between the **software** and **hardware** of a computer: between the set of rules or instructions encoded by a computer program and the different physical systems that instantiate these rules or instructions (Dupuy, 2000). This distinction was a computational variant of Aristotle's functionalist conception of psychological capacities, since it allowed that one and the same program (software) could be multiply realized in a variety of different physical systems (hardware), including biological systems (sometimes known as **wetware**). For example, a variety of different physical machines (such as PCs and Macs) and humans can instantiate the same programs for adding numbers or playing chess.

Von Neumann was also one of the first to draw attention to the analogy between the organization of the brain and the circuitry of digital computers in his paper "The General and Logical Theory of Automata" (1951), first read at the Hixon Symposium in 1948. Although the original ENIAC machine performed operations in parallel as the human brain does, von Neumann later developed a machine that could perform operations serially, called EDVAC (Electronic Discrete Variable Automatic Computer). Von Neumann's design became the standard for computers in the following decades, with the consequence that modern computers, which employ a central control unit to read and execute programmed instructions serially, are often characterized as **von Neumann machines**. These machines were originally employed to perform mathematical operations, but the introduction of information-processing languages (IPLs) stimulated the development of computer programs for problem solving, decision making, and game playing.

Computer Simulation of Cognitive Processes   In 1954, Allen Newell, who worked at the Systems Research Laboratory of the RAND Corporation, began work on the design of a program that would enable a computer to play chess. J. C. Shaw and Herbert A. Simon joined him in 1955. They worked together on the design of programs for JOHNNIAC (John von Neumann's Integrator and Automatic Computer), a computer built for the RAND Corporation in the 1950s. They temporarily abandoned the plan to develop a chess-playing program and instead directed their attention to simpler programs for proving theorems in geometry and logic.

Newell and Simon developed a program known as the **Logic Theorist**, based upon a specially developed information-processing language. The first machine proof of a theorem in symbolic logic, Theorem 2.01 from Russell and Whitehead's *Principia Mathematica*, was produced on the JOHNNIAC computer in August 1956.

---

[2]In contrast to analog computers, which represent variable physical processes (such as changes in temperature) via changes in some physical variable (such as electrical potential).

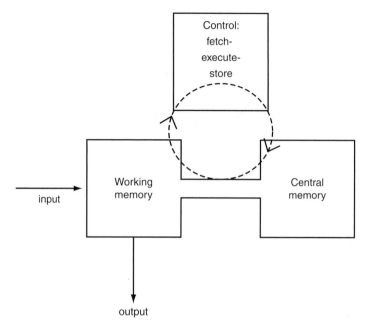

Generic computer architecture (von Neumann machine).

Harnish, R. M. (2002). Minds, brains, computers. Oxford: Basil Blackwell

Newell and Simon first publicized their achievement at the Symposium on Information Theory held at MIT in September 1956, the conference at which the cognitive revolution was born, according to Bruner (1980) and Miller (1989). The following year, Newell, Shaw, and Simon began work on a more complex program, the **General Problem Solver** (GPS), capable of performing a wider range of cognitive tasks, such as playing chess and problem solving, in addition to proving theorems in geometry and logic.

Newell, Shaw, and Simon were convinced of the relevance of their research to the cognitive psychology of human problem solving, and they saw their machine proofs as the simulation of human information processing. They presented their case to psychologists in "Elements of a Theory of Problem Solving," published in *Psychological Review* in 1958. Newell, Shaw, and Simon offered a theory of the "control-systems" of humans and machines to explain their "problem-solving behavior" in terms of "information processing." They explained human and machine problem-solving behavior in terms of the information processes responsible for such behavior: "An explanation of an observed behavior of the organism is provided by a program of primitive information processes that generates this behavior" (1958, p. 151).

Newell, Shaw, and Simon were careful to stress that their theory of information processing in terms of rule-governed operations on symbols had nothing essentially to do with electronic digital computers and that programs specifying such operations could be developed independently of digital computers. They noted that such programs had been developed earlier by Adriaan de Groot (1914–2006), in his classic analysis of problem solving in chess (de Groot, 1946), and by Otto Selz (1922), the last major theorist of the Würzburg school (who was de Groot's teacher):

> Our position is that the appropriate way to describe a piece of problem solving behavior is in terms of a program: a specification of what the organism will do under varying environmental circumstances in terms of certain elementary information processes it is capable of performing. This assertion has nothing to do—directly—with computers. Such programs could be written (now that we have discovered how to do it) if computers had never existed.
>
> —(Newell, Shaw, & Simon, 1958, p. 153)

The Logic Theorist employed a program that comprised four rules of inference (substitution, replacement, detachment, and chaining), which enabled it to employ a variety of methods of "discovering" proofs. With the program and the axioms of *Principia Mathematica* stored in memory, the Logic Theorist was presented with the first 52 theorems of Chapter 2 of *Principia Mathematica*. It succeeded in proving 38 of them.

Like Wiener, Newell, Shaw, and Simon insisted that their theory applied indifferently to humans and machines: "These programs describe both human and machine problem solving at the level of information processes" (1958, p. 153). They claimed that their theory of information-processing was autonomous with respect to human neurophysiology and maintained a functionalist conception of the relation between programs of information-processing and the human brains and machines capable of realizing them:

> Problem solving—at the information-processing level at which we have described it—has nothing specifically "neural" about it, but can be performed by a wide class of mechanisms, including both human brains and digital computers. We do not believe that this functional equivalence between brains and computers implies any structural equivalence at a more minute anatomical level (e.g., equivalence of neurons with circuits). Discovering what neural mechanisms realize these information-processing functions in the human brain is a task for another level of theory construction. Our theory is a theory of the information processes involved in problem solving, and not a theory of neural or electronic mechanisms for information processing.
>
> —(1958, p. 163)

Although Newell, Shaw, and Simon claimed to have offered "a thoroughly operational theory of human problem solving" (1958, p. 166) and to have eliminated "the vaguenesses that have plagued the theory of higher mental processes" (1958, p. 166), they did not offer an operationally defined theory of problem solving. The "operational" in "operational theory" was a reference to the operations performed on symbols by programs, which were defined "in terms of elementary information processes," such as the rules governing the substitution, detachment, replacement, and chaining of logical symbols (1958, p. 157). In contrast to neobehaviorists, Newell, Shaw, and Simon did not believe that the question of "what is learned" in problem solving was a pseudo-issue (Kendler, 1952), but instead offered a specific and substantive answer to the question. They claimed that the Logic Theorist learned theorems, as well as subproblems for proofs that had been previously attempted, and which theorems were useful in conjunction with particular methods.

They maintained that the Logic Theorist simulated problem solving in humans by executing "the same sequences of information processes that humans execute when they are solving problems" (1958, p. 153). As evidence for this, they noted that the Logic Theorist not only succeeded in solving a range of problems solvable by humans (no mean achievement in itself), but that it also manifested many of the characteristics "exhibited by humans in dealing with the same problems" (1958, p. 162). These included dependence on the sequence in which problems were presented, preparatory and directional "set," employment of heuristically governed vicarious trial and error, and hierarchical organization of problems and subproblems (1958, p. 162).

Newell, Shaw, and Simon later recognized that the Logic Theorist did not mimic the behavior of humans particularly well when compared with subject protocols based upon "think-aloud" tapes of human subjects engaged in the solution of logical problems (devised by O. K. Moore and S. B Anderson in their research on human problem solving at Yale University). The program of the later General Problem Solver was specially designed to reproduce the distinctive features of human problem solving revealed through human subject protocols (Newell & Simon, 1972).

Artificial Intelligence The Logic Theorist heralded the development of "information-processing" or "computational" psychology and represented an early achievement of the emerging discipline that came to be known as **artificial intelligence**: the science of intelligent machines (Minsky, 1963). This naturally raised the question of whether cognitive processes, such as those involved in proving theorems, playing chess, or understanding language, can properly be ascribed to machines, in the same sense in which they are paradigmatically ascribed to humans. This question has vexed psychologists as much as it has vexed critical philosophers and humanists.

Turing, the intellectual pioneer of the modern computer, was himself optimistic about the prospect of developing genuinely intelligent computing machines.

In "Computing Machinery and Intelligence" (1950), he described an "imitation game," now known as the **Turing test**, in which a human interrogator poses questions to a machine and another human, whose only contact with them is via a teleprinter link. Turing maintained that we should be prepared to ascribe intelligence to a machine if we could not discriminate the responses of the human communicator from a machine simulating or "imitating" these responses.

The Chinese Room   While many workers in artificial intelligence have accepted this "solution," psychologists and philosophers such as John Searle (1980) and Herbert Dreyfus (1972) have been much less enthusiastic. Searle has argued that the symbols that computers manipulate, such as those processed by computers operating on "story-reading" programs (Schank & Abelson, 1977), mean nothing to them, unlike the symbols that humans employ in language comprehension and communication.

To illustrate his point, Searle imagined a room in which a person who speaks only English receives written questions in Chinese. The person responds with printed answers in Chinese in accord with instructions from an English rulebook, which specifies the appropriate Chinese answers to questions set in Chinese. The person identifies the Chinese questions merely by the shape of the symbols and prints out the set of symbols that the rulebook identifies as the appropriate answer in Chinese. Searle claimed that a person performing such a task could pass the "Turing test," but would not understand Chinese: Such a person would merely "produce the answers by manipulating uninterpreted formal symbols " (Searle, 1980, p. 418). Since such a person would essentially "behave like a computer," performing "computational operations on formally specified elements," Searle concluded that linguistic comprehension and communication should not be ascribed to digital computers.

Searle's argument presents a real challenge to artificial intelligence researchers committed to what Searle calls **strong AI**: the view that we can ascribe cognitive states to computers in exactly the same sense that we ascribe them to humans.[3] Such researchers have been obliged to specify what more is required of mechanical systems for the symbols that they process to have meaning for such systems. Popular candidates are sensory and motor links to the physical world and/or some form of learning or analogue of learning.

However, Searle's challenge presents much less of a problem for cognitive psychologists. Despite the initial enthusiasm for computer simulation among psychologists (Hovland, 1960), Simon's confident prediction that most theories in psychology would eventually take the form of computer programs (Dreyfus, 1972)

---

[3]Strong AI is contrasted with weak AI, the view that computers are useful tools for formulating and testing hypotheses about the mind or the view that we can create machines that can perform tasks such as calculation and industrial product control, which would be described as intelligent if performed by humans.

turned out to be false. Cognitive psychologists never really embraced computer simulation as a means of testing theories of human cognitive processing, even as they developed detailed theories of human cognitive processing inspired by computer models.

Indeed, it may be fairly said that computer simulation and the computer model of cognition proved to be an example of the proverbial ladder that could be thrown away once psychologists were prepared to accept hypothetical theoretical constructs relating to cognitive states and processes (whose meaningful contents were independent of the content of operational definitions). Nonetheless, it would be hard to overestimate the powerful role played by the computer simulation of human cognitive processes in establishing the scientific legitimacy of causal explanatory appeals to cognitive rules and representations. The ability to specify cognitive theories as computer programs and to test them via the mechanical performance of computers gave the lie to behaviorist complaints about the vagueness and untestability of cognitive theoretical constructs. As Margaret Boden put it, the computer model promoted the double discipline of explicitness and testing: "a computer model enables us not only to state and clarify our theoretical ideas, but to find out whether they have the inferential consequences we believe them to have" (Boden, 1997, p. 56).

The demonstration that information-processing programs simulating human cognition could be instantiated in electronic machines completely undermined standard behaviorist complaints about theoretical appeals to cognition as a return to immaterial souls or spirits. Descartes' discredited ontological dualism was replaced by the respectable methodological dualism of von Neumann's distinction between cognitive software and mechanical hardware (or wetware, in the case of animals and humans). For cognitive psychologists, this functionalist conception of cognition enabled them to preserve the autonomy of cognitive psychological explanation without abandoning their common commitment to materialism. While they emphasized that theories about cognitive processes, like theories about computer programs, were not about material systems per se, they granted that they could be instantiated only in material systems of sufficient complexity (such as human and animal brains or computer hardware).

COGNITIVE PSYCHOLOGY

Other forms of cognitive theory were developed within psychology during the 1950s, more or less independently of the work on computer simulation and artificial intelligence, notably by Jerome Bruner, George Miller, and Ulric Neisser, who also played a significant role in the institutional development of cognitive psychology.

Jerome Bruner: Higher Mental Processes

Jerome Bruner, a student of William McDougall's at Duke and Gordon Allport's at Harvard, worked on propaganda, morale, and public opinion research during the Second World War. He explored the influence of cognitive factors such as expectation, emotion, and motivation on perception in a series of experimental studies (Bruner & Postman, 1947a, 1947b; 1949) that came to represent the "new look" in perception (Bruner & Krech, 1950). These studies indicated that subjects who are hungry or poor, for example, tend to see food or money when presented with ambiguous perceptual data. They included studies of perceptual defense (inspired by Freudian notions of repression) that indicated that taboo words are not as readily recognizable in tachiscopic presentations as neutral words, even though they generate measurable affective responses.

Bruner treated perception as an active cognitive process rather than the passive association of sensory stimuli. He developed this emphasis on the active role of cognition in *Studies in Thinking* (Bruner, Goodnow, & Austin, 1956), the first product of the collaborative Cognition Project that Bruner set up at Harvard in 1952. *Studies in Thinking* was an experimentally based study of the cognitive strategies that subjects employ in concept formation (such as "successive scanning," "conservative focusing," and "focus gambling"). This influential work deserves to be classified as the first substantive psychological monograph of the cognitive revolution.[4]

Bruner was explicit about his intentional break with the peripheralist stimulus-response behaviorist tradition and his return to a cognitive orientation or, as he put it, his "revival" of the study of "Higher Mental Processes":

> One need not look far for the origins of the revival. Partly, it has resulted from a recognition of the complex processes that mediate between the classical "stimuli" and "responses" out of which stimulus-response learning theories hoped to fashion a psychology that would by-pass anything smacking of the "mental." The impeccable peripheralism of such theories could not last long. . . .
>
> . . . Information theory is another source of the revival. Its short history in psychology recapitulates the fate of stimulus-response learning theory. The inputs and outputs of a communication system, it soon became apparent, could not be dealt with exclusively in terms of the nature of these inputs and outputs alone nor even in terms of such internal characteristics as channel capacity and noise. The coding and recoding of inputs—how incoming signals are sorted and organized—turns out to be the important secret of the black box that lies athwart the information channel.
>
> —(Bruner et al., 1956, pp. vi–vii)

---

[4]Even though it was predated by Rapaport's *The Organization and Pathology of Thought* (1951) and Vinacke's *The Psychology of Thinking* (1952), not to mention Moore's 1938 *Cognitive Psychology*.

As in the case of other pioneers of the cognitive revolution, the original stimulus for Bruner's work came from outside American psychology. Bruner was influenced by the early work of the British psychologist Sir Frederic C. Bartlett (1886–1969) on memory schemas (Bartlett, 1932) and by the work of the European psychologist Jean Piaget (1896–1980), who had been studying the cognitive development of children since the 1920s (Piaget, 1926, 1927, 1930). Bruner met Bartlett while a visitor at the University of Cambridge from 1955 to 1956, where they organized a conference on cognition in the summer of 1956 (funded by the Rockefeller Foundation), the same year he first visited Piaget in Geneva. Piaget's influence was reflected in *Studies in Cognitive Growth* (Bruner, Oliver, & Greenfield, 1966), a work that promoted a theoretical conception of cognitive development as active and creative in contrast to Piaget's own theory of biologically determined stages. Bruner's account of cognitive development partly reprised earlier criticisms of Piaget's theory developed by the Russian psychologist Lev Vygotsky (1896–1934). Although both Piaget and Vygotsky (1934/1986) advanced cognitive theories in the 1920s, they had little influence on the early development of cognitive psychology in America in the 1950s (Bruner being a notable exception). English translations of the works of both authors became readily available in America only in the 1960s.

Bruner moved to Oxford in 1972, where he continued to work on the cognitive development of children. He returned to the United States in 1981 to take up an appointment at The New School of Social Research and later moved to Rockefeller University.

George Miller: Cognitive Science

George Miller majored in English and speech at the University of Alabama, and gained his PhD in psychology from Harvard in 1946. He was one of the first psychologists to embrace the statistical formulations of information theory developed by Shannon (Miller, 1953), although his early work was very much in the behaviorist tradition. Miller used statistical descriptions of information flow in his analysis of operant conditioning (Frick & Miller, 1951; Miller & Frick, 1949), which he extended to the analysis of verbal communication in *Language and Communication* (1951), one of the earliest sources of Skinner's views on verbal behavior. However, during the 1950s Miller came to treat humans more as (active) processors of information than as (passive) channels of information. He was impressed by the computer simulation of cognitive processes and was strongly influenced by his personal acquaintance with cognitive pioneers such as Bruner and Chomsky. Miller claimed that he abandoned behaviorism as a direct result of meeting Chomsky at a summer seminar at Stanford University (Miller, 1989).

Miller promoted Chomsky's ideas on language in "Some Psychological Studies of Grammar" (1962), having earlier reprised the experimental study of attention pioneered by Wundt (Miller, 1956). By 1965 Miller had abandoned the behaviorist mantra altogether and had joined with Bruner in talking

> about hypothesis testing instead of discrimination learning, about the evaluation of hypotheses instead of the reinforcement of responses, about rules instead of habits, about productivity instead of generalization, about symbols instead of conditioned stimuli, about linguistic structure instead of chains of responses.
>
> —(Miller, 1965, p. 20)

In 1960 Miller and Bruner managed to persuade McGeorge Bundy, the Dean of Faculty at Harvard, to establish the Center for Cognitive Studies (funded by the Carnegie Corporation), which hosted a number of distinguished visiting faculty engaged in the study of language, memory, perception, concept formation, and cognitive development. Although the life of the center was short (it was discontinued after 10 years, due to intellectual fragmentation and departmental politics), it provided temporary institutional legitimization of the cognitive "paradigm" in psychology at a critical period of its development. Miller moved to Rockefeller University and then to Princeton University, where he established a new program and laboratory in **cognitive science**, the name for the newly evolved interdisciplinary matrix of cognitive psychology, artificial intelligence, and linguistics (and associated disciplines such as neurophysiology, logic, mathematics, and philosophy).

Strategies, Programs, and Plans

Although the various programs of theory and research in psycholinguistics, attention, computer simulation, concept development, and cognitive growth proceeded largely independently of each other (at least in the early stages), they were united on the conceptual level by their commitment to a realist construal of theories about cognitive states and processes and by the joint acknowledgment by early cognitive theorists of each other's work. Chomsky, Broadbent, Newell, Shaw, Simon, Bruner, and Miller were committed to a realist conception of theories about cognitive states and processes as autonomous hypothetical constructs and made no attempt to provide operational definitions of them. Bruner cited the work of Herbert Simon (1962) in *Studies in Cognitive Growth* (Bruner, Oliver, & Greenfield, 1966); Newell, Shaw, and Simon treated Bruner's theoretical term "strategy" as referencing essentially the same type of cognitive rule structure as their theoretical term "program" (1958, p. 153); and Chomsky cited Bruner and Newell, Shaw, and Simon (and Lashley) in his 1959 review of Skinner's *Verbal Behavior* (Chomsky, 1959, pp. 55–57).

Miller, Eugene Galanter, and Karl Pribram integrated emerging cognitive theories in *Plans and the Structure of Behavior* (1960). They proposed a general framework for the development of information-processing theory based upon the notion of a *plan*, defined as a "hierarchical process in the organism that can control the order in which a sequence of operations is to be formed" (1960, p. 16). The general orientation of the book was heavily influenced by recent work in computer simulation, and the authors avowed that the term *program* could be substituted for *plan* throughout the work. Rejecting peripheralist accounts of behavior based upon the chaining of stimulus-response sequences, they recommended the TOTE (Test-Operate-Test-Exit) routine as a superior unit of analysis.

Ulric Neisser: Cognitive Psychology

Ulric Neisser's *Cognitive Psychology* (1967), which integrated recent work on perception, attention, concept development, psycholinguistics, and computer simulation, effectively christened the emerging field of cognitive psychology. Neisser's interest in cognitive psychology was stimulated by his work with Miller at Harvard (where he gained his PhD in 1956) and Köhler at Swarthmore (where he gained his MA in 1952). He taught at Brandeis and Cornell University before moving to Emory University in 1983.

Neisser articulated the new "information-processing" approach of cognitive psychology, distinguishing it from alternative physiological, psychoanalytic, and behaviorist approaches. He characterized "cognitive psychology" as the study of "cognitive mechanisms" and defined cognition as "all the processes by which sensory input is transformed, reduced, elaborated, stored, recovered and used":

> Such terms as *sensation, perception, imagery, retention, recall, problem-solving*, and *thinking*, among many others, refer to hypothetical stages or aspects of cognition.
>
> —(1967, p. 4)

Neisser also championed a realist conception of cognitive hypothetical constructs:

> The basic reason for studying the cognitive processes has become as clear as the reason for studying anything else: because they are there. Our knowledge of the world *must* be somehow developed from the stimulus input. . . . Cognitive processes surely exist, so it can hardly be unscientific to study them.
>
> —(1967, p. 5)

Neisser's cognitive psychology developed information-processing psychology beyond the confines of information theory and computer simulation. Like Miller and Broadbent, Neisser recognized that information theory is inadequate as a characterization of cognitive processes, since it treats cognitive systems as "unselective." In contrast, Neisser maintained that human beings "are by no means neutral or passive towards the incoming information. . . . they select some parts for attention at the expense of others, recoding and reformulating them in complex ways" (1967, p. 7). He granted that "the task of the psychologist trying to understand human cognition is analogous to that of a man trying to discover how a computer has been programmed" (1967, p. 6), but his theoretical exploitation of computational concepts did not involve any blind commitment to computer simulation, which he critically dismissed as "simplistic."

The Cognitive Revolution

Neisser's book introduced the cognitive psychological "paradigm" and the "cognitive revolution" (although Neisser himself never used the terms). Yet, like the behaviorist "revolution," the cognitive revolution was not an overnight affair. It began in the 1950s, but progressed slowly throughout the 1960s. This was despite Donald Hebb's call for a "second American revolution" in psychology devoted to the "serious, persistent, and if necessary, daring exploration of the thought processes "(1960, p. 745) and his confident claim that computational cognitive theories had begun to displace behaviorist learning theories:

> It is becoming apparent from such work as that of Broadbent (1958) and of Miller, Galanter and Pribram (1960) that the computer analogy, which can readily include an autonomous central process as a factor in behavior, is a powerful contender for the center of the stage.
>
> —(Hebb, 1960, p. 740)

Stevens's 1951 *Handbook of Experimental Psychology* and Woodworth and Schlosberg's 1954 *Experimental Psychology* had little to say about cognitive processes (Woodworth and Schlosberg's 1954 text had less on cognition than *Woodworth's* 1938 text), and the *Annual Review of Psychology* reported little on cognition throughout the 1950s and early 1960s (Hearnshaw, 1989).

Behaviorism remained institutionally as well as intellectually dominant in the immediate postwar period, when it was very hard to attain an academic position in psychology without at least an avowed commitment to behaviorism. As Miller, who began his career as a behaviorist, recalled,

> The chairmen of all the important departments would tell you they were behaviorists. Membership of the elite Society of Experimental Psychology was limited to people of a behavioristic persuasion. . . . The power, the honors, the authority, the textbooks, the money, everything in psychology was owned by the behaviorists. . . . those of us who wanted to be scientific psychologists couldn't really oppose it. You just wouldn't get a job.
>
> —(Baars, 1986, p. 203)

Yet by the late 1960s cognitive psychology had established itself as a viable theoretical and research program, and it was progressively institutionalized throughout the 1970s. New journals devoted to cognition were founded, such as *Cognitive Psychology* (1970), *Cognition* (1972), *Memory and Cognition* (1973), *Cognitive Science* (1977), and *Cognitive Therapy and Research* (1977). Departments began to hire faculty with specialization in cognitive psychology, undergraduate textbooks began to appear to satisfy the demand generated by new courses in cognitive psychology, and graduate programs in cognitive psychology (and interdisciplinary cognitive science) were introduced at a number of universities. By the late 1970s the cognitive revolution appeared complete, with Lachman, Lachman, and Butterfield (1979) declaring that a Kuhnian "paradigm shift" had occurred in psychology, in which the "information-processing" paradigm had displaced the earlier behaviorist paradigm:

> Information-processing psychology . . . has become the dominant paradigm in the study of adult cognitive processes.
>
> —(1979, p. 6)

They claimed that from the perspective of the "information-processing" paradigm, cognitive psychology was the study of "the way man collects, stores, modifies, and interprets environmental information or information already stored internally" (Lachman, Lachman, & Butterfield, 1979, p. 7).

By the 1980s the cognitive "paradigm" began to penetrate subdisciplines such as social, developmental, and clinical psychology. Social psychologists turned their attention to "social cognition" (Fiske & Taylor, 1982; Nisbett & Ross, 1980), developmental psychologists became engaged in debates over the nature and development of the child's "theory of mind" (Astington, Harris, & Olston, 1988; Perner, Leekam, & Wimmer, 1987; Wellman & Esters, 1986), and "cognitive therapy" became the new fashion in clinical psychology (Beck, 1976; Ellis, 1984).

Whatever their differences, and whatever their degree of commitment to the computer analogy, most cognitive psychologists from the 1970s onward were engaged in the study of cognitive processing. They exemplified the "rules and representations" (Bechtel, 1988) approach to cognition pioneered by Chomsky and given mechanical expression in the computer simulation of cognitive processes by Newell, Shaw, and Simon. This approach was reflected in a variety of seminal works, such as Anderson's *The Architecture of Cognition* (1983), Johnston Laird's *Mental Models: Towards a Cognitive Science of Language, Inference and Consciousness* (1983), Marr's *Vision: A Computational Investigation Into the Human Representation and Processing of Visual Information* (1982), Kosslyn's *Image and Mind* (1980), Schank and Abelson's *Scripts, Plans, Goals and Understanding* (1977), and Rosch and Lloyd's *Cognition and Categorization* (1978).

THE COGNITIVE REVOLUTION

Some have represented the development of cognitive psychology as a genuine revolution in psychological science (Baars, 1986; Gardner, 1985; Lachman, Lachman, & Butterfield, 1979). Others have questioned whether there was a revolution and suggested that cognitive psychology evolved naturally from "liberalized" forms of neobehaviorism that allowed for the introduction of internal intervening variables such as "mediating" r-s connections (Amsel, 1989; Holdstock, 1994; Kendler & Kendler, 1975; Leahey, 1992; Mandler, 2002).

The Cognitive Revolution as "Paradigm Shift"

Some have represented the emergence of cognitive psychology as a Kuhnian "paradigm shift" (Kuhn, 1970), in which the theoretical and methodological schema of behaviorism gave way to the theoretical and methodological schema of cognitivism under the pressure of irresolvable empirical anomalies (Lachman, Lachman, & Butterfield, 1979; Palermo, 1971; Weimer & Palermo, 1973). According to Lachman, Lachman, and Butterfield (1979), the development of information-processing theory in cognitive psychology represented a Kuhnian "scientific revolution," in which the "puzzle-solving" tradition of behaviorism was displaced by the "puzzle-solving" tradition of cognitive psychology:

> The scientific study of cognitive psychology has moved dramatically forward under the pre-theoretical commitments of the information-processing approach. Great progress is reflected in the way in which our discipline has refocused its research effort toward accounting for intelligent human behavior. This refocusing required a revolution. The significant issues simply could not be addressed adequately within the framework of neobehavioristic psychology.
>
> Now information-processing psychology is an established paradigm, and it guides the vast bulk of psychological research in human cognition. Our revolution is complete, and the atmosphere is one of normal science.
>
> —(Lachman, Lachman & Butterfield, 1979, p. 525)

However, for the following reasons, the historical movement from behaviorism to cognitive psychology is not best characterized in terms of a Kuhnian "paradigm shift." The various empirical problems faced by behaviorism, such as the difficulty of explaining linguistic behavior in terms of conditioning theory and the recognition of biological limits on conditioning, did not result in the abandonment of behaviorism. Behaviorists continued to maintain their in-house journals, their own APA division, and a sizable professional membership. Indeed, Skinner's school of radical behaviorism expanded institutionally during the same period in the 1950s that cognitive psychology was being developed (Krantz, 1972). The primary stimulus for the emergence of cognitive psychology came from external developments in information theory, linguistics, and computer simulation, rather than from the internal empirical anomalies faced by behaviorism.

The conflict between behaviorism and cognitive psychology was not a conflict between *exclusive* theoretical paradigms, on a par with the conflict between the physical theories of Newton and Einstein in the early 20th century or between the wave and particle theories of light in the early 19th century. The critical evidence that supported Einstein's physical theory and the wave theory of light appeared to demonstrate the general inadequacy of Newton's physical theory and the particle theory of light and led to their complete rejection by most scientists. Yet few imagined that the empirical problems faced by behaviorism demonstrated the fundamental inadequacy of theories of classical and operant conditioning. The recognized empirical anomalies indicated only a general delimitation of the scope of explanations in terms of conditioning (albeit long overdue) and the extension of biological and cognitive explanations to the range of human and animal behavior for which conditioning theory proved to be inadequate.

It was only because behaviorists had overestimated the scope of conditioning theory and presumed that it was able to accommodate all forms of animal and human behavior, including complex forms of human behavior such as linguistic behavior, that it faced these empirical problems. Earlier animal and comparative psychologists had not been so intellectually imperialistic. Lloyd Morgan had recognized biological limits on learning and the inability of theories of associative learning to explain higher cognitive processes (Morgan, 1894/1977, 1896).

One would be hard put to discriminate a set of core theoretical and methodological schema constitutive of a behaviorist paradigm, other than a commitment to observable behavior as the subject matter of scientific psychology. Watson, Tolman, Hull, and Skinner differed quite radically in their theoretical explanations of human and animal behavior and their advocacy of inductive and hypothetic-deductive approaches to scientific method. It is probably even harder to discriminate a set of theoretical and methodological schema constitutive of a cognitive paradigm, other than a commitment to cognition as a legitimate subject matter of scientific psychology. There are at best only family resemblances between the various theories advanced by Chomsky, Broadbent, Bruner, Simon, Miller, and Neisser, for example.

The cognitive revolution did not represent a revolution in terms of attitudes to the existence of cognitive states and processes. It is commonly supposed that behaviorists denied, whereas cognitive psychologists affirmed, the existence of cognitive states and processes (Baars, 1986; Fodor, 1975). Yet Watson, Tolman, Hull, and Skinner never denied the existence of cognitive states and processes (although all but Tolman denied that cognitive states and processes play a role in the causal explanation of human and animal behavior), and many early cognitive psychologists avowed agnosticism with respect to the existence of cognitive states and processes (Anderson, 1980; Lachman, Lachman, & Butterfield, 1979; Nisbett & Ross, 1981).

From Intervening Variables to Cognitive Hypothetical Constructs

Although the cognitive revolution did not constitute a Kuhnian paradigm shift, it did mark a significant change in the conception of theories of cognitive states and processes: from their treatment as operationally defined *intervening variables* to their treatment as independently meaningful *hypothetical constructs*. Even the most "liberalized" forms of neobehaviorist theory never possessed independent meaning. Theoretical postulates such as "drive," "habit strength," "pure stimulus act," and all the intervening variables of "mediation theory" were provided with rigorous operational definitions, since neobehaviorists avowed that independent (or surplus) meaning has no place in a properly scientific psychology. In contrast, the theories advanced by cognitive psychologists from the 1950s onward did possess independent meaning. Cognitive psychologists provided substantive theoretical definitions of the sensory register, attention, long- and short-term memory, depth grammar, cognitive heuristics, visual perception, propositional and imagery coding, episodic and semantic memory, template-matching, procedural networks, inference, induction, and the like, but eschewed operational definitions (as opposed to specified operational measures) of these cognitive states and processes.

However, the difference between neobehaviorist and cognitive psychological theories was more than a difference between operational definition and independent theoretical meaning. Unlike later cognitive psychological theories, neobehaviorist theories lacked specifically cognitive content. Although neobehaviorists did employ terms like *cognition, concept,* and *representation,* they did not use them to reference the types of contentful representational states that cognitive psychologists maintain are employed in the rule-governed processing of information.

For example, Hull operationally defined concept formation in terms of stimulus discrimination and verbal association. Thus a person was said to grasp the meaning of the concept "dog" when he or she could discriminate dog stimuli and associate the verbal label "dog" with them (Hull, 1920, p. 5). Yet parrots could achieve this form of discriminative learning without any mastery of concepts or linguistic meaning (Goldstein & Scheerer, 1941). Hull's operational definition of a concept in terms of a conditioned (verbal) response was quite different, for example, from the cognitive theoretical definition of a concept advanced by Homer Reed (1946), in terms of a word or idea that stands for any one of a group of things.

Analogously, Osgood (1953) defined a "representational mediation process" as an internal stimulus that elicits a behavior (or "fractional portion" of a behavior) normally elicited by a stimulus, in the absence of that stimulus (or prior to its appearance). For example, he claimed that an "internal stimulus" or "external verbal stimulus" associated with a stimulus such as a hammer comes to represent hammers. Yet such an internal stimulus or verbal label "hammer" only represents hammers in the sense that a tone "represented" food for Pavlov's dogs: It was a conditioned causal sign for it. As Osgood put it, such postulated internal states "represent" objects in the fashion that dark clouds "represent" rain (they are causal indicators of rain):

> The buzzer elicits an "anxiety" reaction—part of the "fear" response originally made to the shock—and it is by virtue of this fact that it means or represents shock.
>
> —(Osgood, 1953, p. 695)

Yet representational states employed in thought, memory, judgment, inference, and the like are symbols of objects, not causal signs for them. The concept of buzzer and the word *buzzer,* for example, represent and mean buzzers, independently of whether or not they have come to be associated with shock via conditioning. Even when they *have* come to be associated with shock via conditioning, the concept of buzzer and word *buzzer* continue to represent buzzers and not shock.

That is, there was nothing cognitive about the internal mediational states (or internal r-s sequences) postulated by neobehaviorists (with the exception of Tolman's cognitive maps). Hull and his followers seem to have supposed that cognitive states are merely internal states capable of generating behavior, which can be instantiated in mechanical devices or "psychic machines" (Hull, 1937). Yet this is plainly not the case. Although programmed computers may be able to simulate cognitive states and processes and generate "artificially intelligent" behavior, traditional mechanical devices, including the hydraulic statues in the Royal Gardens at St. Germain that so impressed Descartes, plainly cannot. The electromechanical models of classical and instrumental conditioning developed in the 1950s (e.g., Walter, 1953), in contrast to the problem-solving programs developed by Newell, Shaw, and Simon (1958), were not models of cognition. Hull seems to have supposed that the only alternative to his account of cognition in terms of conditioned learning was an appeal to "non-physical" entities such as immaterial souls or spirits (Hull, 1937, pp. 31–32), but the cognitive revolution itself demonstrated that it was not.

The development of independently meaningful cognitive theories in contrast to operationally defined theories of internal "mediating" states was not accidentally related to cognitive psychologists' rejection of behaviorist commitments to strong contiguity between cognitive and associative sensory-motor functions. Behaviorists justified their reductive explanations of human language learning and concept formation in terms of principles of conditioned learning derived from animal experimentation by maintaining that human cognitive functions differ only in degree of complexity from associative stimulus-response functions common to humans and animals. In contrast, cognitive theorists such as

Lashley, Chomsky, and Bruner claimed that language learning and concept formation could not be reductively explained as more elaborate forms of associative conditioned learning, but had to be explained in terms of the rule-governed processing of representational states. Behaviorists who treated cognitive states as nothing more than internal states that causally mediate between associated stimuli and responses were naturally inclined to operationally define them in terms of associated stimuli and responses. Cognitive psychologists who treated cognitive states as representational states processed in accord with rules were not even tempted to define them in terms of associated stimuli and responses.

COGNITION AND BEHAVIOR

There is another respect in which the cognitive revolution represented a fundamental discontinuity between earlier behaviorist and later cognitive forms of psychological theory. Cognitive psychologists from the 1950s onward did not merely aim to develop and evaluate cognitive explanations of behavior to replace explanations of behavior in terms of classical and operant conditioning: They also treated cognitive states and processes as legitimate objects of explanation in themselves. Although neobehaviorists treated references to cognitive states and processes as legitimate theoretical posits in the explanation of animal and human behavior, no behaviorist seems to have thought that cognitive states and processes were worthy of explanation or investigation in their own right. This was true even of Tolman, the most cognitive behaviorist, who gave the following examples of the types of behavior studied by behaviorist psychologists:

> A rat running a maze; a cat getting out of a puzzle-box; a man driving home to dinner; a child hiding from a stranger; a woman doing her washing or gossiping over the telephone; a pupil marking a mental-test sheet; a psychologist reciting a list of nonsense syllables; my friend and I telling one another our thoughts and feelings.
>
> —(1932, p. 8)

No reference was made to drawing an inference, solving an arithmetical problem, recalling the order of speakers at a wedding ceremony, or any other form of cognitive process.

The cognitive revolution in psychology involved the rejection of the behaviorist restriction of the subject matter of psychology to observable behavior. Cognitive psychologists since the 1950s have been as much concerned with the explanation of cognitive processing as they have been with the explanation of observable behavior. They have wanted to know whether images are processed phenomenally or sententially, whether semantic memory is accessed via the activation of hierarchically related conceptual nodes or feature lists, whether errors in inference are due to interference or the employment of distorting heuristics, and whether the prediction of the behavior of others is grounded in simulation of their cognitive processes or information-based theoretical modules. These sorts of questions were scarcely even raised, never mind addressed, within behaviorism.

Structuralism and Anthropomorphism

Their treatment of cognitive states and processes as legitimate objects of explanation does not mean that cognitive psychologists have neglected the critical evidential role of observable behavior in the empirical evaluation of theories of cognitive states and processes, and indeed cognitive psychologists often stress their employment of rigorous operational measures of cognitive constructs (Mandler, 1979). It also does not mean that the development of cognitive psychology marks a return to Titchener's structural psychology or Romanes's anthropomorphism, as various behaviorist critics of the cognitive revolution have charged (Amsel, 1989; Skinner, 1985, 1990).

Titchener's form of structural psychology was based upon two critical assumptions of the empiricist associationist tradition in psychology: that cognition is both imagistic and conscious. By contrast, the forms of cognitive psychology that developed from the 1950s onward did not equate cognition and imagery (Pavio, 1971) and did not presume that cognitive states and processes (including imagery) are conscious (Ericsson & Simon, 1980; Kosslyn, 1980). On the contrary, one of the heralded achievements of contemporary cognitive psychology has been the experimental demonstration that subjects have limited introspective access to their own cognitive states and processes:

> The accuracy of subject reports is so poor as to suggest that any introspective access that may exist is not sufficient to produce generally correct or reliable reports.
>
> —(Nisbett & Wilson, 1977, p. 233)

Neobehaviorists have complained that in attributing cognitive states and processes to animals, cognitive psychologists have reintroduced the methodological sins of "subjectivism" and "anthropomorphism" supposedly exorcised through the application of Morgan's canon:

> These animal cognitivists, who recognized a paradigm shift when they saw one, adopted the language and the models of human cognitive psychology and information processing. Consequently, instead of using animals as models for human function, they were now back to the kind of subjectivism and anthropomorphism the behaviorists had rejected. They were using animal behavior as a vehicle for their introspections, for understanding the mind, . . . and they were using humans as

models for animal cognition. This use of humans as models for animals can happen *only in psychology*!

—(Amsel, 1989, pp. 38–39)

Yet there is nothing intrinsically subjective or unscientific about using human cognition as a model for animal cognition. The only basis for calling such theoretical modeling subjective or unscientific is the supposed scientific illegitimacy of ascribing conscious or cognitive states to animals, according to the behaviorist interpretation of Morgan's canon. Yet although Morgan doubted that animals possess cognitive capacities such as means-end reasoning and abstract thought, he never doubted the scientific legitimacy of ascribing these capacities to them and maintained that there are good grounds for ascribing consciousness to animals. Behaviorists interpreted Morgan's canon as a prescription against the cognitive explanation of human and animal behavior only because they presumed that all human and animal behavior could be explained in terms of associative learning. Yet the work of Lashley, Chomsky, the Brelands, Garcia, Bruner, and Miller indicated that it could not.

Cognitive psychologists denied that cognitive processes could be explained in terms of classical and operant conditioning and thus denied the strong continuity between cognitive processes and reflexive associative processes affirmed by behaviorists (and by most late-19th-century physiologists and evolutionary theorists). Yet in ascribing cognitive processes to animals, cognitive psychologists also affirmed the strong continuity between human and animal psychology affirmed by behaviorists (and by most late-19th-century physiologists and evolutionary theorists). They did this without inconsistency because the denial of strong continuity between cognitive and reflexive associative processes does not mandate the denial of strong continuity between human and animal psychology and behavior. Although cognitive psychologists maintained (with Wundt and Morgan) that there are forms of cognition and patterns of behavior characteristic of humans that cannot be reduced to associative processes or conditioning, they also affirmed that many of these can be attributed to higher animals (Griffin, 1976; Premack & Premack, 1983; Roitblat, 1987). They maintained (contra Wundt and Morgan) that some animals had reached a stage of evolution sufficient for the emergence of such forms of cognition and patterns of behavior.

The Cognitive Tradition

Although the cognitive revolution did not represent a return to Titchener's structural psychology, it did represent a return to the "modern investigation of thinking" associated with the Würzburg school (Kulpe, 1912/1964). The Würzburg psychologists developed theories of cognitive processing that anticipated contemporary cognitive psychological theories: They postulated rule-governed operations on representational states without presupposing that such rules and representations were imagistic or conscious. Many pioneers of the cognitive revolution acknowledged the early work of the Würzburg psychologists. Newell, Shaw, and Simon's computer simulation of human problem solving was based upon the "thought-psychology" of Otto Selz, one of the members of the Würzburg school, and the work of his student Adriaan de Groot, who developed prototype "programs" for the analysis of problem solving by chess players (de Groot, 1946).

These early forms of cognitive psychology survived the demise of the Würzburg school in the 1920s. Thomas Vernon Moore (1877–1969), professor of psychology at the Catholic University of America, who visited the Würzburg psychologists in 1915, published *Cognitive Psychology* in 1938 (Knapp, 1985), and Woodworth's *Experimental Psychology* of that same year included a long chapter on "Thinking." A small group of American psychologists continued Wundt's experimental studies of attention throughout the early decades of the 20th century, until Broadbent and Miller returned them to center stage in the 1950s (Lovie, 1983, cited in Knapp, 1986). During the first half of the 20th century, psychologists continued to pursue cognitive psychological areas of research, such as problem solving, reasoning, concept formation, inductive inference, transfer of logical organization, and logical inference (Greenwood, 2001), and most of the experimental studies that supported these forms of research employed human subjects rather than rats and pigeons. A cognitive tradition developed from the 1920s onward that was continuous with contemporary cognitive psychology, albeit decidedly attenuated during the heyday of behaviorism.

Criticism and Connectionism

The cognitive revolution has not progressed entirely smoothly. Over and above behaviorist complaints about a return to subjectivism and anthropomorphism, a number of critics, including some of the early pioneers of the cognitive revolution, have raised concerns about the theoretical and empirical foundations of cognitive psychology. Some have complained about the fragmented nature of the discipline (Jenkins, 1981; Newell, 1973), noting that cognitive psychologists appear to study a wide variety of cognitive states and processes in the absence of any unified theory integrating research in perception, memory, and problem solving, for example. Yet some cognitive psychologists have developed integrative theories (Anderson, 1983), and it is possible that the lack of theoretical integration within cognitive psychology is itself a function of the limited integration of cognitive "modules" within cognitive architectures (Fodor, 1983). Others have complained about the artificiality of much experimental research in cognitive psychology, most notably Neisser, who called for a more "ecological" approach in his 1976 book *Cognition and Reality*. Yet although many critics have exploited his "second thoughts" to their rhetorical advantage, Neisser never questioned the basic theoretical or methodological integrity of cognitive psychology as a form of scientific psychology. He later affirmed that a wide range of current research in cognitive psychology is of "real significance" and that cognitive psychology and related disciplines "have made important and ecologically valid discoveries" (Neisser, 1997, p. 17).

A more interesting complaint was developed by John Anderson (1978, 1981), who claimed that behavioral data are insufficient to adjudicate between competing theories of representation, since a number of different theories of representation (in terms of propositions, images, or schema, for example) can accommodate the same behavioral data. Given this "fundamental indeterminacy" with respect to the empirical adjudication of competing theories, we are never in a position to infer the "psychological reality" of the relevant cognitive states and processes.

Yet the underdetermination of theories by empirical data is a fact of life in any science (Quine, 1960), and it is often possible to develop novel empirical predictions that enable scientists to empirically adjudicate between competing theories—as proved to be the case with respect to the conflict between the Ptolemaic and Copernican theories and the wave and particle theories of light. As Anderson himself acknowledged, competing theories of representation that are empirically underdetermined by behavioral predictions may be adjudicated by reference to neurophysiology (only one theory of cognitive processing may be consistent with the neural architecture of the brain) or by considerations of economy and efficiency. Given their rejection of introspective methods, cognitive psychologists cannot of course appeal to subject reports to establish the "psychological reality" of theories of representation. Yet in this respect they are no worse off than theoretical chemists or biologists, who likewise cannot appeal to the reports of molecules or cells to adjudicate between competing chemical and biological theories that predict the same range of empirical data.

It might turn out that the empirical underdetermination of competing cognitive theories is not a temporary function of the underdeveloped nature of theories of representation, but an enduring problem that cannot be resolved by appeal to novel prediction, neurophysiology, or considerations of economy and efficiency. Yet if this proved to be the case, it would be because a number of competing theories of representation have continued to furnish equally good explanations and predictions of a wide range of empirical behavior, are consistent with known neurophysiological data, and remain closely equivalent with respect to considerations of economy and efficiency. At this point cognitive psychology would have developed to a theoretical stage where it enjoys the luxury of a problem faced by advanced sciences such as subatomic physics.

Connectionism The most significant critique of cognitive psychology was internal and focused upon the reliance of theories of cognitive processing on theories of computation based upon the operation of von Neumann computers, which process information serially at high speeds. During the 1980s cognitive psychologists developed **connectionist** theories of cognitive processing, modeled upon **parallel distributed processing** (PDP) computer architectures, which encode information via the statistical distribution of connection "weights" among units in a nodal network. In a connectionist system, each unit is connected to other units and can send and receive excitatory and inhibitory signals. Connectionist systems process information when patterns of activation in designated "input" units spread through a system of internal units known as "hidden units," and patterns of activation stabilize in designated "output" units. In this fashion connectionist systems can distinguish rocks from mines, discriminate phonemes, and form the past tense of verbs. They excel in pattern recognition and learning, two areas that proved problematic for traditional cognitive systems based upon serial computation. The "Bible" of this new form of cognitive psychology was David Rumelhart and James

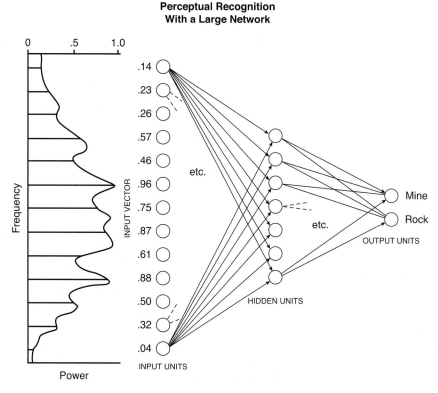

Parallel distributed processing: learning network for discriminating rocks from mines.
Churchland, P. (1988). Matter and consciousness. Cambridge, MA: MIT Press

McClelland's *Parallel Distributed Processing: Explorations in Microcognition,* which was published in 1986.

One of the perceived virtues of connectionist theories was that they were modeled upon the parallel processing of information by interconnected neurons in the brain:

> One reason for the appeal of PDP models is their obvious "physiological" flavor. They seem so much more closely tied to the physiology of the brain than other kinds of information-processing models. The brain consists of a large number of highly inter-connected elements which apparently send very simple excitory and inhibitory mes-sages to each other and update their excitations on the basis of these simple messages.
>
> —(McClelland, Rumelhart, & Hinton, 1986, p. 10)

Some have claimed that the development of connectionist theories has transformed cognitive psychology and marks the demise of traditional compu-tational theories of cognition, since connectionist theories of processing do not presuppose the cognitive representation of rules, a distinctive feature of cognitive theories from Chomsky to Neisser. For example, commenting on the performance of a connectionist network that simulated the acquisition of English past tense, Rumelhart and McClelland claimed that

> We have, we believe, provided a distinct alternative to the view that children learn the rules of English past-tense formulation in any explicit sense. We have shown that a reasonable account of the acquisition of past tense can be provided without recourse to the notion of a rule as anything more than a *description* of the language.
>
> —(Rumelhart & McClelland, 1986, p. 267)

However, connectionist theories do not deny the representation of rules, but only particular theories about how they are encoded and learned. They claim that rules are represented within the distribution of connection "weights" between units and that networks learn via the modular adjustment of the strength of connections between units, in contrast to traditional computational cognitive theories based upon von Neumann architectures, in which a central processing unit controls the processing of information in accord with a set of rules stored in the computer program.

Consequently, it may be argued that connectionism is better represented as a creative development or transformation of traditional cognitive theories than as a displacement of them. This seems to have been the original view of the pioneers of connectionist theory:

> Though the appeal of PDP models is definitely enhanced by their physiological plausi-bility and neural inspiration, these are not the primary basis for their appeal to us. We are, after all, cognitive scientists, and PDP models appeal to us for psychological and

computational reasons. They hold out the hope of offering computationally sufficient and psychologically accurate mechanistic accounts of the phenomena of human cognition which have eluded successful explication in conventional computational formalisms; and they have radically altered the way we think about the time-course of processing, the nature of representation, and the mechanisms of learning.

—(McClelland, Rumelhart, & Hinton, 1986, p. 11)

Defenders of traditional cognitive psychology have maintained that connectionism poses no threat to traditional cognitive theories, either because they doubt the ability of connectionist systems to "scale up" to cover more complex and integrated cognitive processes (Dennett, 1991) or because they treat connectionist theories as merely accounts of how the forms of information processing described by traditional cognitive theories are implemented in the human brain (Fodor & Pylyshyn, 1988). While some have suggested that developments in connectionism and (more recently) "dynamical-systems" theory (Port & Gelder, 1995; Serra & Zanarini, 1990) mark a return to earlier forms of associationist psychology and behaviorism (Haselager, 1997), contemporary connectionist theories based upon computational learning algorithms appear to bear only a very tenuous relation to earlier traditions based upon the correlation of imagistic ideas and conditioned stimulus response connections.

THE SECOND CENTURY

One thing is for sure. The cognitive revolution is an ongoing revolution, and theories of cognitive processing continue to be developed in creative and fertile ways. Moreover, whatever one concludes about the significance of recent developments in connectionist theory, it is clear that contemporary scientific psychology has reached a stage where it does not consider the postulation of cognitive theories (about unconscious and unobservable cognitive states) to be unscientific and no longer maintains that the content of scientific psychological theories should be restricted to the content of operational definitions. Consequently, at the beginning of the 21st century, with psychology having celebrated the first centennial of scientific psychology in 1987 and of the APA in 1992, we may close this conceptual history of psychology on a generally positive note.

Without presuming a presentist perspective on the development of psychological theory and methodology, it can be said that contemporary psychology embraces roughly the same conception of scientific theory as the mature physical sciences, even though it continues to romanticize about its ability to reproduce particular (and arguably inappropriate) features of Newtonian science, such as universal explanation (Kimble, 1995; Shepard, 1987, 1995) and unified theory (Spence, 1987; Staats, 1983). Perhaps in the 21st century psychology will finally free itself of this conceptual baggage from its early protoscientific history.

It may be forced to, since the fate of cognitive psychology is no longer exclusively in the hands of psychologists. Cognitive psychology now forms part of the broader interdisciplinary matrix that is cognitive science, which will undoubtedly be influenced by developments in the other disciplines (such as computer science, neuroscience, linguistics, mathematics, and philosophy) that make up cognitive science. What is true of the fate of cognitive psychology is also true of the fate of institutional psychology, since the APA no longer exclusively determines the future of the discipline.

The APA grew at a phenomenal rate in the postwar period: from over 9,000 in 1950 to over 19,000 in 1960; from over 30,000 in 1970 to over 50,000 in 1980; and from over 70,000 in 1990 to over 83,000 in 2000 (APA, 2001). The charter members of the APA met in G. Stanley Hall's office at Clark University in 1892. Today conference attendees number between 10,000 and 20,000 and occupy a slew of hotels in major cities. APA revenues have grown from just over $60 in 1892 to tens of millions of dollars in the 21st century.

Most of the growth in the postwar period came from professional rather than academic psychology, and the balance between the academic and professional psychologists within the APA began to shift in favor of the professionals (clinical, counseling, industrial, educational, and other applied psychologists). Before the war about two thirds of the APA membership were academics; by the 1980s only about a third were. Throughout the 1960s and 1970s academic psychologists pressed for changes in the structure of the APA that would have given them greater power within an organization increasingly dominated by professionals. When the APA rejected a restructuring plan in 1988, the academics split to form the American Psychological Society (APS). From an initial charter membership of 1,500, the APS grew to 5,000 by 1989, and to 15,000 by 1995 (Brewer, 1994). The membership of the APS, unlike the membership of the APA, includes many biologists, computer scientists, philosophers, linguists, and mathematicians, who are not academically qualified psychologists (who do not have a degree in psychology). Given that the qualified memberships only partially overlap, it is unlikely that the two associations will reunify in the near future.

DISCUSSION QUESTIONS

1. Do you think that some machines are intrinsically purposive? Do we ascribe purpose to machines because they employ feedback or because purposive humans design them? If a machine malfunctioned in a systematic way, would we still call its behavior purposive?

2. Newell, Shaw, and Simon suggested that the adequacy of the computer simulation of human problem solving depends upon the ability to mimic the

cognitive strategies of human problem solvers, as revealed by "think-aloud" subject protocols. Is this a legitimate criterion of adequacy for the computer simulation of cognition? What problems might you anticipate with such an approach?

3. Contemporary cognitive psychology appears to be committed to strong continuity between human and animal psychology but not to strong continuity between higher cognitive and lower reflexive associative processes. Is this position consistent?

4. Would a computer programmed to operate on principles of classical and operant conditioning be able to understand language or engage in purposive behavior?

5. Do you think it possible to reconstruct the cognitive revolution as a Kuhnian "paradigm shift"?

GLOSSARY

artificial intelligence The science of intelligent machines.

bit A binary unit, the elemental unit of information theory, conceived of as the amount of information required to determine between two equiprobable alternatives.

cognitive science The name for the interdisciplinary matrix of cognitive psychology, artificial intelligence, and linguistics (and associated disciplines such as neurophysiology, logic, mathematics, and philosophy) that evolved as a product of the cognitive revolution in psychology.

connectionism Set of cognitive theories developed in the 1980s modeled upon the parallel processing of information in the brain rather than the serial processing of von Neumann computers.

cybernetics The science of control and communication in animals and machines.

digital computer A computer that performs operations on binary units of information.

feedback Signals from a goal that modify goal-directed behavior.

General Problem Solver Computer designed by Allen Newell, J. C. Shaw, and Herbert Simon, capable of cognitive tasks such as playing chess and problem solving.

hardware The physical systems that instantiate the rules or instructions encoded in computer programs.

Logic Theorist Computer program designed by Allen Newell and Herbert Simon, capable of proving theorems in logic.

new logic Form of truth-functional logic developed in the late 19th and 20th centuries, whose sentential operators (such as "if . . . then") are definable in terms of primitive operators such as "and" and "not."

noise Random disturbance superimposed upon a signal, such as electrical noise caused by heat in electrical circuits.

parallel distributed processing Computer architecture in which information is encoded via the statistical distribution of connection "weights" among units in a nodal network.

program A set of rules or instructions stored in the memory of a computer.

servomechanism Term used to describe intrinsically purposive machines such as torpedoes, whose behavior is regulated by feedback.

software The set of rules or instructions encoded by a computer program.

strong AI View that we can ascribe cognitive states to computers in exactly the same sense that we ascribe them to humans.

Turing machine A machine capable of performing elementary operations on symbols in accord with a set of instructions.

Turing test A hypothetical test suggested by Alan Turing as a practical means of deciding whether intelligence should be ascribed to a machine. Turing claimed that we should call a machine intelligent if we could not discriminate the responses of a human communicator from a machine simulating or "imitating" the responses of a human communicator.

universal Turing machine A general-purpose machine capable of performing operations specified by a variety of different Turing machines (defined by their individual sets of instructions).

von Neumann machine Computer that employs a central control unit to read and execute programmed instructions sequentially.

wetware Term used to describe biological systems that can instantiate the rules or instructions encoded in computer programs.

REFERENCES

American Psychological Association. (2001). *Directory of the American Psychological Association: 2001 edition.* Washington, DC: Author.

Amsel, A. (1989). *Behaviorism, neobehaviorism, and cognitivism in learning theory: Historical and contemporary perspectives.* Hillsdale, NJ: Erlbaum.

Anderson, J. (1978). Arguments concerning representations for mental imagery. *Psychological Review, 85,* 249–277.

Anderson, J. (1981). Concepts, propositions, and schemata: What are the cognitive units? In J. H. Flowers (Ed.), *Nebraska symposium on motivation: Vol. 28. Cognitive processes.* Lincoln: University of Nebraska Press.

Anderson, J. (1983). *The architecture of cognition*. Cambridge, MA: Harvard University Press.

Angell, J. R. (1907). The province of functional psychology. *Psychological Review, 14*, 61–91.

Astington, J. W., Olson, D., & Harris, P. (Eds.). (1988). *Developing theories of mind.* Cambridge: Cambridge University Press.

Baars, B. J. (1986). *The cognitive revolution in psychology*. New York: Guilford Press.

Baddeley, A. (1994). The magical number seven: Still magic after all these years? *Psychological Review, 101*, 353–356.

Bartlett, F. C. (1932). *Remembering*. Cambridge: Cambridge University Press.

Bartlett, F. C. (1943). Fatigue following highly skilled work. *Proceedings of the Royal Society, 131*, 247–257.

Bechtel, W. (1988). Connectionism and rules and representation systems: Are they compatible? *Philosophical Psychology, 1*, 5–16.

Beck, A. T. (1976). *Cognitive therapy and emotional disorders*. New York: International Universities Press.

Boden, M. (1997). Promise and achievement in cognitive science. In D. M. Johnson & C. E. Erneling (Eds.), *The future of the cognitive revolution*. New York: Oxford University Press.

Brewer, M. B. (1994). Growing up with APA: The next five years. *APS Observer*, 10.

Broadbent, D. E. (1957). A mechanical model for human attention and immediate memory. *Psychological Review, 64*, 205–215.

Broadbent, D. E. (1958). *Perception and communication*. Oxford: Pergamon Press.

Bruner, J. (1980). Jerome. S. Bruner. In G. Lindzey (Ed.), *A history of psychology in autobiography* (Vol. 7). San Francisco: Freeman.

Bruner, J. S., Goodnow, J., & Austin, G. (1956). *A study of thinking*. New York: Wiley.

Bruner, J. S., & Krech, D. (Eds.). (1950). *Perception and personality*. Durham: University of North Carolina Press.

Bruner, J. S., Oliver, R. R., & Greenfield, P. M. (1966). *Studies in cognitive growth*. New York: Wiley.

Bruner, J. S., & Postman, L. (1947a). Emotional selectivity in perception and reaction. *Journal of Personality, 16*, 69–77.

Bruner, J. S., & Postman, L. (1947b). Tension and tension-release as organizing factors in perception. *Journal of Personality, 15*, 300–308.

Bruner, J. S., & Postman, L. (1949). On perception of incongruity: A paradigm. *Journal of Personality, 18*, 206–223.

Chomsky, N. (1959). Review of B. F. Skinner's *Verbal Behavior. Language, 35*, 26–58.

Cohen, D. (1977). *Psychologists on psychology*. New York: Taplinger.

Craik, K. J. W. (1947). Theory of the human operator in control systems: II. Man as an element in a control system. *British Journal of Psychology, 38*, 142–148.

de Groot, A. D. (1946). *Het denken van denschaker* [*Thought and choice in chess*]. Amsterdam: Noord-Hollandsche Uitgevers Maatschappij.

Dennett, D. C. (1991). Two contrasts: Folk craft versus folk science, and belief versus opinion. In J. D. Greenwood (Ed.), *The future of folk psychology: Intentionality and cognitive science*. Cambridge: Cambridge University Press.

Dreyfus, H. L. (1972). *What computers can't do: A critique of artificial reason*. New York: Harper & Row.

Dupuy, J-P. (2000). *The mechanization of the mind: On the origins of cognitive science* (M. B. DeBevoise, Trans.). Princeton, NJ: Princeton University Press.

Ellis, A. (1984). Rational-emotive therapy. In R. J. Corsini (Ed.), *Current psychotherapies* (3rd ed.). Itasca, IL: Peacock.

Ericsson, K. A., & Simon, H. (1980). Verbal reports as data. *Psychological Review, 87*, 215–281.

Fiske, S. T., & Taylor, S. E. (1982). *Social cognition*. New York: Random House.

Fodor, J. A. (1975). *The language of thought*. Cambridge, MA: Harvard University Press.

Fodor, J. A. (1983). *The modularity of mind*. Cambridge, MA: MIT Press.

Fodor, J. A., & Pylyshyn, Z. W. (1988). Connectionism and cognitive architecture: A critical analysis. *Cognition, 28*, 3–71.

Frick, F. C., & Miller, G. A. (1951). A statistical description of operant conditioning. *American Journal of Psychology, 64*, 20–36.

Gardner, H. (1985). *The mind's new science: A history of the cognitive revolution*. New York: Basic Books.

Garner, W. R. (1962). *Uncertainty and structure as psychological concepts*. New York: Wiley.

Goldstein, K., & Scheerer, M. (1941). Abstract and concrete behavior: An experimental study with special tests. *Psychological Monographs, 53*(2).

Greenwood, J. D. (2001). Understanding the "cognitive revolution" in psychology. *Journal of the History of the Behavioral Sciences, 35*, 1–22.

Griffin, D. R. (1976). *The question of animal awareness: Evolutionary continuity of mental experience*. New York: Rockefeller Press.

Haselager, W. F. G. (1997). *Cognitive psychology and folk psychology: The right frame of mind*. Thousand Oaks, CA: Sage.

Hearnshaw, L. S. (1989). *The shaping of modern psychology: A historical introduction*. London: Routledge.

Hebb, D. O. (1949). *The organization of behavior*. New York: Wiley.

Hebb, D. O. (1960). The second American revolution. *American Psychologist, 15*, 735–745.

Hodges, A. (1992). *Alan Turing: The enigma* (Rev. ed.) London: Vintage.

Holdstock, L. T. (1994). Is the cognitive revolution all it is made up to be? *American Psychologist, 49*, 819–820.

Hovland, C. I. (1952). A "communication analysis" of concept learning. *Psychological Review, 59*, 461–472.

Hovland, C. I. (1960). Computer simulation of thinking. *American Psychologist, 15*, 687–693.

Hull, C. L. (1920). Quantitative aspects of the evolution of concepts: An experimental approach. *Psychological Monographs, 28* (Whole No 123).

Hull, C. L. (1930). Knowledge and purpose as habit mechanisms. *Psychological Review, 36*, 511–525.

Hull, C. L. (1937). Mind, mechanism and adaptive behavior. *Psychological Review, 44*, 1–32.

Hunt, E. B. (1962). *Concept learning: An information processing problem.* New York: Wiley.

Hunt, M. (1994). *The story of psychology.* New York: Anchor Books.

Jenkins, J. J. (1981). Can we find a fruitful cognitive psychology? In J. H. Flowers (Ed.), *Nebraska symposium on motivation, 1980: Vol. 28. Cognitive processes.* Lincoln: University of Nebraska Press.

Kendler, H. H. (1952) What is learned?—A theoretical blind alley. *Psychological Review, 59*, 269–277.

Kendler, H. H., & Kendler, T. S. (1975). From discrimination learning to cognitive development: A neobehaviorist odyssey. In W. K. Estes (Ed.), *Handbook of learning and cognitive processes* (Vol. 1). Hillsdale, NJ: Erlbaum.

Kimble, G. A. (1995). Discussant's remarks: From chaos to coherence in psychology. *International Newsletter of Uninomic Psychology, 15*, 34–38.

Knapp, T. J. (1985). Contributions to the history of psychology: T. V. Moore and his "Cognitive psychology." *Psychological Reports, 357*, 1311–1316.

Knapp, T. J. (1986). The emergence of cognitive psychology in the latter half of the twentieth century. In T. J. Knapp & L. C. Robertson (Eds.), *Approaches to cognition: Contrasts and controversies.* Hillsdale, NJ: Erlbaum.

Kosslyn, S. M. (1980). *Image and mind.* Cambridge, MA: Harvard University Press.

Krantz, D. L. (1972). The mutual isolation of operant and non-operant psychology as a case study. *Journal of the History of the Behavioral Sciences, 8*, 86–102.

Kuhn, T. S. (1970). *The structure of scientific revolutions* (2nd ed.). Chicago: University of Chicago Press.

Külpe, O. (1964). The modern psychology of thinking. In G. Mandler & J. M. Mandler (Eds. and Trans.), *Thinking: From association to Gestalt.* New York: Wiley. (Original work published 1912 in German)

Lachman, J. R., Lachman, J., & Butterfield, E. (1979). *Cognitive psychology and information processing.* Hillsdale, NJ: Erlbaum.

Leahey, T. H. (1992). The mythical revolutions in of American psychology. *American Psychologist, 47*, 308–318.

Lovie, A. D. (1983). Attention and behaviorism—fact and fiction. *British Journal of Psychology, 74*, 301–310.

Mandler, G. (1979). Emotion. In E. Hearst (Ed.), *The first century of experimental psychology*. Hillsdale, NJ: Erlbaum.

Mandler, G. (2002). Origins of the cognitive (r)evolution. *Journal for the History of the Behavioral Sciences, 38*, 339–353.

Marr, D. (1982). *Vision: A computational investigation into the human representation and processing of visual information*. San Francisco: Freeman.

McClelland, J. L. Rumelhart, D. E., & Hinton, G. E. (1986). The appeal of parallel distributed processing. In D. E. Rumelhart, J. L. McClelland, & the PDP Research Group. (Eds.). (1986). *Explorations in the microstructure of cognition: Vol.1. Foundations*. Cambridge, MA: MIT Press.

McCulloch, W. S., & Pitts, W. (1943). A logical calculus of the ideas immanent in nervous activity. *Bulletin of Mathematical Biophysics, 5*, 115–133.

Miller, G. A. (1951). *Language and communication*. New York: McGraw-Hill.

Miller, G. A. (1953). What is information measurement? *American Psychologist, 8*, 3–11.

Miller, G. A. (1956). The magical number seven, plus or minus two: Some limits on our capacity for processing information. *Psychological Review, 63*, 81–97.

Miller, G. A. (1962). Some psychological studies of grammar. *American Psychologist, 17*, 748–762.

Miller, G. A. (1965). Some preliminaries to psycholinguistics. *American Psychologist, 20*, 15–20.

Miller, G. A. (1989). George A. Miller. In G. Lindzey (Ed.), *A history of psychology in autobiography* (Vol. 8). Stanford, CA: Stanford University Press.

Miller, G. A., & Frick, F. C. (1949). Statistical behavioristics and sequences of responses. *Psychological Review, 56*, 311–324.

Miller, G. A., Galanter, E., & Pribram, K. H. (1960). *Plans and the structure of behavior*. New York: Holt.

Miller, N. E. (1959). Liberalization of basic S-R concepts. In S. Koch (Ed.), *Psychology: Study of a science* (Vol. 2). New York: McGraw-Hill.

Minsky, M. (1963). Steps towards artificial intelligence. In E. A. Feigenbaum & J. Feldman (Eds.), *Computers and thought*. New York: McGraw-Hill. (Originally circulated in 1957)

Moore, T. V. (1938). *Cognitive psychology*. Philadelphia: Lippincott.

Morgan, C. L. (1896). *Habit and instinct*. London: Arnold.

Morgan, C. L. (1977). *Introduction to comparative psychology*. In D. N. Robinson (Ed.), *Significant contributions to the history of psychology*, 1750–1920. Series D: *Comparative psychology* (Vol. 2). Washington, DC: University Publications of America. (Original work published 1894)

Neisser, U. (1967). *Cognitive psychology*. New York: Appleton-Century-Crofts.

Neisser, U. (1976). *Cognition and reality*. San Francisco: Freeman.

Neisser, U. (1997). The future of cognitive science: An ecological analysis. In D. M. Johnson & C. E. Erneling (Eds.), *The future of the cognitive revolution*. New York: Oxford University Press.

Newell, A. (1973). You can't play twenty questions with nature and win. In W. G. Chase (Ed.), *Visual information processing*. New York: Academic Press.

Newell, A., Shaw, J. C., & Simon, H. A. (1958). Elements of a theory of problem solving. *Psychological Review, 84*, 231–259.

Newell, A., & Simon, H. (1972). Historical addendum. In A. Newell & H. Simon, *Human problem solving*. Englewood Cliffs, NJ: Prentice-Hall.

Nisbett, R. E., & Ross, L. (1980). *Human inference: Strategies and shortcomings in social judgment*. Englewood Cliffs, NJ: Prentice-Hall.

Nisbett, R. E., & Wilson, T. D, (1977). Telling more than we can know: Verbal reports on mental processes. *Psychological Review, 84*, 231–259.

Osgood, C. E. (1953). *Method and theory in experimental psychology*. New York: Oxford University Press.

Osgood, C. E. (1957). A behaviorist analysis of perception and language as cognitive phenomena. In H. E. Gruber (Ed.), *Contemporary approaches to cognition*. Cambridge, MA: Harvard University Press.

Palermo, D. S. (1971). Is a scientific revolution taking place in psychology? *Science Studies, 1*, 135–155.

Pavio, A. (1971). *Imagery and verbal processes*. New York: Holt, Rinehart & Winston.

Perner, J., Leekam, S. R., & Wimmer, H. (1987). Three-year-olds' difficulty with false belief: The case for a conceptual deficit. *British Journal of Developmental Psychology, 5*, 125–137.

Piaget, J. (1926). *The language and thought of the child*. London: Kegan Paul, Trench & Trubner.

Piaget, J. (1927). *Judgment and reasoning in the child*. London: Kegan Paul, Trench & Trubner.

Piaget, J. (1930). *The child's conception of physical causality*. London: Kegan Paul, Trench & Trubner.

Port, R., & Gelder, T. (Eds.). (1995). *Mind as motion: Explorations in the dynamics of cognition*. Cambridge: MIT Press.

Premack, D., & Premack, A. J. (1983). *The mind of an ape*. New York: Norton.

Quine, W. V. O. (1960). *Word and object*. Cambridge, MA: MIT Press.

Rapaport, D. (1951). *Organization and pathology of thought*. New York: Columbia University Press.

Reed, H. (1940). Factors influencing the learning and retention of concepts: I. The influence of set. *Journal of Experimental Psychology, 36*, 71–87.

Roitblat, H. L. (1987). *Introduction to comparative cognition*. New York: Freeman.

Rosch, E., & Lloyd, B. B. (Eds.). (1978). *Cognition and categorization*. Hillsdale, NJ: Erlbaum.

Rosenblueth, A., Wiener, N., & Bigelow, J. (1943). Behavior, purpose and teleology. *Philosophy of Science, 10*, 18–24.

Rumelhart, D. E., & McClelland, J. L. (1986). On learning the past tense of English verbs. In D. E. Rumelhart, J. L. McClelland, & the PDP Research Group. (Eds.), *Explorations in the microstructure of cognition: Vol. 2. Psychological and biological models*. Cambridge, MA: MIT Press.

Rumelhart, D. E., McClelland, J. L, & the PDP Research Group. (Eds.). (1986). *Explorations in the microstructure of cognition: Vol. 1. Foundations. Vol. 2. Psychological and biological models*. Cambridge, MA: MIT Press.

Russell, B., & Whitehead, A. N. (1910). *Principia mathematica*. Cambridge: The University Press.

Schank, R. C., & Abelson, R. (1977). *Scripts, plans, goals and understanding*. Hillsdale, NJ: Erlbaum.

Searle, J. (1980). Minds, brains, and programs. *The Behavioral and Brain Sciences, 3*, 417–457.

Selz, O. (1922). *Zur Psychologie des produktiven Denkens und des Irrtums* [*About the psychology of productive thinking and error*]. Bonn: Cohen.

Serra, R., & Zanarini, G. (1990). *Complex systems and cognitive processes*. Berlin: Springer-Verlag.

Shannon, C. E. (1938). *A symbolic analysis of relay and switching circuits*. Master's thesis, MIT.

Shannon, C. E. (1948). A mathematical model of communication. *Bell System Technical Journal, 27*, 379–423, 623–656.

Shannon, C. E., & Weaver, W. (1949). *The mathematical theory of communication*. Urbana: University of Illinois Press.

Shepard, R. N. (1987). Toward a universal law of generalization for psychological science. *Science, 237*, 1317–1323.

Shepard, R. N. (1995). Mental universals: Towards a twenty-first century science of mind. In R. L. Solso & D. W. Massaro (Eds.), *The science of the mind: 2001 and beyond*. New York: Oxford University Press.

Simon, H. A. (1962). An information processing theory of intellectual development. In W. Kessen & C. Kuhlman (Eds.), *Thought in the young child. Monographs on Social Research and Child Development, 27*(2), Serial No. 83.

Skinner, B. F. (1985). Cognitive science and behaviorism. *British Journal of Psychology, 76*, 291–301.

Skinner, B. F. (1990). Can psychology be a science of the mind? *American Psychologist, 45*, 1206–1210.

Spence, J. T. (1987). Centrifugal versus centripetal tendencies in psychology: Will the center hold? *American Psychologist, 42*, 1052–1054.

Staats, A. W. (1983). *Psychology's crisis of disunity: Philosophy and method for a unified science*. New York: Praeger.

Stevens, S. S. (Ed.). (1951). *Handbook of experimental psychology*. New York: Wiley.

Tolman, E. C. (1932). *Purposive behavior in animals and men*. New York: Century.

Turing, A. (1936). On computable numbers, with an application to the Entscheidungs-problem. *Proceedings of the London Mathematical Society, 42*, 230–265.

Turing, A. (1950). Computing machinery and intelligence. *Mind, 51*, 433–460.

Turing, A. (1992). Proposed electronic calculator. *National Physical Laboratory Report*. In J. L. Britton, D. C. Ince, & P. T. Saunders (Eds.), *Collected works of Alan Turing*. New York: Elsevier. (Original work published 1946)

Vinacke, W. E. (1952). *The psychology of thinking*. New York: McGraw-Hill.

von Neumann, J. (1951). The general and logical theory of automata. In L. A. Jeffress (Ed.), *Cerebral mechanisms in behavior: The Hixon Symposium*. New York: Wiley.

Vygotsky, L. S. (1986). *Thought and language* (A. Kozulin, Trans.). Cambridge, MA: MIT Press. (Original work published 1934)

Walter, W. G. (1953). *The living brain*. London: Chapman & Hall.

Weimer, W. B., & Palermo, D. S. (1973). Paradigms and normal science in psychology. *Science Studies, 3*, 211–244.

Wellman, H. M., & Esters, D. (1986). Early understanding of mental entities: A reexamination of childhood realism. *Child Development, 57*, 910–923.

Wiener, N. (1948). *Cybernetics, or control and communication in the animal and the machine*. New York: Wiley.

Woodworth, R. S. (1938). *Experimental psychology*. New York: Holt.

Woodworth, R. S., & Schlosberg, R. (1954). *Experimental psychology* (2nd ed.). New York: Holt.

Wundt, W. (1912). *An introduction to psychology*. London: Allen & Unwin.

CHAPTER 13

Abnormal and Clinical Psychology

H ISTORIES OF ABNORMAL AND CLINICAL PSYCHOLOGY TEND TO BE decidedly presentist and generally represent the history of psychological theory and therapy as a progression from superstitious theories of spirit possession and brutal persecution to contemporary scientific theories and humane treatments (Sedgewick, 1982). Often this is based upon little more than condescending assumptions about earlier peoples. For example, when Neolithic skulls were discovered with holes in them, the French neurophysiologist Paul Broca opined that they must have been made "in order to liberate evil spirits" (Ackerknecht, 1982, pp. 8–9), a representation still repeated in contemporary histories of psychology. Yet it is just as likely that such holes were the product of early forms of trepanning, the removal of part of the skull to reduce swelling of the brain caused by injury through war or hunting.

As noted earlier, the ancient and medieval peoples were rather more sophisticated and humane, at least relative to their times, than they are usually given credit for. They recognized depression, mania, and hysteria and attributed most psychological disorders to neural causes. Their psychological treatments, which were usually based upon holistic principles derived from the Hippocratic school and Galen, included fresh air, relaxation, dieting, and music, as well as bloodletting and purgation.

From early Roman times, laws governed the treatment of the psychologically disturbed and provided for family or community guardianship of persons designated as "insane" or "mad" (Neaman, 1975). These laws recognized that such persons were not legally responsible for their actions, because of their diminished or defective powers of reasoning (Maher & Maher, 1985a; Neugebauer, 1978). Institutions devoted to the treatment of the psychologically disturbed were set up in medieval cities such as Baghdad, Valencia, and London, and the common law of many medieval European states included protections for them (Schoeneman, 1977).

Those deemed insane were generally cared for by their families or legally appointed guardians. They were occasionally beaten—the common law of England allowed people to beat their mad relatives (Allderidge, 1979)—and those deemed dangerous were restrained or imprisoned. Although no doubt many were persecuted and exploited, their treatment was not especially cruel relative to the conditions of the time. Michael McDonald's (1981) analysis of the notebooks of Richard Napier (1559–1634), a 17th-century English physician, indicates that less than 1 percent of those who consulted him for psychological problems complained of beatings or other forms of abuse.

Eventually the insane became the legal responsibility of local parishes and urban centers, which were also responsible for the poor and the unemployed. They were housed in asylums, originally created to isolate lepers and later employed to house a wide variety of "degenerates" and "destitutes." This was as much a social as a medical measure, designed to combat the growing problems of begging and vagrancy, as well as occasional acts of violence. For example, the departments of the Hôpital Général of Paris, La Bicêtre for men and Salpêtrière for women, were created to confine beggars, tramps, and prostitutes along with the insane and the immature, by order of a royal edict of 1656 (Rosen, 1968).

While many institutions were originally intended as humane retreats, they evolved into places of incarceration. St. Mary's of Bethlehem in London, founded in 1247, degenerated into the human zoo that came to be known as "Old Bedlam" (after a corruption of the Cockney pronunciation), where inmates were chained

Ramble Gripe restrained by orderlies in Bedlam (Hogarth).

and whipped, regularly "treated" with purgatives, emetics, and bloodletting, and subjected to the indignity of public display before paying visitors. Yet although conditions in places like Bedlam were undoubtedly grim, they were probably not much worse than the working and living conditions of most ordinary people at the time. Although occasionally used as a form of treatment, restraints were generally employed only with violent patients. Those with manageable disorders were allowed out to beg as long as they wore identifying badges, and they became known as "Tom o' Bedlams." The original intent of charging visitors to view the inmates was to raise money to support their treatment.

NEUROSES, ALIENISTS, AND PSYCHIATRY

Robert Burton (1577–1640) was one of the first physicians to develop a systematic classification of psychological disorders and their causes and treatment in *Anatomy of Melancholy* (1621). Although his compilation was based upon Galen's theory of humors and animal spirits, he distinguished mania from melancholy and documented a wide variety of causes of melancholy, such as poor child rearing and education, excessive love, religious fervor, bereavement, poverty, isolation, and old age (Millon, 2004). A chronic depressive himself, Burton believed that it was difficult but not impossible to relieve melancholy through treatment.

William Cullen (1710–1790), professor of medicine at the University of Edinburgh, who produced a comprehensive classification of physical and psychological disorders in *First Lines of the Practice of Physick* (1777), characterized as **neuroses** those physical and psychological disorders caused by damage to or disease of the nervous system. His colleague Robert Whytt described the form of nervous exhaustion later characterized as **neurasthenia** by the American neurologist George Beard (1839–1883). The Swiss physician Felix Plater (1536–1614) used the term **mental alienation** to describe the troubled condition of those suffering from psychological disorders, and up until the early 20th century physicians engaged in their diagnosis were characterized as **alienists** (the term is sometimes still used to characterize forensic psychiatrists). Johann Christian Reil (1759–1813), professor of medicine at the University of Halle, introduced the term **psychiatry** to describe the study and treatment of psychological disorders. Johann Christian Heinroth (1773–1843) was appointed to the first chair in psychiatry at the University of Leipzig in 1811 and revived the ancient term **paranoia** to describe a variety of disorders based upon intellectual and emotional disturbance.

In *Observations on Madness and Melancholy* (1809), the English physician John Haslam (1764–1844) provided detailed descriptions of the phases of manic depression (bipolar disorder) and the symptoms of the degenerative disorder that the Belgian psychiatrist Bénédict-Augustin Morel (1809–1873) later classified as **dementia praecox**, because of its early onset and rapid progression (the disorder had also been recognized by the Roman physician Aretaeus in the first century and by Thomas Willis in the 17th). Morel came to believe that degeneration is characteristic of all psychological disorders and followed the French physician Jacques-Joseph Moreau (1804–1884) in claiming that mental degeneration is determined by heredity and impervious to treatment.

Social Darwinists readily embraced this view and endorsed Morel's claim that degeneracy constituted the "greatest obstacle" to social progress (Morel, 1857). The German psychiatrist Richard von Krafft-Ebing (1840–1902), a follower of Morel's, claimed that hereditary degeneracy was the cause of criminality, sexual perversion, and social unrest among the lower classes (Krafft-Ebing, 1879). Similar views were advanced by Cesare Lombroso (1835–1909), the Italian professor of psychiatry and criminal anthropology, who suggested that degeneracy could be identified via abnormalities in the shape of the head, eyes, ears, and jaw (Lombroso, 1876), and by Felix Voisin (1794–1872), a disciple of the phrenologists Gall and Spurzheim.

Not all theorists held that psychological disorders were a product of inherited degeneracy or that they were especially characteristic of the lower classes. Daniel Noble identified chemical causes of psychological disorder, based upon his own empirical explorations of the effects of alcohol, cannabis, and opium, whose use was by no means limited to the lower classes (Noble, 1853). William Moseley recognized a variety of social causes (Moseley, 1838) and attributed the high rates of psychological disorder in middle- and upper-class women in Victorian society to the lack of exercise of their mental faculties (Maher & Maher, 1985b).

The British physician James Cowles Prichard (1786–1848) was one of the first to adopt an explicitly moral attitude to psychological disorder. He treated "moral insanity" as a defect of character, the result of allowing oneself to be swayed by "affections" rather than by "natural feelings" of rightness and responsibility. Consequently many early-19th-century treatments of psychological disorder were conceived of as forms of **moral management**, directed to the transformation of character through personal counseling and religious training.

THE REFORM OF ASYLUMS

Among those who conceived of the treatment of psychological disorder as a form of moral management was William Battie (1704–1776), the founder of St. Luke's Hospital in London. He distinguished between "original" (inherited) and "consequential" forms of madness in his *Treatise on Madness* (1758). Battie claimed that the latter could be treated by isolation from the influence of family and friends, which he held to be the social cause of madness. Many attributed psychological disorders to the unhealthy conditions of cities, for which reason melancholy was often treated as the English malady (Cheyne, 1734). Consequently many asylums were located in the country and conceived of as retreats from the traumatic conditions of city life.

William Tuke (1732–1822), a retired English tea and coffee merchant, set up a retreat in York as a refuge for psychologically disturbed Quakers in 1796, based upon principles of moral management. He treated inmates at the York retreat with respect and dignity, in a rural setting designed to resemble a farmstead. Tuke developed a treatment regime of exercise and wholesome diet, supplemented by pastoral counseling and occupational therapy. He eliminated barred cells and physical restraints (except in violent cases) and prohibited bloodletting and beating. His son and his grandson Daniel Hack Tuke (1827–1895) continued the York retreat. Daniel traveled to the United States and promoted the humane treatment of the insane through meetings with the superintendents of American asylums, which he considered to be superior to most British and European institutions (Millon, 2004). The York retreat stimulated the creation of similar retreats in Europe and the United States, such as the Friends Asylum for the Use of Persons Deprived of the Use of Their Reason, founded in Philadelphia in 1813.

Juan Luis Vives and Johann Weyer had advocated the humane treatment of the insane in the 16th century (Reisman, 1991), but their noble ideals had been neglected as asylums had degenerated into places of incarceration for the destitute and degenerate as well as those suffering from genuine psychological disorders. By the end of the 18th century, public concern about the conditions in such institutions inspired various reform movements, which resulted in government commissions and regulations governing the treatment of the insane. A British Act of 1774 mandated medical supervision and restricted occupancy to those certified as insane, to exclude the dumping of troublesome relatives. In France the Code Napoléon was modified in 1838 to include regulations governing the certification of the insane and the establishment and inspection of public asylums. Such reforms were more a product of Enlightenment ideals than scientific developments in theory and treatment, although the pioneers of reform did introduce empirical methods of classification and evaluation and emphasized the need for accurate statistical records of the efficacy of treatments (Earle, 1838/1887; Pinel, 1801/1806).

Vincenzo Chiarugi (1759–1820), superintendent of the Ospedale di Bonifazio in Florence, initiated a number of humanitarian reforms, including the limitation of physical restraints on patients. He eliminated shackles and chains and permitted restraint by straitjacket only for the violent and delirious. In *On Insanity and Its Classification,* he avowed that physicians are obliged to "respect the insane individual as a person" (1793/1987, p. 24). The French physician Joseph Daquin (1732–1815) recommended a similar humanitarian approach to the treatment of the mentally ill at the French hospital in Chambery, including the removal of shackles and other forms of physical restraint (Millon, 2004), Like Chiarugi, he recommended that the insane should be treated in isolation from the broader community and those incarcerated for different reasons, such as the poor and the degenerate (Daquin, 1791).

These early contributions were eclipsed by the work of Philippe Pinel (1745–1826), who was appointed head of the Bicêtre Hospital in Paris during the French Revolution. From 1793 to 1795 Pinel initiated a variety of reforms, which included the removal of chains from inmates and the elimination of practices such as blood-letting, beating, and confinement. Although Pinel usually receives the credit, it was Jean-Baptiste Pussin who initiated the practice of removing restraints. Pussin was a former inmate of the Bicêtre who was put in charge of incurable cases (Weiner, 1979).

Pinel continued these reforms when he was appointed director of the Salpêtrière hospital in 1795. This was the Paris asylum for insane women, with around 8,000 inmates. Pinel and Pussin oversaw the removal of chains from inmates and insti-tuted the same humane treatment regimes (which included forms of occupational therapy) that had produced impressive improvement rates at the Bicêtre. Pinel developed a classification of psychological disorders based upon case studies of inmates and their treatment progress (1798, 1801). He instituted a system that assigned inmates to separate wards according to their diagnostic types, which was duplicated by many of his disciples, but criticized by the Belgian alienist Joseph Guislain (1797–1860), who complained that grouping the depressive, the apa-thetic, and the violent together only exacerbated their condition (Millon, 2004).

Jean-Étienne-Dominique Esquirol (1772–1840), Pinel's disciple and succes-sor at the Salpêtrière, tried to promote his humane treatment regime throughout Europe, but with limited success. John Connolly (1784–1860) and Joseph Guislain (1797–1860) initiated similar reforms in England and Belgium, but progress remained slow, given the sustained opposition by most physicians. In the United States, pioneers such as Benjamin Rush (1745–1813) and Eli Todd (1762–1832) championed the humane treatment of the mentally ill and the reform of asylums. Rush, who had trained with Cullen in Edinburgh, deplored the cruelty and cus-todial nature of the institutional treatment of the insane in *Medical Inquiries and Observations Upon the Diseases of the Mind* (1812). He became superintendent of the Pennsylvania Hospital, where he petitioned the governors for better facilities for the treatment of inmates. Yet Rush, who is often treated as the father of American psychiatry, retained many doubtful practices. He remained an enthusiastic sup-porter of bloodletting and promoted the use of restraining and "spinning" chairs, later known as "Rush" chairs, which were supposed to calm patients through induced dizziness.

Eli Todd founded the Connecticut (or Hartford) Retreat for the Insane in 1824 with money raised by public subscription. He introduced a program of moral management based upon the pastoral counseling provided at the York Retreat, which became a model for the type of care provided at a number of institutions founded in the early 19th century. Samuel Woodward (1787–1850), a disciple of Todd's, promoted the moral management of the insane while superintendent of Worcester State Hospital in Massachusetts, as did Pliny Earle (1809–1892), the superintendent of Bloomington Hospital in New York. Earle championed the use of detailed statistical records of psychological treatment to counter what he believed to be overinflated treatment success rates claimed by his colleagues (Earle, 1848) and published an account of the principles of moral management (Earle, 1838/1887). He characterized it as a form of treatment designed to restore the "mental faculties" to their optimal level of functioning through rest, relaxation, and the cultivation of reason and self-control.

However, the sheer numbers of inmates in public asylums, which were inundated with the poor and the criminal, forced many superintendents to abandon moral management and resort to beatings, cold baths, and physical restraint. Appalled by the conditions that had developed in American asylums, Dorothea Dix (1802–1887) devoted her life to their reform. Dix originally worked as a teacher at a Boston prison for women and was moved to press for reform when she discovered that women suffering from psychological disorders were incarcerated along with common criminals. She traveled from state to state for about 40 years, and harnessed the press and public in her effort to persuade legislatures to reform or create new institutions for the insane (Reisman, 1991).

A number of Dix's disciples instituted her reforms while serving as superintendents

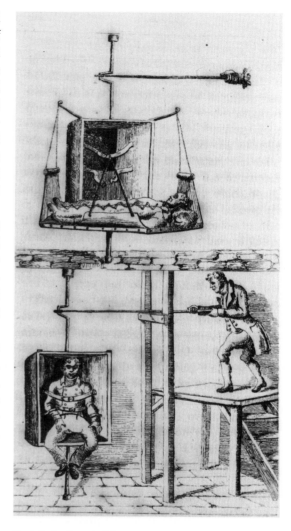

Rush "spinning chair."

at major state institutions: these included John S. Butler (1803–1878) at Boston Lunatic Hospital and Worcester State Hospital and John M. Galt (1819–1862) at the Williamsburg Asylum, the first public institution for the care of the insane, founded in 1773 (Zwelling, 1985). Dix gained her reputation as an American Florence Nightingale when she served as chief of hospital nurses during the American Civil War, and she exploited that reputation when she later toured Europe to promote her cause. She lectured Queen Victoria and Pope Pius IX on the need for reform of the institutional treatment of the insane, with some degree of success. Queen Victoria appointed a royal commission to investigate the treatment of the insane in Britain, and the pope established a new asylum in Rome (Reisman, 1991).

However, her achievements were modest and limited in her own country. American Social Darwinists questioned the wisdom of supporting constitutional mental degenerates, and Dix failed in her attempt to have Congress institute a land-grant bill to finance the establishment of psychiatric hospitals in the way that the Morrill Act supported the development of state universities. Many institutions continued with traditional forms of incarceration and physical restraint, along with "treatments" such as bloodletting, purging, spinning, electrical stimulation, and the ingestion of chemicals such as strychnine and mercury.

MAGNETISM, MESMERISM, AND HYPNOSIS

Although theories of physical and psychological health and disease based upon bodily humors fell out of favor in the 17th and 18th centuries, theories based upon the balance of physical forces remained popular. Luigi Galvani and Alessandro Volta claimed that electricity was the basis of life and mind, a view that gained increasing acceptance with the 19th-century investigation of the electrical nature of neural transmission. Such views formed the basis of Erasmus Darwin's theory of "fluid materialism" and Mary Shelley's *Frankenstein*.

Electrical treatments of physical and psychological disorders became popular, especially in the latter part of the 19th century. The employment of electrical stimulation as a medical treatment goes back to ancient times (the Roman essayist Pliny recorded how electric eels were used to relieve the pain of childbirth) but accelerated in the 19th century through technological advances in the measurement and application of electric current. Electropathic belts and direct electrical stimulation of the body and brain were touted as cures for ailments ranging from headaches to neurasthenia and were employed by physicians such as James and Freud. In the late 19th century John Birch reported improvement after he applied an electric current to the head of a depressed patient at St. Thomas's Hospital in London (Clare, 1976, cited in Maher & Maher, 1985b), a technique developed in the 20th century as electroconvulsive treatment (ECT).

However, at least as influential was the view that magnetic force forms the basis of life and mind. Gilbert had conceived of magnetism as a universal force, and Newton had suggested that gravitation is a form of magnetism. This led to the idea that magnetism is a cosmic force that governs every aspect of the universe, including the body and mind. Physical and psychological health came to be treated as a function of the proper alignment of magnetic forces in the body and brain, and disease and disorder as a product of misalignment. This naturally led to the view that cures of physical and psychological disorders could be affected by the application of magnetic force through the use of physical magnets, a view promoted in the 18th century by Franz Anton Mesmer (1734–1815).

Mesmer gained a medical degree from the University of Vienna in 1766 with a dissertation on planetary influences. He claimed to have identified the invisible "subtle and mobile fluid" that is the medium of magnetic force and that pervades every aspect of the universe. He supposed that the planets influence the distribution of magnetic fluids in the body and that "animal magnetism" is a product of "animal gravitation":

> Those spheres . . . exert a direct action on all the parts that go to make up animate bodies, in particular on the nervous system, by an all-penetrating fluid.

—(1779/1948, p. 3)

Mesmer claimed that physical and psychological disorders are caused by obstructions to the free flow of magnetic fluid in the body and brain and that relief can be attained only through the restoration of magnetic balance. He originally employed steel magnets and other physical media such as magnetized water in his "magnetic" treatments, but eventually claimed that some individuals (including himself) had such strong personal magnetic fields that they were able to manipulate the fields of others by merely moving their hands in the proximity of their bodies.

Mesmer was ridiculed as a charlatan in his native Vienna and condemned by physicians, scientists, and the clergy, who thought him in league with the devil. However, his theory and practice were more enthusiastically received in Paris, where he set up a salon in 1878 and shifted from individual to more lucrative group treatments. These involved elaborate apparatus and ceremonies. To the accompaniment of music, attendants used magnetic rods to connect patients to a bath containing "magnetized water" and instructed them to rub their bodies with the ends of the rods. After an hour or so of this magnetic experience, Mesmer would appear in an elaborate purple silk robe and wave his magnetized wand over them. He claimed great success for this form of treatment, which came to be known as **mesmerism**. It attracted the enthusiastic support of Marie Antoinette, the French queen, and the marquis de Lafayette, the American revolutionary hero.

Mesmer's success in relieving physical and psychological disorders was almost certainly a product of suggestion—he regularly advised patients of the anticipated outcome of their treatments. This was the conclusion of the royal commission that Louis XVI established in 1784 to evaluate the efficacy of mesmerism as a medical treatment. Benjamin Franklin (1706–1790) chaired the commission, whose members were drawn from the French Academy of Sciences. They included the distinguished French scientist Antoine Lavoisier (1743–1794) and Dr. Joseph Ignace Guillotin (1738–1814), who did not invent the instrument of execution that bears his name, but merely recommended it as a more humane form of execution. When the commission published its report in 1784,

Mesmerist represented as manipulating the magnetic field of a subject.

it concluded that Mesmer was a fraud and attributed the positive effects of magnetic treatments to the imagination of patients:

> Imagination apart from magnetism produces convulsions, and . . . magnetism without imagination produces nothing.
>
> —(Beloff, 1975, p. 268)

The report effectively destroyed Mesmer's career, and he left Paris the following year. However, despite vigorous opposition from the medical and religious establishment, many mesmerists remained committed to the view that their form of treatment was grounded in the manipulation of invisible magnetic fluids. As late as the end of the 19th century, Albert Binet, the pioneer of intelligence testing in France, claimed to have demonstrated the transfer and polarization of sensations via the use of magnets (Binet & Féré, 1887). This almost destroyed Binet's own career, when other French researchers demonstrated that similar effects could be attained through mere suggestion.

Others continued to employ mesmeric treatments but abandoned the theory of magnetic fluids. Mesmer had managed to induce a state of trance in patients by merely commanding them to sleep, by staring intently at them and exclaiming "Dormez!" The French nobleman Armand M-J de Chastenet (1751–1825), the marquis de Puységur, rejected the theory of magnetic fluids, but became a successful practitioner of mesmeric techniques. He founded the Society of Harmony in 1785 to promote mesmerism, and his reputation spread throughout Europe, much to Mesmer's displeasure. Puységur discovered that he could induce temporary states of paralysis in patients during periods of "mesmeric" or "artificial" somnambulism: They could be commanded to speak, dance, and perform mechanical tasks, with no recollection of their actions upon awakening. He demonstrated the therapeutic effects of what he called "nervous sleep," including its anesthetic properties: He was able to raise a patient's threshold of pain while in a trance state.

John Elliotson (1791–1868), professor of medicine at University College, London, suggested that such artificially induced trance states could be employed as a surgical anesthetic. He performed a number of operations using the technique, including some amputations (Gravitz, 1988), as did James Esdaile (1808–1859), an East India Company surgeon stationed in Calcutta (Esdaile, 1846, 1852). Yet the medical establishment remained skeptical and critical. The Governing Council of University College admonished Elliotson in 1837 with a resolution banning the use of mesmeric techniques, and he promptly resigned his position. When Esdaile returned home to Scotland and tried to employ mesmeric techniques at Perth Royal Infirmary, the medical authorities proscribed his work (Beloff, 1975). Their early successes were soon forgotten with the development of chemical anesthetic agents such as ether and chloroform, which seemed more reliably effective than induced trance states, and the surgical use of mesmeric techniques was abandoned.

Elliotson later explored the use of mesmeric techniques as forms of treatment for psychological disorders and founded the journal *The Zoist: A Journal of Cerebral Physiology and Mesmerism and Their Application to Human Welfare* in 1843 (Beloff, 1975). He claimed that mesmeric techniques were the most effective treatment for hysterical disorders, such as forms of paralysis or blindness that have no physiological basis, later characterized as "conversion hysterias" (Matarazzo, 1985). The Scottish surgeon James Braid (1795–1860) explained these treatment effects in terms of suggestibility and the operation of unconscious psychological processes. Braid, who had attended a demonstration of mesmeric techniques by a traveling French mesmerist, was originally skeptical, but became convinced of their efficacy when he found that he could induce trance states in members of his own family and command them to perform tasks of which they were consequently amnesic. In *Neurhypnology, or The Rationale of Nervous Sleep, Considered in Relation With Animal Magnetism* (1843), he characterized the trance state as a form of artificial sleep and treated mesmeric techniques as forms of sugges-tion operating on the unconscious mind. Braid introduced the term **hypnosis**, from the Greek *hypnos,* meaning "sleep," to describe the state of "nervous sleep" induced by mesmeric treatments (by dropping the "neur" from " neurhypnol-ogy"). Like Puységur, Braid repudiated the theory of magnetic fluids and claimed that he had "entirely separated Hypnotism from Animal Magnetism" (Braid, 1843, p. 112). His exploration of hypnotic treatment effects lent a degree of respectability to their study, but it was many years before the medical establish-ment took them seriously.

Jean-Martin Charcot (1835–1893), director of the Salpêtrière hospital, made important contributions to the study of multiple sclerosis and "shaking palsy" (Parkinsonism), and he became famous for his weekly public lectures, which attracted physicians from all over Europe and America, including Freud and James. In later years he turned his attention to the investigation of hysteria. Through the use of hypnosis, he dramatically induced hysterical symptoms such as anesthesia, paralysis, and falling fits in his female patients (although there is some suspicion that many of these were staged [Maher & Maher, 2003]).

Charcot believed that hysteria is a form of mental pathology based upon congenital degeneracy of the nervous system and that those subject to such degen-eracy are susceptible to hypnotism. Since he claimed that hysteria and susceptibility to hypnosis are products of the same underlying neurological deficiency, he

Charcot's demonstration of female hysteria at the Salpêtrière.

maintained that susceptibility to hypnosis is a symptom of hysteria and that only hysterical patients can be hypnotized. Although he was one of the first to recognize cases of male hysteria, Charcot thought that hysteria is many times more common in women and believed that female hysteria is related to ovarian compression. (Hippocrates had earlier traced it to the uterus.)

Ambroise-Auguste Liébault (1823–1904), one of the physicians who repudiated Binet's claims about the efficacy of magnetic treatments, challenged Charcot's account of hysteria. Liébault practiced in a rural community near Nancy in France and began to use hypnosis as a therapeutic technique after he heard of Bain's work. He rejected Charcot's treatment of susceptibility to hypnosis as a symptom of hysteria and his theory that both are caused by degeneracy. In *Sleep and Analogous States* (1866), Liébault reported that a good many hysterical patients are resistant to hypnosis and that some perfectly normal, stable, and well-balanced persons are extremely susceptible. Hippolyte Bernheim (1840–1919), professor of medicine at the Nancy School of Medicine, repeated Liébault's challenge. Bernheim was impressed with Liébault's therapeutic achievements and came to employ hypnotic techniques in his own clinic.

Liébauld and Bernheim held that suggestion is the primary vehicle of hypnotism and its therapeutic effects. They claimed that suggestibility is a normal and universal psychological trait and that every person can be hypnotized—although some are more suggestible and easier to hypnotize than others. Bernheim developed this central thesis of what became known as the **Nancy School** in *Hypnosis and Suggestion in Psychotherapy* (1865), which eventually prevailed in medical circles and which Charcot endorsed in later years. Liébauld and Bernheim employed hypnosis extensively in their treatment of hysteria and other psychological disorders and found that later positive suggestions could eliminate the harmful effects of earlier negative or "pathological" suggestions.

This latter insight was developed by Pierre Janet (1859–1947), one of Charcot's students, who became director of the neurophysiological clinic at the Salpêtrière. Janet claimed that certain painful thoughts, feelings, and desires become dissociated from normal consciousness and form separate psychological systems, or dissociated aspects of personality. Although these are normally unconscious, they are manifested in hysterical symptoms such as conversion paralyses—forms of physical paralysis, blindness, or analgesia that do not have discernible physical or physiological bases. Janet speculated that hysterical symptoms are a product of unconscious memories, which have their origin in earlier traumatic incidents. He investigated the medical records of patients at the Salpêtrière and noted that in many cases some physical shock or psychological trauma preceded the onset of hysterical symptoms. He suggested that hysterics have split personalities, one of which operates unconsciously as a secondary personality that can "invade" the primary personality (Janet, 1889, 1893). Janet claimed that this secondary personality could be revealed through hypnosis, which he used to explore patient memories of past traumatic incidents. He discovered that the "psychological analysis" of such memories, during which patients expressed the emotion associated with the trauma, frequently brought relief of their hysterical symptoms—an insight famously developed by Freud (Ellenberger, 1970). In later years Janet claimed that Freud had plagiarized his ideas, and he became a vocal critic of Freud's theory of the sexual etiology of most hysterical symptoms.

FREUD AND PSYCHOANALYSIS

The individual who had the greatest impact on the developing fields of psychiatry and abnormal psychology in the early decades of the 20th century was Sigmund Freud (1856–1939). He was born in the town of Freiberg in Moravia, a province of the Austro-Hungarian Empire, on May 6, 1856, the third of 8 children. Shortly afterward, the family moved to Vienna, where Freud lived until 1938, when he was forced by the Nazis to flee to London. He excelled at school and had a special talent for languages. When the University of Vienna withdrew its policy of excluding Jewish students in the 1860s, Freud seized the opportunity. His reading of Darwin's *Origin of Species* reputedly stimulated his interest in science, and he joined the medical school in 1873.

During his training, Freud took elective courses in psychology with Franz Brentano and became a research assistant to Ernst W. von Brücke, one of the founding members of the Berlin Physical Society. As a student Freud embraced the reductive physicalism of Brücke, du Bois-Reymond, and Helmholtz, although he later abandoned it when he developed his psychodynamic theories. After he received his medical degree in 1881, he worked with the neuroanatomist Theodor Meynert (1833–1892) on the diagnosis of brain damage.

In 1884 Freud began to experiment with the use of cocaine and became an early and enthusiastic advocate of its analgesic and therapeutic properties. He supplied it to his relatives, friends, and fiancée; prescribed it to his patients; and published half a dozen papers lauding its beneficial effects. He was severely criticized by his medical colleagues when the dangers of cocaine addiction became increasingly clear. Freud's incautious celebration of cocaine as a therapeutic agent in the absence of proper empirical evaluation was one reason why many in the medical community were skeptical when he first developed his psychodynamic theories. He managed to avoid the cocaine addiction to which many of his friends and patients succumbed, but never surmounted his addiction to nicotine. He smoked around 20 cigars a day, even after he was diagnosed with cancer of the palate and jaw. He later endured a series of 33 operations during which his jaw was replaced by an artificial device that he called "the monster."

Freud originally planned to continue his work on brain damage, but his research interests changed when he visited Charcot's clinic in the winter of 1885.

He was greatly impressed by Charcot's public demonstrations of female hysteria and his ability to induce and relieve hysterical symptoms through hypnosis. He was also intrigued by Janet's suggestion that hysteria is the product of repressed memories of traumatic events isolated in an unconscious secondary personality. Freud translated Charcot's lectures and became interested in conversion hysteria, which he recognized could not be accommodated by the form of reductive neuro-physiological analysis that he had employed in his years of research with Brücke and Meynert (Bolles, 1993).

Studies on Hysteria

On returning to Vienna, Freud married Martha Bernays and settled down to private practice. He specialized in nervous diseases and employed fashionable electrical and water treatments, as well as explicitly directive and suggestive treatments. His friend Joseph Breuer (1842–1925), an associate of Meynert's whom Freud had met while a research student, referred many of his early patients. Although Freud usually claimed sole credit for the development of psychoanalytic theory and repudiated the suggestion that Janet had anticipated its basic principles, he credited Breuer with the discovery of the psychoanalytic method, through his treatment of a patient known as Anna O.

Anna O had developed a number of hysterical symptoms while nursing her dying father. These included visual impairment, paralysis of her arms and legs, speech disorientation, and refusal to drink water from a glass. During one of the periodic trances into which she frequently lapsed, Anna acted out her emotional response to an episode that had occurred some months earlier, during which she had been disgusted by the sight of a dirty dog drinking water from a glass. When she recovered from the trance, Breuer found that she was now able to drink. He was able to relate her hysterical symptoms to earlier emotional traumas, most of which related to her fear and guilt concerning the impending death of her father. He also found that he could relieve Anna's symptoms by having her discharge her negative emotions through reenactment of the original traumatic episode.

Breuer called this therapeutic method the "talking cure," after Anna's own description, and Freud began to employ a similar method with his own patients. He and Breuer co-authored a paper "On the Psychological Mechanism of Hysterical Phenomena: Preliminary Communication" in 1893, and published *Studies on Hysteria* in 1895. In this latter work they articulated the main theoretical components of psychoanalysis. They claimed that hysterical symptoms are expressions of repressed memories of earlier (often childhood) traumas, which can be relieved through the cathartic expression or **abreaction** of these emotionally charged memories, a process that Anna O called "chimney sweeping." They identified the clinical phenomenon of **transference**, in which feelings originally directed to parents are redirected to the therapist, and **countertransference**, in which the therapist develops an emotional attachment to the patient. The marital tensions generated by these emotional attachments caused Breuer to discontinue Anna's treatment and his general use of the "talking cure."

Still in the grip of Brücke's reductionist approach, Freud completed *Project for a Scientific Psychology* in 1895 (although the work was only published post-humously in 1950), in which he tried to provide a neurophysiological account of the basic psychological processes presupposed by psychoanalytic theory (for example, he treated the emotional charge of a pathological idea as a quantifiable degree of neuronal excitation). He continued to employ the "talking cure" in his treatment of hysterical patients and began to use hypnosis after his visit to Bernheim's Nancy clinic in 1889. Freud was impressed by Bernheim's ability to relieve hysterical symptoms through hypnosis and by his demonstration of post-hypnotic suggestion, which illustrated the power of unconscious ideas to influence behavior. However, Freud abandoned hypnosis when he found he could identify pathogenic ideas by simply having patients relax and describe whatever came into their mind, no matter how apparently trivial or potentially embarrassing it might be—a method he called **free association**. He came to believe that the essential component of psychoanalytic treatment is the cathartic expression of emotions associated with repressed memories, however they may be identified, through spontaneous trance states, hypnosis, free association, or, as he later maintained, through dreams, jokes, and slips of the tongue.

In *Studies on Hysteria* (1895/1953) and "The Etiology of Hysteria," a paper presented to the Psychiatric and Neurological Society in Vienna in 1896, Freud claimed that the repressed memories responsible for neurotic symptoms are invariably memories of childhood sexual abuse—a claim rejected by Breuer, who maintained in a separate conclusion to *Studies on Hysteria* that repressed memories are not necessarily sexual. However, Freud soon abandoned this **seduction theory**. He came to believe that hysterical symptoms are **wish fulfillments**, symbolic expressions of repressed memories and desires that have their source in childhood sexual fantasies. Freud later maintained that this fundamental change in theoretical orientation marked the real beginning of psychoanalysis.

Psychosexual Development

Freud began to employ dream analysis in conjunction with free association in his therapeutic practice, since he came to believe that dreams are also symbolic wish fulfillments. This was a product of his own self-analysis, begun in 1896 to alleviate his extreme depression over the death of his father. In *The Interpretation of Dreams* (1900), Freud claimed that psychoanalysis is able to uncover the repressed **latent content** of dreams, as opposed to their reported apparent or **manifest**

content. Since he believed that the repression of traumatic memories is weaker during dreaming than waking consciousness, Freud characterized dreams as "the royal road to the unconscious." *The Interpretation of Dreams* was followed by the *Psychopathology of Everyday Life* (1901), in which Freud argued that the apparent accidents and errors of everyday life are also symbolic wish fulfillments, now generally known as **Freudian slips**. Freud extended this analysis to jokes in *Jokes and Their Relation to the Unconscious* (Freud, 1905/1966).

One of the avowed discoveries of Freud's self-analysis was the **Oedipus complex**. In his treatment of a recurrent childhood dream, Freud identified his hostility toward his father and desire for his mother and explained his overreaction to his father's death as due to guilt about an earlier death wish relating to his father. He made the Oedipus complex the cornerstone of his theory of psychosexual development. According to Freud, sexual satisfaction is associated with different erogenous zones in the course of child development, during the so-called oral, anal, phallic, latency, and genital stages. He held that too much or too little stimulation at any of these stages leads to fixation of the relevant needs, leading to the development of personality types associated with these stages, such as the celebrated oral and anal personalities.

According to Freud, the most important developmental stage for understanding both normal and abnormal adult behavior is the phallic stage, during which the Oedipal conflict is generated. Between the ages of 3 and 6, male children develop strong sexual desire for their mother and come to treat their father as a rival. The active erogenous zone during this period is the genital area, and the male child experiences castration anxiety, based upon fear of the more powerful father. The Oedipal conflict is resolved through the child's identification with the father, which gains him symbolic access to his mother and removes the fear of castration, although only temporarily, since repressed desires continue to influence adult dreams and behavior. Freud maintained that female children experience a similar but qualitatively distinct form of conflict around the same time, which he originally called the "Electra complex," although he later abandoned the term. They also develop a castration complex, which is resolved in an analogous fashion through identification with the mother.

This process of identification with the parent of the opposite sex was the supposed vehicle for the development of what Freud called the **super-ego**, through the internalization of the moral principles of the parent of the opposite sex. In his theory of personality, Freud distinguished between the id, the ego, and the super-ego. The **id** represents the instinctual engine of human psychology, comprising basic drives and desires, such as hunger, thirst, and sexual desire, which underlie all behavior. The id operates on the **pleasure principle** and strives to attain the gratification of basic drives and desires, which is by nature pleasurable. One of the primitive instinctual mechanisms is symbolic wish fulfillment, in which an image representing an object satisfying a desire is generated. However, basic drives and desires are more effectively and efficiently satiated by the real-world objects that naturally satisfy them. The **ego**, which operates on the **reality principle**, identifies and pursues the real-world objects of instinctual drive and desire. However, the activity of the ego is constrained by the super-ego, which restricts the objects pursued to those that are socially approved (by the relevant parent).

These conflicts generate various forms of anxiety, notably neurotic and moral anxiety—feelings of being overwhelmed by instinctual drives and the shame and guilt associated with disapproved means of satisfying them. To explain how we avoid these forms of anxiety, Freud postulated a set of defense mechanisms employed by the ego, such as repression, identification, projection, and sublimation. Freud maintained that these defense mechanisms are unconscious, but play a major role in the explanation of normal as well as abnormal behavior (such as neurotic behavior). This was one of the distinctive features of his theory. For Freud, all aspects of human life, from the most bizarre dreams to the mundane choices of everyday life, are invested with symbolic meanings that express forms of wish fulfillment relating to early childhood sexual experiences and memories.

The basic elements of Freud's account of unconscious psychological states and processes had been anticipated by a number of earlier theorists. Leibniz and Fechner had acknowledged unconscious states; Mill and Helmholtz had recognized unconscious processes; and Herbart and Drobisch had maintained that some ideas are repressed. Nineteenth-century interest in the unconscious was evidenced by the popularity of Karl von Hartmann's (1842–1906) *Philosophy of the Unconscious* (1869), which ran into many editions. Schopenhauer and Nietzsche had claimed that much of human behavior is governed by irrational instinctual drives and desires, including sexual ones, and Janet had identified the role of pathogenic ideas in hysteria. Freud's genius lay in his integration of these various elements into a comprehensive theory of psychosexual development, personality, and motivation.

The Reception of Freud's Theory

Studies on Hysteria was well received, but the medical establishment dismissed Freud's theory of infant sexuality. However, this was not because it dealt with sexual matters (Sulloway, 1979), which were a lively topic of interest in the late 19th century, as evidenced by the popularity of works such as von Krafft-Ebing's *Psychopathia Sexualis* (1886), a compendium of case histories of sexual perversions, Albert Moll's *Perversions of the Sex Instinct* (1891), and Havelock Ellis's seven-volume *Studies in the Psychology of Sex* (1897–1928). The skepticism with which the medical community received Freud's theories was based partly upon his early advocacy of cocaine as a therapeutic agent, but also upon legitimate concerns about the empirical adequacy of his theory—concerns reprised by many later critics of psychoanalysis.

In the early decades of the 20th century, a select group of physicians in Europe and America adopted Freud's theory. In 1902 Freud established a Wednesday Evening Group devoted to the discussion of psychoanalytic theory and case histories, which was reconstituted as the Vienna Psychoanalytic Society in 1908: Members included Alfred Adler (1870–1937), Abraham A. Brill (1874–1948), Sándor Ferenczi (1873–1933), and Carl Jung 1875–1961). There was sufficient interest in the psychoanalytic movement to support the First International Psychoanalytical Congress in 1908. Brill set up a psychoanalytic practice in New York in 1908 and produced the first English translations of Freud's work in 1909. Loyal disciples such as Ernest Jones (1879–1958) and Freud's daughter Anna Freud (1895–1982) helped create centers of classical psychoanalysis in Toronto, New York, and London.

However, the emerging psychoanalytic movement began to fragment as a result of the defection of Freud's former disciples, who promoted their own psychodynamic theories and therapeutic methods. Adler split in 1911 and developed a form of individual psychology based upon feelings of inferiority. Jung split in 1912 and developed a theory of the collective unconscious as the repository of symbolic meaning, which included but was not restricted to sexual meaning. Ferenczi rejected Freud's account of sexual wish fulfillment and championed the original seduction theory. Karen Horney (1885–1952), Melanie Klein (1882–1960), Erich Fromm (1900–1980), and Henry Stack Sullivan (1892–1949) developed theories that looked to the broader social and cultural contexts of human psychology and behavior as the source of psychodynamic conflict. Erik Erikson (1902–1994) developed a theory of psychosocial development that postulated crises of adjustment from infancy to old age. This fragmentation accelerated from the 1920s onward, when Freud began to drastically revise his own theories, to the point that one commentator could reasonably identify 36 distinct schools of psychoanalysis derived from the original Freudian orthodoxy (Harper, 1959).

In 1924 William Alanson White (1870–1937), then president of the American Psychiatric Association, urged psychiatrists to embrace psychoanalytic theory and practice, and psychoanalysis became the dominant theoretical orientation of most medically trained American psychiatrists in the first half of the 20th century (Routh & Reisman, 2003). However, American psychologists did not so readily embrace psychoanalysis, and their general response to Freud was respectful but critical (Green & Rieber, 1980; Hornstein, 1992). Hall, Münsterberg, and Witmer rejected psychoanalytic theory, although Hall admired Freud enough to invite him to speak at the 20th anniversary celebrations at Clark University in 1909.

Freud's American visit was a significant intellectual event. Accompanied by Brill, Jung, Ferenczi, and Jones, he delivered a series of lectures on psychoanalysis at Clark. These were well received and attended by American luminaries such as Cattell, Goddard, James, Jastrow, Meyer, and Titchener. Freud's theory quickly became the focus of professional and public attention, displacing mesmerism, hypnotism, and other popular fads of the day (Green & Rieber, 1980). Dozens of articles were published in popular magazines and professional journals, leading the Harvard psychiatrist Morton Prince to complain that "Freudian psychology had flooded the field like a full rising tide and the rest of us were left submerged like clams in the sands at low water" (Hale, 1971, p. 434). However, most of the professional psychological response, such as the reviews by Woodworth (1917) and Jastrow (1932), remained critical. McDougall (1926) claimed that Freud's theory was brilliant but wrong, a common judgment among American psychologists. Meyer dismissed Freud's theory as dogmatic, and Prince developed Harvard psychiatry in effective opposition to psychoanalysis.

Freud's lectures at Clark won psychoanalysis a temporary place as a school of American psychology (Murchison, 1930). However, it was almost completely displaced within academic psychology during the behaviorist and neobehaviorist periods. Even the apparent exception, the attempt by neobehaviorists such as John Dollard (1900–1980) and Neal Miller (1909–2002) to integrate psychoanalysis and behaviorist learning theory (Dollard & Miller, 1950; Miller & Dollard, 1941), was little more than a reduction of Freudian concepts to those of conditioning theory (for example, transference was reduced to stimulus generalization). The discipline of clinical psychology that Lightner Witmer founded in 1907 developed independently of and often in opposition to the psychoanalytic movement, as clinical psychologists came to embrace theories and therapies grounded in behaviorist learning theory and cognitive psychology.

At the same time, Freud's theories came to have a significant impact beyond clinical medicine and psychology, when he extended them to society and religion in *Totem and Taboo* (1912–1913) and *The Future of an Illusion* (1927). They also came to have a significant impact on social sciences such as anthropology and sociology, postmodern and feminist critiques, and popular culture at large. This was especially true of American culture, where Freudian terminology quickly entered the vernacular. This latter development was not something that Freud would have welcomed. He was always ambivalent about America and feared that the commercially exploitive aspects of its culture would contaminate his theories. In 1935 he rejected a lucrative offer of $100,000 from MGM to make a movie featuring psychoanalysis (Green & Rieber, 1980).

The Scientific Status of Freud's Theory

Freud always represented psychoanalysis as a scientific theory. However, the scientific credentials of his theory have been frequently questioned, as has Freud's integrity as a scientist. Doubts about his theory were raised almost from the moment of inception—his first paper on hysteria received a frosty reception from fellow scientists, including sexual researchers such as von Krafft-Ebing—but more forcefully as the 20th century progressed. Scientific methodologists criticized Freud for interpreting data to suit his theory, for his tendency to dismiss or ignore alternative theories, and for his general reluctance to submit psychoanalytic theory to critical experimental tests (Cioffi, 1970; Popper, 1963).

There are certainly grounds for such complaints. Freud made the rather ridiculous claim that only psychoanalytically trained physicians could evaluate psychoanalytic theory, given the inevitable bias of untrained critics:

> None but physicians who practice psychoanalysis can have any access whatsoever to this sphere of knowledge or any possibility of forming a judgment that is uninfluenced by their own dislikes and prejudices.
>
> —(Freud, 1905/1953, Preface, p. 43)

He added insult to injury by suggesting that failure to accept psychoanalytic theory is a symptom of repression!

Freud did not appear to care much about the empirical evaluation of his theories. In 1934 Saul Rosenzweig (1907–2004) sent him reprints of his experimental studies of repression (Rosenzweig, 1933; Rosenzweig & Mason, 1934), but Freud's reply was dismissive and condescending:

> I have examined your experimental studies for the verification of psychoanalytic propositions with interest. I cannot put much value on such confirmation because the abundance of reliable observations on which these propositions rest makes them independent of experimental verification. Still, it can do no harm.
>
> —(Letter from Freud to Rosenzweig, cited in Rosenzweig, 1986, pp. 37–38)

Freud rarely took seriously alternative explanations of the clinical cases that provided the "reliable observations" on which psychoanalytic theory was supposed to be based. He explained Little Hans's fear of horses in terms of the projection of his fear of castration by his father (1909/1966, 10, 5–147), but dismissed the child's own account in terms of the fright he got the first time he saw a horse, when it fell down and caused a great commotion—a standard behaviorist explanation in terms of a classically conditioned fear (Wolpe & Rachman, 1960). He dismissed evidence of child abuse after he abandoned the seduction theory and developed the theory of the Oedipal and Electra conflicts. When Jeffrey Masson made this charge in the 1980s, he was promptly fired from his position at the Freud Archives (Masson, 1984).

Some scholars have tried to defend Freud against such charges (Glymour, 1980), and others have claimed that Freudian theory does license testable empirical predictions, some of which have been confirmed (Fisher & Greenberg, 1977;

Kline, 1972). Adolf Grünbaum (1983, 1984) has argued that Freud behaved like a "sophisticated scientific methodologist" in advancing arguments for psychoanalytic theory. Freud maintained that only psychoanalysis could attain a lasting and durable cure for neuroses, since only psychoanalysis could achieve the correct insight necessary for it:

> After all, (a patient's) conflicts will only be successfully solved and his resistances overcome if the anticipatory ideas given (by his analyst) tally with what is real in him.
>
> —(Freud, 1917/1963, 16, p. 452)

This claim, in conjunction with Freud's claim that psychoanalysis is an effective treatment of neuroses, constitutes what Grünbaum calls the **tally argument** for psychoanalytic theory.

Unfortunately for Freud's reputation and legacy, later research did not support these claims. Anna O's treatment is usually represented as an unqualified success, with all her symptoms eliminated. Yet in later years Anna, whose real name was Bertha Pappenheim (1859–1936), disputed this representation, claiming that she had to be admitted to a sanitarium for treatment in 1882, shortly after she completed her "talking cure" with Freud and Breuer. Pappenheim was a social worker and pioneer of women's rights, who founded schools and homes for disadvantaged young girls. She was critically dismissive of psychoanalysis as a theory and therapy and refused to allow any of those in her care to be exposed to it (Ellenberger, 1972).

In a famous study, Hans Eysenck (1916–1997) claimed that the recovery rate for neurotics who receive psychoanalytic therapy is not significantly superior (statistically) to the "spontaneous remission" rates of neurotics who do not (Eysenck, 1952). In response, the American Psychoanalytic Association commissioned its own study of the efficacy of psychoanalysis, but the results were so bad that the association suppressed its publication (Storr, 1966). Later studies indicated that other forms of psychological therapy, such as behavior therapy, achieve recovery rates comparable if not superior to those of psychoanalysis (Eysenck, 1965; Rachman & Wilson, 1971) and that correct insight is not necessary for effective psychotherapy (Wallerstein, 1995). Such findings did considerable damage to the reputation of psychoanalysis among psychologists. The tally argument was Freud's response to the charge that the efficacy of psychoanalysis is best explained in terms of suggestion, commonly held to be the basis of earlier mesmeric and hypnotic treatments. Unfortunately, the charge remains unanswered to the present day (Greenwood, 1996, 1997).

Freud's theory of unconscious psychological states and processes was a critical target for behaviorists from Watson to Skinner, although there was nothing inherently unscientific about it. Karl Pribram and Merton Gill have argued that the basic theoretical systems postulated by Freud in his *Project for a Scientific Psychology* have been confirmed by contemporary cognitive psychology and neurophysiology (Primbram & Gill, 1976).

Freud died in London in 1939, after escaping from the Nazis in 1938 with his daughter Anna; his four sisters perished in the concentration camps. He left a major intellectual and cultural legacy and a legion of psychodynamic schools within medical psychiatry. However, by this time mainstream American psychologists, including clinical psychologists, had largely abandoned his theories.

SCIENTIFIC PSYCHOLOGY AND ABNORMAL PSYCHOLOGY

The development of psychology in Germany in the late 19th century promoted a scientific approach to the assessment and treatment of psychological disorders, despite the fact that Wundt expressed little interest in this area (although he published a paper on hypnosis and suggestion in 1888). Early German abnormal psychology was dominated by Wilhelm Griesinger (1817–1868), the founder of academic psychiatry in Germany, and author of *Mental Pathology and Therapeutics* (1845). Griesinger claimed that since mental disorders are brain diseases, they are the proper subject matter of general medicine. He championed this position in the first issue of *The Archives for Psychiatry and Nervous Diseases,* which he founded in 1868:

> Patients with so-called mental diseases are really individuals with diseases of the nerves and the brain. . . . Psychiatry . . . must become an integral part of general medicine and accessible to all medical circles.
>
> —(1868, p. 12)

Griesinger's reductive neurophysiological conception of psychopathology matched the reductive physicalism of the Berlin Physical Society and was championed by Henry Maudsley (1835–1918) in Britain and by Valentine Magnan (1835–1916) in France.

The German psychiatrist Karl Ludwig Kahlbaum (1828–1899) developed a classificatory system based upon the course and outcome of psychological disorders, rather than their neuropathology. Emil Kraepelin (1856–1926), a student and lifelong friend of Wundt's, who founded laboratories of experimental psychopathology at Heidelberg and Munich, developed a classificatory system that combined the developmental and neurological approaches of Kahlbaum and Griesinger and was avowedly based upon the principles of the new physiological psychology (Kraepelin, 1883). He stressed the importance of identifying the core symptoms of psychological disorders, but held that the only way to discriminate between disorders with similar symptoms was through the developmental analysis of their course and outcome.

Kraepelin's classificatory system, originally published in *Compendium of Psychiatry* (1883) and revised in multivolume editions of his *Textbook of Psychiatry* (1915), included familiar categories such as manic-depressive psychosis and paranoia. It also included novel categories such as dementia praecox, later characterized as **schizophrenia** by the Swiss psychiatrist Eugene Bleuler (1857–1939). Kraepelin (following Wundt) treated dementia praecox as a disorder of attention and maintained that it was a constitutional disease incapable of treatment, although he later admitted that around 10 percent of diagnosed cases make an almost full recovery (Reisman, 1991). In contrast, Bleuler conceived of schizophrenia as a disorder based upon the disassociation of thought and emotion and maintained that it could be treated (Bleuler, 1911/1950).

Kraepelin revised his classification system up until his death in 1926, and aspects of it were later incorporated in the *American Standard Nomenclature of Disease* and the *International Classification of Disease*. In 1952 American psychiatrists established their own diagnostic criteria in the *Diagnostic and Statistical Manual of Mental Disorders* (DSM), published by the American Psychiatric Association. The original manual defined psychological disorders in terms of their theoretical causal etiology (DSM, 1952), but this was abandoned in later editions such as DSM II (1968), DSM III (1980), DSM III-R (revised, 1987), DSM IV (1994), and DSM IV-TR (2000), in which classifications were based upon essential and common symptoms (Mayes & Horwitz, 2005; Wilson, 1993).

Other psychiatrists and psychologists adopted Kraepelin's scientific approach to abnormal psychology. In America, psychological laboratories were set up at medical facilities such as the McLean Hospital in Massachusetts, the Worcester State Hospital, and the New York State Psychiatric Institute (Maher & Maher, 2003). However, while the number of hospitals dedicated to the care of the psychologically abnormal expanded dramatically in the early decades of the 20th century—from around 100 at the turn of the century to between 200 and 300 by the 1930s, with a resident population of over half a million—the control and treatment of patients suffering from psychological disorders remained firmly in the hands of medically trained professionals.

In the 19th century, Americans shared the European enthusiasm for electrical and magnetic treatments, as evidenced by the popularity of the Reverend John Dods's *Electrical Psychology* of 1850. Mesmerism was originally promoted in America by traveling French demonstrators such as Dr. Joseph du Commun, who arrived in 1815 and started a society of magnetizers in New York (Beloff, 1975). For many Americans, mesmerism was associated with spiritualism, because they believed that the somnambulant had clairvoyant powers. Phineas Quimby (1802–1866), a former clockmaker, was one of the first Americans to employ mesmeric techniques for therapeutic purposes: His most famous patient was Mary Patterson (later Mary Baker Eddy), the founder of Christian Science (Beloff, 1975). Mesmerism was also closely associated with religion and formed the basis of the

Emmanuel Movement, a Christian ministry devoted to the treatment of nervous disorders that James christened the "mind-cure" movement. Elwood Worcester (1864–1940), a student of Wundt's, and the physician Isador Coriat (1875–1943), an interpreter of Freud, founded the movement, which was named after Emmanuel Church in Boston, where the original meetings were held.

As academic and applied psychology developed in America, it was initially only medically trained psychologists who concerned themselves with abnormal psychology and psychotherapy. William James, who had originally trained as a physician, took an active interest in the work of Charcot and Janet (both of whom he visited) and was greatly impressed by Breuer and Freud's *Studies on Hysteria* when it appeared in 1895. He began to employ hypnosis in his own therapeutic practice and maintained that hypnosis was the best treatment for nervous diseases such as hysteria. He also employed hypnosis in his analysis of mediums, cementing the early association of mesmeric techniques with spiritualism and religion, which led Joseph Jastrow to lament in his 1901 APA presidential address that psychologists were too often identified with "spook chasers" (Reisman, 1991, p. 47).

Hugo Münsterberg, the medically trained student of Wundt's who took over the psychology laboratory at Harvard from James, employed a variety of directive and suggestive therapeutic techniques, including hypnosis, in his early attempts at psychotherapy. Boris Sidis (1867–1923), a medically trained student of James's, became director of the New York State Psychiatric Institute. In *The Psychology of Suggestion* (1898), he characterized the unconscious mind as uncritical, irrational, amoral, involuntary, animalistic, and suggestible. He employed hypnosis in his treatment of hysterical patients for a number of years, but later abandoned it in favor of a form of therapy based upon sympathetic rapport (Sidis, 1902).

Morton Prince (1854–1929), another medically trained student of James's who studied with Charcot in Paris and Bernheim in Nancy, played a significant role in the early institutional development of abnormal psychology in America. Prince founded the *Journal of Abnormal Psychology* in 1906, the Psychopathological Association (with Sidis) in 1910, and the Harvard Psychological Clinic in 1927. He is perhaps best remembered for his study of dissociation, which he followed Janet in treating as a form of hysteria. In 1906 he published *The Dissociation of Personality*, an analysis of his treatment of Christine Beauchamp, a classic case of "multiple personality." Prince was impressed by Freud's work and helped to introduce psychoanalysis to America, although he developed Harvard psychiatry in opposition to psychoanalytic theory and practice. He was an early proponent of a view that proved enormously popular with later generations of clinical psychologists. Prince claimed that psychological disorders are the product of maladaptive learning, which could be relieved through relearning or "education" (Prince, 1909–1910).

Adolf Meyer (1866–1950), who completed his medical training in Zurich and took up a position at the Illinois Eastern Hospital for the Insane from 1893 to 1895, shared this view. He was later appointed director of clinical research at

Worcester Hospital for the Insane, with an academic appointment at Clark University (he took over from Hall as instructor in psychology at the hospital). Meyer later became professor of psychiatry at Johns Hopkins and director of the Phipps Psychiatric Clinic in Baltimore, where he integrated psychological and biological approaches in the medical training of psychiatrists. He encouraged Watson to work with infants and pioneered the use of developmental case histories. Meyer dismissed Freud's theories, but also rejected Griesinger and Kraepelin's claim that most psychological disorders are products of neural pathology. He treated them as functional disorders: the product of maladaptive responses rather than constitutional degeneracy. Meyer maintained that many psychological disorders, including dementia praecox or schizophrenia, are ineffective "psychobiological reactions" to the difficulties and stresses of everyday life, which lead to the formation of "progressive habit deteriorations" (Meyer, 1912). He claimed that they could be treated through training programs directed toward more adaptive and effective responses.

Meyer was a supporter of the **mental hygiene movement**, originally inspired by the work of Clifford Beers (1876–1943), who founded the first mental hygiene society in Connecticut in 1908. Beers was a former suicidal depressive who described his experience in mental institutions in *The Mind That Found Itself* (1908), with an introduction by William James. The aim of the movement was to increase public awareness of mental illness and promote its effective treatment. Henry Phipps, the Baltimore industrialist, was inspired by Beer's work to endow the psychiatric clinic at Johns Hopkins, later known as the Phipps Clinic. Meyer served as its first director and helped Beers set up the National Committee on Mental Hygiene in 1909, dedicated to the public dissemination of information about the prevention and treatment of mental disorder.

Lightner Witmer, generally recognized as the founder of clinical psychology in America, was highly critically of the therapeutic practices of some of his medically trained psychological colleagues. Conversely, a good many medically trained psychiatrists were skeptical about the therapeutic pretensions of their psychological colleagues. When the psychiatrist Karl Menninger (1893–1990) founded the American Orthopsychiatric Association in 1924, he originally restricted the membership to psychiatrists, although it was later extended to clinical psychologists and other mental health professionals such as Witmer and Goddard.

The work of clinical psychologists in the first four decades of the 20th century was largely devoted to mental testing and diagnosis, remedial education, and forms of training designed to redirect maladaptive behavior. They developed psychometric measures of personality and psychological functioning, such as the Downey-Will Temperament Test, Woodworth's Psychoneurotic Inventory, Symonds Adjustment Questionnaire, and the Woodworth-House Mental Hygiene Inventory. David Levy promoted the use of the Rorschach personality test in America, based upon the inkblot pictures first described by Hermann Rorschach

(1884–1922) in *Psychodiagnostik* (1921). Christiana D. Morgan and Henry Murray introduced the Thematic Apperception Test (TAT), another measure of personality, in 1935. Clinical psychologists developed diagnostic tests such as the Babcock Deterioration Test and eventually won the right to make committals to state institutions and hospitals on the basis of such tests. However, until the Second World War the treatment of psychological disorder remained the exclusive domain of medically trained psychiatrists, who supervised clinical psychologists in hospitals and clinics.

ECT, LOBOTOMY, AND PSYCHOPHARMACOLOGY

As the 20th century advanced, new forms of therapy displaced the eclectic mix of treatments popular in the 19th century. **Electroconvulsive treatment (ECT)**, in which convulsions are induced by passing an electrical current through the brain, was introduced in the late 1930s, although the use of electrical stimulation as a treatment goes back to antiquity, and camphor-induced seizures had been used as a treatment for centuries. The modern treatment regime was developed by Joseph Ladislau von Meduna (1896–1964), a Hungarian physician who used pentylene-tetrazol (metrazol), a synthetic extract of camphor, to artificially induce convulsions in patients suffering from schizophrenia. He reported qualified success and later extended this form of treatment to melancholics and manic-depressives (Meduna, 1935). Ugo Cerletti and Lucio Bini, two Italian psychiatrists who had read reports of Meduna's work, created convulsions in patients by passing an electrical current through their temporal lobes and also reported qualified success (Cerletti & Bini, 1938). Cerletti and Bini first used this treatment on a vagrant who had been brought to them by the police, after he had been found wandering the streets of Rome speaking "incomprehensible gibberish" (Impasato, 1960).

Metrazol shock treatment was widely used in psychiatric hospitals in Europe and America until the 1940s, but was eventually displaced by ECT, which Lothar Kalinowski and Renato Almansi introduced to America in 1939. Originally employed in the treatment of schizophrenia, ECT was later extended to the treatment of forms of depression, particularly those that did not respond well to drug treatments. The use of ECT has been controversial since its inception. Despite the multitude of theories, there is no generally accepted account of its efficacy (Sackheim, 1988), and the often debilitating side effects, from memory loss to brain damage, have led many to question its therapeutic utility. The use of ECT declined during the 1970s, but appears to be on the increase again, although not because of any major developments in theoretical validation or improvement in treatment outcomes (Giles, 2002).

Another controversial treatment that was introduced in the 1930s was **prefrontal lobotomy**, a surgical operation producing lesion of the nerve fibers in the frontal lobes (severing the fiber tracts connecting the prefrontal lobes with the thalamus). The Portuguese physician Egas Moniz (1874–1955), whose original idea had been to inject the frontal lobes with alcohol, pioneered the use of the technique. Although he was disappointed to discover that the surgery did not eliminate chronic delusions in schizophrenics, as he had originally hoped, Moniz claimed that it changed their emotional response from distress to apathy (Moniz, 1937). Reports of the success of these operations were greatly exaggerated and neglected their side effects. Nevertheless, the technique was widely adopted in Europe and America in the late 1940s and early 1950s, when it was extended to the treatment of other psychological disorders (Valenstein, 1986). Moniz won the Nobel Prize for his work in 1949, but it brought him little satisfaction. He was shot by one of his lobotomized patients and remained a paraplegic for the rest of his life.

Walter Freeman and J. W. Watts promoted the operation in the United States (Freeman & Watts, 1942). Freeman reputedly performed over 3,000 lobotomies in his lifetime and championed the surgery as the solution to America's social ills. However, the use of the procedure declined in the late 1950s amid concerns about its serious side effects and ethical questions about the conditions under which lobotomies were performed—sometimes physicians unqualified in neurosurgery conducted them in their offices. Freeman, who once performed the procedure in a motel room, lost his surgical privileges following the death of a lobotomy patient during an operation (Maher & Maher, 2003). As in the case of ECT, lobotomy was employed for many years in the absence of any generally accepted theoretical justification and amid serious doubts about its efficacy. The underlying motivation for continuing both treatments seems to have been to maintain the morale of professional mental health practitioners by doing *something* for their patients (Reisman, 1991).

Psychoactive Drugs and Institutional Care

More effective and enduring was the employment of psychoactive drugs. The tranquilizers chlorpromazine and reserpine (which Avicenna had used in its herbal form rauwolfia) were employed in the treatment of schizophrenia, and lithium and other MAO (monoamine oxidase) inhibitors in the treatment of mania and depression. The theoretical rationale for these and later drug treatments was that psychological disorders are related to the disruption of the balance of chemical neurotransmitters in the brain, such as norepinephrine, dopamine, and serotonin, which the various drug treatments aimed to restore—an old idea in modern neurophysiological guise. These treatments did reduce the severity and frequency of symptoms, but they also created dependencies, and critics complained that they simply managed rather than relieved psychological disorders. Although they transformed the lives of many schizophrenics, schizophrenia remained a debilitating condition for others.

The success of psychoactive drug treatments had a significant impact on institutional care. Many schizophrenics found release from their catatonic states, and restraints were removed from formerly violent patients. In many cases they obviated the need for institutional care; patients who had formerly required hospitalization could now be treated on an outpatient basis. This led to a dramatic drop in the population receiving institutional care, which fell from over 600,000 in the 1940s to less than 150,000 by the 1970s (Reisman, 1991). The process of deinstitutionalization was accelerated by the social policies of the 1960s. The Community Mental Health Centers Act of 1963 provided federal support for community centers offering outpatient mental health services, along with outreach and drug and alcohol treatment programs.

Unfortunately, the community mental health center program was seriously underfunded, and former patients were not always able to manage their drug regimes. The process of deinstitutionalization came to be driven as much by economic as by professional psychological goals, and many of those suffering from psychological disorders joined the populations of homeless persons in major metropolitan centers. The problem was compounded by legal challenges to the committal authority of psychologists and psychiatrists, enabling potentially violent and self-destructive individuals to refuse institutional treatment, including drug and ECT treatment. One of the saddest outcomes of this well-intentioned social experiment was a new generation of Tom o' Bedlams on the streets of New York, London, and Rome, begging on subways and muttering to themselves on city sidewalks.

The Myth of Mental Illness

In 1960 the psychiatrist Thomas Szasz published an article and book with the title "The Myth of Mental Illness." He claimed that most neuroses and psychoses are "problems of living" rather than pathological psychological disorders, although he did recognize that some have their origin in neurological damage and dysfunction. He argued that the treatment of patients as "mentally ill" sanctioned illegitimate exercises of social control: Patients were imprisoned, institutionalized, and subjected to drug, surgical, and behavioral treatments against their will. Szasz claimed that such involuntary treatments were never justified and constituted "crimes against humanity." His views promoted legal challenges that resulted in more stringent conditions and limits on the involuntary incarceration and treatment of psychiatric patients.

Szasz's critique of the moral presumptions of psychiatry and his claim that many treatment practices undermine fundamental principles of individuality and freedom found a responsive audience in the 1960s, as evidenced by the popularity of novels and films such as Ken Kesey's *One Flew Over the Cuckoo's Nest*. However, most of the psychiatric establishment dismissed Szasz as a dangerous radical, in the same league as Timothy Leary, the former Harvard physician turned LSD guru. While damaging to psychiatry, Szasz's critique provided indirect legitimization for clinical psychological treatments, particularly those based upon behaviorism and cognitive psychology, since it was fairly easy to represent "problems in living" as problems of learning and cognitive adjustment.

POSTWAR CLINICAL PSYCHOLOGY

In the First World War, psychologists played only a minor psychotherapeutic role. The applied psychologist Harry Hollingworth (1880–1956) of Barnard College examined soldiers suffering from "shell shock" while serving (with the rank of captain) in the army hospital at Plattsburgh, New York (Hollingworth, 1920), but most psychologists were assigned to personnel selection and intelligence testing. Between the wars clinical psychologists continued to focus on psychometrics and remedial education and generally deferred to psychiatrists in the treatment of psychological disorders. The training of clinical psychologists was haphazard and unregulated, despite the efforts of those clinical and counseling psychologists who petitioned the APA for the development of professional training standards. While some psychology internships were established as part of clinical training (the first at Vineland in 1908), students participating in them were generally restricted to research and psychometric examination (Routh, 2000).

After the Second World War, clinical psychologists continued to develop diagnostic and personality tests, such as the Minnesota Multiphasic Personality Inventory (MMPI), but became more directly engaged in the treatment of psychological disorders, including depression and schizophrenia. This was largely a function of their war experience and the huge demand for clinical services in the aftermath of the war. Although many psychologists were employed in personnel evaluation and assessment during the war, many were also employed in counseling and psychotherapy (Hunter, 1946), since the number of psychological casualties overwhelmed the resources of psychiatry. Consequently, many postwar clinical psychologists came to believe that the provision of psychotherapy was an integral part of their professional role (Krugman, 1945).

When the United States entered the Second World War in December 1941, the government recognized that there were too few psychiatrists to service the psychological needs of soldiers and directed the U.S. Public Health Service (USPHS) and the Veterans Administration (VA) to increase the availability of clinical psychologists. After the war, there was a huge demand for clinical psychologists to accommodate the psychological needs of the 16 million returning veterans (along with the 4 million from previous wars). This led to the rapid development of university training programs, funded by the USPHS, the VA, and the National Institute of Mental Health (founded in 1948). The APA worked with these institutions to establish a set of standards for clinical training and a program of accreditation, first established for clinical psychologists in 1946 and for counseling psychologists in 1952. By 1949, there were 42 graduate schools offering a doctorate in clinical psychology, and about 149 offering some form of clinical training (Reisman, 1991). The numbers of clinical psychologists within the profession began to increase dramatically and was reflected in the divisional affiliation of the presidents of the APA. Carl Rogers was elected president in 1946, the first of many clinical psychologists to hold the office after the war. The Division of Clinical Psychology (Division 12) constituted the largest division of the reconstituted postwar APA, and by 1954 its 1,500 members outnumbered the combined membership of the Divisions of Experimental and General Psychology by two to one (Capshew, 1999).

Clinical Training

The 1947 APA Committee on Training in Clinical Psychology recommended that graduate training programs in clinical psychology should include a solid grounding in theoretical and experimental psychology, with internships and practical training in both diagnosis and therapy: "at least a four-year program which combines academic and clinical training throughout but which includes intensive clinical experience in the form of an internship" (1947, p. 544). This combination of academic research and practical training became known as the **scientist-practitioner** or "Boulder" model of clinical training, after it was officially endorsed at the APA Conference on Clinical Training in Psychology, funded by the Public Health Service and held in Boulder, Colorado, in 1949.

A later APA conference, held at Vail, Colorado, in 1973, reaffirmed the scientific-practitioner model, but also endorsed an alternative "practitioner" model, which stimulated the development of clinical programs offering a Doctor of Psychology degree (PsyD), specifically oriented to professional clinicians. Leta Hollingworth had suggested such a degree in 1918, but it was not instituted until 1968, when the University of Illinois allowed clinical graduate students to pursue either a PhD or PsyD, a practice followed by other graduate schools in the ensuing decades. The alternative practitioner model was also supported by the creation of independent professional schools of psychology, such as the California School of Professional Psychology, founded in 1969 (Routh & Reisman, 2003). By the 1980s there were about 20 professional schools, although some remained affiliated with universities, such as the Rutgers Graduate School of Applied and Professional Psychology.

In the postwar period, the theories and therapies that clinical psychologists developed reflected the influence of behaviorism and cognitivism within academic psychology. Joseph Wolpe (1958) developed "systematic desensitization" as a means of relieving phobias, a form of treatment that had been pioneered by Mary Cover Jones in her extinction of Peter's fear of rabbits (Jones, 1924) and documented by Locke in *Some Thoughts Concerning Education* (1693/1989). Skinnerian operant-conditioning techniques became almost as popular as drug treatments in many hospital wards, with therapists shaping the behavior of patients through token economy programs (Stahl & Leitenberg, 1976). Although legal challenges eventually restricted the use of such programs and aversion therapy, behavioral treatments remained popular among clinical psychologists. The advent of the cognitive revolution in psychology introduced a variety of cognitive and cognitive-behavioral theories and therapies (Bandura, 1977; Beck, 1972; Rotter, 1975; Seligman, 1975).

HUMANISTIC PSYCHOLOGY

Abraham Maslow (1908–1970) and Carl Rogers (1902–1987) raised doubts about scientific approaches to psychological disorders, largely in reaction to some of the more technologically oriented behaviorist treatments. They developed an alternative approach that came to be known as **humanistic psychology**. Maslow was a former behaviorist who came to believe that the behaviorist approach was too narrow, possibly through his contact with European refugees such as Adler, Lewin, and Wertheimer in New York City. He developed his theory of personality as a form of **self-actualization** through an intensive study of the lives of Wertheimer and Ruth Benedict, two especially creative individuals whom he greatly admired. Maslow later maintained that Wertheimer was the inspiration for his theory.

Maslow held that human motivation is grounded in the capacity of all individuals to actualize their potential, although in his own research he focused on individuals who seemed to live especially creative and rewarding lives. Maslow claimed that human motivation is arranged in a hierarchy and that basic human needs, such as the need for security and love, have to be satisfied before people can become true "self-actualizers" and attain their full potential. Few people attain full self-actualization in practice, because they are too engaged with the satisfaction of basic needs or lack the courage and energy to develop their true selves (Maslow, 1943). However, Maslow claimed that all humans have the capacity to enrich their lives by actualizing their higher potential, even if they cannot attain the creative heights of a Wertheimer or Benedict. He developed his brand of humanistic psychology as a "third force" in psychology, in opposition to the dehumanizing scientific objectivity of behaviorism and the "crippled psychology" of psychoanalysis (Maslow, 1954, p. 180). Maslow stressed the values of autonomy and choice in the development of a full human life, including the open expression of feeling. He was elected president of the APA in 1967, but left academia the following year for a research fellowship at the Saga Corporation, where he remained until his death in 1970.

Carl Rogers developed what came to be known as "person-" or **client-centered therapy**, a form of psychotherapy that champions the self-knowledge of the patient and the empathy of the therapist over more detached scientific approaches (Rogers, 1947, 1951, 1966). Like Maslow, Rogers affirmed that all individuals are capable of actualizing their highest potential and that their attempts may be promoted or impeded through personal development and social interaction. He claimed that individual self-fulfillment requires acknowledgment of the unconditioned worth of the person by parents, friends, and therapists. Like Maslow, he lauded human autonomy and spontaneous expression over the constraints of scientific objectivity, although his own research was focused on emotionally disturbed individuals rather than creative self-actualizers. Rogers was elected president of the APA in 1946 and later received its Distinguished Scientific Contribution and Distinguished Professional Contribution Awards.

The roots of humanistic psychology lie in Brentano's phenomenological psychology and philosophy, especially as developed by Edmund Husserl and Martin Heidegger (1889–1976), which focused upon the phenomenological exploration of consciousness and being as the goal of self-knowledge. One branch of phenomenology developed as existential philosophy and psychology, which emphasized the creative role of the individual in the determination of his or her essential being, through the work of Maurice Merleau-Ponty (1908–1961), Ludwig Binswanger (1881–1966), and Jean-Paul Sartre (1905–1980). Rollo May (1909–1994) promoted existential psychology in America and extended basic existentialist principles to psychotherapy and personality theory. Amedeo Giorgi (1931–) claimed that existential psychology is the foundation of a truly human science (Giorgi, 1970). Giorgi was a member of the psychology department at Duquesne University, which became the center of existential-phenomenological psychology in the United States and sponsor of the *Journal of Phenomenological Psychology*. The cause of humanistic psychology was also advanced by the development of personality psychology, which stressed the individuality and variability of personality and resisted the fashion for operationalized theory and rigorous experimentation, notably through the pioneering work of William Stern (1935, 1938) and Gordon Allport (1937, 1955).

Humanistic psychology was a popular movement in psychology throughout the 1960s and 1970s. *The Journal of Humanistic Psychology* was founded in 1961, the American Association for Humanistic Psychology in 1962, and the APA Division of Humanistic Psychology in 1971. Yet although it was respectfully acknowledged and institutionally recognized, few mainstream experimental or clinical psychologists embraced it. The empirical foundation for humanistic psychology was always doubtful, and humanist psychologists never developed a common theoretical or metatheoretical position, as they readily acknowledged. They often claimed that they were not opposed to scientific approaches per se and suggested that these could be "incorporated" within humanistic psychology. However, they had great difficulty in squaring their avowed commitment to causal determination with their hymning of human freedom and autonomy, although Joseph Rychlak made a heroic effort to incorporate humanistic goals within a scientific perspective in works such as *The Psychology of Rigorous Humanism* (1988). Maslow and Rogers lauded the Nietzschian free expression of emotion, but other humanistic psychologists were inspired by the Platonic ideal of the rational control of emotion, as in the case of Albert Ellis's promotion of **rational-emotive therapy** (Ellis, 1958).

INTO THE 21st CENTURY

The introduction of certification and licensing laws extended the professional authority of clinical psychologists. The first certification laws were introduced in Connecticut in 1945, requiring a doctoral degree and a year or more of professional experience. The next year the APA created the American Board of Examiners in Professional Psychology (ABEPP) to ensure the maintenance of national standards in clinical psychology and counseling. Clinical psychologists had earlier won the right to certify patients for institutional and hospital care and to serve as medical staff in hospitals. They later won the right to treat patients and receive third-party insurance payments, as a result of lawsuits such as *Blue Shield of Virginia vs. McCready* (1982).

However, the postwar advancement of the profession was not matched by obvious advances in fundamental theory and therapy. Alternative cognitive, behavioral, neurophysiological, developmental, and constitutional theories of psychological disorder abounded, with little prospect of integration or accommodation. The situation was compounded by disagreements about the scientific classification of psychological disorders and the historical expansion of diagnostic categories. *The Diagnostic and Statistical Manual of Mental Disorders* (DSM) recognized 106 categories when it was first published in 1952. The 1968 edition (DSM-II) recognized 182 categories; by the 1980 edition (DSM III) the number had expanded to 265. Such category expansion did not always appear to be a natural consequence of theoretical refinement. The revised third edition, which appeared in 1987 (DSM-III-R), was judged by many to be inferior to the original third edition.

Forms of psychological therapy continued to proliferate in the postwar period. By the end of the 1970s, Beutler (1979) estimated that there were around 130 different schools of psychological treatment. Whatever their theoretical rationale, they all came to be haunted by the type of critique originally advanced against psychoanalysis by Hans Eysenck (1952), who maintained that the recovery rates for neurotics receiving psychoanalytic treatment were no better than the "spontaneous remission" rates of those left untreated. Around the same time Meehl (1954) complained that clinical psychologists were poor diagnosticians, whose rates of diagnostic success were no better than those based upon statistical actuarial tables relating symptoms and disorders, a charge repeated by Kleinmuntz (1967) with respect to clinicians' interpretations of MMPI, Rorschach, and TAT scores.

Later comparative studies of professional psychological treatments with "no-treatment" groups did suggest that they were effective (Sloane et al., 1975), and later meta-analyses (Luborsky, Singer, & Luborsky, 1975; Smith & Glass, 1977; Smith, Glass, & Miller, 1980) suggested that virtually all forms of psychological treatment are better than no treatment. However, such studies also indicated that most forms of psychological treatment are about equal in efficacy and that none are demonstrably more effective than placebo control treatments. This was a troubling outcome, given the impoverished nature of most placebo control treatments, especially with respect to "nonspecific" factors such as client and therapist expectancy and credibility of treatment (Borcovec & Nau, 1977; Kazdin & Wilcoxon, 1978), which some suggested might account for the efficacy of all forms of psychological treatment (Bergin & Lambert, 1984; Frank, 1974, 1983).

Concerns about the theoretical justification of professional psychological treatments were exacerbated when Congress demanded scientific evidence for them as a condition for endorsing insurance payments to clinical psychologists. Yet despite the plethora of later studies, including the massive National Institute of Mental Health study of depression in the 1990s (Elkin, 1994; Elkin et al., 1989), the suggestibility of clients (and therapists) remains a viable explanation of the efficacy of many forms of psychological treatment (Greenwood, 1997), the type of explanation that Freud's tally argument was designed but failed to refute.

Despite the initial rapport between clinical psychologists and medical psychiatrists, tensions developed as the century progressed, especially with the postwar intrusion of clinical psychologists into the realm of psychotherapy. The profession of medical psychiatry resisted the certification of clinical psychologists and challenged their right to provide psychotherapy and receive insurance payments for their services. They continue to resist the extension of prescription privileges to clinical psychologists (DeLeon & Wiggins, 1996).

Tensions also increased between clinical practitioners and academic psychologists when clinical, consulting, and other professional psychologists came to outnumber the mainstream academic members of the APA in the postwar period. Having for many years been treated as second-class citizens by the academicians, clinical psychologists came to dominate and control the institutions of the APA, including the presidency and the governing committees. They refused to surrender their new powers to the academics, who broke away to form the American Psychological Society (APS) in 1988. Thus at the beginning of the 21st century, the APA is primarily a professional association, dominated by clinical and other applied psychologists, and will likely remain that way for the foreseeable future (Pickren & Fowler, 2003).

DISCUSSION QUESTIONS

1. Why do you think the history of clinical psychology is so presentist? Does the progress of 20th-century clinical psychology justify this stance?

2. To what degree did Janet anticipate Freud? Do you think Janet was justified in accusing Freud of plagiarism?

3. Do you think psychoanalysis and behaviorism can be reconciled, as Dollard and Miller (1950) claimed?

4. Freud maintained that those who reject psychoanalytic theory are repressed. Would it be fair to respond that those who accept it are engaged in wish fulfillment?

5. Can "mental illness" really be characterized as a "myth"?

6. Should clinical psychologists be both scientists and practitioners?

GLOSSARY

abreaction In psychoanalysis, the cathartic expression of emotionally charged memories.

alienist Early name for a physician engaged in the diagnosis and treatment of the mentally disturbed.

dementia praecox Early name for disorder later characterized as schizophrenia, so-called because of its early onset and rapid progression.

client-centered therapy Form of psychotherapy based upon acknowledgment of the intrinsic worth of people, in contrast to more detached scientific approaches.

countertransference Emotional attachment that a therapist develops for a patient in the course of psychoanalysis.

ego In psychoanalytic theory, aspect of personality that identifies and pursues the real-world objects of instinctual drive and desire.

electroconvulsive treatment (ECT) Controversial treatment of schizophrenia and depression in which convulsions are induced by passing an electrical current through the brain.

Emmanuel Movement Christian ministry devoted to the treatment of nervous disorders.

free association In psychoanalysis, method of identifying pathogenic ideas by having the patient relax and describe whatever comes into his or her mind, no matter how apparently trivial or potentially embarrassing it might be.

Freudian slip Symbolic wish fulfillment expressed in everyday accidents and errors.

humanistic psychology An approach to psychological disorders and their treatment that emphasizes the autonomy, potential, and personal feelings of individuals, in contrast to objective scientific approaches.

hypnosis Term coined by the Scottish surgeon James Braid to describe the state of "nervous sleep" induced by mesmeric treatments.

id Instinctual core of personality, comprising basic drives and desires (such as hunger, thirst, and sexual desire).

latent content Repressed content (of dreams).

manifest content Apparent content (of dreams).

mental alienation Early term used to describe the troubled condition of those suffering from psychological disorders.

mental hygiene movement Early-20th-century movement that aimed to increase public awareness of mental illness and promote its effective treatment.

mesmerism Form of treatment developed by Franz Mesmer, supposedly based upon the manipulation of magnetic forces in the body.

moral management Form of 19th-century psychological treatment directed to the transformation of character through personal counseling and religious training.

Nancy school The theoretical position developed by Nancy physicians Ambroise-Auguste Liébault and Hippolyte Bernheim, who claimed that suggestion is the primary vehicle of hypnotism and that suggestibility is a normal and universal psychological trait.

neuroses Term first used by the Edinburgh physician William Cullen to characterize physical or psychological disorders caused by damage to or disease of the nervous system.

neurasthenia Nervous exhaustion.

Oedipus complex In psychoanalytic theory, emotional conflict generated by the male child's sexual desire for his mother and fear of his father, resolved through identification with his father.

paranoia Term employed by Johann Christian Heinroth to describe a variety of disorders based upon intellectual and emotional disturbance.

pleasure principle In psychoanalytic theory, principle directed to the gratification of basic drives and desires.

prefrontal lobotomy Surgical operation producing lesion of the nerve fibers in the frontal lobes, employed as a treatment of schizophrenia and other disorders.

psychiatry Term introduced by Johann Christian Reil to describe the study and treatment of mental disorder.

rational-emotive therapy Form of therapy based upon the rational control of emotion.

reality principle In psychoanalytic theory, principle directed to the identification and pursuit of real-world objects of instinctual drive and desire.

schizophrenia Term introduced by Eugene Bleuler to describe the disorder formerly classified as dementia praecox, which he believed was based upon the dissociation of thought and emotion.

scientist-practitioner model The model of clinical training combining academic research and practical training that was endorsed at the APA conference on clinical training in psychology in Boulder, Colorado, in 1949.

seduction theory Freud's early theory that neurotic symptoms are the product of repressed memories of childhood sexual abuse.

self-actualization In Maslow's personality theory, the capacity every individual has to reach his or her highest potential.

super-ego In psychoanalytic theory, the aspect of personality based upon the internalization of the moral principles of the parent of the opposite sex, which restricts the objects of drive and desire pursued to those that are socially approved.

tally argument Theoretical justification of psychoanalysis attributed to Freud by Adolf Grünbaum, based upon the claim that correct insight is necessary for the cure of neuroses.

transference Redirection of patient feelings for parents to the therapist in the course of psychoanalysis.

wish fulfillment Symbolic expression of repressed memories and desires.

REFERENCES

Ackerknecht, E. H. (1982). *A short history of medicine*. Baltimore, MD: Johns Hopkins University Press.

Allderidge, P. (1979). Hospitals, madhouses and asylums: Cycles in the care of the insane. *British Journal of Psychiatry, 134,* 321–334.

Allport, G. W. (1937). *Personality: A psychological interpretation*. New York: Holt, Rinehart & Winston.

Allport, G. W. (1955). *Becoming: Basic considerations of a psychology of personality*. New Haven: Yale University Press.

American Psychiatric Association. (1952). *Diagnostic and statistical manual of mental disorders*. Washington, DC: Author.

American Psychiatric Association. (1968). *Diagnostic and statistical manual of mental disorders* (2nd ed.). (DSM-II). Washington, DC: Author.

American Psychiatric Association. (1980). *Diagnostic and statistical manual of mental disorders* (3rd ed.). (DSM-III). Washington, DC: Author.

American Psychiatric Association. (1987). *Diagnostic and statistical manual of mental disorders* (3rd ed., rev.). (DSM-III-R). Washington, DC: Author.

American Psychiatric Association. (1994). *Diagnostic and statistical manual of mental disorders* (4th ed.). (DSM-IV). Washington, DC: Author.

American Psychiatric Association. (2000). *Diagnostic and statistical manual of mental disorders.* (4th ed., rev.). (DSM-IV-TR). Washington, DC: Author.

American Psychological Association. (1947). Recommended graduate training program in clinical psychology. *American Psychologist, 2,* 539–558.

Bandura, A. (1977). *Social learning theory.* Englewood Cliffs, NJ: Prentice-Hall.

Battie, W. (1758). *A treatise on madness.* London: J. Whiston & B. White.

Beck, A. T. (1972). *Depression: Causes and treatment.* Philadelphia: University of Pennsylvania Press.

Beers, C. (1908). *The mind that found itself: An autobiography.* New York: Longmans, Green.

Beloff, J. (1975). *Psychological sciences.* London: Crosby Lockwood Staples.

Bergin, A. E., & Lambert, M. J. (1984). The evaluation of therapeutic outcomes. In S. L. Garfield & A. E. Bergin (Eds.), *Handbook of psychotherapy and behavior change* (3rd ed.). New York: Wiley.

Bernheim, H. (1968). *Hypnosis and suggestion in psychotherapy.* New Hyde Park, NY: University Books. (Original work published 1865)

Beutler, L. E. (1979). Toward specific psychological therapies for specific conditions. *Journal of Consulting and Clinical Psychology, 47,* 882–897.

Binet, A., & Féré, C. (1887). *Animal magnetism.* London: Kegan Paul.

Bleuler, E. (1950). *Dementia praecox oder gruppe der schzophrenien* [*Dementia praecox or the groups of schizophrenias*]. Leipzig: Deuticke. (Original work published 1911)

Bolles, R. C. (1993). *The story of psychology: A thematic history.* Belmont, CA: Brooks-Cole.

Borcovec, T. D., & Nau, S. D. (1977). Credibility of analog therapy rationales. *Journal of Behavior Therapy and Experimental Psychiatry, 3,* 257–260.

Braid, J. (1843). *Neurhypnology, or the rationale of nervous sleep, considered in relation with animal magnetism.* London: Churchill.

Burton, R. (1621). *Anatomy of melancholy: What it is.* Oxford: John James Lichfield for Henry Short Cribbs.

Capshew, J. H. (1999). *Psychologists on the march: Science, practice, and professional identity in America, 1929–1969.* Cambridge: Cambridge University Press.

Cerletti, U., & Bini, L. (1938). L'elletroshock [Electric shock]. *Archivo Generale di Neurologia, 19,* 266–268.

Cheyne, G. (1734). *The English malady.* London: Cornhill.

Chiarugi, V. (1987). *On insanity and its classification* (G. Mora, Trans.). Canton, MA: Science History. (Originally published 1793)

Cioffi, F. (1970). Freud and the idea of a pseudo-science. In R. Borger & F. Cioffi (Eds.), *Explanation in the behavioral sciences*. Cambridge: Cambridge University Press.

Clare, A. (1976). *Psychiatry in dissent*. London: Tavistock.

Cullen, W. (1777). *First lines of the practice of physick for the use of students at the University of Edinburgh*. Edinburgh, Scotland: W. Creech.

Daquin, J. (1791). *Philosophie de la folie* [Philosophy of insanity]. Chambery: Gorrin.

DeLeon, P. H., & Wiggins, J. G. (1996). Prescription privileges for psychologists. *American Psychologist, 51*, 225–229.

Dods, J. B. (1850). *Electrical psychology* (2nd ed.). New York: Fowler & Wells.

Dollard, J., & Miller, N. E. (1950). *Personality and psychotherapy*. New York: McGraw-Hill.

Earle, P. (1848). *History, description and statistics of the Bloomingdale asylum*. New York: Egbert, Hovey & King.

Earle, P. (1887). *The curability of insanity*. Philadelphia: Lippincott. (Originally published 1838)

Elkin, I. (1994). The NIMH treatment of depression collaborative research program: Where we are and where we began. In A. E. Bergin & S. L. Garfield (Eds.), *Handbook of psychotherapy and behavior change* (4th ed.). New York: Wiley.

Elkin, I., Shea, M. T., Watkins, J., Imber, S., Sotsky, S., Collins, J., Glass, D., Pilkonis, P., Leber, W., Docherty, J., Fiester, A., & Parloff, M. (1989). National Institute of Mental Health treatment of depression collaborative research program: General effectiveness of treatments. *Archives of General Psychology, 46*, 971–982.

Ellenberger, H. F. (1970). *The discovery of the unconscious: The history and evolution of dynamic psychiatry*. New York: Basic Books.

Ellenberger, H. F. (1972). The story of Anna O: A critical review with new data. *Journal of the History of the Behavioral Sciences, 8*, 267–279.

Ellis, A. (1958). Rational psychotherapy. *Journal of General Psychology, 59*, 35–59.

Ellis, H. (1897–1928). *Studies in the psychology of sex* (Vols. 1–7). Philadelphia: F. A. Davis.

Esdaile, J. (1846). *Mesmerism in India and its practical application in surgery and medicine*. London: Longman, Brown, Green, & Longmans.

Esdaile, J. (1852). *The introduction of mesmerism as an anaesthetic and curative agent into the hospitals of India*. (Pamphlet). Perth, Scotland: Dewar.

Eysenck, H. (1952). The effects of psychotherapy: An evaluation. *Journal of Consulting Psychology, 16*, 319–324.

Eysenck, H. (1965). The effects of psychotherapy. *International Journal of Psychiatry, 1*, 99–142.

Fisher, S., & Greenberg, R. P. (1977). *The scientific credibility of Freud's theories and therapy*. New York: Basic Books.

Frank, J. D. (1974). Psychotherapy: The restoration of morale. *American Journal of Psychotherapy, 131,* 271–274.

Frank, J. D. (1983). The placebo is psychotherapy. *Behavioral and Brain Sciences, 6,* 291–292.

Freeman, W., & Watts, J. W. (1942). *Psychosurgery.* Springfield, IL: Charles C. Thomas.

Freud, S. (1953). *A project for a scientific psychology.* In J. Strachey (Ed.), *The standard edition of the complete psychological works of Sigmund Freud* (Vol. 1). London: Hogarth Press. (Original work published 1895)

Freud, S. (1953). Preface to *Three essays on the theory of sexuality.* In J. Strachey (Ed.), *The standard edition of the complete psychological works of Sigmund Freud* (Vol. 7). London: Hogarth Press. (Original work published 1905)

Freud, S. (1958). *The interpretation of dreams.* In J. Strachey (Ed.), *The standard edition of the complete psychological works of Sigmund Freud* (Vols. 4–5). London: Hogarth Press. (Original work published 1900)

Freud, S. (1960). *The psychopathology of everyday life.* In J. Strachey (Ed.), *The standard edition of the complete psychological works of Sigmund Freud* (Vol. 6). London: Hogarth Press. (Original work published 1901)

Freud, S. (1961). *The future of an illusion.* In J. Strachey (Ed.), *The standard edition of the complete psychological works of Sigmund Freud* (Vol. 21). London: Hogarth Press. (Original work published 1927)

Freud, S. (1962). *The etiology of hysteria.* In J. Strachey (Ed.), *The standard edition of the complete psychological works of Sigmund Freud* (Vol. 3). London: Hogarth Press. (Original work published 1896)

Freud, S. (1963). *Introductory lectures on psychoanalysis.* In J. Strachey (Ed.), *The standard edition of the complete psychological works of Sigmund Freud* (Vols. 15–16). London: Hogarth Press. (Original work published 1917)

Freud, S. (1966). Analysis of a phobia of a nine-year old boy. In J. Strachey (Ed.), *The standard edition of the complete psychological works of Sigmund Freud* (Vol. 10). London: Hogarth Press. (Original work published 1909)

Freud, S. (1966). *Jokes and their relation to the unconscious.* In J. Strachey (Ed.), *The standard edition of the complete psychological works of Sigmund Freud* (Vol. 8). London: Hogarth Press. (Original work published 1905)

Freud, S. (1966). *Totem and taboo.* In J. Strachey (Ed.), *The standard edition of the complete psychological works of Sigmund Freud* (Vol. 13). London: Hogarth Press. (Original work published 1912–1913)

Freud, S., & Breuer, J. (1966). On the psychical mechanism of hysterical phenomena: A preliminary communication. In J. Strachey (Ed.), *The standard edition of the complete psychological works of Sigmund Freud* (Vol. 2). London: Hogarth Press. (Original work published 1893)

Freud, S., & Breuer, J. (1966). *Studies on hysteria.* In J. Strachey (Ed.), *The standard edition of the complete psychological works of Sigmund Freud* (Vol. 2). London: Hogarth Press. (Original work published 1895)

Giles, J. (2002). Electroconvulsive therapy and the fear of deviance. *Journal for the Theory of Social Behaviour, 32,* 61–87.

Giorgi, A. (1970). *Psychology as a human science: A phenomenologically based approach.* New York: Harper & Row.

Glymour, C. (1980). *Theory and evidence.* Princeton: Princeton University Press.

Gravitz, M. A. (1988). Early use of hypnosis as surgical anesthesia. *American Journal of Clinical Hypnosis, 30,* 201–208.

Green, M., & Rieber, R. W. (1980). The assimilation of psychoanalysis in America. In R. W. Rieber & K. Salzinger (Eds.), *Psychology: Theoretical-historical perspectives.* New York: Academic Press.

Greenwood, J. D. (1996). Freud's tally argument, placebo control treatments, and the evaluation of psychotherapy. *Philosophy of Science, 63,* 605–621.

Greenwood, J. D. (1997). Placebo control treatments and the evaluation of psychotherapy. *Philosophy of Science, 64,* 497–510.

Griesinger, W. (1845). *Mental pathology and therapeutics.* London: New Sydenham Society.

Griesinger, W. (1868). Introductory comments. *Archives for Psychiatry and Nervous Diseases, 1,* 12.

Grünbaum, A. (1983). Retrospective versus prospective testing of aetiological hypotheses in Freudian theory. In J. Earman (Ed.), *Minnesota studies in the philosophy of science: Vol. 10. Testing scientific theories.* Minneapolis: University of Minnesota Press.

Grünbaum, A. (1984). *The foundations of psychoanalysis: A philosophical critique.* Berkeley: University of California Press.

Hale, N. G., Jr. (1971). *Freud and the Americans: The beginnings of psychoanalysis in the United States 1876–1917.* New York: Oxford University Press.

Harper, R. A. (1959). *Psychoanalysis and psychotherapy.* Englewood Cliffs, NJ: Prentice-Hall.

Haslam, J. (1809). *Observations on madness and melancholy.* London: J. Callow.

Hollingworth, H. L. (1920). *The psychology of functional neuroses.* New York: Appleton.

Hollingworth, L. (1918). Tentative suggestions for the certification of practicing psychologists. *Journal of Applied Psychology, 2,* 280–284.

Hornstein, G. A. (1992). The return of the repressed: Psychology's problematic relations with psychoanalysis, 1909–1960. *American Psychologist, 47,* 254–263.

Hunter, W. S. (1946). Psychology in the war. *American Psychologist, 1,* 479–492.

Impasato, D. (1960). The story of the first electric shock treatment. *American Journal of Psychiatry, 116,* 1113–1114.

Janet, P. (1889). *L'Automatisme psychologique [Psychological automatism].* Paris: Felix Alcan.

Janet, P. (1893). *L'état mental des hystériques [The mental state of hysterics].* Paris: Rueff & Cie.

Jastrow, J. (1932). *The house that Freud built.* New York: Greenberg.

Jones, M. C. (1924). A laboratory study of fear: The case of Peter. *Pedagogical Seminary, 31,* 308–315.

Kazdin, A. E., & Wilcoxon, L. A. (1978). Systematic desensitization and non-specific treatment effects: A methodological evaluation. *Psychological Bulletin, 5,* 729–758.

Kleinmuntz, B. (1967). Sign and seer: Another example. *Journal of Abnormal Psychology, 72,* 163–165.

Kline, P. (1972). *Fact and fantasy in Freudian theory.* London: Methuen.

Kraepelin, E. (1883). *Compendium of psychiatry.* Leipzig: Abel.

Kraepelin, E. (1915). *Psychiatrie: Ein Lehrbuch* [*Textbook of psychiatry*] (8th ed.). Leipzig: Barth.

Krugman, M. (1945). Recent developments in clinical psychology. *Journal of Consulting Psychology, 9,* 342–353.

Liébault, A. A. (1866). *Du sommeil et des etates analogues* [*Sleep and analogous states*]. Paris: Masson.

Locke, J. (1989). *Some thoughts concerning education* (J. W. Yolton & J. S. Yolton, Eds.). New York: Oxford University Press. (Original work published 1693)

Lombroso, C. (1876). *The delinquent man.* Milano: Hoepli.

Luborsky, L., Singer, R., & Luborsky, L. (1975). Comparative studies of psycho-therapies. *Archives of General Psychiatry, 32,* 995–1008.

Maher, W. B., & Maher, B. E. (1985a). Psychopathology: I. From ancient times to the 18th century. In G. A. Kimble & K. Schlesinger (Eds.), *Topics in the history of psychology* (Vol. 2). Hillsdale, NJ: Erlbaum.

Maher, W. B., & Maher, B. E. (1985b). Psychopathology: II. From the 18th century to modern times. In G. A. Kimble & K. Schlesinger (Eds.), *Topics in the history of psychology* (Vol. 2). Hillsdale, NJ: Erlbaum.

Maher, W. B., & Maher, B. E. (2003). Abnormal psychology. In D. K. Freedheim (Ed.), *Handbook of psychology: Vol. 1. History of psychology.* Hoboken, NJ: Wiley.

Maslow, A. H. (1943). A theory of human motivation. *Psychological Review, 50,* 370–396.

Maslow, A. H. (1954). *Motivation and personality.* New York: Harper.

Masson, J. M. (1984). *The assault on truth: Freud's suppression of the seduction theory.* New York: Farrar, Straus, & Giroux.

Matarazzo, J. D. (1985). Psychotherapy. In G. A. Kimble & K. Schlesinger (Eds.), *Topics in the history of psychology* (Vol. 2). Hillsdale, NJ: Erlbaum.

Mayes, R., & Horwitz, A. V. (2005). DSM-III and the revolution in the classification of mental illness. *Journal of the History of the Behavioral Sciences, 41,* 249–267.

McDonald, M. (1981). *Mystical Bedlam—madness, anxiety and healing in seventeenth-century England.* Cambridge: Cambridge University Press.

McDougall, W. (1926). *Outline of abnormal psychology.* New York: Scribner's.

Meduna, L. V. (1935). Experiments on biological influences on the course of schizophrenia. *Zeitschrift fuer die Gesamte Neurologie und Psychiatrie, 152,* 235–262.

Meehl, P. E. (1954). *Clinical vs statistical prediction: A theoretical analysis and review of the evidence.* Minneapolis: University of Minnesota Press.

Mesmer, A. (1948). *Dissertation on the discovery of animal magnetism* (G. Frankau, Trans.). London: Macdonald. (Original work published 1779)

Meyer, A. (1912). Remarks on habit disorganizations in the essential deteriorations. *Nervous and Mental Diseases Monographs,* 95–109.

Miller, N. E., & Dollard, J. (1941). *Social learning and imitation.* New Haven, CT: Yale University Press.

Millon, T. (2004). *Masters of the mind: Exploring the story of mental illness from ancient times to the new millennium.* Hoboken, NJ: Wiley.

Moll, A. (1891). *Die Konträre Sexualempfindung* [*Perversions of the sex instinct*]. Berlin: Fischer.

Monitz, E. (1937). Psycho-chirugie [Psychosurgery]. *Nervenartz, 10,* 113–118.

Morel, B. A. (1857). *Traité des désgénérescences physiques intellectuelles et morales de l'espece humaine* [*Treatise on physical, intellectual, and moral degeneracy in the human species*]. Paris: Baillière.

Moseley, W. E. (1838). *Eleven chapters on nervous and mental complaints.* London: Simpkin, Marshall.

Murchison, C. (1930). *Psychologies of 1930.* Worcester, MA: Clark University Press.

Neaman, J. S. (1975). *Suggestion of the devil.* New York: Anchor.

Neugebauer, R. (1978). Treatment of the mentally ill in medieval and early modern England: A reappraisal. *Journal of the History of the Behavioral Sciences, 14,* 158–169.

Noble, D. (1853). *Elements of psychological medicine.* London: Churchill.

Pickren, W., & Fowler, R. D. (2003). Professional organizations. In D. K. Freedheim (Ed.), *Handbook of psychology*: *Vol. 1. History of psychology.* Hoboken, NJ: Wiley.

Pinel, P. (1798). *Nosographie philosophique* [*Philosophical nosography*]. Paris: Richard, Caille, & Ravier.

Pinel, P. (1806). *Traite medico-philosophique de l'alienation mentale* [*Medical-philosophical treatise on mental alienation*] (D. D. Davis, Trans.). Sheffield: Todd. (Original work published 1801)

Popper, K. R. (1963). *Conjectures and refutations.* London: Routledge & Kegan Paul.

Primbram, K., & Gill, M. (1976). *Freud's "Project" reassessed.* London: Hutchinson.

Prince, M. (1906). *The dissociation of a personality.* New York: Longmans Green.

Prince, M. (1909–1910). Contribution to *Psychotherapeutics, a symposium.* Boston: Badgers.

Rachman, S. J., & Wilson, G. T. (1971). *The effects of psychological therapy.* Oxford: Pergamon Press.

Reisman, J. M. (1991). *A history of clinical psychology* (2nd ed.). New York: Hemisphere.

Rogers, C. R. (1947). Some observations on the organization of personality. *American Psychologist, 2,* 358–368.

Rogers, C. R. (1951). *Client-centered therapy.* Boston: Houghton-Mifflin.

Rogers, C. R. (1966). Client-centered therapy. In S. Arieti (Ed.), *American handbook of psychiatry.* New York: Basic Books.

Rorschach, H. (1921). *Psychodiagnostik [Psychodiagnostic].* Bern: Huber.

Rosen, G. (1968). *Madness in society: Chapters in the historical sociology of mental illness.* London: Routledge & Kegan Paul.

Rosenzweig, S. (1933). Preferences in the repetition of successful and unsuccessful activities as a function of age and personality. *Journal of Genetic Psychology, 42,* 423–441.

Rosenzweig, S. (1986). *The emergence of idiodynamics.* New York: McGraw-Hill.

Rosenzweig, S., & Mason, G. (1934). An experimental study of memory in relation to the theory of repression. *British Journal of Psychology, 24,* 247–265.

Rotter, J. B. (1975). Some problems and misconceptions related to the construct of internal versus external control of reinforcement. *Journal of Consulting and Clinical Psychology, 43,* 56–67.

Routh, D. K. (2000). Clinical psychology training: A history of ideas and practices prior to 1946. *American Psychologist, 55,* 236–241.

Routh, D. K., & Reisman, J. M. (2003). Clinical psychology. In D. K. Freedheim (Ed.), *Handbook of psychology: Vol. 1. History of psychology.* Hoboken, NJ: Wiley.

Rush, B. (1812). *Medical inquiries and observations upon the diseases of the mind.* Philadelphia: Kimber & Richardson.

Rychlak, J. (1988). *The psychology of rigorous humanism* (2nd ed.). New York: New York University Press.

Sackheim, R. A. (1988). Mechanisms of action in electroconvulsive therapy. In A. J. Frances & R. J. Hales (Eds.), *Annual Review of Psychiatry* (Vol. 7). Washington, DC: American Psychiatric Press.

Schoeneman, T. J. (1977). The role of mental illness in the European witch hunts of the sixteenth and seventeenth centuries: An assessment. *Journal of the History of the Behavioral Sciences, 13,* 337–351.

Sedgewick, P. (1982). *Psychopolitics.* New York: Harper & Row.

Seligman, M. E. (1975). *Helplessness.* San Francisco: Freeman.

Sidis, B. (1898). *The psychology of suggestion.* New York: Appleton.

Sidis, B. (1902). *Psychopathological researches: Studies in mental dissociation.* New York: G. E. Stechert.

Sloane, R., Staples, F., Cristol, A., Yorkston, N., & Whipple, K. (1975). *Psychotherapy versus behavior therapy.* Cambridge, MA: Harvard University Press.

Smith, M. L., & Glass, C. V. (1977). Meta-analysis of psychotherapy outcome studies. *American Psychologist, 32,* 752–760.

Smith, M. L., Glass, C. V., & Miller, T. I. (1980). *The benefits of psychotherapy.* Baltimore: Johns Hopkins University Press.

Stahl, J. R., & Leitenberg, H. (1976). Behavioral treatment of the chronic mental hospital patient. In H. Leitenberg (Ed.), *Handbook of behavior modification and behavior therapy.* Englewood Cliffs, NJ: Prentice-Hall.

Stern, W. (1935). On the nature and structure of character. *Character and Personality, 3,* 270–289.

Stern, W. (1938). *General psychology from the personalist standpoint.* (H. D. Spoerl, Trans.). New York: Macmillan.

Storr, A. (1966). The concept of a cure. In C. Rycroft (Ed.), *Psychoanalysis observed.* London: Constable.

Sulloway, F. J. (1979). *Freud, biologist of the mind: Beyond the psychoanalytic legend.* New York: Basic Books.

Szasz, T. S. (1960a). The myth of mental illness. *American Psychologist, 15,* 113–118.

Szasz, T. S. (1960b). *The myth of mental illness.* New York: Harper & Row.

Valenstein, E. S. (1986). *Great and desperate cures.* New York: Basic Books.

von Hartmann, K. E. (1869). *Philosophy of the unconscious.* Berlin: Duncker.

von Krafft-Ebing, R. (1879). *Lehrbuch der Psychiatrie auf klinischer girundlage* [*Textbook of psychiatry on a clinical foundation*]. Stuttgart: Erike.

von Krafft-Ebing, R. (1969). *Psychopathia sexualis* [*Sexual psychopathology*]. New York: Putnam. (Original work published 1886)

Wallerstein, R. S. (1995). *The talking cures: The psychoanalyses and the psychotherapies.* Yale: Yale University Press.

Weiner, D. B. (1979). The apprenticeship of Philippe Pinel: A new document, "Observations of Citizen Pussin on the Insane." *American Journal of Psychiatry, 136,* 1128–1134.

Wilson, M. (1993). DSM and the transformation of America psychiatry: A history. *American Journal of Psychiatry, 150,* 399–410.

Wolpe, J. (1958). *Psychotherapy by reciprocal inhibition.* Stanford, CA: Stanford University Press.

Wolpe, J., & Rachman, S. (1960). Psychoanalytic "evidence": A critique based upon Freud's case of Little Hans. *Journal of Nervous and Mental Disease, 130,* 135–148.

Woodworth, R. S. (1917). Some criticism of Freudian psychology. *Journal of Abnormal Psychology, 12,* 174–194.

Wundt. W. (1888). Hypnotismus und suggestion [Hypnosis and suggestion]. *Philosophische Studien, 8.*

Zwelling, S. S. (1985). *Quest for a cure: The public hospital in Williamsburg, Virginia, 1773–1885.* Williamsburg, VA: Colonial Williamsburg Foundation.

CHAPTER 14

Social and Developmental Psychology

T HE RECOGNITION OF THE **SOCIAL ORIENTATION** OF HUMAN psychology and behavior—the orientation of some aspects of human thought, emotion, and behavior to the represented thought, emotion, and behavior of members of social groups—goes back to antiquity. Aristotle characterized the human being as a "social animal" (*Politics*, I, 2, 1253a2), and medieval scholars acknowledged the critical role of social community in the shaping of human psychology and behavior. Indeed in medieval times, individuals were primarily conceived of as members of social communities:

> To describe an individual was to give an example of the group of which he was a member, and so to offer a particular description of that group and of the relationships within it.
>
> —(Williams, 1961, p. 91)

Many social theorists from Plato to Émile Durkheim (1858–1917) were **holists** who conceived of social groups as supra-individual entities with emergent properties such as social minds: social forms of mentality not reducible to the mental properties of the individual persons who compose social groups. This notion was challenged by individualist social theorists in the 17th and 18th centuries, notably by Thomas Hobbes (1651/1966), who maintained that social groups are nothing more than collections of individuals and that social thought, emotion, and behavior are nothing more than the aggregate thought, emotion, and behavior of collections of individuals, governed by the pursuit of pleasure and avoidance of pain. In a similar vein, the Scottish economist Adam Smith (1723–1790) famously maintained that the distribution of social goods is a product of the individual pursuit of self-interest (Smith, 1776).

Following the Renaissance and Reformation, the medieval conception of the individual as an inseparable member of social groups was displaced by a conception of the individual as independent of social community, as an autonomous rational agent whose psychology and behavior are self-determined (Farr, 1996). When Émile Durkheim represented the emergent social mentality of social groups as analogous to the emergent properties of cells (Durkheim, 1902/1982), such vitalist biological accounts were already under assault from reductive physiologists such as Brücke, du Bois-Reymond, and Helmholtz, who argued that the properties of cells are reducible to the physical and chemical properties of the molecules that compose them (du Bois-Reymond, 1842/1927). Individualistic social theorists likewise insisted that the properties of social groups are reducible to the psychological properties of the individuals that compose them.

SOCIAL PSYCHOLOGY

The notion of a distinctive social psychology of human thought, emotion, and behavior developed from the theories of Giambattista Vico and Johann Gottfried Herder, who recognized the possibility of different forms of psychology and behavior associated with different social communities in different cultures and historical periods. Johann Friedrich Herbart, famous for his individual psychology of representations bound by attractive and repulsive forces, proposed the idea of a separate social psychology of opinions and actions governed by social forces (Herbart, 1821).

Wilhelm von Humboldt related differences in human psychology and behavior to different social communities and their associated linguistic modes of expression (von Humboldt, 1836). He characterized the study of the forms of language and custom associated with different social communities as *Völkerpsychologie*, a designation Moritz Lazarus (1824–1903) employed in his attempt to inaugurate a discipline devoted to the study of different social forms of human psychology, culture, and language.

In the late 19th century, Émile Durkheim, the founding father of sociology (who visited Wundt's laboratory in Leipzig in the 1880s), distinguished between social and individual forms of thought, emotion, and behavior, which he characterized as the respective subject matters of social and individual psychology (Durkheim, 1895/1982). Durkheim characterized social forms of thought, emotion, and behavior as those associated with the membership of distinctive social groups, such as the forms of thought, emotion, and behavior characteristic of Catholics as opposed to Protestants, or liberal democrats as opposed to socialists, and appealed to such differences to explain the different rates of suicide among different social groups (Durkheim, 1897). Max Weber (1864–1920), the founder of German sociology, similarly characterized social action as action oriented to the represented actions of members of social groups (Weber, 1922/1978).

Around the same time, Gustave Le Bon (1841–1931) and Gabriel Tarde (1843–1904) developed theories of **crowd psychology** (Le Bon, 1895/1896; Tarde,

1890/1903, 1901). Le Bon and Tarde claimed that the irrational and emotional behavior of individuals in crowds is the product of suggestibility and imitation, echoing turn-of-the-century concerns about the threats posed to civilization by democratic assemblies, trial by jury, and universal suffrage (Nye, 1975; van Ginneken, 1985, 1992). Le Bon and Tarde associated the irrational and emotional behavior of crowds with abnormal behavior, likening the behavior of individuals in crowds to individuals in a hypnotic state: "Society is imitation and imitation is a form of somnambulism" (Tarde, 1890, p. 87). The Harvard psychiatrist Morton Prince institutionalized this early association of social and abnormal psychology. He included papers on social psychology in the *Journal of Abnormal Psychology* (founded in 1906) and changed the name of the journal to the *Journal of Abnormal and Social Psychology* in 1917.

Durkheim and Weber rejected the crowd psychology of Le Bon and Tarde by distinguishing between social thought, emotion, and behavior (oriented to the represented thought, emotion, and behavior of members of social groups) and merely imitated behavior. Durkheim insisted that

> Imitation does not always express, indeed never expresses, what is essential and characteristic in the social fact. Doubtless every social fact is imitated and has, as we have just shown, a tendency to become generalized, but this *is because it is social, i.e. obligatory.*
>
> —(1895, p. 59)

Weber claimed that merely imitated actions, such as imitating the manner in which another sets a fishing line, or following another in a crowd, are not instances of social action:

> Mere imitation of the action of others . . . will not be considered a case of specifically social action if it is purely reactive. . . . The mere fact that a person is found to employ some apparently useful procedure which he learned from someone else does not, however, constitute, in the present sense, social action.
>
> —(1922/1978, pp. 23–24)

For Weber, action based upon imitation counts as social action only when "the action of others is imitated because it is fashionable or traditional or exemplary" or when it is based upon "a justified expectation on the part of members of a group that a customary rule will be adhered to" (1922/1978, p. 24).

Albert Schäffle (1831–1903), Ludwig Gumplowicz (1838–1909), and Gustav Ratzenhofer (1842–1904) developed the notion of a distinctive social psychology within sociology, and their work was discussed by early American sociologists and social psychologists (Bogardus, 1922; Small, 1905; Small & Vincent, 1894; Ward, 1883). Albion Small (1854–1926) and George Vincent's (1864–1941)

Introduction to the Study of Society (1894) was largely responsible for the American dissemination of the work of European social theorists, including Georg Simmel (1858–1918), perhaps the most social psychological of the early sociologists (Simmel, 1894, 1908).

Early German and American Social Psychology

The social dimensions of human psychology and behavior were also recognized by the founding fathers of psychology in Germany and America. Wundt maintained that certain forms of human psychology and behavior are grounded in social community:

> All such products of a general character presuppose as a condition the existence of a mental *community* composed of many individuals.
>
> —(Wundt, 1897/1902, p. 23, original emphasis)

Like Durkheim, Wundt distinguished social from individual or experimental psychology on the grounds that the objects of social as opposed to individual or experimental psychology are grounded in the membership of social groups:

> Because of this dependence on the community, in particular the social community, this whole department of psychological investigation is designated as *social psychology*, and distinguished from individual, or as it may be called because of its predominating method, *experimental* psychology.
>
> —(Wundt, 1897/1902, p. 23, original emphasis)

Wundt thought that the experimental study of elemental conscious processes needed to be supplemented by the historical-comparative study of the "mental products" of social communities, such as language, myth, and custom, and spent most of his later years developing this form of psychology in his 10–volume *Völkerpsychologie* (1900–1920).

Wundt's student Oswald Külpe, the founder of the Würzburg School, also acknowledged that socially engaged psychological states and behavior form the subject matter of a distinctive social psychology.

> Social psychology treats of the mental phenomena dependent upon a community of individuals; it is already a special department of study, if not a fully developed science.
>
> —(Külpe, 1895, p. 7)

Few of Wundt's returning American students showed much interest in the development of *Völkerpsychologie*. Yet many early American scientific psychologists, including both structuralist psychologists such as Edward B. Titchener and functionalist psychologists such as James R. Angell, followed Wundt in recognizing the distinct identity as well as the value of social psychology, conceived of as a discipline concerned with those psychological states and behaviors that are grounded in the membership of social groups:

> Just as the scope of psychology extends beyond man to the animals, so too does it extend from the individual man to groups of men, to societies.
>
> —(Titchener, 1910, p. 28)

> Social psychology, in its broadest sense, has to do mainly with the psychological principles involved in those expressions of mental life which take form in social relations, organizations, and practices.
>
> —(Angell, 1908, p. 4)

William James, often represented as the founder of American psychology, also recognized the possibility of a distinctive social psychology of socially oriented psychology and behavior. In a famous section of the *Principles*, James described the various **social selves** that can be attributed to individuals, conceived of as complexes of beliefs, attitudes, emotions, and habits associated with membership in different social groups:

> We may practically say that he has as many social selves as there are distinct *groups* of persons about whose opinion he cares. He generally shows a different side of himself to each of these different groups. Many a youth who is demure enough before his parents and teachers, swears and swaggers like a pirate among his "tough" young friends. We do not show ourselves to our children as to our club companions, to our customers as to the laborers we employ, to our own masters and employers as to our intimate friends. From this there results what practically is a division of the man into several selves; and this may be a discordant splitting, as when one is afraid to let one set of his acquaintances know him as he is elsewhere; or it may be a perfectly harmonious division of labor, as where one tender to his children is stern to the soldiers or prisoners under his command.
>
> —(James, 1890, p. 294)

The psychological tension produced in individuals by the social orientation of much of their psychology and behavior to different social groups (such as family, friends, profession, and religion) was a popular topic for early American social psychologists (Cooley, 1902; Faris, 1925; La Piere, 1938).

The first American textbooks in social psychology were *Social Psychology* (1908) by Edward A. Ross (1866–1951) and *Introduction to Social Psychology* (1908) by William McDougall. In *Social Psychology* (and *Social Control*, 1906), Ross argued that the subtle social influences on human psychology and behavior could be identified and surmounted (or exploited) by a scientific social psychology. McDougall is often represented as having advocated an individualistic biological position in *Introduction to Social Psychology*, but this work was intended as a preliminary to the study of the social orientation of human psychology and behavior, which McDougall considered to be the distinctive subject matter of social psychology, or collective or group psychology.

Although *Introduction to Social Psychology* focused on human instincts, McDougall followed Ross in arguing for the critical importance of the "social environment" in the determination of human psychology and behavior. He maintained that the

> very important advance in psychology toward usefulness is due to the increasing recognition that the adult human mind is the product of the moulding influence exerted by the social environment, and of the fact that the strictly individual human mind, with which alone the older introspective and descriptive psychology concerned itself, is an abstraction merely and has no real existence.
>
> —(McDougall, 1908, p. 16)

McDougall's *Introduction to Social Psychology* dealt with the first part of what he considered to be the "fundamental problem of social psychology":

> For social psychology has to show how, given the native propensities and capacities of the individual human mind, all the complex mental life of societies is shaped by them and in turn reacts upon the course of their development and operation in the individual.
>
> —(McDougall, 1908, p. 18)

The second part McDougall dealt with in *The Group Mind* (1920), which represented his attempt to determine "the general principles of collective mental life which are incapable of being deduced from the laws of the mental life of isolated individuals" (McDougall, 1920, pp. 7–8). McDougall's reference to "isolated individuals" was not to individuals who are physically isolated from each other (the contrast class of theorists of crowd behavior), but to individuals "in the absence of the system of relations that render them a society" (1920, p. 9).

Ross was a sociologist and McDougall a psychologist, and in the early decades of the 20th century the social orientation of human psychology and behavior was explored by social psychologists working in both departments of sociology (Bogardus, 1924a, 1924b; Ellwood, 1924, 1925; Faris, 1925; Thomas, 1904; Thomas & Znaniecki, 1918; Young, 1925, 1930, 1931) and psychology (Dunlap, 1925; Kantor, 1922; Katz & Schanck, 1938; McDougall, 1920; Wallis, 1925, 1935).

These social psychologists all maintained that socially oriented forms of human psychology and behavior constitute the distinctive subject matter of **social** (or group or collective) **psychology**. They distinguished socially oriented psychology and behavior from individual psychology and behavior, the product of reasons or causes operating independently of social orientation, such as self-interest or instinct, and held that such individual psychology and behavior constitute the subject matter of **individual psychology.** Thus Knight Dunlap, for example, maintained that

> One of the outstanding characteristics of the human individual is his associating in groups of various kinds. These groups are not mere collections of people, but possess psychological characteristics binding the individuals together or organizing them in complicated ways.
>
> Human groups are the manifestation of the social nature of man. . . . The psychological study of man is therefore not complete until we have investigated his groupings, and analyzed the mental factors involved therein. This study is *social psychology*, or *group psychology*.
>
> —(Dunlap, 1925, p. 11)

These social psychologists held that human psychology and behavior is socially oriented to a wide range of social groups, from simple friendship dyads to whole societies, including families, clubs, professions, religious groups, unions, political parties, states, and nations (Ellwood, 1925; McDougall, 1920).

A frequent focus of early American social psychology was the study of social attitudes, conceived of as attitudes associated with membership of social groups such as political or religious groups or particular professions or trades, which Emory S. Bogardus (1882–1973) characterized as **occupational attitudes**:

> Each occupation has its characteristic attitudes, which, taken in the large, may be referred to here as the occupational attitude. . . . each occupation is characterized by social attitudes and values peculiar to itself.
>
> —(Bogardus, 1924a, p. 172)

Such social attitudes were frequently appealed to in the explanation of prejudice and stereotypes:

> The individual manifestation of race prejudice cannot be understood apart from a consideration of group attitudes. In collecting data it often happens that the investigator finds cases of the acquisition of a prejudice with astonishing suddenness and as the result of a single experience. But this could only happen in a milieu where there was a pre-existing group attitude. One who has no negro prejudice can acquire

it from a single encounter but it is the group attitude that makes it possible for him to acquire it.

—(Faris, 1925, p. 405)

Individualistic Social Psychology

In the early decades of the 20th century, American social psychologists working in departments of psychology and sociology conceived of social psychology as the study of those aspects of human psychology and behavior that are oriented to the represented psychology and behavior of members of social groups, a conception shared by European psychologists (Bartlett, 1932; Piaget, 1932) and sociologists such as Durkheim, Weber, and Simmel. However, this conception was gradually abandoned by American social psychologists as the 20th century developed, when Floyd Allport (1890–1971), sometimes characterized as the founder of American scientific or experimental social psychology (Katz, 1991), challenged it.

Floyd Allport studied with Hugo Münsterberg, who suggested that Allport write his dissertation on social facilitation, conceived of as interpersonal influences on human psychology and behavior. Allport's work on social facilitation was based upon the comparative experimental study of human performance on a variety of perceptual, motor, and cognitive tasks, in the presence and absence of other persons. Münsterberg had introduced Allport to the work of Walther Moede (1888–1958), who called his own form of experimental social psychology experimental crowd psychology (Moede, 1914, 1920), and educational psychologists such as Ernst Meumann, since much of the early work on social facilitation was based upon the performance of schoolchildren working alone or together (F. Allport, 1974). In his own experimental studies, Allport found that performance on many perceptual and motor tasks improves in the presence of others, while performance on some cognitive tasks deteriorates (F. Allport, 1920). Allport accepted a position at the University of North Carolina at Chapel Hill in 1922, but later moved to Syracuse University, where he spent the majority of his academic career (from 1924 to 1956).

Allport did not directly challenge the original conception of the social orientation of human psychology and behavior, but launched a critical attack on the notion of the social mind frequently associated with it. The notion of a social or group mind figured in the writings of many early social psychologists, including Wundt and McDougall, who titled his second work on social psychology *The Group Mind* (McDougall, 1920). Allport attacked this notion with great vigor and characterized theoretical commitment to the existence of a social or group mind as the **group fallacy**. He claimed that this fallacy derived from the misguided attempt to explain "social phenomena in terms of the group as a whole, whereas the true explanation is to be found only in its component parts, the individuals" (1924b, p. 60). He also claimed that the group fallacy was responsible for the mistaken belief that "it is possible to have a 'group psychology' as distinct from the psychology of individuals" (1924b, p. 62). In *Social Psychology* Allport famously claimed that

> There is no psychology of groups that is not essentially and entirely a psychology of individuals. Social psychology must not be placed in contradistinction to the psychology of the individual; it is part of the psychology of the individual, whose behavior it studies in relation to that sector of his environment comprised by his fellows.
>
> —(1924a, p. 4)

He consequently redefined the subject matter of social psychology, now conceived of as a branch of individual psychology, as **interpersonal psychological states and behavior**—that is, as psychological states and behavior relating to other persons:

> Social psychology is the science which studies the behavior of the individual insofar as his behavior stimulates other individuals, or is itself a reaction to their behavior; and which describes the consciousness of the individuals insofar as it is a consciousness of social objects and social reactions.
>
> —(F. Allport, 1924a, p. 12)

In contrast to the earlier conception of social-psychological states and behavior (in which social and individual behavior were distinguished in terms of their orientation to or independence from the represented behavior of members of social groups), Allport distinguished social and individual behavior in terms of whether or not it is directed toward other persons:

> Social behavior comprises the stimulations and reactions arising between an individual and the *social* portion of his environment; that is, between the individual and his fellows. Examples of such behavior would be the reaction to language, gestures, and other movements of our fellow men, in contrast with our reactions towards nonsocial objects, such as plants, minerals, tools, and inclement weather.
>
> —(Allport, 1924a, p. 3)

The contrast may be illustrated by noting that most early American social psychologists maintained that social behavior need not be directed toward other persons, such as the social behavior of the solitary genuflector or golfer (La Piere, 1938) and can be directed toward nonpersons, such as the social behavior of individuals who avoid walking under ladders or paint landscapes rather than portraits (Thomas & Znaniecki, 1918).

Allport was an avowed behaviorist, but his rejection of the social mind was based more upon his empiricist commitment to the principle of explanatory reduction than upon any behaviorist rejection of cognition or consciousness. Allport maintained that the social psychological is reducible to the individual psychological in precisely the same fashion as the psychological is reducible to the physiological and the physiological to the electrochemical: "In the hierarchy of sciences the field of description of one science becomes the field of explanation for the science immediately above it" (1924b, p. 69). This was a reductive commitment Allport shared with empiricist philosophers such as Hobbes and reductive physiologists such as von Brücke, du Bois-Reymond, and Helmholtz, rather than with behaviorists such as Watson, who in fact insisted on the autonomy of behaviorist explanation with respect to physiology and electrochemistry (Watson, 1919).

Allport's own commitment to behaviorism was lukewarm. He maintained that it was a "serious mistake" to believe that "consciousness has no place in a science of behavior" and suggested that "consciousness accompanying reactions which are not readily observable . . . furnishes us with valuable evidence of these reactions, and thus aids in our selection of explanatory principles" (1924b, p. 3). Although he paid lip service to Watson's famous denial that cognitive states ever function as inner causes (1924a, p. 2), he regularly appealed to cognitive "impressions of universality" and pathological "projections" of beliefs and emotions in the causal explanation of crowd behavior, social behavior, and "conformity behavior" (1924a, 1934). Like many early social psychologists, including other avowed behaviorists such the psychologist Knight Dunlap and the sociologist Emory Bogardus, Allport maintained that a central focus of social psychology should be the study of social attitudes, albeit reconceived as merely "common attitudes" directed toward other persons (1924a, p. 6).

Allport followed those behaviorists who questioned the scope of explanations of human behavior in terms of inherited instincts (Bernard, 1921; Dunlap, 1919; Kuo, 1921; Watson, 1924), notably the multiplicity of human instincts postulated by William McDougall in his *Introduction to Social Psychology* (1908). However, like most social psychologists, he also recognized that instincts play a role in the explanation of behavior, albeit redescribed as "drives" (Dunlap, 1925) or "prepotent reflexes" (Allport, 1924a).

Although Allport's critique of some of the more extreme claims about the social or group mind advanced by theorists such as Wallis (1925, 1935) and McDougall (1920) was warranted, their own advocacy of a distinctive social psychology directed to the study of socially oriented psychology and behavior was independent of their commitment to the notion of an emergent social or group mind. Other social psychologists, such as Dunlap (1925), Kantor (1922), La Piere (1938), and Ross (1908), advocated a distinctive social psychology of socially oriented psychology and behavior while repudiating the notion of a social or group mind. However, many later social psychologists followed Allport in rejecting the notion of a distinctive social psychology along with the notion of an emergent social or group mind. With some justification McDougall later regretted that he had made a "tactical error" in talking about the group mind.

Individualism and Social Psychology   There were other reasons why the notion of a distinctive social psychology of socially oriented psychology and behavior was abandoned. Allport represented the social orientation of thought, emotion, and behavior as a threat to liberal principles of rational self-determination or the "sovereignty of the individual," which had been promoted in the 19th century by John Stuart Mill in Britain and Josiah Warren (1798–1894) in America. Allport likened socially oriented thought, emotion, and behavior to the impetuous and irrational behavior of crowds (as had Le Bon and Tarde). In "The J-Curve Hypothesis of Conforming Behavior" (1934), he noted that the statistical distribution of "conforming" behavior, such as Episcopalians bowing in silent prayer before church service and motorists stopping before a red light, tends to be highly asymmetrical, in contrast to the normal symmetrical distribution of behavior expressive of random personality differences. Allport treated the J-shaped distribution of "conforming" behavior as psychologically as well as statistically abnormal, representing a pathological form of "crowd-like subservience" (1934, p. 396).

In *Institutional Psychology* (1933), Allport railed against socially oriented thought, emotion, and behavior, which he believed posed a threat to society as well as the autonomy of individuals. In a similar vein, his brother Gordon Allport associated socially oriented thought, emotion, and behavior with the ideology of totalitarian states, which he claimed to be a product of commitment to the notion of a supra-individual group mind:

> According to Hegel's idealistic philosophy there is only one Mind. . . . It works itself out in the course of history. Individual men are but its agents. Its principal focus is in the state, which is therefore the chief agent of divine life on earth. Each state has, in fact it *is*, a group mind. It has its own laws of growth and development (the dialectic) and while it makes much use of individuals, it is by no means reducible to their transitory mental life. Marx, as well as Hitler, was among the sinister spiritual children of Hegel. Like him, they equated personal freedom with obedience to the group, morality with discipline, personal growth with the prosperity of the party, class, or state. *Du bist nichts: dein Volk ist alles* was the Nazi rallying cry.
>
> We can trace Hegel's psychological influence in several directions. As we have said, it underlay Karl Marx's exaltation of social class as a superindividual entity. In Britain, Bosanquet and Green were among the political followers who, following Hegel, viewed the state as an organic mind transcending the component minds of individuals, and demanding "sober daily loyalty." It is hardly necessary to point out that psychological apologists for racism and nationalism . . . tend no less than Hegel to apotheosize the group mind, as represented by the state, race, folk, or *Kultur*.
>
> —(1954, pp. 34–35)

Yet this critical association was unfairly directed to advocates of a distinctive social or group psychology such as Wundt and McDougall. The Nazis burnt copies of Wundt's *Völkerpsychologie* (1900–1920) precisely because Nazi apologists such as von Eickstedt (1933) insisted that race should be defined by blood rather than by social community, as Wundt had maintained (Brock, 1992). Moreover, the historical disciples of Wundt, notably the social anthropologist Franz Boas and his followers, were among the staunchest critics of the racist policies of Nazi Germany (Boas, 1934/1945).

McDougall repudiated the association with Hegel's philosophy and totalitarianism and tried to defend a form of **communitarian individualism**, in which human individuality is attained "in and through the community" (1920, p. 17). This he opposed to the form of **autonomy individualism** based upon rational self-determination, associated with utilitarianism and laissez-faire economics, which he claimed promoted an ideal of individual liberty that "was proving destructive of the real liberty of the vast majority" (1920, p. 17). Yet the association stuck, with the consequence that socially oriented forms of human psychology and behavior came to be represented in the later social-psychological literature as individually and socially subversive forms of "other-directed" behavior (Krech, Crutchfield, & Ballachey, 1962, after Riesman, 1950), "group-think" (Janis, 1968), "conformity" (Kiesler & Kiesler, 1969), and "obedience" (Milgram, 1963, 1974).

Of course, the idea that socially oriented thought, emotion, and behavior posed a threat to human individuality and society was no reason for excluding it as the subject matter of a distinctive social psychology. Ross (1908) had maintained that the goal of a distinctive social psychology was precisely to identify such social influences on human psychology and behavior so that individuals could surmount them. Social psychologists such as Daniel Katz (1903–1998) and Richard Schanck (1902–) noted that socially oriented thought and behavior need not be involuntary or regimented, but may be freely embraced by members of a social group: "The uniform activities of a group of people may represent their fundamental wishes very well" (Katz & Schanck, 1938, p. 9).

Experimental Social Psychology   The individualistic and experimental approach to social psychology that Floyd Allport promoted was already well represented by the 1930s in Gardner Murphy (1895–1979) and Lois B. Murphy's (1902–2003) book-length survey *Experimental Social Psychology* (Murphy & Murphy, 1931; Murphy, Murphy, & Newcomb, 1937) and John F. Dashiell's (1888–1975) chapter on experimental social psychology in the 1935 *Handbook of Social Psychology* (Murchison, 1935). Within this evolving experimental tradition, Norman Triplett's (1861–1910) study of pacemaking and competition among cyclists and children playing games (Triplett, 1898) came to be treated as the first experiment in social psychology (Haines & Vaughan, 1979), and the experimental method came to be seen as providing the best hope and promise of a genuinely scientific social psychology:

> From the experiments of Triplett to the appearance of Allport's studies it was becoming steadily clearer that social psychology could advance by the experimental method.
>
> —(Murphy, Murphy, & Newcomb, 1937, p. 13)

An essential feature of this individualistic and experimental approach to social psychology was the denial of any real distinction between social and individual psychology. The assumption that all social behavior could be accommodated by the explanatory resources of individual psychology was clearly if somewhat quaintly expressed by Dashiell in his chapter on experimental social psychology in the 1935 *Handbook of Social Psychology*:

> Particularly it is to be borne in mind that in this objective stimulus-response relationship to his fellows we have to deal with no radically new concepts, no principles essentially different to those applying to non-social situations.
>
> —(1935, p. 1097)

This individual and experimental form of social psychology was grounded more in the crowd psychology of Le Bon, Tarde, and Moede than the socially oriented psychology of Wundt, MacDougall, and Dunlap (as Allport freely acknowledged). For Le Bon, Tarde, and Moede, the "social" behavior of individuals in crowds was contrasted with the behavior of individuals physically isolated from each other. Thus Le Bon maintained that individuals in a crowd

> feel, think and act in a manner quite different from that in which each individual of them would feel, think and act were he in a state of isolation.
>
> —(1895, p. 2)

For Wundt, MacDougall, and Dunlap, socially oriented behavior was contrasted with individual behavior, such as instinctual or rational behavior not oriented to the represented psychology and behavior of members of social groups, irrespective of the physical proximity of other persons. Thus Dunlap insisted that socially oriented thought and behavior can be engaged in the *absence* of other persons, including members of one's own social group:

> "Social consciousness" . . . is the consciousness (in the individual, of course) of others in *the group*. . . . The consciousness of others may be perceptual, or it may be ideational. One may be conscious of one's membership in the Lutheran Church, or

in the group of atheists, when physically alone; and this group consciousness *may* be as important and as vivid under such circumstances as when one is physically surrounded by members of the group.

—(1925, p. 19)

Yet it was the conception of social groups as crowds that shaped the form of experimental social psychology that Allport and later generations of social psychologists embraced. Allport treated experimental "social" groups as "small crowds" (Allport, 1924a, p. 260), as aggregates of individuals assembled for some experimental task. He distinguished between **co-acting** and **face-to-face** experimental groups, without any reference to the social orientation or affiliation of the members of experimental groups, who were normally strangers to each other. Co-acting groups were defined as groups in which "the individuals are primarily occupied with some stimulus rather than one another. The social stimuli in operation [from other persons] are therefore merely *contributory*" (1924a, p. 260). Face-to-face (or "interacting") groups were defined as groups in which "the individuals react mainly or entirely to one another" and so "the social stimulations in effect are of a *direct* order" (1924a, p. 261).

Allport's equation of social and crowd behavior was extended to include the behavior of dispersed populations, which Gabriel Tarde (1901) had called **publics** (King, 1990). Social attitude research came to be replaced by **public opinion** research, which comprised surveys of the common attitudes or opinions of physically dispersed aggregations of individuals, independently of their social orientation or affiliation. This was stimulated in large part by the development of instruments for the measurement of individual attitudes (Likert, 1932; Thurstone, 1931; Thurstone & Chave, 1929).

Nevertheless, the original conception of the social orientation of human psychology and behavior was not abandoned overnight. The 1935 *Handbook of Social Psychology* contained a fairly eclectic set of approaches. This work included Dashiell's chapter on experimental social psychology, but it also included chapters on social attitudes, the comparative psychology of the negro, the white man, the red man, and the yellow man, and the social psychology of primates—not to mention the social psychology of fish and flowers! Moreover, the social orientation of attitudes and behavior continued to be explored from the 1930s to the 1950s through a variety of methods, including experimental methods. Representative studies included Solomon Asch's experimental studies of conformity (1951; Asch, Block, & Hertzman, 1938), Muzafer Sherif's studies of the formation of social norms (1935, 1936), Theodore Newcomb's longitudinal study of attitude change at Bennington College (Newcomb, 1943), and Leon Festinger, H. W. Reiken, and Stanley Schachter's study of millennium cults (Festinger, Reiken, & Schachter, 1956).

Social Psychology in the Postwar Period

The original conception of the social orientation of human psychology and behavior underwent a brief renaissance in the years immediately following the Second World War, notably through the work of Solomon Asch (1907–1996) and Muzafer Sherif (1906–1988). This was largely a product of the interdisciplinary links forged between psychologists and sociologists, psychiatrists, and anthropologists during the war. Social psychologists worked with their social science colleagues in the Army Information and Education Division, the Office of Strategic Services, and the National Research Council. They contributed to the U.S. Strategic Bombing Survey (1946), the study of morale and propaganda (G. Watson, 1942), and the investigation of the attitudes and adjustment of combat troops (Stouffer, Lumsdaine, et al., 1949; Stouffer, Suchman, et al., 1949).

These collaborative efforts generated considerable optimism about the possibility of developing social psychology as a genuinely interdisciplinary science. New research facilities were created, such as the Survey Research Center in Washington, and new interdisciplinary programs were set up, such as the Department of Social Relations at Harvard and the doctoral program in social psychology at the University of Michigan. Wartime work on communication and attitude change (Hovland, Lumsdaine, & Sheffield, 1949) was continued at Yale through the Communication and Attitude Change Program.

Kurt Lewin set up the first doctoral program in group psychology at MIT in 1946, where he initiated a creative experimental program focused on group processes and socially relevant "action research" (Lewin, 1948, 1951). Lewin, who famously maintained "there is nothing so practical as a good theory," was also a political activist. He was instrumental in the founding of the Society for the Psychological Study of Social Issues (SPSSI, now Division 9 of the APA) and worked vigorously for the Commission of Community Interrelations (which he also helped to establish) in New York City. Faculty and students in the MIT program included Leon Festinger, Harold H. Kelley, John Thibaut, Dorwin Cartwright, and Stanley Schachter, all destined to play a significant role in the development of postwar social psychology. When Lewin died in 1947, the program moved to the University of Michigan, where Theodore M. Newcomb headed it.

Postwar texts in social psychology, such as Theodore Newcomb and Eugene L. Hartley's *Readings in Social Psychology* (1947) and David Krech and Richard S. Crutchfield's *Theory and Problems of Social Psychology* (1948), championed an interdisciplinary approach and bemoaned the divergence between "psychological" and "sociological" social psychology that had developed in the years before the war (Newcomb, 1951). The Krech and Crutchfield text, like the Asch (1952) and Sherif (1948) texts, paid homage to the general principles of Gestalt psychology, as did much of the early work of Kurt Lewin. New theoretical concepts such as Herbert

H. Hyman's (1918–1985) notion of social **reference groups** (1942), to which attitudes and behavior are socially oriented, brought hope of a genuine integration of divergent disciplinary perspectives:

> Although this theory is still in the initial stages of development, because of the problems it formulates it promises to be of central importance to social psychology. In particular it is important to those social scientists who desire to interpret the development of attitudes, to predict their expression under different social conditions, to understand the social basis of their stability or resistance to change, or to devise means of increasing or overcoming this resistance. . . . Through . . . research and conceptual development . . . we may expect great advances in our understanding of the social basis of attitudes.
>
> —(Kelley, 1952)

However, the postwar interdisciplinary enthusiasm was short-lived. The scramble for research funds by psychologists and sociologists encouraged as much competition as cooperation. Psychologists continued to dominate the institutional academic delivery of social psychology, including the journals and textbooks, as they had done prior to the war. Sociologists naturally resented this, and many of the interdisciplinary programs created after the war fractured along disciplinary lines (such the programs at Michigan and Harvard). Beyond the interdisciplinary rhetoric, graduate students had to specialize in psychology or sociology (or anthropology or psychiatry) and prepare themselves for an institutional academic world still rigidly divided along traditional disciplinary lines (Collier, Minton, & Reynolds, 1991). Most chose to specialize in psychology, and even within sociology, "psychological" forms of social psychology came to dominate (Burgess, 1977; Liska, 1977). While early sociological social psychologists such as Baldwin, Cooley, and Mead had followed James in recognizing the social dimensions of the self (Baldwin, 1897; Cooley, 1902; Mead, 1934), in the postwar period sociological social psychologists such as Harold Blumer (1900–1987) focused primarily on interpersonal interaction (Blumer, 1969, 1984), developing what became known as the "symbolic interactionist" tradition in sociological social psychology.

Moreover, even the most enthusiastic advocates of interdisciplinary integration, such as Krech and Crutchfield (1948), maintained the Allport line that social psychology is just a branch of individual psychology. The explosion of experimental studies of "small group" processes in the 1950s and early 1960s, largely inspired by Lewin's program of research on "group processes" (Cartwright & Zandler, 1953), was followed by a precipitous decline in the late 1960s and early 1970s (McGrath, 1978; Steiner, 1974). Social psychologists quickly lost interest in social reference groups (Singer, 1988), and many of Lewin's former associates and colleagues pursued their own individualistic cognitive programs of research

(Patnoe, 1988). Leon Festinger, one of Lewin's former students at the University of Iowa and later his colleague at MIT, abandoned his earlier interest in social groups and developed his influential theory of "cognitive dissonance" (Festinger, 1957). By the late 1960s most social psychologists had come to endorse Gordon Allport's oft-quoted interpersonal definition of the subject matter of social psychology, in terms of the relation of thought, emotion, and behavior to other persons:

> With few exceptions, social psychologists attempt to understand and explain how the thought, feeling, and behavior of individuals are influenced by the actual, imagined, or implied presence of other human beings.
>
> —(G. Allport, 1954, p. 5)

The dominant research programs of the postwar decades were individualistic and cognitive in orientation, such as those developed from cognitive consistency theory (Abelson & Rosenberg, 1958), exchange theory (Thibaut & Kelley, 1959), attribution theory (Bem, 1967), interpersonal attraction (Kelley, 1950), and person perception (Heider, 1958). The *Journal of Abnormal and Social Psychology* abandoned its link with social psychology in 1965, and the *Journal of Personality and Social Psychology* was instituted as the premier journal in social psychology. The *Journal of Experimental Social Psychology* was also founded in 1965.

Although research continued on "social" groups, it focused almost exclusively on the reaction of individuals in experimental groups to manipulated independent variables. Subjects in experimental groups in social psychology were randomly assigned to different treatment conditions. In consequence, very few studies were able to explore the social orientation of human psychology and behavior, since subjects were rarely selected according to their social group orientation or affiliation. Thus McGrath's 1978 review of the "small-group" experimental literature could exhaustively classify the experimental research surveyed under Allport's categories of "co-acting" and "interacting" ("face-to-face") groups (McGrath, 1978).

Although prewar research had employed a variety of methodologies, postwar research became dominated by experimentation, which came to be perceived as the most (or only) reliable means of evaluating causal explanations in social psychology. Christie (1965) contrasted the 30 percent of experimental studies reported in the *Journal of Abnormal and Social Psychology* in 1948 with the 83 percent reported in 1958. Higbee and Wells (1972) compared articles published in the 1969 *Journal of Personality and Social Psychology* with Christie's (1965) study of the *Journal of Abnormal and Social Psychology*, and noted that 87 percent of the *Journal of Personality and Social Psychology* studies employed experimental manipulation. The later study by Higbee, Millard, and Folkman (1982) confirmed that the trend continued throughout the 1970s.

According to Winston (1990), the common definition of experimentation in psychology in terms of the manipulation of independent variables (while holding other variables constant, and observing the effects upon dependent variables) was first introduced by Edwin G. Boring in *The Physical Dimensions of Consciousness* (1933, pp. 9–10) and popularized in psychology through Robert Woodworth's *Experimental Psychology* (1938). Woodworth also promoted the notion that experimentation is the best, if not the only means of identifying causes, by distinguishing experimentation from other comparative and correlational methods. The use of this definition of experimentation (in terms of the manipulation of independent variables) in psychology texts increased dramatically from the 1930s to the 1970s, from around 5 percent in the 1930s to around 95 percent in the 1970s (Winston & Blais, 1996). More remarkably, the use of this definition of experimentation increased earlier and more dramatically in social psychology than in general experimental psychology (Danziger & Dzinas, 1997).

In the early postwar years, social psychologists accepted that social-group orientation could be explored experimentally, since they allowed that social-group orientation could be treated as an independent variable. For example, A. L. Edwards (1954) and Leon Festinger (1953) treated the preselection of subjects according to political party and religious affiliation as the experimental manipulation of variables, as in Edwards's (1941) study of political orientation and recognition and Festinger's (1947) study of "group-belongingness" and voting behavior. The first and second editions of *Research Methods in Social Relations* allowed that from a "logical point of view" the manipulation of variables is not strictly necessary for experimental inquiry (Jahoda, Deutsch, & Cook, 1951, p. 59) and that "equality" of experimental treatment groups could be attained via methods other than randomization, such as subject matching or frequency-distribution control (Selltiz, Jahoda, Deutsch, & Cook, 1959, pp. 77–80).

However, the social-psychological definition of experimentation became increasingly restrictive as the postwar decades progressed. By the third and fourth editions of *Research Methods in Social Relations*, "true experiments" were defined as those in which potential confounding variables are excluded via randomization (Selltiz, Wrightsman, & Cook, 1976), and "subject" or "organismic" variables, including social variables such as political- or religious-group affiliation, were treated as confounding variables (Kidder, 1981, p. 19). Crano and Brewer's *Principles of Research in Social Psychology* (1973, p. 33) defined "true experiments" as manipulations involving the random assignment of subjects to "treatment" groups. This restrictive conception of the experiment was enshrined in the later editions of the *Handbook of Social Psychology*. The random assignment of subjects to experimental conditions was originally seen as a "major advantage" of experimentation (Aronson & Carlsmith, 1968, p. 7), but the later handbooks affirmed that "the essence of an experiment is the random assignment of participants to experimental conditions" (Aronson, Wilson & Brewer, 1998, p. 112). Recent studies of research trends in social psychology from the 1960s to the 1990s have documented the increasing dominance of "true experiments" employing the random assignment of subjects to experimental treatment conditions (Reis & Stiller, 1992; Sherman et al., 1999; West, Newsom, & Fenaughty, 1992), which effectively precluded the experimental study of the social orientation of human psychology and behavior, since such social variables were treated as confounding variables (Greenwood, 2004).

The Crisis in Social Psychology Not everyone was happy with the way social psychology developed in the postwar decades. Some lamented the abandonment of the integrative visions of the 1950s and expressed concern about "the continuing and growing fragmentation of the discipline" (Katz, 1967, p. 341). Others complained about the increasingly asocial nature of the discipline (Sherif, 1977; Tajfel, 1972). However, the specifically social focus of these critical voices was almost obliterated by the cacophony of metatheoretical, methodological, and moral critiques that constituted the 1970s **crisis in social psychology** (Elms, 1975).

Over and above complaints about the impoverished and fragmented nature of social-psychological theory, there were serious doubts raised about the empirical progress of the discipline, despite the plethora of experimental studies. Gordon Allport (1968, p. 3) expressed concern over the "slender achievements" of social psychology, and Muzafer Sherif (1977, pp. 368–389) complained that very few "golden kernels" could be extracted from the experimental "chaff" of the preceding decades. More radically, critics such as Kenneth Gergen and Harry C. Triandis complained about the culturally and historically bounded nature of experimental findings in social psychology (Gergen 1973; Triandis, 1976). They maintained that such findings were restricted to temporary phases of American culture and not generalizable beyond them. For example, studies of competition and conflict were doubtfully generalizable beyond the individualistic and capitalist culture of America (Plon, 1974), or conformity studies in the Asch paradigm beyond the McCarthy era in the United States (Gergen, 1973).

There were doubts raised about the social relevance of much research (Ring, 1967) and moral and methodological concerns expressed about the use of deception experiments (Kelman, 1967). Many of these critiques focused upon Stanley Milgram's controversial experimental studies of "destructive obedience" (Milgram, 1963), in which "teachers" inflicted potentially dangerous electric shocks on "learners" (Baumrind, 1964). However, perhaps the most common complaint focused on the "artificiality" of laboratory experiments in social psychology (Babbie, 1975; Harré & Secord, 1972). Many critics questioned the generalizability and "real-world" relevance of isolative laboratory studies:

> The greatest weakness of laboratory experiments lies in their artificiality. Social processes observed to occur within a laboratory setting might not necessarily occur within more natural settings.
>
> —(Babbie, 1975, p. 254)

Concerns were also expressed about the various **interaction effects** that appeared to plague experimentation in social psychology (Miller, 1972). These interaction effects included contaminating or confounding variables such as "experimenter expectancy effect" (Rosenthal, 1966), "demand characteristics" (Orne, 1962), and "evaluation apprehension" (Rosenberg, 1969). Further doubts were raised about the generalizability of findings based upon experimental populations of volunteers (Rosenthal & Rosnow, 1969)—and largely (psychology) student volunteers to boot (Higbee, Millard, & Folkman, 1982; Higbee & Wells, 1972). These complaints led some to call for alternatives to deceptive laboratory experiments, such as field experiments (Silverman, 1977) or role-playing experiments (Kelman, 1967).

However, little changed as a result of the crisis. Mainstream social psychologists renewed their allegiance to the experimental tradition and maintained that an increased commitment to methodological and statistical rigor would resolve most of the problems (Suls & Gastorf, 1980; Suls & Rosnow, 1988). More radical critics, unsatisfied by this approach, became associated with the postmodernist **social constructionist** movement in social psychology (Gergen, 1985), according to which the adoption of scientific theories is a matter of social rhetoric and negotiation rather than a product of empirical evaluation. However, the social constructionist denial of the objective empirical evaluation of scientific theories (in any domain, including physics and biology as well as social psychology) limited the appeal of this position for the majority of practicing social psychologists.

A lot of ink was needlessly spilt on the question of the generality of findings in social psychology, since it is a question that can be resolved only by empirical research on the cultural and historical scope of actual social-psychological explanations. Much of the "artificiality of experiments" debate focused on technical, philosophical, and moral issues, but largely ignored the very real problems of experimental attempts to isolate aspects of relational social-psychological phenomena, such as the judgments of trial jurors, or to study the social orientation of attitudes when "true experiments" mandated the random assignment of subjects to experimental groups. Sherman et al.'s (1999) study of research methods represented in *Journal of Personality and Social Psychology* and *Personality and Social Psychology Bulletin* between 1976 and 1996 recorded the continuing dominance of experimentation over all other methods of research.

Social Cognition The crisis was effectively resolved by the adoption of the *social-cognition* paradigm in the late 1970s and 1980s, propelled by the dramatic success of the cognitive revolution in psychology. Many agreed that the scientific promise of social psychology could be fulfilled by "getting inside the head" (Taylor & Fiske, 1981) to experimentally explore social forms of cognition. The social-cognition paradigm appeared to satisfy both those committed to an experimental psychology and those who wished to have a more cognitive and "social" social psychology.

Social cognition was the dominant topic of conferences in the late 1970s, and of edited collections in the early 1980s. Susan Fiske and Shelley Taylor's definitive text *Social Cognition* came out in 1982. The journal *Social Cognition* was instituted in the early 1980s, along with the "Attitudes and Social Cognition" section of the *Journal of Personality and Social Psychology*. Markus and Zajonc (1985) claimed that social psychology and cognitive psychology are "nearly synonymous" and reaffirmed that social psychology is just a branch of individual psychology. Jones (1985) critically dismissed "crisis" talk as not merely overstated, but as damaging and downright disloyal to the scientific institution of social psychology. McGuire (1985) reaffirmed the commitment of mainstream social psychology to the theoretical and methodological paradigm initiated with Floyd Allport's (1924a) individual and experimental reorientation of social psychology.

Yet the 1980s conception of social cognition was no more social than Floyd Allport's (1924a) conception of "social behavior." **Social cognition** was conceived of and defined in terms of cognitive states and processes directed toward other persons and social groups (rather than socially oriented to the represented psychology and behavior of members of social groups):

> The study of social cognition concerns how people make sense of other people and themselves.
>
> —(Fiske & Taylor, 1991, p. 17)

It was presumed that the same individual modes of information processing that underlie our perception and cognition of nonsocial objects such as tables, trees, and tarantulas also underlie our perception and cognition of social objects such as people and social groups:

> As one reviews research on social cognition, the analogy between the perception of things and the perception of people becomes increasingly clear. The argument is made repeatedly: the principles that describe how people think in general also describe how people think about people.
>
> —(Fiske & Taylor, 1991, p. 5)

This was precisely the individualistic assumption that underpinned Floyd Allport's (1924a) and John P. Dashiell's (1935) conception of social psychology.

However, in the last few decades there appears to have been a revival of interest in the social (and cultural) orientation of human psychology and behavior, as evidenced by a spate of books with titles such as *Socially Shared Cognition* (Resnick, Levine, & Teasley, 1991), *What's Social About Social Cognition?* (Nye & Brower, 1996), and *Group Beliefs* (Bar-Tel, 1990). Considerable interest has been expressed in the European work of Serge Moscovici and his colleagues on "social representations" (Farr & Moscovici, 1984; Moscovici, 1961) and of Henri Tajfel and J. C. Turner on "social identity" theory (Tajfel, 1981; Tajfel & Turner, 1986; Turner, 1987). Significantly, some of the proponents of the new discipline of "cultural psychology" have explicitly represented themselves as reconstituting the original form of social psychology developed by Durkheim, Wundt, and McDougall (Cole, 1996).

DEVELOPMENTAL PSYCHOLOGY

Speculation about the early "ages of man" goes back to antiquity. Ancient and medieval theorists generally treated children as young adults and believed that their basic cognitive, moral, and motivational capacities were fully developed by around age 5. They held that children differed from adults primarily in terms of their limited physique and knowledge (Aries, 1962), but were capable of gainful employment, sex, and marriage (Rush, 1980).

Empirically grounded theories of childhood were a product of the Enlightenment. In 1785 Joachim Heinrich Campe (1746–1818), a German educational reformer, called upon parents to record accounts of

> the entire moral and physical treatment of the child, including the observed effects and consequences; observations of the first expressions of independence, attention, joy and pain; advances in physical and mental development; gradual formation of language and the child's own very simple grammar; the beginnings of individual differences and emotions; basic patterns of future personality; etc.
>
> —(1785, p. xxvii, cited in Bringmann, Hewett, & Ungerer, 1997, p. 37)

Various parents took up Campe's suggestion and produced what came to be known as **baby diaries**. These included Dietrich Tiedemann's (1748–1803) "Observations on the Development of Mental Abilities in Children" (Tiedemann, 1787), a record of the first two and half years of his son's development, Hippolyte Taine's (1828–1893) record of his daughters' linguistic development (Taine, 1876), and Charles Darwin's "Biographical Sketch of an Infant" (Darwin, 1897). Such developmental records later fell out of favor and came to be treated as amateurish and unscientific, although Millicent Shinn (1858–1940) received the first PhD in psychology from the University of California at Berkeley in 1898 for her dissertation documenting the first two years of the development of her niece Ruth (Scarborough & Furumoto, 1987), later published as *Biography of a Baby* (1900).

Adolf Kussmaul (1822–1902) adopted a more experimental approach in *Investigations of the Mental Life of Newborn Children* (Kussmaul, 1859). Kussmaul, a German internist, did experimental studies of the sensory responses of newborns while working as a public health physician in Heidelberg (Bringmann, Balance, & Bringmann, 1997). William T. Preyer's (1841–1897) publication of *The Mind of the Child* in 1882 is usually held to mark the beginning of scientific approaches to the study of child development. A professor of physiology at the University of Vienna, Preyer documented the development of "the separate vital processes" of his own son from birth to age 3, and provided a set of methodological guidelines for the objective study and recording of child development (Preyer, 1882).

Scientific Psychology and Developmental Psychology

Early scientific psychological conceptions of child development were linked to theoretical perspectives in education, psychiatry, and biology. Many theories were based upon Haeckel's (1876) account of developmental recapitulation ("ontogeny recapitulates phylogeny"), which anticipated the modern concept of maturation. This was certainly true of the developmental theories propounded by G. Stanley Hall, generally recognized as the founder of developmental psychology in America. Hall pioneered the use of questionnaires in his study of child development (White, 1992) and quickly established links with educators (as did John Dewey at the University of Chicago and Teachers College). Hall was one of the founders of the child-study movement and published a number of articles and books on child development (Hall, 1893, Hall & Browne, 1904). He also pioneered the study of adolescence (Hall, 1904), a term he coined, and of old age (Hall, 1922). He founded *Pedagogical Seminary* in 1891, later retitled *The Journal of Genetic Psychology*.

Hall brought Freud to America in 1909, where he delivered a set of lectures on psychoanalysis at the 20th anniversary celebrations at Clark University. Although Freud's detailed psychosexual theory of child development was generally rejected by developmental psychologists (Berndt & Zigler, 1985), the critical discussion of his theory established many of the research goals of early developmental psychology, which included the study of aggression, sex roles, morality, breast-feeding, and toilet training (Parke & Clarke-Stewart, 2003). Moreover, the **social-learning** approach to child development, which played a significant role in developmental psychology from the 1930s to the 1970s, was originally based upon the attempt by some of Hull's students—notably John Dollard, Neal Miller, and Robert Sears—to integrate neobehaviorist learning theory and psychoanalytic theory (albeit in terms of the effective reduction of psychoanalytic theory to learning theory). They proposed neobehaviorist explanations of sex typing, childhood aggression, dependency, and moral development in terms of reinforcement through drive reduction (Dollard et al., 1939; Miller & Dollard, 1941) and explored child-rearing practices (such as toilet training and discipline) through extensive interviews with mothers (Sears, Maccoby, & Levin, 1957).

James Mark Baldwin was another pioneer of developmental psychology, who stressed the social dimensions of development and whose account of child development in terms of assimilation and accommodation (1895, 1897) influenced Jean

Piaget's (1926, 1932) studies of the cognitive development of the child (Berndt & Zigler, 1985). Other early accounts of child development also emphasized the social dimensions of development. The Russian psychologist Lev Vygotsky (1896–1934) accounted for the development of cognition in terms of the appropriation of the social form of language (Vygotsky, 1929, 1934). In Vygotsky's account, differences in social conditions lead to differences in psychological functions and patterns of cognitive development. Vygotsky's student and colleague, Alexander Luria (1902–1977), explored this implication. He documented cognitive-developmental changes associated with educational, economic, and industrial changes in the Soviet Republics of Central Asia (Luria, 1931, 1976). Piaget's early work also emphasized the role of social factors in child development (Piaget, 1932).

However, later theorists tended to neglect the social dimensions of child development (as social psychologists came to neglect the social orientation of human psychology and behavior), although they continued to stress the importance of interpersonal interaction, particularly with parents and other adults. This was especially true of the social-learning theories developed in the 1930s and 1940s (Dollard et al., 1939; Miller & Dollard, 1941), which came to dominate research in developmental psychology in the 1950s and 1960s. Social-learning theories focused on interpersonal rather than socially oriented learning and were variants of the theories of imitative learning first developed by Le Bon and Tarde. Yet like social psychologists, developmental psychologists never abandoned their theoretical focus on cognitive states and processes, even during the period of the hegemony of behaviorism.

Studies of child development in the early decades of the 20th century were strongly influenced by the mental testing movement. Arnold Gesell (1880–1961) worked at the Yale Clinic for Child Development from 1911 to 1961. He constructed a **developmental quotient** (Gesell, 1928), a measure of child development modeled upon Terman's intelligence quotient and based upon longitudinal studies of motor, linguistic, adaptive, and personal-social behavior (Berndt & Zigler, 1985). Gesell developed the notion of maturational stages introduced by earlier theorists such as Hall and maintained that learning plays a relatively minor role in child development.

John B. Watson championed the opposite view, that learning is the primary determinant of child development, although the few experiments he conducted on conditioned learning in young children (Watson, 1926; Watson & Rayner, 1920) provided rather weak evidential support for his grandiose environmentalist claims. Nonetheless, Watson had probably the greatest impact on child-rearing practices, largely through his popular works on child rearing, such as *Psychological Care of Infant and Child* (Watson & Watson, 1928), a field to which Gesell and his colleagues also contributed (Gesell & Ilg, 1946).

Watson's experimental studies of infants at the Phipps Clinic in Baltimore were supported by a grant from the **Laura Spelman Rockefeller Memorial Fund**, which also funded institutes of developmental research at major universities such

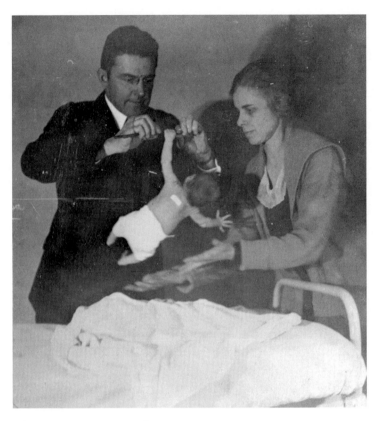

John B. Watson testing newborns.

as Yale, Columbia, Iowa, Minnesota, and UC Berkeley (Lomax, 1977). These were modeled upon the successful agricultural research stations of Midwestern state universities (at the University of Iowa, for example, the institute was called the Child Welfare Research Station). The Rockefeller Foundation also supported the work of Karl and Charlotte Bühler at the Vienna Institute of Psychology and Institute of Child Psychology. Charlotte Bühler visited the United States in 1924–1925 as a fellow of the Rockefeller Fund, where she met with Arnold Gesell and Edward L. Thorndike.

Rockefeller fellowships in child study and parent education also provided a unique opportunity for women, since in the early years the fund specifically directed its recruitment to women, advertising their fellowships under the rubric "For women only." Of the 212 fellowship appointments made between 1924 and 1931, 205 were awarded to women, and women came to be well represented in the emerging discipline of developmental psychology (Cahan, 2005).

Large-scale longitudinal studies of cognitive, moral, social, and linguistic development were carried out in the 1930s and 1940s (Bayley, 1933, 1935,

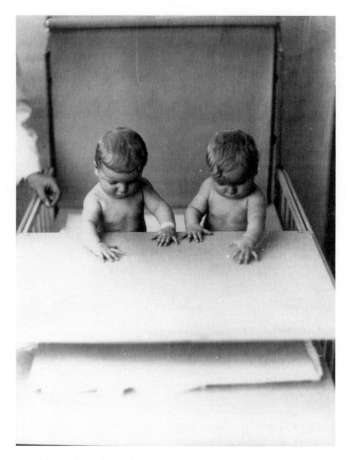

Arnold Gesell study of identical twins.

1949). The theoretical debates about development initiated by Gesell and Watson continued, with Galton's method of twin studies employed to assess the relative contributions of maturation and learning (McGraw, 1935; Newman, Freeman, & Holzinger, 1937).

The first *Handbook of Child Psychology* was published in 1931 (Murchison, 1931), and the Society for Research in Child Development was founded in 1934. The Society became responsible for the publication of *Child Development* and *Child Developmental Abstracts and Bibliography*, the two premier journals in developmental psychology, and instituted the series *Monographs of the Society for Research in Child Development*. The APA Division of Developmental Psychology was founded in 1954, and the APA journal *Developmental Psychology* was launched in 1967.

Social learning theories remained influential throughout the 1960s and 1970s, although later theories were based upon cognitive modeling rather than reinforcement (Bandura, Ross & Ross, 1961). The critical importance of maternal support and contact was demonstrated by John Bowlby's (1907–1990) research on maternal deprivation (Bowlby, 1958, 1969) and Harry Harlow's (1905–1981) research on infant monkeys and surrogate mothers (Harlow & Zimmerman, 1959).

Cognitive Development

Research on cognitive development came to dominate developmental psychology from the 1960s onward, in line with the cognitive revolution in psychology and stimulated by the resurgence of interest in the work of Jean Piaget (1896–1980). Piaget had been developing his theory of child development since the 1920s, although reactions to his early work (Piaget, 1926) were critical and unenthusiastic. However, interest in Piaget's biological-maturational account of cognitive development grew as critics came to question the explanatory range of neobehaviorist learning theory, and Chomsky's (1957) work on the child's acquisition of language stimulated interest in the programmed acquisition of cognitive capacities and skills. Piaget's work was reintroduced to American psychologists through J. McVicker Hunt's *Intelligence and Experience* (1961) and John Flavell's *The Developmental Psychology of John Piaget* (1963).

Piaget was a former student of the psychiatrist Eugene Bleuler (1857–1939) and had worked with Theodore Simon on the elaboration of Binet's intelligence tests. He advanced a **stage theory** of cognitive development based upon detailed longitudinal studies of his own children (Piaget, 1952, 1954; Piaget & Inhelder, 1958). According to Piaget, children attain mastery of cognitive structures through assimilation and accommodation. As children mature, they acquire increasingly more complex cognitive structures as they pass through the sensorimotor (birth to 2 years), preoperational (2 to 7 years), concrete operational (7 to 11 years), and formal operational (11 to 15 years) stages. While Piaget stressed the child's active contribution, he also maintained that the stages of development are fixed by biological maturation and that each developmental stage is characterized by the simultaneous acquisition of an integrated range of cognitive skills. One distinctive feature of Piaget's theory was that he maintained that later cognitive stages are discontinuous with earlier stages (analogous to the discontinuity of theoretical stages in the development of Western science [Piaget & Garcia, 1989]), in contrast to both Gesell and Watson, who maintained that development is a continuous accumulation of increasingly complex capacities and skills.

Piaget's theory was enormously influential and stimulated a great deal of research. In recognition of his unique contribution to developmental psychology, he was awarded the APA's Distinguished Scientific Contribution Award in 1969. This is not to say that Piaget's theories were universally accepted. Some critics questioned Piaget's claim that stages of development are fixed and maintained that cognitive development can be accelerated through educational training, while others raised doubts about the cross-cultural applicability of Piaget's theory (Berndt & Zigler, 1985). Similar doubts about cross-cultural applicability were raised concerning Lawrence Kohlberg's (1927–1987) extension of Piaget's stage theory of moral development (Kohlberg, 1969, 1984; Piaget, 1932). Kohlberg's theory also stimulated a great deal of research, including Carol Gilligan's studies of the development of the "care" perspective, which she maintained was distinctive of female moral development (Gilligan, 1982). Eventually research on cognitive and moral development transcended the original Piagetian orientation, and developmental psychologists began to investigate the development of cognitive, emotional, and social capacities and skills not covered by the Piaget and Kohlberg stage paradigms (Flavell, 1994).

Since the 1980s, one of the hot topics has been the study of the development of the **child's theory of mind**, which has focused on the development of young children's ability to explain and predict their own and others' behavior in terms of mental states such as beliefs, desires, and emotion (Astington, Olson, & Harris, 1988; Carruthers & Smith, 1996). Research has suggested that a major transformation in the child's theory of mind occurs around age 4, when children move from an elementary "copy" theory of mind to a fully "representational" theory of mind, which allows them to acknowledge the explanatory role of false beliefs (Wellman, 1990). This research has been largely based upon the "false-belief" experimental paradigm, in which an imaginary scenario is acted out with child dolls. For example, one doll—Sally—hides her marble in a box and goes away for a walk. While she is away, another doll—Anne—removes the marble from the box and hides it in a basket. Children are asked where Sally will look for her marble when she returns and wants it. In most cases, 3-year-olds answer that Sally will look for her marble in the basket, where it really is, rather than in the box, where she should believe it is. In contrast, 4- to 5-year-olds and adults generally answer that Sally will look for the marble in the box, where she falsely believes it to be (Hogrefe, Wimmer, & Perner, 1986).

As developmental psychology became an established and recognized subdiscipline of psychology, developmental psychologists began to apply their findings to broader social issues. They were instrumental in the promotion of the **Head Start** program, a government program aimed at enriching the educational and social experience of economically disadvantaged children during the critical early years of development. The expert advice of developmental psychologists was sought by government agencies on the influence of television, the effects of day care, and the efficacy of reading programs (Berndt & Zigler, 1985).

Like their colleagues in social psychology, developmental psychologists have tended to neglect the social orientation of human psychology and behavior, with most research on "socialization" focusing on imitative interpersonal behavior and interaction. However, unlike their colleagues in social psychology, developmental psychologists never became committed to experimentation as the sine qua non of scientific psychology. Although there has been an increase in the proportion of experimental studies in recent decades, developmental psychologists have continued to employ a variety of empirical methods, such as longitudinal studies, naturalistic observation, field experiments, participant observation and interviews, alongside controlled laboratory studies.

DISCUSSION QUESTIONS

1. Try to identify socially oriented forms of thought, emotion, and behavior that are not directed to social objects (other persons and groups) and forms of thought, emotion, and behavior directed to social objects (other persons and social groups) that are not socially oriented.

2. Try to identity some occupational (social) attitudes. Can you identify any occupational attitudes associated with contemporary social psychologists?

3. Is it possible to do experiments in social psychology, given the various methodological and moral problems identified during the "crisis" in social psychology? Can the experimental study of socially oriented psychology and behavior be reconciled with the demand for randomization?

4. Are "baby diaries" a legitimate method of empirical study in developmental psychology? Consider the advantages and disadvantages of having child caregivers as child observers.

5. Has the subject matter of developmental psychology changed in the 20th century to the same degree as the subject matter of social psychology?

GLOSSARY

autonomy individualism Conception of individualism in which individuality is considered in terms of rational self-determination, associated with utilitarianism and laissez-faire economics.

baby diary Descriptive record of early child development based upon parental observations.

child's theory of mind The ability of children to explain and predict their own and others' behavior in terms of mental states such as beliefs, desires, and emotions.

co-acting group For Floyd Allport, an experimental group in which subjects are primarily engaged with some common stimulus.

communitarian individualism Conception of individualism in which individuality is considered in terms of relations to social community.

crisis in social psychology Period in the 1970s during which social psychology was subjected to a variety of metatheoretical, methodological, and moral critiques.

crowd psychology Theories of the irrational and emotional behavior of members of crowds (based upon suggestibility and imitation) developed by Le Bon and Tarde at the turn of the century.

developmental quotient Arnold Gesell's measure of development modeled upon Terman's intelligence quotient and based upon longitudinal studies of motor, linguistic, adaptive, and personal-social behavior.

face-to-face (interacting) group Experimental group in which subjects interact with one another.

group fallacy According to Floyd Allport, the misguided attempt to explain social phenomena in terms of the group as a whole, rather than in terms of the individuals who compose it.

Head Start program Government program aimed at enriching the educational and social experience of economically disadvantaged children during the critical early years of development.

holism Theory that social groups are supra-individual entities with emergent properties, not reducible to the properties of the individual persons that compose them.

interaction effects Interactions between experimenters and subjects that introduce contaminating or confounding variables.

individual psychology Study of psychology and behavior that is the product of reasons or causes operating independently of social orientation.

interpersonal psychological states and behavior Psychological states and behavior directed toward other persons.

Laura Spelman Rockefeller Memorial Fund Major source of funding for institutes of developmental research at American universities.

occupational attitude Term employed by Emory Bogardus to characterize attitudes associated with membership of particular professions or trades.

public Term introduced by Gabriel Tarde to describe physically dispersed populations of individuals.

public opinion research Surveys of the common attitudes or opinions of physically dispersed aggregations of individuals, independently of their social orientation or affiliation.

reference group Term introduced by Herbert Hyman to reference the different social groups to which an individual's attitudes and behavior may be oriented.

social cognition Cognitive states and processes directed toward other persons and social groups.

social learning theory A theory of learning and development based upon imitation and cognitive modeling.

social orientation The orientation of human psychology and behavior to the represented psychology and behavior of members of social groups.

social psychology As originally conceived, the study of the socially oriented forms of human psychology and behavior.

social constructionism Postmodern conception of theory adoption as a matter of social rhetoric and negotiation rather than a product of empirical evaluation.

social self Term employed by James to characterize those aspects of self that are associated with membership of social groups.

stage theory A theory of development that postulates different stages of development.

REFERENCES

Abelson, R. P., & Rosenberg, M. J. (1958). Symbolic psychologic: A model of attitudinal cognition. *Behavioral Science, 3,* 1–13.

Allport, F. H. (1920). The influence of the group upon association and thought. *Journal of Experimental Psychology, 3,* 159–182.

Allport, F. H. (1924a). *Social psychology.* Boston: Houghton Mifflin.

Allport, F. H. (1924b). The group fallacy in relation to social science. *Journal of Abnormal and Social Psychology, 19,* 60–73.

Allport, F. H. (1933). *Institutional behavior.* Chapel Hill, NC: University of North Carolina Press.

Allport, F. H. (1934). The J-curve hypothesis of conforming behavior. *Journal of Social Psychology, 5,* 141–181.

Allport, F. H. (1974). Autobiography. In G. Lindzey (Ed.), *A history of psychology in autobiography* (Vol. 6). Englewood Cliffs, NJ: Prentice-Hall.

Allport, G. W. (1954). The historical background of modern social psychology. In G. Lindzey (Ed.), *Handbook of social psychology* (Vol. 1). Reading, MA: Addison-Wesley.

Allport, G. W. (1968). Six decades of social psychology. In Sven Lundstedt (Ed.), *Higher education in social psychology.* Cleveland: Case Western Reserve University Press.

Angell, J. R. (1908). *Psychology.* New York: Holt.

Aries, P. (1962). *Centuries of childhood: A social history of family life* (R. Bladick, Trans.). New York: Random House.

Aristotle. (1984). *Politics.* In Jonathan Barnes (Ed.), *Complete works of Aristotle: The revised Oxford translation.* Princeton, NJ: Princeton University Press. (Original work from fourth century BCE)

Aronson, E., & Carlsmith, J. M. (1968). Experimentation in social psychology. In G. Lindzey & E. Aronson (Eds.), *The handbook of social psychology* (2nd ed.). Reading, MA: Addison-Wesley.

Aronson, E., Wilson, T. D., & Brewer, M. B. (1998). Experimentation in social psychology. In D. T. Gilbert, S. T. Fiske, & G. Lindzey (Eds.), *The handbook of social psychology* (4th ed.). New York: Oxford University Press.

Asch, S. E. (1951). Effects of group pressure upon the modification and distortion of judgements. In H. Guetzkow (Ed.), *Groups, leadership, and men.* Pittsburgh: Carnegie Press.

Asch, S. E. (1952). *Social psychology.* Englewood Cliffs, NJ: Prentice-Hall.

Asch, S. E., Block, H., & Hertzman, M. (1938). Studies in the principles of judgments and attitudes: I. Two principles of judgment. *Journal of Psychology, 5,* 219–251.

Astington, J. W., Olson, D., & Harris, P. (Eds.). (1988). *Developing theories of mind.* Cambridge: Cambridge University Press.

Babbie, E. R. (1975). *The practice of social research.* Belmont, CA: Wadsworth.

Baldwin, J. M. (1895). *Mental development in the child and the race.* New York: Macmillan.

Baldwin, J. M. (1897). *Social and ethical interpretations in mental development.* New York: Macmillan.

Bandura, A., Ross, D., & Ross, S. A. (1961). Transmission of aggression through imitation of aggressive models. *Journal of Abnormal and Social Psychology, 63,* 575–582.

Bar-Tel, D. (1990). *Group beliefs.* New York: Springer-Verlag.

Bartlett, F. C. (1932). *Remembering: A study in experimental and social psychology.* New York: Macmillan.

Baumrind, D. (1964). Some thoughts on ethics of research: After reading Milgram's "Behavioral study of obedience." *Journal of Abnormal and Social Psychology, 51,* 616–623.

Bayley, N. (1933). The development of motor abilities during the first three years. A developmental study of 61 children by repeated tests. *Genetic Psychology Monographs, 14,* 1–92.

Bayley, N. (1935). Mental growth during the first three years. A developmental study of 61 children by repeated tests. *Monographs of the Society for Research in Child Development*, No. 1.

Bayley, N. (1949). Consistency and variability in the growth of intelligence from birth to eighteen years. *Journal of Genetic Psychology, 75,* 165–196.

Bem, D. J. (1967). Self-perception: An alternative interpretation of cognitive dissonance phenomena. *Psychological Review, 74,* 183–200.

Bernard, L. L. (1921). The misuse of instinct in the social sciences. *Psychological Review, 28,* 96–119.

Berndt, T. J., & Zigler, E. F. (1985). Developmental psychology. In G. A Kimble & K. Schlesinger (Eds.), *Topics in the history of psychology* (Vol. 2). Hillsdale, NJ: Erlbaum.

Blumer, H. (1969). *Symbolic interactionism: Perspective and method.* Englewood Cliffs, NJ: Prentice-Hall.

Blumer, H. (1984). *Symbolic interactionism.* Englewood Cliffs, NJ: Prentice-Hall.

Boas, F. (1945). Aryans and non-Aryans. In *Race and democratic society.* New York: Augustin. (Original work published 1934)

Bogardus, E. S. (1922). *A history of social thought.* Los Angeles, CA: University of Southern California Press.

Bogardus, E. S. (1924a). The occupational attitude. *Journal of Applied Sociology, 8,* 171–177.

Bogardus, E. S. (1924b). *Fundamentals of social psychology.* New York: Century.

Boring, E. G. (1933). *The physical dimensions of consciousness.* New York: Century.

Bowlby, J. (1958). The nature of the child's tie to his mother. *International Journal of Psycho-Analysis, 39,* 350–373.

Bowlby, J. (1969). *Attachment and loss: Vol. 1. Attachment.* London: Hogarth Press.

Bringmann, W. G., Balance, W. D. G., & Bringmann, N. J. (1997). The mental life of newborn children. In W. G. Bringmann, H. E. Lück, R. Miller, & C. E. Early (Eds.), *A pictorial history of psychology.* Chicago: Quintessence.

Bringmann, W. G., Hewett, P., & Ungerer, G. A. (1997). An 18th-century baby biography. In W. G. Bringmann, H. E. Lück, R. Miller, & C. E. Early (Eds.), *A pictorial history of psychology.* Chicago: Quintessence.

Brock, A. (1992). Was Wundt a "Nazi"?: Völkerpsychologie, racism, and anti-Semitism. *Theory & Psychology, 2,* 205-223.

Burgess, R. (1977). The withering away of social psychology. *American Sociologist, 12,* 12–13.

Cahan, E. (2005). *Science, practice, and gender roles in early child psychology.* Paper presented at the 37th Annual Meeting of *Cheiron,* University of California at Berkeley, June 23–26.

Campe, J. H. (Ed.). (1785-1791). *Allgemeine Revision des gesampten Schul- und Erziehungswesens von einer Gesellschaft praktischer Erzieher* [General revision of the complete school and educational systems of a society of practical educators] (Vols. 1–16). Hamburg: Bohn.

Carruthers, P. K., & Smith, P. K. (1996). *Theories of theories of mind.* Cambridge: Cambridge University Press.

Cartwright, D., & Zander, A. (Eds.). (1953). *Group dynamics: Research and theory.* Elsmford, NY: Row, Peterson.

Chomsky, N. (1957). *Syntactic structures.* The Hague: Mouton.

Christie, R. (1965). Some implications of recent trends in social psychology. In O. Klineberg & R. Christie (Eds.), *Perspectives in social psychology.* New York: Holt, Rinehart & Winston.

Cole, M. (1996). *Cultural psychology: The once and future discipline.* Cambridge, MA: Harvard University Press.

Collier, G., Minton, H. L., & Reynolds, G. (1991). *Currents of thought in American social psychology.* Oxford: Oxford University Press.

Cooley, C. H. (1902). *Human nature and the social order.* New York: Scribner's.

Crano, W. D., & Brewer, M. B. (1973). *Principles of research in social psychology.* New York: McGraw-Hill.

Danziger, K., & Dzinas, K. (1997). How psychology got its variables. *Canadian Psychologist, 38,* 43–48.

Darwin, C. (1897). Biographical sketch of an infant. *Mind, 2,* 285–294.

Dashiell, J. F. (1935). Experimental studies of the influence of social situations on the behavior of individual human adults. In C. A. Murchison (Ed.), *Handbook of social psychology.* Worcester, MA: Clark University Press.

Dollard, J., Doob, L. W., Miller, N. E., Mowrer, O. H., & Sears, R. R. (1939). *Frustration and aggression.* New Haven, CT: Yale University Press.

du Bois-Reymond, E. (1842). *Zwei grosse Naturforscher des 19 Jahrhunderts: Ein Briefwechsel zwischen Emil Du Bois-Reymond und Karl Ludwig* [*Two major scientists of the 19th century: Emil Du Bois-Reymond and Karl Ludwig*]. Leipzig: Barth, 1927.

Dunlap, K. (1919). Are there any instincts? *Journal of Abnormal and Social Psychology, 14,* 307–311.

Dunlap, K. (1925) *Social psychology.* Baltimore: Williams & Wilkins.

Durkheim, E. (1897). *Suicide* (J. A. Spaulding & G. Simpson, Trans.). New York: Free Press.

Durkheim, E. (1982). Preface to second edition of *The rules of sociological method.* In S. Lukes (Ed.) & W. D. Halls (Trans.), *Durkheim: The rules of sociological method and selected texts on sociology.* New York: Macmillan. (Original work published 1902)

Durkheim, E. (1982). *The rules of sociological method.* In S. Lukes (Ed.) & W. D. Halls (Trans.), *Durkheim: The rules of sociological method and selected texts on sociology.* New York: Macmillan. (Original work published 1895)

Edwards, A. L. (1941) Political frames of reference as a factor influencing recognition. *Journal of Abnormal and Social Psychology, 36,* 34–61.

Edwards, A. L. (1954). Experiments: Their planning and execution. In G. Lindzey (Ed.), *The handbook of social psychology.* Reading, MA: Addison-Wesley.

Ellwood, C. A. (1924). The relations of sociology and social psychology. *Journal of Abnormal and Social Psychology, 19,* 3–12.

Ellwood, C. A. (1925). *The psychology of human society.* New York: Appleton.

Elms, A. C. (1975). The crisis of confidence in social psychology. *American Psychologist, 30,* 967–976.

Faris, E. (1925). The concept of social attitudes. *Journal of Applied Sociology, 9,* 404–409.

Farr, R. M. (1996). *The roots of modern social psychology 1872–1954*. Oxford: Blackwell.

Farr, R. M., & Moscovici, S. (Eds.). (1984). *Social representations*. Cambridge: Cambridge University Press.

Festinger, L. (1947). The role of group-belongingness in a voting situation. *Human Relations*, 154–180.

Festinger, L. (1953). Laboratory experiments. In L. Festinger & D. Katz (Eds.), *Research methods in the behavioral sciences*. New York: Holt, Rinehart & Winston.

Festinger, L. (1957). *A theory of cognitive dissonance*. Stanford, CA: Stanford University Press.

Festinger, L., Riecken, H. W., & Schachter, S. (1956). *When prophecy fails*. Minneapolis: University of Minnesota Press.

Fiske, S. T., & Taylor, S. E. (1982). *Social cognition*. New York: Random House.

Fiske, S. T., & Taylor, S. E. (1991). *Social cognition* (2nd ed.). New York: McGraw-Hill.

Flavell, J. H. (1963). *The developmental psychology of Jean Piaget*. New York: Van Nostrand.

Flavell, J. H. (1994). Cognitive development: Past, present, and future. In R. D. Parke, P. A. Ornstein, J. J. Rieser, & Zahn-Waxler, C. (Eds.), *A century of developmental psychology*. Washington, DC: American Philosophical Association.

Gergen, K. J. (1973). Social psychology as history. *Journal of Personality and Social Psychology, 26,* 309–320.

Gergen, K. J. (1985). The social constructionist movement in modern psychology. *American Psychologist, 40,* 266–275.

Gesell, A. (1928). *Infancy and human growth*. New York: Macmillan.

Gesell, A., & Ilg, F. L. (1946). *The child from five to ten*. New York: Harper.

Gilligan, C. (1982). *In a different voice: Psychological theory and women's development*. Cambridge, MA: Harvard University Press.

Greenwood, J. D. (2004). *The disappearance of the social in American social psychology*. New York: Cambridge University Press.

Haeckel, E. (1876). *The history of creation* (Vols. 1–2). New York: Appleton.

Haines, H., & Vaughan, G. M. (1979). Was 1898 a "great date" in the history of experimental social psychology? *Journal of the History of the Behavioral Sciences, 15,* 323–332.

Hall, G. S. (1893). *The content of children's minds when entering school*. New York: Kellogg.

Hall, G. S. (1904). *Adolescence: Its psychology and its relations to physiology, anthropology, sociology, sex, crime, religion and education*. New York: Appleton.

Hall, G. S. (1922). *Senescence*. New York: Appleton.

Hall, G. S., & Browne, C. E. (1904). The cat and the child. *Pedagogical Seminary, 11,* 3–29.

Harlow, H. F., & Zimmerman, R., R. (1959). Affectional responses in the infant monkey. *Science, 130,* 421–432.

Harré, R., & Secord, P. F. (1972). *The explanation of social behavior.* Totowa, NJ: Rowman & Littlefield.

Heider, F. (1958). *The psychology of interpersonal relations.* New York: Wiley.

Herbart, J. F. (1821). Über einige Beziehungen zwischen Psychologie und Staatswissenschaft [About several relationships between psychology and political science]. In K. Kehrbach (Ed.), *Herbart's Sämtliche Werke* (Vol. 5). Langensalza: Beyer, 1890.

Higbee, K. L., Millard, R. J., & Folkman, J. R. (1982). Social psychology research during the 1970's: Predominance of experimentation and college students. *Personality and Social Psychology Bulletin, 8,* 180–183.

Higbee, K. L., & Wells, M. G. (1972). Some research trends in social psychology during the 1960's. *American Psychologist, 27,* 963–966.

Hobbes, T. (1966). *Leviathan.* In W. Molesworth (Ed.), *The English works of Thomas Hobbes.* Darmstadt, Germany: Scientia Verlag Aalen. (Original work published 1651)

Hogrefe, G. J., Wimmer, H., & Perner, J. (1986). Ignorance versus false belief: A developmental lag in attribution of epistemic states. *Child Development, 57,* 567–582.

Hovland, C. I., Lumsdaine, A. A., & Sheffield, F. D. (Eds.). (1949). *Experiments in mass communication.* (Studies in Social Psychology in World War II, Vol. 3.) Princeton, NJ: Princeton University Press.

Hunt, J. M. (1961). *Intelligence and experience.* New York: Ronald Press.

Hyman, H. (1942). The psychology of status. *Archives of Psychology,* No. 269.

Jahoda, M., Deutsch, M., & Cook, S. W. (1951). *Research methods in social relations.* New York: Dryden Press.

James, W. (1890). *The principles of psychology.* New York: Holt.

Janis, I. L. (1968). *Victims of groupthink.* New York: Harcourt Brace & Jovanovich.

Jones, E. E. (1985). Major developments in social psychology during the past five decades. In G. Lindzey & E. Aronson (Eds.), *The handbook of social psychology* (3rd ed.). New York: Random House/Erlbaum.

Kantor, J. R. (1922). How is social psychology possible? *Journal of Abnormal and Social Psychology, 17,* 62–78.

Katz, D. (1967). Editorial. *Journal of Personality and Social Psychology, 7,* 341–344.

Katz, D. (1991). Floyd Henry Allport: Founder of social psychology as a behavioral science. In G. A. Kimble, M. Wertheimer, & C. White (Eds.), *Portraits of pioneers in psychology* (Vol. 1). Hillsdale, NJ: Erlbaum.

Katz. D., & Schanck, R. (1938). *Social psychology.* New York: Wiley.

Kelley, H. H. (1950). The warm-cold variable in first impressions of persons. *Journal of Personality, 18,* 431–439.

Kelley, H. H. (1952). Two functions of reference groups. In G. E. Swanson, T. M. Newcomb, & E. L. Hartley (Eds.), *Readings in social psychology* (2nd ed.). New York: Holt.

Kelman, H. C. (1967). Human use of human subjects: The problem of deception in social psychological experiments. *Psychological Bulletin, 67,* 1–11.

Kidder, L. H. (1981). *Selltiz, Wrightsman and Cook's research methods in social relations* (4th ed.). New York: Holt, Rinehart & Winston.

Kiesler, C. A., & Kiesler, S. B. (1969). *Conformity.* Reading, MA: Addison-Wesley.

King, E. G. (1990). Reconciling democracy and crowd in turn-of-the-century American social psychological thought. *Journal of the History of the Behavioral Sciences, 26,* 335-343.

Kohlberg, L. (1969). *Stages in the development of moral thought and action.* New York: Holt, Rinehart & Winston.

Kohlberg, L. (1984). *The psychology of moral development: The nature and validity of moral stages.* San Francisco: Harper & Row.

Krech, D., & Crutchfield, R. S. (1948). *Theory and problems of social psychology.* New York: McGraw-Hill.

Krech, D., Crutchfield, R. S., & Ballachey, E. L. (1962). *Individual in society: A textbook of social psychology.* New York: McGraw-Hill.

Külpe, O. (1895). *Outlines of psychology* (E. B. Titchener, Trans.). New York: Macmillan.

Kuo, Z. Y. (1921). Giving up instincts in psychology. *Journal of Philosophy, 18,* 645–666.

Kussmaul, A. (1859). *Untersuchungen über die sinneswahrnehmungen des neugeborenen Menschen [Investigations of the mental life of newborn children].* Heidelberg: Winter.

La Piere, R. T. (1938). *Collective psychology.* New York: McGraw-Hill.

Le Bon, G. (1896). *The crowd: A study of the popular mind.* London: T. Fisher Unwin. (Original work published 1895 in French)

Lewin, K. (1948). *Resolving social conflicts: Selected papers on group dynamics.* New York: Harper.

Lewin, K. (1951). *Field theory in social science.* New York: Harper.

Likert, R. (1932). A technique for the measurement of attitudes. *Archives of Psychology, 140,* 1–55.

Liska, F. (1977). The dissipation of sociological social psychology. In L. H. Strickland, F. E. Aboud, & K. J. Gergen (Eds.), *Social psychology in transition.* New York: Plenum.

Lomax, E. (1977). The Laura Spelman Rockefeller Memorial: Some of its contributions to early research in child development. *Journal of the History of the Behavioral Sciences, 13,* 283–293.

Luria, A. R. (1931) Psychological expedition to Central Asia. *Science, 74,* 383–384.

Luria, A. R. (1976). *Cognitive development: Its cultural and social foundations.* Cambridge, MA: Harvard University Press.

Markus, H., & Zajonc, R. B. (1985). The cognitive perspective in social psychology. In G. Lindzey & E. Aronson, (Eds.), *Handbook of social psychology* (3rd ed.). New York: Random House.

McDougall, W. (1908). *Introduction to social psychology.* New York: John W. Luce.

McDougall, W. (1920). *The group mind.* New York: Putnam.

McGrath, J. (1978). Small group research. *American Behavioral Scientist, 21,* 651–673.

McGraw, M. (1935). *Growth, a study of Johnny and Jimmy.* New York: Appleton Century.

McGuire, W. J. (1985). Toward social psychology's second century. In S. Koch & D. E. Leary (Eds.), *A century of psychology as science.* New York: McGraw-Hill.

Mead, G. H. (1934). *Mind, self and society: From the standpoint of a social behaviorist.* (C. W. Morris, Ed.). Chicago: University of Chicago Press.

Milgram, S. (1963). Behavioral study of obedience. *Journal of Abnormal and Social Psychology, 67,* 371–378.

Milgram, S. (1974). *Obedience to authority.* New York: Harper & Row.

Miller, A. G. (Ed.). (1972). *The social psychology of psychological research.* New York: Free Press.

Miller, N. E., & Dollard, J. (1941). *Social learning and imitation.* New Haven, CT: Yale University Press.

Moede, W. (1914). Der Wetteifer, seine Struktur und sein Ausmass [On rivalry, its structure and extent]. *Zeitschrift für pädagogische Psychologie, 15,* 353–368.

Moede, W. (1920). *Experimentelle Massenpsychologie [Experimental mass psychology].* Leipzig: Hirzel.

Moscovici, S. (1961). *La psychanalyse, son image et son public [Psychoanalysis, its image and its public].* Paris: Presses Universitaires de France.

Murchison, C. A. (Ed.). (1931). *Handbook of child psychology.* Worcester, MA: Clark University Press.

Murchison, C. A. (Ed.). (1935). *Handbook of social psychology.* Worcester, MA: Clark University Press.

Murphy, G., & Murphy, L. B. (1931). *Experimental social psychology.* New York: Harper.

Murphy, G., Murphy, L. B., & Newcomb, T. M. (1937). *Experimental social psychology* (Rev. ed.). New York: Harper.

Newcomb, T. M. (1943). *Personality and social change: Attitude formation in a student community.* New York: Holt.

Newcomb, T. M. (1951). Social psychological theory: Integrating individual and social approaches. In J. M. Rohrer & M. Sherif (Eds.), *Social psychology at the crossroads.* New York: Harper.

Newcomb, T. M., & Hartley, E. L. (Eds.). (1947). *Readings in social psychology.* New York: Holt.

Newman, H. H., Freeman, F. N., & Holzinger, K. J. (1937). *Twins: A study of heredity and environment.* Chicago: University of Chicago Press.

Nye, J. L., & Brower, A. M. (Eds.). (1996). *What's social about social cognition? Research on socially shared cognition in small groups.* Thousand Oaks, CA: Sage.

Nye, R. A. (1975). *The origins of crowd psychology: Gustav Le Bon and the crisis of mass democracy in the Third Republic.* London: Sage.

Orne, M. T. (1962). On the social psychology of the psychological experiment: With particular reference to demand characteristics and their implications. *American Psychologist, 17,* 776–783.

Parke, R. D., & Clarke-Stewart, A. (2003). Developmental psychology. In D. K. Freedheim (Ed.), *Handbook of psychology: Vol. 1. History of psychology.* Hoboken, NJ: Wiley.

Patnoe, S. (1988). *A narrative history of experimental social psychology.* New York: Springer-Verlag.

Piaget, J. (1926). *The language and thought of the child.* New York: Harcourt, Brace.

Piaget, J. (1932). *The moral judgment of the child.* New York: Free Press.

Piaget, J. (1952). *The origin of intelligence in children.* New York: International Universities Press.

Piaget, J. (1954). *The construction of reality in the child.* New York: Basic Books.

Piaget, J., & Garcia, J. (1989). Psychogenesis and the history of science. (H. Frieder, Trans.). New York: Columbia University Press.

Piaget, J., & Inhelder, B. (1958). *The growth of logical thinking from childhood to adolescence.* New York: Basic Books.

Plon, M. (1974). On the meaning of the notion of conflict and its study in social psychology. *European Journal of Social Psychology, 4,* 389–436.

Preyer, W. T. (1882). *Die Seele des Kindes* [*The mind of a child*]. Stuttgart: Bonz.

Reis, H. T., & Stiller, J. (1992). Publication trends in JPSP: A three-decade review. *Personality and Social Psychology Bulletin, 18,* 465–472.

Resnick, L. B., Levine, J., & Teasley, S. D. (Eds.). (1991). *Perspectives on socially shared cognition.* Washington, DC: American Philosophical Association.

Riesman, D. (1950). *The lonely crowd.* New Haven, CT: Yale University Press.

Ring, K. (1967). Experimental social psychology: Some sober questions about some frivolous values. *Journal of Experimental Social Psychology, 3,* 113–123.

Rosenberg, M. J. (1969). The conditions and consequences of evaluation apprehension. In R. Rosenthal & R. L. Rosnow (Eds.), *Artifact in behavioral research.* New York: Academic Press.

Rosenthal, R. (1966). *Experimenter effects on behavioral research.* New York: Appleton-Century-Crofts.

Rosenthal, R., & Rosnow, R. (1969). The volunteer subject. In R. Rosenthal & R. L. Rosnow (Eds.), *Artifact in behavioral research.* New York: Academic Press.

Ross, E. A. (1906). *Social control.* New York: Macmillan.

Ross, E. A. (1908). *Social psychology: An outline and source book.* New York: Macmillan.

Rush, F. (1980). *The best-kept secret: Sexual abuse of children.* Bradenton, FL: The Human Services Institute.

Scarborough, E., & Furumoto, L. (1987). *Untold lives: The first generation of American women psychologists.* New York: Columbia University Press.

Sears, R. R., Maccoby, E. E., & Levin, H. (1957). *Patterns of child rearing.* Evanston, IL: Row, Peterson.

Selltiz, C., Jahoda, M., Deutsch, M., & Cook, S. W. (1959). *Research methods in social relations* (2nd ed.). New York: Holt, Rinehart & Winston.

Selltiz, C., Wrightsman, L. R., & Cook, S. W. (1976). *Research methods in social relations* (3rd ed.). New York: Holt, Rinehart & Winston.

Sherif, M. (1935). A study of some social factors in perception. *Archive of Psychology*, No. 187.

Sherif, M. (1936). *The psychology of social norms*. New York: Harper.

Sherif, M. (1948). *An outline of social psychology*. New York: Harper.

Sherif, M. (1977). Crisis in social psychology: Some remarks towards breaking through the crisis. *Personality and Social Psychology Bulletin, 3,* 368–382.

Sherman, R. C., Buddie, A. M., Dragan, K. L., End, C. M., & Finney, L. J. (1999). Twenty years of PSPB: Trends in content, design, and analysis. *Personality and Social Psychology Bulletin, 25,* 177–187.

Shinn, M. W. (1900). *The biography of a baby*. Boston: Houghton Mifflin.

Silverman, I. (1977). *The human subject in the psychological laboratory*. New York: Pergamon.

Simmel, G. (1894). Das problem der Soziologie. *Jahrbuch für Gesetzgebung, Verwaltung und Volkswissenschaft, 18,* 271–277.

Simmel, G. (1959). How is society possible? In Kurt H. Wolff (Ed.), *Georg Simmel, 1858–1918: A collection of essays, with translations and a bibliography.* Columbus: Ohio State University Press. (Original work published 1908)

Singer, E. (1988). Reference groups and social evaluations. In M. Rosenberg & R. H. Turner (Eds.), *Social psychology: Sociological perspectives*. New York: Basic Books.

Small, A. W. (1905). *General sociology*. Chicago: University of Chicago Press.

Small, A. W., & Vincent, G. E. (1894). *Introduction to the study of society*. New York: American Book.

Smith, A. (1776). *An inquiry into the nature and causes of the wealth of nations* (Vols. 1–2). London: W. Strahan & T. Cadell.

Steiner, I. D. (1974). Whatever happened to the group in social psychology? *Journal of Experimental Social Psychology, 10,* 94–108.

Stouffer, S. A., Lumsdaine, A. A., Lumsdaine, M. H., Williams, R. M., Smith, M. B., Janis, I. L., Star, S. A., & Cottrell, I. S. (Eds.). (1949). *The American soldier: Combat and its aftermath.* (Studies in Social Psychology in World War II, Vol. 2). Princeton, NJ: Princeton University Press.

Stouffer, S. A., Suchman, E. A., De Vinney, L. C., Star, S. A., & Williams, R. B., Jr. (Eds.). (1949). *The American soldier: Adjustment during army life* (Studies in Social Psychology in World War II, Vol. 1). Princeton, NJ: Princeton University Press.

Suls, J. M., & Gastorf, J. (1980). Has the social psychology of the experiment influenced how research is conducted? *European Journal of Social Psychology, 10,* 291–294.

Suls, J. M., & Rosnow, R. L. (1988). Concerns about artifacts in psychological experiments. In J. G. Morawski (Ed.), *The rise of experimentation in American psychology*. New Haven: Yale University Press.

Taine, H. (1876). Note sur l'acquisition de language chez les enfants et dans l'espèce humaine [Note on the acquisition of language by infants and in the human species]. *Revue Philosophique, 1,* 3–23.

Tajfel, H. (1972). Experiments in a vacuum. In J. Israel & H. Tajfel (Eds.), *The context of social psychology: A critical assessment*. London: Academic Press.

Tajfel, H. (1981). *Human groups and social categories*. Cambridge: Cambridge University Press.

Tajfel, H., & Turner, J. C. (1986). The social identity theory of intergroup behavior. In S. Worchel & W. G. Austin (Eds.), *Psychology of intergroup relations* (2nd ed.). Chicago: Nelson-Hall.

Tarde, G. (1901). *L'opinion et la foule* [*The opinion of the crowd*]. Paris: F. Alcan.

Tarde, G. (1903). *The laws of imitation* (E. C. Parsons, Trans.). New York: Holt.

Taylor, S. E., & Fiske, S. T. (1981). Getting inside the head: Methodologies for process analysis in attribution and social cognition. In J. H. Harvey, W. Ickes, & R. F. Kidd (Eds.), *New directions in attribution research*. Hillsdale, NJ: Erlbaum.

Thibaut, J. W., & Kelley, H. H. (1959). *The social psychology of groups*. New York: Wiley.

Thomas, W. I. (1904). The province of social psychology. *American Journal of Sociology, 10,* 445–455.

Thomas, W. I., & Znaniecki, F. (1918). Methodological note. In *The Polish peasant in Europe and America* (Vol. 1). Chicago: University of Chicago Press.

Thurstone, L. L. (1931). The measurement of social attitudes. *Journal of Abnormal and Social Psychology, 26,* 249–269.

Thurstone, L. L., & Chave, E. J. (1929). *The measurement of attitude*. Chicago: University of Chicago Press.

Tiedemann, D. (1787). Beobachtung über die Entwicklung der Seelenfähigkeiten bei Kindern. [Observations on the development of mental abilities in children]. *Hessische Beiträge zur Gelehrsamkeit und Kunst, 2,* 313–333; *3,* 486–502.

Titchener, E. B. (1910). *A textbook of psychology*. New York: Macmillan.

Triandis, H. C. (1976). Social psychology and cultural analysis. In L. H. Strickland, F. E. Aboud, & K. J. Gergen (Eds.), *Social psychology in transition*. New York: Plenum Press.

Triplett, N. (1898). The dynamogenic factors in pacemaking and competition. *American Journal of Psychology, 9,* 507–533.

Turner, J. C. (1987). *Discovering the social group: A self-categorization theory*. Oxford: Blackwell.

United States Strategic Bombing Survey. (1946). *The effects of bombing on German morale*. Washington, DC: U.S. Government Printing Office.

van Ginneken, J. (1985). The 1878 debate on the origins of crowd psychology. *Journal of the History of the Behavioral Sciences, 21*, 375–382.

van Ginneken, J. (1992). *Crowds, psychology and politics, 1871–1899.* Cambridge: Cambridge University Press.

von Eickstedt, E. (1936). *Grundlagen der Rassenpsychologie [Fundamentals of racial psychology].* Stuttgart: Enke.

von Humboldt, W. (1836). *Über die Verschiedenheit des menschlichen Sprachbaus und ihren Einfluss auf die geistige Entwicklung des Menschengeschlechts [The diversity of human language structure and its influence on the mental development of mankind].* Berlin: Acadamie der Wissenchaften.

Vygotsky, L. (1929). *Pedologija podrostka* (Vol. 1). Moscow: Rabotnik Prosveshchenija.

Vygotsky, L. (1934). *Thought and language.* Cambridge, MA: MIT Press.

Wallis, W. D. (1925). The independence of social psychology. *Journal of Abnormal and Social Psychology, 20*, 147–150.

Wallis, W. D. (1935). The social group as an entity. *Journal of Abnormal and Social Psychology, 29*, 367–370.

Ward, L. (1883) *Dynamic sociology.* New York: Appleton.

Watson, G. (Ed.). (1942). *Civilian morale.* Boston: Houghton Mifflin.

Watson, J. B. (1919). *Psychology from the standpoint of a behaviorist.* Philadelphia: Lippincott.

Watson, J. B. (1924). *Behaviorism.* New York: Norton.

Watson, J. B. (1926). Experimental studies of the growth of the emotions. In C. Murchison (Ed.), *Psychologies of 1925.* Worcester, MA: Clark University Press.

Watson, J. B., & Rayner, R. R. (1920). Conditioned emotional reactions. *Journal of Experimental Psychology, 3*, 1–14.

Watson, J. B., & Watson, R. R. (1928). *The psychological care of infant and child.* New York: Norton.

Weber, M. (1978). *Economy and society* (Vols. 1–2; G. Roth & C. Wittich, Eds.). Berkeley: University of California Press. (Original work published 1922)

Wellman, H. M. (1990). *The child's theory of mind.* Cambridge, MA: MIT Press.

West, S. G., Newsom, J. T., & Fenaughty, A. M. (1992). Publication trends in JPSP: Stability and change in topics, methods and theories across two decades. *Personality and Social Psychology Bulletin, 18*, 473–484.

White, S. H. (1992). G. Stanley Hall: From philosophy to developmental psychology. *Developmental Psychology, 28*, 25–34.

Williams, R. (1961). *The long revolution.* New York: Columbia University Press.

Winston, A. S. (1990). Robert Sessions Woodworth and the "Columbia Bible": How the psychological experiment was redefined. *American Journal of Psychology, 103*, 391–401.

Winston, A. S., & Blais, D. J. (1996). What counts as an experiment?: A transdisciplinary analysis of textbooks, 1930–1970. *American Journal of Psychology, 109*, 599–616.

Woodworth, R. S. (1938). *Experimental psychology*. New York: Holt.

Wundt, W. (1900–1920). *Völkerpsychologie* (Vols. 1–10). Leipzig: W. Engelmann.

Wundt, W. (1902). *Outlines of psychology* (C. H. Judd, Trans.). St Claires Shores, MI: Scholarly Press. (Original work published 1897)

Young, K. (1925). Social psychology. In H. E. Barnes (Ed.), *The history and prospects of social sciences*. New York: Knopf.

Young, K. (1930). *Social psychology*. New York: Crofts.

Young, K. (Ed.). (1931). *Social attitudes*. New York: Holt.

The Past and Future of Scientific Psychology

T HE LAST TWO CHAPTERS DEMONSTRATE AN IMPORTANT FEATURE OF the historical development of clinical, social, and developmental psychology in relation to the general development of psychology in America in the 20th century. The development of these subdisciplines of psychology did not simply parallel the general development of psychology in terms of the historical progression from structural to functional psychology, and from behaviorism to cognitive psychology. While theories and therapies based upon behaviorist learning theory and cognitive processing were developed in clinical psychology, they were developed together in the postwar period, which marked the end of the behaviorist hegemony in general psychology. While some social psychologists called themselves behaviorists, they remained committed to the study of social attitudes and public opinion from the beginning to the end of the 20th century. Developmental psychologists never embraced the general commitment by psychologists (including social psychologists) to experimentation as the essence of scientific psychology.

This illustrates the contingency of the development of American psychology. Although one may trace the conceptual continuities and discontinuities between the development of structural and functional psychology, and behaviorism and cognitive psychology, it is well to remember that the development of American psychology depended upon the particularities and peculiarities of the social, cultural, political, and institutional context and the vagaries of the careers of individual psychologists.

This contingency becomes especially apparent when one compares the 20th-century development of American psychology with the development of psychology in other countries (Sexton & Misiak, 1976). To take but a few illustrative examples, Italian psychology embraced cognitive psychology in the early 1920s and never looked back (Mecacci, 1992). When George Miller critiqued the behaviorist position at a talk he gave in London in the 1960s, his host pointed out that there were only three behaviorists in Britain and apologized for the fact that none were in attendance (Baars, 1986). Henri Pieron (1881–1964) articulated the behaviorist position in France in 1908 (Pieron, 1908), but considered cognitive psychology to be an essential component of experimental psychology (Pieron, 1929).

From its inception, French psychology was closely linked to medicine and clinical psychology, through the work of Charcot, Janet, and George Dumas (1866–1946). The development of psychology in Latin America was based upon a peculiar mix of Wundtian physiological psychology and Freudian psychoanalysis (Stubbe & Ramon, 1997), and Russian psychology prior to the revolution comprised an eclectic mix of cognitive psychology, musicology, psychophysics, physiology, linguistics, and social and development psychology, as well as the objective psychology of Sechenov, Bechterev, and Pavlov (Zinchenko, 1997).

This should remind us that the future of scientific psychology, as much as the past, depends upon the contingencies of historical circumstance and personality.

REFERENCES

Baars, B. J. (1986). *The cognitive revolution in psychology.* New York: Guilford Press.

Mecacci, L. (1992). *Storia della psicologia italiana.* Rome: Instituto della Enciclopedia Italiana.

Pieron, H. (1908). L'evolution du psychisme. *Revue Du Mois.*

Pieron, H. (1929). *Principles of experimental psychology* (J. B. Miner, Trans.). London: Kegan Paul, Trench, Trubner.

Sexton, V. S., & Misiak, H. (1976). *Psychology around the world.* Belmont, CA: Wadsworth.

Stubbe, H., & Ramon, L. (1997). Psychology in Latin America. In W. G. Bringmann, H. E. Lück, R. Miller, & C. E. Early (Eds.), *A pictorial history of psychology.* Chicago: Quintessence.

Zinchenko, V. P. (1997). Russian psychology. In W. G. Bringmann, H. E. Lück, R. Miller, & C. E. Early (Eds.), *A pictorial history of psychology.* Chicago: Quintessence.

CREDITS

NAME INDEX

Wedgwood, J., 251
Wedgwood, S., 251
Weiner, D.B., 570
Weiss, P., 411, 424
Weissman, A., 246
Wellman, H.M., 542, 638
Wells, M.G., 627, 630
Wells, S., 208
Wertheimer, M., 307, 326, 327–329, 333, 335, 336, 596
West, S.G., 629
Weyer, J., 89, 569
Whewell, W., 21
Whipple, K., 599
White, A.D., 353
White, S.H., 633
White, W.A., 583
Whytt, R., 4, 101, 141, 142, 211, 220, 567
Wiener, N., 59, 525–526
Wiggam, A., 458
Wiggins, J.G., 599
Wigmore, J., 368
Wilberforce, B.S., 257, 258, 260
Wilcoxon, L.A., 599
Wilkes, K.V., 60, 156
William of Orange, 153
Williams, L., 356
Williams, R., 611
Williams, R.B., Jr., 503, 625

Williams, R.M., 503, 625
Willis, T., 133, 141, 568
Wilson, E., 265
Wilson, G.T., 586
Wilson, M., 588
Wilson, T.D., 628
Wimmer, H., 542, 638
Windelband, W., 311, 336–337
Winston, A.S., 19, 627–628
Wirth, W., 302, 307, 308, 312
Wissler, C., 382, 452
Witasek, S., 334
Witherspoon, J., 181
Witmer, L., 367, 368, 383–386, 397, 584
Wittmer, L., 313
Wolfe, H.K., 308, 313, 388
Wolff, C., 296
Wolpe, J., 158, 449, 585, 595–596
Woodward, S., 570
Woodward, W.R., 3
Woodworth, R.S., 11, 19, 316, 322, 325–326, 365, 382, 396–397, 398, 409, 420–421, 541, 550, 584, 628
Woolley, H.T., 264, 354
Worcester, E., 589
Wozniak, R.H., 337
Wright, C., 363
Wrightsman, L.R., 628

Wundt, M., 298
Wundt, W., 2, 3, 23, 185, 221, 287, 295. *see also* Wundt, William in Subject Index

Xenophanes, 41
Xenophon, 32

Yeats, W.B., 159
Yerkes, R.M., 367, 397, 425, 426, 427, 428, 433, 455, 459, 460, 462, 502
Yorkston, N., 599
Young, K., 616
Young, R.M., 10, 205, 206, 209, 210, 212, 213, 216, 222, 241

Zajonc, R.B., 631
Zanarini, G., 554
Zander, A., 626
Zax, M., 88
Zeigarnik, B., 334
Zenderland, L., 454, 461
Zeno of Citium, 70–71
Zeno of Elea, 41–42
Zigler, E.F., 633, 634, 638
Zimmerman, R.R., 637
Zinchenko, V.P., 655
Znaniecki, F., 616, 619
Zwelling, S.S., 571

SUBJECT INDEX